# THE READER'S
# BIBLE
## A NARRATIVE

Selections from
the King James Version

# THE READER'S
# BIBLE
# A NARRATIVE

Selections from
the King James Version

Edited with an Introduction
and Notes by
ROLAND MUSHAT FRYE

Princeton University Press
Princeton, New Jersey

Originally published 1965 under the title **The Bible:
Selections from the King James Version for Study as
Literature** by Houghton Mifflin Company in Riverside
Editions under the General Editorship of Gordon N. Ray.
Reissued 1977 under the same title by Princeton
University Press in Princeton Paperback edition.

# Preface

Among the books which an educated man should know, none is more important than the Bible. Surely no other book has affected the life of society so deeply and at so many different points. The purpose of this edition is to present the Old and New Testaments in representative selections, so that we can study the literary greatness of the Bible and seek to understand something of its impact upon our culture. For such a literary study the so-called King James or Authorized Version of 1611 has been chosen, for it is almost unanimously regarded as being literarily the greatest English translation. (The text used here of course embodies the standard and universally adopted modernizations of the original 1611 text.)

The Bible is here reduced to approximately one-fourth or one-fifth of its length so as to be put within range of study in a single course in literature. An earnest effort has been made to abridge in such a way that the whole is fairly represented by what is presented. Thus, though much has been eliminated, what remains should provide the reader with a firm impression of the depth, sweep, and greatness of the whole Bible.

By kind permission of the Westminster Press, the verse lineation of poetic passages follows the usage of the *Westminster Study Edition of the Bible*, King James Version. The six maps appear by permission of Thomas Nelson and Sons.

I have been very fortunate indeed in having the editorial help and guidance of Miss Marie Edel, the editor of this book in its first edition, and I wish to express the gratitude I feel to her for all that she has done to make this book more useful.

R. M. F.

# Preface to the Princeton Paperback Edition

In the years since the original publication of this book, changing judgments about Biblical scholarship have for the most part concerned relatively minor points of emphasis and understanding. The one major exception concerns the source relationships and chronology of the gospels in the New Testament. In 1963 it was possible to write that "it is now generally believed among New Testament scholars that Mark's Gospel was one of the sources used by Matthew and Luke" and that Matthew and Luke also used an early collection of the sayings of Jesus called "Q" (see below, pp. xi-xii). That general agreement has since been disrupted, and a new consensus has yet to emerge. Various critiques of this once-accepted model of gospel relationships have appeared over the past dozen or so years, among the most important of which is William R. Farmer's *The Synoptic Problem: A Critical Analysis* (New York: Macmillan, 1964). By a combination of literary-historical, logical, and textual analyses, Farmer has proposed a return to the earliest view of Matthew as the first of the gospels, and he has gone on to argue cogently for the later succession of Luke and Mark, in that order. A number of notable younger scholars have been persuaded to Farmer's view, but even among those who have not been convinced of his chronological ordering, many now recognize that the so-called "two document" hypothesis (that is, Matthew and Luke separately developed but in dependence upon Mark and the hypothetical "Q") is of highly dubious value.

The excitement was further compounded with the appearance of John A. T. Robinson's *Redating the New Testament* (Philadelphia: Westminster Press, 1976). Robinson's earlier *Honest to God* had called for a readjustment of theological understanding in the direction of modern patterns of thought, and now he presented a cogent argument for regarding all four gospels as having been composed more or less synchronously during about twenty-five years, beginning in the late thirties and extending no later than the mid sixties of the Christian Era. There would appear to be few advantages from discussing source relations in the once-fashionable manner, if the compilation of all the gospels was proceeding at the same time and with complex but varying degrees of interchange.

These developments should be recorded, for those who wish to pursue them further, but they do not alter the literary focus upon the Biblical texts, nor of the guides to their study, which are presented here.

# Preface

Although not revolutionary in the same sense as Farmer and Robinson, other scholars have contributed importantly over the past dozen years. A supplementary volume to the *Interpreter's Dictionary of the Bible* has appeared under the general editorship of Keith Crim (Nashville, Tennessee: Abingdon, 1976). M. Barclay has provided an updated and intelligent summary of criticism in his *Introduction to the First Three Gospels* (Philadelphia: Westminster Press, 1975), and his *Introduction to John and the Acts of the Apostles* (Philadelphia: Westminster Press, 1976), and there is a useful *Handbook of Biblical Criticism* by Richard N. Soulen (Atlanta: John Knox Press, 1976). For historical correlations, Jack Finegan has provided the very valuable *Handbook of Biblical Chronology* (Princeton: Princeton University Press, 1964).

More general treatments may be found in Samuel Sandmel, *The Enjoyment of Scripture: The Law, The Prophets, and The Writings* (New York: Oxford University Press, 1972), in T. R. Henn, *The Bible as Literature* (New York: Oxford University Press, 1970), and in Leland Ryken, *The Literature of the Bible* (Grand Rapids, Michigan: Zondervan Publishing House, 1974). Fascinating for its subject is Ward Allen's *Translating for King James: Notes Made By A Translator of King James's Bible* (Nashville, Tennessee: Vanderbilt University Press, 1969). Suggestions for the use of standard literary critical techniques for analyses of the Bible may be found in Roland Mushat Frye, "A Literary Perspective for the Criticism of the Gospels," *Jesus and Man's Hope* (ed. Donald G. Miller and Dikran Y. Hadidian), Pittsburgh, 1971, pp. 193-221, and "On the Historical-Critical Method in New Testament Studies," *Perspective* 14 (1973), pp. 28-33.

October 1977                                                R. M. F.

# Contents

❖ Selections from the New Testament

# Introduction: *The Bible as Literature*

## I. Form and Content

The Bible is characterized from beginning to end by a remarkable literary dynamism. The events treated and the literary forms in which they are recounted create a complex texture made up of many and varied threads. The reader is left, as a result, with an impression of vast sweep and vitality in which virtually all forms of human experience and literary expression have a place.

That this great, sprawling, diverse whole is essentially unified upon certain basic themes, we shall see as our study proceeds, but our first impression as serious readers of the Bible is of diversity, and so it is on the subject of diversity that we shall begin our discussion here. The Bible opens upon a scene of vast primordial chaos, with the spirit of God brooding dove-like upon the abyss to bring forth life and all that lives, in a vision which the great Greek critic Longinus cited as the essence of the sublime in literature.[1] The Bible closes upon a vision of a new heaven and a new earth, reconstituted and everlasting, in which the forces of evil which are so prominent in the body of the book are reduced to impotence and replaced by universal justice and love, harmony and beauty.

This beginning, which looks back beyond the first writing of human history, and this conclusion, which looks forward beyond the last syllable of recorded time, should show us that the Bible is concerned with far more significant matters than the accurate recounting of past happenings. It is nonetheless true that history is one of the most characteristic modes of Hebrew thought, and modern archaeology has repeatedly demonstrated the historical reliability of the Biblical tradition, a reliability which surpasses that of the histories of any other ancient people. Thus we have in both testaments supreme narrative accounts of actual events which occurred in the past. But these events are never merely retold in factual terms: they are always told in terms of their meaning for understanding the present and shaping the future. Thus history is always kept within a framework of interpretive significance, as the events are seen not merely in reference to themselves but also in reference to a continuously heuristic meaning for men and societies.[2]

[1] Longinus, *On the Sublime*, trans. Benedict Einarson (Chicago: Packard and Company, 1945), p. 18.

[2] In this sense of an event in the past which continually assumes normative importance for later generations, interpretive history may be called "myth,"

Within such a concern for history, the Hebrew writers found it necessary to employ not only the events of history but also certain other literary forms which, though they are not in our terms strictly historical, appealed to the Biblical writers as useful for contributing to an understanding of history in any terms. Thus we find, alongside remarkably accurate treatments of the past, accounts which fit more nearly into the categories of parable and story and legend. The parables in the New Testament, and the treatments of Adam and Eve, of Noah, and of Jonah in the Old, for example, are not necessarily accounts of particular historical events which may be located in chronology and geography, but they are nonetheless significant uses of plot and story to interpret man's historical existence. Fitting somewhere between such uses of fiction in the interest of truth and such historical accounts as we find, say, in the book of Kings, there are stories like that of Job which may or may not be based in historical events, but whose value as dramatized encounter between man and man and between man and God is unaffected by the question of their literal historicity. There are also such tales as those about Samson, where we have an ancient folk hero whose deeds, however real, have been preserved in the literary forms generally associated with historic legend. And in the beautiful story of Ruth we have a perfect pastoral idyll where form and action unite to present a human truth within a setting of simple rural life and deep religious conviction.

The question of historicity in Ruth is patently immaterial, but with Ruth's descendant, David, the matter of history is again central. In the accounts of David's life we find ourselves in contact with past actions and events, often as real as the battles of Hastings, Bunker Hill, and Bull Run. But here the significance is not restricted to the time of David's life, or even to the history of David's people, for the events are so related as to achieve epic status and universality of meaning.

If the story of David constitutes a magnificent prose epic, the Psalms achieve the personal intensity and pervasive beauty so characteristic of great lyric poetry. And if the Psalms preserve lyrics of personal devotion and of encounter with God, the Song of Songs is a lyric of human love, of the sexual relation between man and woman, presented with great power and beauty. In the New Testament epistles, on the other hand, we have some of the greatest letters of all time, and also (especially with Paul) the development of highly intellectual essays.

The Bible presents man as being engaged in every circumstance of life in repeated, persistent, and unremitting relationships with God, and these relationships (whether of acceptance or rejection) are presented in many different and appropriate literary forms. If the literary forms of the Bible are many, so too were the manners of developing the various books of the Bible as we know them. Some books — and

---

but the word "myth" has so many conflicting meanings both among scholars and among laymen that I find its use creates more confusion than clarity and so prefer not to employ it at all.

Job is an example — represent the adaptation of tales common not only to the Hebrews but to other Near Eastern peoples. Other books — and the books treating Moses and the exodus from Egypt into the promised land are examples — represent a uniquely Hebrew experience. At times the general and the unique merge, as in many aspects of the Old Testament law where widespread ethical ideals (ancient, but also modern) are united with quite distinctive Hebrew orientations. In the Bible, then, we have the joining of many different literary forms, sources, and ideas; the presence side by side of historical fact, traditional story, and imaginative fiction; and the treatment both of universal human wisdom and preeminently Hebrew understanding.

We know a great deal — though by no means all that we should like to know — about the long historical process of acceptance, rejection, and incorporation by which the Biblical books assumed their present shape. The books of the Old Testament, which were of course written in Hebrew, were taking on their present form during the thousand years before the birth of Jesus, while the New Testament books were written in Greek during the period of some hundred years after that time. In the Old Testament, furthermore, twenty-four Hebrew books are explicitly mentioned which are unknown to us except by name. Even had they been preserved intact, they would probably not have won a place in the canon, for most of the valuable material in them seems to have been integrated into the Old Testament books we now have.

The course of editorial selection and inclusion may be briefly illustrated by reference to the first five books of the Old Testament, or the Pentateuch. Scholars have traced in these books various stages of editing which led to the establishment of the text as we now know it. The history of this particular recension covers a period of several hundred years, between the ninth and fifth centuries B.C. The most obvious signs of the process of uniting several sources may be seen in doublet and triplet versions of what appears to be the same incident, as in the posing of a wife as a sister in Genesis 12:10–20, 20:1–16, and 26:6–11, or in the disagreement as to how many animals were to be taken on the ark between the accounts in Genesis 6:19–20 and 7:2–3. This development of the text by writing, selection, and merging is thought by many to have gone through four stages, denoted by the letters J, E, D, and P, depending upon whether the deity was referred to as Jahweh or Elohim, and upon whether the editorial work was carried out by the Deuteronomist or the Priestly school.

In the Gospel records of the New Testament, there are somewhat similar signs of the bringing together of various source materials, though here the process of formation took only several decades rather than several centuries. The first verse of Luke's Gospel refers to the existence of "many" accounts, which Luke evidently used as he felt was appropriate in addition to more personal knowledge which he acquired from eyewitnesses. It is now generally believed among New Testament scholars that Mark's Gospel was one of the sources used by Matthew and Luke, though scholars in earlier centuries (Saint Augustine, for example) have believed that the reverse was the case, and that Mark's Gospel was merely an abridgment of Matthew's. Modern scholars, furthermore, hold that Luke and Matthew both used an early collection of the sayings of Jesus. This collection is called "Q" as an abbreviation of the German word for "source," *Quelle*. Other materials, certainly oral and probably written, were also available for use.

The choice of Greek as the language of the New Testament was not so radical a break with Jewish culture as might at first sight appear, for Jews in the first century of the Christian era were no longer speaking classical Hebrew, but rather Aramaic and Greek. By the beginning of the Christian era the Old Testament had been completely translated into Greek and was used in this form by Gentile converts and by many Jews who, as a cosmopolitan people living throughout the known world spoke Greek, the international language of the time. That the New Testament should have been composed in Greek would have appeared natural, whether from the Jewish or the Gentile point of view. The Bible developed, then, not only over a long span of history and in different literary forms, but also in different languages.

Somewhat more will be said about the development of the Bible in the introductions to the particular selections, but it is important to recognize at the outset that the Bible as we know it today is the product of a long and complex history of composition and compilation, bringing together many different literary strata and genres. Readers may therefore expect to find a very wide variety of style and contents. But at least one element is present which we often assume to be absent, and two elements are absent which are sometimes assumed to be present. Let us turn first to the commonly ignored element of the book which I should like to underscore here simply because it is so little noted: this is its humor, of which there is a surprising amount. The humor is never flippant or frivolous, but is of the kind about which G. B. Shaw advised us that "when a thing is funny, search it for a hidden truth."[3] In the teachings of Jesus, especially in his response to questions and objections, we find the humor of the well-turned phrase and the apt repartee which is close to the heart of true wit. Even Peter can be made the butt of a significant thrust of humor which throws light on the imperceptive response of even the most faithful men to Jesus' entire ministry when, at the Last Supper, Jesus comes to wash Peter's feet, and Peter impetuously asks him to wash "not my feet only, but also my hands and head" (John 13:6–10). Indeed, a remarkable element in Peter's greatness as the leader of the apostles is shown by the fact that his fellow Christians not only preserved accounts of his betrayal of Jesus but also treasured the story of his ridiculous reaction to the transfigura-

[3] *Back to Methuselah* in *Selected Plays*, Vol. II (New York: Dodd, Mead and Company, 1948), p. 247.

tion of Jesus in the presence of Moses and Elijah. (See Luke 22:55–62 and 9:33.) If the one instance was tragic and utterly unfunny, the other preserved an attractively humorous insight into Peter's complex character. It was possible not only to admire and even revere Peter, but to see his weakness and to smile at his follies.

But humor is not restricted to the New Testament. In the story of Balaam preserved in Numbers 22–24 there is a wry satire of pagan diviners who thought that magic incantations could control the will of God. The basic situation is, of course, utterly serious, but there is a fine irony in the treatment of aspects of it. So, too, in the encounter on Mount Carmel when the lone Elijah confronts the many prophets of Baal: mocking the absurd and fruitless gyrations and shouts of the servants of Baal, Elijah caustically advises them to call louder to Baal, for "either he is talking, or he is pursuing, or he is in a journey, or peradventure he sleepeth, and must be awaked" (I Kings 18:27). If there is anywhere a more effective satiric line than this one, I do not know it.

But it is in Jonah, I suggest, that we have the finest example of satiric humor in the Bible and one of the finest in any literature. Jonah is at once a deadly serious and a very funny book. These two qualities are inseparably joined together, for the seriousness concerns the judgment and the mercy of God, while the humor evolves from the assumption on Jonah's part that he really knows better than God. Thus Jonah attempts to evade God and God's commands by flying to another country aboard a ship. Jonah's massive self-confidence is never quite pompous, for he does have a kind of integrity which impels him to tell his shipmates that his presence on the ship is the cause of the storm, and to accept being cast overboard. Though he is not pompous, he tends toward the mock-heroic, and his being swallowed and vomited up by the whale provides an appropriately tragi-comic nemesis, admirably suited to his character. Similarly, when he does preach to Nineveh and the city repents, Jonah sulks, even pouts, because God shows mercy to a city which Jonah had declared to be doomed. "I do well to be angry, even unto death," he tells the Lord, but the Lord replies through the incident of the gourd to deflate the smug self-righteousness of this intensely human figure who assumes that his own judgment and integrity are superior to the judgment and integrity of God. The fact that we laugh at Jonah (or at least should laugh at him) does not minimize the utter seriousness of the book, for in recognizing that Jonah is ridiculous we can see the ridiculous aspect of all human pretensions, including our own. And we should also remember that the Nineveh which Jonah so despises here was the capital of the hated empire of Assyria, which God — happily unencumbered with Jonah's self-righteousness — was able to love and willing to redeem.

What we have just been saying indicates the breadth of the Bible, including as it does many forms of human concern. But we must be careful not to regard it as an all-inclusive book, for that it certainly is not. We must, indeed, be as careful to note what the Bible excludes as we are to note what it includes. Here there are two concerns which, we must remember, are quite outside the scope of the Bible, though they are sometimes assumed to be within it. There are also other matters with which the Bible is not dealing, but it is especially important to understand the relation of the Bible to these two in particular.

First, the Bible does not claim, either implicitly or explicitly, to be a book of science. The first chapters of Genesis, for example, do not provide and were not intended to provide a geological and biological account of the origins and development of the created universe. The late Henry Norris Russell, perhaps the greatest American astronomer of our century, once said that the early chapters of Genesis would have been written precisely as they were even if their ancient author had been aware of all the developments of modern science. When the problem is stated in this way, we can see the basic differences between a scientific and a Biblical account of the origins of the world in which man lives. The Bible is not concerned with the assemblage of atoms, but with man's nature, conduct, and destiny. The story of Adam and Eve is a parable intended to give man an understanding of himself, not a literal and scientific account of his distant ancestors. A knowledge of the original Hebrew is important here, for though "Adam" and "Eve" have become proper names in English and are applied to individuals, they were not proper names at all in Hebrew, but common nouns. "Adam" meant "man," and "Eve" meant something like "life," the word being used interchangeably with "woman." When we understand this, we are able to see that the story of the fall is based upon man's unwillingness to accept existence in the image of God and his desire instead to accept the temptation to be "as gods." Man's unwillingness to accept and follow the will of God, and his contrary will to establish himself and his own individual desires as "god," precipitates the evils with which men plague themselves and each other. Thus, in the words of the great twentieth-century Jewish scholar Martin Buber, we are all engaged in "Adam's fall," which "continually happens here and now in all its reality."[4]

Just as the Bible is not intent upon supplying definitive scientific information, neither does it pretend to provide a unified philosophical system. It is, of course, true that the root meaning of the word "philosophy" as the love of truth or the love of wisdom may be applied to the Bible, but if on the other hand the word is taken in its usual sense of a unified system of abstractions, statements, and propositions, then the Bible is not at all philosophical. The knowledge of God and of man with which the Bible is concerned is not transmitted abstractly, but in terms of concrete symbols and historical events. Even the epistles of the Apostle Paul are not systematic analyses of

4 *The Writings of Martin Buber* (New York: Meridian Books, 1956), p. 28.

abstract ideas, but are explorations of the mystery and meaning and message of Jesus, interpreted as the final representation of God in history. Neither in Paul nor elsewhere in the Bible is there a definition of God in formal philosophical or propositional terms. God is not understood by means of definitions and syllogisms, but in terms of events in the lives of men and societies.

Biblical understandings as to man, God, and the relations between them are not reached by deduction from abstractions defining God and man, but by reference to the experiences of human communities and individuals who lived in faithful or unfaithful relation to God. The Biblical writers do not refer for their authority to major and minor premises in a syllogistic way, but rather to the experiences of men whose relations to God and to each other were regarded as profoundly indicative of the truth about God and man. The Bible thus, not only refuses to yield a unified philosophical system, but reveals a pervasive and persistent suspicion of philosophical system-building.

From the philosophical point of view, indeed, the Bible seems to maintain a number of irreconcilable contradictions, as in a sense it does. But the Biblical approach is not for that reason to be branded as in itself disorderly, for in its own terms it is an orderly concern with truth. The Bible preserves and interprets the mixed texture of human experience, and thus finds it necessary to affirm apparent contradictions as common elements of the ultimate truth. We thus find paradoxical affirmations that free will and foreordination, mercy and justice, compassion and condemnation are all parts of a larger truth as to the relations between God and man. These affirmations, furthermore, are never philosophically reconciled to each other and are rarely if ever put in the form of universal "laws," but are preserved in intimate association with particular events, individual experiences, and special occasions. The movements of Biblical thought are through concrete images and symbols, intimately associated with human existence — which is to say that the Bible does not represent a philosophical or scientific but primarily a literary approach to truth.

But that, in turn, is not to say that the Bible can be understood apart from its religious and ethical concerns, for these concerns are integral to its literary intent and content. To read the Bible apart from these primary issues is not to read it at all, and is comparable to reading *Hamlet* without the prince. The religion and the poetry of the Bible are in fact inseparable. Our task here is to approach the Bible in its full literary dimension, divorcing ourselves temporarily from the urge to proselytize either for or against it. In this study, our purpose is not either to affirm or deny, but rather to understand.

# II. Characterization and Plot

To understand any literary work, it is necessary to know something at least about its forms and development, about what has been included in its text and what is outside its range of interests, subjects which we have been discussing up until this point. An even more basic issue concerns the work's overall unifying theme, for it is only in terms of this theme that its treatment of character, plot, and incident can be appropriately understood. The pervasive theme of the Bible is the interaction between individuals, societies, and God, and one of the pervasive purposes of the Bible is to derive out of these interactions a clarification of each of the constituent elements. Throughout it is assumed that man cannot understand himself apart from God and from his own society, nor can he understand society apart from God and the individual, and it is finally assumed that man by virtue both of human limitation and human greatness cannot understand God apart from himself and his society.

Of what I have called the three constituent elements, the dominant one is, of course, God. The characterization of God may indeed be said to be the central literary concern of the Bible, and it is pursued from beginning to end, for the principal character, or actor, or protagonist of the Bible is God. Not even the most seemingly insignificant action in the Bible can be understood apart from the emerging characterization of the deity. With this great protagonist and his designs, all other characters and events interact, as history becomes the great arena for God's characteristic and characterizing actions. The origin of this characterization is always understood to be God himself, for in the Biblical perspective it is only from God himself that an appropriate idea of God may arise.

The Biblical writers thus display a remarkable and persistent, though implicit, agnosticism: man left to himself can scarcely form a valid conception of God, though he can and does create idols. Scorn for man-made images of God is encountered throughout the Bible. To the Biblical writers, it seems axiomatic that if God is to be known by man, the initiative must come from God himself. And God's self-disclosure is never understood by the Biblical writers as providing an anatomical sketch or accurate portrait of God. God is above all human categories, and the use of anthropomorphic descriptions is not to provide men with a blueprint of the deity, but rather to help men to understand God in terms which men can assimilate. Thus, though God is described as having eyes to see with and arms to act with, the Bible strictly prohibits translating these figurative symbols into literal equivalents in a brazen image of God. Similarly, the description of God as "above" the earth, "in heaven," does not mean that God can be located on an astronomer's chart of the stellar spaces, or that heaven can. The point is that God does exist and that he exists beyond the reach of man. One cannot read these and other Biblical treatments of God without a lively recognition of the place and role of figurative and symbolic language.

The most useful understanding of God is provided, according to the Biblical writers, in God's various actions in history. By encountering individual men and human communities, God provides for his own characterization, and is his own characterizer. The very marked differences between the various human personalities to whom God discloses himself in the Bible provides for a universality of relevance. The great human characters of the Bible are almost all highly individualistic, and their individualism is not minimized by their encounters with God. Indeed, the expectation of everlasting life which can be found in the Bible is not at all concerned with the absorption of the soul of men into the soul of the divine, for the Biblical Heaven is not thought of as a Nirvana in which all individuality is lost, but as a community in which individual personalities are granted everlasting existence. The characterization of God is intimately related with the characterization of humanity, and that in turn concerns the establishment of the integrity of the individual human personality, which in its turn involves the righteousness of a community. All of this is rooted and grounded in God, whose developing self-disclosure and characterization supplies the unity of the Bible. Here again we would do well to note the comment of Martin Buber:

> *Biblia,* books, is the name of a book composed of many books. It is really one book, for one basic theme unites all the stories and songs, sayings and prophecies contained within it. The theme of the Bible is the encounter between a group of people and the Lord of the world in the course of history, the sequence of events occurring on earth.[5]

That the characterization of God should occur on earth, in the course of history, is a significant feature of the Bible. God is not known to man through any process by which man elevates himself above the earth and outside of time, but rather by a process of God's dramatic action in connection with man on the earth and in the context of time. We thus must return once more to the central fact that God is not defined in any philosophical or statemental sense, but is rather represented as being at work with men and communities. Furthermore, information about God is not the central issue: what counts is relationship with God. The Hebrew writers thus choose as the word to apply to man's "knowledge" of God a metaphorical adaptation of the word applied to the "knowledge" of a woman by her husband or of a husband by his wife. The context of the use of this metaphor, and the careful limits imposed upon it, clearly show that no fertility rites were involved. The words, used in this fashion, are not to be understood literally but rather metaphorically. The only valid knowledge of God on man's part is like the only valid knowledge of each other which a married couple has: it is "existential," not abstract. When this is understood we can see why it was possible, from very early times, for that magnificent poem of married love, the Song of Songs, to be interpreted allegorically as the story of the relationship between God and his people. Relationship, intimacy, actuality are the key factors.

[5] *The Writings of Martin Buber,* p. 239.

In the Bible, the self-disclosure of God the protagonist comes at the point where man is, and it is primarily developed through the course of man's existence in the theater of this world. However miraculous the entrances of the protagonist upon this stage may appear to be, and they are often dramatically miraculous, they do constitute entrances into the ordinary affairs of men. Thus God speaks to Moses as Moses is leading his flock near Horeb, he speaks to David in the course of ruling his people, and he speaks to the New Testament magi as they are about their business of observing the stars. The encounters of God and man, in which both are increasingly understood, come at work, in action, in the events of time, and the invitation is to look through these events to what lies both within and beyond them — to look, in short, at God and ourselves.

Two things must be said at this point about the literary characterization of a great protagonist. In the first place, if the character of the protagonist is more than flat and one-sided, that character cannot be altogether disclosed at the outset of the action, but can only be developed in the course of the action. We cannot, for example, fully understand Hamlet or King Lear as Shakespeare presents them merely in terms of the first acts of the dramas in which they appear. Neither can we understand the Biblical protagonist God only on the basis of the first (or the last) books of the Bible, for there is a considerable development of characterization from first to last. The parallel which I have suggested is, to be sure, only partially valid, but it should help us to recognize that our understanding of the protagonist becomes richer, fuller, and better rounded as the book develops its total vision from the merging of the various insights of saga, history, parable, law, song, prophecy, gospel, and epistle.

This brings us to the second observation which must be made: no matter how complete the characterization of a great protagonist may be, it cannot be expected to achieve a total consistency, or to provide a set of totally self-contained and self-explanatory insights in which contradictory traits and puzzling issues are eliminated entirely. Small characters may be quite predictable, quite easily and snugly pigeonholed, but great characters simply cannot be — witness Shakespeare's great heroes, for example. And what applies to the human heroes of Shakespeare must be allowed to apply with a multiple factor to the Biblical characterization of God. If there is forever an element of uncertainty about Hamlet, there must be a far greater sense of the numinous about God: if it were not so, the Biblical characterization would be ridiculous, and whether we regard it as true or false no sane man can regard it as ridiculous. As Albert Schweitzer has written, "the highest knowledge is to know that we are surrounded by mystery."[6] The Biblical characterization of God moves forward within an atmosphere mixed of mystery and clarity.

[6] *Christianity and the Religions of the World* (London: George Allen and Unwin, 1951), p. 80.

## Introduction

This characterization of God is integrally related to individual men and to human society. The knowledge of God as he exists *per se* holds very little if any interest for the Biblical writers: what matters is not what God is in himself but what he is towards men and what he expects of men.

God's disclosure of himself and of his demands is the great theme of the Bible: we may call it "the speech of God." But there is, parallel to this, a minor theme of "the silence of God," for God repeatedly declares that he will withdraw from men who have abandoned righteousness and justice in human society. By his very silence, by his refusal to communicate with men who actively support or passively condone evil practices in society, God announces his condemnation of men because of their relations within the community. This silence of God can be even more appalling than the thunder of the prophets, for so long as the prophets speak there is some communication between the people and God. But whether through prophecy or silence, the point is the same. Men are, to be sure, related directly to God as individuals, but this is not all: they are also related to God through each other and through human community. These two avenues of relationship are coordinate, and the first cannot function without the second.

It is for this reason that we find so much emphasis in the Bible upon the relationship between people. In the first books of the Bible, the so-called "Books of Moses," there is a careful attempt to provide for a just as well as a holy society. Some of the laws through which this concern is expressed may seem strange or even picayunish to us on first reading, but a little reflection will reveal their basic purpose. A sufficient number of these ancient laws are included in our selections so as to convey an impression of the scope of the Old Testament legal code. Rarely if ever has such a careful attempt been made to devise a system which would protect all elements of society, and not merely those who held power. The law, of course, was not able to guarantee a righteous nation, and the prophets came to supplement it with their powerful addresses. Both the law and the prophets, in differing ways, sought to achieve a relationship between men which was worthy of those who would be related faithfully with God. For the Biblical writers, religion was as much social and ethical as it was devotional. When Jesus spoke in the New Testament of the two great commandments, he was summarizing the Old Testament tradition of the law and the prophets: that men should love God with all their beings, and their neighbors as themselves.

This conjunction of concerns runs through the Bible from beginning to end. When Adam and Eve eat the fruit of knowledge, it is an explicit usurpation upon deity, as they attempt to "be as gods," assuming to themselves the determination of good and evil. Once that step has been taken, the murder of Abel by Cain follows inevitably, and what should be a garden of productive and harmonious relationships between men has been succeeded by a wilderness of violence and predation. Evil multiplies upon itself until the world as a whole is no longer worthy of preservation, and God condemns it in the flood. Here, though, the individual righteous man is preserved, and Noah is commissioned with his family to make a fresh start at a society of order and righteousness. But soon again man attempts to usurp upon the deity, the usurpation this time being expressed through building the tower of Babel which will reach up to heaven itself. Again the result of attempted self-deification leads to the alienation of men from each other, and the men who could communicate with each other on the basis of a common allegiance to God now find that they are unable to understand each other, as they are radically separated by the barrier of language. The sequence of events is obviously parabolic, intended to attribute the fragmentation of mankind into rival camps to the very fact of men's attempts to put themselves in the place of God.

As the early chapters of the Bible move more and more out of the realm of parable and into the realm of history, we see the continuing union of a concern for God, as the Bible characterizes God, and a concern for righteousness in human society. When Abraham is called, he is called as an individual, but his individual call is to found a nation through which all nations will be benefited. Even at the most chauvinistic moments in the establishment of the nation of Israel, there was a concern for "the stranger within the gates," and throughout the history of Israel there is presented the divine concern for justice and for mercy.

The most intensely individual characters in the Bible are always put into vital relation with their communities as well as with their God, for the consistent patterns of Biblical characterization indicate that personalities can be firmly grounded only in these terms. Thus Moses is not called to a solitary communion with God, but rather to the freeing and establishment of his people. His relationships to God and to the community are of course distinct, but they are never dissociated, and when he claims as his own prerogative that power to work wonders which has been delegated to him by God, he is incapacitated from leading into the land of promise the people whom he had already freed. With David, the next great leader of Israel, the relationship to community and to God are similarly close, but David's great sin is in usurping the place of a man while Moses' was in usurping the powers of God. When David becomes infatuated with Uriah's wife, Bathsheba, he does not hesitate to have Uriah placed where he will be killed in battle, and he proceeds to marry the woman whose chastity he had already violated. By this infringement of human rights and human integrity, David is incapacitated from building the temple just as Moses had earlier been incapacitated from leading the people into Canaan.

Both Moses and David stand out among the most clearly delineated characters in human history and literature. In the Bible they are painted, as Oliver Cromwell wanted himself painted, "warts and all."

But even more remarkable is the fact that in times when magic power and royal power were extravagantly honored, Moses was condemned for his misuse of the one and David for his abuse of the other. And these two men, we must remember, were the greatest heroes of Israel. The presentation of their faults and weaknesses and defeats is therefore all the more interesting, and it indicates from but another point of view the fact that in the Bible the real hero is not any man — no matter how heroic or noble — but rather the Lord God.

The development of the characterization of God as the protagonist of the Bible is cumulative. His character cannot be understood on the basis of any one book of the Bible, much less on the basis of an isolated verse or two. We see him first as the creator of the universe in the magnificent opening of Genesis, but here the universe is obviously only a backdrop against which the drama of man is to be played out. The initial panorama of humanity shows Everyman and Everywoman endowed with a harmonious existence in a garden, an existence which they can maintain by accepting the primacy of God. When they repudiate this primacy, chaos replaces harmony and they find themselves in a wilderness rather than a garden. God's first attempt to provide mankind with a good existence has failed, because man refused to accept it. The second attempt comes after the flood, and it too fails for essentially the same reason.

At this point God turns from attempting to create a righteous, harmonious, and peaceful order for all mankind, and begins to concentrate upon one race — the race of Abraham — and the Bible focuses upon the experience of this one people. The chosen people became a kind of laboratory school for the development of a conception of human personality and human society which may serve as a pattern to all of mankind. The dramatic movement then is this: a concern for all mankind is narrowed in focus — without losing its universal intent in the mind of God — to one segment of mankind, whose experiences and insights will later be used as a means of enlightening the entire human race as to the meaning and purpose of true humanity.

It is not that Israel achieves and maintains the ideal humanity, for it repeatedly falls short of doing so in a mixed pattern of failure and success. But out of these successes and failures there emerge standards which make possible a viable understanding of God, of the individual man, and of human society. The motley surface of human experience is evident throughout. It is a long way from the early Israelitish hatred of Moab to the assertion in the book of Ruth that the great King David himself was descended from a Moabite woman, just as there is a great distance from the psalmist's prayer that God would dash the little ones of his enemy against the rocks (Psalms 137:9) to the prayer of Jesus on the cross, "Father, forgive them; for they know not what they do" (Luke 23:34). Even within the same generation, there is an infinite distance separating the inhumanity of Ahab and Jezebel from the human concern of Elijah, or the arrogant luxuriousness of a Jehoiakim from the self-sacrifice of a Jeremiah. Throughout, however, as the Bible characterizes men and God in terms of their encounters with each other, there is the rising crescendo of a central theme and conviction about God and about humanity:

> He hath showed thee, O man, what is good;
> And what doth the Lord require of thee,
> But to do justly, and to love mercy,
> And to walk humbly with thy God? (Micah 6:8)

These themes are all present in the Old Testament, and many feel that they are sufficiently delineated there. When we come to the New Testament, however, we encounter a group of writers who are convinced that more needs to be said, and who declare that the Old Testament themes are both summarized and completed in the life and work of Jesus. It is clear that the New Testament writers regarded the work of Jesus in both particular and universal terms. Here, they believed, the particular tradition of Israel came to its climax and fruition, here the teachings of the law and the prophets were fulfilled. Beyond these particular terms, they also held that what happened in and through Jesus was of universal significance, affecting not only the Jewish race but all races of men. Particularity and universality are not, however, to be separated too severely, for the Old Testament repeatedly affirmed that the particular people Israel were to be a blessing to mankind universally. Jesus inherited this understanding from the past, just as he inherited Daniel's phrase describing the coming savior or messiah as the Son of Man, and the conception of Second Isaiah that the messiah should be a suffering servant.

In these and other ways Jesus and his disciples consciously carried on the central traditions of the Old Testament. Even at the point of their most radical breaks with the Judaic community of the first century A.D., the early Christians believed themselves to be merely testifying to the fulfillment by God's action of what had been carried on through the Old Testament period. In what they regarded as the unique and incomparable person of Jesus the Christ, they found the dramatic continuation and culmination of the whole former process of God's disclosure of himself, and of his will for individuals and communities. Thus, whether or not a person regards the New Testament as a valid religious culmination to the Old Testament (and honest men differ on this question), it does unmistakably maintain a literary and dramatic continuity with it.

We can see this literary continuity in the preservation of the pervasive Biblical emphasis on the characterization of God, of man, and of human community. The New Testament writers find these three elements brought to a final clarification in the person of Jesus Christ and the events of his life on earth. It is here, they hold, that men can find the fullest understanding of God. The God who had previously acted through history now enters directly into history to disclose his true character to man, so that man may have an immediate and assured experience of God, but without idolatry. This is not to say that everything about God is revealed to man in the person of Jesus Christ, for the New Testament never says that. Indeed, it is careful not to draw a simple equation between Jesus of Nazareth and God: in Christianity such an exclusive definition is heresy.

The New Testament writers clearly understood themselves to be dealing with a unique and unprecedented disclosure of God: Jesus Christ was undoubtedly human, and yet he was more than even the greatest human beings through whom God had spoken in the past — Abraham, Moses, David, the prophets. In view of all of this, Jesus was not only called the Christ, but also the Son of God and the Word of God made flesh. It was in him that the ultimate characterization of God for man took place. Henceforth, according to this conviction, men may find what God is like in the New Testament's graphic and dramatic presentation of Jesus Christ.

We have referred to the suspicion on the part of the Biblical writers of any abstract, philosophical definition of God: throughout, the Bible prefers to present the characterization of God in terms of actions and in terms of vivid figurative language. What the New Testament writers maintain is that such means have been ultimately dramatized in a single person, Jesus Christ. Though God is not to be defined in statemental forms, he has defined himself dramatically in and through Jesus Christ. It is this conviction which permeates and gives form to the various literary developments of the New Testament.

But, according to the New Testament, the other constituent elements of the Bible's concern — man and society — are also definitively characterized in the person of Jesus Christ. Of these, let us first consider the relevance of Christ for the characterization of man. Here we must remember that in the Christian tradition, the humanity of Christ has been asserted as strongly as the divinity. The first heresy to challenge the Christian Church held that Jesus was entirely divine, without any human nature at all, but this heresy was condemned quite early. The New Testament Christians persistently emphasized the human nature as well as the divinity of their Lord. In him as the incarnate Word of God, they saw a divine sanction for the kind of humanity which he displayed. In Jesus of Nazareth, then, they saw the ideal man, the man by whose pattern all humanity should be judged. In other words, they discovered in Jesus the characterization of man as he should be. Though other men could not attain this perfection of manliness, their humanity could be judged by its approximation to the master pattern in the person of Christ.

In the Bible, the individual is never dissociated from the community. Thus, once the character of God has been disclosed and once the ideal or archetypal pattern for the individual has been established, we may expect these to have direct relevance for the community, and this is just what we do find. In what the New Testament writers thought of as direct continuity with the "old Israel," a "new Israel" is established, a new community which is to reach beyond race and nation to embrace all men who accept the new understanding of God and man "in Christ." This new community is referred to as "the body of Christ," in a graphic metaphor expressing its ideal character: thus understood, human community is to be judged as to how well it expresses service and love, rather than the obvious worldly values of self-assertion, success, and power.

The New Testament says a great deal about this ideal for human community. The development of various New Testament individuals is quite exciting to observe, as they come to understand God, themselves, and human society in fresh and enfranchising ways. There is, however, no indication in the New Testament that anyone was able to "imitate" Christ perfectly, and there is repeated acknowledgment in the developing story of the New Testament church that it was far from representing in practice the ideal "body of Christ." What we find, then, is not the actual creation of a perfect new society of perfect men, but rather the striking response of a group of interesting and often highly individual persons to their expanding recognition of the significance of Jesus Christ.

In the New Testament, these responses and experiences are vividly recounted, but the story does not end there. Throughout the New Testament, there is a vision of the conclusion of all history. This vision is important not only for the future, but also for the present. What it says about the present is this: the career of Jesus Christ is the central watershed of human history; Christ himself is not a mere accident or statistically explainable product of the course of history, but is instead the central figure of all history, the keystone in the arch of God's design and man's destiny. When the world ends, all things present and past will be judged by their conformity to this supreme standard. At the point of this final judgment, there will be established a new future of unending duration. in which a new heaven and a new earth will be consummated according to God's design as expressed through Jesus Christ.

This confident expectation pervades the New Testament, and may be seen repeatedly in its various books. It reaches its final expression at the end of the last New Testament book, the Apocalypse, or Book of Revelation, in the passages with which this edition closes. Here we see the burning lake of perdition, a description which is drawn directly from the garbage pit in the Valley of Hinnom or Gehenna where the city of Jerusalem burned its refuse and useless waste. The symbolism is apt and easily understood: sin and evil will be as utterly destroyed as refuse. This, we are told, is "the second death." Then above the starkly described smoking dump in the valley is a great and high mountain — an obvious allusion to the Mount Zion where Jerusalem stood above the valley of Hinnom. But what appears now is not the old Jerusalem, with its many defections, but "the holy Jerusalem descending out of heaven from God." Continuity is observed in the relationships, but a radically new community is now called into being. Here in the final culmination, man and society are perfectly established in community with and under God. This perfection is conveyed through rich and luxuriant symbols of dimensions, design, and decoration. We are not much accustomed, in the twentieth century, to such symbolic opulence, and it may strike some readers at first as too "oriental" or even baroque, but it is utterly magnificent. The quality of its richness is set in sharp contrast — and I think purposely so — with the stark simplicity of the opening verses of the Bible. The purpose of the contrast is to indicate that here men will find completion in the most ultimate sense of which their imagination is now capable and of which their purified personalities will eventually become capable. With this vision of the establishment of faithful men within a community of the life everlasting under God, the Biblical epic comes to its incomparable close.

The movement from the beginning of Genesis to the end of Revelation is carried out with a clear sense of dramatic purpose. When understood within the total perspective of the Bible, human history is not a drama of the absurd, but a story with a plot: it has both direction and meaning. At times it may appear to participants and to observers to be a mystery story, but as in a well-constructed mystery the purpose and the plot are always there, even when concealed, and the Biblical writers find a key to the mystery in the unfolding purposes of God.

We have already seen how closely the Biblical writers associated the characterization of God the protagonist with the actions and events through which he chose to disclose himself. When considered in literary terms, this means that character and plot are intimately co-ordinated, and what was true of God also applied to man. The Biblical understanding of man closely connected what a man was with what he did. The modern dramatic poet Christopher Fry, in his play based upon the Exodus, has Moses wish "to do what I am" and say "I was born this action."[7] These words dramatize a major Biblical conception.

In the Bible, man's problems are not posed as arising out of the material world. "Matter" is not regarded as an obstacle or enemy, for it is a part of the created order and was pronounced to be good by God the creator. Man's difficulties do not arise out of the hostility of inanimate "things," but out of the operation of human choices in history. In literary terms, both man's successes and his failures may be seen as the interaction of character and plot, enacted against the background of divine purpose and meaning. This basic conception pervades the Bible: man's responsible choices in history are the heart of the matter — not the cycles of nature and the myths based in these cycles, nor abstractions arranged according to philosophical patterns.

 The phrase "man's responsible choices in history" does not imply that man can choose the challenges with which he will be faced, for his range of choice in that area is obviously limited on any count. What man can do is to choose his response to the conditions with

[7] *The Firstborn* (London: Oxford University Press, 1954), pp. 43, 42.

which he is faced in his existence. Not all of these choices involve clear-cut moral or religious decisions, but the character of mind which underlies the choice may nonetheless be religious and ethical, or the reverse, even when the alternatives for action are not of much apparent significance in themselves. In the earlier stages of Biblical history there seems to have been a greater tendency to see the alternatives for action largely in black and white terms, whereas in the New Testament there is considerably greater consciousness of shades of grey in the action and of the even more crucial importance of the interior attitudes which lead to making choices between possible actions. Whether seen in terms of the character of the action chosen, or the attitude underlying the choice, or more likely both, the Bible places primary emphasis upon man's response to the historical conditions and challenges which arise during the normal course of his existence. It is through these responses that a man is related to God, and the quality of his relation is controlled by the cumulative effect of his choices. When we consider the number of choices, large and small, of action or reaction or inaction which each person has to make in the course of one day, and that each of these choices involves the individual's relationship with God, then it becomes apparent with just how vast a significance the Bible invests ordinary life.

Under this view, nothing in life is meaningless: affliction, sickness, and failure are all significant, as are power, health, and success, whether on a great scale or a small. Even boredom takes on meaning, for one must respond to that, too. Everything that happens to a person represents an opportunity to serve or to repudiate God. History — as the succession of great and small events in time — thus assumes very great importance, for it is the realm in which individuals and societies relate themselves to God. Obviously, this understanding of life is intensely dramatic, and the Bible is constantly concerned with the movement of events in sequence, and the human response to these events. In literary terms, this means that the Bible is intensely concerned with plot and character. This concern is evident throughout: the prophets speak directly to historical events and challenges; the lyrics of the psalmists have clear relevance to the response of men to particular experiences; the writers of the New Testament epistles are advising men how to deal with actual problems in a godly way. In these literary forms, as well as in the narrative and historical books, we are never far removed from men responding to the challenges which come in the history of their own lives.

The Biblical literature thus focuses upon choice and action of many different kinds in many different contexts by many different characters — in short, there are many subplots within the larger plot of God's design — so that the Bible provides a sweeping panorama of man, a meaningful mosaic made up of particular events joined into a whole. Within the sweep of this whole, many diversities are recognized and many different interpretations remain possible. For example, what have been called "the everlasting antinomies" of God's omnipotent providence and man's responsible freedom of choice are not resolved in a way which would satisfy philosophical logic, and it is at least doubtful whether any solution is possible in such terms. What the Bible does provide is a literarily satisfactory correlation: man's will and God's purpose are coordinated upon the grid of dramatic action in history, as character interacts with character, and plot with character. Man makes his choices and is responsible for them, and yet at the same time God maintains a providential oversight and direction of events. These two emphases — somewhat like the physicist Heysenberg's two complementary assertions about the properties of light — are not subject to logical fusion, but exist together because both are regarded as inescapable parts of human experience. To the Biblical writers, who were very practical people, the only sensible approach to an insoluble paradox was to preserve both of its elements, in balance, and go on with the business of living.

It is with this business of living that the Biblical histories and stories are concerned, and the different units are brought together in such a way as to provide cumulative insight into man's nature and destiny. The various particular incidents are usually so related as to show a clear sense of plot, structure, and progression within themselves. In the early chapters of Genesis, for example, the repudiation by Adam and Eve of a divinely established order of the knowledge of good and evil leads directly and with dramatic logic to the dissension between Cain and Abel, and eventuates in Cain's murder of Abel as Cain assumes to himself the role of sole arbiter of good and evil. In other instances, different stories follow each other in the Bible without such an integral relation, but display rather the random qualities of sequence apparent in everyday life. But however the particular incidents may be related to each other, all are related to a larger unity of design: the unfolding purpose of God for men and societies. This is the epic theme of the Bible, to which all the episodes are related, just as in the *Iliad* all episodes are unified about the siege of Troy.

Of the different episodes which make up the Bible, each contributes something to the total purpose and design, without losing its particularity in the process. Particular and universal are related in the Bible according to a literary pattern which is distinctively poetic and essentially non-allegorical. Goethe has something to say about this relationship which, though Goethe was not directing his remark to the Scriptures, directly applies to the technique of the Biblical writers:

> It matters a great deal whether the poet is seeking the particular for the universal, or seeing the universal in the particular. The former process gives rise to allegory, in which the particular serves only as an instance or example of the universal; the latter, on the other hand, is the true nature of poetry: it gives expression to the particular without in any way thinking of, or referring to, the

universal. He who vividly grasps the particular will at the same time grasp the universal. . . .[8]

That is the nature of the Biblical treatment of history and of story, and according to Goethe it is also "the true nature of poetry." In the Bible, the real and the imaginary experiences of an ancient people are written with such power and skill that they will always seem relevant to modern men, no matter what may be the time or setting of their modernity. In the Bible, the particular becomes recognized as universal through a transformation which is one of the marks of great literature. The convictions of the Bible, to be sure, are the convictions of religion and ethics, but the methods are the methods of literature. On a literary analysis alone, the Bible is one of a relative small number of very great books. If, in addition, its central religious convictions are regarded as valid, then it is incomparably the greatest single literary possession of the human race. On either count, it is eminently worth the careful reading which students are invited to give it here, within a literary context.

Such a reading should result in the broadening of understanding, of humane sympathy, and of insight, the sharpening of standards of choice and action, rather than any mere accumulation of clichés and platitudes. It should not consist so much in the amassing of information as in the development of wisdom so that men and actions and events may be seen in perspective and evaluated. What the Bible, considered as literature, conveys, is transmitted experience, or perhaps it would be better to say vicarious experience. When the Bible is perceptively read, the reader stands somewhere between being a spectator and being a participant; in short, the reader becomes involved with the action and the words. When a society has been schooled in this way, as our society has been schooled in the Bible or as Greek society was schooled in Homer, it has available to it a vast range of intelligible common references, an available reservoir of values, allusions, and understood forms. In this way the dignifying and ennobling influence of great literary conceptions enters into the intimate consciousness of a culture.

# III. The Bible in English

According to Hugh Blair, the great eighteenth-century literary critic, "the style of the poetical books of the Old Testament is, beyond the style of all other poetical works, fervid, bold, and animated." That sentence superbly characterizes the literary quality of that period in England which produced Shakespeare, Spenser, Donne, and the King

[8] "Reflections and Maxims," trans. W. B. Rönnfeldt, in *Great Writings of Goethe*, ed. Stephen Spender (New York: New American Library, 1958), pp. 274–75.

James Version of the Bible. No other age in the history of English or American literature has been so admirably suited to reproducing the tone of the Biblical literature in appropriate English. The Augustan period, for example, lacked the spontaneity, the aggressiveness of spirit: its conception of regular and correct expression could scarcely have done justice to the verve and direct involvement of the Jewish writers. The Romantics could, and did, appreciate the Bible both in the original and in the Authorized Version, but Romanticism lacked the sense of the austere, the controlled majesty which was so important in the Biblical materials. The literature of our own time moves usually on a different plane, and though it can sound many of the depths of human existence, it rarely manages to reach the heights of the human spirit and has been singularly lacking in its ability to convey awe, reverence, and mystery. Of all the periods in our literary history, only the English Renaissance contained within itself so full an appreciation of literary style and expression as to allow its translators and editors to do full justice to the tone as well as the meaning of the Bible.

The structural character of Hebrew poetry is particularly suited to translation. For poetry such as our own which relies heavily on meter and rhyme, the problems of reproducing the poetic structure in a different language are immense and perhaps even insuperable. Translators of such poetry find it impossible to reproduce meaning, rhyme, and meter: almost always, one or more important elements must be sacrificed. Of course, something must be sacrificed in all translation, for as there are no perfect and complete synonyms within a single language, so there are even less adequate synonyms between languages. But the basic formal principle of Hebrew literature is far better suited to translation than that of almost any other literature, for Hebrew poetry is structured on parallel thoughts in successive lines or half lines, so that thought and form itself are in fact one. This poetic method is known as parallelism of members.

Psalm 24 is a fine example of this poetic system, in which a succession of carefully constructed parallels beautifully conveys the development of the psalmist's sense. In the opening verses of the psalm, we see the exaltation of God set forth in parallel phrases and followed by parallel questions which involve man's relationship with God:

> The earth is the Lord's, and the fulness thereof;
> The world, and they that dwell therein.
> For he hath founded it upon the seas,
> And established it upon the floods.
> Who shall ascend into the hill of the Lord?
> Or who shall stand in his holy place?

Here we begin with the exaltation of God in the earth and among his creatures, and move to a question involving man's place before God. The central use of the question as a device is significant and representative, for no literature with which I am familiar employs questions so frequently and so pivotally as does the literature of the Bible. The answer to the question moves us into the central portion of the psalm:

> He that hath clean hands, and a pure heart;
> Who hath not lifted up his soul unto vanity,
> Nor sworn deceitfully,
> He shall receive the blessing from the Lord,
> And righteousness from the God of his salvation.

Advancing still by the movement of corresponding ideas, the psalmist clarifies the character of the just individual, and then moves into the character of the righteous community, the ideal Israel or Jacob:

> This is the generation of them that seek him,
> That seek thy face, O Jacob.

Seeking God and seeking a righteous community (here personified as Jacob, after the name of the founding patriarch) are not equated but are inseparably related by the parallel structure. It is on the basis of this relationship that the Lord God may be expected to come to the community which seeks the divine and which also pursues human righteousness. God is thus expected to enter into Jerusalem, and even the gates are commanded to prepare for him, as the righteousness of the people becomes the gate for God's entrance:

> Lift up your heads, O ye gates;
> And be ye lifted up, ye everlasting doors;
> And the King of glory shall come in.

What follows now employs not merely parallelism, but the interlocking of parallels and the repetition of former phrases:

> Who is this King of glory?
> The Lord strong and mighty,
> The Lord mighty in battle.
> Lift up your heads, O ye gates;
> Even lift them up, ye everlasting doors,
> And the King of glory shall come in.
> Who is this King of glory?
> The Lord of hosts,
> He is the King of glory.

As the basis of Biblical poetic form, parallelism of members is capable of an almost infinite variation in use, complexity, and effect. It also makes possible translations of Hebrew poetry which are characterized at once by beauty of English form and essential faithfulness to the original. "The effect of Hebrew poetry can be preserved and transferred in a foreign language as the effect of other great poetry cannot," Matthew Arnold wrote, for it "is a poetry, as is well known, of parallelism; it depends not on meter and rhyme but on a balance of thought, conveyed by a corresponding balance of sentence; and the effect of this can be transferred to another language."[9]

Another striking characteristic of Biblical literature which facilitates translation is the concreteness of its imagery and allusion. We are rarely dealing with abstractions and abstract nouns, which are so nearly impossible to translate from one language to another, for the Biblical writers persistently define, illustrate, and present their message through the most concrete symbols. The Biblical themes, even when unique in meaning, are expressed through universally relevant and understandable means. For a Greek, God might be a vast, noble, and impersonal abstraction, but for the Jew he was intimately personal — a father caring for his children, or a husband for his wife, or a shepherd for his sheep. Faithful men are not described as well-adjusted or mature, but are said to feast at a table prepared for them by God in the presence of their enemies, and are pictured as drinking from a cup which runs over. The symbols of the Bible are simple and universal symbols, such as men and women everywhere can understand: food and drink, hunger and thirst, love and hatred, pilgrimage towards a goal or aimless wandering, light and darkness, laughter and tears, birth and death, and myriads of others in fascinating and meaningful combinations.

These symbols are as intelligible in English as they were in Hebrew and Greek. Coleridge, who was among the finest poets and was the finest literary critic produced in England, declared that "after reading Isaiah, or St. Paul's Epistle to the Hebrews, Homer and Virgil are disgustingly tame to me, and Milton himself barely tolerable."[10] It is the great good fortune of English-speaking people to have an English version of the Bible which stands with the original in literary power and excellence. Sir Arthur Quiller-Couch, editor of Shakespeare and of the Oxford Books of Verse, judged that the Authorized or King James Version of the Bible was the greatest literary achievement in the English language, with the possible exception of Shakespeare, and that it had influenced our literature "far more deeply" even than Shakespeare.[11] Discussing qualities of style, Matthew Arnold wrote that there is "one English book, and one only where, as in the *Iliad* itself, perfect plainness of speech is allied with perfect nobleness, and that book is the Bible."[12]

The history of the English Bible, honored as it is for style as well as for content, is both interesting and significant. The King James Version, presented here, bears the name of the English sovereign who in 1604 authorized work to begin on an improved and "perfected" Eng-

[9] *Isaiah of Jerusalem* (London: Macmillan and Company, 1883), p. 4.

[10] Quoted in *In Praise of the Bible*, ed. Geoffrey Murray (London: Frederick Muller, 1955), p. 38.

[11] "On Reading the Bible," in *The English Bible: Essays by Various Writers* (London: Methuen and Company, 1938), p. 101.

[12] *On the Study of Celtic Literature and On Translating Homer* (London: Macmillan and Company, 1903), pp. 239–40.

lish Bible. Under the King's authorization, the work was divided among forty-seven of the leading Biblical scholars of the time, who were formed into panels or committees, three for the Old Testament, two for the New, and one for the Apocrypha. The work of these separate committees was then submitted to a twelve-man committee of the whole, made up of two men drawn from each of the panels. These men reviewed the entire work before its appearance in print in 1611. They did not, however, attempt to achieve an absolute uniformity of translation, as we can see in the treatment of Old Testament proper names in the New Testament, for example. Thus the Hebrew prophet who appears in the Old Testament under the name "Elijah" is referred to in the New Testament as "Elias," and even greater confusion occurs when Moses' successor Joshua is referred to as "Jesus" in the translation of Stephen's sermon at Acts 7:45. While the original names could justifiably be Anglicized in either of these ways, the confusion arises from the failure to hold consistently to one form. There are remarkably few instances of confusion of this kind, however, when we consider the scope of the work and the number of men engaged upon it.

King James' committee of "learned men" did not regard their task as the creation of a new translation, nor did they claim to have introduced a new translation. The tradition of English Bibles upon which they drew extended back to William Tyndale, whose English New Testament appeared in its first version in 1526. In the succeeding three-quarters of a century a considerable number of Bibles appeared in English. Tyndale himself carefully revised his New Testament before his final version appeared in 1535, and produced as well a translation of the Pentateuch and of Jonah. After his death there appeared a translation of the Old Testament historical books from Joshua to Second Chronicles which most scholars attribute to him. His work as the greatest English translator of the Bible came to an end in 1535 when he was betrayed into the hands of the Inquisition by a friend, and he was executed in 1536.

After Tyndale's arrest, the translation of the Old Testament was completed by Miles Coverdale. Relying heavily on the version of those Biblical books which Tyndale had been able to complete, Coverdale in 1535 brought forth on the continent the first English rendering of the complete Bible. Coverdale was not of the same stature as Tyndale in learning, but he ranks directly after him in influencing the development of the English Bible. Whereas Tyndale had worked from the original Hebrew and Greek, though also consulting the Latin of Erasmus and the Vulgate along with the German of Luther, Miles Coverdale translated from the Vulgate and the recent Latin translation of the Dominican Father Pagninus, as well as from the German versions of Luther and of Zwingli. Coverdale's work has distinctive stylistic qualities of its own, of course, but he did follow the general tone of elegant simplicity established by Tyndale. Between these two pioneers, the noble style of the English Bible was firmly established.

Neither Tyndale's translations nor Coverdale's had been properly licensed for printing in England either by church authority or by the royal approval of King Henry VIII. The first English Bible to appear under royal permission was the so-called Matthew Bible, printed in 1537. The "Thomas Matthew" whose name appeared on the title page of this Bible appears actually to have been Tyndale's former associate, John Rogers, who for this volume merged the translations of Tyndale and of Coverdale. The use of the pseudonym seems to have made it possible for King Henry now to permit the appearance of those Biblical translations which had formerly appeared without his authorization and even in defiance of his government's prohibition.

The Matthew Bible was published with notes, explanations, and certain phrases in the text itself which some conservative readers found offensive, and so the authorities decided to have it revised. The revision began in the spring of 1538 and was entrusted to Miles Coverdale himself, now granted both royal and ecclesiastical favor. Coverdale revised the text with some thoroughness, but still in basic reliance upon his own translations and those of Tyndale. The result was called the Great Bible because of its size. It appeared first in 1539, and went through a number of editions. From 1540 onwards it carried a preface by Archbishop Thomas Cranmer, and is therefore sometimes known as Cranmer's Bible.

The next major version of the English Bible was undertaken by a group of scholarly English refugees who had fled from Queen Mary's England to Geneva. The Geneva Version was to become the most popular version in Elizabethan England, and was the version which Shakespeare principally knew. It went through over a hundred editions in its various forms from the appearance of the New Testament in 1557, and of the whole Bible in 1560 to the end of Elizabeth's reign in 1603. Its scholarly excellence was acknowledged even among those who disagreed with the Calvinist theology of its marginal notes and explanations.

The marginal comments of the Geneva Version made it too partisan for official use in the Church of England services, though its high quality at the same time rendered the Great Bible obsolete. Hence in 1561 Elizabeth's Archbishop of Canterbury, Matthew Parker, led a number of his bishops in revising the Great Bible. The resulting Bible, known as the Bishops' Bible, appeared in 1568, and was further revised in an edition of 1572. Though never officially recognized by the Queen, this Bible was appointed for official use by the Convocation of Canterbury in 1571 and continued in such use until the appearance of the King James Version of 1611. It was not able, however, to displace the Geneva Version in popular favor and as time passed there was increasing demand for a new version which could attain more nearly universal use.

This need was not met until the appearance in 1611 of the King James Version, but meanwhile another significant development was taking place among English Roman Catholic refugees on the continent.

## Introduction

As the Geneva Version had been produced by Protestants living in exile from the Roman Catholic Queen Mary, so a Roman Catholic translation was prepared by Father Gregory Martin who was living in exile from the Protestant Queen Elizabeth. Martin had completed his English translation of both Testaments by 1582, but though his New Testament appeared in that year, his complete English Bible was not published until 1609–10. The work was carried out at the English College founded on the continent by Cardinal William Allen for the preservation of English Roman Catholicism. As the College was located in Rheims when the New Testament appeared and at Douai when the Old Testament was issued, the translation is generally known as the Rheims-Douai. It was based on the Latin Vulgate as the officially accepted text of the Bible for Roman Catholics, and represented an original translation which stands apart from all the versions thus far discussed. Martin's translation did, however, occasionally contribute important readings to the King James Version, and so has a place in this account. After Martin's completion of his translation, there was no significant development in English Biblical translation until after the death of Elizabeth I and the accession of James I in 1603.

Early in 1604 a group of churchmen representing various shades of theological opinion within the Church of England met with King James at Hampton Court, and in the course of the conference considered Dr. John Reynolds' proposal that a new version of the English Bible be prepared. The proposal met with James' hearty approval, for he found the explanatory notes of the popular Geneva Version "seditious and savoring too much of dangerous and traitorous conceits," and yet was aware of the drawbacks of the Bishops' Bible. It was thus determined that a new version should be prepared "of the whole Bible, as consonant as can be to the original Hebrew and Greek, and this to be set out and printed without any marginal notes."[13]

It was to this task that the forty-seven leading scholars, to whom we have already referred, devoted themselves. Their basic method was to work both with the Biblical texts in the original languages and with the existing English versions, principally traceable to Tyndale and Coverdale; to select the best readings; and, where necessary, to introduce new readings which seemed preferable to those already existing. To think of them as original translators of the Hebrew and Greek is quite false, and to expect that as a large committee working through various subcommittees they could produce a great work of art belies not only the facts of the case but also common sense. No committee has ever by itself *created* a great work of art. What they did was to *perfect* a great work of art.

To say this is to clarify, not diminish, their achievement. They were not only men of learning, but also men of rare taste and discernment.

---

[13] F. F. Bruce, *The English Bible: A History of Translations* (New York: Oxford University Press, 1961), pp. 96–97.

As such they were able to bring out of the basic work of Tyndale and Coverdale — along with the improvements which had already been made upon that work by later versions, and also in honest consultation with the independent Roman Catholic translation — a version which was superior to anything that had yet appeared in English. Of their own work the King James translators declared that "we never thought from the beginning that we should need to make a new translation, nor yet to make of a bad one a good one; . . . but to make a good one better, or out of many good ones one principal good one, not justly to be excepted against; that hath been our endeavor, that our mark."[14]

We may get a clearer impression of the development of the English Bible if we turn now from this brief and generalized account and examine certain specific passages as they appeared in the principal versions which we have been considering. There were, of course, other English translations both prior to and after Tyndale and Coverdale, but we are concerned here only with the major work leading up to the King James Version. The following tables will allow a comparison of well-known verses in these different renditions. To the left of each verse there is an identifying mark, "T" standing for Tyndale, "C" for Coverdale, "M" for Matthew, "Gr" for Great Bible, "Ge" for Geneva Bible, "B¹" for Bishops' Bible of 1568, "B²" for Bishops' Bible of 1572, and "B³" for the Bishops' Bible of 1602, "R-D" for Rheims-Douai, and "KJV" for the King James Version.

### *Psalms 23:1–2a*

C. The Lord is my shepherd, I can want nothing. He feedeth me in a green pasture,

M. The Lord is my shepherd, I can want nothing. He feedeth me in a green pasture,

Gr. The Lord is my shepherd, therefore can I lack nothing. He shall feed me in a green pasture,

Ge. The Lord is my shepherd, I shall not want. He maketh me to rest in green pasture,

B¹. God is my sheepherd, therefore I can lack nothing: He will cause me to repose myself in pasture full of grass,

R-D. Our Lord ruleth me, and nothing shall be wanting to me: in place of pasture there he hath placed me,

KJV. The Lord is my shepherd, I shall not want. He maketh me to lie down in green pastures:

The base in the King James Version lies in Coverdale and Geneva, but a very great improvement is made by substituting "to lie down" for "to rest" and by introducing the plural "green pastures." The treatments of the next verse and a half of the same Psalm are also instructive.

[14] *Ibid.*, p. 101.

## *Psalms 23:2b–3a*

C. and leadeth me to a fresh water. He quickeneth my soul,

M. and leadeth me to a fresh water. He quickeneth my soul,

Gr. and lead me forth beside the waters of comfort. He shall convert my soul,

Ge. and leadeth me by the still waters. He restoreth my soul.

B¹. and he will lead me unto calm waters. He will convert my soul.

R-D. Upon the water of reflection he hath brought me up, he hath converted my soul.

KJV. He leadeth me beside the still waters. He restoreth my soul:

Here the Authorized Version has adopted the reading of Geneva, but with one very telling change: the connective "and" is dropped, and "He" is substituted, thus providing a considerably more forceful expression.

Let us now take a descriptive passage and note its development through the principal versions. The passage is from Luke's account of the nativity.

## *Luke 2:8*

T. And there were in the same region shepherds abiding in the field and watching their flock by night.

Gr. And there were in the same region shepherds, watching and keeping their flock by night.

Ge. And there were in the same country shepherds, abiding in the field, and keeping watch by night because of the flock.

B³. There were in the same country shepherds abiding in the field, keeping watch over their flock by night.

R-D. And there were in the same country shepherds watching, and keeping the night watches over their flock.

KJV. And there were in the same country shepherds abiding in the field, keeping watch over their flock by night.

Here the 1611 editors simply took over the Bishops' wording. A few verses later comes the song of the angels.

## *Luke 2:14*

T. Glory to God on high, and peace on earth: and unto men rejoicing.

C. Glory be unto God on high, and peace upon earth, and unto men a good will.

M. Glory to God on high, and peace on earth, and unto men rejoicing.

Gr. Glory to God on high, and peace on earth, and unto men a good will.

Ge. Glory be to God in the high heavens, and peace in earth, and towards men good will.

B¹. Glory be to God on high, and peace on the earth, and unto men a good will.

B². Glory to God in the highest, and peace on earth, and among men a good will.

R-D. Glory in the highest to God, and in earth peace to men of good will.

KJV. Glory to God in the highest, and on earth peace, good will towards men.

There is some difference of meaning between several of the translations of the final phrase here, and none of these versions quite captures what modern scholars regard as the meaning of the Greek text — that peace is granted among men with whom God is well pleased. But this advance in understanding is due to the advances which have taken place in the knowledge of New Testament Greek in the course of several centuries of study. Having taken this fact into account, we can still see the consummate literary taste which led to the final wording and (no less important) order of words in the King James rendering. Here the editors took the initial phrase from the second editions of Bishops', followed the second phrase of Rheims-Douai with very slight variation, and inverted Geneva's rendering of the final phrase. At other times our editors would simply take the best single rendering of a passage, and follow it with little or no change, as we have seen with the description of the shepherds and as with the opening words of the Lord's Prayer shown below.

## *Matthew 6:9b–10a*

T. O, our father which art in heaven, hallowed be thy name. Let thy kingdom come.

Gr. Our father, which art in heaven, hallowed be thy name. Let thy kingdom come.

Ge. Our father which art in heaven, hallowed be thy name. Thy kingdom come.

B³. Our father which art in heaven, hallowed be thy name. Let thy kingdom come.

R-D. Our father which art in heaven, sanctified be thy name. Let thy kingdom come.

KJV. Our father which art in heaven, hallowed be thy name. Thy kingdom come.

Here the Authorized Version has merely incorporated Geneva, while Geneva had in turn but slightly modified Tyndale. Let us turn next to one of the most famous passages from the Epistles, and examine the treatment of Paul's definition of charity.

## First Corinthians 13:4–5a

T. Love suffereth long, and is courteous. . . . Love doth not frowardly, swelleth not.

C. Love is patient and courteous. . . . Love doth not frowardly,
is not puffed up.

M. Love suffereth long, and is courteous. . . . Love doth not frowardly, swelleth not.

Gr. Love suffereth long, and is courteous. . . . Love doth not frowardly, swelleth not.

Ge. Love suffereth long, and is bountiful. . . . Love doth not boast
itself; it is not puffed up.

B¹. Love suffereth long, and is courteous. . . . Love doth not frowardly, swelleth not.

B². Charity suffereth long, and is courteous. . . . Charity doth not
frowardly, swelleth not.

R-D. Charity is patient, is benign; . . . dealeth not perversely, is not
puffed up.

KJV. Charity suffereth long and is kind . . . charity vaunteth not
itself, is not puffed up.

A number of comments are in order here. In the first place, the substitution of "charity" for "love" resulted from a growing recognition
that the English word "love," with its vast ambiguities, was not a
suitable vehicle for conveying the sense of the Greek *agape*, and so
the translators returned to using an Anglicized form of the Vulgate's
word *caritas*. In this, the King James Version followed its two immediate predecessors. Beyond this point, however, we see two quite
original translations — "is kind" and "vaunteth not itself" — which
are less stilted, more simple, and more graphic than the previously used
words.

The selections which we have been studying here were chosen to
illustrate the process by which the Authorized Version was developed.
That process, as the forty-seven editors themselves affirmed, was more
a matter of choosing from available riches than of creating something
absolutely original. At every point, of course, they acknowledged their
responsibility, whether for introducing new translations or relying on
the translations of others, and we must also acknowledge not only the
good taste but the good scholarship which lay behind their work. That
a precise accuracy must be denied to the Authorized Version at certain
points does not reflect unfavorably upon the editors and their predecessors so much as it reflects favorably upon the development of the
knowledge of the original languages and advances in discovery and
reconstruction of earlier texts which have come since their time. The
work of King James' editors has certainly been surpassed in accuracy
by a number of modern translations, though not to such an extent as
to impugn the essential and overall validity of their work. Nor can any

more recent translation be said to equal or even approach the literary stature of their achievement. Their achievement, and that of their predecessors, was to impart to the English Bible what Longinus had found in Genesis: the highest quality of sublimity. Indeed, whatever flaws we may find in it, the King James Version is pervasively marked by what Aristotle called "the perfection of style," which is "to be clear without being mean."[15]

[15] *The Art of Poetry,* trans. Lane Cooper (Ithaca: Cornell University Press, 1947), p. 71 (22.1).

# Suggestions for Further Reading

## I. Commentaries, Background Works, and Reference Books

The most popular of the recent commentaries is *The Interpreter's Bible*, edited by George A. Buttrick, Nolan B. Harmon, and others (12 vols., 1952–57). Though this commentary too often lacks literary sensitivity and discernment, it contains a wealth of scholarly information. A *Catholic Commentary on Holy Scripture*, edited by B. Orchard, E. F. Sutcliffe and others (1953), should also be noted, along with the *Soncino Books of the Bible* prepared by a number of Jewish scholars. The *Moffatt New Testament Commentary*, in several volumes, contains a number of helpful studies. The publication of the multivolume *Anchor Bible* was launched in 1965 under the general editorship of William F. Albright and David N. Freedman with a distinguished interfaith board of editors and translators for the various books of the Bible; this edition promises to be an indispensable aid to all serious students. Recently completed is the series known as *The Layman's Bible Commentary*, designed for the use of Protestant laymen rather than professional theologians. *The Abington Bible Commentary* (1942) is a well-known one-volume work.

*The Bible in the Church* by R. M. Grant (1948) traces the history of Biblical influence and interpretation within the church, while two other books supplement this study in terms of modern thought and scholarship: A. M. Hunter's *Interpreting the New Testament: 1900–1950* (1951) and J. D. Smart's *The Interpretation of Scripture* (1960).

The best among the readily available atlases of the Bible are probably the *Westminster Historical Atlas to the Bible* by G. E. Wright and F. V. Filson (1945), and *Atlas of the Bible* by L. H. Grollenberg (1956). Several fascinating and reliable archaeological studies are available, including *What Mean These Stones* by Millar Burroughs (1941), *Light from the Ancient Past* by Jack Finegan (1946), *Biblical Archaeology* by G. Ernest Wright (1957), and the exciting reports of the great Jewish archaeologist Nelson Glueck: *The River Jordan* (1941) and *Rivers in the Desert* (1959). For the history of ideas and institutions relevant to the Bible, the reader should study W. F. Albright's *From Stone Age to Christianity: Monotheism and the Historical Process* (1940). For those interested in comparing Biblical with other contemporary writings of the Near East, there is J. B. Pritchard's *Ancient Near Eastern Texts Relating to the Old Testament*

(1950). For the relation between the Bible and the Dead Sea Scrolls, two studies by Millar Burroughs are especially recommended: *The Dead Sea Scrolls* (1955) and *More Light on the Dead Sea Scrolls* (1958). A shorter, but also reliable, treatment is *The Ancient Library of Qumran* by Frank M. Cross, Jr. (1958).

Under the editorship of James Hastings, a number of now slightly dated but still quite useful dictionaries and encyclopedias were compiled: *Dictionary of the Bible* (1898) in one volume; *Dictionary of the Bible* (5 vols., 1898–1904); *Dictionary of Christ and the Gospels* (2 vols., 1906–8); and *Encyclopedia of Religion and Ethics* (13 vols., 1908–26). The most recent encyclopedic work is *The Interpreter's Dictionary of the Bible*, edited by George A. Buttrick (4 vols., 1962). Alan Richardson's *Theological Word Book of the Bible* (1950) is helpful in its field, as are William Barclay's two small volumes *A New Testament Wordbook* and *More New Testament Words* (1958). Various translations into English are also available from Gerhard Kittel's *Theological Wordbook of the New Testament*, while valuable insight may be gained from Singer's *The Jewish Encyclopedia* (12 vols., 1901–6) and from *The Catholic Encyclopedia*, edited by C. G. Herbermann and others (15 vols., 1907–14). *The Westminster Dictionary of the Bible* (1944) and *Harper's Bible Dictionary* (1952) are useful one-volume works.

James Strong's *Exhaustive Concordance of the Bible* (1894) is the most comprehensive single concordance of the Authorized or King James Version. For those who are interested in comparing this version with the Revised Standard Version, there is the *Complete Concordance of the Revised Standard Version of the Bible* (1957), which was compiled by electronic computer and published within five years of the Revised Standard Version itself.

## II. THE ENGLISH VERSIONS

There are a number of useful reprints of the early English translations of the Bible. F. Fry's *The First New Testament Printed in the English Language* (1862) and A. W. Pollard's *The Beginning of the New Testament translated by William Tyndale* (1926) both deal with Tyndale's 1525 New Testament, while N. H. Wallis edited Tyndale's 1534 New Testament with the original prefaces and notes and the variants of the 1525 edition (1938). *William Tyndale's Pentateuch* was edited by J. I. Mombert (1884), while for Coverdale's work there is *Miles Coverdale, Biblia 1535* (1838). A. W. Pollard (1911) brought out an exact reprint of the 1611 King James Version. *The New Testament Hexapla* (1841) presents six translations in parallel columns (the medieval Wycliffe-Purvey, the 1534 Tyndale, the Great Bible of 1539, the Geneva Version of 1557, the Rheims, and the King James Version). A more recent effort along similar lines is *The New Testament Octapla*, edited by L. Weigle (1962), which contains eight versions in parallel columns (Tyndale, Great Bible, Geneva, Bishops', Rheims, King James, American Standard, and Revised Standard). The latter two volumes together greatly facilitate a comparative study of Biblical translations. It is regrettable that no similar parallel text editions have been prepared of various Old Testament translations.

C. C. Butterworth's *The Literary Lineage of the King James Bible: 1340–1611* (1941) and F. H. A. Scrivener's *The Authorized Version, Its Subsequent Reprints and Modern Representatives* (1884) together cover the background, development, and subsequent changes of the King James Version. Of many histories of English versions of the Bible, three will be mentioned here: *The English Bible* by F. F. Bruce (1961) and *The English New Testament from Tyndale to the Revised Standard Version* by L. A. Weigle (1949) are fairly extensive treatments by recognized Biblical scholars, while *The English Bible* by Sir Herbert Grierson (1947) is a briefer survey by a well-known authority on English literature. A. W. Pollard's *Records of the English Bible* (1911) should also be mentioned, while J. F. Mozley has separate studies of the two formative translators, *William Tyndale* (1937) and *Coverdale and His Bibles* (1953). A fine general study, made up of various essays by different authorities, is *The Cambridge History of the Bible: The West from the Reformation to the Present Day*, edited by S. L. Greenslade (1963). Of special interest is the work of David Daiches, well described in its title: *The King James Version of the Bible: An Account of the Development and Sources of the English Bible of 1611 with Special Reference to the Hebrew Tradition* (1941). Valuable studies from the Roman Catholic point of view are *On Englishing the Bible* by R. Knox (1949) and *English Versions of the Bible* by H. Pope, revised by Sebastian Bullough (1952). In this connection, see also *The Part of Rheims in the Making of the English Bible* by J. G. Carleton (1902).

III. INFLUENCE OF THE BIBLE ON ENGLISH LITERATURE

A remarkable renascence of Biblical drama has taken place in our own time. Christopher Frye's *The Firstborn* (1946) concerns Moses and the Exodus from Egypt, while Archibald MacLeish's *J.B.* (1956) is a contemporary treatment of the Job situation, and Clifford Odets makes similar use of the story of Noah and his family in *The Flowering Peach* (1954). Paddy Chayefsky in his *Gideon* (1962) develops the relations between the Old Testament hero and Jehovah in terms of a fairly secular version of modern Judaism, while Jonah's story is wittily recreated in *It Should Happen to a Dog* (1956) by Wolf Mankowitz. Marc Connelly's *The Green Pastures* (1929) combines simplicity with subtlety in a play which incorporates many Biblical themes, and George Bernard Shaw's *Back to Methuselah* (1922) constitutes a Shavian rewriting of the Bible. Two volumes edited by

Marvin Halverson in the *Religious Drama* series (1957–59) contain modern morality, Biblical, and other religiously oriented plays, including works by Auden, Fry, Sayers, Mankowitz, Williams, and Lagerkvist. Notable in modern fiction, too, is Thomas Mann's group of four novels entitled *Joseph and His Brothers* (1934–44).

The Middle Ages were especially productive of Biblical drama, much of which is readily available in print today. See, for example, *Religious Drama II: Twenty-one Mystery and Morality Plays*, edited by E. Martin Browne (1958), *Everyman and Medieval Miracle Plays*, edited by A. C. Cawley (1959), as well as the collection in Everyman's Library. For the relevant Old English literature, only one modern English rendering can be heartily recommended, and this is Charles W. Kennedy's splendid alliterative verse translation entitled *Early English Christian Poetry* (1952). Of the many literary treatments of Biblical themes in English, the crowning achievements are surely John Milton's *Paradise Lost* (1667), *Paradise Regained* (1671), and *Samson Agonistes* (1671), and John Bunyan's *Pilgrim's Progress* (1678).

Notable poetical anthologies are the *Oxford Book of Christian Verse* (1940) and the *Oxford Book of Mystical Verse* (1916), along with *Masterpieces of Religious Verse*, edited by J. D. Morrison (1948), and *The World's Great Religious Poetry*, edited by C. M. Hill (1939). Edward Wagenknecht's *The Story of Jesus in the World's Literature* (1946) includes prose as well as verse. As with most anthologies, the quality of the individual selections varies considerably in each of these volumes, but each contains much work by excellent writers.

The influence of the Bible upon English literature has been far more pervasive than can be suggested by any list of works which are concerned with retelling Biblical incidents. Students wishing to study particular phases of this influence will find ample references in the standard bibliographies of individual authors, of periods, and of genres, and by consulting the card-catalogue of any good library.


IV. LITERARY ANALYSIS OF THE ENGLISH BIBLE

As for treatments of the literary quality of the English Bible, the reader is referred to two useful anthologies: *The English Bible: Essays by Various Hands*, edited by V. F. Storr (1938), and *The Bible Read as Literature*, edited by Mary E. Reid (1959). The latter contains C. S. Lewis' controversial essay suggesting that both the literary quality and the literary influence of the King James Version have been overestimated. *In Praise of the Bible* (1955), compiled by Geoffrey Murray, contains suggestive, brief comments by a wide range of prominent persons but frustrates the reader by failing to provide documentation. The reader is also referred to J. H. Penniman's *A Book about the English Bible* (1919), C. A. Dinsmore's *The English Bible as Literature* (1931), and W. O. Sypherd's *The Literature of the English Bible* (1938) for various useful literary analyses. Stimulating suggestions for literary study are also found in R. G. Moulton's *The Literary Study of the Bible: An Account of the Leading Forms of Literature Represented in the Sacred Writings* (1899). Of particular interest are lengthy analyses by two great poets and critics: Matthew Arnold's editions of *Isaiah of Jerusalem* (1883) and *Isaiah XL–LXVI* (1875), and Samuel Taylor Coleridge's *Confessions of an Inquiring Spirit* (1840), while many stimulating literary comments about the Bible are scattered throughout the writings of both men.

# Chronological Outline
## of Major Periods and Events

| | |
|---|---|
| c. 2000–1700 B.C. | Abraham, Isaac, and Jacob |
| c. 1700–1300 B.C. | The Hebrews in Egypt |
| c. 1300–1250 B.C. | The Epic of Moses |
| c. 1250–1025 B.C. | Conquest and Chaos |
| c. 1025–960 B.C. | The Epic of David |
| c. 960–750 B.C. | The Age of Kings |
| c. 750–600 B.C. | The Age of Prophets |
| c. 600–400 B.C. | Exile and Return |
| c. 4 B.C. | Birth of Jesus |
| c. A.D. 30 | Crucifixion of Jesus |
| c. A.D. 37–40 | Conversion of Paul |

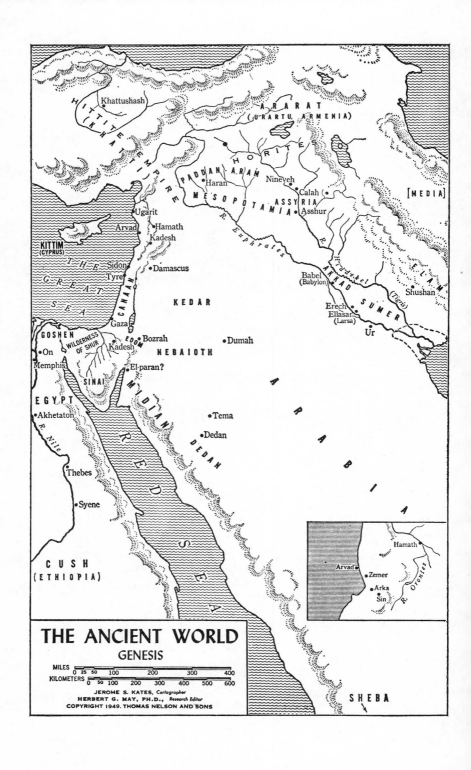

THE ANCIENT WORLD
GENESIS

MILES 0 25 50 100 200 300 400
KILOMETERS 0 50 100 200 300 400 500 600

JEROME S. KATES, *Cartographer*
HERBERT G. MAY, PH.D., *Research Editor*
COPYRIGHT 1949. THOMAS NELSON AND SONS

*Selections from*

# THE OLD TESTAMENT

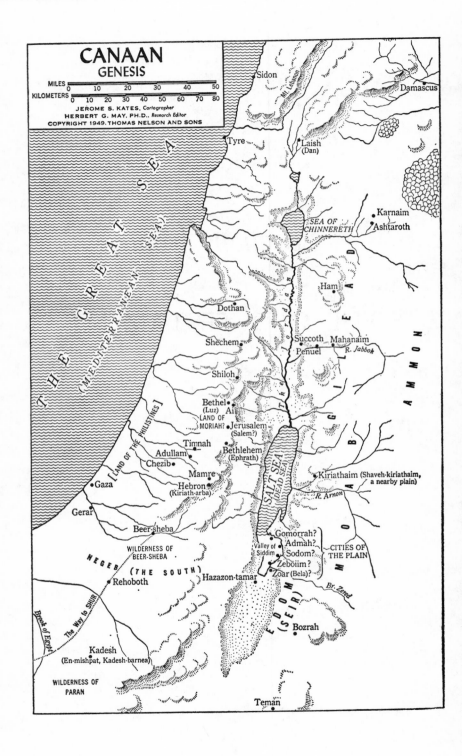

# CANAAN
## GENESIS

MILES
0  10  20  30  40  50

KILOMETERS
0  10  20  30  40  50  60  70  80

JEROME S. KATES, *Cartographer*
HERBERT G. MAY, PH.D., *Research Editor*
COPYRIGHT 1949, THOMAS NELSON AND SONS

Sidon

Damascus

THE GREAT SEA

(MEDITERRANEAN SEA)

Mt. Lebanon

Tyre

Laish
(Dan)

Karnaim

Ashtaroth

SEA OF
CHINNERETH

Ham

Dothan

Succoth
Penuel
Mahanaim
R. Jabbok

Shechem

Shiloh

Bethel
(Luz) Ai
LAND OF
MORIAH?
Jerusalem
(Salem?)

Timnah
Bethlehem
(Ephrath)

Adullam

Chezib

Mamre
Hebron
(Kiriath-arba)

Gaza

Gerar

Beer-sheba

WILDERNESS OF
BEER-SHEBA

NEGEB (THE SOUTH)

Rehoboth

Kiriathaim (Shaveh-kiriathaim,
a nearby plain)

R. Arnon

SALT SEA
(DEAD SEA)

Gomorrah?
Admah?
Valley of
Siddim
Sodom?

Zeboiim?
Zoar (Bela)?

CITIES OF
THE PLAIN

Hazazon-tamar

Br. Zered

Brook of Egypt

The Way to SHUR

Kadesh
(En-mishpat, Kadesh-barnea)

Bozrah

EDOM (SEIR)

WILDERNESS OF
PARAN

Teman

LAND OF THE PHILISTINES

GILEAD

AMMON

MOAB

Jordan R.

# From Eden to Egypt: *Genesis*

Against the background of a majestic poetic account of the creation of the universe, the book of Genesis first considers the nature of man and of human society under the parables of Adam, Eve, and their descendants. The repeated defections of men in attempting to command for themselves the place of the Deity, and in assuming to themselves alone the determination of good and evil, lead to an increasing conflict between men who would make themselves gods over each other. After the parabolic incident of the Tower of Babel, there comes a climactic alienation as the division of language separates men symbolically from any common human community.

It is at this point that the drama of the chosen people begins, as God calls Abraham to establish a holy nation through which all mankind may be blessed. With Abraham, Isaac, and Jacob we begin to move into the shadowy world of the earliest history, a blending of literary imagination and historic memory. The social and cultural picture of the Age of the Patriarchs which is provided in Genesis corresponds strikingly with the findings of modern archaeology, but the figures treated here have about them a universal humanity which makes them close kin to us even after almost four thousand years of great cultural and religious change.

## *Genesis*

### THE CREATION

1 In the beginning God created the heaven and the earth. 2 And the earth was without form, and void; and darkness was upon the face of the deep. And the Spirit of God moved upon the face of the waters. 3 And God said, Let there be light: and there was light. 4 And God saw the light, that it was good: and God divided the light from the darkness. 5 And God called the light Day, and the darkness he called Night. And the evening and the morning were the first day.

6 And God said, Let there be a firmament in the midst of the waters, and let it divide the waters from the waters. 7 And God made the firmament, and divided the waters which were under the firmament from the waters which were above the firmament: and it was

so. 8 And God called the firmament Heaven. And the evening and the morning were the second day.

9 And God said, Let the waters under the heaven be gathered together unto one place, and let the dry land appear: and it was so. 10 And God called the dry land Earth; and the gathering together of the waters called he Seas: and God saw that it was good. 11 And God said, Let the earth bring forth grass, the herb yielding seed, and the fruit tree yielding fruit after his kind, whose seed is in itself, upon the earth: and it was so. 12 And the earth brought forth grass, and herb yielding seed after his kind, and the tree yielding fruit, whose seed was in itself, after his kind: and God saw that it was good. 13 And the evening and the morning were the third day.

14 And God said, Let there be lights in the firmament of the heaven to divide the day from the night; and let them be for signs, and for seasons, and for days, and years: 15 And let them be for lights in the firmament of the heaven to give light upon the earth: and it was so. 16 And God made two great lights; the greater light to rule the day, and the lesser light to rule the night: he made the stars also. 17 And God set them in the firmament of the heaven to give light upon the earth, 18 And to rule over the day and over the night, and to divide the light from the darkness: and God saw that it was good. 19 And the evening and the morning were the fourth day.

20 And God said, Let the waters bring forth abundantly the moving creature that hath life, and fowl that may fly above the earth in the open firmament of heaven. 21 And God created great whales, and every living creature that moveth, which the waters brought forth abundantly, after their kind, and every winged fowl after his kind: and God saw that it was good. 22 And God blessed them, saying, Be fruitful, and multiply, and fill the waters in the seas, and let fowl multiply in the earth. 23 And the evening and the morning were the fifth day.

24 And God said, Let the earth bring forth the living creature after his kind, cattle, and creeping thing, and beast of the earth after his kind: and it was so. 25 And God made the beast of the earth after his kind, and cattle after their kind, and every thing that creepeth upon the earth after his kind: and God saw that it was good.

26 And God said, Let us make man in our image, after our likeness: and let them have dominion over the fish of the sea, and over the fowl of the air, and over the cattle, and over all the earth, and over every creeping thing that creepeth upon the earth. 27 So God created man in his own image, in the image of God created he him; male and female created he them. 28 And God blessed them, and God said unto them, Be fruitful and multiply, and replenish the earth, and subdue it: and have dominion over the fish of the sea, and over the fowl of the air, and over every living thing that moveth upon the earth.

29 And God said, Behold, I have given you every herb bearing seed, which is upon the face of all the earth, and every tree, in the which is the fruit of a tree yielding seed; to you it shall be for meat. 30 And to every beast of the earth, and to every fowl of the air, and to every

thing that creepeth upon the earth, wherein there is life, I have given every green herb for meat: and it was so. 31 And God saw every thing that he had made, and behold, it was very good. And the evening and the morning were the sixth day.

2 Thus the heavens and the earth were finished, and all the host of them. 2 And on the seventh day God ended his work which he had made; and he rested on the seventh day from all his work which he had made. 3 And God blessed the seventh day, and sanctified it: because that in it he had rested from all his work which God created and made.

4 These are the generations of the heavens and of the earth when they were created, in the day that the Lord God made the earth and the heavens, 5 And every plant of the field before it was in the earth, and every herb of the field before it grew: for the Lord God had not caused it to rain upon the earth, and there was not a man to till the ground. 6 But there went up a mist from the earth, and watered the whole face of the ground. 7 And the Lord God formed man of the dust of the ground, and breathed into his nostrils the breath of life; and man became a living soul.

8 And the Lord God planted a garden eastward in Eden; and there he put the man whom he had formed. 9 And out of the ground made the Lord God to grow every tree that is pleasant to the sight, and good for food; the tree of life also in the midst of the garden, and the tree of knowledge of good and evil. 10 And a river went out of Eden to water the garden; and from thence it was parted, and became into four heads. 11 The name of the first is Pison: that is it which compasseth the whole land of Havilah, where there is gold; 12 And the gold of that land is good: there is bdellium and the onyx stone. 13 And the name of the second river is Gihon: the same is it that compasseth the whole land of Ethiopia. 14 And the name of the third river is Hiddekel: that is it which goeth toward the east of Assyria. And the fourth river is Euphrates. 15 And the Lord God took the man, and put him into the garden of Eden to dress it and to keep it. 16 And the Lord God commanded the man, saying, Of every tree of the garden thou mayest freely eat: 17 But of the tree of the knowledge of good and evil, thou shalt not eat of it: for in the day that thou eatest thereof thou shalt surely die.

18 And the Lord God said, It is not good that the man should be alone; I will make him a help meet for him. 19 And out of the ground the Lord God formed every beast of the field, and every fowl of the air; and brought them unto Adam to see what he would call them: and whatsoever Adam called every living creature, that was the name thereof. 20 And Adam gave names to all cattle, and to the fowl of the air, and to every beast of the field; but for Adam there was not found a help meet for him. 21 And the Lord God caused a deep sleep to fall upon Adam, and he slept; and he took one of his ribs, and closed up the flesh instead thereof. 22 And the rib, which the Lord God had

5

taken from man, made he a woman, and brought her unto the man. 23 And Adam said, This is now bone of my bones, and flesh of my flesh: she shall be called Woman, because she was taken out of man. 24 Therefore shall a man leave his father and his mother, and shall cleave unto his wife: and they shall be one flesh. 25 And they were both naked, the man and his wife, and were not ashamed.

## MAN'S SELF-DEIFICATION

3 Now the serpent was more subtile than any beast of the field which the Lord God had made. And he said unto the woman, Yea, hath God said, Ye shall not eat of every tree of the garden? 2 And the woman said unto the serpent, We may eat of the fruit of the trees of the garden: 3 But of the fruit of the tree which is in the midst of the garden, God hath said, Ye shall not eat of it, neither shall ye touch it, lest ye die. 4 And the serpent said unto the woman, Ye shall not surely die: 5 For God doth know that in the day ye eat thereof, then your eyes shall be opened, and ye shall be as gods, knowing good and evil. 6 And when the woman saw that the tree was good for food, and that it was pleasant to the eyes, and a tree to be desired to make one wise, she took of the fruit thereof, and did eat, and gave also unto her husband with her; and he did eat. 7 And the eyes of them both were opened, and they knew that they were naked; and they sewed fig leaves together, and made themselves aprons. 8 And they heard the voice of the Lord God walking in the garden in the cool of the day: and Adam and his wife hid themselves from the presence of the Lord God amongst the trees of the garden.

9 And the Lord God called unto Adam, and said unto him, Where art thou? 10 And he said, I heard thy voice in the garden, and I was afraid, because I was naked; and I hid myself. 11 And he said, Who told thee that thou wast naked? Hast thou eaten of the tree, whereof I commanded thee that thou shouldest not eat? 12 And the man said, The woman whom thou gavest to be with me, she gave me of the tree, and I did eat. 13 And the Lord God said unto the woman, What is this that thou hast done? And the woman said, The serpent beguiled me, and I did eat. 14 And the Lord God said unto the serpent, Because thou hast done this, thou art cursed above all cattle, and above every beast of the field; upon thy belly shalt thou go, and dust shalt thou eat all the days of thy life: 15 And I will put enmity between thee and the woman, and between thy seed and her seed; it shall bruise thy head, and thou shalt bruise his heel. 16 Unto the woman he said, I will greatly multiply thy sorrow and thy conception; in sorrow thou shalt bring forth children; and thy desire shall be to thy husband, and he shall rule over thee.

17 And unto Adam he said, Because thou hast hearkened unto the voice of thy wife, and hast eaten of the tree, of which I commanded thee, saying, Thou shalt not eat of it: cursed is the ground for thy sake; in sorrow shalt thou eat of it all the days of thy life; 18 Thorns also

6

and thistles shall it bring forth to thee; and thou shalt eat the herb of the field: 19 In the sweat of thy face shalt thou eat bread, till thou return unto the ground; for out of it wast thou taken: for dust thou art, and unto dust shalt thou return. 20 And Adam called his wife's name Eve; because she was the mother of all living. 21 Unto Adam also and to his wife did the Lord God make coats of skins, and clothed them.

22 And the Lord God said, Behold, the man is become as one of us, to know good and evil: and now, lest he put forth his hand, and take also of the tree of life, and eat, and live for ever: 23 Therefore the Lord God sent him forth from the garden of Eden, to till the ground from whence he was taken. 24 So he drove out the man: and he placed at the east of the garden of Eden cherubim, and a flaming sword which turned every way, to keep the way of the tree of life.

## THE PROGRESS OF SIN

4 And Adam knew Eve his wife; and she conceived, and bare Cain, and said, I have gotten a man from the Lord. 2 And she again bare his brother Abel. And Abel was a keeper of sheep, but Cain was a tiller of the ground. 3 And in process of time it came to pass, that Cain brought of the fruit of the ground an offering unto the Lord. 4 And Abel, he also brought of the firstlings of his flock and of the fat thereof. And the Lord had respect unto Abel and to his offering: 5 But unto Cain and to his offering he had not respect. And Cain was very wroth, and his countenance fell. 6 And the Lord said unto Cain, Why art thou wroth? and why is thy countenance fallen? 7 If thou doest well, shalt thou not be accepted? And if thou doest not well, sin lieth at the door: and unto thee shall be his desire, and thou shalt rule over him. 8 And Cain talked with Abel his brother: and it came to pass, when they were in the field, that Cain rose up against Abel his brother, and slew him.

9 And the Lord said unto Cain, Where is Abel thy brother? And he said, I know not: Am I my brother's keeper? 10 And he said, What hast thou done? the voice of thy brother's blood crieth unto me from the ground. 11 And now art thou cursed from the earth, which hath opened her mouth to receive thy brother's blood from thy hand. 12 When thou tillest the ground, it shall not henceforth yield unto thee her strength; a fugitive and a vagabond shalt thou be in the earth. 13 And Cain said unto the Lord, My punishment is greater than I can bear. 14 Behold, thou hast driven me out this day from the face of the earth; and from thy face shall I be hid; and I shall be a fugitive and a vagabond in the earth; and it shall come to pass, that every one that findeth me shall slay me. 15 And the Lord said unto him, Therefore whosoever slayeth Cain, vengeance shall be taken on him sevenfold. And the Lord set a mark upon Cain, lest any finding him should kill him.

16 And Cain went out from the presence of the Lord, and dwelt in the land of Nod, on the east of Eden. 17 And Cain knew his wife; and

she conceived, and bare Enoch: and he builded a city, and called the name of the city, after the name of his son, Enoch. 18 And unto Enoch was born Irad: and Irad begat Mehujael: and Mehujael begat Methusael: and Methusael begat Lamech. 19 And Lamech took unto him two wives: the name of the one was Adah, and the name of the other Zillah. 20 And Adah bare Jabal: he was the father of such as dwell in tents, and of such as have cattle. 21 And his brother's name was Jubal: he was the father of all such as handle the harp and organ. 22 And Zillah, she also bare Tubal-cain, an instructor of every artificer in brass and iron; and the sister of Tubal-cain was Naamah. 23 And Lamech said unto his wives,

> Adah and Zillah, hear my voice;
> Ye wives of Lamech, hearken unto my speech:
> For I have slain a man to my wounding,
> And a young man to my hurt.

24 If Cain shall be avenged sevenfold,
> Truly Lamech seventy and sevenfold.

25 And Adam knew his wife again; and she bare a son, and called his name Seth: For God, said she, hath appointed me another seed instead of Abel, whom Cain slew. 26 And to Seth, to him also there was born a son; and he called his name Enos: then began men to call upon the name of the Lord.

6 And it came to pass, when men began to multiply on the face of the earth, and daughters were born unto them, 2 That the sons of God saw the daughters of men that they were fair; and they took them wives of all which they chose. 3 And the Lord said, My Spirit shall not always strive with man, for that he also is flesh; yet his days shall be a hundred and twenty years. 4 There were giants in the earth in those days; and also after that, when the sons of God came in unto the daughters of men, and they bare children to them, the same became mighty men which were of old, men of renown.

5 And God saw that the wickedness of man was great in the earth, and that every imagination of the thoughts of his heart was only evil continually. 6 And it repented the Lord that he had made man on the earth, and it grieved him at his heart. 7 And the Lord said, I will destroy man whom I have created from the face of the earth; both man, and beast, and the creeping thing, and the fowls of the air; for it repenteth me that I have made them. 8 But Noah found grace in the eyes of the Lord.

## NOAH AND THE FLOOD

9 These are the generations of Noah: Noah was a just man and perfect in his generations, and Noah walked with God. 10 And Noah begat three sons, Shem, Ham, and Japheth. 11 The earth also was corrupt before God; and the earth was filled with violence. 12 And

God looked upon the earth, and, behold, it was corrupt; for all flesh had corrupted his way upon the earth.

13 And God said unto Noah, The end of all flesh is come before me; for the earth is filled with violence through them; and, behold, I will destroy them with the earth. 14 Make thee an ark of gopher wood; rooms shalt thou make in the ark, and shalt pitch it within and without with pitch. 15 And this is the fashion which thou shalt make it of: The length of the ark shall be three hundred cubits, the breadth of it fifty cubits, and the height of it thirty cubits. 16 A window shalt thou make to the ark, and in a cubit shalt thou finish it above; and the door of the ark shalt thou set in the side thereof; with lower, second, and third stories shalt thou make it. 17 And, behold, I, even I, do bring a flood of waters upon the earth, to destroy all flesh, wherein is the breath of life, from under heaven; and every thing that is in the earth shall die. 18 But with thee will I establish my covenant; and thou shalt come into the ark, thou, and thy sons, and thy wife, and thy son's wives with thee. 19 And of every living thing of all flesh, two of every sort shalt thou bring into the ark, to keep them alive with thee; they shall be male and female. 20 Of fowls after their kind, and of cattle after their kind, of every creeping thing of the earth after his kind; two of every sort shall come unto thee, to keep them alive. 21 And take thou unto thee of all food that is eaten, and thou shalt gather it to thee; and it shall be for food for thee, and for them. 22 Thus did Noah; according to all that God commanded him, so did he.

7 And the Lord said unto Noah, Come thou and all thy house into the ark; for thee have I seen righteous before me in this generation. 2 Of every clean beast thou shalt take to thee by sevens, the male and his female: and of beasts that are not clean by two, the male and his female. 3 Of fowls also of the air by sevens, the male and the female; to keep seed alive upon the face of all the earth. 4 For yet seven days, and I will cause it to rain upon the earth forty days and forty nights; and every living substance that I have made will I destroy from off the face of the earth. 5 And Noah did according unto all that the Lord commanded him.

6 And Noah was six hundred years old when the flood of waters was upon the earth. 7 And Noah went in, and his sons, and his wife, and his sons' wives with him, into the ark, because of the waters of the flood. 8 Of clean beasts, and of beasts that are not clean, and of fowls, and of every thing that creepeth upon the earth, 9 There went in two and two unto Noah into the ark, the male and the female, as God had commanded Noah. 10 And it came to pass after seven days, that the waters of the flood were upon the earth. 11 In the six hundredth year of Noah's life, in the second month, the seventeenth day of the month, the same day were all the fountains of the great deep broken up, and the windows of heaven were opened. 12 And the rain was upon the earth forty days and forty nights.

13 In the selfsame day entered Noah, and Shem, and Ham, and Japheth, the sons of Noah, and Noah's wife, and the three wives of his sons with them, into the ark; 14 They, and every beast after his kind, and all the cattle after their kind, and every creeping thing that creepeth upon the earth after his kind, and every fowl after his kind, every bird of every sort. 15 And they went in unto Noah into the ark, two and two of all flesh, wherein is the breath of life. 16 And they that went in, went in male and female of all flesh, as God had commanded him: and the Lord shut him in.

17 And the flood was forty days upon the earth; and the waters increased, and bare up the ark, and it was lifted up above the earth. 18 And the waters prevailed, and were increased greatly upon the earth; and the ark went upon the face of the waters. 19 And the waters prevailed exceedingly upon the earth; and all the high hills, that were under the whole heaven, were covered. 20 Fifteen cubits upward did the waters prevail; and the mountains were covered. 21 And all flesh died that moved upon the earth, both of fowl, and of cattle, and of beast, and of every creeping thing that creepeth upon the earth, and every man: 22 All in whose nostrils was the breath of life, of all that was in the dry land, died. 23 And every living substance was destroyed which was upon the face of the ground, both man, and cattle, and the creeping things, and the fowl of the heaven; and they were destroyed from the earth: and Noah only remained alive, and they that were with him in the ark. 24 And the waters prevailed upon the earth a hundred and fifty days.

8   And God remembered Noah, and every living thing, and all the cattle that was with him in the ark: and God made a wind to pass over the earth, and the waters assuaged. 2 The fountains also of the deep and the windows of heaven were stopped, and the rain from heaven was restrained. 3 And the waters returned from off the earth continually: and after the end of the hundred and fifty days the waters were abated. 4 And the ark rested in the seventh month, on the seventeenth day of the month, upon the mountains of Ararat. 5 And the waters decreased continually until the tenth month: in the tenth month, on the first day of the month, were the tops of the mountains seen.

6 And it came to pass at the end of forty days, that Noah opened the window of the ark which he had made: 7 And he sent forth a raven, which went forth to and fro, until the waters were dried up from off the earth. 8 Also he sent forth a dove from him, to see if the waters were abated from off the face of the ground. 9 But the dove found no rest for the sole of her foot, and she returned unto him into the ark; for the waters were on the face of the whole earth. Then he put forth his hand, and took her, and pulled her in unto him into the ark. 10 And he stayed yet other seven days; and again he sent forth the dove out of the ark. 11 And the dove came in to him in the evening, and, lo, in her mouth was an olive leaf plucked off: so Noah knew that the waters were

abated from off the earth. 12 And he stayed yet other seven days, and sent forth the dove, which returned not again unto him any more.

13 And it came to pass in the six hundredth and first year, in the first month, the first day of the month, the waters were dried up from off the earth: and Noah removed the covering of the ark, and looked, and, behold, the face of the ground was dry. 14 And in the second month, on the seven and twentieth day of the month, was the earth dried.

15 And God spake unto Noah, saying, 16 Go forth of the ark, thou, and thy wife, and thy sons, and thy sons' wives with thee. 17 Bring forth with thee every living thing that is with thee, of all flesh, both of fowl, and of cattle, and of every creeping thing that creepeth upon the earth; that they may breed abundantly in the earth, and be fruitful, and multiply upon the earth. 18 And Noah went forth, and his sons, and his wife, and his sons' wives with him: 19 Every beast, every creeping thing, and every fowl, and whatsoever creepeth upon the earth, after their kinds, went forth out of the ark.

20 And Noah builded an altar unto the Lord; and took of every clean beast, and of every clean fowl, and offered burnt offerings on the altar. 21 And the Lord smelled a sweet savor; and the Lord said in his heart, I will not again curse the ground any more for man's sake; for the imagination of man's heart is evil from his youth: neither will I again smite any more every thing living, as I have done. 22 While the earth remaineth, seedtime and harvest, and cold and heat, and summer and winter, and day and night shall not cease.

9   And God blessed Noah and his sons, and said unto them, Be fruitful, and multiply, and replenish the earth. 2 And the fear of you and the dread of you shall be upon every beast of the earth, and upon every fowl of the air, upon all that moveth upon the earth, and upon all the fishes of the sea; into your hand are they delivered. 3 Every moving thing that liveth shall be meat for you; even as the green herb have I given you all things. 4 But flesh with the life thereof, which is the blood thereof, shall ye not eat. 5 And surely your blood of your lives will I require: at the hand of every beast will I require it, and at the hand of man; at the hand of every man's brother will I require the life of man. 6 Whoso sheddeth man's blood, by man shall his blood be shed: for in the image of God made he man. 7 And you, be ye fruitful, and multiply; bring forth abundantly in the earth, and multiply therein.

8 And God spake unto Noah, and to his sons with him, saying, 9 And I, behold, I establish my covenant with you, and with your seed after you; 10 And with every living creature that is with you, of the fowl, of the cattle, and of every beast of the earth with you; from all that go out of the ark, to every beast of the earth. 11 And I will establish my covenant with you; neither shall all flesh be cut off any more by the waters of a flood; neither shall there any more be a flood to

destroy the earth. 12 And God said, This is the token of the covenant which I make between me and you, and every living creature that is with you, for perpetual generations: 13 I do set my bow in the cloud, and it shall be for a token of a covenant between me and the earth. 14 And it shall come to pass, when I bring a cloud over the earth, that the bow shall be seen in the cloud: 15 And I will remember my covenant, which is between me and you and every living creature of all flesh; and the waters shall no more become a flood to destroy all flesh. 16 And the bow shall be in the cloud; and I will look upon it, that I may remember the everlasting covenant between God and every living creature of all flesh that is upon the earth. 17 And God said unto Noah, This is the token of the covenant, which I have established between me and all flesh that is upon the earth.

18 And the sons of Noah, that went forth of the ark, were Shem, and Ham, and Japheth: and Ham is the father of Canaan. 19 These are the three sons of Noah: and of them was the whole earth overspread.

20 And Noah began to be a husbandman, and he planted a vineyard: 21 And he drank of the wine, and was drunken; and he was uncovered within his tent. 22 And Ham, the father of Canaan, saw the nakedness of his father, and told his two brethren without. 23 And Shem and Japheth took a garment, and laid it upon both their shoulders, and went backward, and covered the nakedness of their father; and their faces were backward, and they saw not their father's nakedness. 24 And Noah awoke from his wine, and knew what his younger son had done unto him. 25 And he said,

Cursed be Canaan;
A servant of servants shall he be unto his brethren.
26 And he said,
Blessed be the Lord God of Shem;
And Canaan shall be his servant.
27 God shall enlarge Japheth,
And he shall dwell in the tents of Shem;
And Canaan shall be his servant.

28 And Noah lived after the flood three hundred and fifty years. 29 And all the days of Noah were nine hundred and fifty years: and he died.

### THE TOWER OF PRIDE

11 And the whole earth was of one language, and of one speech. 2 And it came to pass, as they journeyed from the east, that they found a plain in the land of Shinar; and they dwelt there. 3 And they said one to another, Go to, let us make brick, and burn them thoroughly. And they had brick for stone, and slime had they for mortar. 4 And they said, Go to, let us build us a city, and a tower, whose top may reach unto heaven; and let us make us a name, lest we be scattered abroad upon the face of the whole earth.

5 And the Lord came down to see the city and the tower, which the children of men builded. 6 And the Lord said, Behold, the people is one, and they have all one language; and this they begin to do: and now nothing will be restrained from them, which they have imagined to do. 7 Go to, let us go down, and there confound their language, that they may not understand one another's speech. 8 So the Lord scattered them abroad from thence upon the face of all the earth: and they left off to build the city. 9 Therefore is the name of it called Babel; because the Lord did there confound the language of all the earth: and from thence did the Lord scatter them abroad upon the face of all the earth.

## A PEOPLE CHOSEN: ABRAHAM

12 Now the Lord had said unto Abram, Get thee out of thy country, and from thy kindred, and from thy father's house, unto a land that I will show thee: 2 And I will make of thee a great nation, and I will bless thee, and make thy name great; and thou shalt be a blessing: 3 And I will bless them that bless thee, and curse him that curseth thee: and in thee shall all families of the earth be blessed. 4 So Abram departed, as the Lord had spoken unto him; and Lot went with him: and Abram was seventy and five years old when he departed out of Haran. 5 And Abram took Sarai his wife, and Lot his brother's son, and all their substance that they had gathered, and the souls that they had gotten in Haran; and they went forth to go into the land of Canaan; and into the land of Canaan they came. 6 And Abram passed through the land unto the place of Sichem, unto the plain of Moreh. And the Canaanite was then in the land. 7 And the Lord appeared unto Abram, and said, Unto thy seed will I give this land: and there builded he an altar unto the Lord, who appeared unto him. 8 And he removed from thence unto a mountain on the east of Beth-el, and pitched his tent, having Beth-el on the west, and Hai on the east: and there he builded an altar unto the Lord, and called upon the name of the Lord.

13 2 And Abram was very rich in cattle, in silver, and in gold. 3 And he went on his journeys from the south even to Beth-el, unto the place where his tent had been at the beginning, between Beth-el and Hai; 4 Unto the place of the altar, which he had made there at the first: and there Abram called on the name of the Lord. 5 And Lot also, which went with Abram, had flocks, and herds, and tents. 6 And the land was not able to bear them, that they might dwell together: for their substance was great, so that they could not dwell together. 7 And there was a strife between the herdmen of Abram's cattle and the herdmen of Lot's cattle: and the Canaanite and the Perizzite dwelt then in the land. 8 And Abram said unto Lot, Let there be no strife, I pray thee, between me and thee, and between my herdmen and thy herdmen; for we be brethren. 9 Is not the whole

land before thee? separate thyself, I pray thee, from me: if thou wilt take the left hand, then I will go to the right; or if thou depart to the right hand, then I will go to the left. 10 And Lot lifted up his eyes, and beheld all the plain of Jordan, that it was well watered every where, before the Lord destroyed Sodom and Gomorrah, even as the garden of the Lord, like the land of Egypt, as thou comest unto Zoar. 11 Then Lot chose him all the plain of Jordan; and Lot journeyed east: and they separated themselves the one from the other. 12 Abram dwelt in the land of Canaan, and Lot dwelt in the cities of the plain, and pitched his tent toward Sodom. 13 But the men of Sodom were wicked and sinners before the Lord exceedingly.

15 After these things the word of the Lord came unto Abram in a vision, saying, Fear not, Abram: I am thy shield, and thy exceeding great reward. 2 And Abram said, Lord God, what wilt thou give me, seeing I go childless, and the steward of my house is this Eliezer of Damascus? 3 And Abram said, Behold, to me thou hast given no seed: and, lo, one born in my house is mine heir.[1] 4 And, behold, the word of the Lord came unto him, saying, This shall not be thine heir; but he that shall come forth out of thine own bowels shall be thine heir. 5 And he brought him forth abroad, and said, Look now toward heaven, and tell the stars, if thou be able to number them: and he said unto him, So shall thy seed be. 6 And he believed in the Lord; and he counted it to him for righteousness. 7 And he said unto him, I am the Lord that brought thee out of Ur of the Chaldees, to give thee this land to inherit it. 8 And he said, Lord God, whereby shall I know that I shall inherit it? 9 And he said unto him, Take me a heifer of three years old, and a she goat of three years old, and a ram of three years old, and a turtledove, and a young pigeon. 10 And he took unto him all these, and divided them in the midst, and laid each piece one against another: but the birds divided he not. 11 And when the fowls came down upon the carcasses, Abram drove them away. 12 And when the sun was going down, a deep sleep fell upon Abram; and, lo, a horror of great darkness fell upon him. 13 And he said unto Abram, Know of a surety that thy seed shall be a stranger in a land that is not theirs, and shall serve them; and they shall afflict them four hundred years; 14 And also that nation, whom they shall serve, will I judge: and afterward shall they come out with great substance. 15 And thou shalt go to thy fathers in peace; thou shalt be buried in a good old age. 16 But in the fourth generation they shall come hither again: for the iniquity of the Amorites is not yet full. 17 And it came to pass, that, when the sun went down, and it was dark, behold a smoking furnace, and a burning lamp that passed between those pieces. 18 In that same day the Lord made a covenant with Abram, saying, Unto thy seed have I given this land, from the river of Egypt unto the

[1] Abraham's only heir is a hired retainer.

great river, the river Euphrates: 19 The Kenites, and the Kenizzites, and the Kadmonites, 20 And the Hittites, and the Perizzites, and the Rephaim, 21 And the Amorites, and the Canaanites, and the Girgashites, and the Jebusites.

## ABRAHAM'S SONS

16 Now Sarai, Abram's wife, bare him no children: and she had a handmaid, an Egyptian, whose name was Hagar. 2 And Sarai said unto Abram, Behold now, the Lord hath restrained me from bearing: I pray thee, go in unto my maid; it may be that I may obtain children by her. And Abram hearkened to the voice of Sarai. 3 And Sarai, Abram's wife, took Hagar her maid the Egyptian, after Abram had dwelt ten years in the land of Canaan, and gave her to her husband Abram to be his wife. 4 And he went in unto Hagar, and she conceived: and when she saw that she had conceived, her mistress was despised in her eyes. 5 And Sarai said unto Abram, My wrong be upon thee: I have given my maid into thy bosom; and when she saw that she had conceived, I was despised in her eyes: the Lord judge between me and thee. 6 But Abram said unto Sarai, Behold, thy maid is in thy hand; do to her as it pleaseth thee. And when Sarai dealt hardly with her, she fled from her face.

7 And the angel of the Lord found her by a fountain of water in the wilderness, by the fountain in the way to Shur. 8 And he said, Hagar, Sarai's maid, whence camest thou? and whither wilt thou go? And she said, I flee from the face of my mistress Sarai. 9 And the angel of the Lord said unto her, Return to thy mistress, and submit thyself under her hands. 10 And the angel of the Lord said unto her, I will multiply thy seed exceedingly, that it shall not be numbered for multitude. 11 And the angel of the Lord said unto her, Behold, thou art with child, and shalt bear a son, and shalt call his name Ishmael; because the Lord hath heard thy affliction. 12 And he will be a wild man; his hand will be against every man, and every man's hand against him: and he shall dwell in the presence of all his brethren. 15 And Hagar bare Abram a son: and Abram called his son's name, which Hagar bare, Ishmael. 16 And Abram was fourscore and six years old, when Hagar bare Ishmael to Abram.

17 And when Abram was ninety years old and nine, the Lord appeared to Abram, and said unto him, I am the Almighty God; walk before me, and be thou perfect. 2 And I will make my covenant between me and thee, and will multiply thee exceedingly. 3 And Abram fell on his face: and God talked with him, saying, 4 As for me, behold, my covenant is with thee, and thou shalt be a father of many nations. 5 Neither shall thy name any more be called Abram, but thy name shall be Abraham; for a father of many nations have I made thee. 6 And I will make thee exceeding fruitful, and I will make

15

nations of thee, and kings shall come out of thee. 7 And I will establish my covenant between me and thee and thy seed after thee in their generations, for an everlasting covenant, to be a God unto thee and to thy seed after thee. 8 And I will give unto thee, and to thy seed after thee, the land wherein thou art a stranger, all the land of Canaan, for an everlasting possession; and I will be their God. 9 And God said unto Abraham, Thou shalt keep my covenant therefore, thou, and thy seed after thee in their generations. 10 This is my covenant, which ye shall keep, between me and you and thy seed after thee; Every man child among you shall be circumcised. 11 And ye shall circumcise the flesh of your foreskin; and it shall be a token of the covenant betwixt me and you. 12 And he that is eight days old shall be circumcised among you, every man child in your generations, he that is born in the house, or bought with money of any stranger, which is not of thy seed. 13 He that is born in thy house, and he that is bought with thy money, must needs be circumcised: and my covenant shall be in your flesh for an everlasting covenant. 14 And the uncircumcised man child whose flesh of his foreskin is not circumcised, that soul shall be cut off from his people; he hath broken my covenant.

15 And God said unto Abraham, As for Sarai thy wife, thou shalt not call her name Sarai, but Sarah shall her name be. 16 And I will bless her, and give thee a son also of her: yea, I will bless her, and she shall be a mother of nations; kings of people shall be of her. 17 Then Abraham fell upon his face, and laughed, and said in his heart, Shall a child be born unto him that is a hundred years old? and shall Sarah, that is ninety years old, bear? 18 And Abraham said unto God, O that Ishmael might live before thee! 19 And God said, Sarah thy wife shall bear thee a son indeed; and thou shalt call his name Isaac: and I will establish my covenant with him for an everlasting covenant, and with his seed after him. 20 And as for Ishmael, I have heard thee: Behold, I have blessed him, and will make him fruitful, and will multiply him exceedingly; twelve princes shall he beget, and I will make him a great nation. 21 But my covenant will I establish with Isaac, which Sarah shall bear unto thee at this set time in the next year. 22 And he left off talking with him, and God went up from Abraham.

23 And Abraham took Ishmael his son, and all that were born in his house, and all that were bought with his money, every male among the men of Abraham's house; and circumcised the flesh of their foreskin in the selfsame day, as God had said unto him. 24 And Abraham was ninety years old and nine, when he was circumcised in the flesh of his foreskin. 25 And Ishmael his son was thirteen years old, when he was circumcised in the flesh of his foreskin. 26 In the selfsame day was Abraham circumcised, and Ishmael his son. 27 And all the men of his house, born in the house, and bought with money of the stranger, were circumcised with him.

## SODOM AND GOMORRAH

18 And the Lord appeared unto him in the plains of Mamre: and he sat in the tent door in the heat of the day; 2 And he lifted up his eyes and looked, and, lo, three men stood by him: and when he saw them, he ran to meet them from the tent door, and bowed himself toward the ground, 3 And said, My Lord, if now I have found favor in thy sight, pass not away, I pray thee, from thy servant: 4 Let a little water, I pray you, be fetched, and wash your feet, and rest yourselves under the tree: 5 And I will fetch a morsel of bread, and comfort ye your hearts; after that ye shall pass on: for therefore are ye come to your servant. And they said, So do, as thou hast said. 6 And Abraham hastened into the tent unto Sarah, and said, Make ready quickly three measures of fine meal, knead it, and make cakes upon the hearth. 7 And Abraham ran unto the herd, and fetched a calf tender and good, and gave it unto a young man; and he hasted to dress it. 8 And he took butter, and milk, and the calf which he had dressed, and set it before them; and he stood by them under the tree, and they did eat. 9 And they said unto him, Where is Sarah thy wife? And he said, Behold, in the tent. 10 And he said, I will certainly return unto thee according to the time of life; and, lo, Sarah thy wife shall have a son. And Sarah heard it in the tent door, which was behind him. 11 Now Abraham and Sarah were old and well stricken in age; and it ceased to be with Sarah after the manner of women. 12 Therefore Sarah laughed within herself, saying, After I am waxed old shall I have pleasure, my lord being old also? 13 And the Lord said unto Abraham, Wherefore did Sarah laugh, saying, Shall I of a surety bear a child, which am old? 14 Is any thing too hard for the Lord? At the time appointed I will return unto thee, according to the time of life, and Sarah shall have a son. 15 Then Sarah denied, saying, I laughed not; for she was afraid. And he said, Nay; but thou didst laugh.

16 And the men rose up from thence, and looked toward Sodom: and Abraham went with them to bring them on the way. 17 And the Lord said, Shall I hide from Abraham that thing which I do; 18 Seeing that Abraham shall surely become a great and mighty nation, and all the nations of the earth shall be blessed in him? 19 For I know him, that he will command his children and his household after him, and they shall keep the way of the Lord, to do justice and judgment; that the Lord may bring upon Abraham that which he hath spoken of him. 20 And the Lord said, Because the cry of Sodom and Gomorrah is great, and because their sin is very grievous, 21 I will go down now, and see whether they have done altogether according to the cry of it, which is come unto me; and if not, I will know. 22 And the men turned their faces from thence, and went toward Sodom: but Abraham stood yet before the Lord.

23 And Abraham drew near, and said, Wilt thou also destroy the righteous with the wicked? 24 Peradventure there be fifty righteous

within the city: wilt thou also destroy and not spare the place for the fifty righteous that are therein? 25 That be far from thee to do after this manner, to slay the righteous with the wicked; and that the righteous should be as the wicked, that be far from thee: Shall not the Judge of all the earth do right? 26 And the Lord said, If I find in Sodom fifty righteous within the city, then I will spare all the place for their sakes. 27 And Abraham answered and said, Behold now, I have taken upon me to speak unto the Lord, which am but dust and ashes: 28 Peradventure there shall lack five of the fifty righteous: wilt thou destroy all the city for lack of five? And he said, If I find there forty and five, I will not destroy it. 29 And he spake unto him yet again, and said, Peradventure there shall be forty found there. And he said, I will not do it for forty's sake. 30 And he said unto him, Oh let not the Lord be angry, and I will speak: Peradventure there shall thirty be found there. And he said, I will not do it, if I find thirty there. 31 And he said, Behold now, I have taken upon me to speak unto the Lord: Peradventure there shall be twenty found there. And he said, I will not destroy it for twenty's sake. 32 And he said, Oh let not the Lord be angry, and I will speak yet but this once: Peradventure ten shall be found there. And he said, I will not destroy it for ten's sake. 33 And the Lord went his way, as soon as he had left communing with Abraham: and Abraham returned unto his place.

19   And there came two angels to Sodom at even; and Lot sat in the gate of Sodom: and Lot seeing them rose up to meet them; and he bowed himself with his face toward the ground; 2 And he said, Behold now, my lords, turn in, I pray you, into your servant's house, and tarry all night, and wash your feet, and ye shall rise up early, and go on your ways. And they said, Nay; but we will abide in the street all night. 3 And he pressed upon them greatly; and they turned in unto him, and entered into his house; and he made them a feast, and did bake unleavened bread, and they did eat. 4 But before they lay down, the men of the city, even the men of Sodom, compassed the house round, both old and young, all the people from every quarter: 5 And they called unto Lot, and said unto him, Where are the men which came in to thee this night? bring them out unto us, that we may know them.[1]

6 And Lot went out at the door unto them, and shut the door after him, 7 And said, I pray you, brethren, do not so wickedly. 8 Behold now, I have two daughters which have not known man; let me, I pray you, bring them out unto you, and do ye to them as is good in your eyes: only unto these men do nothing; for therefore came they under the shadow of my roof. 9 And they said, Stand back. And they said again, This one fellow came in to sojourn, and he will needs be a judge: now will we deal worse with thee than with them. And they pressed sore upon the man, even Lot, and came near to break the door.

1 "To know" is a common Biblical expression for having sexual relations, in this instance sodomy.

10 But the men put forth their hand, and pulled Lot into the house to them, and shut to the door. 11 And they smote the men that were at the door of the house with blindness, both small and great: so that they wearied themselves to find the door. 12 And the men said unto Lot, Hast thou here any besides? son-in-law, and thy sons, and thy daughters, and whatsoever thou hast in the city, bring them out of this place: 13 For we will destroy this place, because the cry of them is waxen great before the face of the Lord; and the Lord hath sent us to destroy it. 14 And Lot went out, and spake unto his sons-in-law, which married his daughters, and said, Up, get you out of this place; for the Lord will destroy this city, But he seemed as one that mocked unto his sons-in-law.

15 And when the morning arose, then the angels hastened Lot, saying, Arise, take thy wife, and thy two daughters, which are here; lest thou be consumed in the iniquity of the city. 16 And while he lingered, the men laid hold upon his hand, and upon the hand of his wife, and upon the hand of his two daughters; the Lord being merciful unto him: and they brought him forth, and set him without the city. 17 And it came to pass, when they had brought them forth abroad, that he said, Escape for thy life; look not behind thee, neither stay thou in all the plain; escape to the mountain, lest thou be consumed. 18 And Lot said unto them, Oh, not so, my Lord: 19 Behold now, thy servant hath found grace in thy sight, and thou hast magnified thy mercy, which thou hast showed unto me in saving my life; and I cannot escape to the mountain, lest some evil take me, and I die: 20 Behold now, this city is near to flee unto, and it is a little one: O, let me escape thither, (is it not a little one?) and my soul shall live. 21 And he said unto him, See, I have accepted thee concerning this thing also, that I will not overthrow this city, for the which thou hast spoken. 22 Haste thee, escape thither; for I cannot do any thing till thou be come thither. Therefore the name of the city was called Zoar.

23 The sun was risen upon the earth when Lot entered into Zoar. 24 Then the Lord rained upon Sodom and upon Gomorrah brimstone and fire from the Lord out of heaven; 25 And he overthrew those cities, and all the plain, and all the inhabitants of the cities, and that which grew upon the ground. 26 But his wife looked back from behind him, and she became a pillar of salt. 27 And Abraham gat up early in the morning to the place where he stood before the Lord: 28 And he looked toward Sodom and Gomorrah, and toward all the land of the plain, and beheld, and, lo, the smoke of the country went up as the smoke of a furnace.

29 And it came to pass, when God destroyed the cities of the plain, that God remembered Abraham, and sent Lot out of the midst of the overthrow, when he overthrew the cities in the which Lot dwelt.

30 And Lot went up out of Zoar, and dwelt in the mountain, and his two daughters with him; for he feared to dwell in Zoar: and he dwelt in a cave, he and his two daughters. 31 And the firstborn said unto the younger, Our father is old, and there is not a man in the earth

to come in unto us after the manner of all the earth: 32 Come, let us make our father drink wine, and we will lie with him, that we may preserve seed of our father. 33 And they made their father drink wine that night: and the firstborn went in, and lay with her father; and he perceived not when she lay down, nor when she arose. 34 And it came to pass on the morrow, that the firstborn said unto the younger, Behold, I lay yesternight with my father: let us make him drink wine this night also; and go thou in, and lie with him, that we may preserve seed of our father. 35 And they made their father drink wine that night also: and the younger arose, and lay with him; and he perceived not when she lay down, nor when she arose. 36 Thus were both the daughters of Lot with child by their father. 37 And the firstborn bare a son, and called his name Moab: the same is the father of the Moabites unto this day. 38 And the younger, she also bare a son, and called his name Ben-ammi: the same is the father of the children of Ammon unto this day.

## ISAAC

21 And the Lord visited Sarah as he had said, and the Lord did unto Sarah as he had spoken. 2 For Sarah conceived, and bare Abraham a son in his old age, at the set time of which God had spoken to him. 3 And Abraham called the name of his son that was born unto him, whom Sarah bare to him, Isaac. 4 And Abraham circumcised his son Isaac being eight days old, as God had commanded him. 5 And Abraham was a hundred years old, when his son Isaac was born unto him. 6 And Sarah said, God hath made me to laugh, so that all that hear will laugh with me. 7 And she said, Who would have said unto Abraham, that Sarah should have given children suck? for I have borne him a son in his old age.

8 And the child grew, and was weaned: and Abraham made a great feast the same day that Isaac was weaned. 9 And Sarah saw the son of Hagar the Egyptian, which she had borne unto Abraham, mocking. 10 Wherefore she said unto Abraham, Cast out this bondwoman and her son: for the son of this bondwoman shall not be heir with my son, even with Isaac. 11 And the thing was very grievous in Abraham's sight because of his son. 12 And God said unto Abraham, Let it not be grievous in thy sight because of the lad, and because of thy bondwoman; in all that Sarah hath said unto thee, hearken unto her voice; for in Isaac shall thy seed be called. 13 And also of the son of the bondwoman will I make a nation, because he is thy seed.

14 And Abraham rose up early in the morning, and took bread, and a bottle of water, and gave it unto Hagar, putting it on her shoulder, and the child, and sent her away: and she departed, and wandered in the wilderness of Beer-sheba. 15 And the water was spent in the bottle, and she cast the child under one of the shrubs. 16 And she went, and sat her down over against him a good way off, as it were a bowshot: for she said, Let me not see the death of the child. And she sat over against him, and lifted up her voice, and wept. 17 And God heard the

voice of the lad; and the angel of God called to Hagar out of heaven, and said unto her, What aileth thee, Hagar? fear not; for God hath heard the voice of the lad where he is. 18 Arise, lift up the lad, and hold him in thine hand; for I will make him a great nation. 19 And God opened her eyes, and she saw a well of water; and she went, and filled the bottle with water, and gave the lad drink. 20 And God was with the lad; and he grew, and dwelt in the wilderness, and became an archer. 21 And he dwelt in the wilderness of Paran: and his mother took him a wife out of the land of Egypt.

22 And it came to pass at that time, that Abimelech and Phichol the chief captain of his host spake unto Abraham, saying, God is with thee in all that thou doest: 23 Now therefore swear unto me here by God, that thou wilt not deal falsely with me, nor with my son, nor with my son's son: but according to the kindness that I have done unto thee, thou shalt do unto me, and to the land wherein thou hast so-journed. 24 And Abraham said, I will swear. 25 And Abraham reproved Abimelech because of a well of water, which Abimelech's servants had violently taken away. 26 And Abimelech said, I wot not who hath done this thing: neither didst thou tell me, neither yet heard I of it, but to-day. 27 And Abraham took sheep and oxen, and gave them unto Abimelech; and both of them made a covenant. 28 And Abraham set seven ewe lambs of the flock by themselves. 29 And Abimelech said unto Abraham, What mean these seven ewe lambs which thou hast set by themselves? 30 And he said, For these seven ewe lambs shalt thou take of my hand, that they may be a witness unto me, that I have digged this well. 31 Wherefore he called that place Beer-sheba; because there they sware both of them. 32 Thus they made a covenant at Beer-sheba: then Abimelech rose up, and Phichol the chief captain of his host, and they returned into the land of the Philistines. 33 And Abraham planted a grove in Beer-sheba, and called there on the name of the Lord, the everlasting God. 34 And Abraham sojourned in the Philistines' land many days.

22 And it came to pass after these things, that God did tempt Abraham, and said unto him, Abraham: and he said, Behold, here I am. 2 And he said, Take now thy son, thine only son Isaac, whom thou lovest, and get thee into the land of Moriah; and offer him there for a burnt offering upon one of the mountains which I will tell thee of. 3 And Abraham rose up early in the morning, and saddled his ass, and took two of his young men with him, and Isaac his son, and clave the wood for the burnt offering, and rose up, and went unto the place of which God had told him. 4 Then on the third day Abraham lifted up his eyes, and saw the place afar off. 5 And Abraham said unto his young men, Abide ye here with the ass; and I and the lad will go yonder and worship, and come again to you. 6 And Abraham took the wood of the burnt offering, and laid it upon Isaac his son; and he took the fire in his hand, and a knife; and they went both of them together. 7 And Isaac spake unto Abraham his father, and said,

My father: and he said, Here am I, my son. And he said, Behold the fire and the wood: but where is the lamb for a burnt offering? 8 And Abraham said, My son, God will provide himself a lamb for a burnt offering: so they went both of them together.

9 And they came to the place which God had told him of; and Abraham built an altar there, and laid the wood in order, and bound Isaac his son, and laid him on the altar upon the wood. 10 And Abraham stretched forth his hand, and took the knife to slay his son. 11 And the Angel of the Lord called unto him out of heaven, and said, Abraham, Abraham: and he said, Here am I. 12 And he said, Lay not thine hand upon the lad, neither do thou any thing unto him: for now I know that thou fearest God, seeing thou hast not withheld thy son, thine only son, from me. 13 And Abraham lifted up his eyes, and looked, and behold behind him a ram caught in a thicket by his horns: and Abraham went and took the ram, and offered him up for a burnt offering in the stead of his son. 14 And Abraham called the name of that place Jehovah-jireh: as it is said to this day, In the mount of the Lord it shall be seen. 15 And the Angel of the Lord called unto Abraham out of heaven the second time, 16 And said, By myself have I sworn, saith the Lord, for because thou hast done this thing, and hast not withheld thy son, thine only son, 17 That in blessing I will bless thee, and in multiplying I will multiply thy seed as the stars of the heaven, and as the sand which is upon the seashore; and thy seed shall possess the gate of his enemies; 18 And in thy seed shall all the nations of the earth be blessed; because thou hast obeyed my voice. 19 So Abraham returned unto his young men, and they rose up and went together to Beer-sheba; and Abraham dwelt at Beer-sheba.

20 And it came to pass after these things, that it was told Abraham, saying, Behold, Milcah, she hath also borne children unto thy brother Nahor; 21 Huz his firstborn, and Buz his brother, and Kemuel the father of Aram, 22 And Chesed, and Hazo, and Pildash, and Jidlaph, and Bethuel. 23 And Bethuel begat Rebekah: these eight Milcah did bear to Nahor, Abraham's brother. 24 And his concubine, whose name was Reumah, she bare also Tebah, and Gaham, and Thahash, and Maachah.

### SARAH'S DEATH

23 And Sarah was a hundred and seven and twenty years old: these were the years of the life of Sarah. 2 And Sarah died in Kirjath-arba; the same is Hebron in the land of Canaan: and Abraham came to mourn for Sarah, and to weep for her. 3 And Abraham stood up from before his dead, and spake unto the sons of Heth, saying, 4 I am a stranger and a sojourner with you: give me a possession of a burying-place with you, that I may bury my dead out of my sight. 5 And the children of Heth answered Abraham, saying unto him, 6 Hear us, my lord: thou art a mighty prince among us: in the choice of our sepulchres bury thy dead; none of us shall withhold from thee his sepulchre,

but that thou mayest bury thy dead. 7 And Abraham stood up, and bowed himself to the people of the land, even to the children of Heth. 8 And he communed with them, saying, If it be your mind that I should bury my dead out of my sight, hear me, and entreat for me to Ephron the son of Zohar, 9 That he may give me the cave of Machpelah, which he hath, which is in the end of his field; for as much money as it is worth he shall give it me for a possession of a buryingplace amongst you.

10 And Ephron dwelt among the children of Heth: and Ephron the Hittite answered Abraham in the audience of the children of Heth, even of all that went in at the gate of his city, saying, 11 Nay, my lord, hear me: the field give I thee, and the cave that is therein, I give it thee; in the presence of the sons of my people give I it thee: bury thy dead. 12 And Abraham bowed down himself before the people of the land. 13 And he spake unto Ephron in the audience of the people of the land, saying, But if thou wilt give it, I pray thee, hear me: I will give thee money for the field; take it of me, and I will bury my dead there. 14 And Ephron answered Abraham, saying unto him, 15 My lord, hearken unto me: the land is worth four hundred shekels of silver; what is that betwixt me and thee? bury therefore thy dead. 16 And Abraham hearkened unto Ephron; and Abraham weighed to Ephron the silver, which he had named in the audience of the sons of Heth, four hundred shekels of silver, current money with the merchant. 17 And the field of Ephron, which was in Machpelah, which was before Mamre, the field, and the cave which was therein, and all the trees that were in the field, that were in all the borders round about, were made sure 18 Unto Abraham for a possession in the presence of the children of Heth, before all that went in at the gate of his city. 19 And after this, Abraham buried Sarah his wife in the cave of the field of Machpelah before Mamre: the same is Hebron in the land of Canaan. 20 And the field, and the cave that is therein, were made sure unto Abraham for a possession of a buryingplace by the sons of Heth.

## ISAAC'S MARRIAGE

24 And Abraham was old, and well stricken in age: and the Lord had blessed Abraham in all things. 2 And Abraham said unto his eldest servant of his house, that ruled over all that he had, Put, I pray thee, thy hand under my thigh:[1] 3 And I will make thee swear by the Lord, the God of heaven, and the God of the earth, that thou shalt not take a wife unto my son of the daughters of the Canaanites, among whom I dwell: 4 But thou shalt go unto my country, and to my kindred, and take a wife unto my son Isaac. 5 And the servant said unto him, Peradventure the woman will not be willing to follow me unto this land: must I needs bring thy son again unto the land from whence

---

[1] A very ancient method of solemnizing an oath.

thou camest? 6 And Abraham said unto him, Beware thou that thou bring not my son thither again. 7 The Lord God of heaven, which took me from my father's house, and from the land of my kindred, and which spake unto me, and that sware unto me, saying, Unto thy seed will I give this land; he shall send his angel before thee, and thou shalt take a wife unto my son from thence. 8 And if the woman will not be willing to follow thee, then thou shalt be clear from this my oath: only bring not my son thither again. 9 And the servant put his hand under the thigh of Abraham his master, and sware to him concerning that matter.

10 And the servant took ten camels of the camels of his master, and departed; for all the goods of his master were in his hand: and he arose, and went to Mesopotamia, unto the city of Nahor. 11 And he made his camels to kneel down without the city by a well of water at the time of the evening, even the time that women go out to draw water. 12 And he said, O Lord God of my master Abraham, I pray thee, send me good speed this day, and show kindness unto my master Abraham. 13 Behold, I stand here by the well of water; and the daughters of the men of the city come out to draw water: 14 And let it come to pass, that the damsel to whom I shall say, Let down thy pitcher, I pray thee, that I may drink; and she shall say, Drink, and I will give thy camels drink also: let the same be she that thou hast appointed for thy servant Isaac; and thereby shall I know that thou hast showed kindness unto my master.

15 And it came to pass, before he had done speaking, that, behold, Rebekah came out, who was born to Bethuel, son of Milcah, the wife of Nahor, Abraham's brother, with her pitcher upon her shoulder. 16 And the damsel was very fair to look upon, a virgin, neither had any man known her: and she went down to the well, and filled her pitcher, and came up. 17 And the servant ran to meet her, and said, Let me, I pray thee, drink a little water of thy pitcher. 18 And she said, Drink, my lord: and she hasted, and let down her pitcher upon her hand, and gave him drink. 19 And when she had done giving him drink, she said, I will draw water for thy camels also, until they have done drinking. 20 And she hasted, and emptied her pitcher into the trough, and ran again unto the well to draw water, and drew for all his camels. 21 And the man wondering at her held his peace, to wit whether the Lord had made his journey prosperous or not. 22 And it came to pass, as the camels had done drinking, that the man took a golden earring of half a shekel weight, and two bracelets for her hands of ten shekels weight of gold; 23 And said, Whose daughter art thou? tell me, I pray thee: is there room in thy father's house for us to lodge in? 24 And she said unto him, I am the daughter of Bethuel the son of Milcah, which she bare unto Nahor. 25 She said moreover unto him, We have both straw and provender enough, and room to lodge in. 26 And the man bowed down his head, and worshipped the Lord. 27 And he said, Blessed be the Lord God of my master Abraham, who hath not left destitute my master of his mercy and his truth: I

being in the way, the Lord led me to the house of my master's brethren. 28 And the damsel ran, and told them of her mother's house these things.

29 And Rebekah had a brother, and his name was Laban: and Laban ran out unto the man, unto the well. 30 And it came to pass, when he saw the earring, and bracelets upon his sister's hands, and when he heard the words of Rebekah his sister, saying, Thus spake the man unto me, that he came unto the man; and, behold, he stood by the camels at the well. 31 And he said, Come in, thou blessed of the Lord; wherefore standest thou without? for I have prepared the house, and room for the camels. 32 And the man came into the house: and he ungirded his camels, and gave straw and provender for the camels, and water to wash his feet, and the men's feet that were with him. 33 And there was set meat before him to eat: but he said, I will not eat, until I have told mine errand. And he said, Speak on. 34 And he said, I am Abraham's servant. 35 And the Lord hath blessed my master greatly, and he is become great: and he hath given him flocks, and herds, and silver, and gold, and menservants, and maidservants, and camels, and asses. 36 And Sarah my master's wife bare a son to my master when she was old: and unto him hath he given all that he hath. 37 And my master made me swear, saying, Thou shalt not take a wife to my son of the daughters of the Canaanites, in whose land I dwell: 38 But thou shalt go unto my father's house, and to my kindred, and take a wife unto my son. 39 And I said unto my master, Peradventure the woman will not follow me. 40 And he said unto me, The Lord, before whom I walk, will send his angel with thee, and prosper thy way; and thou shalt take a wife for my son of my kindred, and of my father's house: 41 Then shalt thou be clear from this my oath, when thou comest to my kindred; and if they give not thee one, thou shalt be clear from my oath. 42 And I came this day unto the well, and said, O Lord God of my master Abraham, if now thou do prosper my way which I go: 43 Behold, I stand by the well of water; and it shall come to pass, that when the virgin cometh forth to draw water, and I say to her, Give me, I pray thee, a little water of thy pitcher to drink; 44 And she say to me, Both drink thou, and I will also draw for thy camels: let the same be the woman whom the Lord hath appointed out for my master's son. 45 And before I had done speaking in mine heart, behold, Rebekah came forth with her pitcher on her shoulder; and she went down unto the well, and drew water: and I said unto her, Let me drink, I pray thee. 46 And she made haste, and let down her pitcher from her shoulder, and said, Drink, and I will give thy camels drink also: so I drank, and she made the camels drink also. 47 And I asked her, and said, Whose daughter art thou? And she said, The daughter of Bethuel, Nahor's son, whom Milcah bare unto him: and I put the earring upon her face, and the bracelets upon her hands. 48 And I bowed down my head, and worshipped the Lord, and blessed the Lord God of my master Abraham, which had led me in the right way to take my master's brother's

daughter unto his son. 49 And now, if ye will deal kindly and truly with my master, tell me: and if not, tell me; that I may turn to the right hand, or to the left.

50 Then Laban and Bethuel answered and said, The thing proceedeth from the Lord: we cannot speak unto thee bad or good. 51 Behold, Rebekah is before thee; take her, and go, and let her be thy master's son's wife, as the Lord hath spoken. 52 And it came to pass, that, when Abraham's servant heard their words, he worshipped the Lord, bowing himself to the earth. 53 And the servant brought forth jewels of silver, and jewels of gold, and raiment, and gave them to Rebekah: he gave also to her brother and to her mother precious things. 54 And they did eat and drink, he and the men that were with him, and tarried all night; and they rose up in the morning, and he said, Send me away unto my master. 55 And her brother and her mother said, Let the damsel abide with us a few days, at the least ten; after that she shall go. 56 And he said unto them, Hinder me not, seeing the Lord hath prospered my way; send me away that I may go to my master. 57 And they said, We will call the damsel, and inquire at her mouth. 58 And they called Rebekah, and said unto her, Wilt thou go with this man? And she said, I will go. 59 And they sent away Rebekah their sister, and her nurse, and Abraham's servant, and his men. 60 And they blessed Rebekah, and said unto her,

Thou art our sister;
Be thou the mother of thousands of millions,
And let thy seed possess the gate[1] of those which hate them.

61 And Rebekah arose, and her damsels, and they rode upon the camels, and followed the man: and the servant took Rebekah, and went his way. 62 And Isaac came from the way of the well Lahai-roi; for he dwelt in the south country. 63 And Isaac went out to meditate in the field at the eventide: and he lifted up his eyes, and saw, and, behold, the camels were coming. 64 And Rebekah lifted up her eyes, and when she saw Isaac, she lighted off the camel. 65 For she had said unto the servant, What man is this that walketh in the field to meet us? And the servant had said, It is my master: therefore she took a veil, and covered herself. 66 And the servant told Isaac all things that he had done. 67 And Isaac brought her into his mother Sarah's tent, and took Rebekah, and she became his wife; and he loved her: and Isaac was comforted after his mother's death.

## ABRAHAM'S DEATH

25 5 And Abraham gave all that he had unto Isaac. 6 But unto the sons of the concubines, which Abraham had, Abraham gave gifts, and sent them away from Isaac his son, while he yet lived, eastward, unto the east country. 7 And these are the days of the years of Abraham's life which he lived, a hundred threescore and fifteen years.

---

[1] The seat of judgment and authority was traditionally at the gate of a city.

8 Then Abraham gave up the ghost, and died in a good old age, an old man, and full of years; and was gathered to his people. 9 And his sons Isaac and Ishmael buried him in the cave of Machpelah, in the field of Ephron the son of Zohar the Hittite, which is before Mamre; 10 The field which Abraham purchased of the sons of Heth: there was Abraham buried, and Sarah his wife. 11 And it came to pass after the death of Abraham, that God blessed his son Isaac; and Isaac dwelt by the well Lahai-roi.

12 Now these are the generations of Ishmael, Abraham's son, whom Hagar the Egyptian, Sarah's handmaid, bare unto Abraham: 13 And these are the names of the sons of Ishmael, by their names, according to their generations: the firstborn of Ishmael, Nebajoth; and Kedar, and Adbeel, and Mibsam, 14 And Mishma, and Dumah, and Massa, 15 Hadar, and Tema, Jetur, Naphish, and Kedemah: 16 These are the sons of Ishmael, and these are their names, by their towns, and by their castles; twelve princes according to their nations. 17 And these are the years of the life of Ishmael, a hundred and thirty and seven years: and he gave up the ghost and died, and was gathered unto his people. 18 And they dwelt from Havilah unto Shur, that is before Egypt, as thou goest toward Assyria: and he died in the presence of all his brethren.

## ISAAC'S SONS

19 And these are the generations of Isaac, Abraham's son: Abraham begat Isaac. 20 And Isaac was forty years old when he took Rebekah to wife, the daughter of Bethuel the Syrian of Padan-aram, the sister to Laban the Syrian. 21 And Isaac entreated the Lord for his wife, because she was barren: and the Lord was entreated of him, and Rebekah his wife conceived. 22 And the children struggled together within her; and she said, If it be so, why am I thus? And she went to inquire of the Lord. 23 And the Lord said unto her,

Two nations are in thy womb,
And two manner of people shall be separated from thy bowels;
And the one people shall be stronger than the other people;
And the elder shall serve the younger.

24 And when her days to be delivered were fulfilled, behold, there were twins in her womb. 25 And the first came out red, all over like a hairy garment; and they called his name Esau. 26 And after that came his brother out, and his hand took hold on Esau's heel; and his name was called Jacob: and Isaac was threescore years old when she bare them.

27 And the boys grew: and Esau was a cunning hunter, a man of the field; and Jacob was a plain man, dwelling in tents. 28 And Isaac loved Esau, because he did eat of his venison: but Rebekah loved Jacob. 29 And Jacob sod[1] pottage: and Esau came from the field, and

[1] Cooked.

he was faint: 30 And Esau said to Jacob, Feed me, I pray thee, with that same red pottage; for I am faint: therefore was his name called Edom. 31 And Jacob said, Sell me this day thy birthright. 32 And Esau said, Behold, I am at the point to die: and what profit shall this birthright do to me? 33 And Jacob said, Swear to me this day; and he sware unto him: and he sold his birthright unto Jacob. 34 Then Jacob gave Esau bread and pottage of lentils; and he did eat and drink, and rose up, and went his way. Thus Esau despised his birthright.

26 And there was a famine in the land, besides the first famine that was in the days of Abraham. And Isaac went unto Abimelech king of the Philistines unto Gerar. 2 And the Lord appeared unto him, and said, Go not down into Egypt; dwell in the land which I shall tell thee of. 3 Sojourn in this land, and I will be with thee, and will bless thee; for unto thee, and unto thy seed, I will give all these countries, and I will perform the oath which I sware unto Abraham thy father; 4 And I will make thy seed to multiply as the stars of heaven, and will give unto thy seed all these countries; and in thy seed shall all the nations of the earth be blessed: 5 Because that Abraham obeyed my voice, and kept my charge, my commandments, my statutes, and my laws.

6 And Isaac dwelt in Gerar. 7 And the men of the place asked him of his wife; and he said, She is my sister: for he feared to say, She is my wife; lest, said he, the men of the place should kill me for Rebekah; because she was fair to look upon. 8 And it came to pass, when he had been there a long time, that Abimelech king of the Philistines looked out at a window, and saw, and, behold, Isaac was sporting with Rebekah his wife. 9 And Abimelech called Isaac, and said, Behold, of a surety she is thy wife: and how saidst thou, She is my sister? And Isaac said unto him, Because I said, Lest I die for her. 10 And Abimelech said, What is this thou hast done unto us? one of the people might lightly have lain with thy wife, and thou shouldest have brought guiltiness upon us. 11 And Abimelech charged all his people, saying, He that toucheth this man or his wife shall surely be put to death. 12 Then Isaac sowed in that land, and received in the same year a hundredfold: and the Lord blessed him. 13 And the man waxed great, and went forward, and grew until he became very great: 14 For he had possession of flocks, and possession of herds, and great store of servants: and the Philistines envied him. 15 For all the wells which his father's servants had digged in the days of Abraham his father, the Philistines had stopped them, and filled them with earth. 16 And Abimelech said unto Isaac, Go from us; for thou art much mightier than we.

17 And Isaac departed thence, and pitched his tent in the valley of Gerar, and dwelt there. 18 And Isaac digged again the wells of water, which they had digged in the days of Abraham his father; for the Philistines had stopped them after the death of Abraham: and he called their names after the names by which his father had called

them. 19 And Isaac's servants digged in the valley, and found there a well of springing water. 20 And the herdmen of Gerar did strive with Isaac's herdmen, saying, The water is ours: and he called the name of the well Esek; because they strove with him. 21 And they digged another well, and strove for that also: and he called the name of it Sitnah. 22 And he removed from thence, and digged another well; and for that they strove not: and he called the name of it Rehoboth; and he said, For now the Lord hath made room for us, and we shall be fruitful in the land.

23 And he went up from thence to Beer-sheba. 24 And the Lord appeared unto him the same night, and said, I am the God of Abraham thy father: fear not, for I am with thee, and will bless thee, and multiply thy seed for my servant Abraham's sake. 25 And he builded an altar there, and called upon the name of the Lord, and pitched his tent there: and there Isaac's servants digged a well.

26 Then Abimelech went to him from Gerar, and Ahuzzath one of his friends, and Phichol the chief captain of his army. 27 And Isaac said unto them, Wherefore come ye to me, seeing ye hate me, and have sent me away from you? 28 And they said, We saw certainly that the Lord was with thee: and we said, Let there be now an oath betwixt us, even betwixt us and thee, and let us make a covenant with thee; 29 That thou wilt do us no hurt, as we have not touched thee, and as we have done unto thee nothing but good, and have sent thee away in peace: thou art now the blessed of the Lord. 30 And he made them a feast, and they did eat and drink. 31 And they rose up betimes in the morning, and sware one to another: and Isaac sent them away, and they departed from him in peace. 32 And it came to pass the same day, that Isaac's servants came, and told him concerning the well which they had digged, and said unto him, We have found water. 33 And he called it Shebah: therefore the name of the city is Beersheba unto this day.

34 And Esau was forty years old when he took to wife Judith the daughter of Beeri the Hittite, and Bashemath the daughter of Elon the Hittite: 35 Which were a grief of mind unto Isaac and to Rebekah.

## JACOB THE TRICKSTER

27 And it came to pass, that when Isaac was old, and his eyes were dim, so that he could not see, he called Esau his eldest son, and said unto him, My son: and he said unto him, Behold, here am I. 2 And he said, Behold now, I am old, I know not the day of my death: 3 Now therefore take, I pray thee, thy weapons, thy quiver and thy bow, and go out to the field, and take me some venison; 4 And make me savory meat, such as I love, and bring it to me, that I may eat; that my soul may bless thee before I die.

5 And Rebekah heard when Isaac spake to Esau his son. And Esau went to the field to hunt for venison, and to bring it. 6 And Rebekah

spake unto Jacob her son, saying, Behold, I heard thy father speak unto Esau thy brother, saying, 7 Bring me venison, and make me savory meat, that I may eat, and bless thee before the Lord before my death. 8 Now therefore, my son, obey my voice according to that which I command thee. 9 Go now to the flock, and fetch me from thence two good kids of the goats; and I will make them savory meat for thy father, such as he loveth: 10 And thou shalt bring it to thy father, that he may eat, and that he may bless thee before his death. 11 And Jacob said to Rebekah his mother, Behold, Esau my brother is a hairy man, and I am a smooth man: 12 My father peradventure will feel me, and I shall seem to him as a deceiver; and I shall bring a curse upon me, and not a blessing. 13 And his mother said unto him, Upon me be thy curse, my son: only obey my voice, and go fetch me them. 14 And he went, and fetched, and brought them to his mother: and his mother made savory meat, such as his father loved. 15 And Rebekah took goodly raiment of her eldest son Esau, which were with her in the house, and put them upon Jacob her younger son: 16 And she put the skins of the kids of the goats upon his hands, and upon the smooth of his neck: 17 And she gave the savory meat and the bread, which she had prepared, into the hand of her son Jacob.

18 And he came unto his father, and said, My father: and he said, Here am I; who art thou, my son? 19 And Jacob said unto his father, I am Esau thy firstborn; I have done according as thou badest me: arise, I pray thee, sit and eat of my venison, that thy soul may bless me. 20 And Isaac said unto his son, How is it that thou hast found it so quickly, my son? And he said, Because the Lord thy God brought it to me. 21 And Isaac said unto Jacob, Come near, I pray thee, that I may feel thee, my son, whether thou be my very son Esau or not. 22 And Jacob went near unto Isaac his father; and he felt him, and said, The voice is Jacob's voice, but the hands are the hands of Esau. 23 And he discerned him not, because his hands were hairy, as his brother Esau's hands: so he blessed him. 24 And he said, Art thou my very son Esau? And he said, I am. 25 And he said, Bring it near to me, and I will eat of my son's venison, that my soul may bless thee. And he brought it near to him, and he did eat: and he brought him wine, and he drank. 26 And his father Isaac said unto him, Come near now, and kiss me, my son. 27 And he came near, and kissed him: and he smelled the smell of his raiment, and blessed him, and said,

> See, the smell of my son
> Is as the smell of a field
> Which the Lord hath blessed:

28 Therefore God give thee
> Of the dew of heaven,
> And the fatness of the earth,
> And plenty of corn and wine:

29 Let people serve thee,
> And nations bow down to thee:
> Be lord over thy brethren,

And let thy mother's sons bow down to thee:
Cursed be every one that curseth thee,
And blessed be he that blesseth thee.

30 And it came to pass, as soon as Isaac had made an end of blessing Jacob, and Jacob was yet scarce gone out from the presence of Isaac his father, that Esau his brother came in from his hunting. 31 And he also had made savory meat, and brought it unto his father, and said unto his father, Let my father arise, and eat of his son's venison, that thy soul may bless me. 32 And Isaac his father said unto him, Who art thou? And he said, I am thy son, thy firstborn, Esau. 33 And Isaac trembled very exceedingly, and said, Who? where is he that hath taken venison, and brought it me, and I have eaten of all before thou camest, and have blessed him? yea, and he shall be blessed. 34 And when Esau heard the words of his father, he cried with a great and exceeding bitter cry, and said unto his father, Bless me, even me also, O my father. 35 And he said, Thy brother came with subtilty, and hath taken away thy blessing. 36 And he said, Is not he rightly named Jacob? for he hath supplanted me these two times: he took away my birthright; and, behold, now he hath taken away my blessing. And he said, Hast thou not reserved a blessing for me? 37 And Isaac answered and said unto Esau, Behold, I have made him thy lord, and all his brethren have I given to him for servants; and with corn and wine have I sustained him: and what shall I do now unto thee, my son? 38 And Esau said unto his father, Hast thou but one blessing, my father? bless me, even me also, O my father. And Esau lifted up his voice, and wept. 39 And Isaac his father answered and said unto him,

Behold, thy dwelling shall be the fatness of the earth,
And of the dew of heaven from above;
40 And by thy sword shalt thou live,
And shalt serve thy brother:
And it shall come to pass when thou shalt have the dominion,
That thou shalt break his yoke from off thy neck.

## JACOB'S FLIGHT

41 And Esau hated Jacob because of the blessing wherewith his father blessed him: and Esau said in his heart, The days of mourning for my father are at hand; then will I slay my brother Jacob. 42 And these words of Esau her elder son were told to Rebekah: and she sent and called Jacob her younger son, and said unto him, Behold, thy brother Esau, as touching thee, doth comfort himself, purposing to kill thee. 43 Now therefore, my son, obey my voice; and arise, flee thou to Laban my brother to Haran;

44 And tarry with him a few days, until thy brother's fury turn away; 45 Until thy brother's anger turn away from thee, and he forget that which thou hast done to him: then I will send, and fetch thee from thence: why should I be deprived also of you both in one day?

46 And Rebekah said to Isaac, I am weary of my life because of the daughters of Heth: if Jacob take a wife of the daughters of Heth, such as these which are of the daughters of the land, what good shall my life do me?

28 And Isaac called Jacob, and blessed him, and charged him, and said unto him, Thou shalt not take a wife of the daughters of Canaan. 2 Arise, go to Padan-aram, to the house of Bethuel thy mother's father; and take thee a wife from thence of the daughters of Laban thy mother's brother. 3 And God Almighty bless thee, and make thee fruitful, and multiply thee, that thou mayest be a multitude of people; 4 And give thee the blessing of Abraham, to thee, and to thy seed with thee; that thou mayest inherit the land wherein thou art a stranger, which God gave unto Abraham. 5 And Isaac sent away Jacob: and he went to Padan-aram unto Laban, son of Bethuel the Syrian, the brother of Rebekah, Jacob's and Esau's mother.

6 When Esau saw that Isaac had blessed Jacob, and sent him away to Padan-aram, to take him a wife from thence; and that as he blessed him he gave him a charge, saying, Thou shalt not take a wife of the daughters of Canaan; 7 And that Jacob obeyed his father and his mother, and was gone to Padan-aram; 8 And Esau seeing that the daughters of Canaan pleased not Isaac his father; 9 Then went Esau unto Ishmael, and took unto the wives which he had Mahalath the daughter of Ishmael Abraham's son, the sister of Nebajoth, to be his wife.

10 And Jacob went out from Beer-sheba, and went toward Haran. 11 And he lighted upon a certain place, and tarried there all night, because the sun was set; and he took of the stones of that place, and put them for his pillows, and lay down in that place to sleep. 12 And he dreamed, and behold a ladder set up on the earth, and the top of it reached to heaven: and behold the angels of God ascending and descending on it. 13 And, behold, the Lord stood above it, and said, I am the Lord God of Abraham thy father, and the God of Isaac: the land whereon thou liest, to thee will I give it, and to thy seed; 14 And thy seed shall be as the dust of the earth; and thou shalt spread abroad to the west, and to the east, and to the north, and to the south: and in thee and in thy seed shall all the families of the earth be blessed. 15 And, behold, I am with thee, and will keep thee in all places whither thou goest, and will bring thee again into this land; for I will not leave thee, until I have done that which I have spoken to thee of. 16 And Jacob awaked out of his sleep, and he said, Surely the Lord is in this place; and I knew it not. 17 And he was afraid, and said, How dreadful is this place! this is none other but the house of God, and this is the gate of heaven.

18 And Jacob rose up early in the morning, and took the stone that he had put for his pillows, and set it up for a pillar, and poured oil upon the top of it. 19 And he called the name of that place Beth-el: but the name of that city was called Luz at the first. 20 And Jacob vowed

a vow, saying, If God will be with me, and will keep me in this way that I go, and will give me bread to eat, and raiment to put on, 21 So that I come again to my father's house in peace; then shall the Lord be my God: 22 And this stone, which I have set for a pillar, shall be God's house: and of all that thou shalt give me I will surely give the tenth unto thee.

## JACOB'S MARRIAGE

29 Then Jacob went on his journey, and came into the land of the people of the east. 2 And he looked, and behold a well in the field, and, lo, there were three flocks of sheep lying by it; for out of that well they watered the flocks: and a great stone was upon the well's mouth. 3 And thither were all the flocks gathered: and they rolled the stone from the well's mouth, and watered the sheep, and put the stone again upon the well's mouth in his place. 4 And Jacob said unto them, My brethren, whence be ye? And they said, Of Haran are we. 5 And he said unto them, Know ye Laban the son of Nahor? And they said, We know him. 6 And he said unto them, Is he well? And they said, He is well: and, behold, Rachel his daughter cometh with the sheep. 7 And he said, Lo, it is yet high day, neither is it time that the cattle should be gathered together: water ye the sheep, and go and feed them. 8 And they said, We cannot, until all the flocks be gathered together, and till they roll the stone from the well's mouth; then we water the sheep. 9 And while he yet spake with them, Rachel came with her father's sheep: for she kept them. 10 And it came to pass, when Jacob saw Rachel the daughter of Laban his mother's brother, and the sheep of Laban his mother's brother, that Jacob went near, and rolled the stone from the well's mouth, and watered the flock of Laban his mother's brother. 11 And Jacob kissed Rachel, and lifted up his voice, and wept. 12 And Jacob told Rachel that he was her father's brother, and that he was Rebekah's son: and she ran and told her father.

13 And it came to pass, when Laban heard the tidings of Jacob his sister's son, that he ran to meet him, and embraced him, and kissed him, and brought him to his house. And he told Laban all these things. 14 And Laban said to him, Surely thou art my bone and my flesh. And he abode with him the space of a month. 15 And Laban said unto Jacob, Because thou art my brother, shouldest thou therefore serve me for nought? tell me, what shall thy wages be? 16 And Laban had two daughters: the name of the elder was Leah, and the name of the younger was Rachel. 17 Leah was tender eyed[1]; but Rachel was beautiful and well-favored. 18 And Jacob loved Rachel; and said, I will serve thee seven years for Rachel thy younger daughter. 19 And Laban said, It is better that I give her to thee, than that I should give her to another man: abide with me. 20 And Jacob served seven

---

[1] I.e., had weak eyes.

years for Rachel; and they seemed unto him but a few days, for the love he had to her.

21 And Jacob said unto Laban, Give me my wife, for my days are fulfilled, that I may go in unto her. 22 And Laban gathered together all the men of the place, and made a feast. 23 And it came to pass in the evening, that he took Leah his daughter, and brought her to him; and he went in unto her. 24 And Laban gave unto his daughter Leah Zilpah his maid for a handmaid. 25 And it came to pass, that in the morning, behold, it was Leah: and he said to Laban, What is this thou hast done unto me? did not I serve with thee for Rachel? wherefore then hast thou beguiled me? 26 And Laban said, It must not be so done in our country, to give the younger before the firstborn. 27 Fulfil her week, and we will give thee this also for the service which thou shalt serve with me yet seven other years. 28 And Jacob did so, and fulfilled her week: and he gave him Rachel his daughter to wife also. 29 And Laban gave to Rachel his daughter Bilhah his handmaid to be her maid. 30 And he went in also unto Rachel, and he loved also Rachel more than Leah, and served with him yet seven other years.

31 And when the Lord saw that Leah was hated, he opened her womb: but Rachel was barren. 32 And Leah conceived, and bare a son; and she called his name Reuben: for she said, Surely the Lord hath looked upon my affliction; now therefore my husband will love me. 33 And she conceived again, and bare a son; and said, Because the Lord hath heard that I was hated, he hath therefore given me this son also: and she called his name Simeon. 34 And she conceived again, and bare a son; and said, Now this time will my husband be joined unto me, because I have borne him three sons: therefore was his name called Levi. 35 And she conceived again, and bare a son; and she said, Now will I praise the Lord: therefore she called his name Judah; and left bearing.

30 And when Rachel saw that she bare Jacob no children, Rachel envied her sister; and said unto Jacob, Give me children, or else I die. 2 And Jacob's anger was kindled against Rachel; and he said, Am I in God's stead, who hath withheld from thee the fruit of the womb? 3 And she said, Behold my maid Bilhah, go in unto her; and she shall bear upon my knees, that I may also have children by her. 4 And she gave him Bilhah her handmaid to wife: and Jacob went in unto her. 5 And Bilhah conceived, and bare Jacob a son. 6 And Rachel said, God hath judged me, and hath also heard my voice, and hath given me a son: therefore called she his name Dan. 7 And Bilhah Rachel's maid conceived again, and bare Jacob a second son. 8 And Rachel said, With great wrestlings have I wrestled with my sister, and I have prevailed: and she called his name Naphtali. 9 When Leah saw that she had left bearing, she took Zilpah her maid, and gave her Jacob to wife. 10 And Zilpah Leah's maid bare Jacob a son. 11 And Leah said, A troop cometh: and she called his name Gad. 12 And Zilpah Leah's maid bare Jacob a second son. 13 And Leah said, Happy am I,

for the daughters will call me blessed: and she called his name Asher.

14 And Reuben went in the days of wheat harvest, and found mandrakes[1] in the field, and brought them unto his mother Leah. Then Rachel said to Leah, Give me, I pray thee, of thy son's mandrakes. 15 And she said unto her, Is it a small matter that thou hast taken my husband? and wouldest thou take away my son's mandrakes also? And Rachel said, Therefore he shall lie with thee to-night for thy son's mandrakes. 16 And Jacob came out of the field in the evening, and Leah went out to meet him, and said, Thou must come in unto me; for surely I have hired thee with my son's mandrakes. And he lay with her that night. 17 And God hearkened unto Leah, and she conceived, and bare Jacob the fifth son. 18 And Leah said, God hath given me my hire because I have given my maiden to my husband: and she called his name Issachar. 19 And Leah conceived again, and bare Jacob the sixth son. 20 And Leah said, God hath endued me with a good dowry; now will my husband dwell with me, because I have borne him six sons: and she called his name Zebulun. 21 And afterward she bare a daughter, and called her name Dinah. 22 And God remembered Rachel, and God hearkened to her, and opened her womb. 23 And she conceived, and bare a son; and said, God hath taken away my reproach. 24 And she called his name Joseph; and said, The Lord shall add to me another son.

## JACOB OUTWITS LABAN AT LAST

25 And it came to pass, when Rachel had borne Joseph, that Jacob said unto Laban, Send me away, that I may go unto mine own place, and to my country. 26 Give me my wives and my children, for whom I have served thee, and let me go: for thou knowest my service which I have done thee. 27 And Laban said unto him, I pray thee, if I have found favor in thine eyes, tarry: for I have learned by experience that the Lord hath blessed me for thy sake. 28 And he said, Appoint me thy wages, and I will give it. 29 And he said unto him, Thou knowest how I have served thee, and how thy cattle was with me. 30 For it was little which thou hadst before I came, and it is now increased unto a multitude; and the Lord hath blessed thee since my coming: and now, when shall I provide for mine own house also? 31 And he said, What shall I give thee? And Jacob said, Thou shalt not give me any thing: if thou wilt do this thing for me, I will again feed and keep thy flock. 32 I will pass through all thy flock to-day, removing from thence all the speckled and spotted cattle, and all the brown cattle among the sheep, and the spotted and speckled among the goats: and of such shall be my hire. 33 So shall my righteousness answer for me in time to come, when it shall come for my hire before thy face: every one that is not speckled and spotted among the goats, and brown among the sheep, that shall be counted stolen with me.

---

[1] Used to make a love potion.

34 And Laban said, Behold, I would it might be according to thy word. 35 And he removed that day the he goats that were ring-streaked and spotted, and all the she goats that were speckled and spotted, and every one that had some white in it, and all the brown among the sheep, and gave them into the hand of his sons. 36 And he set three days' journey betwixt himself and Jacob: and Jacob fed the rest of Laban's flocks.

37 And Jacob took him rods of green poplar, and of the hazel and chestnut tree; and pilled[1] white streaks in them, and made the white appear which was in the rods. 38 And he set the rods which he had pilled before the flocks in the gutters in the watering troughs when the flocks came to drink, that they should conceive when they came to drink. 39 And the flocks conceived before the rods, and brought forth cattle ring-streaked, speckled, and spotted. 40 And Jacob did separate the lambs, and set the faces of the flocks toward the ring-streaked, and all the brown in the flock of Laban; and he put his own flocks by themselves, and put them not unto Laban's cattle. 41 And it came to pass, whensoever the stronger cattle did conceive, that Jacob laid the rods before the eyes of the cattle in the gutters, that they might conceive among the rods. 42 But when the cattle were feeble, he put them not in: so the feebler were Laban's, and the stronger Jacob's. 43 And the man increased exceedingly, and had much cattle, and maidservants, and menservants, and camels, and asses.

31 And he heard the words of Laban's sons, saying, Jacob hath taken away all that was our father's; and of that which was our father's hath he gotten all this glory. 2 And Jacob beheld the countenance of Laban, and, behold, it was not toward him as before. 3 And the Lord said unto Jacob, Return unto the land of thy fathers, and to thy kindred; and I will be with thee. 4 And Jacob sent and called Rachel and Leah to the field unto his flock, 5 And said unto them, I see your father's countenance, that it is not toward me as before; but the God of my father hath been with me. 6 And ye know that with all my power I have served your father. 7 And your father hath deceived me, and changed my wages ten times; but God suffered him not to hurt me. 8 If he said thus, The speckled shall be thy wages; then all the cattle bare speckled: and if he said thus, the ring-streaked shall be thy hire; then bare all the cattle ring-streaked. 9 Thus God hath taken away the cattle of your father, and given them to me. 10 And it came to pass at the time that the cattle conceived, that I lifted up mine eyes, and saw in a dream, and, behold, the rams which leaped upon the cattle were ring-streaked, speckled and grizzled. 11 And the angel of God spake unto me in a dream, saying, Jacob: and I said, Here am I. 12 And he said, Lift up now thine eyes, and see, all the rams which leap upon the cattle are ring-streaked, speckled,

[1] Pilled. This use of sticks was thought by ancient herdsmen to be very effective in breeding cattle.

and grizzled: for I have seen all that Laban doeth unto thee. 13 I am the God of Beth-el, where thou anointedst the pillar, and where thou vowedst a vow unto me: now arise, get thee out from this land, and return unto the land of thy kindred. 14 And Rachel and Leah answered and said unto him, Is there yet any portion or inheritance for us in our father's house? 15 Are we not counted of him strangers? for he hath sold us, and hath quite devoured also our money. 16 For all the riches which God hath taken from our father, that is ours, and our children's: now then, whatsoever God hath said unto thee, do.

17 Then Jacob rose up, and set his sons and his wives upon camels; 18 And he carried away all his cattle, and all his goods which he had gotten, the cattle of his getting, which he had gotten in Padan-aram, for to go to Isaac his father in the land of Canaan. 19 And Laban went to shear his sheep: and Rachel had stolen the images that were her father's. 20 And Jacob stole away unawares to Laban the Syrian, in that he told him not that he fled. 21 So he fled with all that he had; and he rose up, and passed over the river, and set his face toward the mount Gilead.

22 And it was told Laban on the third day, that Jacob was fled. 23 And he took his brethren with him, and pursued after him seven days' journey; and they overtook him in the mount Gilead. 24 And God came to Laban the Syrian in a dream by night, and said unto him, Take heed that thou speak not to Jacob either good or bad. 25 Then Laban overtook Jacob. Now Jacob had pitched his tent in the mount: and Laban with his brethren pitched in the mount of Gilead. 26 And Laban said to Jacob, What hast thou done, that thou hast stolen away unawares to me, and carried away my daughters, as captives taken with the sword? 27 Wherefore didst thou flee away secretly, and steal away from me; and didst not tell me, that I might have sent thee away with mirth, and with songs, with tabret, and with harp? 28 And has not suffered me to kiss my sons and my daughters? thou hast now done foolishly in so doing. 29 It is in the power of my hand to do you hurt: but the God of your father spake unto me yesternight, saying, Take thou heed that thou speak not to Jacob either good or bad. 30 And now, though thou wouldest needs be gone, because thou sore longedst after thy father's house, yet wherefore hast thou stolen my gods? 31 And Jacob answered and said to Laban, Because I was afraid: for I said, Peradventure thou wouldest take by force thy daughters from me. 32 With whomsoever thou findest thy gods, let him not live: before our brethren discern thou what is thine with me, and take it to thee. For Jacob knew not that Rachel had stolen them.

33 And Laban went into Jacob's tent, and into Leah's tent, and into the two maidservants' tents; but he found them not. Then went he out of Leah's tent, and entered into Rachel's tent. 34 Now Rachel had taken the images, and put them in the camel's furniture, and sat upon them. And Laban searched all the tent, but found them not. 35 And

she said to her father, Let it not displease my lord that I cannot rise up before thee; for the custom of women is upon me. And he searched, but found not the images.

36 And Jacob was wroth, and chode with Laban: and Jacob answered and said to Laban, What is my trespass? what is my sin, that thou hast so hotly pursued after me? 37 Whereas thou hast searched all my stuff, what hast thou found of all thy household stuff? set it here before my brethren and thy brethren, that they may judge betwixt us both. 38 This twenty years have I been with thee; thy ewes and thy she goats have not cast their young, and the rams of thy flock have I not eaten. 39 That which was torn of beasts I brought not unto thee; I bare the loss of it; of my hand didst thou require it, whether stolen by day, or stolen by night. 40 Thus I was; in the day the drought consumed me, and the frost by night; and my sleep departed from mine eyes. 41 Thus have I been twenty years in thy house: I served thee fourteen years for thy two daughters, and six years for thy cattle, and thou hast changed my wages ten times. 42 Except the God of my father, the God of Abraham, and the fear of Isaac, had been with me, surely thou hadst sent me away now empty. God hath seen mine affliction and the labor of my hands, and rebuked thee yesternight.

43 And Laban answered and said unto Jacob, These daughters are my daughters, and these children are my children, and these cattle are my cattle, and all that thou seest is mine: and what can I do this day unto these my daughters, or unto their children which they have borne? 44 Now therefore come thou, let us make a covenant, I and thou; and let it be for a witness between me and thee. 45 And Jacob took a stone, and set it up for a pillar. 46 And Jacob said unto his brethren, Gather stones, and they took stones, and made a heap: and they did eat there upon the heap. 47 And Laban called it Jegarsahadutha: but Jacob called it Galeed. 48 And Laban said, This heap is a witness between me and thee this day. Therefore was the name of it called Galeed. 49 And Mizpah; for he said, The Lord watch between me and thee, when we are absent one from another. 50 If thou shalt afflict my daughters, or if thou shalt take other wives beside my daughters, no man is with us; see, God is witness betwixt me and thee. 51 And Laban said to Jacob, Behold this heap, and behold this pillar, which I have cast betwixt me and thee; 52 This heap be witness, and this pillar be witness, that I will not pass over this heap to thee, and that thou shalt not pass over this heap and this pillar unto me, for harm. 53 The God of Abraham, and the God of Nahor, the God of their father, judge betwixt us. And Jacob sware by the fear of his father Isaac. 54 Then Jacob offered sacrifice upon the mount, and called his brethren to eat bread: and they did eat bread, and tarried all night in the mount. 55 And early in the morning Laban rose up, and kissed his sons and his daughters, and blessed them: and Laban departed, and returned unto his place.

## JACOB RETURNS HOME

**32** And Jacob went on his way, and the angels of God met him. 2 And when Jacob saw them, he said, This is God's host: and he called the name of that place Mahanaim.

3 And Jacob sent messengers before him to Esau his brother unto the land of Seir, the country of Edom. 4 And he commanded them, saying, Thus shall ye speak unto my lord Esau; Thy servant Jacob saith thus, I have sojourned with Laban, and stayed there until now: 5 And I have oxen, and asses, flocks, and menservants, and womenservants: and I have sent to tell my lord, that I may find grace in thy sight. 6 And the messengers returned to Jacob, saying, We came to thy brother Esau, and also he cometh to meet thee, and four hundred men with him. 7 Then Jacob was greatly afraid and distressed: and he divided the people that was with him, and the flocks, and herds, and the camels, into two bands; 8 And said, If Esau come to the one company, and smite it, then the other company which is left shall escape.

9 And Jacob said, O God of my father Abraham, and God of my father Isaac, the Lord which saidst unto me, Return unto thy country, and to thy kindred, and I will deal well with thee: 10 I am not worthy of the least of all the mercies, and of all the truth, which thou hast showed unto thy servant; for with my staff I passed over this Jordan; and now I am become two bands. 11 Deliver me, I pray thee, from the hand of my brother, from the hand of Esau: for I fear him, lest he will come and smite me, and the mother with the children. 12 And thou saidst, I will surely do thee good, and make thy seed as the sand of the sea, which cannot be numbered for multitude.

13 And he lodged there that same night; and took of that which came to his hand a present for Esau his brother; 14 Two hundred she goats and twenty he goats, two hundred ewes and twenty rams, 15 Thirty milch camels with their colts, forty kine and ten bulls, twenty she asses and ten foals. 16 And he delivered them into the hand of his servants, every drove by themselves; and said unto his servants, Pass over before me, and put a space betwixt drove and drove. 17 And he commanded the foremost, saying, When Esau my brother meeteth thee, and asketh thee, saying, Whose art thou? and whither goest thou? and whose are these before thee? 18 Then thou shalt say, They be thy servant Jacob's; it is a present sent unto my lord Esau: and, behold, also he is behind us. 19 And so commanded he the second, and the third, and all that followed the droves, saying, On this manner shall ye speak unto Esau, when ye find him. 20 And say ye moreover, Behold, thy servant Jacob is behind us. For he said, I will appease him with the present that goeth before me, and afterward I will see his face; peradventure he will accept of me. 21 So went the present over before him; and himself lodged that night in the company. 22 And he rose up that night, and took his two wives, and his

two womenservants, and his eleven sons, and passed over the ford Jabbok. 23 And he took them, and sent them over the brook, and sent over that he had.

24 And Jacob was left alone; and there wrestled a man with him until the breaking of the day. 25 And when he saw that he prevailed not against him, he touched the hollow of his thigh; and the hollow of Jacob's thigh was out of joint, as he wrestled with him. 26 And he said, Let me go, for the day breaketh. And he said, I will not let thee go, except thou bless me. 27 And he said unto him, What is thy name? And he said, Jacob. 28 And he said, Thy name shall be called no more Jacob, but Israel: for as a prince hast thou power with God and with men, and hast prevailed. 29 And Jacob asked him, and said, Tell me, I pray thee, thy name. And he said, Wherefore is it that thou dost ask after my name? And he blessed him there. 30 And Jacob called the name of the place Peniel: for I have seen God face to face, and my life is preserved. 31 And as he passed over Penuel the sun rose upon him, and he halted upon his thigh.

33    And Jacob lifted up his eyes, and looked, and, behold, Esau came, and with him four hundred men. And he divided the children unto Leah, and unto Rachel, and unto the two handmaids. 2 And he put the handmaids and their children foremost, and Leah and her children after, and Rachel and Joseph hindermost. 3 And he passed over before them, and bowed himself to the ground seven times, until he came near to his brother. 4 And Esau ran to meet him, and embraced him, and fell on his neck, and kissed him: and they wept. 5 And he lifted up his eyes, and saw the women and the children, and said, Who are those with thee? And he said, The children which God hath graciously given thy servant. 6 Then the handmaidens came near, they and their children, and they bowed themselves. 7 And Leah also with her children came near, and bowed themselves: and after came Joseph near and Rachel, and they bowed themselves. 8 And he said, What meanest thou by all this drove which I met? And he said, These are to find grace in the sight of my lord. 9 And Esau said, I have enough, my brother; keep that thou hast unto thyself. 10 And Jacob said, Nay, I pray thee, if now I have found grace in thy sight, then receive my present at my hand: for therefore I have seen thy face, as though I had seen the face of God, and thou wast pleased with me. 11 Take, I pray thee, my blessing that is brought to thee; because God hath dealt graciously with me, and because I have enough. And he urged him, and he took it. 12 And he said, Let us take our journey, and let us go, and I will go before thee. 13 And he said unto him, My lord knoweth that the children are tender, and the flocks and herds with young are with me; and if men should overdrive them one day, all the flock will die. 14 Let my lord, I pray thee, pass over before his servant; and I will lead on softly, according as the cattle that goeth before me and the children be able to endure, until I come unto my lord unto Seir. 15 And Esau said, Let me now leave with thee some

of the folk that are with me. And he said, What needeth it? let me find grace in the sight of my lord. 16 So Esau returned that day on his way unto Seir. 17 And Jacob journeyed to Succoth, and built him a house, and made booths for his cattle: therefore the name of the place is called Succoth.

18 And Jacob came to Shalem, a city of Shechem, which is in the land of Canaan, when he came from Padan-aram; and pitched his tent before the city. 19 And he bought a parcel of a field, where he had spread his tent, at the hand of the children of Hamor, Shechem's father, for a hundred pieces of money. 20 And he erected there an altar, and called it El-Elohe-Israel.

## DINAH AND HER BROTHERS

34 And Dinah the daughter of Leah, which she bare unto Jacob, went out to see the daughters of the land. 2 And when Shechem the son of Hamor the Hivite, prince of the country, saw her, he took her, and lay with her, and defiled her. 3 And his soul clave unto Dinah the daughter of Jacob, and he loved the damsel, and spake kindly unto the damsel. 4 And Shechem spake unto his father Hamor, saying, Get me this damsel to wife. 5 And Jacob heard that he had defiled Dinah his daughter: now his sons were with his cattle in the field: and Jacob held his peace until they were come. 6 And Hamor the father of Shechem went out unto Jacob to commune with him. 7 And the sons of Jacob came out of the field when they heard it: and the men were grieved, and they were very wroth, because he had wrought folly in Israel in lying with Jacob's daughter; which thing ought not to be done. 8 And Hamor communed with them, saying, The soul of my son Shechem longeth for your daughter: I pray you give her him to wife. 9 And make ye marriages with us, and give your daughters unto us, and take our daughters unto you. 10 And ye shall dwell with us: and the land shall be before you; dwell and trade ye therein, and get you possessions therein. 11 And Shechem said unto her father and unto her brethren, Let me find grace in your eyes, and what ye shall say unto me I will give. 12 Ask me never so much dowry and gift, and I will give according as ye shall say unto me: but give me the damsel to wife. 13 And the sons of Jacob answered Shechem and Hamor his father deceitfully, and said, because he had defiled Dinah their sister: 14 And they said unto them, We cannot do this thing, to give our sister to one that is uncircumcised; for that were a reproach unto us: 15 But in this will we consent unto you: If ye will be as we be, that every male of you be circumcised; 16 Then will we give our daughters unto you, and we will take your daughters to us, and we will dwell with you, and we will become one people. 17 But if ye will not hearken unto us, to be circumcised; then will we take our daughter, and we will be gone.

18 And their words pleased Hamor and Shechem Hamor's son. 19 And the young man deferred not to do the thing, because he had

delight in Jacob's daughter: and he was more honorable than all the house of his father. 20 And Hamor and Shechem his son came unto the gate of their city, and communed with the men of their city, saying, 21 These men are peaceable with us; therefore let them dwell in the land, and trade therein; for the land, behold, it is large enough for them; let us take their daughters to us for wives, and let us give them our daughters. 22 Only herein will the men consent unto us for to dwell with us, to be one people, if every male among us be circumcised, as they are circumcised. 23 Shall not their cattle and their substance and every beast of theirs be ours? only let us consent unto them, and they will dwell with us. 24 And unto Hamor and unto Shechem his son hearkened all that went out of the gate of his city; and every male was circumcised, all that went out of the gate of his city. 25 And it came to pass on the third day, when they were sore, that two of the sons of Jacob, Simeon and Levi, Dinah's brethren, took each man his sword, and came upon the city boldly, and slew all the males. 26 And they slew Hamor and Shechem his son with the edge of the sword, and took Dinah out of Shechem's house, and went out. 27 The sons of Jacob came upon the slain, and spoiled the city, because they had defiled their sister. 28 They took their sheep, and their oxen, and their asses, and that which was in the city, and that which was in the field, 29 And all their wealth, and all their little ones, and their wives took they captive, and spoiled even all that was in the house.

30 And Jacob said to Simeon and Levi, Ye have troubled me to make me to stink among the inhabitants of the land, among the Canaanites and the Perizzites: and I being few in number, they shall gather themselves together against me, and slay me; and I shall be destroyed, I and my house. 31 And they said, Should he deal with our sister as with a harlot?

## JACOB'S RETURN TO BETH-EL

35 And God said unto Jacob, Arise, go up to Beth-el, and dwell there: and make there an altar unto God, that appeared unto thee when thou fleddest from the face of Esau thy brother. 2 Then Jacob said unto his household, and to all that were with him, Put away the strange gods that are among you, and be clean, and change your garments: 3 And let us arise, and go up to Beth-el; and I will make there an altar unto God, who answered me in the day of my distress, and was with me in the way which I went. 4 And they gave unto Jacob all the strange gods which were in their hand, and all their earrings which were in their ears; and Jacob hid them under the oak which was by Shechem. 5 And they journeyed: and the terror of God was upon the cities that were round about them, and they did not pursue after the sons of Jacob. 6 So Jacob came to Luz which is in the land of Canaan, that is, Beth-el, he and all the people that were with him. 7 And he built there an altar, and called the place El-beth-el; because there God

appeared unto him, when he fled from the face of his brother. 8 But Deborah Rebekah's nurse died, and she was buried beneath Beth-el under an oak: and the name of it was called Allon-bachuth.

9 And God appeared unto Jacob again, when he came out of Padan-aram, and blessed him. 10 And God said unto him, Thy name is Jacob: thy name shall not be called any more Jacob, but Israel shall be thy name; and he called his name Israel. 11 And God said unto him, I am God Almighty: be fruitful and multiply; a nation and a company of nations shall be of thee, and kings shall come out of thy loins; 12 And the land which I gave Abraham and Isaac, to thee I will give it, and to thy seed after thee will I give the land. 13 And God went up from him in the place where he talked with him. 14 And Jacob set up a pillar in the place where he talked with him, even a pillar of stone: and he poured a drink offering thereon, and he poured oil thereon. 15 And Jacob called the name of the place where God spake with him, Beth-el.

16 And they journeyed from Beth-el; and there was but a little way to come to Ephrath: and Rachel travailed, and she had hard labor. 17 And it came to pass, when she was in hard labor, that the midwife said unto her, Fear not; thou shalt have this son also. 18 And it came to pass, as her soul was in departing, (for she died,) that she called his name Ben-oni: but his father called him Benjamin. 19 And Rachel died, and was buried in the way to Ephrath, which is Bethlehem. 20 And Jacob set a pillar upon her grave: that is the pillar of Rachel's grave unto this day. 21 And Israel journeyed, and spread his tent beyond the tower of Edar. 22 And it came to pass, when Israel dwelt in that land, that Reuben went and lay with Bilhah his father's concubine: and Israel heard it.

Now the sons of Jacob were twelve: 23 The sons of Leah; Reuben, Jacob's first-born, and Simeon, and Levi, and Judah, and Issachar, and Zebulun: 24 The sons of Rachel; Joseph, and Benjamin: 25 And the sons of Bilhah, Rachel's handmaid; Dan, and Naphtali: 26 And the sons of Zilpah, Leah's handmaid; Gad, and Asher. These are the sons of Jacob, which were born to him in Padan-aram.

37 And Jacob dwelt in the land wherein his father was a stranger, in the land of Canaan. 2 These are the generations of Jacob.

## THE STORY OF JOSEPH

Joseph, being seventeen years old, was feeding the flock with his brethren; and the lad was with the sons of Bilhah, and with the sons of Zilpah, his father's wives: and Joseph brought unto his father their evil report. 3 Now Israel loved Joseph more than all his children, because he was the son of his old age: and he made him a coat of many colors. 4 And when his brethren saw that their father loved him more than all his brethren, they hated him, and could not speak peaceably unto him.

5 And Joseph dreamed a dream, and he told it his brethren: and they hated him yet the more. 6 And he said unto them, Hear, I pray you, this dream which I have dreamed: 7 For, behold, we were binding sheaves in the field, and, lo, my sheaf arose, and also stood upright; and, behold, your sheaves stood round about, and made obeisance to my sheaf. 8 And his brethren said to him, Shalt thou indeed reign over us? or shalt thou indeed have dominion over us? And they hated him yet the more for his dreams, and for his words. 9 And he dreamed yet another dream, and told it his brethren, and said, Behold, I have dreamed a dream more; and, behold, the sun and the moon and the eleven stars made obeisance to me. 10 And he told it to his father, and to his brethren: and his father rebuked him, and said unto him, What is this dream that thou hast dreamed? Shall I and thy mother and thy brethren indeed come to bow down ourselves to thee to the earth? 11 And his brethren envied him; but his father observed the saying.

12 And his brethren went to feed their father's flock in Shechem. 13 And Israel said unto Joseph, Do not thy brethren feed the flock in Shechem? come, and I will send thee unto them. And he said to him, Here am I. 14 And he said to him, Go, I pray thee, see whether it be well with thy brethren, and well with the flocks; and bring me word again. So he sent him out of the vale of Hebron, and he came to Shechem. 15 And a certain man found him, and, behold, he was wandering in the field: and the man asked him, saying, What seekest thou? 16 And he said, I seek my brethren: tell me, I pray thee, where they feed their flocks. 17 And the man said, They are departed hence; for I heard them say, Let us go to Dothan. And Joseph went after his brethren, and found them in Dothan.

18 And when they saw him afar off, even before he came near unto them, they conspired against him to slay him. 19 And they said one to another, Behold, this dreamer cometh. 20 Come now therefore, and let us slay him, and cast him into some pit, and we will say, Some evil beast hath devoured him; and we shall see what will become of his dreams. 21 And Reuben heard it, and he delivered him out of their hands; and said, Let us not kill him. 22 And Reuben said unto them, Shed no blood, but cast him into this pit that is in the wilderness, and lay no hand upon him; that he might rid him out of their hands, to deliver him to his father again.

23 And it came to pass, when Joseph was come unto his brethren, that they stripped Joseph out of his coat, his coat of many colors that was on him; 24 And they took him, and cast him into a pit: and the pit was empty, there was no water in it. 25 And they sat down to eat bread: and they lifted up their eyes and looked, and, behold, a company of Ishmaelites came from Gilead, with their camels bearing spicery and balm and myrrh, going to carry it down to Egypt. 26 And Judah said unto his brethren, What profit is it if we slay our brother, and conceal his blood? 27 Come, and let us sell him to the Ishmaelites, and let not our hand be upon him; for he is our brother and our flesh: and his brethren were content. 28 Then there passed by Midianites

merchantmen; and they drew and lifted up Joseph out of the pit, and sold Joseph to the Ishmaelites for twenty pieces of silver: and they brought Joseph into Egypt.

29 And Reuben returned unto the pit; and, behold, Joseph was not in the pit; and he rent his clothes. 30 And he returned unto his brethren, and said, The child is not; and I, whither shall I go? 31 And they took Joseph's coat, and killed a kid of the goats, and dipped the coat in the blood; 32 And they sent the coat of many colors, and they brought it to their father; and said, This have we found: know now whether it be thy son's coat or no. 33 And he knew it, and said, It is my son's coat; an evil beast hath devoured him; Joseph is without doubt rent in pieces. 34 And Jacob rent his clothes, and put sackcloth upon his loins, and mourned for his son many days. 35 And all his sons and all his daughters rose up to comfort him; but he refused to be comforted; and he said, For I will go down into the grave unto my son mourning. Thus his father wept for him.

### JOSEPH IN EGYPT

39 And Joseph was brought down to Egypt; and Potiphar, an officer of Pharaoh, captain of the guard, an Egyptian, bought him of the hands of the Ishmaelites, which had brought him down thither. 2 And the Lord was with Joseph, and he was a prosperous man; and he was in the house of his master the Egyptian. 3 And his master saw that the Lord was with him, and the Lord made all that he did to prosper in his hand. 4 And Joseph found grace in his sight, and he served him: and he made him overseer over his house, and all that he had he put into his hand. 5 And it came to pass from the time that he had made him overseer in his house, and over all that he had, that the Lord blessed the Egyptian's house for Joseph's sake; and the blessing of the Lord was upon all that he had in the house, and in the field. 6 And he left all that he had in Joseph's hand; and he knew not aught he had, save the bread which he did eat. And Joseph was a goodly person, and well-favored.

7 And it came to pass after these things, that his master's wife cast her eyes upon Joseph; and she said, Lie with me. 8 But he refused, and said unto his master's wife, Behold, my master wotteth not what is with me in the house, and he hath committed all that he hath to my hand; 9 There is none greater in this house than I; neither hath he kept back any thing from me but thee, because thou art his wife: how then can I do this great wickedness, and sin against God? 10 And it came to pass, as she spake to Joseph day by day, that he hearkened not unto her, to lie by her, or to be with her. 11 And it came to pass about this time, that Joseph went into the house to do his business; and there was none of the men of the house there within. 12 And she caught him by his garment, saying, Lie with me: and he left his garment in her hand, and fled, and got him out. 13 And it came to pass, when she saw that he had left his garment in her hand, and was fled forth,

14 That she called unto the men of her house, and spake unto them, saying, See, he hath brought in a Hebrew unto us to mock us; he came in unto me to lie with me, and I cried with a loud voice: 15 And it came to pass, when he heard that I lifted up my voice and cried, that he left his garment with me, and fled, and got him out. 16 And she laid up his garment by her, until his lord came home. 17 And she spake unto him according to these words, saying, The Hebrew servant, which thou hast brought unto us, came in unto me to mock me: 18 And it came to pass, as I lifted up my voice and cried, that he left his garment with me, and fled out. 19 And it came to pass, when his master heard the words of his wife, which she spake unto him, saying, After this manner did thy servant to me; that his wrath was kindled. 20 And Joseph's master took him, and put him into the prison, a place where the king's prisoners were bound: and he was there in the prison.

21 But the Lord was with Joseph, and showed him mercy, and gave him favor in the sight of the keeper of the prison. 22 And the keeper of the prison committed to Joseph's hand all the prisoners that were in the prison; and whatsoever they did there, he was the doer of it. 23 The keeper of the prison looked not to any thing that was under his hand; because the Lord was with him, and that which he did, the Lord made it to prosper.

40 And it came to pass after these things, that the butler of the king of Egypt and his baker had offended their lord the king of Egypt. 2 And Pharaoh was wroth against two of his officers, against the chief of the butlers, and against the chief of the bakers. 3 And he put them in ward in the house of the captain of the guard, into the prison, the place where Joseph was bound. 4 And the captain of the guard charged Joseph with them, and he served them: and they continued a season in ward. 5 And they dreamed a dream both of them, each man his dream in one night, each man according to the interpretation of his dream, the butler and the baker of the king of Egypt, which were bound in the prison. 6 And Joseph came in unto them in the morning, and looked upon them, and, behold, they were sad. 7 And he asked Pharaoh's officers that were with him in the ward of his lord's house, saying, Wherefore look ye so sadly to-day? 8 And they said unto him, We have dreamed a dream, and there is no interpreter of it. And Joseph said unto them, Do not interpretations belong to God? tell me them, I pray you.

9 And the chief butler told his dream to Joseph, and said to him, In my dream, behold, a vine was before me; 10 And in the vine were three branches: and it was as though it budded, and her blossoms shot forth; and the clusters thereof brought forth ripe grapes: 11 And Pharaoh's cup was in my hand: and I took the grapes, and pressed them into Pharaoh's cup, and I gave the cup into Pharaoh's hand. 12 And Joseph said unto him, This is the interpretation of it: The three branches are three days: 13 Yet within three days shall Pharaoh

lift up thine head, and restore thee unto thy place; and thou shalt deliver Pharaoh's cup into his hand, after the former manner when thou wast his butler. 14 But think on me when it shall be well with thee, and show kindness, I pray thee, unto me, and make mention of me unto Pharaoh, and bring me out of this house: 15 For indeed I was stolen away out of the land of the Hebrews: and here also have I done nothing that they should put me into the dungeon.

16 When the chief baker saw that the interpretation was good, he said unto Joseph, I also was in my dream, and, behold, I had three white baskets on my head: 17 And in the uppermost basket there was of all manner of bakemeats for Pharaoh; and the birds did eat them out of the basket upon my head. 18 And Joseph answered and said, This is the interpretation thereof: The three baskets are three days: 19 Yet within three days shall Pharaoh lift up thy head from off thee, and shall hang thee on a tree; and the birds shall eat thy flesh from off thee.

20 And it came to pass the third day, which was Pharaoh's birthday, that he made a feast unto all his servants: and he lifted up the head of the chief butler and of the chief baker among his servants. 21 And he restored the chief butler unto his butlership again; and he gave the cup into Pharaoh's hand: 22 But he hanged the chief baker: as Joseph had interpreted to them. 23 Yet did not the chief butler remember Joseph, but forgat him.

41 And it came to pass at the end of two full years, that Pharaoh dreamed: and, behold, he stood by the river. 2 And, behold, there came up out of the river seven well-favored kine and fat-fleshed; and they fed in a meadow. 3 And, behold, seven other kine came up after them out of the river, ill-favored and lean-fleshed; and stood by the other kine upon the brink of the river. 4 And the ill-favored and lean-fleshed kine did eat up the seven well-favored and fat kine. So Pharaoh awoke. 5 And he slept and dreamed the second time: and, behold, seven ears of corn came up upon one stalk, rank and good. 6 And, behold, seven thin ears and blasted with the east wind sprung up after them. 7 And the seven thin ears devoured the seven rank and full ears. And Pharaoh awoke, and, behold, it was a dream. 8 And it came to pass in the morning that his spirit was troubled; and he sent and called for all the magicians of Egypt, and all the wise men thereof: and Pharaoh told them his dream; but there was none that could interpret them unto Pharaoh.

9 Then spake the chief butler unto Pharaoh, saying, I do remember my faults this day: 10 Pharaoh was wroth with his servants, and put me in ward in the captain of the guard's house, both me and the chief baker: 11 And we dreamed a dream in one night, I and he; we dreamed each man according to the interpretation of his dream. 12 And there was there with us a young man, a Hebrew, servant to the captain of the guard; and we told him, and he interpreted to us our dreams; to each man according to his dream he did interpret.

13 And it came to pass, as he interpreted to us, so it was; me he restored unto mine office, and him he hanged.

14 Then Pharaoh sent and called Joseph, and they brought him hastily out of the dungeon: and he shaved himself, and changed his raiment, and came in unto Pharaoh. 15 And Pharaoh said unto Joseph, I have dreamed a dream, and there is none that can interpret it: and I have heard say of thee, that thou canst understand a dream to interpret it. 16 And Joseph answered Pharaoh, saying, It is not in me: God shall give Pharaoh an answer of peace. 17 And Pharaoh said unto Joseph, In my dream, behold, I stood upon the bank of the river: 18 And, behold, there came up out of the river seven kine, fat-fleshed and well-favored; and they fed in a meadow: 19 And, behold, seven other kine came up after them, poor and very ill-favored and lean-fleshed, such as I never saw in all the land of Egypt for badness: 20 And the lean and the ill-favored kine did eat up the first seven fat kine: 21 And when they had eaten them up, it could not be known that they had eaten them; but they were still ill-favored, as at the beginning. So I awoke. 22 And I saw in my dream, and, behold, seven ears came up in one stalk, full and good: 23 And, behold, seven ears, withered, thin, and blasted with the east wind, sprung up after them: 24 And the thin ears devoured the seven good ears: and I told this unto the magicians; but there was none that could declare it to me.

25 And Joseph said unto Pharaoh, The dream of Pharaoh is one: God hath showed Pharaoh what he is about to do. 26 The seven good kine are seven years; and the seven good ears are seven years: the dream is one. 27 And the seven thin and ill-favored kine that came up after them are seven years; and the seven empty ears blasted with the east wind shall be seven years of famine. 28 This is the thing which I have spoken unto Pharaoh: What God is about to do he showeth unto Pharaoh. 29 Behold, there come seven years of great plenty throughout all the land of Egypt: 30 And there shall arise after them seven years of famine; and all the plenty shall be forgotten in the land of Egypt; and the famine shall consume the land; 31 And the plenty shall not be known in the land by reason of that famine following; for it shall be very grievous. 32 And for that the dream was doubled unto Pharaoh twice; it is because the thing is established by God, and God will shortly bring it to pass. 33 Now therefore let Pharaoh look out a man discreet and wise, and set him over the land of Egypt. 34 Let Pharaoh do this, and let him appoint officers over the land, and take up the fifth part of the land of Egypt in the seven plenteous years. 35 And let them gather all the food of those good years that come, and lay up corn under the hand of Pharaoh, and let them keep food in the cities. 36 And that food shall be for store to the land against the seven years of famine, which shall be in the land of Egypt; that the land perish not through the famine.

37 And the thing was good in the eyes of Pharaoh, and in the eyes of all his servants. 38 And Pharaoh said unto his servants, Can we

find such a one as this is, a man in whom the Spirit of God is? 39 And Pharaoh said unto Joseph, Forasmuch as God hath showed thee all this, there is none so discreet and wise as thou art: 40 Thou shalt be over my house, and according unto thy word shall all my people be ruled: only in the throne will I be greater than thou. 41 And Pharaoh said unto Joseph, See, I have set thee over all the land of Egypt. 42 And Pharaoh took off his ring from his hand, and put it upon Joseph's hand, and arrayed him in vestures of fine linen, and put a gold chain about his neck; 43 And he made him to ride in the second chariot which he had; and they cried before him, Bow the knee: and he made him ruler over all the land of Egypt. 44 And Pharaoh said unto Joseph, I am Pharaoh, and without thee shall no man lift up his hand or foot in all the land of Egypt. 45 And Pharaoh called Joseph's name Zaphnath-paaneah; and he gave him to wife Asenath the daughter of Poti-pherah priest of On. And Joseph went out over all the land of Egypt.

46 And Joseph was thirty years old when he stood before Pharaoh king of Egypt. And Joseph went out from the presence of Pharaoh, and went throughout all the land of Egypt. 47 And in the seven plenteous years the earth brought forth by handfuls. 48 And he gathered up all the food of the seven years, which were in the land of Egypt, and laid up the food in the cities: the food of the field, which was round about every city, laid he up in the same. 49 And Joseph gathered corn as the sand of the sea, very much, until he left numbering; for it was without number. 50 And unto Joseph were born two sons, before the years of famine came: which Asenath the daughter of Poti-pherah priest of On bare unto him. 51 And Joseph called the name of the firstborn Manasseh: For God, said he, hath made me forget all my toil, and all my father's house. 52 And the name of the second called he Ephraim: For God hath caused me to be fruitful in the land of my affliction.

53 And the seven years of plenteousness, that was in the land of Egypt, were ended. 54 And the seven years of dearth began to come, according as Joseph had said: and the dearth was in all lands; but in all the land of Egypt there was bread. 55 And when all the land of Egypt was famished, the people cried to Pharaoh for bread: and Pharaoh said unto all the Egyptians, Go unto Joseph; what he saith to you, do. 56 And the famine was over all the face of the earth: and Joseph opened all the storehouses, and sold unto the Egyptians; and the famine waxed sore in the land of Egypt. 57 And all countries came into Egypt to Joseph for to buy corn; because that the famine was so sore in all lands.

## JOSEPH AND HIS BROTHERS

42 Now when Jacob saw that there was corn in Egypt, Jacob said unto his sons, Why do ye look one upon another? 2 And he said, Behold, I have heard that there is corn in Egypt: get you down thither,

and buy for us from thence; that we may live, and not die. 3 And Joseph's ten brethren went down to buy corn in Egypt. 4 But Benjamin, Joseph's brother, Jacob sent not with his brethren; for he said, Lest peradventure mischief befall him. 5 And the sons of Israel came to buy corn among those that came: for the famine was in the land of Canaan.

6 And Joseph was the governor over the land, and he it was that sold to all the people of the land: and Joseph's brethren came, and bowed down themselves before him with their faces to the earth. 7 And Joseph saw his brethren, and he knew them, but made himself strange unto them, and spake roughly unto them; and he said unto them, Whence come ye? And they said, From the land of Canaan to buy food. 8 And Joseph knew his brethren, but they knew not him. 9 And Joseph remembered the dreams which he dreamed of them, and said unto them, Ye are spies; to see the nakedness of the land ye are come. 10 And they said unto him, Nay, my lord, but to buy food are thy servants come. 11 We are all one man's sons; we are true men; thy servants are no spies. 12 And he said unto them, Nay, but to see the nakedness of the land ye are come. 13 And they said, Thy servants are twelve brethren, the sons of one man in the land of Canaan; and, behold, the youngest is this day with our father, and one is not. 14 And Joseph said unto them, That is it that I spake unto you, saying, Ye are spies: 15 Hereby ye shall be proved: By the life of Pharaoh ye shall not go forth hence, except your youngest brother come hither. 16 Send one of you, and let him fetch your brother, and ye shall be kept in prison, that your words may be proved, whether there be any truth in you: or else by the life of Pharaoh surely ye are spies. 17 And he put them all together into ward three days.

18 And Joseph said unto them the third day, This do, and live; for I fear God: 19 If ye be true men, let one of your brethren be bound in the house of your prison: go ye, carry corn for the famine of your houses: 20 But bring your youngest brother unto me; so shall your words be verified, and ye shall not die. And they did so. 21 And they said one to another, We are verily guilty concerning our brother, in that we saw the anguish of his soul, when he besought us, and we would not hear; therefore is this distress come upon us. 22 And Reuben answered them, saying, Spake I not unto you, saying, Do not sin against the child; and ye would not hear? therefore, behold, also his blood is required. 23 And they knew not that Joseph understood them; for he spake unto them by an interpreter. 24 And he turned himself about from them, and wept; and returned to them again, and communed with them, and took from them Simeon, and bound him before their eyes.

25 Then Joseph commanded to fill their sacks with corn, and to restore every man's money into his sack, and to give them provision for the way: and thus did he unto them.

26 And they laded their asses with the corn, and departed thence. 27 And as one of them opened his sack to give his ass provender in

the inn, he espied his money; for, behold, it was in his sack's mouth. 28 And he said unto his brethren, My money is restored; and, lo, it is even in my sack: and their heart failed them, and they were afraid, saying one to another, What is this that God hath done unto us?

29 And they came unto Jacob their father unto the land of Canaan, and told him all that befell unto them; saying, 30 The man, who is the lord of the land, spake roughly to us, and took us for spies of the country. 31 And we said unto him, We are true men; we are no spies: 32 We be twelve brethren, sons of our father; one is not, and the youngest is this day with our father in the land of Canaan. 33 And the man, the lord of the country, said unto us, Hereby shall I know that ye are true men; leave one of your brethren here with me, and take food for the famine of your households, and be gone: 34 And bring your youngest brother unto me: then shall I know that ye are no spies, but that ye are true men: so will I deliver you your brother, and ye shall traffic in the land.

35 And it came to pass as they emptied their sacks, that, behold, every man's bundle of money was in his sack: and when both they and their father saw the bundles of money, they were afraid. 36 And Jacob their father said unto them, Me have ye bereaved of my children: Joseph is not, and Simeon is not, and ye will take Benjamin away: all these things are against me. 37 And Reuben spake unto his father, saying, Slay my two sons, if I bring him not to thee: deliver him into my hand, and I will bring him to thee again. 38 And he said, My son shall not go down with you; for his brother is dead, and he is left alone: if mischief befall him by the way in the which ye go, then shall ye bring down my gray hairs with sorrow to the grave.

43 And the famine was sore in the land. 2 And it came to pass, when they had eaten up the corn which they had brought out of Egypt, their father said unto them, Go again, buy us a little food. 3 And Judah spake unto him, saying, The man did solemnly protest unto us, saying, Ye shall not see my face, except your brother be with you. 4 If thou wilt send our brother with us, we will go down and buy thee food: 5 But if thou wilt not send him, we will not go down: for the man said unto us, Ye shall not see my face, except your brother be with you. 6 And Israel said, Wherefore dealt ye so ill with me, as to tell the man whether ye had yet a brother? 7 And they said, The man asked us straitly of our state, and of our kindred, saying, Is your father yet alive? have ye another brother? and we told him according to the tenor of these words: Could we certainly know that he would say, Bring your brother down? 8 And Judah said unto Israel his father, Send the lad with me, and we will arise and go; that we may live, and not die, both we, and thou, and also our little ones. 9 I will be surety for him; of my hand shalt thou require him: if I bring him not unto thee, and set him before thee, then let me bear the blame for ever: 10 For except we had lingered, surely now we had returned this second time. 11 And their father Israel said unto them, If it must

be so now, do this; take of the best fruits in the land in your vessels, and carry down the man a present, a little balm, and a little honey, spices and myrrh, nuts and almonds: 12 And take double money in your hand; and the money that was brought again in the mouth of your sacks, carry it again in your hand; peradventure it was an oversight. 13 Take also your brother, and arise, go again unto the man: 14 And God Almighty give you mercy before the man, that he may send away your other brother, and Benjamin. If I be bereaved of my children, I am bereaved.

15 And the men took that present, and they took double money in their hand, and Benjamin; and rose up, and went down to Egypt, and stood before Joseph. 16 And when Joseph saw Benjamin with them, he said to the ruler of his house, Bring these men home, and slay, and make ready; for these men shall dine with me at noon. 17 And the man did as Joseph bade; and the man brought the men into Joseph's house. 18 And the men were afraid, because they were brought into Joseph's house; and they said, Because of the money that was returned in our sacks at the first time are we brought in; that he may seek occasion against us, and fall upon us, and take us for bondmen, and our asses.

19 And they came near to the steward of Joseph's house, and they communed with him at the door of the house, 20 And said, O sir, we came indeed down at the first time to buy food: 21 And it came to pass, when we came to the inn, that we opened our sacks, and, behold, every man's money was in the mouth of his sack, our money in full weight: and we have brought it again in our hand. 22 And other money have we brought down in our hands to buy food: we cannot tell who put our money in our sacks. 23 And he said, Peace be to you, fear not: your God, and the God of your father, hath given you treasure in your sacks: I had your money. And he brought Simeon out unto them. 24 And the man brought the men into Joseph's house, and gave them water, and they washed their feet; and he gave their asses provender. 25 And they made ready the present against Joseph came at noon: for they heard that they should eat bread there.

26 And when Joseph came home, they brought him the present which was in their hand into the house, and bowed themselves to him to the earth. 27 And he asked them of their welfare, and said, Is your father well, the old man of whom ye spake? Is he yet alive? 28 And they answered, Thy servant our father is in good health, he is yet alive. And they bowed down their heads, and made obeisance. 29 And he lifted up his eyes, and saw his brother Benjamin, his mother's son, and said, Is this your younger brother, of whom ye spake unto me? And he said, God be gracious unto thee, my son. 30 And Joseph made haste; for his bowels did yearn upon his brother: and he sought where to weep; and he entered into his chamber, and wept there. 31 And he washed his face, and went out, and refrained himself, and said, Set on bread. 32 And they set on for him by himself, and for them by themselves, and for the Egyptians, which

did eat with him, by themselves: because the Egyptians might not eat bread with the Hebrews; for that is an abomination unto the Egyptians. 33 And they sat before him, the firstborn according to his birthright, and the youngest according to his youth: and the men marveled one at another. 34 And he took and sent messes unto them from before him: but Benjamin's mess was five times so much as any of theirs. And they drank, and were merry with him.

44 And he commanded the steward of his house, saying, Fill the men's sacks with food, as much as they can carry, and put every man's money in his sack's mouth. 2 And put my cup, the silver cup, in the sack's mouth of the youngest, and his corn money. And he did according to the word that Joseph had spoken. 3 As soon as the morning was light, the men were sent away, they and their asses. 4 And when they were gone out of the city, and not yet far off, Joseph said unto his steward, Up, follow after the men; and when thou dost overtake them, say unto them, Wherefore have ye rewarded evil for good? 5 Is not this it in which my lord drinketh, and whereby indeed he divineth? ye have done evil in so doing. 6 And he overtook them, and he spake unto them these same words. 7 And they said unto him, Wherefore saith my lord these words? God forbid that thy servants should do according to this thing: 8 Behold, the money, which we found in our sacks' mouths, we brought again unto thee out of the land of Canaan: how then should we steal out of thy lord's house silver or gold? 9 With whomsoever of thy servants it be found, both let him die, and we also will be my lord's bondmen. 10 And he said, Now also let it be according unto your words: he with whom it is found shall be my servant; and ye shall be blameless. 11 Then they speedily took down every man his sack to the ground, and opened every man his sack. 12 And he searched, and began at the eldest, and left at the youngest: and the cup was found in Benjamin's sack. 13 Then they rent their clothes, and laded every man his ass, and returned to the city.
14 And Judah and his brethren came to Joseph's house; for he was yet there: and they fell before him on the ground. 15 And Joseph said unto them, What deed is this that ye have done? wot ye not that such a man as I can certainly divine? 16 And Judah said, What shall we say unto my lord? what shall we speak? or how shall we clear ourselves? God hath found out the iniquity of thy servants: behold, we are my lord's servants, both we, and he also with whom the cup is found. 17 And he said, God forbid that I should do so: but the man in whose hand the cup is found, he shall be my servant; and as for you, get you up in peace unto your father.
18 Then Judah came near unto him, and said, O my lord, let thy servant, I pray thee, speak a word in my lord's ears, and let not thine anger burn against thy servant: for thou art even as Pharaoh. 19 My lord asked his servants, saying, Have ye a father, or a brother? 20 And we said unto my lord, We have a father, an old man, and a child of his old age, a little one; and his brother is dead, and he alone is left

of his mother, and his father loveth him. 21 And thou saidst unto thy servants, Bring him down unto me, that I may set mine eyes upon him. 22 And we said unto my lord, The lad cannot leave his father: for if he should leave his father, his father would die. 23 And thou saidst unto thy servants, Except your youngest brother come down with you, ye shall see my face no more. 24 And it came to pass when we came up unto thy servant my father, we told him the words of my lord. 25 And our father said, Go again, and buy us a little food. 26 And we said, We cannot go down: if our youngest brother be with us, then will we go down: for we may not see the man's face, except our youngest brother be with us. 27 And thy servant my father said unto us, Ye know that my wife bare me two sons: 28 And the one went out from me, and I said, Surely he is torn in pieces; and I saw him not since: 29 And if ye take this also from me, and mischief befall him, ye shall bring down my gray hairs with sorrow to the grave. 30 Now therefore when I come to thy servant my father, and the lad be not with us; seeing that his life is bound up in the lad's life; 31 It shall come to pass, when he seeth that the lad is not with us, that he will die: and thy servants shall bring down the gray hairs of thy servant our father with sorrow to the grave. 32 For thy servant became surety for the lad unto my father, saying, If I bring him not unto thee, then I shall bear the blame to my father for ever. 33 Now therefore, I pray thee, let thy servant abide instead of the lad a bondman to my lord; and let the lad go up with his brethren. 34 For how shall I go up to my father, and the lad be not with me? lest peradventure I see the evil that shall come on my father.

## JOSEPH SAVES HIS PEOPLE

45 Then Joseph could not refrain himself before all them that stood by him; and he cried, Cause every man to go out from me. And there stood no man with him, while Joseph made himself known unto his brethren. 2 And he wept aloud: and the Egyptians and the house of Pharaoh heard. 3 And Joseph said unto his brethren, I am Joseph; doth my father yet live? And his brethren could not answer him; for they were troubled at his presence. 4 And Joseph said unto his brethren, Come near to me, I pray you. And they came near. And he said, I am Joseph your brother, whom ye sold into Egypt. 5 Now therefore be not grieved, nor angry with yourselves, that ye sold me hither: for God did send me before you to preserve life. 6 For these two years hath the famine been in the land: and yet there are five years, in the which there shall neither be earing nor harvest. 7 And God sent me before you to preserve you a posterity in the earth, and to save your lives by a great deliverance. 8 So now it was not you that sent me hither, but God: and he hath made me a father to Pharaoh, and lord of all his house, and a ruler throughout all the land of Egypt. 9 Haste ye, and go up to my father, and say unto him, Thus saith thy son Joseph, God hath made me lord of all Egypt: come down

unto me, tarry not: 10 And thou shalt dwell in the land of Goshen, and thou shalt be near unto me, thou, and thy children, and thy children's children, and thy flocks, and thy herds, and all that thou hast: 11 And there will I nourish thee; for yet there are five years of famine; lest thou, and thy household, and all that thou hast, come to poverty. 12 And, behold, your eyes see, and the eyes of my brother Benjamin, that it is my mouth that speaketh unto you. 13 And ye shall tell my father of all my glory in Egypt, and of all that ye have seen; and ye shall haste and bring down my father hither. 14 And he fell upon his brother Benjamin's neck, and wept; and Benjamin wept upon his neck. 15 Moreover he kissed all his brethren, and wept upon them: and after that his brethren talked with him.

16 And the fame thereof was heard in Pharaoh's house, saying, Joseph's brethren are come: and it pleased Pharaoh well, and his servants. 17 And Pharaoh said unto Joseph, Say unto thy brethren, This do ye; lade your beasts, and go, get you unto the land of Canaan; 18 And take your father and your households, and come unto me: and I will give you the good of the land of Egypt, and ye shall eat the fat of the land. 19 Now thou art commanded, this do ye; take you wagons out of the land of Egypt for your little ones, and for your wives, and bring your father, and come. 20 Also regard not your stuff; for the good of all the land of Egypt is yours. 21 And the children of Israel did so: and Joseph gave them wagons, according to the commandment of Pharaoh, and gave them provision for the way. 22 To all of them he gave each man changes of raiment; but to Benjamin he gave three hundred pieces of silver, and five changes of raiment. 23 And to his father he sent after this manner; ten asses laden with the good things of Egypt, and ten she asses laden with corn and bread and meat for his father by the way. 24 So he sent his brethren away, and they departed: and he said unto them, See that ye fall not out by the way. 25 And they went up out of Egypt, and came into the land of Canaan unto Jacob their father, 26 And told him, saying, Joseph is yet alive, and he is governor over all the land of Egypt. And Jacob's heart fainted, for he believed them not. 27 And they told him all the words of Joseph, which he had said unto them: and when he saw the wagons which Joseph had sent to carry him, the spirit of Jacob their father revived. 28 And Israel said, It is enough; Joseph my son is yet alive: I will go and see him before I die.

46 And Israel took his journey with all that he had, and came to Beer-sheba, and offered sacrifices unto the God of his father Isaac. 2 And God spake unto Israel in the visions of the night, and said, Jacob, Jacob. And he said, Here am I. 3 And he said, I am God, the God of thy father: fear not to go down into Egypt; for I will there make of thee a great nation. 4 I will go down with thee into Egypt; and I will also surely bring thee up again: and Joseph shall put his hand upon thine eyes. 5 And Jacob rose up from Beer-sheba: and the sons of Israel carried Jacob their father, and their little ones, and their

wives, in the wagons which Pharaoh had sent to carry him. 6 And they took their cattle, and their goods, which they had gotten in the land of Canaan, and came into Egypt, Jacob, and all his seed with him: 7 His sons, and his sons' sons with him, his daughters, and his sons' daughters, and all his seed brought he with him into Egypt.

28 And he sent Judah before him unto Joseph, to direct his face unto Goshen; and they came into the land of Goshen. 29 And Joseph made ready his chariot, and went up to meet Israel his father, to Goshen, and presented himself unto him; and he fell on his neck, and wept on his neck a good while. 30 And Israel said unto Joseph, Now let me die, since I have seen thy face, because thou art yet alive. 31 And Joseph said unto his brethren, and unto his father's house, I will go up, and show Pharaoh, and say unto him, My brethren, and my father's house, which were in the land of Canaan, are come unto me; 32 And the men are shepherds, for their trade hath been to feed cattle; and they have brought their flocks, and their herds, and all that they have. 33 And it shall come to pass, when Pharaoh shall call you, and shall say, What is your occupation? 34 That ye shall say, Thy servants' trade hath been about cattle from our youth even until now, both we, and also our fathers: that ye may dwell in the land of Goshen; for every shepherd is an abomination unto the Egyptians.

47   Then Joseph came and told Pharaoh, and said, My father and my brethren, and their flocks, and their herds, and all that they have, are come out of the land of Canaan; and, behold, they are in the land of Goshen. 2 And he took some of his brethren, even five men, and presented them unto Pharaoh. 3 And Pharaoh said unto his brethren, What is your occupation? And they said unto Pharaoh, Thy servants are shepherds, both we, and also our fathers. 4 They said moreover unto Pharaoh, For to sojourn in the land are we come; for thy servants have no pasture for their flocks; for the famine is sore in the land of Canaan: now therefore, we pray thee, let thy servants dwell in the land of Goshen. 5 And Pharaoh spake unto Joseph, saying, Thy father and thy brethren are come unto thee: 6 The land of Egypt is before thee; in the best of the land make thy father and brethren to dwell; in the land of Goshen let them dwell: and if thou knowest any men of activity among them, then make them rulers over my cattle. 7 And Joseph brought in Jacob his father, and set him before Pharaoh: and Jacob blessed Pharaoh. 8 And Pharaoh said unto Jacob, How old art thou? 9 And Jacob said unto Pharaoh, The days of the years of my pilgrimage are a hundred and thirty years: few and evil have the days of the years of my life been, and have not attained unto the days of the years of the life of my fathers in the days of their pilgrimage. 10 And Jacob blessed Pharaoh, and went out from before Pharaoh. 11 And Joseph placed his father and his brethren, and gave them a possession in the land of Egypt, in the best of the land, in the land of Rameses, as Pharaoh had commanded. 12 And Joseph nourished his

father, and his brethren, and all his father's household, with bread, according to their families.

13 And there was no bread in all the land; for the famine was very sore, so that the land of Egypt and all the land of Canaan fainted by reason of the famine. 14 And Joseph gathered up all the money that was found in the land of Egypt, and in the land of Canaan, for the corn which they bought: and Joseph brought the money into Pharaoh's house. 15 And when money failed in the land of Egypt, and in the land of Canaan, all the Egyptians came unto Joseph, and said, Give us bread: for why should we die in thy presence? for the money faileth. 16 And Joseph said, Give your cattle; and I will give you for your cattle, if money fail. 17 And they brought their cattle unto Joseph: and Joseph gave them bread in exchange for horses, and for the flocks, and for the cattle of the herds, and for the asses; and he fed them with bread for all their cattle for that year. 18 When that year was ended, they came unto him the second year, and said unto him, We will not hide it from my lord, how that our money is spent; my lord also hath our herds of cattle; there is not aught left in the sight of my lord, but our bodies, and our lands: 19 Wherefore shall we die before thine eyes, both we and our land? buy us and our land for bread, and we and our land will be servants unto Pharaoh: and give us seed, that we may live, and not die, that the land be not desolate. 20 And Joseph bought all the land of Egypt for Pharaoh; for the Egyptians sold every man his field, because the famine prevailed over them: so the land became Pharaoh's. 21 And as for the people, he removed them to cities from one end of the borders of Egypt even to the other end thereof. 22 Only the land of the priests bought he not; for the priests had a portion assigned them of Pharaoh, and did eat their portion which Pharaoh gave them: wherefore they sold not their lands. 23 Then Joseph said unto the people, Behold, I have bought you this day and your land for Pharaoh: lo, here is seed for you, and ye shall sow the land. 24 And it shall come to pass in the increase, that ye shall give the fifth part unto Pharaoh, and four parts shall be your own, for seed of the field, and for your food, and for them of your households, and for food for your little ones. 25 And they said, Thou hast saved our lives: let us find grace in the sight of my lord, and we will be Pharaoh's servants. 26 And Joseph made it a law over the land of Egypt unto this day, that Pharaoh should have the fifth part; except the land of the priests only, which became not Pharaoh's.

27 And Israel dwelt in the land of Egypt, in the country of Goshen; and they had possessions therein, and grew, and multiplied exceedingly.

## JACOB'S DEATH

28 And Jacob lived in the land of Egypt seventeen years: so the whole age of Jacob was a hundred forty and seven years. 29 And the time drew nigh that Israel must die: and he called his son Joseph, and

said unto him, If now I have found grace in thy sight, put, I pray thee, thy hand under my thigh, and deal kindly and truly with me; bury me not, I pray thee, in Egypt: 30 But I will lie with my fathers, and thou shalt carry me out of Egypt, and bury me in their buryingplace. And he said, I will do as thou hast said. 31 And he said, Swear unto me. And he sware unto him. And Israel bowed himself upon the bed's head.

48 And it came to pass after these things, that one told Joseph, Behold, thy father is sick: and he took with him his two sons, Manasseh and Ephraim. 2 And one told Jacob, and said, Behold, thy son Joseph cometh unto thee: and Israel strengthened himself, and sat upon the bed. 3 And Jacob said unto Joseph, God Almighty appeared unto me at Luz in the land of Canaan, and blessed me, 4 And said unto me, Behold, I will make thee fruitful, and multiply thee, and I will make of thee a multitude of people; and will give this land to thy seed after thee for an everlasting possession. 5 And now thy two sons, Ephraim and Manasseh, which were born unto thee in the land of Egypt, before I came unto thee into Egypt, are mine; as Reuben and Simeon, they shall be mine. 6 And thy issue, which thou begettest after them, shall be thine, and shall be called after the name of their brethren in their inheritance. 7 And as for me, when I came from Padan, Rachel died by me in the land of Canaan in the way, when yet there was but a little way to come unto Ephrath: and I buried her there in the way of Ephrath; the same is Bethlehem.

8 And Israel beheld Joseph's sons, and said, Who are these? 9 And Joseph said unto his father, They are my sons, whom God hath given me in this place. And he said, Bring them, I pray thee, unto me, and I will bless them. 10 Now the eyes of Israel were dim for age, so that he could not see. And he brought them near unto him; and he kissed them, and embraced them. 11 And Israel said unto Joseph, I had not thought to see thy face: and, lo, God hath showed me also thy seed. 12 And Joseph brought them out from between his knees, and he bowed himself with his face to the earth. 13 And Joseph took them both, Ephraim in his right hand toward Israel's left hand, and Manasseh in his left hand toward Israel's right hand, and brought them near unto him. 14 And Israel stretched out his right hand, and laid it upon Ephraim's head, who was the younger, and his left hand upon Manasseh's head, guiding his hands wittingly; for Manasseh was the firstborn. 15 And he blessed Joseph, and said, God, before whom my fathers Abraham and Isaac did walk, the God which fed me all my life long unto this day, 16 The Angel which redeemed me from all evil, bless the lads; and let my name be named on them, and the name of my fathers Abraham and Isaac; and let them grow into a multitude in the midst of the earth. 17 And when Joseph saw that his father laid his right hand upon the head of Ephraim, it displeased him: and he held up his father's hand, to remove it from Ephraim's head unto Manasseh's head. 18 And Joseph said unto his father, Not so, my

father: for this is the firstborn; put thy right hand upon his head. 19 And his father refused, and said, I know it, my son, I know it: he also shall become a people, and he also shall be great: but truly his younger brother shall be greater than he, and his seed shall become a multitude of nations. 20 And he blessed them that day, saying, In thee shall Israel bless, saying, God make thee as Ephraim and as Manasseh: and he set Ephraim before Manasseh. 21 And Israel said unto Joseph, Behold, I die; but God shall be with you, and bring you again unto the land of your fathers. 22 Moreover I have given to thee one portion above thy brethren, which I took out of the hand of the Amorite with my sword and with my bow.

49 And Jacob called unto his sons, and said, Gather yourselves together, that I may tell you that which shall befall you in the last days.

2 Gather yourselves together, and hear, ye sons of Jacob;
And hearken unto Israel your father.
3 Reuben, thou art my firstborn,
My might, and the beginning of my strength,
The excellency of dignity, and the excellency of power:
4 Unstable as water, thou shalt not excel;
Because thou wentest up to thy father's bed;
Then defiledst thou it: he went up to my couch.
5 Simeon and Levi are brethren;
Instruments of cruelty are in their habitations.
6 O my soul, come not thou into their secret;
Unto their assembly, mine honor, be not thou united:
For in their anger they slew a man,
And in their self-will they digged down a wall.
7 Cursed be their anger, for it was fierce;
And their wrath, for it was cruel:
I will divide them in Jacob,
And scatter them in Israel.
8 Judah, thou art he whom thy brethren shall praise:
Thy hand shall be in the neck of thine enemies;
Thy father's children shall bow down before thee.
9 Judah is a lion's whelp:
From the prey, my son, thou art gone up:
He stooped down, he couched as a lion,
And as an old lion; who shall rouse him up?
10 The sceptre shall not depart from Judah,
Nor a lawgiver from between his feet,
Until Shiloh come;
And unto him shall the gathering of the people be.
11 Binding his foal unto the vine,
And his ass's colt unto the choice vine;
He washed his garments in wine,
And his clothes in the blood of grapes:

12 His eyes shall be red with wine,
  And his teeth white with milk.
13 Zebulun shall dwell at the haven of the sea;
  And he shall be for a haven of ships;
  And his border shall be unto Zidon.
14 Issachar is a strong ass
  Couching down between two burdens:
15 And he saw that rest was good,
  And the land that it was pleasant;
  And bowed his shoulder to bear,
  And became a servant unto tribute.
16 Dan shall judge his people,
  As one of the tribes of Israel.
17 Dan shall be a serpent by the way,
  An adder in the path,
  That biteth the horse heels,
  So that his rider shall fall backward.
18 I have waited for thy salvation, O Lord.
19 Gad, a troop shall overcome him:
  But he shall overcome at the last.
20 Out of Asher his bread shall be fat,
  And he shall yield royal dainties.
21 Naphtali is a hind let loose:
  He giveth goodly words.
22 Joseph is a fruitful bough,
  Even a fruitful bough by a well;
  Whose branches run over the wall:
23 The archers have sorely grieved him,
  And shot at him, and hated him:
24 But his bow abode in strength,
  And the arms of his hands were made strong
  By the hands of the mighty God of Jacob;
  (From thence is the shepherd, the stone of Israel;)
25 Even by the God of thy father, who shall help thee;
  And by the Almighty, who shall bless thee
  With blessings of heaven above,
  Blessings of the deep that lieth under,
  Blessings of the breasts, and of the womb:
26 The blessings of thy father have prevailed
  Above the blessings of my progenitors
  Unto the utmost bound of the everlasting hills:
  They shall be on the head of Joseph,
  And on the crown of the head of him that was separate from
    his brethren.
27 Benjamin shall raven as a wolf:
  In the morning he shall devour the prey,
  And at night he shall divide the spoil.

28 All these are the twelve tribes of Israel: and this is it that their father spake unto them, and blessed them; every one according to his blessing he blessed them. 29 And he charged them, and said unto them, I am to be gathered unto my people: bury me with my fathers in the cave that is in the field of Ephron the Hittite, 30 In the cave that is in the field of Machpelah, which is before Mamre, in the land of Canaan, which Abraham bought with the field of Ephron the Hittite for a possession of a buryingplace. 31 There they buried Abraham and Sarah his wife; there they buried Isaac and Rebekah his wife; and there I buried Leah. 32 The purchase of the field and of the cave that is therein was from the children of Heth. 33 And when Jacob had made an end of commanding his sons, he gathered up his feet into the bed, and yielded up the ghost, and was gathered unto his people.

50 And Joseph fell upon his father's face, and wept upon him, and kissed him. 2 And Joseph commanded his servants the physicians to embalm his father: and the physicians embalmed Israel. 3 And forty days were fulfilled for him; for so are fulfilled the days of those which are embalmed: and the Egyptians mourned for him threescore and ten days.

4 And when the days of his mourning were past, Joseph spake unto the house of Pharaoh, saying, If now I have found grace in your eyes, speak, I pray you, in the ears of Pharaoh, saying, 5 My father made me swear, saying, Lo, I die: in my grave which I have digged for me in the land of Canaan, there shalt thou bury me. Now therefore let me go up, I pray thee, and bury my father, and I will come again. 6 And Pharaoh said, Go up, and bury thy father, according as he made thee swear. 7 And Joseph went up to bury his father: and with him went up all the servants of Pharaoh, the elders of his house, and all the elders of the land of Egypt, 8 And all the house of Joseph, and his brethren, and his father's house: only their little ones, and their flocks, and their herds, they left in the land of Goshen. 9 And there went up with him both chariots and horsemen: and it was a very great company. 10 And they came to the threshingfloor of Atad, which is beyond Jordan; and there they mourned with a great and very sore lamentation: and he made a mourning for his father seven days. 11 And when the inhabitants of the land, the Canaanites, saw the mourning in the floor of Atad, they said, This is a grievous mourning to the Egyptians: wherefore the name of it was called Abel-mizraim, which is beyond Jordan. 12 And his sons did unto him according as he commanded them: 13 For his sons carried him into the land of Canaan, and buried him in the cave of the field of Machpelah, which Abraham bought with the field for a possession of a buryingplace of Ephron the Hittite, before Mamre. 14 And Joseph returned into Egypt, he, and his brethren, and all that went up with him to bury his father, after he had buried his father.

15 And when Joseph's brethren saw that their father was dead, they said, Joseph will peradventure hate us, and will certainly requite us all the evil which we did unto him. 16 And they sent a messenger unto Joseph, saying, Thy father did command before he died, saying, 17 So shall ye say unto Joseph, Forgive, I pray thee now, the trespass of thy brethren, and their sin; for they did unto thee evil: and now, we pray thee, forgive the trespass of the servants of the God of thy father. And Joseph wept when they spake unto him. 18 And his brethren also went and fell down before his face; and they said, Behold, we be thy servants. 19 And Joseph said unto them, Fear not: for am I in the place of God? 20 But as for you, ye thought evil against me; but God meant it unto good, to bring to pass, as it is this day, to save much people alive. 21 Now therefore fear ye not: I will nourish you, and your little ones. And he comforted them, and spake kindly unto them.

### JOSEPH'S DYING PROPHECY

22 And Joseph dwelt in Egypt, he, and his father's house: and Joseph lived a hundred and ten years. 23 And Joseph saw Ephraim's children of the third generation: the children also of Machir the son of Manasseh were brought up upon Joseph's knees. 24 And Joseph said unto his brethren, I die; and God will surely visit you, and bring you out of this land unto the land which he sware to Abraham, to Isaac, and to Jacob. 25 And Joseph took an oath of the children of Israel, saying, God will surely visit you, and ye shall carry up my bones from hence. 26 So Joseph died, being a hundred and ten years old: and they embalmed him, and he was put in a coffin in Egypt.

# The Epic of Moses: *Exodus,*
## *Leviticus, Numbers, Deuteronomy*

After Genesis, the next four books of the Bible — Exodus, Leviticus, Numbers, and Deuteronomy — are focused upon the person of Moses. Various strata of editing are apparent in these books, as we have noted in the Introduction, but throughout we have a concentration upon the great leader and lawgiver Moses, who abandoned a princely station in Egypt to defend his people from oppression. Yet even here, even with Moses, the real hero or protagonist is God. From the time when Moses was keeping his flock in the desert near Mount Horeb to the time of his death on Mount Pisgah, his life was a working out of the relations between a man, his God, and his community, but God remained the key figure.

In these books, narratives about the escape of the Israelites from bondage and their approach to the land of promise are interspersed with codes of conduct to govern their lives in society. The most famous of these codes is, of course, the Ten Commandments, but this is only one part of an elaborate system of religious observances and social justice. Representative selections are given here from both the ritual and the civil law, and something should be said about each.

The civil law was a careful attempt to establish a society on the basis of the will of God for humane justice and mercy. Some of the provisions will be immediately understandable to us even today, for they deal with precepts which are timeless and essential to any system of justice — like the condemnation of false witness, for example. Other provisions will seem strange at first reading, for they apply to a form of society radically different from anything which most of us know and would have very little apparent bearing upon human relations under modern urban conditions. Here, however, a little reflection will show that most of these provisions were directly relevant to life in a nation made up largely of herdsmen and farmers. Thus certain laws prohibit overworking the land and the mistreating of animals, while others expressly provide against oppression of women and of the poor in ways directly pertinent to the conditions of Old Testament Israel. Few if any among human societies have ever so carefully guarded the rights of all men, especially the poor and unfortunate. These laws do not, however, represent the Bible's final word on

63

human relations, and some things here will strike us as typical products of a brutal age when viewed from the compassionate perspective of the prophetic and New Testament writings.

The religious law is quite complex. Its major purpose was to provide for the development of a holy community, conscious of its obligation to God. Idolatry of every kind was rigorously prohibited, as was the infiltration from surrounding nations of the practice of human sacrifice and the cult prostitution of the fertility rites. The provisions laid down against such influences may seem to us today to be overly rigorous and even cruel, but it is historically unlikely that the small and often weak nation of Israel could have preserved its religious integrity without such stringent measures, faced as Israel always was with the threats of powerful nations and the rivalry of less demanding religions.

Something should surely be said about the system of sacrifices, though whatever is said here will inevitably oversimplify. Some offerings were made purely as praise to God, while others had to do with the purging away of human sin. As for these latter, the expiatory sacrifices were never divorced from the requirement that an individual should do all within his power to correct his fault and to make amends for such harm as his sin had caused. Once this was done, the individual or group of individuals was able to have an animal sacrifice ordered by the priest. It was a system of objectifying and dispelling guilt quite different from modern man's habit of internalizing his guilt, and may well have been more effective. The theme is continued in the New Testament in direct connection with the sacrifice of Christ on the cross.

Legal codes may scarcely be expected to attain high literary merit in their own right. The treatment of Moses, however, is of a high order of merit, as is the treatment of various minor characters, while the narrative moves with a great sweeping dignity and attains a level of epic significance.

# *Exodus*

## BONDAGE IN EGYPT

1 Now these are the names of the children of Israel, which came into Egypt; every man and his household came with Jacob. 2 Reuben, Simeon, Levi, and Judah, 3 Issachar, Zebulun, and Benjamin, 4 Dan, and Naphtali, Gad, and Asher. 5 And all the souls that came out of the loins of Jacob were seventy souls: for Joseph was in Egypt already. 6 And Joseph died, and all his brethren, and all that generation.

7 And the children of Israel were fruitful, and increased abundantly, and multiplied, and waxed exceeding mighty; and the land was filled

with them. 8 Now there arose up a new king over Egypt, which knew not Joseph. 9 And he said unto his people, Behold, the people of the children of Israel are more and mightier than we: 10 Come on, let us deal wisely with them; lest they multiply, and it come to pass, that, when there falleth out any war, they join also unto our enemies, and fight against us, and so get them up out of the land. 11 Therefore they did set over them taskmasters to afflict them with their burdens. And they built for Pharaoh treasure cities, Pithom and Raamses. 12 But the more they afflicted them, the more they multiplied and grew. And they were grieved because of the children of Israel. 13 And the Egyptians made the children of Israel to serve with rigor: 14 And they made their lives bitter with hard bondage, in mortar, and in brick, and in all manner of service in the field: all their service, wherein they made them serve, was with rigor.

15 And the king of Egypt spake to the Hebrew midwives, of which the name of the one was Shiphrah, and the name of the other Puah; 16 And he said, When ye do the office of a midwife to the Hebrew women, and see them upon the stools, if it be a son, then ye shall kill him; but if it be a daughter, then she shall live. 17 But the midwives feared God, and did not as the king of Egypt commanded them, but saved the men children alive. 18 And the king of Egypt called for the midwives, and said unto them, Why have ye done this thing, and have saved the men children alive? 19 And the midwives said unto Pharaoh, Because the Hebrew women are not as the Egyptian women; for they are lively, and are delivered ere the midwives come in unto them. 20 Therefore God dealt well with the midwives: and the people multiplied, and waxed very mighty. 21 And it came to pass, because the midwives feared God, that he made them houses. 22 And Pharaoh charged all his people, saying, Every son that is born ye shall cast into the river, and every daughter ye shall save alive.

## MOSES

2 And there went a man of the house of Levi, and took to wife a daughter of Levi. 2 And the woman conceived, and bare a son: and when she saw him that he was a goodly child, she hid him three months. 3 And when she could not longer hide him, she took for him an ark of bulrushes, and daubed it with slime and with pitch, and put the child therein; and she laid it in the flags by the river's brink. 4 And his sister stood afar off, to wit what would be done to him. 5 And the daughter of Pharaoh came down to wash herself at the river; and her maidens walked along by the river's side: and when she saw the ark among the flags, she sent her maid to fetch it. 6 And when she had opened it, she saw the child: and, behold, the babe wept. And she had compassion on him, and said, This is one of the Hebrews' children. 7 Then said his sister to Pharaoh's daughter, Shall I go and call to thee a nurse of the Hebrew women, that she may nurse the child for thee? 8 And Pharaoh's daughter said to her, Go. And the

maid went and called the child's mother. 9 And Pharaoh's daughter said unto her, Take this child away, and nurse it for me, and I will give thee thy wages. And the woman took the child, and nursed it. 10 And the child grew, and she brought him unto Pharaoh's daughter, and he became her son. And she called his name Moses: and she said, Because I drew him out of the water.

11 And it came to pass in those days, when Moses was grown, that he went out unto his brethren, and looked on their burdens: and he spied an Egyptian smiting a Hebrew, one of his brethren. 12 And he looked this way and that way, and when he saw that there was no man, he slew the Egyptian, and hid him in the sand. 13 And when he went out the second day, behold, two men of the Hebrews strove together: and he said to him that did the wrong, Wherefore smitest thou thy fellow? 14 And he said, Who made thee a prince and a judge over us? intendest thou to kill me, as thou killedst the Egyptian? And Moses feared, and said, Surely this thing is known.

15 Now when Pharaoh heard this thing, he sought to slay Moses. But Moses fled from the face of Pharaoh, and dwelt in the land of Midian: and he sat down by a well. 16 Now the priest of Midian had seven daughters: and they came and drew water, and filled the troughs to water their father's flock. 17 And the shepherds came and drove them away: but Moses stood up and helped them, and watered their flock. 18 And when they came to Reuel their father, he said, How is it that ye are come so soon to-day? 19 And they said, An Egyptian delivered us out of the hand of the shepherds, and also drew water enough for us, and watered the flock. 20 And he said unto his daughters, And where is he? why is it that ye have left the man? call him, that he may eat bread. 21 And Moses was content to dwell with the man: and he gave Moses Zipporah his daughter. 22 And she bare him a son, and he called his name Gershom: for he said, I have been a stranger in a strange land.

23 And it came to pass in process of time, that the king of Egypt died: and the children of Israel sighed by reason of the bondage, and they cried, and their cry came up unto God by reason of the bondage. 24 And God heard their groaning, and God remembered his covenant with Abraham, with Isaac, and with Jacob. 25 And God looked upon the children of Israel, and God had respect unto them.

## GOD CALLS MOSES

3 Now Moses kept the flock of Jethro his father-in-law, the priest of Midian: and he led the flock to the back side of the desert, and came to the mountain of God, even to Horeb. 2 And the Angel of the Lord appeared unto him in a flame of fire out of the midst of a bush: and he looked, and, behold, the bush burned with fire, and the bush was not consumed. 3 And Moses said, I will now turn aside, and see this great sight, why the bush is not burnt. 4 And when the Lord saw that he turned aside to see, God called unto him out of the midst of the

bush, and said, Moses, Moses. And he said, Here am I. 5 And he said, Draw not nigh hither: put off thy shoes from off thy feet; for the place whereon thou standest is holy ground. 6 Moreover he said, I am the God of thy father, the God of Abraham, the God of Isaac, and the God of Jacob. And Moses hid his face; for he was afraid to look upon God.

7 And the Lord said, I have surely seen the affliction of my people which are in Egypt, and have heard their cry by reason of their taskmasters; for I know their sorrows; 8 And I am come down to deliver them out of the hand of the Egyptians, and to bring them up out of that land unto a good land and a large, unto a land flowing with milk and honey; unto the place of the Canaanites, and the Hittites, and the Amorites, and the Perizzites, and the Hivites, and the Jebusites. 9 Now therefore, behold, the cry of the children of Israel is come unto me: and I have also seen the oppression wherewith the Egyptians oppress them. 10 Come now therefore, and I will send thee unto Pharaoh, that thou mayest bring forth my people the children of Israel out of Egypt. 11 And Moses said unto God, Who am I, that I should go unto Pharaoh, and that I should bring forth the children of Israel out of Egypt? 12 And he said, Certainly I will be with thee; and this shall be a token unto thee, that I have sent thee: When thou hast brought forth the people out of Egypt, ye shall serve God upon this mountain.

13 And Moses said unto God, Behold, when I come unto the children of Israel, and shall say unto them, The God of your fathers hath sent me unto you; and they shall say to me, What is his name? what shall I say unto them? 14 And God said unto Moses, I Am That I Am: and he said, Thus shalt thou say unto the children of Israel, I Am hath sent me unto you. 15 And God said moreover unto Moses, Thus shalt thou say unto the children of Israel, The Lord God of your fathers, the God of Abraham, the God of Isaac, and the God of Jacob, hath sent me unto you: this is my name for ever, and this is my memorial unto all generations. 16 Go, and gather the elders of Israel together, and say unto them, The Lord God of your fathers, the God of Abraham, of Isaac, and of Jacob, appeared unto me, saying, I have surely visited you, and seen that which is done to you in Egypt: 17 And I have said, I will bring you up out of the affliction of Egypt unto the land of the Canaanites, and the Hittites, and the Amorites, and the Perizzites, and the Hivites, and the Jebusites, unto a land flowing with milk and honey. 18 And they shall hearken to thy voice: and thou shalt come, thou and the elders of Israel, unto the king of Egypt, and ye shall say unto him, The Lord God of the Hebrews hath met with us: and now let us go, we beseech thee, three days' journey into the wilderness, that we may sacrifice to the Lord our God.

19 And I am sure that the king of Egypt will not let you go, no, not by a mighty hand. 20 And I will stretch out my hand, and smite Egypt with all my wonders which I will do in the midst thereof: and after that he will let you go. 21 And I will give this people favor in the sight of the Egyptians: and it shall come to pass, that, when ye go,

ye shall not go empty: 22 But every woman shall borrow of her neighbor, and of her that sojourneth in her house, jewels of silver, and jewels of gold, and raiment: and ye shall put them upon your sons, and upon your daughters; and ye shall spoil the Egyptians.

4 And Moses answered and said, But, behold, they will not believe me, nor hearken unto my voice: for they will say, The Lord hath not appeared unto thee. 2 And the Lord said unto him, What is that in thine hand? And he said, A rod. 3 And he said, Cast it on the ground. And he cast it on the ground, and it became a serpent; and Moses fled from before it. 4 And the Lord said unto Moses, Put forth thine hand, and take it by the tail. And he put forth his hand, and caught it, and it became a rod in his hand: 5 That they may believe that the Lord God of their fathers, the God of Abraham, the God of Isaac, and the God of Jacob, hath appeared unto thee. 6 And the Lord said furthermore unto him, Put now thine hand into thy bosom. And he put his hand into his bosom: and when he took it out, behold, his hand was leprous as snow. 7 And he said, Put thine hand into thy bosom again. And he put his hand into his bosom again; and plucked it out of his bosom, and, behold, it was turned again as his other flesh. 8 And it shall come to pass, if they will not believe thee, neither hearken to the voice of the first sign, that they will believe the voice of the latter sign. 9 And it shall come to pass, if they will not believe also these two signs, neither hearken unto thy voice, that thou shalt take of the water of the river, and pour it upon the dry land: and the water which thou takest out of the river shall become blood upon the dry land.

10 And Moses said unto the Lord, O my Lord, I am not eloquent, neither heretofore, nor since thou hast spoken unto thy servant; but I am slow of speech, and of a slow tongue. 11 And the Lord said unto him, Who hath made man's mouth? or who maketh the dumb, or deaf, or the seeing, or the blind? have not I the Lord? 12 Now therefore go, and I will be with thy mouth, and teach thee what thou shalt say. 13 And he said, O my Lord, send, I pray thee, by the hand of him whom thou wilt send. 14 And the anger of the Lord was kindled against Moses, and he said, Is not Aaron the Levite thy brother? I know that he can speak well. And also, behold, he cometh forth to meet thee: and when he seeth thee, he will be glad in his heart. 15 And thou shalt speak unto him, and put words in his mouth: and I will be with thy mouth, and with his mouth, and will teach you what ye shall do. 16 And he shall be thy spokesman unto the people: and he shall be, even he shall be to thee instead of a mouth, and thou shalt be to him instead of God. 17 And thou shalt take this rod in thine hand, wherewith thou shalt do signs.

18 And Moses went and returned to Jethro his father-in-law, and said unto him, Let me go, I pray thee, and return unto my brethren which are in Egypt, and see whether they be yet alive. And Jethro said to Moses, Go in peace. 19 And the Lord said unto Moses in Midian, Go, return into Egypt: for all the men are dead which sought

thy life. 20 And Moses took his wife and his sons, and set them upon an ass, and he returned to the land of Egypt: and Moses took the rod of God in his hand. 21 And the Lord said unto Moses, When thou goest to return into Egypt, see that thou do all those wonders before Pharaoh, which I have put in thine hand: but I will harden his heart, that he shall not let the people go. 22 And thou shalt say unto Pharaoh, Thus saith the Lord, Israel is my son, even my firstborn: 23 And I say unto thee, Let my son go, that he may serve me: and if thou refuse to let him go, behold, I will slay thy son, even thy firstborn. 24 And it came to pass by the way in the inn, that the Lord met him, and sought to kill him. 25 Then Zipporah took a sharp stone, and cut off the foreskin of her son, and cast it at his feet, and said, Surely a bloody husband art thou to me. 26 So he let him go: then she said, A bloody husband thou art, because of the circumcision.

## MOSES CALLS THE PEOPLE

27 And the Lord said to Aaron, Go into the wilderness to meet Moses. And he went, and met him in the mount of God, and kissed him. 28 And Moses told Aaron all the words of the Lord who had sent him, and all the signs which he had commanded him. 29 And Moses and Aaron went and gathered together all the elders of the children of Israel: 30 And Aaron spake all the words which the Lord had spoken unto Moses, and did the signs in the sight of the people. 31 And the people believed: and when they heard that the Lord had visited the children of Israel, and that he had looked upon their affliction, then they bowed their heads and worshipped.

5  And afterward Moses and Aaron went in, and told Pharaoh, Thus saith the Lord God of Israel, Let my people go, that they may hold a feast unto me in the wilderness. 2 And Pharaoh said, Who is the Lord, that I should obey his voice to let Israel go? I know not the Lord, neither will I let Israel go. 3 And they said, The God of the Hebrews hath met with us: let us go, we pray thee, three days' journey into the desert, and sacrifice unto the Lord our God; lest he fall upon us with pestilence, or with the sword. 4 And the king of Egypt said unto them, Wherefore do ye, Moses and Aaron, let the people from their works? get you unto your burdens. 5 And Pharaoh said, Behold, the people of the land now are many, and ye make them rest from their burdens. 6 And Pharaoh commanded the same day the taskmasters of the people, and their officers, saying, 7 Ye shall no more give the people straw to make brick, as heretofore: let them go and gather straw for themselves. 8 And the tale[1] of the bricks, which they did make heretofore, ye shall lay upon them; ye shall not diminish aught thereof: for they be idle; therefore they cry, saying, Let us go and sacrifice to our God. 9 Let there more work be laid upon the men, that they may labor therein; and let them not regard vain words.

[1] Tally, number.

10 And the taskmasters of the people went out, and their officers, and they spake to the people, saying, Thus saith Pharaoh, I will not give you straw. 11 Go ye, get you straw where you can find it: yet not aught of your work shall be diminished. 12 So the people were scattered abroad throughout all the land of Egypt to gather stubble instead of straw. 13 And the taskmasters hasted them, saying, Fulfil your works, your daily tasks, as when there was straw. 14 And the officers of the children of Israel, which Pharaoh's taskmasters had set over them, were beaten, and demanded, Wherefore have ye not fulfilled your task in making brick both yesterday and to-day, as heretofore?

15 Then the officers of the children of Israel came and cried unto Pharaoh, saying, Wherefore dealest thou thus with thy servants? 16 There is no straw given unto thy servants, and they say to us, Make brick: and, behold, thy servants are beaten; but the fault is in thine own people. 17 But he said, Ye are idle, ye are idle: therefore ye say, Let us go and do sacrifice to the Lord. 18 Go therefore now, and work; for there shall no straw be given you, yet shall ye deliver the tale of bricks. 19 And the officers of the children of Israel did see that they were in evil case, after it was said, Ye shall not minish aught from your bricks of your daily task.

20 And they met Moses and Aaron, who stood in the way, as they came forth from Pharaoh: 21 And they said unto them, The Lord look upon you, and judge; because ye have made our savor to be abhorred in the eyes of Pharaoh, and in the eyes of his servants, to put a sword in their hand to slay us. 22 And Moses returned unto the Lord, and said, Lord, wherefore hast thou so evil entreated this people? why is it that thou hast sent me? 23 For since I came to Pharaoh to speak in thy name, he hath done evil to this people; neither hast thou delivered thy people at all.

6 Then the Lord said unto Moses, Now shalt thou see what I will do to Pharaoh: for with a strong hand shall he let them go, and with a strong hand shall he drive them out of his land. 2 And God spake unto Moses, and said unto him, I am the Lord: 3 And I appeared unto Abraham, unto Isaac, and unto Jacob, by the name of God Almighty; but by my name Jehovah was I not known to them. 4 And I have also established my covenant with them, to give them the land of Canaan, the land of their pilgrimage, wherein they were strangers. 5 And I have also heard the groaning of the children of Israel, whom the Egyptians keep in bondage; and I have remembered my covenant. 6 Wherefore say unto the children of Israel, I am the Lord, and I will bring you out from under the burdens of the Egyptians, and I will rid you out of their bondage, and I will redeem you with a stretched out arm, and with great judgments: 7 And I will take you to me for a people, and I will be to you a God: and ye shall know that I am the Lord your God, which bringeth you out from under the burdens of the Egyptians. 8 And I will bring you in unto the land, con-

cerning the which I did swear to give it to Abraham, to Isaac, and to Jacob; and I will give it you for a heritage: I am the Lord. 9 And Moses spake so unto the children of Israel: but they hearkened not unto Moses for anguish of spirit, and for cruel bondage.

10 And the Lord spake unto Moses, saying, 11 Go in, speak unto Pharaoh king of Egypt, that he let the children of Israel go out of his land. 12 And Moses spake before the Lord, saying, Behold, the children of Israel have not hearkened unto me; how then shall Pharaoh hear me, who am of uncircumcised lips? 13 And the Lord spake unto Moses and unto Aaron, and gave them a charge unto the children of Israel, and unto Pharaoh king of Egypt, to bring the children of Israel out of the land of Egypt.

14 These be the heads of their fathers' houses: The sons of Reuben the firstborn of Israel; Hanoch, and Pallu, Hezron, and Carmi: these be the families of Reuben. 15 And the sons of Simeon; Jemuel, and Jamin, and Ohad, and Jachin, and Zohar, and Shaul the son of a Canaanitish woman: these are the families of Simeon. 16 And these are the names of the sons of Levi according to their generations; Gershon, and Kohath, and Merari: and the years of the life of Levi were a hundred thirty and seven years. 17 The sons of Gershon; Libni, and Shimi, according to their families. 18 And the sons of Kohath; Amram, and Izhar, and Hebron, and Uzziel: and the years of the life of Kohath were a hundred thirty and three years. 19 And the sons of Merari; Mahali and Mushi: these are the families of Levi according to their generations. 20 And Amram took him Jochebed his father's sister to wife; and she bare him Aaron and Moses: and the years of the life of Amram were a hundred and thirty and seven years. 21 And the sons of Izhar; Korah, and Nepheg, and Zichri. 22 And the sons of Uzziel; Mishael, and Elzaphan, and Zithri. 23 And Aaron took him Elisheba, daughter of Amminadab, sister of Naashon, to wife; and she bare him Nadab and Abihu, Eleazar and Ithamar. 24 And the sons of Korah; Assir, and Elkanah, and Abiasaph: these are the families of the Korhites. 25 And Eleazar Aaron's son took him one of the daughters of Putiel to wife; and she bare him Phinehas: these are the heads of the fathers of the Levites according to their families. 26 These are that Aaron and Moses, to whom the Lord said, Bring out the children of Israel from the land of Egypt according to their armies. 27 These are they which spake to Pharaoh king of Egypt, to bring out the children of Israel from Egypt: these are that Moses and Aaron.

## THE PLAGUES

28 And it came to pass on the day when the Lord spake unto Moses in the land of Egypt, 29 That the Lord spake unto Moses, saying, I am the Lord: speak thou unto Pharaoh king of Egypt all that I say unto thee. 30 And Moses said before the Lord, Behold, I am of uncircumcised lips, and how shall Pharaoh hearken unto me?

7 And the Lord said unto Moses, See, I have made thee a god to Pharaoh; and Aaron thy brother shall be thy prophet. 2 Thou shalt speak all that I command thee; and Aaron thy brother shall speak unto Pharaoh, that he send the children of Israel out of his land. 3 And I will harden Pharaoh's heart, and multiply my signs and my wonders in the land of Egypt. 4 But Pharaoh shall not hearken unto you, that I may lay my hand upon Egypt, and bring forth mine armies, and my people the children of Israel, out of the land of Egypt by great judgments. 5 And the Egyptians shall know that I am the Lord, when I stretch forth mine hand upon Egypt, and bring out the children of Israel from among them. 6 And Moses and Aaron did as the Lord commanded them, so did they. 7 And Moses was fourscore years old, and Aaron fourscore and three years old, when they spake unto Pharaoh. 8 And the Lord spake unto Moses and unto Aaron, saying, 9 When Pharaoh shall speak unto you, saying, Show a miracle for you: then thou shalt say unto Aaron, Take thy rod, and cast it before Pharaoh, and it shall become a serpent.

10 And Moses and Aaron went in unto Pharaoh, and they did so as the Lord commanded: and Aaron cast down his rod before Pharaoh, and before his servants, and it became a serpent. 11 Then Pharaoh also called the wise men and the sorcerers: now the magicians of Egypt, they also did in like manner with their enchantments. 12 For they cast down every man his rod, and they became serpents: but Aaron's rod swallowed up their rods. 13 And he hardened Pharaoh's heart, that he hearkened not unto them; as the Lord had said.

14 And the Lord said unto Moses, Pharaoh's heart is hardened, he refuseth to let the people go. 15 Get thee unto Pharaoh in the morning; lo, he goeth out unto the water; and thou shalt stand by the river's brink against he come; and the rod which was turned to a serpent shalt thou take in thine hand. 16 And thou shalt say unto him, The Lord God of the Hebrews hath sent me unto thee, saying, Let my people go, that they may serve me in the wilderness: and, behold, hitherto thou wouldest not hear. 17 Thus saith the Lord, In this thou shalt know that I am the Lord: behold, I will smite with the rod that is in mine hand upon the waters which are in the river, and they shall be turned to blood. 18 And the fish that is in the river shall die, and the river shall stink; and the Egyptians shall loathe to drink of the water of the river. 19 And the Lord spake unto Moses, Say unto Aaron, Take thy rod, and stretch out thine hand upon the waters of Egypt, upon their streams, upon their rivers, and upon their ponds, and upon all their pools of water, that they may become blood; and that there may be blood throughout all the land of Egypt, both in vessels of wood, and in vessels of stone.

20 And Moses and Aaron did so, as the Lord commanded; and he lifted up the rod, and smote the waters that were in the river, in the sight of Pharaoh, and in the sight of his servants; and all the waters that were in the river were turned to blood. 21 And the fish that was

in the river died; and the river stank, and the Egyptians could not drink of the water of the river; and there was blood throughout all the land of Egypt. 22 And the magicians of Egypt did so with their enchantments: and Pharaoh's heart was hardened, neither did he hearken unto them; as the Lord had said. 23 And Pharaoh turned and went into his house, neither did he set his heart to this also. 24 And all the Egyptians digged round about the river for water to drink; for they could not drink of the water of the river. 25 And seven days were fulfilled, after that the Lord had smitten the river.

8 And the Lord spake unto Moses, Go unto Pharaoh, and say unto him, Thus saith the Lord, Let my people go, that they may serve me. 2 And if thou refuse to let them go, behold, I will smite all thy borders with frogs: 3 And the river shall bring forth frogs abundantly, which shall go up and come into thine house, and into thy bed-chamber, and upon thy bed, and into the house of thy servants, and upon thy people, and into thine ovens, and into thy kneadingtroughs: 4 And the frogs shall come up both on thee, and upon thy people, and upon all thy servants. 5 And the Lord spake unto Moses, Say unto Aaron, Stretch forth thine hand with thy rod over the streams, over the rivers, and over the ponds, and cause frogs to come up upon the land of Egypt. 6 And Aaron stretched out his hand over the waters of Egypt; and the frogs came up, and covered the land of Egypt. 7 And the magicians did so with their enchantments, and brought up frogs upon the land of Egypt.

8 Then Pharaoh called for Moses and Aaron, and said, Entreat the Lord, that he may take away the frogs from me, and from my people; and I will let the people go, that they may do sacrifice unto the Lord. 9 And Moses said unto Pharaoh, Glory over me: when shall I entreat for thee, and for thy servants, and for thy people, to destroy the frogs from thee and thy houses, that they may remain in the river only? 10 And he said, To-morrow. And he said, Be it according to thy word; that thou mayest know that there is none like unto the Lord our God. 11 And the frogs shall depart from thee, and from thy houses, and from thy servants, and from thy people; they shall remain in the river only. 12 And Moses and Aaron went out from Pharaoh: and Moses cried unto the Lord because of the frogs which he had brought against Pharaoh. 13 And the Lord did according to the word of Moses; and the frogs died out of the houses, out of the villages, and out of the fields. 14 And they gathered them together upon heaps; and the land stank. 15 But when Pharaoh saw that there was respite, he hardened his heart, and hearkened not unto them; as the Lord had said.

16 And the Lord said unto Moses, Say unto Aaron, Stretch out thy rod, and smite the dust of the land, that it may become lice throughout all the land of Egypt. 17 And they did so; for Aaron stretched out his hand with his rod, and smote the dust of the earth, and it became lice in man, and in beast; all the dust of the land became lice throughout all the land of Egypt. 18 And the magicians did so with their enchant-

ments to bring forth lice, but they could not: so there were lice upon man, and upon beast. 19 Then the magicians said unto Pharaoh, This is the finger of God: and Pharaoh's heart was hardened, and he hearkened not unto them; as the Lord had said.

20 And the Lord said unto Moses, Rise up early in the morning, and stand before Pharaoh; lo, he cometh forth to the water; and say unto him, Thus saith the Lord, Let my people go, that they may serve me. 21 Else, if thou wilt not let my people go, behold, I will send swarms of flies upon thee, and upon thy servants, and upon thy people, and into thy houses: and the houses of the Egyptians shall be full of swarms of flies, and also the ground whereon they are. 22 And I will sever in that day the land of Goshen, in which my people dwell, that no swarms of flies shall be there; to the end thou mayest know that I am the Lord in the midst of the earth. 23 And I will put a division between my people and thy people: to-morrow shall this sign be. 24 And the Lord did so; and there came a grievous swarm of flies into the house of Pharaoh, and into his servants' houses, and into all the land of Egypt: the land was corrupted by reason of the swarm of flies.

25 And Pharaoh called for Moses and for Aaron, and said, Go ye, sacrifice to your God in the land. 26 And Moses said, It is not meet so to do; for we shall sacrifice the abomination of the Egyptians to the Lord our God: lo, shall we sacrifice the abomination of the Egyptians before their eyes, and will they not stone us? 27 We will go three days' journey into the wilderness, and sacrifice to the Lord our God, as he shall command us. 28 And Pharaoh said, I will let you go, that ye may sacrifice to the Lord your God in the wilderness; only ye shall not go very far away: entreat for me. 29 And Moses said, Behold, I go out from thee, and I will entreat the Lord that the swarms of flies may depart from Pharaoh, from his servants, and from his people, to-morrow: but let not Pharaoh deal deceitfully any more in not letting the people go to sacrifice to the Lord. 30 And Moses went out from Pharaoh, and entreated the Lord. 31 And the Lord did according to the word of Moses; and he removed the swarms of flies from Pharaoh, from his servants, and from his people; there remained not one. 32 And Pharaoh hardened his heart at his time also, neither would he let the people go.

9 Then the Lord said unto Moses, Go in unto Pharaoh, and tell him, Thus saith the Lord God of the Hebrews, Let my people go, that they may serve me. 2 For if thou refuse to let them go, and wilt hold them still, 3 Behold, the hand of the Lord is upon thy cattle which is in the field, upon the horses, upon the asses, upon the camels, upon the oxen, and upon the sheep: there shall be a very grievous murrain. 4. And the Lord shall sever between the cattle of Israel and the cattle of Egypt: and there shall nothing die of all that is the children's of Israel. 5 And the Lord appointed a set time, saying, To-morrow the Lord shall do this thing in the land. 6 And the Lord did that thing on the morrow, and all the cattle of Egypt died: but of the cattle of the children of

Israel died not one. 7 And Pharaoh sent, and, behold, there was not one of the cattle of the Israelites dead. And the heart of Pharaoh was hardened, and he did not let the people go.

8 And the Lord said unto Moses and unto Aaron, Take to you handfuls of ashes of the furnace, and let Moses sprinkle it toward the heaven in the sight of Pharaoh. 9 And it shall become small dust in all the land of Egypt, and shall be a boil breaking forth with blains upon man, and upon beast, throughout all the land of Egypt. 10 And they took ashes of the furnace, and stood before Pharaoh; and Moses sprinkled it up toward heaven; and it became a boil breaking forth with blains upon man, and upon beast. 11 And the magicians could not stand before Moses because of the boils; for the boil was upon the magicians, and upon all the Egyptians. 12 And the Lord hardened the heart of Pharaoh, and he hearkened not unto them; as the Lord had spoken unto Moses.

13 And the Lord said unto Moses, Rise up early in the morning, and stand before Pharaoh, and say unto him, Thus saith the Lord God of the Hebrews, Let my people go, that they may serve me. 14 For I will at this time send all my plagues upon thine heart, and upon thy servants, and upon thy people; that thou mayest know that there is none like me in all the earth. 15 For now I will stretch out my hand, that I may smite thee and thy people with pestilence; and thou shalt be cut off from the earth. 16 And in very deed for this cause I have raised thee up, for to show in thee my power; and that my name may be declared throughout all the earth. 17 As yet exaltest thou thyself against my people, that thou wilt not let them go? 18 Behold, to-morrow about this time I will cause it to rain a very grievous hail, such as hath not been in Egypt since the foundation thereof even until now. 19 Send therefore now, and gather thy cattle, and all that thou hast in the field; for upon every man and beast which shall be found in the field, and shall not be brought home, the hail shall come down upon them, and they shall die. 20 He that feared the word of the Lord among the servants of Pharaoh made his servants and his cattle flee into the houses: 21 And he that regarded not the word of the Lord left his servants and his cattle in the field.

22 And the Lord said unto Moses, Stretch forth thine hand toward heaven, that there may be hail in all the land of Egypt, upon man, and upon beast, and upon every herb of the field, throughout the land of Egypt. 23 And Moses stretched forth his rod toward heaven: and the Lord sent thunder and hail, and the fire ran along upon the ground; and the Lord rained hail upon the land of Egypt. 24 So there was hail, and fire mingled with the hail, very grievous, such as there was none like it in all the land of Egypt since it became a nation. 25 And the hail smote throughout all the land of Egypt all that was in the field, both man and beast; and the hail smote every herb of the field, and brake every tree of the field. 26 Only in the land of Goshen, where the children of Israel were, was there no hail.

27 And Pharaoh sent, and called for Moses and Aaron, and said

unto them, I have sinned this time: the Lord is righteous, and I and my people are wicked. 28 Entreat the Lord (for it is enough) that there be no more mighty thunderings and hail; and I will let you go, and ye shall stay no longer. 29 And Moses said unto him, As soon as I am gone out of the city, I will spread abroad my hands unto the Lord; and the thunder shall cease, neither shall there be any more hail; that thou mayest know how that the earth is the Lord's. 30 But as for thee and thy servants, I know that ye will not yet fear the Lord God. 31 And the flax and the barley was smitten: for the barley was in the ear, and the flax was bolled. 32 But the wheat and the rye were not smitten: for they were not grown up. 33 And Moses went out of the city from Pharaoh, and spread abroad his hands unto the Lord: and the thunders and hail ceased, and the rain was not poured upon the earth. 34 And when Pharaoh saw that the rain and the hail and the thunders were ceased, he sinned yet more, and hardened his heart, he and his servants. 35 And the heart of Pharaoh was hardened, neither would he let the children of Israel go; as the Lord had spoken by Moses.

10 And the Lord said unto Moses, Go in unto Pharaoh: for I have hardened his heart, and the heart of his servants, that I might show these my signs before him: 2 And that thou mayest tell in the ears of thy son, and of thy son's son, what things I have wrought in Egypt, and my signs which I have done among them; that ye may know how that I am the Lord. 3 And Moses and Aaron came in unto Pharaoh, and said unto him, Thus saith the Lord God of the Hebrews, How long wilt thou refuse to humble thyself before me? let my people go, that they may serve me. 4 Else, if thou refuse to let my people go, behold, to-morrow will I bring the locusts into thy coast: 5 And they shall cover the face of the earth, that one cannot be able to see the earth: and they shall eat the residue of that which is escaped, which remaineth unto you from the hail, and shall eat every tree which groweth for you out of the field: 6 And they shall fill thy houses, and the houses of all thy servants, and the houses of all the Egyptians; which neither thy fathers, nor thy fathers' fathers have seen, since the day that they were upon the earth unto this day. And he turned himself, and went out from Pharaoh. 7 And Pharaoh's servants said unto him, How long shall this man be a snare unto us? let the men go, that they may serve the Lord their God: knowest thou not yet that Egypt is destroyed? 8 And Moses and Aaron were brought again unto Pharaoh: and he said unto them, Go, serve the Lord your God: but who are they that shall go? 9 And Moses said, We will go with our young and with our old, with our sons and with our daughters, with our flocks and with our herds will we go; for we must hold a feast unto the Lord. 10 And he said unto them, Let the Lord be so with you, as I will let you go, and your little ones: look to it; for evil is before you. 11 Not so: go now ye that are men, and serve the Lord; for that ye did desire. And they were driven out from Pharaoh's presence.

12 And the Lord said unto Moses, Stretch out thine hand over the land of Egypt for the locusts, that they may come up upon the land of Egypt, and eat every herb of the land, even all that the hail hath left. 13 And Moses stretched forth his rod over the land of Egypt, and the Lord brought an east wind upon the land all that day, and all that night; and when it was morning, the east wind brought the locusts. 14 And the locusts went up over all the land of Egypt, and rested in all the coasts of Egypt: very grievous were they; before them there were no such locusts as they, neither after them shall be such. 15 For they covered the face of the whole earth, so that the land was darkened; and they did eat every herb of the land, and all the fruit of the trees which the hail had left: and there remained not any green thing in the trees, or in the herbs of the field, through all the land of Egypt.

16 Then Pharaoh called for Moses and Aaron in haste; and he said, I have sinned against the Lord your God, and against you. 17 Now therefore forgive, I pray thee, my sin only this once, and entreat the Lord your God, that he may take away from me this death only. 18 And he went out from Pharaoh, and entreated the Lord. 19 And the Lord turned a mighty strong west wind, which took away the locusts, and cast them into the Red sea; there remained not one locust in all the coasts of Egypt. 20 But the Lord hardened Pharaoh's heart, so that he would not let the children of Israel go.

21 And the Lord said unto Moses, Stretch out thine hand toward heaven, that there may be darkness over the land of Egypt, even darkness which may be felt. 22 And Moses stretched forth his hand toward heaven; and there was a thick darkness in all the land of Egypt three days: 23 They saw not one another, neither rose any from his place for three days: but all the children of Israel had light in their dwellings.

24 And Pharaoh called unto Moses, and said, Go ye, serve the Lord; only let your flocks and your herds be stayed: let your little ones also go with you. 25 And Moses said, Thou must give us also sacrifices and burnt offerings, that we may sacrifice unto the Lord our God. 26 Our cattle also shall go with us; there shall not a hoof be left behind; for thereof must we take to serve the Lord our God; and we know not with what we must serve the Lord, until we come thither. 27 But the Lord hardened Pharaoh's heart, and he would not let them go.

28 And Pharaoh said unto him, Get thee from me, take heed to thyself, see my face no more; for in that day thou seest my face thou shalt die. 29 And Moses said, Thou hast spoken well, I will see thy face again no more.

11 And the Lord said unto Moses, Yet will I bring one plague more upon Pharaoh, and upon Egypt; afterward he will let you go hence: when he shall let you go, he shall surely thrust you out hence altogether. 2 Speak now in the ears of the people, and let every man borrow of his neighbor, and every woman of her neighbor, jewels of silver, and jewels of gold. 3 And the Lord gave the people favor in the sight of the Egyptians. Moreover, the man Moses was very great in

the land of Egypt, in the sight of Pharaoh's servants, and in the sight of the people.

4 And Moses said, Thus saith the Lord, About midnight will I go out into the midst of Egypt: 5 And all the firstborn in the land of Egypt shall die, from the firstborn of Pharaoh that sitteth upon his throne, even unto the firstborn of the maidservant that is behind the mill; and all the firstborn of beasts. 6 And there shall be a great cry throughout all the land of Egypt, such as there was none like it, nor shall be like it any more. 7 But against any of the children of Israel shall not a dog move his tongue, against man or beast: that ye may know how that the Lord doth put a difference between the Egyptians and Israel. 8 And all these thy servants shall come down unto me, and bow down themselves unto me, saying, Get thee out, and all the people that follow thee: and after that I will go out. And he went out from Pharaoh in a great anger. 9 And the Lord said unto Moses, Pharaoh shall not hearken unto you; that my wonders may be multiplied in the land of Egypt. 10 And Moses and Aaron did all these wonders before Pharaoh: and the Lord hardened Pharaoh's heart, so that he would not let the children of Israel go out of his land.

## THE PASSOVER

12 And the Lord spake unto Moses and Aaron in the land of Egypt, saying, 2 This month shall be unto you the beginning of months: it shall be the first month of the year to you. 3 Speak ye unto all the congregation of Israel, saying, In the tenth day of this month they shall take to them every man a lamb, according to the house of their fathers, a lamb for a house: 4 And if the household be too little for the lamb, let him and his neighbor next unto his house take it according to the number of the souls; every man according to his eating shall make your count for the lamb. 5 Your lamb shall be without blemish, a male of the first year: ye shall take it out from the sheep, or from the goats: 6 And ye shall keep it up until the fourteenth day of the same month: and the whole assembly of the congregation of Israel shall kill it in the evening. 7 And they shall take of the blood, and strike it on the two side posts and on the upper doorpost of the houses, wherein they shall eat it. 8 And they shall eat the flesh in that night, roast with fire, and unleavened bread; and with bitter herbs they shall eat it. 9 Eat not of it raw, nor sodden at all with water, but roast with fire; his head with his legs, and with the purtenance thereof. 10 And ye shall let nothing of it remain until the morning; and that which remaineth of it until the morning ye shall burn with fire. 11 And thus shall ye eat it; with your loins girded, your shoes on your feet, and your staff in your hand; and ye shall eat it in haste: it is the Lord's passover. 12 For I will pass through the land of Egypt this night, and will smite all the firstborn in the land of Egypt, both man and beast; and against all the gods of Egypt I will execute judgment: I am the Lord. 13 And the blood shall

be to you for a token upon the houses where ye are: and when I see the blood, I will pass over you, and the plague shall not be upon you to destroy you, when I smite the land of Egypt. 14 And this day shall be unto you for a memorial; and ye shall keep it a feast to the Lord throughout your generations: ye shall keep it a feast by an ordinance for ever.

15 Seven days shall ye eat unleavened bread; even the first day ye shall put away leaven out of your houses: for whosoever eateth leavened bread from the first day until the seventh day, that soul shall be cut off from Israel. 16 And in the first day there shall be a holy convocation, and in the seventh day there shall be a holy convocation to you; no manner of work shall be done in them, save that which every man must eat, that only may be done of you. 17 And ye shall observe the feast of unleavened bread; for in this selfsame day have I brought your armies out of the land of Egypt: therefore shall ye observe this day in your generations by an ordinance for ever. 18 In the first month, on the fourteenth day of the month at even, ye shall eat unleavened bread, until the one and twentieth day of the month at even. 19 Seven days shall there be no leaven found in your houses: for whosoever eateth that which is leavened, even that soul shall be cut off from the congregation of Israel, whether he be a stranger, or born in the land. 20 Ye shall eat nothing leavened; in all your habitations shall ye eat unleavened bread.

21 Then Moses called for all the elders of Israel, and said unto them, Draw out and take you a lamb according to your families, and kill the passover. 22 And ye shall take a bunch of hyssop, and dip it in the blood that is in the basin, and strike the lintel and the two side posts with the blood that is in the basin; and none of you shall go out at the door of his house until the morning. 23 For the Lord will pass through to smite the Egyptians; and when he seeth the blood upon the lintel, and on the two side posts, the Lord will pass over the door, and will not suffer the destroyer to come in unto your houses to smite you. 24 And ye shall observe this thing for an ordinance to thee and to thy sons for ever. 25 And it shall come to pass, when ye be come to the land which the Lord will give you, according as he hath promised, that ye shall keep this service. 26 And it shall come to pass, when your children shall say unto you, What mean ye by this service? 27 That ye shall say, It is the sacrifice of the Lord's passover, who passed over the houses of the children of Israel in Egypt, when he smote the Egyptians, and delivered our houses. And the people bowed the head and worshipped. 28 And the children of Israel went away, and did as the Lord had commanded Moses and Aaron, so did they.

29 And it came to pass, that at midnight the Lord smote all the firstborn in the land of Egypt, from the firstborn of Pharaoh that sat on his throne unto the firstborn of the captive that was in the dungeon; and all the firstborn of cattle. 30 And Pharaoh rose up in the night, he, and all his servants, and all the Egyptians; and there was a great

cry in Egypt: for there was not a house where there was not one dead. 31 And he called for Moses and Aaron by night, and said, Rise up, and get you forth from among my people, both ye and the children of Israel; and go, serve the Lord, as ye have said. 32 Also take your flocks and your herds, as ye have said, and be gone; and bless me also. 33 And the Egyptians were urgent upon the people, that they might send them out of the land in haste; for they said, We be all dead men. 34 And the people took their dough before it was leavened, their kneading-troughs being bound up in their clothes upon their shoulders. 35 And the children of Israel did according to the word of Moses; and they borrowed of the Egyptians jewels of silver, and jewels of gold, and raiment: 36 And the Lord gave the people favor in the sight of the Egyptians, so that they lent unto them such things as they required: and they spoiled the Egyptians.

## DELIVERANCE

37 And the children of Israel journeyed from Rameses to Succoth, about six hundred thousand on foot that were men, beside children. 38 And a mixed multitude went up also with them; and flocks, and herds, even very much cattle. 39 And they baked unleavened cakes of the dough which they brought forth out of Egypt, for it was not leavened; because they were thrust out of Egypt, and could not tarry, neither had they prepared for themselves any victuals.

40 Now the sojourning of the children of Israel, who dwelt in Egypt, was four hundred and thirty years. 41 And it came to pass at the end of the four hundred and thirty years, even the selfsame day it came to pass, that all the hosts of the Lord went out from the land of Egypt. 42 It is a night to be much observed unto the Lord for bringing them out from the land of Egypt: this is that night of the Lord to be observed of all the children of Israel in their generations.

43 And the Lord said unto Moses and Aaron, This is the ordinance of the passover: There shall no stranger eat thereof: 44 But every man's servant that is bought for money, when thou hast circumcised him, then shall he eat thereof. 45 A foreigner and a hired servant shall not eat thereof. 46 In one house shall it be eaten; thou shalt not carry forth aught of the flesh abroad out of the house; neither shall ye break a bone thereof. 47 All the congregation of Israel shall keep it. 48 And when a stranger shall sojourn with thee, and will keep the passover to the Lord, let all his males be circumcised, and then let him come near and keep it; and he shall be as one that is born in the land: for no uncircumcised person shall eat thereof. 49 One law shall be to him that is homeborn, and unto the stranger that sojourneth among you. 50 Thus did all the children of Israel; as the Lord commanded Moses and Aaron, so did they. 51 And it came to pass the selfsame day, that the Lord did bring the children of Israel out of the land of Egypt by their armies.

13 And the Lord spake unto Moses, saying, 2 Sanctify unto me all the firstborn, whatsoever openeth the womb among the children of Israel, both of man and of beast: it is mine.

3 And Moses said unto the people, Remember this day, in which ye came out from Egypt, out of the house of bondage; for by strength of hand the Lord brought you out from this place: there shall no leavened bread be eaten. 4 This day came ye out in the month Abib. 5 And it shall be when the Lord shall bring thee into the land of the Canaanites, and the Hittites, and the Amorites, and the Hivites, and the Jebusites, which he sware unto thy fathers to give thee, a land flowing with milk and honey, that thou shalt keep this service in this month. 6 Seven days thou shalt eat unleavened bread, and in the seventh day shall be a feast to the Lord. 7 Unleavened bread shall be eaten seven days; and there shall no leavened bread be seen with thee, neither shall there be leaven seen with thee in all thy quarters. 8 And thou shalt show thy son in that day, saying, This is done because of that which the Lord did unto me when I came forth out of Egypt. 9 And it shall be for a sign unto thee upon thine hand, and for a memorial between thine eyes, that the Lord's law may be in thy mouth: for with a strong hand hath the Lord brought thee out of Egypt. 10 Thou shalt therefore keep this ordinance in his season from year to year.

11 And it shall be when the Lord shall bring thee into the land of the Canaanites, as he sware unto thee and to thy fathers, and shall give it thee, 12 That thou shalt set apart unto the Lord all that openeth the matrix, and every firstling that cometh of a beast which thou hast; the male shall be the Lord's. 13 And every firstling of an ass thou shalt redeem with a lamb; and if thou wilt not redeem it, then thou shalt break his neck: and all the firstborn of man among thy children shalt thou redeem. 14 And it shall be when thy son asketh thee in time to come, saying, What is this? that thou shalt say unto him, By strength of hand the Lord brought us out from Egypt, from the house of bondage: 15 And it came to pass, when Pharaoh would hardly let us go, that the Lord slew all the firstborn in the land of Egypt, both the firstborn of man, and the firstborn of beast: therefore I sacrifice to the Lord all that openeth the matrix, being males; but all the firstborn of my children I redeem. 16 And it shall be for a token upon thine hand, and for frontlets between thine eyes: for by strength of hand the Lord brought us forth out of Egypt.

17 And it came to pass, when Pharaoh had let the people go, that God led them not through the way of the land of the Philistines, although that was near; for God said, Lest peradventure the people repent when they see war, and they return to Egypt: 18 But God led the people about, through the way of the wilderness of the Red sea: and the children of Israel went up harnessed out of the land of Egypt. 19 And Moses took the bones of Joseph with him: for he had

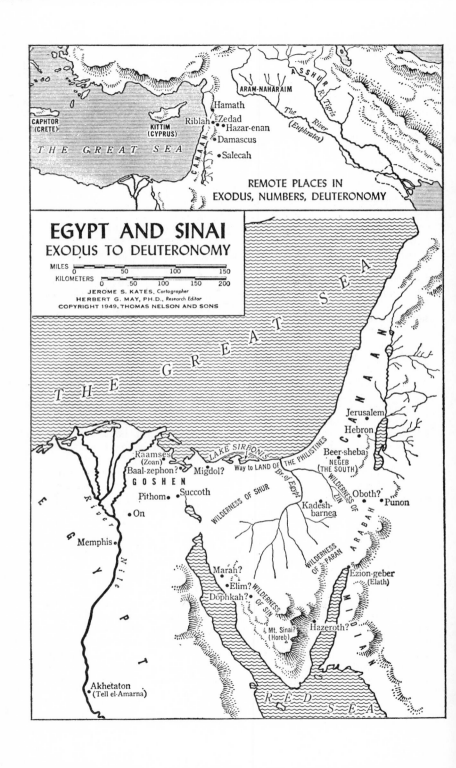

REMOTE PLACES IN
EXODUS, NUMBERS, DEUTERONOMY

# EGYPT AND SINAI
## EXODUS TO DEUTERONOMY

MILES
0        50        100        150

KILOMETERS
0     50     100     150     200

JEROME S. KATES, Cartographer
HERBERT G. MAY, PH.D., Research Editor
COPYRIGHT 1949, THOMAS NELSON AND SONS

straitly sworn the children of Israel, saying, God will surely visit you; and ye shall carry up my bones away hence with you. 20 And they took their journey from Succoth, and encamped in Etham, in the edge of the wilderness. 21 And the Lord went before them by day in a pillar of a cloud, to lead them the way; and by night in a pillar of fire, to give them light; to go by day and night. 22 He took not away the pillar of the cloud by day, nor the pillar of fire by night, from before the people.

14 And the Lord spake unto Moses, saying, 2 Speak unto the children of Israel, that they turn and encamp before Pi-hahiroth, between Migdol and the sea, over against Baal-zephon: before it shall ye encamp by the sea. 3 For Pharaoh will say of the children of Israel, They are entangled in the land, the wilderness hath shut them in. 4 And I will harden Pharaoh's heart, that he shall follow after them; and I will be honored upon Pharaoh, and upon all his host; that the Egyptians may know that I am the Lord. And they did so. 5 And it was told the king of Egypt that the people fled: and the heart of Pharaoh and of his servants was turned against the people, and they said, Why have we done this, that we have let Israel go from serving us? 6 And he made ready his chariot, and took his people with him: 7 And he took six hundred chosen chariots, and all the chariots of Egypt, and captains over every one of them. 8 And the Lord hardened the heart of Pharaoh king of Egypt, and he pursued after the children of Israel: and the children of Israel went out with a high hand. 9 But the Egyptians pursued after them, all the horses and chariots of Pharaoh, and his horsemen, and his army, and overtook them encamping by the sea, beside Pi-hahiroth, before Baal-zephon.

10 And when Pharaoh drew nigh, the children of Israel lifted up their eyes, and, behold, the Egyptians marched after them; and they were sore afraid: and the children of Israel cried out unto the Lord. 11 And they said unto Moses, Because there were no graves in Egypt, hast thou taken us away to die in the wilderness? wherefore hast thou dealt thus with us, to carry us forth out of Egypt? 12 Is not this the word that we did tell thee in Egypt, saying, Let us alone, that we may serve the Egyptians? For it had been better for us to serve the Egyptians, than that we should die in the wilderness. 13 And Moses said unto the people, Fear ye not, stand still, and see the salvation of the Lord, which he will show to you to-day: for the Egyptians whom ye have seen to-day, ye shall see them again no more for ever. 14 The Lord shall fight for you, and ye shall hold your peace.

15 And the Lord said unto Moses, Wherefore criest thou unto me? speak unto the children of Israel, that they go forward: 16 But lift thou up thy rod, and stretch out thine hand over the sea, and divide it: and the children of Israel shall go on dry ground through the midst of the sea. 17 And I, behold, I will harden the hearts of the Egyptians, and they shall follow them: and I will get me honor upon Pharaoh, and upon all his host, upon his chariots, and upon his horsemen. 18 And

the Egyptians shall know that I am the Lord, when I have gotten me honor upon Pharaoh, upon his chariots, and upon his horsemen. 19 And the Angel of God, which went before the camp of Israel, removed and went behind them; and the pillar of the cloud went from before their face, and stood behind them: 20 And it came between the camp of the Egyptians and the camp of Israel; and it was a cloud and darkness to them, but it gave light by night to these: so that the one came not near the other all the night.

21 And Moses stretched out his hand over the sea; and the Lord caused the sea to go back by a strong east wind all that night, and made the sea dry land, and the waters were divided. 22 And the children of Israel went into the midst of the sea upon the dry ground: and the waters were a wall unto them on their right hand, and on their left. 23 And the Egyptians pursued, and went in after them to the midst of the sea, even all Pharaoh's horses, his chariots, and his horsemen. 24 And it came to pass, that in the morning watch the Lord looked unto the host of the Egyptians through the pillar of fire and of the cloud, and troubled the host of the Egyptians, 25 And took off their chariot wheels, that they drave them heavily: so that the Egyptians said, Let us flee from the face of Israel; for the Lord fighteth for them against the Egyptians.

26 And the Lord said unto Moses, Stretch out thine hand over the sea, that the waters may come again upon the Egyptians, upon their chariots, and upon their horsemen. 27 And Moses stretched forth his hand over the sea, and the sea returned to his strength when the morning appeared; and the Egyptians fled against it; and the Lord overthrew the Egyptians in the midst of the sea. 28 And the waters returned, and covered the chariots, and the horsemen, and all the host of Pharaoh that came into the sea after them; there remained not so much as one of them. 29 But the children of Israel walked upon dry land in the midst of the sea; and the waters were a wall unto them on their right hand, and on their left. 30 Thus the Lord saved Israel that day out of the hand of the Egyptians; and Israel saw the Egyptians dead upon the seashore. 31 And Israel saw that great work which the Lord did upon the Egyptians: and the people feared the Lord, and believed the Lord, and his servant Moses.

## SONG OF VICTORY

15 Then sang Moses and the children of Israel this song unto the Lord, and spake, saying,

> I will sing unto the Lord, for he hath triumphed gloriously:
> The horse and his rider hath he thrown into the sea.
> 2 The Lord is my strength and song,
> And he is become my salvation:
> He is my God, and I will prepare him a habitation;
> My father's God, and I will exalt him.

3 The Lord is a man of war:
The Lord is his name.
4 Pharaoh's chariots and his host hath he cast into the sea:
His chosen captains also are drowned in the Red sea.
5 The depths have covered them:
They sank into the bottom as a stone.
6 Thy right hand, O Lord, is become glorious in power:
Thy right hand, O Lord, hath dashed in pieces the enemy.
7 And in the greatness of thine excellency thou hast overthrown
them that rose up against thee:
Thou sentest forth thy wrath, which consumed them as
stubble.
8 And with the blast of thy nostrils the waters were gathered
together,
The floods stood upright as a heap,
And the depths were congealed in the heart of the sea.
9 The enemy said,
I will pursue, I will overtake,
I will divide the spoil; my lust shall be satisfied upon them;
I will draw my sword, my hand shall destroy them.
10 Thou didst blow with thy wind, the sea covered them:
They sank as lead in the mighty waters.
11 Who is like unto thee, O Lord, among the gods?
Who is like thee, glorious in holiness,
Fearful in praises, doing wonders?
12 Thou stretchedst out thy right hand,
The earth swallowed them.
13 Thou in thy mercy hast led forth the people which thou hast
redeemed:
Thou hast guided them in thy strength unto thy holy habi-
tation.
14 The people shall hear, and be afraid:
Sorrow shall take hold on the inhabitants of Palestina.
15 Then the dukes of Edom shall be amazed;
The mighty men of Moab, trembling shall take hold upon
them;
All the inhabitants of Canaan shall melt away.
16 Fear and dread shall fall upon them;
By the greatness of thine arm they shall be as still as a stone;
Till thy people pass over, O Lord,
Till the people pass over, which thou hast purchased.
17 Thou shalt bring them in, and plant them in the mountain of
thine inheritance,
In the place, O Lord, which thou hast made for thee to dwell
in;
In the sanctuary, O Lord, which thy hands have established.
18 The Lord shall reign for ever and ever.

19 For the horse of Pharaoh went in with his chariots and with his horsemen into the sea, and the Lord brought again the waters of the sea upon them; but the children of Israel went on dry land in the midst of the sea. 20 And Miriam the prophetess, the sister of Aaron, took a timbrel in her hand; and all the women went out after her with timbrels and with dances. 21 And Miriam answered them,

Sing ye to the Lord, for he hath triumphed gloriously:
The horse and his rider hath he thrown into the sea.

22 So Moses brought Israel from the Red sea, and they went out into the wilderness of Shur; and they went three days in the wilderness, and found no water. 23 And when they came to Marah, they could not drink of the waters of Marah, for they were bitter: therefore the name of it was called Marah. 24 And the people murmured against Moses, saying, What shall we drink? 25 And he cried unto the Lord; and the Lord showed him a tree, which when he had cast into the waters, the waters were made sweet: there he made for them a statute and an ordinance, and there he proved them, 26 And said, If thou wilt diligently hearken to the voice of the Lord thy God, and wilt do that which is right in his sight, and wilt give ear to his commandments, and keep all his statutes, I will put none of these diseases upon thee, which I have brought upon the Egyptians: for I am the Lord that healeth thee. 27 And they came to Elim, where were twelve wells of water, and threescore and ten palm trees: and they encamped there by the waters.

## MANNA AND THE WILDERNESS

16 And they took their journey from Elim, and all the congregation of the children of Israel came unto the wilderness of Sin, which is between Elim and Sinai, on the fifteenth day of the second month after their departing out of the land of Egypt. 2 And the whole congregation of the children of Israel murmured against Moses and Aaron in the wilderness: 3 And the children of Israel said unto them, Would to God we had died by the hand of the Lord in the land of Egypt, when we sat by the flesh-pots, and when we did eat bread to the full; for ye have brought us forth into this wilderness, to kill this whole assembly with hunger.

4 Then said the Lord unto Moses, Behold, I will rain bread from heaven for you; and the people shall go out and gather a certain rate every day, that I may prove them, whether they will walk in my law, or no. 5 And it shall come to pass, that on the sixth day they shall prepare that which they bring in; and it shall be twice as much as they gather daily. 6 And Moses and Aaron said unto all the children of Israel, At even, then ye shall know that the Lord hath brought you out from the land of Egypt: 7 And in the morning, then ye shall see the glory of the Lord; for that he heareth your murmurings against the Lord: and what are we, that ye murmur against us? 8 And Moses said, This shall be, when the Lord shall give you in the evening flesh to eat,

and in the morning bread to the full; for that the Lord heareth your murmurings which ye murmur against him: and what are we? your murmurings are not against us, but against the Lord.

9 And Moses spake unto Aaron, Say unto all the congregation of the children of Israel, Come near before the Lord: for he hath heard your murmurings. 10 And it came to pass, as Aaron spake unto the whole congregation of the children of Israel, that they looked toward the wilderness, and, behold, the glory of the Lord appeared in the cloud. 11 And the Lord spake unto Moses, saying, 12 I have heard the murmurings of the children of Israel: speak unto them, saying, At even ye shall eat flesh, and in the morning ye shall be filled with bread; and ye shall know that I am the Lord your God.

13 And it came to pass, that at even the quails came up, and covered the camp: and in the morning the dew lay round about the host. 14 And when the dew that lay was gone up, behold, upon the face of the wilderness there lay a small round thing, as small as the hoar frost on the ground. 15 And when the children of Israel saw it, they said one to another, It is manna: for they wist not what it was. And Moses said unto them, This is the bread which the Lord hath given you to eat. 16 This is the thing which the Lord hath commanded, Gather of it every man according to his eating, an omer for every man, according to the number of your persons; take ye every man for them which are in his tents. 17 And the children of Israel did so, and gathered, some more, some less. 18 And when they did mete it with an omer, he that gathered much had nothing over, and he that gathered little had no lack; they gathered every man according to his eating. 19 And Moses said, Let no man leave of it till the morning. 20 Notwithstanding they hearkened not unto Moses; but some of them left of it until the morning, and it bred worms, and stank: and Moses was wroth with them. 21 And they gathered it every morning, every man according to his eating: and when the sun waxed hot, it melted. 31 And the house of Israel called the name thereof Manna: and it was like coriander seed, white; and the taste of it was like wafers made with honey.

17    8 Then came Amalek, and fought with Israel in Rephidim. 9 And Moses said unto Joshua, Choose us out men, and go out, fight with Amalek: to-morrow I will stand on the top of the hill with the rod of God in mine hand. 10 So Joshua did as Moses had said to him, and fought with Amalek: and Moses, Aaron, and Hur went up to the top of the hill. 11 And it came to pass, when Moses held up his hand, that Israel prevailed: and when he let down his hand, Amalek prevailed. 12 But Moses' hands were heavy; and they took a stone, and put it under him, and he sat thereon; and Aaron and Hur stayed up his hands, the one on the one side, and other on the other side; and his hands were steady until the going down of the sun. 13 And Joshua discomfited Amalek and his people with the edge of the sword.

14 And the Lord said unto Moses, Write this for a memorial in a

book, and rehearse it in the ears of Joshua: for I will utterly put out the remembrance of Amalek from under heaven. 15 And Moses built an altar, and called the name of it Jehovah-nissi: 16 For he said, Because the Lord hath sworn that the Lord will have war with Amalek from generation to generation.

18 When Jethro, the priest of Midian, Moses' father-in-law, heard of all that God had done for Moses, and for Israel his people, and that the Lord had brought Israel out of Egypt; 2 Then Jethro, Moses' father-in-law, took Zipporah, Moses' wife, after he had sent her back, 3 And her two sons; of which the name of the one was Gershom; for he said, I have been an alien in a strange land: 4 And the name of the other was Eliezer; for the God of my father, said he, was mine help, and delivered me from the sword of Pharaoh: 5 And Jethro, Moses' father-in-law, came with his sons and his wife unto Moses into the wilderness, where he encamped at the mount of God: 6 And he said unto Moses, I thy father-in-law Jethro am come unto thee, and thy wife, and her two sons with her. 7 And Moses went out to meet his father-in-law, and did obeisance, and kissed him; and they asked each other of their welfare; and they came into the tent. 8 And Moses told his father-in-law all that the Lord had done unto Pharaoh and to the Egyptians for Israel's sake, and all the travail that had come upon them by the way, and how the Lord delivered them. 9 And Jethro rejoiced for all the goodness which the Lord had done to Israel, whom he had delivered out of the hand of the Egyptians. 10 And Jethro said, Blessed be the Lord, who hath delivered you out of the hand of the Egyptians, and out of the hand of Pharaoh, who hath delivered the people from under the hand of the Egyptians. 11 Now I know that the Lord is greater than all gods: for in the thing wherein they dealt proudly he was above them. 12 And Jethro, Moses' father-in-law, took a burnt offering and sacrifices for God: and Aaron came, and all the elders of Israel, to eat bread with Moses' father-in-law before God.

13 And it came to pass on the morrow, that Moses sat to judge the people: and the people stood by Moses from the morning unto the evening. 14 And when Moses' father-in-law saw all that he did to the people, he said, What is this thing that thou doest to the people? Why sittest thou thyself alone, and all the people stand by thee from morning unto even? 15 And Moses said unto his father-in-law, Because the people come unto me to inquire of God: 16 When they have a matter, they come unto me; and I judge between one and another, and I do make them know the statutes of God, and his laws.

17 And Moses' father-in-law said unto him, The thing that thou doest is not good. 18 Thou wilt surely wear away, both thou, and this people that is with thee: for this thing is too heavy for thee; thou art not able to perform it thyself alone. 19 Hearken now unto my voice, I will give thee counsel, and God shall be with thee: Be thou for the people to God-ward, that thou mayest bring the causes unto God: 20 And thou shalt teach them ordinances and laws, and shalt show

them the way wherein they must walk, and the work that they must do. 21 Moreover thou shalt provide out of all the people able men, such as fear God, men of truth, hating covetousness; and place such over them, to be rulers of thousands, and rulers of hundreds, rulers of fifties, and rulers of tens: 22 And let them judge the people at all seasons: and it shall be, that every great matter they shall bring unto thee, but every small matter they shall judge: so shall it be easier for thyself, and they shall bear the burden with thee. 23 If thou shalt do this thing, and God command thee so, then thou shalt be able to endure, and all this people shall also go to their place in peace.

24 So Moses hearkened to the voice of his father-in-law, and did all that he had said. 25 And Moses chose able men out of all Israel, and made them heads over the people, rulers of thousands, rulers of hundreds, rulers of fifties, and rulers of tens. 26 And they judged the people at all seasons: the hard causes they brought unto Moses, but every small matter they judged themselves. 27 And Moses let his father-in-law depart; and he went his way into his own land.

## THE COVENANT

19 In the third month, when the children of Israel were gone forth out of the land of Egypt, the same day came they into the wilderness of Sinai. 2 For they were departed from Rephidim, and were come to the desert of Sinai, and had pitched in the wilderness; and there Israel camped before the mount. 3 And Moses went up unto God, and the Lord called unto him out of the mountain, saying, Thus shalt thou say to the house of Jacob, and tell the children of Israel; 4 Ye have seen what I did unto the Egyptians, and how I bare you on eagles' wings, and brought you unto myself. 5 Now therefore, if ye will obey my voice indeed, and keep my covenant, then ye shall be a peculiar treasure unto me above all people: for all the earth is mine: 6 And ye shall be unto me a kingdom of priests, and a holy nation. These are the words which thou shalt speak unto the children of Israel.

7 And Moses came and called for the elders of the people, and laid before their faces all these words which the Lord commanded him. 8 And all the people answered together, and said, All that the Lord hath spoken we will do. And Moses returned the words of the people unto the Lord. 9 And the Lord said unto Moses, Lo, I come unto thee in a thick cloud, that the people may hear when I speak with thee, and believe thee for ever. And Moses told the words of the people unto the Lord. 10 And the Lord said unto Moses, Go unto the people, and sanctify them to-day and to-morrow, and let them wash their clothes, 11 And be ready against the third day: for the third day the Lord will come down in the sight of all the people upon mount Sinai. 12 And thou shalt set bounds unto the people round about, saying, Take heed to yourselves, that ye go not up into the mount, or touch the border of it: whosoever toucheth the mount shall be surely put to death. 13 There shall not a hand touch it, but he shall surely

be stoned, or shot through; whether it be beast or man, it shall not live: when the trumpet soundeth long, they shall come up to the mount. 14 And Moses went down from the mount unto the people, and sanctified the people; and they washed their clothes. 15 And he said unto the people, Be ready against the third day: come not at your wives.

16 And it came to pass on the third day in the morning, that there were thunders and lightnings, and a thick cloud upon the mount, and the voice of the trumpet exceeding loud; so that all the people that was in the camp trembled. 17 And Moses brought forth the people out of the camp to meet with God; and they stood at the nether part of the mount. 18 And mount Sinai was altogether on a smoke, because the Lord descended upon it in fire: and the smoke thereof ascended as the smoke of a furnace, and the whole mount quaked greatly. 19 And when the voice of the trumpet sounded long, and waxed louder and louder, Moses spake, and God answered him by a voice. 20 And the Lord came down upon mount Sinai, on the top of the mount: and the Lord called Moses up to the top of the mount; and Moses went up. 21 And the Lord said unto Moses, Go down, charge the people, lest they break through unto the Lord to gaze, and many of them perish. 22 And let the priests also, which come near to the Lord, sanctify themselves, lest the Lord break forth upon them. 23 And Moses said unto the Lord, The people cannot come up to mount Sinai: for thou chargedst us, saying, Set bounds about the mount, and sanctify it. 24 And the Lord said unto him, Away, get thee down, and thou shalt come up, thou, and Aaron with thee: but let not the priests and the people break through to come up unto the Lord, lest he break forth upon them. 25 So Moses went down unto the people, and spake unto them.

## THE TEN COMMANDMENTS

20 And God spake all these words, saying.

2 I am the Lord thy God, which have brought thee out of the land of Egypt, out of the house of bondage. 3 Thou shalt have no other gods before me.

4 Thou shalt not make unto thee any graven image, or any likeness of any thing that is in heaven above, or that is in the earth beneath, or that is in the water under the earth: 5 Thou shalt not bow down thyself to them, nor serve them: for I the Lord thy God am a jealous God, visiting the iniquity of the fathers upon the children unto the third and fourth generation of them that hate me; 6 And showing mercy unto thousands of them that love me, and keep my commandments.

7 Thou shalt not take the name of the Lord thy God in vain: for the Lord will not hold him guiltless that taketh his name in vain.

8 Remember the sabbath day, to keep it holy. 9 Six days shalt thou labor, and do all thy work: 10 But the seventh day is the sabbath of

the Lord thy God: in it thou shalt not do any work, thou, nor thy son, nor thy daughter, thy manservant, nor thy maidservant, nor thy cattle, nor thy stranger that is within thy gates: 11 For in six days the Lord made heaven and earth, the sea, and all that in them is, and rested the seventh day: wherefore the Lord blessed the sabbath day, and hallowed it.

12 Honor thy father and thy mother: that thy days may be long upon the land which the Lord thy God giveth thee.

13 Thou shalt not kill.

14 Thou shalt not commit adultery.

15 Thou shalt not steal.

16 Thou shalt not bear false witness against thy neighbor.

17 Thou shalt not covet thy neighbor's house, thou shalt not covet thy neighbor's wife, nor his manservant, nor his maidservant, nor his ox, nor his ass, nor any thing that is thy neighbor's.

18 And all the people saw the thunderings, and the lightnings, and the noise of the trumpet, and the mountain smoking: and when the people saw it, they removed, and stood afar off. 19 And they said unto Moses, Speak thou with us, and we will hear: but let not God speak with us, lest we die. 20 And Moses said unto the people, Fear not: for God is come to prove you, and that his fear may be before your faces, that ye sin not. 21 And the people stood afar off, and Moses drew near unto the thick darkness where God was.

## OTHER COMMANDMENTS

20  22 And the Lord said unto Moses, Thus thou shalt say unto the children of Israel, Ye have seen that I have talked with you from heaven. 23 Ye shall not make with me gods of silver, neither shall ye make unto you gods of gold.

21  Now these are the judgments which thou shalt set before them. 2 If thou buy a Hebrew servant, six years he shall serve: and in the seventh he shall go out free for nothing. 3 If he came in by himself, he shall go out by himself: if he were married, then his wife shall go out with him.

22  25 If thou lend money to any of my people that is poor by thee, thou shalt not be to him as a usurer, neither shalt thou lay upon him usury. 26 If thou at all take thy neighbor's raiment to pledge, thou shalt deliver it unto him by that the sun goeth down: 27 For that is his covering only, it is his raiment for his skin: wherein shall he sleep? and it shall come to pass, when he crieth unto me, that I will hear; for I am gracious.

23  Thou shalt not raise a false report: put not thine hand with the wicked to be an unrighteous witness. 2 Thou shalt not follow a multitude to do evil; neither shalt thou speak in a cause to decline after

many to wrest judgment: 3 Neither shalt thou countenance[1] a poor man in his cause.

4 If thou meet thine enemy's ox or his ass going astray, thou shalt surely bring it back to him again. 5 If thou see the ass of him that hateth thee lying under his burden, and wouldest forbear to help him, thou shalt surely help with him.

6 Thou shalt not wrest the judgment of thy poor in his cause. 7 Keep thee far from a false matter; and the innocent and righteous slay thou not: for I will not justify the wicked. 8 And thou shalt take no gift: for the gift blindeth the wise, and perverteth the words of the righteous. 9 Also thou shalt not oppress a stranger: for ye know the heart of a stranger, seeing ye were strangers in the land of Egypt.

10 And six years thou shalt sow thy land, and shalt gather in the fruits thereof: 11 But the seventh year thou shalt let it rest and lie still; that the poor of thy people may eat: and what they leave the beasts of the field shall eat. In like manner thou shalt deal with thy vineyard, and with thy oliveyard. 12 Six days thou shalt do thy work, and on the seventh day thou shalt rest: that thine ox and thine ass may rest, and the son of thy handmaid, and the stranger, may be refreshed. 13 And in all things that I have said unto you be circumspect: and make no mention of the name of other gods, neither let it be heard out of thy mouth.

## MOSES ON THE MOUNT

24   12 And the Lord said unto Moses, Come up to me into the mount, and be there: and I will give thee tables of stone, and a law, and commandments which I have written; that thou mayest teach them. 13 And Moses rose up, and his minister Joshua; and Moses went up into the mount of God. 14 And he said unto the elders, Tarry ye here for us, until we come again unto you: and, behold, Aaron and Hur are with you: if any man have any matters to do, let him come unto them. 15 And Moses went up into the mount, and a cloud covered the mount. 16 And the glory of the Lord abode upon mount Sinai, and the cloud covered it six days: and the seventh day he called unto Moses out of the midst of the cloud. 17 And the sight of the glory of the Lord was like devouring fire on the top of the mount in the eyes of the children of Israel. 18 And Moses went into the midst of the cloud, and gat him up into the mount: and Moses was in the mount forty days and forty nights.

25   And the Lord spake unto Moses, saying, 2 Speak unto the children of Israel, that they bring me an offering: of every man that giveth it willingly with his heart ye shall take my offering. 3 And this is the offering which ye shall take of them; gold, and silver, and brass, 4 And blue, and purple, and scarlet, and fine linen, and goats' hair, 5 And

---

[1] Judge haughtily or partially.

rams' skins dyed red, and badgers' skins, and shittim wood, 6 Oil for
the light, spices for anointing oil, and for sweet incense, 7 Onyx
stones, and stones to be set in the ephod, and in the breastplate.
8 And let them make me a sanctuary; that I may dwell among them.
9 According to all that I show thee, after the pattern of the tabernacle,
and the pattern of all the instruments thereof, even so shall ye make it.

28 And take thou unto thee Aaron thy brother, and his sons with
him, from among the children of Israel, that he may minister unto
me in the priest's office, even Aaron, Nadab, and Abihu, Eleazar and
Ithamar, Aaron's sons. 2 And thou shalt make holy garments for
Aaron thy brother, for glory and for beauty. 3 And thou shalt speak
unto all that are wise-hearted, whom I have filled with the spirit of
wisdom, that they may make Aaron's garments to consecrate him, that
he may minister unto me in the priest's office. 4 And these are the
garments which they shall make; a breastplate, and an ephod, and a
robe, and a broidered coat, a mitre, and a girdle: and they shall make
holy garments for Aaron thy brother, and his sons, that he may minister unto me in the priest's office.

31 2 See, I have called by name Bezaleel the son of Uri, the son
of Hur, of the tribe of Judah: 3 And I have filled him with the spirit
of God, in wisdom, and in understanding, and in knowledge, and in
all manner of workmanship, 4 To devise cunning works, to work in
gold, and in silver, and in brass, 5 And in cutting of stones, to set
them, and in carving of timber, to work in all manner of workmanship.
6 And I, behold, I have given with him Aholiab, the son of Ahisamach,
of the tribe of Dan: and in the hearts of all that are wise-hearted I
have put wisdom, that they may make all that I have commanded thee;
7 The tabernacle of the congregation, and the ark of the testimony,
and the mercy seat that is thereupon, and all the furniture of the
tabernacle, 8 And the table and his furniture, and the pure candlestick with all his furniture, and the altar of incense, 9 And the altar
of burnt offering with all his furniture, and the laver and his foot,
10 And the clothes of service, and the holy garments for Aaron the
priest, and the garments of his sons, to minister in the priest's office,
11 And the anointing oil, and sweet incense for the holy place: according to all that I have commanded thee shall they do.

18 And he gave unto Moses, when he had made an end of communing with him upon mount Sinai, two tables of testimony, tables
of stone, written with the finger of God.

## ISRAEL REBELS

32 And when the people saw that Moses delayed to come down
out of the mount, the people gathered themselves together unto Aaron,
and said unto him, Up, make us gods, which shall go before us; for as
for this Moses, the man that brought us up out of the land of Egypt,

we wot not what is become of him. 2 And Aaron said unto them, Break off the golden earrings, which are in the ears of your wives, of your sons, and of your daughters, and bring them unto me. 3 And all the people brake off the golden earrings which were in their ears, and brought them unto Aaron. 4 And he received them at their hand, and fashioned it with a graving tool, after he had made it a molten calf: and they said, These be thy gods, O Israel, which brought thee up out of the land of Egypt. 5 And when Aaron saw it, he built an altar before it; and Aaron made proclamation, and said, To-morrow is a feast to the Lord. 6 And they rose up early on the morrow, and offered burnt offerings, and brought peace offerings; and the people sat down to eat and to drink, and rose up to play.

7 And the Lord said unto Moses, Go, get thee down; for thy people, which thou broughtest out of the land of Egypt, have corrupted themselves: 8 They have turned aside quickly out of the way which I commanded them: they have made them a molten calf, and have worshipped it, and have sacrificed thereunto, and said, These be thy gods, O Israel, which have brought thee up out of the land of Egypt. 9 And the Lord said unto Moses, I have seen this people, and, behold, it is a stiffnecked people: 10 Now therefore let me alone, that my wrath may wax hot against them, and that I may consume them: and I will make of thee a great nation. 11 And Moses besought the Lord his God, and said, Lord, why doth thy wrath wax hot against thy people, which thou hast brought forth out of the land of Egypt with great power, and with a mighty hand? 12 Wherefore should the Egyptians speak, and say, For mischief did he bring them out, to slay them in the mountains, and to consume them from the face of the earth? Turn from thy fierce wrath, and repent of this evil against thy people. 13 Remember Abraham, Isaac, and Israel, thy servants, to whom thou swarest by thine own self, and saidst unto them, I will multiply your seed as the stars of heaven, and all this land that I have spoken of will I give unto your seed, and they shall inherit it for ever. 14 And the Lord repented of the evil which he thought to do unto his people.

15 And Moses turned, and went down from the mount, and the two tables of the testimony were in his hand: the tables were written on both their sides; on the one side and on the other were they written. 16 And the tables were the work of God, and the writing was the writing of God, graven upon the tables. 17 And when Joshua heard the noise of the people as they shouted, he said unto Moses, There is a noise of war in the camp. 18 And he said, It is not the voice of them that shout for mastery, neither is it the voice of them that cry for being overcome; but the noise of them that sing do I hear.

19 And it came to pass, as soon as he came nigh unto the camp, that he saw the calf, and the dancing: and Moses' anger waxed hot, and he cast the tables out of his hands, and brake them beneath the mount. 20 And he took the calf which they had made, and burnt it in the fire, and ground it to powder, and strewed it upon the water, and made the children of Israel drink of it.

21 And Moses said unto Aaron, What did this people unto thee, that thou hast brought so great a sin upon them? 22 And Aaron said, Let not the anger of my lord wax hot: thou knowest the people, that they are set on mischief. 23 For they said unto me, Make us gods, which shall go before us: for as for this Moses, the man that brought us up out of the land of Egypt, we wot not what is become of him. 24 And I said unto them, Whosoever hath any gold, let them break it off. So they gave it me: then I cast it into the fire, and there came out this calf.

25 And when Moses saw that the people were naked, (for Aaron had made them naked unto their shame among their enemies,) 26 Then Moses stood in the gate of the camp, and said, Who is on the Lord's side? let him come unto me. And all the sons of Levi gathered themselves together unto him. 27 And he said unto them, Thus saith the Lord God of Israel, Put every man his sword by his side, and go in and out from gate to gate throughout the camp, and slay every man his brother, and every man his companion, and every man his neighbor. 28 And the children of Levi did according to the word of Moses: and there fell of the people that day about three thousand men. 29 For Moses had said, Consecrate yourselves to-day to the Lord, even every man upon his son, and upon his brother; that he may bestow upon you a blessing this day.

30 And it came to pass on the morrow, that Moses said unto the people, Ye have sinned a great sin: and now I will go up unto the Lord; peradventure I shall make an atonement for your sin. 31 And Moses returned unto the Lord, and said, Oh, this people have sinned a great sin, and have made them gods of gold. 32 Yet now, if thou wilt forgive their sin — ; and if not, blot me, I pray thee, out of thy book which thou hast written. 33 And the Lord said unto Moses, Whosoever hath sinned against me, him will I blot out of my book. 34 Therefore now go, lead the people unto the place of which I have spoken unto thee: behold, mine Angel shall go before thee: nevertheless, in the day when I visit, I will visit their sin upon them. 35 And the Lord plagued the people, because they made the calf, which Aaron made.

## THE COVENANT RENEWED

34 And the Lord said unto Moses, Hew thee two tables of stone like unto the first: and I will write upon these tables the words that were in the first tables, which thou brakest. 2 And be ready in the morning, and come up in the morning unto mount Sinai, and present thyself there to me in the top of the mount. 3 And no man shall come up with thee, neither let any man be seen throughout all the mount; neither let the flocks nor herds feed before that mount. 4 And he hewed two tables of stone like unto the first; and Moses rose up early in the morning, and went up unto mount Sinai, as the Lord had commanded him, and took in his hand the two tables of stone. 5 And the

Lord descended in the cloud, and stood with him there, and proclaimed the name of the Lord. 6 And the Lord passed by before him, and proclaimed, The Lord, The Lord God, merciful and gracious, longsuffering, and abundant in goodness and truth, 7 Keeping mercy for thousands, forgiving iniquity and transgression and sin, and that will by no means clear the guilty; visiting the iniquity of the fathers upon the children, and upon the children's children, unto the third and to the fourth generation. 8 And Moses made haste, and bowed his head toward the earth, and worshipped. 9 And he said, If now I have found grace in thy sight, O Lord, let my Lord, I pray thee, go among us; for it is a stiffnecked people; and pardon our iniquity and our sin, and take us for thine inheritance.

27 And the Lord said unto Moses, Write thou these words: for after the tenor of these words I have made a covenant with thee and with Israel. 28 And he was there with the Lord forty days and forty nights; he did neither eat bread, nor drink water. And he wrote upon the tables the words of the covenant, the ten commandments.

29 And it came to pass, when Moses came down from mount Sinai with the two tables of testimony in Moses' hand, when he came down from the mount, that Moses wist not that the skin of his face shone while he talked with him. 30 And when Aaron and all the children of Israel saw Moses, behold, the skin of his face shone; and they were afraid to come nigh him. 31 And Moses called unto them; and Aaron and all the rulers of the congregation returned unto him: and Moses talked with them. 32 And afterward all the children of Israel came nigh: and he gave them in commandment all that the Lord had spoken with him in mount Sinai. 33 And till Moses had done speaking with them, he put a veil on his face. 34 But when Moses went in before the Lord to speak with him, he took the veil off, until he came out. And he came out, and spake unto the children of Israel that which he was commanded. 35 And the children of Israel saw the face of Moses, that the skin of Moses' face shone: and Moses put the veil upon his face again, until he went in to speak with him.

## THE TABERNACLE: ART AND ARTIFICE

3 5 4 And Moses spake unto all the congregation of the children of Israel, saying, This is the thing which the Lord commanded, saying, 5 Take ye from among you an offering unto the Lord: whosoever is of a willing heart, let him bring it, an offering of the Lord; gold, and silver, and brass, 6 And blue, and purple, and scarlet, and fine linen, and goats' hair, 7 And rams' skins dyed red, and badgers' skins, and shittim wood, 8 And oil for the light, and spices for anointing oil, and for the sweet incense, 9 And onyx stones, and stones to be set for the ephod, and for the breastplate. 10 And every wise-hearted among you shall come, and make all that the Lord hath commanded; 11 The tabernacle, his tent, and his covering, his taches, and his boards, his bars, his pillars, and his sockets; 12 The ark, and the staves thereof,

with the mercy seat, and the veil of the covering; 13 The table, and his staves, and all his vessels, and the showbread; 14 The candlestick also for the light, and his furniture, and his lamps, with the oil for the light; 15 And the incense altar, and his staves, and the anointing oil, and the sweet incense, and the hanging for the door at the entering in of the tabernacle; 16 The altar of burnt offering, with his brazen grate, his staves, and all his vessels, the laver and his foot; 17 The hangings of the court, his pillars, and their sockets, and the hanging for the door of the court; 18 The pins of the tabernacle, and the pins of the court, and their cords; 19 The clothes of service, to do service in the holy place, the holy garments for Aaron the priest, and the garments of his sons, to minister in the priest's office.

20 And all the congregation of the children of Israel departed from the presence of Moses. 21 And they came, every one whose heart stirred him up, and every one whom his spirit made willing, and they brought the Lord's offering to the work of the tabernacle of the congregation, and for all his service, and for the holy garments.

30 And Moses said unto the children of Israel, See, the Lord hath called by name Bezaleel the son of Uri, the son of Hur, of the tribe of Judah; 31 And he hath filled him with the spirit of God, in wisdom, in understanding, and in knowledge, and in all manner of workmanship; 32 And to devise curious works, to work in gold, and in silver, and in brass, 33 And in the cutting of stones, to set them, and in carving of wood, to make any manner of cunning work. 34 And he hath put in his heart that he may teach, both he, and Aholiab, the son of Ahisamach, of the tribe of Dan. 35 Them hath he filled with wisdom of heart, to work all manner of work, of the engraver, and of the cunning workman, and of the embroiderer, in blue, and in purple, in scarlet, and in fine linen, and of the weaver, even of them that do any work, and of those that devise cunning work.

36 Then wrought Bezaleel and Aholiab, and every wise-hearted man, in whom the Lord put wisdom and understanding to know how to work all manner of work for the service of the sanctuary, according to all that the Lord had commanded.

2 And Moses called Bezaleel and Aholiab, and every wise-hearted man, in whose heart the Lord had put wisdom, even every one whose heart stirred him up to come unto the work to do it: 3 And they received of Moses all the offering, which the children of Israel had brought for the work of the service of the sanctuary, to make it withal. And they brought yet unto him free offerings every morning. 4 And all the wise men, that wrought all the work of the sanctuary, came every man from his work which they made; 5 And they spake unto Moses, saying, The people bring much more than enough for the service of the work, which the Lord commanded to make. 6 And Moses gave commandment, and they caused it to be proclaimed throughout the camp, saying, Let neither man nor woman make any more work for the offering of the sanctuary. So the people were re-

strained from bringing. 7 For the stuff they had was sufficient for all the work to make it, and too much.

40   17 And it came to pass in the first month in the second year, on the first day of the month, that the tabernacle was reared up. 18 And Moses reared up the tabernacle, and fastened his sockets, and set up the boards thereof, and put in the bars thereof, and reared up his pillars. 19 And he spread abroad the tent over the tabernacle, and put the covering of the tent above upon it; as the Lord commanded Moses.

20 And he took and put the testimony into the ark, and set the staves on the ark, and put the mercy seat above upon the ark: 21 And he brought the ark into the tabernacle, and set up the veil of the covering, and covered the ark of the testimony; as the Lord commanded Moses. 22 And he put the table in the tent of the congregation, upon the side of the tabernacle northward, without the veil. 23 And he set the bread in order upon it before the Lord; as the Lord had commanded Moses. 24 And he put the candlestick in the tent of the congregation, over against the table, on the side of the tabernacle southward. 25 And he lighted the lamps before the Lord; as the Lord commanded Moses. 26 And he put the golden altar in the tent of the congregation before the veil: 27 And he burnt sweet incense thereon; as the Lord commanded Moses. 28 And he set up the hanging at the door of the tabernacle. 29 And he put the altar of burnt offering by the door of the tabernacle of the tent of the congregation, and offered upon it the burnt offering and the meat offering; as the Lord commanded Moses. 30 And he set the laver between the tent of the congregation and the altar, and put water there, to wash withal. 31 And Moses and Aaron and his sons washed their hands and their feet thereat: 32 When they went into the tent of the congregation, and when they came near unto the altar, they washed; as the Lord commanded Moses. 33 And he reared up the court round about the tabernacle and the altar, and set up the hanging of the court gate. So Moses finished the work. 34 Then a cloud covered the tent of the congregation, and the glory of the Lord filled the tabernacle.

# *Leviticus*

## RITUAL LAWS: SACRIFICES

1   And the Lord called unto Moses, and spake unto him out of the tabernacle of the congregation, saying, 2 Speak unto the children of Israel, and say unto them, If any man of you bring an offering unto the Lord, ye shall bring your offering of the cattle, even of the herd, and of the flock.

3 If his offering be a burnt sacrifice of the herd, let him offer a male

without blemish: he shall offer it of his own voluntary will at the door of the tabernacle of the congregation before the Lord. 4 And he shall put his hand upon the head of the burnt offering; and it shall be accepted for him to make atonement for him. 5 And he shall kill the bullock before the Lord: and the priests, Aaron's sons, shall bring the blood, and sprinkle the blood round about upon the altar that is by the door of the tabernacle of the congregation. 6 And he shall flay the burnt offering, and cut it into his pieces. 7 And the sons of Aaron the priest shall put fire upon the altar, and lay the wood in order upon the fire: 8 And the priests, Aaron's sons, shall lay the parts, the head, and the fat, in order upon the wood that is on the fire which is upon the altar: 9 But his inwards and his legs shall he wash in water: and the priest shall burn all on the altar, to be a burnt sacrifice, an offering made by fire, of a sweet savor unto the Lord.

5 14 And the Lord spake unto Moses, saying, 15 If a soul commit a trespass, and sin through ignorance, in the holy things of the Lord; then he shall bring for his trespass unto the Lord a ram without blemish out of the flocks, with thy estimation by shekels of silver, after the shekel of the sanctuary, for a trespass offering: 16 And he shall make amends for the harm that he hath done in the holy thing, and shall add the fifth part thereto, and give it unto the priest: and the priest shall make an atonement for him with the ram of the trespass offering, and it shall be forgiven him.

6 And the Lord spake unto Moses, saying, 2 If a soul sin, and commit a trespass against the Lord, and lie unto his neighbor in that which was delivered him to keep, or in fellowship, or in a thing taken away by violence, or hath deceived his neighbor; 3 Or have found that which was lost, and lieth concerning it, and sweareth falsely; in any of all these that a man doeth, sinning therein: 4 Then it shall be, because he hath sinned, and is guilty, that he shall restore that which he took violently away, or the thing which he hath deceitfully gotten, or that which was delivered him to keep, or the lost thing which he found, 5 Or all that about which he hath sworn falsely; he shall even restore it in the principal, and shall add the fifth part more thereto, and give it unto him to whom it appertaineth, in the day of his trespass offering. 6 And he shall bring his trespass offering unto the Lord, a ram without blemish out of the flock, with thy estimation, for a trespass offering, unto the priest: 7 And the priest shall make an atonement for him before the Lord: and it shall be forgiven him for any thing of all that he hath done in trespassing therein.

## CLEAN AND UNCLEAN FOODS

11 And the Lord spake unto Moses and to Aaron, saying unto them, 2 Speak unto the children of Israel, saying, These are the beasts which ye shall eat among all the beasts that are on the earth. 3 What-

soever parteth the hoof, and is cloven-footed, and cheweth the cud, among the beasts, that shall ye eat. 4 Nevertheless, these shall ye not eat of them that chew the cud, or of them that divide the hoof: as the camel, because he cheweth the cud, but divideth not the hoof; he is unclean unto you. 5 And the coney, because he cheweth the cud, but divideth not the hoof; he is unclean unto you. 6 And the hare, because he cheweth the cud, but divideth not the hoof; he is unclean unto you. 7 And the swine, though he divide the hoof, and be cloven-footed, yet he cheweth not the cud; he is unclean to you. 8 Of their flesh shall ye not eat, and their carcass shall ye not touch; they are unclean to you.

9 These shall ye eat of all that are in the waters: whatsoever hath fins and scales in the waters, in the seas, and in the rivers, them shall ye eat. 10 And all that have not fins and scales in the seas, and in the rivers, of all that move in the waters, and of any living thing which is in the waters, they shall be an abomination unto you: 11 They shall be even an abomination unto you; ye shall not eat of their flesh, but ye shall have their carcasses in abomination. 12 Whatsoever hath no fins nor scales in the waters, that shall be an abomination unto you.

13 And these are they which ye shall have in abomination among the fowls; they shall not be eaten, they are an abomination: the eagle, and the ossifrage, and the ospray, 14 And the vulture, and the kite after his kind; 15 Every raven after his kind; 16 And the owl, and the nighthawk, and the cuckoo, and the hawk after his kind, 17 And the little owl, and the cormorant, and the great owl, 18 And the swan, and the pelican, and the gier-eagle, 19 And the stork, the heron after her kind, and the lapwing, and the bat.

20 All fowls that creep, going upon all four, shall be an abomination unto you. 21 Yet these may ye eat of every flying creeping thing that goeth upon all four, which have legs above their feet, to leap withal upon the earth; 22 Even these of them ye may eat; the locust after his kind, and the bald locust after his kind, and the beetle after his kind, and the grasshopper after his kind. 23 But all other flying creeping things, which have four feet, shall be an abomination unto you.

46 This is the law of the beasts, and of the fowl, and of every living creature that moveth in the waters, and of every creature that creepeth upon the earth: 47 To make a difference between the unclean and the clean, and between the beast that may be eaten and the beast that may not be eaten.

## ATONEMENT

16    2 And the Lord said unto Moses, Speak unto Aaron thy brother, that he come not at all times into the holy place within the veil before the mercy seat, which is upon the ark; that he die not: for I will appear in the cloud upon the mercy seat. 3 Thus shall Aaron come into the holy place; with a young bullock for a sin offering, and a ram for a burnt offering. 4 He shall put on the holy linen coat, and he shall

have the linen breeches upon his flesh, and shall be girded with a linen girdle, and with the linen mitre shall he be attired: these are holy garments; therefore shall he wash his flesh in water, and so put them on. 5 And he shall take of the congregation of the children of Israel two kids of the goats for a sin offering, and one ram for a burnt offering.

11 And Aaron shall bring the bullock of the sin offering, which is for himself, and shall make an atonement for himself, and for his house, and shall kill the bullock of the sin offering which is for himself. 15 Then shall he kill the goat of the sin offering, that is for the people, and bring his blood within the veil, and do with that blood as he did with the blood of the bullock, and sprinkle it upon the mercy seat, and before the mercy seat: 16 And he shall make an atonement for the holy place, because of the uncleanness of the children of Israel, and because of their transgressions in all their sins: and so shall he do for the tabernacle of the congregation, that remaineth among them in the midst of their uncleanness.

20 And when he hath made an end of reconciling the holy place, and the tabernacle of the congregation, and the altar, he shall bring the live goat: 21 And Aaron shall lay both his hands upon the head of the live goat, and confess over him all the iniquities of the children of Israel, and all their transgressions in all their sins, putting them upon the head of the goat, and shall send him away by the hand of a fit man into the wilderness: 22 And the goat shall bear upon him all their iniquities unto a land not inhabited: and he shall let go the goat in the wilderness.

23 And Aaron shall come into the tabernacle of the congregation, and shall put off the linen garments, which he put on when he went into the holy place, and shall leave them there: 24 And he shall wash his flesh with water in the holy place, and put on his garments, and come forth, and offer his burnt offering, and the burnt offering of the people, and make an atonement for himself, and for the people.

29 And this shall be a statute for ever unto you: that in the seventh month, on the tenth day of the month, ye shall afflict your souls, and do no work at all, whether it be one of your own country, or a stranger that sojourneth among you: 30 For on that day shall the priest make an atonement for you, to cleanse you, that ye may be clean from all your sins before the Lord. 31 It shall be a sabbath of rest unto you, and ye shall afflict your souls, by a statute for ever. 32 And the priest, whom he shall anoint, and whom he shall consecrate to minister in the priest's office in his father's stead, shall make the atonement, and shall put on the linen clothes, even the holy garments: 33 And he shall make an atonement for the holy sanctuary, and he shall make an atonement for the tabernacle of the congregation, and for the altar: and he shall make an atonement for the priests, and for all the people of the congregation. 34 And this shall be an everlasting statute unto you, to make an atonement for the children of Israel for all their sins once a year. And he did as the Lord commanded Moses.

# *Numbers*

### RESUMING THE MARCH

9  15 And on the day that the tabernacle was reared up the cloud covered the tabernacle, namely, the tent of the testimony: and at even there was upon the tabernacle as it were the appearance of fire, until the morning. 16 So it was alway: the cloud covered it by day, and the appearance of fire by night. 17 And when the cloud was taken up from the tabernacle, then after that the children of Israel journeyed: and in the place where the cloud abode, there the children of Israel pitched their tents. 18 At the commandment of the Lord the children of Israel journeyed, and at the commandment of the Lord they pitched: as long as the cloud abode upon the tabernacle they rested in their tents. 19 And when the cloud tarried long upon the tabernacle many days, then the children of Israel kept the charge of the Lord, and journeyed not. 20 And so it was, when the cloud was a few days upon the tabernacle; according to the commandment of the Lord they abode in their tents, and according to the commandment of the Lord they journeyed. 21 And so it was, when the cloud abode from even unto the morning, and that the cloud was taken up in the morning, then they journeyed: whether it was by day or by night that the cloud was taken up, they journeyed. 22 Or whether it were two days, or a month, or a year, that the cloud tarried upon the tabernacle, remaining thereon, the children of Israel abode in their tents, and journeyed not: but when it was taken up, they journeyed. 23 At the commandment of the Lord they rested in their tents, and at the commandment of the Lord they journeyed: they kept the charge of the Lord, at the commandment of the Lord by the hand of Moses.

10  11 And it came to pass on the twentieth day of the second month, in the second year, that the cloud was taken up from off the tabernacle of the testimony. 12 And the children of Israel took their journeys out of the wilderness of Sinai; and the cloud rested in the wilderness of Paran. 13 And they first took their journey according to the commandment of the Lord by the hand of Moses.

33 And they departed from the mount of the Lord three days' journey: and the ark of the covenant of the Lord went before them in the three days' journey, to search out a resting place for them. 34 And the cloud of the Lord was upon them by day, when they went out of the camp. 35 And it came to pass, when the ark set forward, that Moses said,

Rise up, Lord, and let thine enemies be scattered;
And let them that hate thee flee before thee.

36 And when it rested, he said,

Return, O Lord, unto the many thousands of Israel.

## GRUMBLING AND OPPOSITION

**11** 4 And the mixed multitude that was among them fell a lusting:[1] and the children of Israel also wept again, and said, Who shall give us flesh to eat? 5 We remember the fish, which we did eat in Egypt freely; the cucumbers, and the melons, and the leeks, and the onions, and the garlic: 6 But now our soul is dried away: there is nothing at all, besides this manna, before our eyes. 7 And the manna was as coriander seed, and the color thereof as the color of bdellium. 8 And the people went about, and gathered it, and ground it in mills, or beat it in a mortar, and baked it in pans, and made cakes of it: and the taste of it was as the taste of fresh oil. 9 And when the dew fell upon the camp in the night, the manna fell upon it.

10 Then Moses heard the people weep throughout their families, every man in the door of his tent: and the anger of the Lord was kindled greatly; Moses also was displeased. 11 And Moses said unto the Lord, Wherefore hast thou afflicted thy servant? and wherefore have I not found favor in thy sight, that thou layest the burden of all this people upon me? 12 Have I conceived all this people? have I begotten them, that thou shouldest say unto me, Carry them in thy bosom, as a nursing father beareth the sucking child, unto the land which thou swarest unto their fathers? 13 Whence should I have flesh to give unto all this people? for they weep unto me, saying, Give us flesh, that we may eat. 14 I am not able to bear all this people alone, because it is too heavy for me. 15 And if thou deal thus with me, kill me, I pray thee, out of hand, if I have found favor in thy sight; and let me not see my wretchedness.

16 And the Lord said unto Moses, Gather unto me seventy men of the elders of Israel, whom thou knowest to be the elders of the people, and officers over them; and bring them unto the tabernacle of the congregation, that they may stand there with thee. 17 And I will come down and talk with thee there: and I will take of the spirit which is upon thee, and will put it upon them; and they shall bear the burden of the people with thee, that thou bear it not thyself alone.

24 And Moses went out, and told the people the words of the Lord, and gathered the seventy men of the elders of the people, and set them round about the tabernacle. 25 And the Lord came down in a cloud, and spake unto him, and took of the spirit that was upon him, and gave it unto the seventy elders: and it came to pass, that, when the spirit rested upon them, they prophesied, and did not cease. 26 But there remained two of the men in the camp, the name of the one was Eldad, and the name of the other Medad: and the spirit rested upon them; and they were of them that were written, but went not out unto the tabernacle: and they prophesied in the camp. 27 And there ran a young man, and told Moses, and said, Eldad and Medad do prophesy in the camp. 28 And Joshua the son of Nun, the servant

[1] "Lust" often has a broader meaning in the Bible than it has in modern usage.

of Moses, one of his young men, answered and said, My lord Moses,
forbid them. 29 And Moses said unto him, Enviest thou for my sake?
would God that all the Lord's people were prophets, and that the Lord
would put his Spirit upon them. 30 And Moses gat him into the camp,
he and the elders of Israel.

12 And Miriam and Aaron spake against Moses because of the
Ethiopian woman whom he had married: for he had married an
Ethiopian woman. 2 And they said, Hath the Lord indeed spoken
only by Moses? hath he not spoken also by us? And the Lord heard it.
3 (Now the man Moses was very meek,[1] above all the men which
were upon the face of the earth.)
4 And the Lord spake suddenly unto Moses, and unto Aaron, and
unto Miriam, Come out ye three unto the tabernacle of the congregation. And they three came out. 5 And the Lord came down in the
pillar of the cloud, and stood in the door of the tabernacle, and called
Aaron and Miriam: and they both came forth. 6 And he said,

> Hear now my words:
> If there be a prophet among you,
> I the Lord will make myself known unto him in a vision,
> And will speak unto him in a dream.
> 7 My servant Moses is not so,
> Who is faithful in all mine house.
> 8 With him will I speak mouth to mouth,
> Even apparently, and not in dark speeches;
> And the similitude of the Lord shall he behold:
> Wherefore then were ye not afraid
> To speak against my servant Moses?

9 And the anger of the Lord was kindled against them; and he departed. 10 And the cloud departed from off the tabernacle; and, behold, Miriam became leprous, white as snow: and Aaron looked upon
Miriam, and, behold, she was leprous. 11 And Aaron said unto Moses,
Alas, my lord, I beseech thee, lay not the sin upon us, wherein we
have done foolishly, and wherein we have sinned. 12 Let her not be
as one dead, of whom the flesh is half consumed when he cometh out
of his mother's womb. 13 And Moses cried unto the Lord, saying,
Heal her now, O God, I beseech thee. 14 And the Lord said unto
Moses, If her father had but spit in her face, should she not be
ashamed seven days? let her be shut out from the camp seven days,
and after that let her be received in again. 15 And Miriam was shut
out from the camp seven days: and the people journeyed not till
Miriam was brought in again. 16 And afterward the people removed
from Hazeroth, and pitched in the wilderness of Paran.

---

[1] Not self-seeking.

## RECONNAISSANCE INTO CANAAN

13 And the Lord spake unto Moses, saying, 2 Send thou men, that they may search the land of Canaan, which I give unto the children of Israel: of every tribe of their fathers shall ye send a man, every one a ruler among them. 3 And Moses by the commandment of the Lord sent them from the wilderness of Paran: all those men were heads of the children of Israel. 17 And Moses sent them to spy out the land of Canaan, and said unto them, Get you up this way southward, and go up into the mountain: 18 And see the land, what it is; and the people that dwelleth therein, whether they be strong or weak, few or many; 19 And what the land is that they dwell in, whether it be good or bad; and what cities they be that they dwell in, whether in tents, or in strongholds; 20 And what the land is, whether it be fat or lean, whether there be wood therein, or not. And be ye of good courage, and bring of the fruit of the land. Now the time was the time of the first ripe grapes.

21 So they went up, and searched the land from the wilderness of Zin unto Rehob, as men come to Hamath. 22 And they ascended by the south, and came unto Hebron; where Ahiman, Sheshai, and Talmai, the children of Anak, were. (Now Hebron was built seven years before Zoan in Egypt.) 23 And they came unto the brook of Eshcol, and cut down from thence a branch with one cluster of grapes, and they bare it between two upon a staff; and they brought of the pomegranates, and of the figs. 24 The place was called the brook Eshcol, because of the cluster of grapes which the children of Israel cut down from thence.

25 And they returned from searching of the land after forty days. 26 And they went and came to Moses, and to Aaron, and to all the congregation of the children of Israel, unto the wilderness of Paran, to Kadesh; and brought back word unto them, and unto all the congregation, and showed them the fruit of the land. 27 And they told him, and said, We came unto the land whither thou sentest us, and surely it floweth with milk and honey; and this is the fruit of it. 28 Nevertheless the people be strong that dwell in the land, and the cities are walled, and very great: and moreover we saw the children of Anak there. 29 The Amalekites dwell in the land of the south: and the Hittites, and the Jebusites, and the Amorites, dwell in the mountains: and the Canaanites dwell by the sea, and by the coast of Jordan. 30 And Caleb stilled the people before Moses, and said, Let us go up at once, and possess it; for we are well able to overcome it. 31 But the men that went up with him said, We be not able to go up against the people; for they are stronger than we. 32 And they brought up an evil report of the land which they had searched unto the children of Israel, saying, The land, through which we have gone to search it, is a land that eateth up the inhabitants thereof; and all the people that we saw in it are men of a great stature. 33 And there we saw

the giants, the sons of Anak, which come of the giants: and we were in our own sight as grasshoppers, and so we were in their sight.

## MOSES REPUDIATED

14 And all the congregation lifted up their voice, and cried; and the people wept that night. 2 And all the children of Israel murmured against Moses and against Aaron: and the whole congregation said unto them, Would God that we had died in the land of Egypt! or would God we had died in this wilderness! 3 And wherefore hath the Lord brought us unto this land, to fall by the sword, that our wives and our children should be a prey? were it not better for us to return into Egypt? 4 And they said one to another, Let us make a captain, and let us return into Egypt. 5 Then Moses and Aaron fell on their faces before all the assembly of the congregation of the children of Israel.

6 And Joshua the son of Nun, and Caleb the son of Jephunneh, which were of them that searched the land, rent their clothes: 7 And they spake unto all the company of the children of Israel, saying, The land, which we passed through to search it, is an exceeding good land. 8 If the Lord delight in us, then he will bring us into this land, and give it us; a land which floweth with milk and honey. 9 Only rebel not ye against the Lord, neither fear ye the people of the land; for they are bread for us: their defense is departed from them, and the Lord is with us: fear them not. 10 But all the congregation bade stone them with stones. And the glory of the Lord appeared in the tabernacle of the congregation before all the children of Israel.

11 And the Lord said unto Moses, How long will this people provoke me? and how long will it be ere they believe me, for all the signs which I have showed among them? 12 I will smite them with the pestilence, and disinherit them, and will make of thee a greater nation and mightier than they. 13 And Moses said unto the Lord, Then the Egyptians shall hear it, (for thou broughtest up this people in thy might from among them;) 15 Now if thou shalt kill all this people as one man, then the nations which have heard the fame of thee will speak, saying, 16 Because the Lord was not able to bring this people into the land which he sware unto them, therefore he hath slain them in the wilderness. 17 And now, I beseech thee, let the power of my Lord be great, according as thou hast spoken, saying, 18 The Lord is long-suffering, and of great mercy, forgiving iniquity and transgression, and by no means clearing the guilty, visiting the iniquity of the fathers upon the children unto the third and fourth generation. 19 Pardon, I beseech thee, the iniquity of this people according unto the greatness of thy mercy, and as thou hast forgiven this people, from Egypt even until now.

20 And the Lord said, I have pardoned according to thy word: 21 But as truly as I live, all the earth shall be filled with the glory of the Lord. 22 Because all those men which have seen my glory, and

my miracles, which I did in Egypt and in the wilderness, and have
tempted me now these ten times, and have not hearkened to my voice;
23 Surely they shall not see the land which I sware unto their fathers,
neither shall any of them that provoked me see it, 30 Save Caleb the
son of Jephunneh, and Joshua the son of Nun. 31 But your little ones,
which ye said should be a prey, them will I bring in, and they shall
know the land which ye have despised. 32 But as for you, your carcasses, they shall fall in this wilderness. 33 And your children shall
wander in the wilderness forty years, and bear your whoredoms, until
your carcasses be wasted in the wilderness. 34 After the number of
the days in which ye searched the land, even forty days, each day for
a year, shall ye bear your iniquities, even forty years, and ye shall
know my breach of promise. 35 I the Lord have said, I will surely
do it unto all this evil congregation, that are gathered together against
me: in this wilderness they shall be consumed, and there they shall
die.

36 And the men which Moses sent to search the land, who returned,
and made all the congregation to murmur against him, by bringing up
a slander upon the land, 37 Even those men that did bring up the evil
report upon the land, died by the plague before the Lord. 38 But
Joshua the son of Nun, and Caleb, the son of Jephunneh, which were
of the men that went to search the land, lived still. 39 And Moses told
these sayings unto all the children of Israel: and the people mourned
greatly.

40 And they rose up early in the morning, and gat them up into
the top of the mountain, saying, Lo, we be here, and will go up unto
the place which the Lord hath promised: for we have sinned. 41 And
Moses said, Wherefore now do ye transgress the commandment of the
Lord? but it shall not prosper. 42 Go not up, for the Lord is not
among you; that ye be not smitten before your enemies. 43 For the
Amalekites and the Canaanites are there before you, and ye shall fall
by the sword: because ye are turned away from the Lord, therefore the
Lord will not be with you. 44 But they presumed to go up unto the
hilltop: nevertheless the ark of the covenant of the Lord, and Moses,
departed not out of the camp. 45 Then the Amalekites came down,
and the Canaanites which dwelt in that hill, and smote them, and
discomfited them, even unto Hormah.

### MOSES' SIN OF PRESUMPTION

20 Then came the children of Israel, even the whole congregation,
into the desert of Zin in the first month: and the people abode in
Kadesh; and Miriam died there, and was buried there. 2 And there
was no water for the congregation: and they gathered themselves together against Moses and against Aaron. 3 And the people chode with
Moses, and spake, saying, Would God that we had died when our
brethren died before the Lord! 4 And why have ye brought up the
congregation of the Lord into this wilderness, that we and our cattle

should die there? 5 And wherefore have ye made us to come up out of Egypt, to bring us in unto this evil place? it is no place of seed, or of figs, or of vines, or of pomegranates; neither is there any water to drink. 6 And Moses and Aaron went from the presence of the assembly unto the door of the tabernacle of the congregation, and they fell upon their faces: and the glory of the Lord appeared unto them. 7 And the Lord spake unto Moses, saying, 8 Take the rod, and gather thou the assembly together, thou and Aaron thy brother, and speak ye unto the rock before their eyes; and it shall give forth his water, and thou shalt bring forth to them water out of the rock: so thou shalt give the congregation and their beasts drink. 9 And Moses took the rod from before the Lord, as he commanded him. 10 And Moses and Aaron gathered the congregation together before the rock, and he said unto them, Hear now, ye rebels; must we fetch you water out of this rock? 11 And Moses lifted up his hand, and with his rod he smote the rock twice: and the water came out abundantly, and the congregation drank, and their beasts also. 12 And the Lord spake unto Moses and Aaron, Because ye believed me not, to sanctify me in the eyes of the children of Israel, therefore ye shall not bring this congregation into the land which I have given them. 13 This is the water of Meribah; because the children of Israel strove with the Lord, and he was sanctified in them.

## THE ADVANCE RESUMED

14 And Moses sent messengers from Kadesh unto the king of Edom, Thus saith thy brother Israel, Thou knowest all the travail that hath befallen us: 15 How our fathers went down into Egypt, and we have dwelt in Egypt a long time; and the Egyptians vexed us, and our fathers: 16 And when we cried unto the Lord, he heard our voice, and sent an angel, and hath brought us forth out of Egypt: and, behold, we are in Kadesh, a city in the uttermost of thy border. 17 Let us pass, I pray thee, through thy country: we will not pass through the fields, or through the vineyards, neither will we drink of the water of the wells: we will go by the king's high way, we will not turn to the right hand nor to the left, until we have passed thy borders. 18 And Edom said unto him, Thou shalt not pass by me, lest I come out against thee with the sword. 19 And the children of Israel said unto him, We will go by the high way: and if I and my cattle drink of thy water, then I will pay for it: I will only, without doing any thing else, go through on my feet. 20 And he said, Thou shalt not go through. And Edom came out against him with much people, and with a strong hand. 21 Thus Edom refused to give Israel passage through his border: wherefore Israel turned away from him.

22 And the children of Israel, even the whole congregation, journeyed from Kadesh, and came unto mount Hor. 23 And the Lord spake unto Moses and Aaron in mount Hor, by the coast of the land of Edom, saying, 24 Aaron shall be gathered unto his people: for he

shall not enter into the land which I have given unto the children of Israel, because ye rebelled against my word at the water of Meribah. 25 Take Aaron and Eleazar his son and bring them up unto mount Hor: 26 And strip Aaron of his garments, and put them upon Eleazar his son: and Aaron shall be gathered unto his people, and shall die there. 27 And Moses did as the Lord commanded: and they went up into mount Hor in the sight of all the congregation. 28 And Moses stripped Aaron of his garments, and put them upon Eleazar his son; and Aaron died there in the top of the mount: and Moses and Eleazar came down from the mount. 29 And when all the congregation saw that Aaron was dead, they mourned for Aaron thirty days, even all the house of Israel.

21 21 And Israel sent messengers unto Sihon king of the Amorites, saying, 22 Let me pass through thy land: we will not turn into the fields, or into the vineyards; we will not drink of the waters of the well: but we will go along by the king's high way, until we be past thy borders. 23 And Sihon would not suffer Israel to pass through his border: but Sihon gathered all his people together, and went out against Israel into the wilderness: and he came to Jahaz, and fought against Israel. 24 And Israel smote him with the edge of the sword, and possessed his land from Arnon unto Jabbok, even unto the children of Ammon: for the border of the children of Ammon was strong. 25 And Israel took all these cities: and Israel dwelt in all the cities of the Amorites, in Heshbon, and in all the villages thereof.

31 Thus Israel dwelt in the land of the Amorites. 32 And Moses sent to spy out Jaazer, and they took the villages thereof, and drove out the Amorites that were there. 33 And they turned and went up by the way of Bashan: and Og the king of Bashan went out against them, he, and all his people, to the battle at Edrei. 34 And the Lord said unto Moses, Fear him not: for I have delivered him into thy hand, and all his people, and his land; and thou shalt do to him as thou didst unto Sihon king of the Amorites, which dwelt at Heshbon. 35 So they smote him, and his sons, and all his people, until there was none left him alive: and they possessed his land.

## BALAAM AND BALAK

22 And the children of Israel set forward, and pitched in the plains of Moab on this side Jordan by Jericho. 2 And Balak the son of Zippor saw all that Israel had done to the Amorites. 3 And Moab was sore afraid of the people, because they were many: and Moab was distressed because of the children of Israel. 4 And Moab said unto the elders of Midian, Now shall this company lick up all that are round about us, as the ox licketh up the grass of the field. And Balak the son of Zippor was king of the Moabites at that time. 5 He sent messengers therefore unto Balaam the son of Beor to Pethor, which is by the river of the land of the children of his people, to call him, saying,

Behold, there is a people come out from Egypt: behold, they cover the face of the earth, and they abide over against me: 6 Come now therefore, I pray thee, curse me this people; for they are too mighty for me: peradventure I shall prevail, that we may smite them, and that I may drive them out of the land: for I wot that he whom thou blessest is blessed, and he whom thou cursest is cursed.

7 And the elders of Moab and the elders of Midian departed with the rewards of divination in their hand; and they came unto Balaam, and spake unto him the words of Balak. 21 And Balaam rose up in the morning, and saddled his ass, and went with the princes of Moab. 22 And God's anger was kindled because he went: and the angel of the Lord stood in the way for an adversary against him. Now he was riding upon his ass, and his two servants were with him. 23 And the ass saw the angel of the Lord standing in the way, and his sword drawn in his hand: and the ass turned aside out of the way, and went into the field: and Balaam smote the ass, to turn her into the way. 24 But the angel of the Lord stood in a path of the vineyards, a wall being on this side, and a wall on that side. 25 And when the ass saw the angel of the Lord, she thrust herself unto the wall, and crushed Balaam's foot against the wall: and he smote her again. 26 And the angel of the Lord went further, and stood in a narrow place, where was no way to turn either to the right hand or to the left. 27 And when the ass saw the angel of the Lord, she fell down under Balaam: and Balaam's anger was kindled, and he smote the ass with a staff. 28 And the Lord opened the mouth of the ass, and she said unto Balaam, What have I done unto thee, that thou hast smitten me these three times? 29 And Balaam said unto the ass, Because thou hast mocked me: I would there were a sword in mine hand, for now would I kill thee. 30 And the ass said unto Balaam, Am not I thine ass, upon which thou hast ridden ever since I was thine unto this day? was I ever wont to do so unto thee? And he said, Nay. 31 Then the Lord opened the eyes of Balaam, and he saw the angel of the Lord standing in the way, and his sword drawn in his hand: and he bowed down his head, and fell flat on his face. 32 And the angel of the Lord said unto him, Wherefore hast thou smitten thine ass these three times? Behold, I went out to withstand thee, because thy way is perverse before me: 33 And the ass saw me, and turned from me these three times: unless she had turned from me, surely now also I had slain thee, and saved her alive. 34 And Balaam said unto the angel of the Lord, I have sinned; for I knew not that thou stoodest in the way against me: now therefore, if it displease thee, I will get me back again. 35 And the angel of the Lord said unto Balaam, Go with the men: but only the word that I shall speak unto thee, that thou shalt speak. So Balaam went with the princes of Balak.

36 And when Balak heard that Balaam was come, he went out to meet him unto a city of Moab, which is in the border of Arnon, which is in the utmost coast. 38 And Balaam said unto Balak, Lo, I am come unto thee: have I now any power at all to say any thing?

the word that God putteth in my mouth, that shall I speak. 39 And Balaam went with Balak, and they came unto Kirjath-huzoth. 40 And Balak offered oxen and sheep, and sent to Balaam, and to the princes that were with him. 41 And it came to pass on the morrow, that Balak took Balaam, and brought him up into the high places of Baal, that thence he might see the utmost part of the people.

23 And Balaam said unto Balak, Build me here seven altars, and prepare me here seven oxen and seven rams. 2 And Balak did as Balaam had spoken; and Balak and Balaam offered on every altar a bullock and a ram. 3 And Balaam said unto Balak, Stand by thy burnt offering, and I will go: peradventure the Lord will come to meet me; and whatsoever he showeth me I will tell thee. And he went to a high place. 4 And God met Balaam: and he said unto him, I have prepared seven altars, and I have offered upon every altar a bullock and a ram. 5 And the Lord put a word in Balaam's mouth, and said, Return unto Balak, and thus thou shalt speak. 6 And he returned unto him, and, lo, he stood by his burnt sacrifice, he, and all the princes of Moab. 7 And he took up his parable, and said,

> Balak the king of Moab hath brought me from Aram,
> Out of the mountains of the east, saying,
> Come, curse me Jacob,
> And come, defy Israel.
> 8 How shall I curse, whom God hath not cursed?
> Or how shall I defy, whom the Lord hath not defied?
> 9 For from the top of the rocks I see him,
> And from the hills I behold him:
> Lo, the people shall dwell alone,
> And shall not be reckoned among the nations.
> 10 Who can count the dust of Jacob,
> And the number of the fourth part of Israel?
> Let me die the death of the righteous,
> And let my last end be like his!

11 And Balak said unto Balaam, What hast thou done unto me? I took thee to curse mine enemies, and, behold, thou hast blessed them altogether. 12 And he answered and said, Must I not take heed to speak that which the Lord hath put in my mouth? 13 And Balak said unto him, Come, I pray thee, with me unto another place, from whence thou mayest see them: thou shalt see but the utmost part of them, and shalt not see them all: and curse me them from thence. 14 And he brought him into the field of Zophim, to the top of Pisgah, and built seven altars, and offered a bullock and a ram on every altar. 15 And he said unto Balak, Stand here by thy burnt offering, while I meet the Lord yonder. 16 And the Lord met Balaam, and put a word in his mouth, and said, Go again unto Balak, and say thus. 17 And when he came to him, behold, he stood by his burnt offering, and the princes of Moab with him. And Balak said unto him, What hath the Lord spoken? 18 And he took up his parable, and said,

Rise up, Balak, and hear;
Hearken unto me, thou son of Zippor:
19 God is not a man, that he should lie;
Neither the son of man, that he should repent:
Hath he said, and shall he not do it?
Or hath he spoken, and shall he not make it good?
20 Behold, I have received commandment to bless:
And he hath blessed; and I cannot reverse it.
21 He hath not beheld iniquity in Jacob,
Neither hath he seen perverseness in Israel:
The Lord his God is with him,
And the shout of a king is among them.
22 God brought them out of Egypt;
He hath as it were the strength of a unicorn.
23 Surely there is no enchantment against Jacob,
Neither is there any divination against Israel:
According to this time it shall be said of Jacob
And of Israel, What hath God wrought!
24 Behold, the people shall rise up as a great lion,
And lift up himself as a young lion:
He shall not lie down until he eat of the prey,
And drink the blood of the slain.

25 And Balak said unto Balaam, Neither curse them at all, nor bless them at all. 26 But Balaam answered and said unto Balak, Told not I thee, saying, All that the Lord speaketh, that I must do? 27 And Balak said unto Balaam, Come, I pray thee, I will bring thee unto another place; peradventure it will please God that thou mayest curse me them from thence. 28 And Balak brought Balaam unto the top of Peor, that looketh toward Jeshimon. 29 And Balaam said unto Balak, Build me here seven altars, and prepare me here seven bullocks and seven rams. 30 And Balak did as Balaam had said, and offered a bullock and a ram on every altar.

24 And when Balaam saw that it pleased the Lord to bless Israel, he went not, as at other times, to seek for enchantments, but he set his face toward the wilderness. 2 And Balaam lifted up his eyes, and he saw Israel abiding in his tents according to their tribes; and the Spirit of God came upon him. 3 And he took up his parable, and said,
Balaam the son of Beor hath said,
And the man whose eyes are open hath said:
4 He hath said, which heard the words of God,
Which saw the vision of the Almighty,
Falling into a trance, but having his eyes open:
5 How goodly are thy tents, O Jacob,
And thy tabernacles, O Israel!
6 As the valleys are they spread forth,
As gardens by the river's side,

As the trees of lignaloes which the Lord hath planted,
And as cedar trees beside the waters.
7 He shall pour the water out of his buckets,
And his seed shall be in many waters,
And his king shall be higher than Agag,
And his kingdom shall be exalted.
8 God brought him forth out of Egypt;
He hath as it were the strength of a unicorn:
He shall eat up the nations his enemies,
And shall break their bones,
And pierce them through with his arrows.
9 He couched, he lay down as a lion,
And as a great lion: who shall stir him up?
Blessed is he that blesseth thee,
And cursed is he that curseth thee.

10 And Balak's anger was kindled against Balaam, and he smote his hands together: and Balak said unto Balaam, I called thee to curse mine enemies, and, behold, thou hast altogether blessed them these three times. 11 Therefore now flee thou to thy place: I thought to promote thee unto great honor; but, lo, the Lord hath kept thee back from honor. 12 And Balaam said unto Balak, . . . 13 If Balak would give me his house full of silver and gold, I cannot go beyond the commandment of the Lord, to do either good or bad of mine own mind; but what the Lord saith, that will I speak. 25 And Balaam rose up, and went and returned to his place: and Balak also went his way.

# *Deuteronomy*

## THE LAST ORATION OF MOSES

1    3 And it came to pass in the fortieth year, in the eleventh month, on the first day of the month, that Moses spake unto the children of Israel, according unto all that the Lord had given him in commandment unto them; 4 After he had slain Sihon the king of the Amorites, which dwelt in Heshbon, and Og the king of Bashan, which dwelt at Astaroth in Edrei: 5 On this side Jordan, in the land of Moab, began Moses to declare this law, saying,

6    4 Hear, O Israel: The Lord our God is one Lord: 5 And thou shalt love the Lord thy God with all thine heart, and with all thy soul, and with all thy might. 6 And these words, which I command thee this day, shall be in thine heart: 7 And thou shalt teach them diligently unto thy children, and shalt talk of them when thou sittest in thine house, and when thou walkest by the way, and when thou liest down, and when thou risest up. 8 And thou shalt bind them for a

sign upon thine hand, and they shall be as frontlets between thine eyes. 9 And thou shalt write them upon the posts of thy house, and on thy gates.

## HISTORY AND MEANING

20 And when thy son asketh thee in time to come, saying, What mean the testimonies, and the statutes, and the judgments, which the Lord our God hath commanded you? 21 Then thou shalt say unto thy son, We were Pharaoh's bondmen in Egypt; and the Lord brought us out of Egypt with a mighty hand: 22 And the Lord showed signs and wonders, great and sore, upon Egypt, upon Pharaoh, and upon all his household, before our eyes: 23 And he brought us out from thence, that he might bring us in, to give us the land which he sware unto our fathers. 24 And the Lord commanded us to do all these statutes, to fear the Lord our God, for our good always, that he might preserve us alive, as it is at this day. 25 And it shall be our righteousness, if we observe to do all these commandments before the Lord our God, as he hath commanded us.

7    6 For thou art a holy people unto the Lord thy God: the Lord thy God hath chosen thee to be a special people unto himself, above all people that are upon the face of the earth. 7 The Lord did not set his love upon you, nor choose you, because ye were more in number than any people; for ye were the fewest of all people: 8 But because the Lord loved you, and because he would keep the oath which he had sworn unto your fathers, hath the Lord brought you out with a mighty hand, and redeemed you out of the house of bondmen, from the hand of Pharaoh king of Egypt. 9 Know therefore that the Lord thy God, he is God, the faithful God, which keepeth covenant and mercy with them that love him and keep his commandments to a thousand generations; 10 And repayeth them that hate him to their face, to destroy them: he will not be slack to him that hateth him, he will repay him to his face. 11 Thou shalt therefore keep the commandments, and the statutes, and the judgments, which I command thee this day, to do them.

17 If thou shalt say in thine heart, These nations are more than I; how can I dispossess them? 18 Thou shalt not be afraid of them: but shalt well remember what the Lord thy God did unto Pharaoh, and unto all Egypt; 19 The great temptations which thine eyes saw, and the signs, and the wonders, and the mighty hand, and the stretched out arm, whereby the Lord thy God brought thee out: so shall the Lord thy God do unto all the people of whom thou art afraid. 20 Moreover the Lord thy God will send the hornet among them, until they that are left, and hide themselves from thee, be destroyed. 21 Thou shalt not be affrighted at them: for the Lord thy God is among you, a mighty God and terrible. 22 And the Lord thy God will put those nations before thee by little and little: thou mayest not con-

sume them at once, lest the beasts of the field increase upon thee.
23 But the Lord thy God shall deliver them unto thee, and shall destroy them with a mighty destruction, until they be destroyed. 24 And
he shall deliver their kings into thine hand, and thou shalt destroy
their name from under heaven: there shall no man be able to stand
before thee, until thou have destroyed them. 25 The graven images of
their gods shall ye burn with fire: thou shalt not desire the silver or
gold that is on them, nor take it unto thee, lest thou be snared therein:
for it is an abomination to the Lord thy God. 26 Neither shalt thou
bring an abomination into thine house, lest thou be a cursed thing
like it: but thou shalt utterly detest it, and thou shalt utterly abhor
it; for it is a cursed thing.

8 All the commandments which I command thee this day shall ye
observe to do, that ye may live, and multiply, and go in and possess
the land which the Lord sware unto your fathers. 2 And thou shalt
remember all the way which the Lord thy God led thee these forty
years in the wilderness, to humble thee, and to prove thee, to know
what was in thine heart, whether thou wouldest keep his commandments, or no. 3 And he humbled thee, and suffered thee to hunger,
and fed thee with manna, which thou knewest not, neither did thy
fathers know; that he might make thee know that man doth not live
by bread only, but by every word that proceedeth out of the mouth
of the Lord doth man live. 4 Thy raiment waxed not old upon thee,
neither did thy foot swell, these forty years. 5 Thou shalt also consider in thine heart, that, as a man chasteneth his son, so the Lord
thy God chasteneth thee. 6 Therefore thou shalt keep the commandments of the Lord thy God, to walk in his ways, and to fear him.
7 For the Lord thy God bringeth thee into a good land, a land of
brooks of water, of fountains and depths that spring out of valleys
and hills; 8 A land of wheat, and barley, and vines, and fig trees, and
pomegranates; a land of oil olive, and honey; 9 A land wherein thou
shalt eat bread without scarceness, thou shalt not lack any thing in it;
a land whose stones are iron, and out of whose hills thou mayest dig
brass. 10 When thou hast eaten and art full, then thou shalt bless
the Lord thy God for the good land which he hath given thee.

9 Hear, O Israel: Thou art to pass over Jordan this day, to go in
to possess nations greater and mightier than thyself, cities great and
fenced up to heaven, 2 A people great and tall, the children of the
Anakim, whom thou knowest, and of whom thou hast heard say,
Who can stand before the children of Anak! 3 Understand therefore
this day, that the Lord thy God is he which goeth over before thee;
as a consuming fire he shall destroy them, and he shall bring them
them down before thy face: so shalt thou drive them out, and destroy
them quickly, as the Lord hath said unto thee. 4 Speak not thou in
thine heart, after that the Lord thy God hath cast them out from
before thee, saying, For my righteousness the Lord hath brought me

in to possess this land: but for the wickedness of these nations the Lord doth drive them out from before thee. 5 Nor for thy righteousness, or for the uprightness of thine heart, dost thou go to possess their land: but for the wickedness of these nations the Lord thy God doth drive them out from before thee, and that he may perform the word which the Lord sware unto thy fathers, Abraham, Isaac, and Jacob. 6 Understand therefore, that the Lord thy God giveth thee not this good land to possess it for thy righteousness; for thou art a stiffnecked people.

## PRECEPTS FOR PEACE AND FOR WAR

10 12 And now, Israel, what doth the Lord thy God require of thee, but to fear the Lord thy God, to walk in all his ways, and to love him, and to serve the Lord thy God with all thy heart and with all thy soul, 13 To keep the commandments of the Lord, and his statutes, which I command thee this day for thy good? 14 Behold, the heaven and the heaven of heavens is the Lord's thy God, the earth also, with all that therein is. 15 Only the Lord had a delight in thy fathers to love them, and he chose their seed after them, even you above all people, as it is this day. 16 Circumcise therefore the foreskin of your heart, and be no more stiffnecked. 17 For the Lord your God is God of gods, and Lord of lords, a great God, a mighty, and a terrible, which regardeth not persons, nor taketh reward: 18 He doth execute the judgment of the fatherless and widow, and loveth the stranger, in giving him food and raiment. 19 Love ye therefore the stranger: for ye were strangers in the land of Egypt. 20 Thou shalt fear the Lord thy God; him shalt thou serve, and to him shalt thou cleave, and swear by his name. 21 He is thy praise, and he is thy God, that hath done for thee these great and terrible things, which thine eyes have seen. 22 Thy fathers went down into Egypt with threescore and ten persons; and now the Lord thy God hath made thee as the stars of heaven for multitude.

18 9 When thou art come into the land which the Lord thy God giveth thee, thou shalt not learn to do after the abominations of those nations. 10 There shall not be found among you any one that maketh his son or his daughter to pass through the fire,[1] or that useth divination, or an observer of times, or an enchanter, or a witch, 11 Or a charmer, or a consulter with familiar spirits, or a wizard, or a necromancer. 12 For all that do these things are an abomination unto the Lord: and because of these abominations the Lord thy God doth drive them out from before thee. 13 Thou shalt be perfect with the Lord thy God. 14 For these nations, which thou shalt possess, hearken unto observers of times, and unto diviners: but as for thee, the Lord thy God hath not suffered thee so to do.

[1] This condemnation of child-sacrifice, after the Canaanite fashion of idolatry, is repeatedly found in the Bible.

20   10 When thou comest nigh unto a city to fight against it, then proclaim peace unto it. 11 And it shall be, if it make thee answer of peace, and open unto thee, then it shall be, that all the people that is found therein shall be tributaries unto thee, and they shall serve thee. 12 And if it will make no peace with thee, but will make war against thee, then thou shalt besiege it: 13 And when the Lord thy God hath delivered it into thine hands, thou shalt smite every male thereof with the edge of the sword: 14 But the women, and the little ones, and the cattle, and all that is in the city, even all the spoil thereof, shalt thou take unto thyself; and thou shalt eat the spoil of thine enemies, which the Lord thy God hath given thee. 15 Thus shalt thou do unto all the cities which are very far off from thee, which are not of the cities of these nations. 16 But of the cities of these people, which the Lord thy God doth give thee for an inheritance, thou shalt save alive nothing that breatheth: 17 But thou shalt utterly destroy them; namely the Hittites, and the Amorites, the Canaanites, and the Perizzites, the Hivites, and the Jebusites; as the Lord thy God hath commanded thee: 18 That they teach you not to do after all their abominations, which they have done unto their gods; so should ye sin against the Lord your God.

21   10 When thou goest forth to war against thine enemies, and the Lord thy God hath delivered them into thine hands, and thou hast taken them captive, 11 And seest among the captives a beautiful woman, and hast a desire unto her, that thou wouldest have her to thy wife; 12 Then thou shalt bring her home to thine house; and she shall shave her head, and pare her nails; 13 And she shall put the raiment of her captivity from off her, and shall remain in thine house, and bewail her father and her mother a full month: and after that thou shalt go in unto her, and be her husband, and she shall be thy wife. 14 And it shall be, if thou have no delight in her, then thou shalt let her go whither she will; but thou shalt not sell her at all for money, thou shalt not make merchandise of her, because thou hast humbled her.

23   24 When thou comest into thy neighbor's vineyard, then thou mayest eat grapes thy fill at thine own pleasure; but thou shalt not put any in thy vessel. 25 When thou comest into the standing corn of thy neighbor, then thou mayest pluck the ears with thine hand; but thou shalt not move a sickle unto thy neighbor's standing corn.

24   5 When a man hath taken a new wife, he shall not go out to war, neither shall he be charged with any business: but he shall be free at home one year, and shall cheer up his wife which he hath taken.

14 Thou shalt not oppress a hired servant that is poor and needy, whether he be of thy brethren, or of thy strangers that are in thy land

within thy gates: 15 At his day thou shalt give him his hire, neither shall the sun go down upon it; for he is poor, and setteth his heart upon it: lest he cry against thee unto the Lord, and it be sin unto thee.

16 The fathers shall not be put to death for the children, neither shall the children be put to death for the fathers: every man shall be put to death for his own sin.

17 Thou shalt not pervert the judgment of the stranger, nor of the fatherless; nor take a widow's raiment to pledge: 18 But thou shalt remember that thou wast a bondman in Egypt, and the Lord thy God redeemed thee thence: therefore I command thee to do this thing.

2 5  13 Thou shalt not have in thy bag divers weights, a great and a small: 14 Thou shalt not have in thine house divers measures, a great and a small: 15 But thou shalt have a perfect and just weight, a perfect and just measure shalt thou have: that thy days may be lengthened in the land which the Lord thy God giveth thee. 16 For all that do such things, and all that do unrighteously, are an abomination unto the Lord thy God.

### THE CHOICE BEFORE ISRAEL: LIFE OR DEATH

2 9  These are the words of the covenant, which the Lord commanded Moses to make with the children of Israel in the land of Moab, besides the covenant which he made with them in Horeb.

2 And Moses called unto all Israel, and said unto them,

3 0  11 For this commandment which I command thee this day, it is not hidden from thee, neither is it far off. 12 It is not in heaven, that thou shouldest say, Who shall go up for us to heaven, and bring it unto us, that we may hear it, and do it? 13 Neither is it beyond the sea, that thou shouldest say, Who shall go over the sea for us, and bring it unto us, that we may hear it, and do it? 14 But the word is very nigh unto thee, in thy mouth, and in thy heart, that thou mayest do it.

15 See, I have set before thee this day life and good, and death and evil; 16 In that I command thee this day to love the Lord thy God, to walk in his ways, and to keep his commandments, and his statutes, and his judgments, that thou mayest live and multiply: and the Lord thy God shall bless thee in the land whither thou goest to possess it. 17 But if thine heart turn away, so that thou wilt not hear, but shalt be drawn away, and worship other gods, and serve them; 18 I denounce unto you this day, that ye shall surely perish, and that ye shall not prolong your days upon the land, whither thou passest over Jordan to go to possess it. 19 I call heaven and earth to record this day against you, that I have set before you life and death, blessing and cursing: therefore choose life, that both thou and thy seed may live: 20 That thou mayest love the Lord thy God, and that thou mayest obey his voice, and that thou mayest cleave unto him: for

he is thy life, and the length of thy days: that thou mayest dwell in the land which the Lord sware unto thy fathers, to Abraham, to Isaac, and to Jacob, to give them.

## THE DEATH OF MOSES

32 48 And the Lord spake unto Moses that selfsame day, saying, 49 Get thee up into this mountain Abarim, unto mount Nebo, which is in the land of Moab, that is over against Jericho; and behold the land of Canaan, which I give unto the children of Israel for a possession: 50 And die in the mount whither thou goest up, and be gathered unto thy people; as Aaron thy brother died in mount Hor, and was gathered unto his people: 51 Because ye trespassed against me among the children of Israel at the waters of Meribah-Kadesh, in the wilderness of Zin; because ye sanctified me not in the midst of the children of Israel. 52 Yet thou shalt see the land before thee; but thou shalt not go thither unto the land which I give the children of Israel.

34 And Moses went up from the plains of Moab unto the mountain of Nebo, to the top of Pisgah, that is over against Jericho: and the Lord showed him all the land of Gilead, unto Dan, 2 And all Naphtali, and the land of Ephraim, and Manasseh, and all the land of Judah, unto the utmost sea, 3 And the south, and the plain of the valley of Jericho, the city of palm trees, unto Zoar. 4 And the Lord said unto him, This is the land which I sware unto Abraham, unto Isaac, and unto Jacob, saying, I will give it unto thy seed: I have caused thee to see it with thine eyes, but thou shalt not go over thither. 5 So Moses the servant of the Lord died there in the land of Moab, according to the word of the Lord. 6 And he buried him in a valley in the land of Moab, over against Beth-peor: but no man knoweth of his sepulchre unto this day. 7 And Moses was a hundred and twenty years old when he died: his eye was not dim, nor his natural force abated. 8 And the children of Israel wept for Moses in the plains of Moab thirty days: so the days of weeping and mourning for Moses were ended.

9 And Joshua the son of Nun was full of the spirit of wisdom; for Moses had laid his hands upon him: and the children of Israel hearkened unto him, and did as the Lord commanded Moses.

10 And there arose not a prophet since in Israel like unto Moses, whom the Lord knew face to face, 11 In all the signs and the wonders which the Lord sent him to do in the land of Egypt, to Pharaoh, and to all his servants, and to all his land, 12 And in all that mighty hand, and in all the great terror which Moses showed in the sight of all Israel.

# Conquest and Chaos:
## Joshua, Judges, Ruth

Like many other great men, Moses did not live to see the completion of the work which he had begun. He was succeeded by Joshua, who, though impressive in his own right, was a lesser figure than Moses. It was under Joshua that the actual conquest of the promised land of Canaan began. Here as elsewhere, the saga of Israel is told with a great honesty which does not seek to blur the faults of either the people or their leaders. The book of Joshua ends with Joshua's moving appeal to the Israelites to choose "this day whom ye will serve," underscoring the pervasive Biblical emphasis on conscious choice.

The conquest was neither completed nor solidified under Joshua, and after his death there ensued a long period of confusion in which the Israelites sometimes consolidated their holdings and at other times became subject to the surrounding Canaanites. The book of Judges treats this era, and conveys an impression of near chaos as each man did what was right in his own eyes. The dark story of brutality and barbarism is partially interrupted from time to time by the rise of some spectacular leader, and a succession of tales of these folk heroes is printed here, but it is clear that their efforts at best had little lasting effect.

Throughout we are conscious of the infiltration into Israelite religion of the worship of Baal and other Canaanite deities. The cut of Baal was associated with the land and the well-being of those who farmed it. Herdsmen such as the Israelites, who were now taking to agriculture for the first time, would inevitably be tempted to accept the religious practices so closely associated with the ways of planting and reaping which they were learning. Throughout the ancient Near East, it was universally regarded as both common sense and common decency to respect the gods of the land, which would differ from land to land. Many Israelites followed the same practice and accepted both Baal and the God of Abraham. Following Moses, however, prophets and many other influential leaders recognized the exclusive claims of the God who had disclosed himself to them. At first there was the demand for strict monolatry, the worship of this God only, but in the course of history Biblical religion solidified a position of strict monothe-

120

ism, the belief in only one God. This characterization of the Deity developed rather slowly, however, and in the period covered by the book of Judges, the God of the Israelites was a warrior god battling other gods as the people were a warrior people battling other peoples.

After the book of Judges, but set in the same period, comes the book of Ruth. This story is an idyllic interlude set in a violent time. The figure of Ruth is surely one of the most attractive in the Bible, as she brings devotion and grace into her distraught world. The book is a marvelous story of religious faith and human love, but it is something more, as well. Ruth was one of the hated Moabites; yet, as the anonymous author is careful to point out, she was the great-grandmother of King David. That fact would not have been lost upon Israelite hearers of the tale. Here was a woman of a hated race who abandoned her people and her gods to serve the one God of Israel, and became the ancestress of Israel's greatest king. The story is an important episode in the expanding Biblical characterizaton of God, of man, and of human community.

# *Joshua*

## THE THRESHOLD OF PROMISE

1 Now after the death of Moses the servant of the Lord, it came to pass, that the Lord spake unto Joshua the son of Nun, Moses' minister, saying, 2 Moses my servant is dead; now therefore arise, go over this Jordan, thou, and all this people, unto the land which I do give to them, even to the children of Israel. 3 Every place that the sole of your foot shall tread upon, that have I given unto you, as I said unto Moses. 4 From the wilderness and this Lebanon even unto the great river, the river Euphrates, all the land of the Hittites, and unto the great sea toward the going down of the sun, shall be your coast. 5 There shall not any man be able to stand before thee all the days of thy life: as I was with Moses, so I will be with thee: I will not fail thee, nor forsake thee. 6 Be strong and of a good courage: for unto this people shalt thou divide for an inheritance the land, which I sware unto their fathers to give them. 7 Only be thou strong and very courageous, that thou mayest observe to do according to all the law, which Moses my servant commanded thee: turn not from it to the right hand or to the left, that thou mayest prosper whithersoever thou goest. 8 This book of the law shall not depart out of thy mouth; but thou shalt meditate therein day and night, that thou mayest observe to do according to all that is written therein: for then thou shalt make thy way prosperous, and then thou shalt have good

success. 9 Have not I commanded thee? Be strong and of a good courage; be not afraid, neither be thou dismayed: for the Lord thy God is with thee whithersoever thou goest.

10 Then Joshua commanded the officers of the people, saying, 11 Pass through the host, and command the people, saying, Prepare you victuals; for within three days ye shall pass over this Jordan, to go in to possess the land, which the Lord your God giveth you to possess it.

12 And to the Reubenites, and to the Gadites, and to half the tribe of Manasseh, spake Joshua, saying, 13 Remember the word which Moses the servant of the Lord commanded you, saying, The Lord your God hath given you rest, and hath given you this land. 14 Your wives, your little ones, and your cattle, shall remain in the land which Moses gave you on this side Jordan; but ye shall pass before your brethren armed, all the mighty men of valor, and help them; 15 Until the Lord have given your brethren rest, as he hath given you, and they also have possessed the land which the Lord your God giveth them: then ye shall return unto the land of your possession, and enjoy it, which Moses the Lord's servant gave you on this side Jordan toward the sunrising.

16 And they answered Joshua, saying, All that thou commandest us we will do, and whithersoever thou sendest us, we will go. 17 According as we hearkened unto Moses in all things, so will we hearken unto thee: only the Lord thy God be with thee, as he was with Moses. 18 Whosoever he be that doth rebel against thy commandment, and will not hearken unto thy words in all that thou commandest him, he shall be put to death: only be strong and of a good courage.

2 And Joshua the son of Nun sent out of Shittim two men to spy secretly, saying, Go view the land, even Jericho. And they went, and came into a harlot's house, named Rahab, and lodged there. 2 And it was told the king of Jericho, saying, Behold, there came men in hither to-night of the children of Israel to search out the country. 3 And the king of Jericho sent unto Rahab, saying, Bring forth the men that are come to thee, which are entered into thine house: for they be come to search out all the country. 4 And the woman took the two men, and hid them, and said thus, There came men unto me, but I wist not whence they were: 5 And it came to pass about the time of shutting of the gate, when it was dark, that the men went out; whither the men went, I wot not: pursue after them quickly; for ye shall overtake them. 6 But she had brought them up to the roof of the house, and hid them with the stalks of flax, which she had laid in order upon the roof. 7 And the men pursued after them the way to Jordan unto the fords: and as soon as they which pursued after them were gone out, they shut the gate.

8 And before they were laid down, she came up unto them upon the roof; 9 And she said unto the men, I know that the Lord hath given you the land, and that your terror is fallen upon us, and that

all the inhabitants of the land faint because of you. 10 For we have heard how the Lord dried up the water of the Red sea for you, when ye came out of Egypt; and what ye did unto the two kings of the Amorites, that were on the other side Jordan, Sihon and Og, whom ye utterly destroyed. 11 And as soon as we had heard these things, our hearts did melt, neither did there remain any more courage in any man, because of you: for the Lord your God, he is God in heaven above, and in earth beneath. 12 Now therefore, I pray you, swear unto me by the Lord, since I have showed you kindness, that ye will also show kindness unto my father's house, and give me a true token: 13 And that ye will save alive my father, and my mother, and my brethren, and my sisters, and all that they have, and deliver our lives from death. 14 And the men answered her, Our life for yours, if ye utter not this our business. And it shall be, when the Lord hath given us the land, that we will deal kindly and truly with thee.

15 Then she let them down by a cord through the window: for her house was upon the town wall, and she dwelt upon the wall. 16 And she said unto them, Get you to the mountain, lest the pursuers meet you; and hide yourselves there three days, until the pursuers be returned: and afterward may ye go your way. 17 And the men said unto her, We will be blameless of this thine oath which thou hast made us swear. 18 Behold, when we come into the land, thou shalt bind this line of scarlet thread in the window which thou didst let us down by: and thou shalt bring thy father, and thy mother, and thy brethren, and all thy father's household, home unto thee. 19 And it shall be, that whosoever shall go out of the doors of thy house into the street, his blood shall be upon his head, and we will be guiltless: and whosoever shall be with thee in the house, his blood shall be on our head, if any hand be upon him. 20 And if thou utter this our business, then we will be quit of thine oath which thou hast made us to swear. 21 And she said, According unto your words, so be it. And she sent them away, and they departed: and she bound the scarlet line in the window.

22 And they went, and came unto the mountain, and abode there three days, until the pursuers were returned: and the pursuers sought them throughout all the way, but found them not. 23 So the two men returned, and descended from the mountain, and passed over, and came to Joshua the son of Nun, and told him all things that befell them: 24 And they said unto Joshua, Truly the Lord hath delivered into our hands all the land; for even all the inhabitants of the country do faint because of us.

## CROSSING THE JORDAN

3 And Joshua rose early in the morning; and they removed from Shittim, and came to Jordan, he and all the children of Israel, and lodged there before they passed over. 2 And it came to pass after three days, that the officers went through the host; 3 And they com-

manded the people, saying, When ye see the ark of the covenant of the Lord your God, and the priests the Levites bearing it, then ye shall remove from your place, and go after it. 4 Yet there shall be a space between you and it, about two thousand cubits by measure: come not near unto it, that ye may know the way by which ye must go: for ye have not passed this way heretofore. 5 And Joshua said unto the people, Sanctify yourselves: for to-morrow the Lord will do wonders among you. 6 And Joshua spake unto the priests, saying, Take up the ark of the covenant, and pass over before the people. And they took up the ark of the covenant, and went before the people.

7 And the Lord said unto Joshua, This day will I begin to magnify thee in the sight of all Israel, that they may know that, as I was with Moses, so I will be with thee. 8 And thou shalt command the priests that bear the ark of the covenant, saying, When ye are come to the brink of the water of Jordan, ye shall stand still in Jordan.

9 And Joshua said unto the children of Israel, Come hither, and hear the words of the Lord your God. 10 And Joshua said, Hereby ye shall know that the living God is among you, and that he will without fail drive out from before you the Canaanites, and the Hittites, and the Hivites, and the Perizzites, and the Girgashites, and the Amorites, and the Jebusites. 11 Behold, the ark of the covenant of the Lord of all the earth passeth over before you into Jordan. 12 Now therefore take you twelve men out of the tribes of Israel, out of every tribe a man. 13 And it shall come to pass, as soon as the soles of the feet of the priests that bear the ark of the Lord, the Lord of all the earth, shall rest in the waters of Jordan, that the waters of Jordan shall be cut off from the waters that come down from above; and they shall stand upon a heap.

14 And it came to pass, when the people removed from their tents, to pass over Jordan, and the priests bearing the ark of the covenant before the people; 15 And as they that bare the ark were come unto Jordan, and the feet of the priests that bare the ark were dipped in the brim of the water, (for Jordan overfloweth all his banks all the time of harvest,) 16 That the waters which came down from above stood and rose up upon a heap very far from the city Adam, that is beside Zaretan; and those that came down toward the sea of the plain, even the salt sea, failed, and were cut off: and the people passed over right against Jericho. 17 And the priests that bare the ark of the covenant of the Lord stood firm on dry ground in the midst of Jordan, and all the Israelites passed over on dry ground, until all the people were passed clean over Jordan.

4 And it came to pass, when all the people were clean passed over Jordan, that the Lord spake unto Joshua, saying, 2 Take you twelve men out of the people, out of every tribe a man, 3 And command ye them, saying, Take you hence out of the midst of Jordan, out of the place where the priests' feet stood firm, twelve stones, and ye shall carry them over with you, and leave them in the lodging place, where

ye shall lodge this night. 4 Then Joshua called the twelve men, whom he had prepared of the children of Israel, out of every tribe a man: 5 And Joshua said unto them, Pass over before the ark of the Lord your God into the midst of Jordan, and take you up every man of you a stone upon his shoulder, according unto the number of the tribes of the children of Israel: 6 That this may be a sign among you, that when your children ask their fathers in time to come, saying, What mean ye by these stones? 7 Then ye shall answer them, That the waters of Jordan were cut off before the ark of the covenant of the Lord; when it passed over Jordan, the waters of Jordan were cut off: and these stones shall be for a memorial unto the children of Israel for ever.

8 And the children of Israel did so as Joshua commanded, and took up twelve stones out of the midst of Jordan, as the Lord spake unto Joshua, according to the number of the tribes of the children of Israel, and carried them over with them unto the place where they lodged, and laid them down there. 9 And Joshua set up twelve stones in the midst of Jordan, in the place where the feet of the priests which bare the ark of the covenant stood: and they are there unto this day. 10 For the priests which bare the ark stood in the midst of Jordan, until every thing was finished that the Lord commanded Joshua to speak unto the people, according to all that Moses commanded Joshua: and the people hasted and passed over.

11 And it came to pass, when all the people were clean passed over, that the ark of the Lord passed over, and the priests, in the presence of the people. 12 And the children of Reuben, and the children of Gad, and half the tribe of Manasseh, passed over armed before the children of Israel, as Moses spake unto them: 13 About forty thousand prepared for war passed over before the Lord unto battle, to the plains of Jericho. 14 On that day the Lord magnified Joshua in the sight of all Israel; and they feared him, as they feared Moses, all the days of his life.

15 And the Lord spake unto Joshua, saying, 16 Command the priests that bear the ark of the testimony, that they come up out of Jordan. 17 Joshua therefore commanded the priests, saying, Come ye up out of Jordan. 18 And it came to pass, when the priests that bare the ark of the covenant of the Lord were come up out of the midst of Jordan, and the soles of the priests' feet were lifted up unto the dry land, that the waters of Jordan returned unto their place, and flowed over all his banks, as they did before. 19 And the people came up out of Jordan on the tenth day of the first month, and encamped in Gilgal, in the east border of Jericho.

5    And it came to pass, when all the kings of the Amorites, which were on the side of Jordan westward, and all the kings of the Canaanites, which were by the sea, heard that the Lord had dried up the waters of Jordan from before the children of Israel, until we were passed over, that their heart melted, neither was there spirit in them any more, because of the children of Israel.

2 At that time the Lord said unto Joshua, Make thee sharp knives, and circumcise again the children of Israel the second time. 3 And Joshua made him sharp knives, and circumcised the children of Israel at the hill of the foreskins. 4 And this is the cause why Joshua did circumcise: All the people that came out of Egypt, that were males, even all the men of war, died in the wilderness by the way, after they came out of Egypt. 5 Now all the people that came out were circumcised; but all the people that were born in the wilderness by the way as they came forth out of Egypt, them they had not circumcised. 6 For the children of Israel walked forty years in the wilderness, till all the people that were men of war, which came out of Egypt, were consumed, because they obeyed not the voice of the Lord: unto whom the Lord sware that he would not show them the land, which the Lord sware unto their fathers that he would give us, a land that floweth with milk and honey. 7 And their children, whom he raised up in their stead, them Joshua circumcised: for they were uncircumcised, because they had not circumcised them by the way. 8 And it came to pass, when they had done circumcising all the people, that they abode in their places in the camp, till they were whole. 9 And the Lord said unto Joshua, This day have I rolled away the reproach of Egypt from off you. Wherefore the name of the place is called Gilgal unto this day.

10 And the children of Israel encamped in Gilgal, and kept the passover on the fourteenth day of the month at even in the plains of Jericho. 11 And they did eat of the old corn of the land on the morrow after the passover, unleavened cakes, and parched corn in the selfsame day. 12 And the manna ceased on the morrow after they had eaten of the old corn of the land; neither had the children of Israel manna any more; but they did eat of the fruit of the land of Canaan that year.

13 And it came to pass, when Joshua was by Jericho, that he lifted up his eyes and looked, and, behold, there stood a man over against him with his sword drawn in his hand: and Joshua went unto him, and said unto him, Art thou for us, or for our adversaries? 14 And he said, Nay; but as captain of the host of the Lord am I now come. And Joshua fell on his face to the earth, and did worship, and said unto him, What saith my lord unto his servant? 15 And the captain of the Lord's host said unto Joshua, Loose thy shoe from off thy foot; for the place whereon thou standest is holy. And Joshua did so.

6 Now Jericho was straitly shut up because of the children of Israel: none went out, and none came in. 2 And the Lord said unto Joshua, See, I have given into thine hand Jericho, and the king thereof, and the mighty men of valor. 3 And ye shall compass the city, all ye men of war, and go round about the city once. Thus shalt thou do six days. 4 And seven priests shall bear before the ark seven trumpets of rams' horns: and the seventh day ye shall compass the city seven times, and

the priests shall blow with the trumpets. 5 And it shall come to pass, that when they make a long blast with the ram's horn, and when ye hear the sound of the trumpet, all the people shall shout with a great shout; and the wall of the city shall fall down flat, and the people shall ascend up every man straight before him.

## THE FALL OF JERICHO

6 And Joshua the son of Nun called the priests, and said unto them, Take up the ark of the covenant, and let seven priests bear seven trumpets of rams' horns before the ark of the Lord. 7 And he said unto the people, Pass on, and compass the city, and let him that is armed pass on before the ark of the Lord. 8 And it came to pass, when Joshua had spoken unto the people, that the seven priests bearing the seven trumpets of rams' horns passed on before the Lord, and blew with the trumpets: and the ark of the covenant of the Lord followed them. 9 And the armed men went before the priests that blew with the trumpets, and the rearward came after the ark, the priests going on, and blowing with the trumpets. 10 And Joshua had commanded the people, saying, Ye shall not shout, nor make any noise with your voice, neither shall any word proceed out of your mouth, until the day I bid you shout; then shall ye shout. 11 So the ark of the Lord compassed the city, going about it once: and they came into the camp, and lodged in the camp. 12 And Joshua rose early in the morning, and the priests took up the ark of the Lord. 13 And seven priests bearing seven trumpets of rams' horns before the ark of the Lord went on continually, and blew with the trumpets: and the armed men went before them; but the rearward came after the ark of the Lord, the priests going on, and blowing with the trumpets. 14 And the second day they compassed the city once, and returned into the camp. So they did six days.

15 And it came to pass on the seventh day, that they rose early about the dawning of the day, and compassed the city after the same manner seven times: only on that day they compassed the city seven times. 16 And it came to pass at the seventh time, when the priests blew with the trumpets, Joshua said unto the people, Shout; for the Lord hath given you the city. 17 And the city shall be accursed, even it, and all that are therein, to the Lord: only Rahab the harlot shall live, she and all that are with her in the house, because she hid the messengers that we sent. 18 And ye, in any wise keep yourselves from the accursed thing,[1] lest ye make yourselves accursed, when ye take of the accursed thing, and make the camp of Israel a curse, and trouble it. 19 But all the silver, and gold, and vessels of brass and iron, are consecrated unto the Lord: they shall come into the treasury of the Lord. 20 So the people shouted when the priests blew with the trum-

---

[1] The curse or taboo is against loot.

pets: and it came to pass, when the people heard the sound of the trumpet, and the people shouted with a great shout, that the wall fell down flat, so that the people went up into the city, every man straight before him, and they took the city. 21 And they utterly destroyed all that was in the city, both man and woman, young and old, and ox, and sheep, and ass, with the edge of the sword.

22 But Joshua had said unto the two men that had spied out the country, Go into the harlot's house, and bring out thence the woman, and all that she hath, as ye sware unto her. 23 And the young men that were spies went in, and brought out Rahab, and her father, and her mother, and her brethren, and all that she had; and they brought out all her kindred, and left them without the camp of Israel. 24 And they burnt the city with fire, and all that was therein: only the silver, and the gold, and the vessels of brass and of iron, they put into the treasury of the house of the Lord. 25 And Joshua saved Rahab the harlot alive, and her father's household, and all that she had; and she dwelleth in Israel even unto this day; because she hid the messengers, which Joshua sent to spy out Jericho.

26 And Joshua adjured them at that time, saying, Cursed be the man before the Lord, that riseth up and buildeth this city Jericho: he shall lay the foundation thereof in his firstborn, and in his youngest son shall he set up the gates of it. 27 So the Lord was with Joshua; and his fame was noised throughout all the country.

## CONTINUING CONQUEST

11  16 So Joshua took all that land, the hills, and all the south country, and all the land of Goshen, and the valley, and the plain, and the mountain of Israel, and the valley of the same; 17 Even from the mount Halak, that goeth up to Seir, even unto Baal-gad in the valley of Lebanon under mount Hermon: and all their kings he took, and smote them, and slew them. 18 Joshua made war a long time with all those kings. 19 There was not a city that made peace with the children of Israel, save the Hivites the inhabitants of Gibeon: all other they took in battle. 20 For it was of the Lord to harden their hearts, that they should come against Israel in battle, that he might destroy them utterly, and that they might have no favor, but that he might destroy them, as the Lord commanded Moses. 21 And at that time came Joshua, and cut off the Anakim from the mountains, from Hebron, from Debir, from Anab, and from all the mountains of Judah, and from all the mountains of Israel: Joshua destroyed them utterly with their cities. 22 There was none of the Anakim left in the land of the children of Israel: only in Gaza, in Gath, and in Ashdod, there remained.

13  Now Joshua was old and stricken in years; and the Lord said unto him, Thou art old and stricken in years, and there remaineth yet very much land to be possessed. 2 This is the land that yet remaineth:

all the borders of the Philistines, and all Geshuri, 3 From Sihor, which
is before Egypt, even unto the borders of Ekron northward, which is
counted to the Canaanite: five lords of the Philistines; the Gazathites,
and the Ashdothites, the Eshkalonites, the Gittites, and the Ekronites;
also the Avites: 4 From the south, all the land of the Canaanites,
and Mearah that is beside the Sidonians, unto Aphek, to the borders
of the Amorites: 5 And the land of the Giblites, and all Lebanon
toward the sunrising, from Baal-gad under mount Hermon unto the
entering into Hamath. 6 All the inhabitants of the hill country from
Lebanon unto Misrephothmaim, and all the Sidonians, them will I
drive out from before the children of Israel: only divide thou it by
lot unto the Israelites for an inheritance, as I have commanded thee.
7 Now therefore divide this land for an inheritance unto the nine
tribes, and the half tribe of Manasseh, 8 With whom the Reubenites
and the Gadites have received their inheritance, which Moses gave
them, beyond Jordan eastward, even as Moses the servant of the Lord
gave them.

## JOSHUA'S FAREWELL ADDRESS

23    And it came to pass, a long time after that the Lord had given
rest unto Israel from all their enemies round about, that Joshua waxed
old and stricken in age.

24    And Joshua gathered all the tribes of Israel to Shechem, and
called for the elders of Israel, and for their heads, and for their judges,
and for their officers; and they presented themselves before God. 2
And Joshua said unto all the people, Thus saith the Lord God of Israel,
Your fathers dwelt on the other side of the flood in old time, even
Terah, the father of Abraham, and the father of Nachor: and they
served other gods. 3 And I took your father Abraham from the other
side of the flood, and led him throughout all the land of Canaan, and
multiplied his seed, and gave him Isaac. 4 And I gave unto Isaac
Jacob and Esau: and I gave unto Esau mount Seir, to possess it; but
Jacob and his children went down into Egypt. 5 I sent Moses also
and Aaron, and I plagued Egypt, according to that which I did among
them: and afterward I brought you out. 6 And I brought your fathers
out of Egypt: and ye came unto the sea; and the Egyptians pursued
after your fathers with chariots and horsemen unto the Red sea.
7 And when they cried unto the Lord, he put darkness between you
and the Egyptians, and brought the sea upon them, and covered them;
and your eyes have seen what I have done in Egypt: and ye dwelt in
the wilderness a long season. 8 And I brought you into the land of the
Amorites, which dwelt on the other side Jordan; and they fought with
you: and I gave them into your hand, that ye might possess their
land; and I destroyed them from before you. 9 Then Balak the son
of Zippor, king of Moab, arose and warred against Israel, and sent and
called Balaam the son of Beor to curse you: 10 But I would not

hearken unto Balaam, therefore he blessed you still: so I delivered you out of his hand. 11 And ye went over Jordan, and came unto Jericho: and the men of Jericho fought against you, the Amorites, and the Perizzites, and the Canaanites, and the Hittites, and the Girgashites, the Hivites, and the Jebusites; and I delivered them into your hand. 12 And I sent the hornet before you, which drave them out from before you, even the two kings of the Amorites; but not with thy sword, nor with thy bow. 13 And I have given you a land for which ye did not labor, and cities which ye built not, and ye dwell in them; of the vineyards and oliveyards which ye planted not do ye eat.

14 Now therefore fear the Lord, and serve him in sincerity and in truth; and put away the gods which your fathers served on the other side of the flood, and in Egypt; and serve ye the Lord. 15 And if it seem evil unto you to serve the Lord, choose you this day whom ye will serve; whether the gods which your fathers served that were on the other side of the flood, or the gods of the Amorites, in whose land ye dwell: but as for me and my house, we will serve the Lord.

16 And the people answered and said, God forbid that we should forsake the Lord, to serve other gods; 17 For the Lord our God, he it is that brought us up and our fathers out of the land of Egypt, from the house of bondage, and which did those great signs in our sight, and preserved us in all the way wherein we went, and among all the people through whom we passed: 18 And the Lord drave out from before us all the people, even the Amorites which dwelt in the land: therefore will we also serve the Lord; for he is our God.

19 And Joshua said unto the people, Ye cannot serve the Lord: for he is a holy God; he is a jealous God; he will not forgive your transgressions nor your sins. 20 If ye forsake the Lord, and serve strange gods, then he will turn and do you hurt, and consume you, after that he hath done you good. 21 And the people said unto Joshua, Nay; but we will serve the Lord. 22 And Joshua said unto the people, Ye are witnesses against yourselves that ye have chosen you the Lord, to serve him. And they said, We are witnesses. 23 Now therefore put away, said he, the strange gods which are among you, and incline your heart unto the Lord God of Israel. 24 And the people said unto Joshua, The Lord our God will we serve, and his voice will we obey.

25 So Joshua made a covenant with the people that day, and set them a statute and an ordinance in Shechem. 26 And Joshua wrote these words in the book of the law of God, and took a great stone, and set it up there under an oak, that was by the sanctuary of the Lord. 27 And Joshua said unto all the people, Behold, this stone shall be a witness unto us; for it hath heard all the words of the Lord which he spake unto us: it shall be therefore a witness unto you, lest ye deny your God. 28 So Joshua let the people depart, every man unto his inheritance.

# *Judges*

## CHAOS AND THE DELIVERERS

2 7 And the people served the Lord all the days of Joshua, and all the days of the elders that outlived Joshua, who had seen all the great works of the Lord, that he did for Israel. 8 And Joshua the son of Nun, the servant of the Lord, died, being a hundred and ten years old. 9 And they buried him in the border of his inheritance in Timnath-heres, in the mount of Ephraim, on the north side of the hill Gaash. 10 And also all that generation were gathered unto their fathers: and there arose another generation after them, which knew not the Lord, nor yet the works which he had done for Israel.

11 And the children of Israel did evil in the sight of the Lord, and served Baalim: 12 And they forsook the Lord God of their fathers, which brought them out of the land of Egypt, and followed other gods, of the gods of the people that were round about them, and bowed themselves unto them, and provoked the Lord to anger. 13 And they forsook the Lord, and served Baal and Ashtaroth. 14 And the anger of the Lord was hot against Israel, and he delivered them into the hands of spoilers that spoiled them, and he sold them into the hands of their enemies round about, so that they could not any longer stand before their enemies. 15 Whithersoever they went out, the hand of the Lord was against them for evil, as the Lord had said, and as the Lord had sworn unto them: and they were greatly distressed.

16 Nevertheless the Lord raised up judges, which delivered them out of the hand of those that spoiled them. 17 And yet they would not hearken unto their judges, but they went a whoring after other gods, and bowed themselves unto them: they turned quickly out of the way which their fathers walked in, obeying the commandments of the Lord; but they did not so. 18 And when the Lord raised them up judges, then the Lord was with the judge, and delivered them out of the hand of their enemies all the days of the judge: for it repented the Lord because of their groanings by reason of them that oppressed them and vexed them. 19 And it came to pass, when the judge was dead, that they returned, and corrupted themselves more than their fathers, in following other gods to serve them, and to bow down unto them; they ceased not from their own doings, nor from their stubborn way. 20 And the anger of the Lord was hot against Israel; and he said, Because that this people hath transgressed my covenant which I commanded their fathers, and have not hearkened unto my voice; 21 I also will not henceforth drive out any from before them of the nations which Joshua left when he died: 22 That through them I may prove Israel, whether they will keep the way of the Lord to walk therein, as their fathers did keep it, or not. 23 Therefore the Lord left

those nations, without driving them out hastily; neither delivered he them into the hand of Joshua.

3 Now these are the nations which the Lord left, to prove Israel by them, even as many of Israel as had not known all the wars of Canaan; 2 Only that the generations of the children of Israel might know to teach them war, at the least such as before knew nothing thereof; 3 Namely, five lords of the Philistines, and all the Canaanites, and the Sidonians, and the Hivites that dwelt in mount Lebanon, from mount Baal-hermon unto the entering in of Hamath. 4 And they were to prove Israel by them, to know whether they would hearken unto the commandments of the Lord, which he commanded their fathers by the hand of Moses. 5 And the children of Israel dwelt among the Canaanites, Hittites, and Amorites, and Perizzites, and Hivites, and Jebusites: 6 And they took their daughters to be their wives, and gave their daughters to their sons, and served their gods.

### EHUD AND SHAMGAR

12 And the children of Israel did evil again in the sight of the Lord: and the Lord strengthened Eglon the king of Moab against Israel, because they had done evil in the sight of the Lord. 13 And he gathered unto him the children of Ammon and Amalek, and went and smote Israel, and possessed the city of palm trees. 14 So the children of Israel served Eglon the king of Moab eighteen years.

15 But when the children of Israel cried unto the Lord, the Lord raised them up a deliverer, Ehud the son of Gera, a Benjamite, a man left-handed: and by him the children of Israel sent a present unto Eglon the king of Moab. 16 But Ehud made him a dagger which had two edges, of a cubit length; and he did gird it under his raiment upon his right thigh. 17 And he brought the present unto Eglon king of Moab: and Eglon was a very fat man. 18 And when he had made an end to offer the present, he sent away the people that bare the present. 19 But he himself turned again from the quarries that were by Gilgal, and said, I have a secret errand unto thee, O king: who said, Keep silence. And all that stood by him went out from him. 20 And Ehud came unto him; and he was sitting in a summer parlor, which he had for himself alone. And Ehud said, I have a message from God unto thee. And he arose out of his seat. 21 And Ehud put forth his left hand, and took the dagger from his right thigh, and thrust it into his belly: 22 And the haft also went in after the blade; and the fat closed upon the blade, so that he could not draw the dagger out of his belly; and the dirt came out. 23 Then Ehud went forth through the porch, and shut the doors of the parlor upon him, and locked them.

24 When he was gone out, his servants came; and when they saw that, behold, the doors of the parlor were locked, they said, Surely he covereth his feet in his summer chamber. 25 And they tarried till they were ashamed: and, behold, he opened not the doors of the

parlor; therefore they took a key, and opened them: and, behold, their lord was fallen down dead on the earth. 26 And Ehud escaped while they tarried, and passed beyond the quarries, and escaped into Seirath. 27 And it came to pass, when he was come, that he blew a trumpet in the mountain of Ephraim, and the children of Israel went down with him from the mount, and he before them. 28 And he said unto them, Follow after me: for the Lord hath delivered your enemies the Moabites into your hand. And they went down after him, and took the fords of Jordan toward Moab, and suffered not a man to pass over. 29 And they slew of Moab at that time about ten thousand men, all lusty, and all men of valor; and there escaped not a man. 30 So Moab was subdued that day under the hand of Israel. And the land had rest fourscore years.

31 And after him was Shamgar the son of Anath, which slew of the Philistines six hundred men with an oxgoad: and he also delivered Israel.

### DEBORAH AND BARAK

4 And the children of Israel again did evil in the sight of the Lord, when Ehud was dead. 2 And the Lord sold them into the hand of Jabin king of Canaan, that reigned in Hazor; the captain of whose host was Sisera, which dwelt in Harosheth of the Gentiles. 3 And the children of Israel cried unto the Lord: for he had nine hundred chariots of iron; and twenty years he mightily oppressed the children of Israel.

4 And Deborah, a prophetess, the wife of Lapidoth, she judged Israel at that time. 5 And she dwelt under the palm tree of Deborah, between Ramah and Beth-el in mount Ephraim: and the children of Israel came up to her for judgment. 6 And she sent and called Barak the son of Abinoam out of Kedesh-naphtali, and said unto him, Hath not the Lord God of Israel commanded, saying, Go and draw toward mount Tabor, and take with thee ten thousand men of the children of Naphtali and of the children of Zebulun? 7 And I will draw unto thee, to the river Kishon, Sisera the captain of Jabin's army, with his chariots and his multitude; and I will deliver him into thine hand. 8 And Barak said unto her, If thou wilt go with me, then I will go: but if thou wilt not go with me, then I will not go. 9 And she said, I will surely go with thee: notwithstanding the journey that thou takest shall not be for thine honor; for the Lord shall sell Sisera into the hand of a woman. And Deborah arose and went with Barak to Kedesh. 10 And Barak called Zebulun and Naphtali to Kedesh; and he went up with ten thousand men at his feet: and Deborah went up with him.

11 Now Heber the Kenite, which was of the children of Hobab the father-in-law of Moses, had severed himself from the Kenites, and pitched his tent unto the plain of Zaanaim, which is by Kedesh.

12 And they showed Sisera that Barak the son of Abinoam was gone up to mount Tabor. 13 And Sisera gathered together all his chariots, even nine hundred chariots of iron, and all the people that

were with him, from Harosheth of the Gentiles unto the river of Kishon. 14 And Deborah said unto Barak, Up; for this is the day in which the Lord hath delivered Sisera into thine hand: is not the Lord gone out before thee? So Barak went down from mount Tabor, and ten thousand men after him. 15 And the Lord discomfited Sisera, and all his chariots, and all his host, with the edge of the sword before Barak; so that Sisera lighted down off his chariot, and fled away on his feet. 16 But Barak pursued after the chariots, and after the host, unto Harosheth of the Gentiles: and all the host of Sisera fell upon the edge of the sword; and there was not a man left.

17 Howbeit Sisera fled away on his feet to the tent of Jael the wife of Heber the Kenite: for there was peace between Jabin the king of Hazor and the house of Heber the Kenite. 18 And Jael went out to meet Sisera, and said unto him, Turn in, my lord, turn in to me; fear not. And when he had turned in unto her into the tent, she covered him with a mantle. 19 And he said unto her, Give me, I pray thee, a little water to drink; for I am thirsty. And she opened a bottle of milk, and gave him drink, and covered him. 20 Again he said unto her, Stand in the door of the tent, and it shall be, when any man doth come and inquire of thee, and say, Is there any man here? that thou shalt say, No. 21 Then Jael Heber's wife took a nail of the tent, and took a hammer in her hand, and went softly unto him, and smote the nail into his temples, and fastened it into the ground: for he was fast asleep and weary. So he died. 22 And, behold, as Barak pursued Sisera, Jael came out to meet him, and said unto him, Come, and I will show thee the man whom thou seekest. And when he came into her tent, behold, Sisera lay dead, and the nail was in his temples. 23 So God subdued on that day Jabin the king of Canaan before the children of Israel. 24 And the hand of the children of Israel prospered, and prevailed against Jabin the king of Canaan, until they had destroyed Jabin king of Canaan.

5 Then sang Deborah and Barak the son of Abinoam on that day, saying,

    2 Praise ye the Lord for the avenging of Israel,
      When the people willingly offered themselves.
    3 Hear, O ye kings; give ear, O ye princes;
      I, even I, will sing unto the Lord;
      I will sing praise to the Lord God of Israel.
    4 Lord, when thou wentest out of Seir,
      When thou marchedst out of the field of Edom,
      The earth trembled, and the heavens dropped,
      The clouds also dropped water.
    5 The mountains melted from before the Lord,
      Even that Sinai from before the Lord God of Israel.
    6 In the days of Shamgar the son of Anath,
      In the days of Jael, the highways were unoccupied,
      And the travelers walked through byways.

7 The inhabitants of the villages ceased, they ceased in Israel,
Until that I Deborah arose,
That I arose a mother in Israel.
8 They chose new gods;
Then was war in the gates:
Was there a shield or spear seen
Among forty thousand in Israel?
9 My heart is toward the governors of Israel,
That offered themselves willingly among the people.
Bless ye the Lord.
10 Speak, ye that ride on white asses,
Ye that sit in judgment,
And walk by the way.
11 They that are delivered from the noise of archers in the places
of drawing water,
There shall they rehearse the righteous acts of the Lord,
Even the righteous acts toward the inhabitants of his villages
in Israel:
Then shall the people of the Lord go down to the gates.
12 Awake, awake, Deborah:
Awake, awake, utter a song:
Arise, Barak, and lead thy captivity captive,
Thou son of Abinoam.
13 Then he made him that remaineth have dominion over the
nobles among the people:
The Lord made me have dominion over the mighty.
14 Out of Ephraim was there a root of them against Amalek;
After thee, Benjamin, among thy people;
Out of Machir came down governors, and out of Zebulun they
that handle the pen of the writer.
15 And the princes of Issachar were with Deborah;
Even Issachar, and also Barak:
He was sent on foot into the valley.
For the divisions of Reuben
There were great thoughts of heart.
16 Why abodest thou among the sheepfolds,
To hear the bleatings of the flocks?
For the divisions of Reuben
There were great searchings of heart.
17 Gilead abode beyond Jordan:
And why did Dan remain in ships?
Asher continued on the seashore,
And abode in his breaches.
18 Zebulun and Naphtali were a people that jeopardized their
lives unto the death
In the high places of the field.
19 The kings came and fought;
Then fought the kings of Canaan

In Taanach by the waters of Megiddo;
They took no gain of money.
20 They fought from heaven;
The stars in their courses fought against Sisera.
21 The river of Kishon swept them away,
That ancient river, the river Kishon.
O my soul, thou hast trodden down strength.
22 Then were the horsehoofs broken
By the means of the prancings, the prancings of their mighty ones.
23 Curse ye Meroz, said the angel of the Lord,
Curse ye bitterly the inhabitants thereof;
Because they came not to the help of the Lord,
To the help of the Lord against the mighty.
24 Blessed above women shall Jael the wife of Heber the Kenite be;
Blessed shall she be above women in the tent.
25 He asked water, and she gave him milk;
She brought forth butter in a lordly dish.
26 She put her hand to the nail,
And her right hand to the workmen's hammer;
And with the hammer she smote Sisera, she smote off his head,
When she had pierced and stricken through his temples.
27 At her feet he bowed, he fell, he lay down:
At her feet he bowed, he fell:
Where he bowed, there he fell down dead.
28 The mother of Sisera looked out at a window,
And cried through the lattice,
Why is his chariot so long in coming?
Why tarry the wheels of his chariots?
29 Her wise ladies answered her,
Yea, she returned answer to herself,
30 Have they not sped? have they not divided the prey;
To every man a damsel or two;
To Sisera a prey of divers colors,
A prey of divers colors of needlework,
Of divers colors of needlework on both sides,
Meet for the necks of them that take the spoil?
31 So let all thine enemies perish, O Lord:
But let them that love him be as the sun when he goeth forth
in his might.
And the land had rest forty years.

### GIDEON

6 And the children of Israel did evil in the sight of the Lord: and the Lord delivered them into the hand of Midian seven years. 2 And the hand of Midian prevailed against Israel: and because of the Midi-

anites the children of Israel made them the dens which are in the mountains, and caves, and strongholds. 3 And so it was, when Israel had sown, that the Midianites came up, and the Amalekites, and the children of the east, even they came up against them; 4 And they encamped against them, and destroyed the increase of the earth, till thou come unto Gaza, and left no sustenance for Israel, neither sheep, nor ox, nor ass. 5 For they came up with their cattle and their tents, and they came as grasshoppers for multitude; for both they and their camels were without number: and they entered into the land to destroy it. 6 And Israel was greatly impoverished because of the Midianites; and the children of Israel cried unto the Lord.

7 And it came to pass, when the children of Israel cried unto the Lord because of the Midianites, 8 That the Lord sent a prophet unto the children of Israel, which said unto them, Thus saith the Lord God of Israel, I brought you up from Egypt, and brought you forth out of the house of bondage; 9 And I delivered you out of the hand of the Egyptians, and out of the hand of all that oppressed you, and drave them out from before you, and gave you their land; 10 And I said unto you, I am the Lord your God; fear not the gods of the Amorites, in whose land ye dwell: but ye have not obeyed my voice.

11 And there came an angel of the Lord, and sat under an oak which was in Ophrah, that pertained unto Joash the Abi-ezrite: and his son Gideon threshed wheat by the winepress, to hide it from the Midianites. 12 And the angel of the Lord appeared unto him, and said unto him, The Lord is with thee, thou mighty man of valor. 13 And Gideon said unto him, O my Lord, if the Lord be with us, why then is all this befallen us? and where be all his miracles which our fathers told us of, saying, Did not the Lord bring us up from Egypt? but now the Lord hath forsaken us, and delivered us into the hands of the Midianites. 14 And the Lord looked upon him, and said, Go in this thy might, and thou shalt save Israel from the hand of the Midianites: have not I sent thee? 15 And he said unto him, O my Lord, wherewith shall I save Israel? behold, my family is poor in Manasseh, and I am the least in my father's house. 16 And the Lord said unto him, Surely I will be with thee, and thou shalt smite the Midianites as one man. 17 And he said unto him, If now I have found grace in thy sight, then show me a sign that thou talkest with me. 18 Depart not hence, I pray thee, until I come unto thee, and bring forth my present, and set it before thee. And he said, I will tarry until thou come again.

19 And Gideon went in, and made ready a kid, and unleavened cakes of an ephah of flour: the flesh he put in a basket, and he put the broth in a pot, and brought it out unto him under the oak, and presented it. 20 And the angel of God said unto him, Take the flesh and the unleavened cakes, and lay them upon this rock, and pour out the broth. And he did so. 21 Then the angel of the Lord put forth the end of the staff that was in his hand, and touched the flesh and the unleavened cakes; and there rose up fire out of the rock, and consumed

the flesh and the unleavened cakes. Then the angel of the Lord departed out of his sight. 22 And when Gideon perceived that he was an angel of the Lord, Gideon said, Alas, O Lord God! for because I have seen an angel of the Lord face to face. 23 And the Lord said unto him, Peace be unto thee; fear not: thou shalt not die. 24 Then Gideon built an altar there unto the Lord, and called it Jehovah-shalom: unto this day it is yet in Ophrah of the Abi-ezrites.

25 And it came to pass the same night, that the Lord said unto him, Take thy father's young bullock, even the second bullock of seven years old, and throw down the altar of Baal that thy father hath, and cut down the grove that is by it: 26 And build an altar unto the Lord thy God upon the top of this rock, in the ordered place, and take the second bullock, and offer a burnt sacrifice with the wood of the grove which thou shalt cut down. 27 Then Gideon took ten men of his servants, and did as the Lord had said unto him: and so it was, because he feared his father's household, and the men of the city, that he could not do it by day, that he did it by night.

28 And when the men of the city arose early in the morning, behold, the altar of Baal was cast down, and the grove was cut down that was by it, and the second bullock was offered upon the altar that was built. 29 And they said one to another, Who hath done this thing? And when they inquired and asked, they said, Gideon the son of Joash hath done this thing. 30 Then the men of the city said unto Joash, Bring out thy son, that he may die: because he hath cast down the altar of Baal, and because he hath cut down the grove that was by it. 31 And Joash said unto all that stood against him, Will ye plead for Baal? will ye save him? he that will plead for him, let him be put to death whilst it is yet morning: if he be a god, let him plead for himself, because one hath cast down his altar. 32 Therefore on that day he called him Jerubbaal, saying, Let Baal plead against him, because he hath thrown down his altar.

33 Then all the Midianites and the Amalekites and the children of the east were gathered together, and went over, and pitched in the valley of Jezreel. 34 But the Spirit of the Lord came upon Gideon, and he blew a trumpet; and Abiezer was gathered after him. 35 And he sent messengers throughout all Manasseh; who also was gathered after him: and he sent messengers unto Asher, and unto Zebulun, and unto Naphtali; and they came up to meet them.

36 And Gideon said unto God, If thou wilt save Israel by mine hand, as thou hast said, 37 Behold, I will put a fleece of wool in the floor; and if the dew be on the fleece only, and it be dry upon all the earth besides, then shall I know that thou wilt save Israel by mine hand, as thou hast said. 38 And it was so: for he rose up early on the morrow, and thrust the fleece together, and wringed the dew out of the fleece, a bowlful of water. 39 And Gideon said unto God, Let not thine anger be hot against me, and I will speak but this once: let me prove, I pray thee, but this once with the fleece; let it now be dry only upon the fleece, and upon all the ground let there be dew. 40 And

God did so that night: for it was dry upon the fleece only, and there was dew on all the ground.

7 Then Jerubbaal, who is Gideon, and all the people that were with him, rose up early, and pitched beside the well of Harod: so that the host of the Midianites were on the north side of them, by the hill of Moreh, in the valley. 2 And the Lord said unto Gideon, The people that are with thee are too many for me to give the Midianites into their hands, lest Israel vaunt themselves against me, saying, Mine own hand hath saved me. 3 Now therefore go to, proclaim in the ears of the people, saying, Whosoever is fearful and afraid, let him return and depart early from mount Gilead. And there returned of the people twenty and two thousand; and there remained ten thousand.

4 And the Lord said unto Gideon, The people are yet too many; bring them down unto the water, and I will try them for thee there: and it shall be, that of whom I say unto thee, This shall go with thee, the same shall go with thee; and of whomsoever I say unto thee, This shall not go with thee, the same shall not go. 5 So he brought down the people unto the water: and the Lord said unto Gideon, Every one that lappeth of the water with his tongue, as a dog lappeth, him shalt thou set by himself; likewise every one that boweth down upon his knees to drink. 6 And the number of them that lapped, putting their hand to their mouth, were three hundred men: but all the rest of the people bowed down upon their knees to drink water. 7 And the Lord said unto Gideon, By the three hundred men that lapped will I save you, and deliver the Midianites into thine hand: and let all the other people go every man unto his place. 8 So the people took victuals in their hand, and their trumpets: and he sent all the rest of Israel every man unto his tent, and retained those three hundred men: and the host of Midian was beneath him in the valley.

9 And it came to pass the same night, that the Lord said unto him, Arise, get thee down unto the host; for I have delivered it into thine hand. 10 But if thou fear to go down, go thou with Phurah thy servant down to the host: 11 And thou shalt hear what they say; and afterward shall thine hands be strengthened to go down unto the host. Then went he down with Phurah his servant unto the outside of the armed men that were in the host. 12 And the Midianites and the Amalekites and all the children of the east lay along in the valley like grasshoppers for multitude; and their camels were without number, as the sand by the sea side for multitude. 13 And when Gideon was come, behold, there was a man that told a dream unto his fellow, and said, Behold, I dreamed a dream, and, lo, a cake of barley bread tumbled into the host of Midian, and came unto a tent, and smote it that it fell, and overturned it, that the tent lay along. 14 And his fellow answered and said, This is nothing else save the sword of Gideon the son of Joash, a man of Israel: for into his hand hath God delivered Midian, and all the host.

15 And it was so, when Gideon heard the telling of the dream, and the interpretation thereof, that he worshipped, and returned into the host of Israel, and said, Arise; for the Lord hath delivered into your hand the host of Midian. 16 And he divided the three hundred men into three companies, and he put a trumpet in every man's hand, with empty pitchers, and lamps within the pitchers. 17 And he said unto them, Look on me, and do likewise: and, behold, when I come to the outside of the camp, it shall be that, as I do, so shall ye do. 18 When I blow with a trumpet, I and all that are with me, then blow ye the trumpets also on every side of all the camp, and say, The sword of the Lord, and of Gideon.

19 So Gideon, and the hundred men that were with him, came unto the outside of the camp in the beginning of the middle watch; and they had but newly set the watch: and they blew the trumpets, and brake the pitchers that were in their hands. 20 And the three companies blew the trumpets, and brake the pitchers, and held the lamps in their left hands, and the trumpets in their right hands to blow withal: and they cried, The sword of the Lord, and of Gideon. 21 And they stood every man in his place round about the camp: and all the host ran, and cried, and fled. 22 And the three hundred blew the trumpets, and the Lord set every man's sword against his fellow, even throughout all the host: and the host fled to Beth-shittah in Zererath, and to the border of Abel-meholah, unto Tabbath. 23 And the men of Israel gathered themselves together out of Naphtali, and out of Asher, and out of all Manasseh, and pursued after the Midianites.

24 And Gideon sent messengers throughout all mount Ephraim, saying, Come down against the Midianites, and take before them the waters unto Beth-barah and Jordan. Then all the men of Ephraim gathered themselves together, and took the waters unto Beth-barah and Jordan. 25 And they took two princes of the Midianites, Oreb and Zeeb; and they slew Oreb upon the rock Oreb, and Zeeb they slew at the winepress of Zeeb, and pursued Midian, and brought the heads of Oreb and Zeeb to Gideon on the other side Jordan.

8 And the men of Ephraim said unto him, Why hast thou served us thus, that thou calledst us not, when thou wentest to fight with the Midianites? And they did chide with him sharply. 2 And he said unto them, What have I done now in comparison of you? Is not the gleaning of the grapes of Ephraim better than the vintage of Abiezer? 3 God hath delivered into your hands the princes of Midian, Oreb and Zeeb: and what was I able to do in comparison of you? Then their anger was abated toward him, when he had said that.

4 And Gideon came to Jordan, and passed over, he, and the three hundred men that were with him, faint, yet pursuing them. 5 And he said unto the men of Succoth, Give, I pray you, loaves of bread unto the people that follow me; for they be faint, and I am pursuing after Zebah and Zalmunna, kings of Midian. 6 And the princes of Succoth said, Are the hands of Zebah and Zalmunna now in thine hand, that

we should give bread unto thine army? 7 And Gideon said, Therefore when the Lord hath delivered Zebah and Zalmunna into mine hand, then I will tear your flesh with the thorns of the wilderness and with briers. 8 And he went up thence to Penuel, and spake unto them likewise: and the men of Penuel answered him as the men of Succoth had answered him. 9 And he spake also unto the men of Penuel, saying, When I come again in peace, I will break down this tower.

10 Now Zebah and Zalmunna were in Karkor, and their hosts with them, about fifteen thousand men, all that were left of all the hosts of the children of the east: for there fell a hundred and twenty thousand men that drew sword. 11 And Gideon went up by the way of them that dwelt in tents on the east of Nobah and Jogbehah, and smote the host: for the host was secure. 12 And when Zebah and Zalmunna fled, he pursued after them, and took the two kings of Midian, Zebah and Zalmunna, and discomfited all the host.

13 And Gideon the son of Joash returned from battle before the sun was up, 14 And caught a young man of the men of Succoth, and inquired of him: and he described unto him the princes of Succoth, and the elders thereof, even threescore and seventeen men. 15 And he came unto the men of Succoth, and said, Behold Zebah and Zalmunna, with whom ye did upbraid me, saying, Are the hands of Zebah and Zalmunna now in thine hand, that we should give bread unto thy men that are weary? 16 And he took the elders of the city, and thorns of the wilderness, and briers, and with them he taught the men of Succoth. 17 And he beat down the tower of Penuel, and slew the men of the city.

18 Then said he unto Zebah and Zalmunna, What manner of men were they whom ye slew at Tabor? And they answered, As thou art, so were they; each one resembled the children of a king. 19 And he said, They were my brethren, even the sons of my mother: as the Lord liveth, if ye had saved them alive, I would not slay you. 20 And he said unto Jether his firstborn, Up, and slay them. But the youth drew not his sword: for he feared, because he was yet a youth. 21 Then Zebah and Zalmunna said, Rise thou, and fall upon us: for as the man is, so is his strength. And Gideon arose, and slew Zebah and Zalmunna, and took away the ornaments that were on their camels' necks.

22 Then the men of Israel said unto Gideon, Rule thou over us, both thou, and thy son, and thy son's son also: for thou hast delivered us from the hand of Midian. 23 And Gideon said unto them, I will not rule over you, neither shall my son rule over you: the Lord shall rule over you. 24 And Gideon said unto them, I would desire a request of you, that ye would give me every man the earrings of his prey. (For they had golden earrings, because they were Ishmaelites.) 25 And they answered, We will willingly give them. And they spread a garment, and did cast therein every man the earrings of his prey. 26 And the weight of the golden earrings that he requested was a thousand and seven hundred shekels of gold; besides ornaments, and collars, and purple raiment that was on the kings of Midian, and be-

sides the chains that were about their camels' necks. 27 And Gideon made an ephod thereof, and put it in his city, even in Ophrah: and all Israel went thither a whoring after it: which thing became a snare unto Gideon, and to his house. 28 Thus was Midian subdued before the children of Israel, so that they lifted up their heads no more. And the country was in quietness forty years in the days of Gideon.

29 And Jerubbaal the son of Joash went and dwelt in his own house. 30 And Gideon had threescore and ten sons of his body begotten: for he had many wives. 31 And his concubine that was in Shechem, she also bare him a son, whose name he called Abimelech. 32 And Gideon the son of Joash died in a good old age, and was buried in the sepulchre of Joash his father, in Ophrah of the Abiezrites.

33 And it came to pass, as soon as Gideon was dead, that the children of Israel turned again, and went a whoring after Baalim, and make Baal-berith their god. 34 And the children of Israel remembered not the Lord their God, who had delivered them out of the hands of all their enemies on every side: 35 Neither showed they kindness to the house of Jerubbaal, namely, Gideon, according to all the goodness which he had showed unto Israel.

## SAMSON

13 And the children of Israel did evil again in the sight of the Lord; and the Lord delivered them into the hand of the Philistines forty years. 2 And there was a certain man of Zorah, of the family of the Danites, whose name was Manoah; and his wife was barren, and bare not. 3 And the angel of the Lord appeared unto the woman, and said unto her, Behold now, thou art barren, and bearest not: but thou shalt conceive, and bear a son. 4 Now therefore beware, I pray thee, and drink not wine nor strong drink, and eat not any unclean thing: 5 For, lo, thou shalt conceive, and bear a son; and no razor shall come on his head: for the child shall be a Nazarite unto God from the womb: and he shall begin to deliver Israel out of the hand of the Philistines. 6 Then the woman came and told her husband, saying, A man of God came unto me, and his countenance was like the countenance of an angel of God, very terrible: but I asked him not whence he was, neither told he me his name: 7 But he said unto me, Behold, thou shalt conceive, and bear a son; and now drink no wine nor strong drink, neither eat any unclean thing: for the child shall be a Nazarite to God from the womb to the day of his death.

8 Then Manoah entreated the Lord, and said, O my Lord, let the man of God which thou didst send come again unto us, and teach us what we shall do unto the child that shall be born. 9 And God hearkened to the voice of Manoah; and the angel of God came again unto the woman as she sat in the field: but Manoah her husband was not with her. 10 And the woman made haste, and ran, and showed her husband, and said unto him, Behold, the man hath appeared unto me,

that came unto me the other day. 11 And Manoah arose, and went after his wife, and came to the man, and said unto him, Art thou the man that spakest unto the woman? And he said, I am. 12 And Manoah said, Now let thy words come to pass. How shall we order the child, and how shall we do unto him? 13 And the angel of the Lord said unto Manoah, Of all that I said unto the woman let her beware. 14 She may not eat of any thing that cometh of the vine, neither let her drink wine or strong drink, nor eat any unclean thing: all that I commanded her let her observe.

15 And Manoah said unto the angel of the Lord, I pray thee, let us detain thee, until we shall have made ready a kid for thee. 16 And the angel of the Lord said unto Manoah, Though thou detain me, I will not eat of thy bread: and if thou wilt offer a burnt offering, thou must offer it unto the Lord. For Manoah knew not that he was an angel of the Lord. 17 And Manoah said unto the angel of the Lord, What is thy name, that when thy sayings come to pass we may do thee honor? 18 And the angel of the Lord said unto him, Why askest thou thus after my name, seeing it is secret? 19 So Manoah took a kid with a meat offering, and offered it upon a rock unto the Lord: and the angel did wondrously; and Manoah and his wife looked on. 20 For it came to pass, when the flame went up toward heaven from off the altar, that the angel of the Lord ascended in the flame of the altar: and Manoah and his wife looked on it, and fell on their faces to the ground. 21 But the angel of the Lord did no more appear to Manoah and to his wife. Then Manoah knew that he was an angel of the Lord. 22 And Manoah said unto his wife, We shall surely die, because we have seen God. 23 But his wife said unto him, If the Lord were pleased to kill us, he would not have received a burnt offering and a meat offering at our hands, neither would he have showed us all these things, nor would as at this time have told us such things as these.

24 And the woman bare a son, and called his name Samson: and the child grew, and the Lord blessed him. 25 And the Spirit of the Lord began to move him at times in the camp of Dan between Zorah and Eshtaol.

14 And Samson went down to Timnath, and saw a woman in Timnath of the daughters of the Philistines. 2 And he came up, and told his father and his mother, and said, I have seen a woman in Timnath of the daughters of the Philistines: now therefore get her for me to wife. 3 Then his father and his mother said unto him, Is there never a woman among the daughters of thy brethren, or among all my people, that thou goest to take a wife of the uncircumcised Philistines? And Samson said unto his father, Get her for me; for she pleaseth me well. 4 But his father and his mother knew not that it was of the Lord, that he sought an occasion against the Philistines: for at that time the Philistines had dominion over Israel.

5 Then went Samson down, and his father and his mother, to

Timnath, and came to the vineyards of Timnath: and, behold, a young lion roared against him. 6 And the Spirit of the Lord came mightily upon him, and he rent him as he would have rent a kid, and he had nothing in his hand: but he told not his father or his mother what he had done. 7 And he went down, and talked with the woman; and she pleased Samson well. 8 And after a time he returned to take her, and he turned aside to see the carcass of the lion: and, behold, there was a swarm of bees and honey in the carcass of the lion. 9 And he took thereof in his hands, and went on eating, and came to his father and mother, and he gave them, and they did eat: but he told not them that he had taken the honey out of the carcass of the lion.

10 So his father went down unto the woman: and Samson made there a feast; for so used the young men to do. 11 And it came to pass, when they saw him, that they brought thirty companions to be with him. 12 And Samson said unto them, I will now put forth a riddle unto you: if ye can certainly declare it me within the seven days of the feast, and find it out, then I will give you thirty sheets and thirty change of garments: 13 But if ye cannot declare it me, then shall ye give me thirty sheets and thirty change of garments. And they said unto him, Put forth thy riddle, that we may hear it. 14 And he said unto them,

> Out of the eater came forth meat,
> And out of the strong came forth sweetness.

And they could not in three days expound the riddle.

15 And it came to pass on the seventh day, that they said unto Samson's wife, Entice thy husband, that he may declare unto us the riddle, lest we burn thee and thy father's house with fire: have ye called us to take that we have? is it not so? 16 And Samson's wife wept before him, and said, Thou dost but hate me, and lovest me not: thou hast put forth a riddle unto the children of my people, and hast not told it me. And he said unto her, Behold, I have not told it my father nor my mother, and shall I tell it thee? 17 And she wept before him the seven days, while their feast lasted: and it came to pass on the seventh day, that he told her, because she lay sore upon him: and she told the riddle to the children of her people.

18 And the men of the city said unto him on the seventh day before the sun went down,

> What is sweeter than honey?
> And what is stronger than a lion?

And he said unto them,

> If ye had not plowed with my heifer,
> Ye had not found out my riddle.

19 And the Spirit of the Lord came upon him, and he went down to Ashkelon, and slew thirty men of them, and took their spoil, and gave change of garments unto them which expounded the riddle. And his anger was kindled, and he went up to his father's house. 20 But Samson's wife was given to his companion, whom he had used as his friend.

144

15 But it came to pass within a while after, in the time of wheat harvest, that Samson visited his wife with a kid; and he said, I will go in to my wife into the chamber. But her father would not suffer him to go in. 2 And her father said, I verily thought that thou hadst utterly hated her; therefore I gave her to thy companion: is not her younger sister fairer than she? take her, I pray thee, instead of her. 3 And Samson said concerning them, Now shall I be more blameless than the Philistines, though I do them a displeasure. 4 And Samson went and caught three hundred foxes, and took firebrands, and turned tail to tail, and put a firebrand in the midst between two tails. 5 And when he had set the brands on fire, he let them go into the standing corn of the Philistines, and burnt up both the shocks, and also the standing corn, with the vineyards and olives. 6 Then the Philistines said, Who hath done this? And they answered, Samson, the son-in-law of the Timnite, because he had taken his wife, and given her to his companion. And the Philistines came up, and burnt her and her father with fire. 7 And Samson said unto them, Though ye have done this, yet will I be avenged of you, and after that I will cease. 8 And he smote them hip and thigh with a great slaughter: and he went down and dwelt in the top of the rock Etam.

9 Then the Philistines went up, and pitched in Judah, and spread themselves in Lehi. 10 And the men of Judah said, Why are ye come up against us? And they answered, To bind Samson are we come up, to do to him as he hath done to us. 11 Then three thousand men of Judah went to the top of the rock Etam, and said to Samson, Knowest thou not that the Philistines are rulers over us? what is this that thou hast done unto us? And he said unto them, As they did unto me, so have I done unto them. 12 And they said unto him, We are come down to bind thee, that we may deliver thee into the hand of the Philistines. And Samson said unto them, Swear unto me, that ye will not fall upon me yourselves. 13 And they spake unto him, saying, No; but we will bind thee fast, and deliver thee into their hand: but surely we will not kill thee. And they bound him with two new cords, and brought him up from the rock.

14 And when he came unto Lehi, the Philistines shouted against him: and the Spirit of the Lord came mightily upon him, and the cords that were upon his arms became as flax that was burnt with fire, and his bands loosed from off his hands. 15 And he found a new jawbone of an ass, and put forth his hand, and took it, and slew a thousand men therewith. 16 And Samson said,

With the jawbone of an ass, heaps upon heaps,
With the jaw of an ass have I slain a thousand men.

17 And it came to pass, when he had made an end of speaking, that he cast away the jawbone out of his hand, and called that place Ramath-lehi. 18 And he was sore athirst, and called on the Lord, and said, Thou hast given this great deliverance into the hand of thy servant: and now shall I die for thirst, and fall into the hand of the

uncircumcised? 19 But God clave a hollow place that was in the jaw, and there came water thereout; and when he had drunk, his spirit came again, and he revived: wherefore he called the name thereof En-hakkore, which is in Lehi unto this day. 20 And he judged Israel in the days of the Philistines twenty years.

16 Then went Samson to Gaza, and saw there a harlot, and went in unto her. 2 And it was told the Gazites, saying, Samson is come hither. And they compassed him in, and laid wait for him all night in the gate of the city, and were quiet all the night, saying, In the morning, when it is day, we shall kill him. 3 And Samson lay till midnight, and arose at midnight, and took the doors of the gate of the city, and the two posts, and went away with them, bar and all, and put them upon his shoulders, and carried them up to the top of a hill that is before Hebron.

4 And it came to pass afterward, that he loved a woman in the valley of Sorek, whose name was Delilah. 5 And the lords of the Philistines came up unto her, and said unto her, Entice him, and see wherein his great strength lieth, and by what means we may prevail against him, that we may bind him to afflict him: and we will give thee every one of us eleven hundred pieces of silver. 6 And Delilah said to Samson, Tell me, I pray thee, wherein thy great strength lieth, and wherewith thou mightest be bound to afflict thee. 7 And Samson said unto her, If they bind me with seven green withes that were never dried, then shall I be weak, and be as another man. 8 Then the lords of the Philistines brought up to her seven green withes which had not been dried, and she bound him with them. 9 Now there were men lying in wait, abiding with her in the chamber. And she said unto him, The Philistines be upon thee, Samson. And he brake the withes, as a thread of tow is broken when it toucheth the fire. So his strength was not known.

10 And Delilah said unto Samson, Behold, thou hast mocked me, and told me lies: now tell me, I pray thee, wherewith thou mightest be bound. 11 And he said unto her, If they bind me fast with new ropes that never were occupied, then shall I be weak, and be as another man. 12 Delilah therefore took new ropes, and bound him therewith, and said unto him, The Philistines be upon thee, Samson. And there were liers in wait abiding in the chamber. And he brake them from off his arms like a thread.

13 And Delilah said unto Samson, Hitherto thou hast mocked me, and told me lies: tell me wherewith thou mightest be bound. And he said unto her, If thou weavest the seven locks of my head with the web. 14 And she fastened it with the pin, and said unto him, The Philistines be upon thee, Samson. And he awaked out of his sleep, and went away with the pin of the beam, and with the web.

15 And she said unto him, How canst thou say, I love thee, when thine heart is not with me? Thou hast mocked me these three times, and hast not told me wherein thy great strength lieth. 16 And it came

to pass, when she pressed him daily with her words, and urged him, so that his soul was vexed unto death; 17 That he told her all his heart, and said unto her, There hath not come a razor upon mine head; for I have been a Nazarite unto God from my mother's womb: if I be shaven, then my strength will go from me, and I shall become weak, and be like any other man.

18 And when Delilah saw that he had told her all his heart, she sent and called for the lords of the Philistines, saying, Come up this once, for he hath showed me all his heart. Then the lords of the Philistines came up unto her, and brought money in their hand. 19 And she made him sleep upon her knees; and she called for a man, and she caused him to shave off the seven locks of his head; and she began to afflict him, and his strength went from him. 20 And she said, The Philistines be upon thee, Samson. And he awoke out of his sleep, and said, I will go out as at other times before, and shake myself. And he wist not that the Lord was departed from him. 21 But the Philistines took him, and put out his eyes, and brought him down to Gaza, and bound him with fetters of brass; and he did grind in the prison house. 22 Howbeit the hair of his head began to grow again after he was shaven.

23 Then the lords of the Philistines gathered them together for to offer a great sacrifice unto Dagon their god, and to rejoice: for they said, Our god hath delivered Samson our enemy into our hand. 24 And when the people saw him, they praised their god: for they said, Our god hath delivered into our hands our enemy, and the destroyer of our country, which slew many of us. 25 And it came to pass, when their hearts were merry, that they said, Call for Samson, that he may make us sport. And they called for Samson out of the prison house; and he made them sport: and they set him between the pillars. 26 And Samson said unto the lad that held him by the hand, Suffer me that I may feel the pillars whereupon the house standeth, that I may lean upon them. 27 Now the house was full of men and women; and all the lords of the Philistines were there; and there were upon the roof about three thousand men and women, that beheld while Samson made sport.

28 And Samson called unto the Lord, and said, O Lord God, remember me, I pray thee, and strengthen me, I pray thee, only this once, O God, that I may be at once avenged of the Philistines for my two eyes. 29 And Samson took hold of the two middle pillars upon which the house stood, and on which it was borne up, of the one with his right hand, and of the other with his left. 30 And Samson said, Let me die with the Philistines. And he bowed himself with all his might; and the house fell upon the lords, and upon all the people that were therein. So the dead which he slew at his death were more than they which he slew in his life. 31 Then his brethren and all the house of his father came down, and took him, and brought him up, and buried him between Zorah and Eshtaol in the buryingplace of Manoah his father. And he judged Israel twenty years.

# Ruth

1 Now it came to pass in the days when the judges ruled, that there was a famine in the land. And a certain man of Bethlehem-judah went to sojourn in the country of Moab, he, and his wife, and his two sons. 2 And the name of the man was Elimelech, and the name of his wife Naomi, and the name of his two sons Mahlon and Chilion, Ephrathites of Bethlehem-judah. And they came into the country of Moab, and continued there. 3 And Elimelech Naomi's husband died; and she was left, and her two sons. 4 And they took them wives of the women of Moab; the name of the one was Orpah, and the name of the other Ruth: and they dwelt there about ten years. 5 And Mahlon and Chilion died also both of them; and the woman was left of her two sons and her husband.

6 Then she arose with her daughters-in-law, that she might return from the country of Moab: for she had heard in the country of Moab how that the Lord had visited his people in giving them bread. 7 Wherefore she went forth out of the place where she was, and her two daughters-in-law with her; and they went on the way to return unto the land of Judah. 8 And Naomi said unto her two daughters-in-law, Go, return each to her mother's house: the Lord deal kindly with you, as ye have dealt with the dead, and with me. 9 The Lord grant you that ye may find rest, each of you in the house of her husband. Then she kissed them; and they lifted up their voice, and wept. 10 And they said unto her, Surely we will return with thee unto thy people. 11 And Naomi said, Turn again, my daughters: why will ye go with me? are there yet any more sons in my womb, that they may be your husbands? 12 Turn again, my daughters, go your way; for I am too old to have a husband. If I should say, I have hope, if I should have a husband also to-night, and should also bear sons; 13 Would ye tarry for them till they were grown? would ye stay for them from having husbands? nay, my daughters; for it grieveth me much for your sakes that the hand of the Lord is gone out against me. 14 And they lifted up their voice, and wept again: and Orpah kissed her mother-in-law; but Ruth clave unto her.

15 And she said, Behold, thy sister-in-law is gone back unto her people, and unto her gods: return thou after thy sister-in-law. 16 And Ruth said, Entreat me not to leave thee, or to return from following after thee: for whither thou goest, I will go; and where thou lodgest, I will lodge: thy people shall be my people, and thy God my God: 17 Where thou diest, will I die, and there will I be buried: the Lord do so to me, and more also, if aught but death part thee and me. 18 When she saw that she was steadfastly minded to go with her, then she left speaking unto her.

19 So they two went until they came to Bethlehem. And it came to pass, when they were come to Bethlehem, that all the city was

moved about them, and they said, Is this Naomi? 20 And she said unto them, Call me not Naomi, call me Mara: for the Almighty hath dealt very bitterly with me. 21 I went out full, and the Lord hath brought me home again empty: why then call ye me Naomi, seeing the Lord hath testified against me, and the Almighty hath afflicted me? 22 So Naomi returned, and Ruth the Moabitess, her daughter-in-law, with her, which returned out of the country of Moab: and they came to Bethlehem in the beginning of barley harvest.

2 And Naomi had a kinsman of her husband's, a mighty man of wealth, of the family of Elimelech; and his name was Boaz. 2 And Ruth the Moabitess said unto Naomi, Let me now go to the field, and glean ears of corn after him in whose sight I shall find grace. And she said unto her, Go, my daughter. 3 And she went, and came, and gleaned in the field after the reapers: and her hap was to light on a part of the field belonging unto Boaz, who was of the kindred of Elimelech. 4 And, behold, Boaz came from Bethlehem, and said unto the reapers, The Lord be with you. And they answered him, The Lord bless thee. 5 Then said Boaz unto his servant that was set over the reapers, Whose damsel is this? 6 And the servant that was set over the reapers answered and said, It is the Moabitish damsel that came back with Naomi out of the country of Moab: 7 And she said, I pray you, let me glean and gather after the reapers among the sheaves: so she came, and hath continued even from the morning until now, that she tarried a little in the house.

8 Then said Boaz unto Ruth, Hearest thou not, my daughter? Go not to glean in another field, neither go from hence, but abide here fast by my maidens: 9 Let thine eyes be on the field that they do reap, and go thou after them: have I not charged the young men that they shall not touch thee? and when thou art athirst, go unto the vessels, and drink of that which the young men have drawn. 10 Then she fell on her face, and bowed herself to the ground, and said unto him, Why have I found grace in thine eyes, that thou shouldest take knowledge of me, seeing I am a stranger? 11 And Boaz answered and said unto her, It hath fully been showed me, all that thou hast done unto thy mother-in-law since the death of thine husband; and how thou hast left thy father and thy mother, and the land of thy nativity, and art come unto a people which thou knewest not heretofore. 12 The Lord recompense thy work, and a full reward be given thee of the Lord God of Israel, under whose wings thou art come to trust. 13 Then she said, Let me find favor in thy sight, my lord; for that thou hast comforted me, and for that thou hast spoken friendly unto thine handmaid, though I be not like unto one of thine handmaidens.

14 And Boaz said unto her, At mealtime come thou hither, and eat of the bread, and dip thy morsel in the vinegar. And she sat beside the reapers: and he reached her parched corn, and she did eat, and was sufficed, and left. 15 And when she was risen up to glean, Boaz commanded his young men, saying, Let her glean even among the

sheaves, and reproach her not: 16 And let fall also some of the hand-fuls of purpose for her, and leave them, that she may glean them, and rebuke her not.

17 So she gleaned in the field until even, and beat out that she had gleaned: and it was about an ephah of barley. 18 And she took it up, and went into the city; and her mother-in-law saw what she had gleaned: and she brought forth, and gave to her that she had reserved after she was sufficed. 19 And her mother-in-law said unto her, Where hast thou gleaned to-day? and where wroughtest thou? blessed be he that did take knowledge of thee. And she showed her mother-in-law with whom she had wrought, and said, The man's name with whom I wrought to-day is Boaz. 20 And Naomi said unto her daughter-in-law, Blessed be he of the Lord, who hath not left off his kindness to the living and to the dead. And Naomi said unto her, The man is near of kin unto us, one of our next kinsmen. 21 And Ruth the Moabitess said, He said unto me also, Thou shalt keep fast by my young men, until they have ended all my harvest. 22 And Naomi said unto Ruth her daughter-in-law, It is good, my daughter, that thou go out with his maidens, that they meet thee not in any other field. 23 So she kept fast by the maidens of Boaz to glean unto the end of barley harvest and of wheat harvest; and dwelt with her mother-in-law.

3   Then Naomi her mother-in-law said unto her, My daughter, shall I not seek rest for thee, that it may be well with thee? 2 And now is not Boaz of our kindred, with whose maidens thou wast? Behold, he winnoweth barley to-night in the threshingfloor. 3 Wash thyself therefore, and anoint thee, and put thy raiment upon thee, and get thee down to the floor: but make not thyself known unto the man, until he shall have done eating and drinking. 4 And it shall be, when he lieth down, that thou shalt mark the place where he shall lie, and thou shalt go in, and uncover his feet, and lay thee down; and he will tell thee what thou shalt do. 5 And she said unto her, All that thou sayest unto me I will do.

6 And she went down unto the floor, and did according to all that her mother-in-law bade her. 7 And when Boaz had eaten and drunk, and his heart was merry, he went to lie down at the end of the heap of corn: and she came softly, and uncovered his feet, and laid her down. 8 And it came to pass at midnight, that the man was afraid, and turned himself: and, behold, a woman lay at his feet. 9 And he said, Who art thou? And she answered, I am Ruth thine handmaid: spread therefore thy skirt over thine handmaid; for thou art a near kinsman. 10 And he said, Blessed be thou of the Lord, my daughter; for thou hast showed more kindness in the latter end than at the beginning, inasmuch as thou followedst not young men, whether poor or rich. 11 And now, my daughter, fear not; I will do to thee all that thou requirest: for all the city of my people doth know that thou art a virtuous woman. 12 And now it is true that I am thy near kinsman: howbeit there is a kinsman nearer than I. 13 Tarry this night, and it

shall be in the morning, that if he will perform unto thee the part of a kinsman, well; let him do the kinsman's part: but if he will not do the part of a kinsman to thee, then will I do the part of a kinsman to thee, as the Lord liveth: lie down until the morning.

14 And she lay at his feet until the morning: and she rose up before one could know another. And he said, Let it not be known that a woman came into the floor. 15 Also he said, Bring the veil that thou hast upon thee, and hold it. And when she held it, he measured six measures of barley, and laid it on her: and she went into the city. 16 And when she came to her mother-in-law, she said, Who art thou, my daughter? And she told her all that the man had done to her. 17 And she said, These six measures of barley gave he me; for he said to me, Go not empty unto thy mother-in-law. 18 Then said she, Sit still, my daughter, until thou know how the matter will fall: for the man will not be in rest, until he have finished the thing this day.

4 Then went Boaz up to the gate, and sat him down there: and, behold, the kinsman of whom Boaz spake came by; unto whom he said, Ho, such a one! turn aside, sit down here. And he turned aside, and sat down. 2 And he took ten men of the elders of the city, and said, Sit ye down here. And they sat down. 3 And he said unto the kinsman, Naomi, that is come again out of the country of Moab, selleth a parcel of land, which was our brother Elimelech's: 4 And I thought to advertise thee, saying, Buy it before the inhabitants, and before the elders of my people. If thou wilt redeem it, redeem it: but if thou wilt not redeem it, then tell me, that I may know: for there is none to redeem it besides thee; and I am after thee. And he said, I will redeem it. 5 Then said Boaz, What day thou buyest the field of the hand of Naomi, thou must buy it also of Ruth the Moabitess, the wife of the dead, to raise up the name of the dead upon his inheritance. 6 And the kinsman said, I cannot redeem it for myself, lest I mar mine own inheritance: redeem thou my right to thyself; for I cannot redeem it.

7 Now this was the manner in former time in Israel concerning redeeming and concerning changing, for to confirm all things; a man plucked off his shoe, and gave it to his neighbor: and this was a testimony in Israel. 8 Therefore the kinsman said unto Boaz, Buy it for thee. So he drew off his shoe. 9 And Boaz said unto the elders, and unto all the people, Ye are witnesses this day, that I have bought all that was Elimelech's, and all that was Chilion's and Mahlon's, of the hand of Naomi. 10 Moreover Ruth the Moabitess, the wife of Mahlon, have I purchased to be my wife, to raise up the name of the dead upon his inheritance, that the name of the dead be not cut off from among his brethren, and from the gate of his place: ye are witnesses this day. 11 And all the people that were in the gate, and the elders, said, We are witnesses. The Lord make the woman that is come into thine house like Rachel and like Leah, which two did build the house of Israel: and do thou worthily in Ephratah, and be famous

in Bethlehem: 12 And let thy house be like the house of Pharez, whom Tamar bare unto Judah, of the seed which the Lord shall give thee of this young woman.

13 So Boaz took Ruth, and she was his wife: and when he went in unto her, the Lord gave her conception, and she bare a son. 14 And the women said unto Naomi, Blessed be the Lord, which hath not left thee this day without a kinsman, that his name may be famous in Israel. 15 And he shall be unto thee a restorer of thy life, and a nourisher of thine old age: for thy daughter-in-law, which loveth thee, which is better to thee than seven sons, hath borne him. 16 And Naomi took the child, and laid it in her bosom, and became nurse unto it. 17 And the women her neighbors gave it a name, saying, There is a son born to Naomi; and they called his name Obed: he is the father of Jesse, the father of David.

18 Now these are the generations of Pharez: Pharez begat Hezron, 19 And Hezron begat Ram, and Ram begat Amminadab, 20 And Amminadab begat Nahshon, and Nahshon begat Salmon, 21 And Salmon begat Boaz, and Boaz begat Obed, 22 And Obed begat Jesse, and Jesse begat David.

# The Epic of David:
## *First and Second Samuel, First Kings*

The great epic hero of Israel was, in my judgment, King David. In him was summarized the best of Hebrew life and faith, along with the kind of human qualities which makes a man loved as well as honored. His characterization is etched with such clarity and credibility that we can know him, as Shakespeare says of the elder Hamlet, "in his habit as he lived."

The early years of David were intimately associated with the reign of Saul, the first king of Israel, and Saul's story in its turn was closely related to the story of Samuel, the last great judge of Israel. It is with Samuel, then, that we begin. There is about Samuel the aura of a great figure who leads his people so effectively that they are prepared to go beyond the limits of his vision. When the Israelites come to Samuel to ask him to anoint a king for them, he protests with the vehemence of one to whom the old days seem necessarily good, though it is hard to see how the chaos of the rule of Judges could have appealed to a man of Samuel's wisdom. He does, however, anoint Saul to be King, and here begins the moving story of Saul's unrealized opportunities. From the beauty and promise of his early days to the erratic madness and bitter jealousies of his last years, Saul is an appealing and tragic figure. What Shakespeare has Brutus say of Caesar might also be said of Saul:

> The abuse of greatness is, when it disjoins
> Remorse from power.

When David makes his first appearance, it is as an adolescent youngster tending his father's sheep. Though already anointed by Samuel to succeed Saul as King of Israel, David does not command the center of our attention until his dramatic encounter with Goliath, the Philistine giant. His first public utterance is his response to the contemptuous challenge of Goliath, and then he speaks in words which are characteristic of his whole outlook. In its modesty and reliance upon God rather than upon the might of his own right arm, his speech stands in marked contrast with "the heroic boast" of the epic warriors of the Classical and Teutonic traditions, and serves to underscore the typically Biblical conception of the hero. He never postures, never poses as an ideal man. His concern for others is obviously genuine, and he can release one of his mercenary captains from his fealty as he retreats before the rebel forces of his own son Absalom, just as he can patiently endure the taunts of Shimei because he knows that he has not been able to retain the loyalty of his own favorite child. His generosity towards King Saul, whether dead or alive, is constant, and his care for Jonathan's crippled son Mephibosheth is one of the brightest signs in a dark and cruel age. His repeated reaction to his own enemies is to treat them with clemency, but as a practical man he knows that his son and successor, Solomon, cannot in his youth and inexperience afford to show the tolerance which has marked David's own reign, and he advises Solomon to execute dangerous opponents and unpredictable supporters alike, in order to avoid the return of chaos. He is far from perfect: in his later days he can anger God by yielding to the temptations inherent in his power by numbering his people, as a gesture of reliance upon his own great might, while in the days of his prime he arranged the assassination of a faithful army captain so as to steal his wife. What is most remarkable is not that he did these things, but rather that he never extenuated his guilt or sought to explain it away. The great leader of a religion with radically exclusive claims, he was yet able to entrust the keeping of the sacred Ark of the Covenant to a converted Philistine, and he consistently attracted to his own side many of his one-time enemies. With all his dignity and concern for others, he was able to reduce an enemy commander to a laughingstock before two armies, when it was necessary to do so in order to preserve the peace.

In sum, David is a tremendous figure: mighty in his anger, and yet essentially and repeatedly compassionate; greatly ambitious, yet startlingly scrupulous in his unwillingness to destroy Saul, or even lesser enemies and opponents; a passionate lover, yet ethically concerned for his own actions; totally dedicated to the welfare of Israel, yet capable of remarkable friendships with the surrounding peoples. Throughout, he is intimately related to his God, and lives consciously in his presence. The personalities surrounding him are vitally and credibly portrayed to provide a sweeping panorama of individuals and communities, above all of which towers the epic figure of David, under God.

# First Samuel

## THE YOUNG SAMUEL

1 Now there was a certain man of Ramathaim-zophim, of mount Ephraim, and his name was Elkanah, the son of Jeroham, the son of Elihu, the son of Tohu, the son of Zuph, an Ephrathite: 2 And he

had two wives; the name of the one was Hannah, and the name of the other Peninnah: and Peninnah had children, but Hannah had no children. 3 And this man went up out of his city yearly to worship and to sacrifice unto the Lord of hosts in Shiloh. And the two sons of Eli, Hophni and Phinehas, the priests of the Lord, were there. 4 And when the time was that Elkanah offered, he gave to Peninnah his wife, and to all her sons and her daughters, portions: 5 But unto Hannah he gave a worthy portion; for he loved Hannah: but the Lord had shut up her womb. 6 And her adversary also provoked her sore, for to make her fret, because the Lord had shut up her womb. 7 And as he did so year by year, when she went up to the house of the Lord, so she provoked her; therefore she wept, and did not eat. 8 Then said Elkanah her husband to her, Hannah, why weepest thou? and why eatest thou not? and why is thy heart grieved? am not I better to thee than ten sons?

9 So Hannah rose up after they had eaten in Shiloh, and after they had drunk. Now Eli the priest sat upon a seat by a post of the temple of the Lord. 10 And she was in bitterness of soul, and prayed unto the Lord, and wept sore. 11 And she vowed a vow, and said, O Lord of hosts, if thou wilt indeed look on the affliction of thine handmaid, and remember me, and not forget thine handmaid, but wilt give unto thine handmaid a man child, then I will give him unto the Lord all the days of his life, and there shall no razor come upon his head. 12 And it came to pass, as she continued praying before the Lord, that Eli marked her mouth. 13 Now Hannah, she spake in her heart; only her lips moved, but her voice was not heard: therefore Eli thought she had been drunken. 14 And Eli said unto her, How long wilt thou be drunken? put away thy wine from thee. 15 And Hannah answered and said, No, my lord, I am a woman of a sorrowful spirit: I have drunk neither wine nor strong drink, but have poured out my soul before the Lord. 16 Count not thine handmaid for a daughter of Belial: for out of the abundance of my complaint and grief have I spoken hitherto. 17 Then Eli answered and said, Go in peace: and the God of Israel grant thee thy petition that thou hast asked of him. 18 And she said, Let thine handmaid find grace in thy sight. So the woman went her way, and did eat, and her countenance was no more sad. 19 And they rose up in the morning early, and worshipped before the Lord, and returned, and came to their house to Ramah: and Elkanah knew Hannah his wife; and the Lord remembered her. 20 Wherefore it came to pass, when the time was come about after Hannah had conceived, that she bare a son, and called his name Samuel, saying, Because I have asked him of the Lord.

21 And the man Elkanah, and all his house, went up to offer unto the Lord the yearly sacrifice, and his vow. 22 But Hannah went not up; for she said unto her husband, I will not go up until the child be weaned, and then I will bring him, that he may appear before the Lord, and there abide for ever. 23 And Elkanah her husband said unto her, Do what seemeth thee good; tarry until thou have weaned him;

only the Lord establish his word. So the woman abode, and gave her son suck until she weaned him. 24 And when she had weaned him, she took him up with her, with three bullocks, and one ephah of flour, and a bottle of wine, and brought him unto the house of the Lord in Shiloh: and the child was young. 25 And they slew a bullock, and brought the child to Eli. 26 And she said, O my lord, as thy soul liveth, my lord, I am the woman that stood by thee here, praying unto the Lord. 27 For this child I prayed; and the Lord hath given me my petition which I asked of him: 28 Therefore also I have lent him to the Lord; as long as he liveth he shall be lent to the Lord. And he worshipped the Lord there.

2 And Hannah prayed, and said,
 My heart rejoiceth in the Lord,
 Mine horn is exalted in the Lord;
 My mouth is enlarged over mine enemies;
 Because I rejoice in thy salvation.
2 There is none holy as the Lord:
 For there is none besides thee:
 Neither is there any rock like our God.
3 Talk no more so exceeding proudly;
 Let not arrogancy come out of your mouth:
 For the Lord is a God of knowledge,
 And by him actions are weighed.
4 The bows of the mighty men are broken,
 And they that stumbled are girded with strength.
5 They that were full have hired out themselves for bread;
 And they that were hungry ceased:
 So that the barren hath borne seven;
 And she that hath many children is waxed feeble.
6 The Lord killeth, and maketh alive:
 He bringeth down to the grave, and bringeth up.
7 The Lord maketh poor, and maketh rich:
 He bringeth low, and lifteth up.
8 He raiseth up the poor out of the dust,
 And lifteth up the beggar from the dunghill,
 To set them among princes,
 And to make them inherit the throne of glory:
 For the pillars of the earth are the Lord's,
 And he hath set the world upon them.
9 He will keep the feet of his saints,
 And the wicked shall be silent in darkness;
 For by strength shall no man prevail.
10 The adversaries of the Lord shall be broken to pieces;
 Out of heaven shall he thunder upon them:
 The Lord shall judge the ends of the earth;
 And he shall give strength unto his king,
 And exalt the horn of his anointed.

11 And Elkanah went to Ramah to his house. And the child did minister unto the Lord before Eli the priest.

12 Now the sons of Eli were sons of Belial; they knew not the Lord. 13 And the priest's custom with the people was, that, when any man offered sacrifice, the priest's servant came, while the flesh was in seething, with a fleshhook of three teeth in his hand; 14 And he struck it into the pan, or kettle, or caldron, or pot; all that the fleshhook brought up the priest took for himself. So they did in Shiloh unto all the Israelites that came thither. 15 Also before they burnt the fat, the priest's servant came, and said to the man that sacrificed, Give flesh to roast for the priest; for he will not have sodden flesh of thee, but raw. 16 And if any man said unto him, Let them not fail to burn the fat presently, and then take as much as thy soul desireth; then he would answer him, Nay; but thou shalt give it me now: and if not, I will take it by force. 17 Wherefore the sin of the young men was very great before the Lord: for men abhorred the offering of the Lord.

18 But Samuel ministered before the Lord, being a child, girded with a linen ephod. 19 Moreover his mother made him a little coat, and brought it to him from year to year, when she came up with her husband to offer the yearly sacrifice. 20 And Eli blessed Elkanah and his wife, and said, The Lord give thee seed of this woman for the loan which is lent to the Lord. And they went unto their own home. 21 And the Lord visited Hannah, so that she conceived, and bare three sons and two daughters. And the child Samuel grew before the Lord.

22 Now Eli was very old, and heard all that his sons did unto all Israel; and how they lay with the women that assembled at the door of the tabernacle of the congregation. 23 And he said unto them, Why do ye such things? for I hear of your evil dealings by all this people. 24 Nay, my sons; for it is no good report that I hear: ye make the Lord's people to transgress. 25 If one man sin against another, the judge shall judge him: but if a man sin against the Lord, who shall entreat for him? Notwithstanding, they hearkened not unto the voice of their father, because the Lord would slay them. 26 And the child Samuel grew on, and was in favor both with the Lord, and also with men.

27 And there came a man of God unto Eli, and said unto him, Thus saith the Lord, Did I plainly appear unto the house of thy father, when they were in Egypt in Pharaoh's house? 28 And did I choose him out of all the tribes of Israel to be my priest, to offer upon mine altar, to burn incense, to wear an ephod before me? and did I give unto the house of thy father all the offerings made by fire of the children of Israel? 29 Wherefore kick ye at my sacrifice and at mine offering, which I have commanded in my habitation; and honorest thy sons above me, to make yourselves fat with the chiefest of all the offerings of Israel my people? 30 Wherefore the Lord God of Israel saith, I said indeed that thy house, and the house of thy father, should walk before me for ever: but now the Lord saith, Be it far from me; for them that honor me I will honor, and they that despise me shall

be lightly esteemed. 31 Behold, the days come, that I will cut off thine arm, and the arm of thy father's house, that there shall not be an old man in thine house. 32 And thou shalt see an enemy in my habitation in all the wealth which God shall give Israel: and there shall not be an old man in thine house for ever. 33 And the man of thine, whom I shall not cut off from mine altar, shall be to consume thine eyes, and to grieve thine heart: and all the increase of thine house shall die in the flower of their age. 34 And this shall be a sign unto thee, that shall come upon thy two sons, on Hophni and Phinehas; in one day they shall die both of them. 35 And I will raise me up a faithful priest, that shall do according to that which is in mine heart and in my mind: and I will build him a sure house; and he shall walk before mine anointed for ever. 36 And it shall come to pass, that every one that is left in thine house shall come and crouch to him for a piece of silver and a morsel of bread, and shall say, Put me, I pray thee, into one of the priests' offices, that I may eat a piece of bread.

3 And the child Samuel ministered unto the Lord before Eli. And the word of the Lord was precious in those days; there was no open vision. 2 And it came to pass at that time, when Eli was laid down in his place, and his eyes began to wax dim, that he could not see; 3 And ere the lamp of God went out in the temple of the Lord, where the ark of God was, and Samuel was laid down to sleep; 4 That the Lord called Samuel: and he answered, Here am I. 5 And he ran unto Eli, and said, Here am I; for thou calledst me. And he said, I called not; lie down again. And he went and lay down. 6 And the Lord called yet again, Samuel. And Samuel arose and went to Eli, and said, Here am I; for thou didst call me. And he answered, I called not, my son; lie down again. 7 Now Samuel did not yet know the Lord, neither was the word of the Lord yet revealed unto him. 8 And the Lord called Samuel again the third time. And he arose and went to Eli, and said, Here am I; for thou didst call me. And Eli perceived that the Lord had called the child. 9 Therefore Eli said unto Samuel, Go, lie down: and it shall be, if he call thee, that thou shalt say, Speak, Lord; for thy servant heareth. So Samuel went and lay down in his place.

10 And the Lord came, and stood, and called as at other times, Samuel, Samuel. Then Samuel answered, Speak; for thy servant heareth. 11 And the Lord said to Samuel, Behold, I will do a thing in Israel, at which both the ears of every one that heareth it shall tingle. 12 In that day I will perform against Eli all things which I have spoken concerning his house: when I begin, I will also make an end. 13 For I have told him that I will judge his house for ever for the iniquity which he knoweth; because his sons made themselves vile, and he restrained them not. 14 And therefore I have sworn unto the house of Eli, that the iniquity of Eli's house shall not be purged with sacrifice nor offering for ever. 15 And Samuel lay until the morning, and opened the doors of the house of the Lord. And Samuel feared to

show Eli the vision. 16 Then Eli called Samuel, and said, Samuel, my son. And he answered, Here am I. 17 And he said, What is the thing that the Lord hath said unto thee? I pray thee hide it not from me: God do so to thee, and more also, if thou hide any thing from me of all the things that he said unto thee. 18 And Samuel told him every whit, and hid nothing from him. And he said, It is the Lord: let him do what seemeth him good.

19 And Samuel grew, and the Lord was with him, and did let none of his words fall to the ground. 20 And all Israel from Dan even to Beer-sheba knew that Samuel was established to be a prophet of the Lord. 21 And the Lord appeared again in Shiloh: for the Lord revealed himself to Samuel in Shiloh by the word of the Lord.

4 And the word of Samuel came to all Israel.

### PHILISTINE WARS

Now Israel went out against the Philistines to battle, and pitched beside Ebenezer: and the Philistines pitched in Aphek. 2 And the Philistines put themselves in array against Israel: and when they joined battle, Israel was smitten before the Philistines: and they slew of the army in the field about four thousand men. 3 And when the people were come into the camp, the elders of Israel said, Wherefore hath the Lord smitten us to-day before the Philistines? Let us fetch the ark of the covenant of the Lord out of Shiloh unto us, that, when it cometh among us, it may save us out of the hand of our enemies. 4 So the people sent to Shiloh, that they might bring from thence the ark of the covenant of the Lord of hosts, which dwelleth between the cherubim: and the two sons of Eli, Hophni and Phinehas, were there with the ark of the covenant of God. 5 And when the ark of the covenant of the Lord came into the camp, all Israel shouted with a great shout, so that the earth rang again. 6 And when the Philistines heard the noise of the shout, they said, What meaneth the noise of this great shout in the camp of the Hebrews? And they understood that the ark of the Lord was come into the camp. 7 And the Philistines were afraid; for they said, God is come into the camp. And they said, Woe unto us! for there hath not been such a thing heretofore. 8 Woe unto us! who shall deliver us out of the hand of these mighty Gods? these are the Gods that smote the Egyptians with all the plagues in the wilderness. 9 Be strong, and quit yourselves like men, O ye Philistines, that ye be not servants unto the Hebrews, as they have been to you: quit yourselves like men, and fight. 10 And the Philistines fought, and Israel was smitten, and they fled every man into his tent: and there was a very great slaughter; for there fell of Israel thirty thousand footmen. 11 And the ark of God was taken; and the two sons of Eli, Hophni and Phinehas, were slain.

12 And there ran a man of Benjamin out of the army, and came to Shiloh the same day with his clothes rent, and with earth upon his

head. 13 And when he came, lo, Eli sat upon a seat by the wayside watching: for his heart trembled for the ark of God. And when the man came into the city, and told it, all the city cried out. 14 And when Eli heard the noise of the crying, he said, What meaneth the noise of this tumult? And the man came in hastily, and told Eli. 15 Now Eli was ninety and eight years old; and his eyes were dim, that he could not see. 16 And the man said unto Eli, I am he that came out of the army, and I fled to-day out of the army. And he said, What is there done, my son? 17 And the messenger answered and said, Israel is fled before the Philistines, and there hath been also a great slaughter among the people, and thy two sons also, Hophni and Phinehas, are dead, and the ark of God is taken. 18 And it came to pass, when he made mention of the ark of God, that he fell from off the seat backward by the side of the gate, and his neck brake, and he died: for he was an old man, and heavy. And he had judged Israel forty years.

19 And his daughter-in-law, Phinehas' wife, was with child, near to be delivered: and when she heard the tidings that the ark of God was taken, and that her father-in-law and her husband were dead, she bowed herself and travailed; for her pains came upon her. 20 And about the time of her death the women that stood by her said unto her, Fear not; for thou hast borne a son. But she answered not, neither did she regard it. 21 And she named the child I-chabod, saying, The glory is departed from Israel: because the ark of God was taken, and because of her father-in-law and her husband. 22 And she said, The glory is departed from Israel: for the ark of God is taken.

5 And the Philistines took the ark of God, and brought it from Eben-ezer unto Ashdod. 2 When the Philistines took the ark of God, they brought it into the house of Dagon, and set it by Dagon. 3 And when they of Ashdod arose early on the morrow, behold, Dagon was fallen upon his face to the earth before the ark of the Lord. And they took Dagon, and set him in his place again. 4 And when they arose early on the morrow morning, behold, Dagon was fallen upon his face to the ground before the ark of the Lord; and the head of Dagon and both the palms of his hands were cut off upon the threshold; only the stump of Dagon was left to him. 5 Therefore neither the priests of Dagon, nor any that come into Dagon's house, tread on the threshold of Dagon in Ashdod unto this day.

6 But the hand of the Lord was heavy upon them of Ashdod, and he destroyed them, and smote them with emerods,[1] even Ashdod and the coasts thereof. 11 So they sent and gathered together all the lords of the Philistines, and said, Send away the ark of the God of Israel, and let it go again to his own place, that it slay us not, and our people: for there was a deadly destruction throughout all the city; the hand of God was very heavy there. 12 And the men that died not

---

[1] Perhaps, tumors.

were smitten with the emerods: and the cry of the city went up to heaven.

6 And the ark of the Lord was in the country of the Philistines seven months. 2 And the Philistines called for the priests and the diviners, saying, What shall we do to the ark of the Lord? tell us wherewith we shall send it to his place. 3 And they said, If ye send away the ark of the God of Israel, send it not empty; but in any wise return him a trespass offering: then ye shall be healed, and it shall be known to you why his hand is not removed from you. 4 Then said they, What shall be the trespass offering which we shall return to him? They answered, Five golden emerods, and five golden mice, according to the number of the lords of the Philistines: for one plague was on you all, and on your lords. 5 Wherefore ye shall make images of your emerods, and images of your mice that mar the land; and ye shall give glory unto the God of Israel: peradventure he will lighten his hand from off you, and from off your gods, and from off your land. 6 Wherefore then do ye harden your hearts, as the Egyptians and Pharaoh hardened their hearts? when he had wrought wonderfully among them, did they not let the people go, and they departed? 7 Now therefore make a new cart, and take two milch kine, on which there hath come no yoke, and tie the kine to the cart, and bring their calves home from them: 8 And take the ark of the Lord, and lay it upon the cart; and put the jewels of gold, which ye return him for a trespass offering, in a coffer by the side thereof; and send it away, that it may go. 9 And see, if it goeth up by the way of his own coast to Beth-shemesh, then he hath done us this great evil: but if not, then we shall know that it is not his hand that smote us; it was a chance that happened to us.

10 And the men did so; and took two milch kine, and tied them to the cart, and shut up their calves at home: 11 And they laid the ark of the Lord upon the cart, and the coffer with the mice of gold and the images of their emerods. 12 And the kine took the straight way to the way of Beth-shemesh, and went along the highway, lowing as they went, and turned not aside to the right hand or to the left; and the lords of the Philistines went after them unto the border of Beth-shemesh. 13 And they of Beth-shemesh were reaping their wheat harvest in the valley: and they lifted up their eyes, and saw the ark, and rejoiced to see it. 14 And the cart came into the field of Joshua, a Beth-shemite, and stood there, where there was a great stone: and they clave the wood of the cart, and offered the kine a burnt offering unto the Lord. 15 And the Levites took down the ark of the Lord, and the coffer that was with it, wherein the jewels of gold were, and put them on the great stone: and the men of Beth-shemesh offered burnt offerings and sacrificed sacrifices the same day unto the Lord. 16 And when the five lords of the Philistines had seen it, they returned to Ekron the same day.

7 And the men of Kirjath-jearim came, and fetched up the ark of the Lord, and brought it into the house of Abinadab in the hill, and sanctified Eleazar his son to keep the ark of the Lord. 2 And it came to pass, while the ark abode in Kirjath-jearim, that the time was long; for it was twenty years: and all the house of Israel lamented after the Lord.

## SAMUEL AS THE LAST OF THE JUDGES

3 And Samuel spake unto all the house of Israel, saying, If ye do return unto the Lord with all your hearts, then put away the strange gods and Ashtaroth from among you, and prepare your hearts unto the Lord, and serve him only: and he will deliver you out of the hand of the Philistines. 4 Then the children of Israel did put away Baalim and Ashtaroth, and served the Lord only.

5 And Samuel said, Gather all Israel to Mizpeh, and I will pray for you unto the Lord. 6 And they gathered together to Mizpeh, and drew water, and poured it out before the Lord, and fasted on that day, and said there, We have sinned against the Lord. And Samuel judged the children of Israel in Mizpeh. 7 And when the Philistines heard that the children of Israel were gathered together to Mizpeh, the lords of the Philistines went up against Israel. And when the children of Israel heard it, they were afraid of the Philistines. 8 And the children of Israel said to Samuel, Cease not to cry unto the Lord our God for us, that he will save us out of the hand of the Philistines. 9 And Samuel took a sucking lamb, and offered it for a burnt offering wholly unto the Lord: and Samuel cried unto the Lord for Israel; and the Lord heard him. 10 And as Samuel was offering up the burnt offering, the Philistines drew near to battle against Israel: but the Lord thundered with a great thunder on that day upon the Philistines, and discomfited them; and they were smitten before Israel. 11 And the men of Israel went out of Mizpeh, and pursued the Philistines, and smote them, until they came under Beth-car. 12 Then Samuel took a stone, and set it between Mizpeh and Shen, and called the name of it Eben-ezer, saying, Hitherto hath the Lord helped us.

13 So the Philistines were subdued, and they came no more into the coast of Israel: and the hand of the Lord was against the Philistines all the days of Samuel. 14 And the cities which the Philistines had taken from Israel were restored to Israel, from Ekron even unto Gath; and the coasts thereof did Israel deliver out of the hands of the Philistines. And there was peace between Israel and the Amorites. 15 And Samuel judged Israel all the days of his life. 16 And he went from year to year in circuit to Beth-el, and Gilgal, and Mizpeh, and judged Israel in all those places. 17 And his return was to Ramah, for there was his house; and there he judged Israel; and there he built an altar unto the Lord.

8 And it came to pass, when Samuel was old, that he made his sons judges over Israel. 2 Now the name of his firstborn was Joel; and the name of his second, Abiah: they were judges in Beer-sheba. 3 And his sons walked not in his ways, but turned aside after lucre, and took bribes, and perverted judgment.

4 Then all the elders of Israel gathered themselves together, and came to Samuel unto Ramah, 5 And said unto him, Behold, thou art old, and thy sons walk not in thy ways: now make us a king to judge us like all the nations. 6 But the thing displeased Samuel, when they said, Give us a king to judge us. And Samuel prayed unto the Lord. 7 And the Lord said unto Samuel, Hearken unto the voice of the people in all that they say unto thee: for they have not rejected thee, but they have rejected me, that I should not reign over them. 8 According to all the works which they have done since the day that I brought them up out of Egypt even unto this day, wherewith they have forsaken me, and served other gods, so do they also unto thee. 9 Now therefore hearken unto their voice: howbeit yet protest solemnly unto them, and show them the manner of the king that shall reign over them.

10 And Samuel told all the words of the Lord unto the people that asked of him a king. 11 And he said, This will be the manner of the king that shall reign over you: He will take your sons, and appoint them for himself, for his chariots, and to be his horsemen; and some shall run before his chariots. 12 And he will appoint him captains over thousands, and captains over fifties; and will set them to ear[1] his ground, and to reap his harvest, and to make his instruments of war, and instruments of his chariots. 13 And he will take your daughters to be confectionaries, and to be cooks, and to be bakers. 14 And he will take your fields, and your vineyards, and your oliveyards, even the best of them, and give them to his servants. 15 And he will take the tenth of your seed, and of your vineyards, and give to his officers, and to his servants. 16 And he will take your menservants, and your maidservants, and your goodliest young men, and your asses, and put them to his work. 17 He will take the tenth of your sheep: and ye shall be his servants. 18 And ye shall cry out in that day because of your king which ye shall have chosen you; and the Lord will not hear you in that day. 19 Nevertheless the people refused to obey the voice of Samuel; and they said, Nay; but we will have a king over us; 20 That we also may be like all the nations; and that our king may judge us, and go out before us, and fight our battles. 21 And Samuel heard all the words of the people, and he rehearsed them in the ears of the Lord. 22 And the Lord said to Samuel, Hearken unto their voice, and make them a king. And Samuel said unto the men of Israel, Go ye every man unto his city.

[1] Plow.

### SAMUEL AND SAUL

9 Now there was a man of Benjamin, whose name was Kish, the son of Abiel, the son of Zeror, the son of Bechorath, the son of Aphiah, a Benjamite, a mighty man of power. 2 And he had a son, whose name was Saul, a choice young man, and a goodly: and there was not among the children of Israel a goodlier person than he: from his shoulders and upward he was higher than any of the people. 3 And the asses of Kish Saul's father were lost. And Kish said to Saul his son, Take now one of the servants with thee, and arise, go seek the asses. 4 And he passed through mount Ephraim, and passed through the land of Shalisha, but they found them not: then they passed through the land of Shalim, and there they were not: and he passed through the land of the Benjamites, but they found them not.

5 And when they were come to the land of Zuph, Saul said to his servant that was with him, Come, and let us return; lest my father leave caring for the asses, and take thought for us. 6 And he said unto him, Behold now, there is in this city a man of God, and he is an honorable man; all that he saith cometh surely to pass: now let us go thither; peradventure he can show us our way that we should go. 7 Then said Saul to his servant, But, behold, if we go, what shall we bring the man? for the bread is spent in our vessels, and there is not a present to bring to the man of God: what have we? 8 And the servant answered Saul again, and said, Behold, I have here at hand the fourth part of a shekel of silver: that will I give to the man of God, to tell us our way. 9 (Beforetime in Israel, when a man went to inquire of God, thus he spake, Come, and let us go to the seer: for he that is now called a Prophet was beforetime called a Seer.) 10 Then said Saul to his servant, Well said; come, let us go. So they went unto the city where the man of God was. 11 And as they went up the hill to the city, they found young maidens going out to draw water, and said unto them, Is the seer here? 12 And they answered them, and said, He is; behold, he is before you: make haste now, for he came to-day to the city; for there is a sacrifice of the people to-day in the high place: 13 As soon as ye be come into the city, ye shall straightway find him, before he go up to the high place to eat: for the people will not eat until he come, because he doth bless the sacrifice; and afterward they eat that be bidden. Now therefore get you up; for about this time ye shall find him. 14 And they went up into the city: and when they were come into the city, behold, Samuel came out against them, for to go up to the high place.

15 Now the Lord had told Samuel in his ear a day before Saul came, saying, 16 To-morrow about this time I will send thee a man out of the land of Benjamin, and thou shalt anoint him to be captain over my people Israel, that he may save my people out of the hand of the Philistines: for I have looked upon my people, because their cry is come unto me. 17 And when Samuel saw Saul, the Lord said unto him, Behold the man whom I spake to thee of! this same shall reign

over my people. 18 Then Saul drew near to Samuel in the gate, and said, Tell me, I pray thee, where the seer's house is. 19 And Samuel answered Saul, and said, I am the seer: go up before me unto the high place; for ye shall eat with me to-day, and to-morrow I will let thee go, and will tell thee all that is in thine heart. 20 And as for thine asses that were lost three days ago, set not thy mind on them; for they are found. And on whom is all the desire of Israel? Is it not on thee, and on all thy father's house? 21 And Saul answered and said, Am not I a Benjamite, of the smallest of the tribes of Israel? and my family the least of all the families of the tribe of Benjamin? wherefore then speakest thou so to me?

22 And Samuel took Saul and his servant, and brought them into the parlor, and made them sit in the chiefest place among them that were bidden, which were about thirty persons. 23 And Samuel said unto the cook, Bring the portion which I gave thee, of which I said unto thee, Set it by thee. 24 And the cook took up the shoulder, and that which was upon it, and set it before Saul. And Samuel said, Behold that which is left! set it before thee, and eat: for unto this time hath it been kept for thee since I said, I have invited the people. So Saul did eat with Samuel that day. 25 And when they were come down from the high place into the city, Samuel communed with Saul upon the top of the house. 26 And they arose early: and it came to pass about the spring of the day, that Samuel called Saul to the top of the house, saying, Up, that I may send thee away. And Saul arose, and they went out both of them, he and Samuel, abroad. 27 And as they were going down to the end of the city, Samuel said to Saul, Bid the servant pass on before us, (and he passed on,) but stand thou still a while, that I may show thee the word of God.

10 Then Samuel took a vial of oil, and poured it upon his head, and kissed him, and said, Is it not because the Lord hath anointed thee to be captain over his inheritance? 2 When thou art departed from me to-day, then thou shalt find two men by Rachel's sepulchre in the border of Benjamin at Zelzah; and they will say unto thee, The asses which thou wentest to seek are found: and, lo, thy father hath left the care of the asses, and sorroweth for you, saying, What shall I do for my son? 3 Then shalt thou go on forward from thence, and thou shalt come to the plain of Tabor, and there shall meet thee three men going up to God to Beth-el, one carrying three kids, and another carrying three loaves of bread, and another carrying a bottle of wine: 4 And they will salute thee, and give thee two loaves of bread; which thou shalt receive of their hands. 5 After that thou shalt come to the hill of God, where is the garrison of the Philistines: and it shall come to pass, when thou art come thither to the city, that thou shalt meet a company of prophets coming down from the high place with a psaltery, and a tabret, and a pipe, and a harp, before them; and they shall prophesy: 6 And the Spirit of the Lord will come upon thee, and thou shalt prophesy with them, and shalt be turned into another

man. 7 And let it be, when these signs are come unto thee, that thou do as occasion serve thee; for God is with thee. 8 And thou shalt go down before me to Gilgal; and, behold, I will come down unto thee, to offer burnt offerings, and to sacrifice sacrifices of peace offerings: seven days shalt thou tarry, till I come to thee, and show thee what thou shalt do.

9 And it was so, that, when he had turned his back to go from Samuel, God gave him another heart: and all those signs came to pass that day. 10 And when they came thither to the hill, behold, a company of prophets met him; and the Spirit of God came upon him, and he prophesied among them. 11 And it came to pass, when all that knew him beforetime saw that, behold, he prophesied among the prophets, then the people said one to another, What is this that is come unto the son of Kish? Is Saul also among the prophets? 12 And one of the same place answered and said, But who is their father? Therefore it became a proverb, Is Saul also among the prophets? 13 And when he had made an end of prophesying, he came to the high place.

14 And Saul's uncle said unto him and to his servant, Whither went ye? And he said, To seek the asses: and when we saw that they were no where, we came to Samuel. 15 And Saul's uncle said, Tell me, I pray thee, what Samuel said unto you. 16 And Saul said unto his uncle, He told us plainly that the asses were found. But of the matter of the kingdom, whereof Samuel spake, he told him not.

17 And Samuel called the people together unto the Lord to Mizpeh; 18 And said unto the children of Israel, Thus saith the Lord God of Israel, I brought up Israel out of Egypt, and delivered you out of the hand of the Egyptians, and out of the hand of all kingdoms, and of them that oppressed you: 19 And ye have this day rejected your God, who himself saved you out of all your adversities and your tribulations; and ye have said unto him, Nay, but set a king over us. Now therefore present yourselves before the Lord by your tribes, and by your thousands. 20 And when Samuel had caused all the tribes of Israel to come near, the tribe of Benjamin was taken. 21 When he had caused the tribe of Benjamin to come near by their families, the family of Matri was taken, and Saul the son of Kish was taken: and when they sought him, he could not be found. 22 Therefore they inquired of the Lord further, if the man should yet come thither. And the Lord answered, Behold, he hath hid himself among the stuff. 23 And they ran and fetched him thence: and when he stood among the people, he was higher than any of the people from his shoulders and upward. 24 And Samuel said to all the people, See ye him whom the Lord hath chosen, that there is none like him among all the people? And all the people shouted, and said, God save the king.

25 Then Samuel told the people the manner of the kingdom, and wrote it in a book, and laid it up before the Lord. And Samuel sent all the people away, every man to his house. 26 And Saul also went

home to Gibeah; and there went with him a band of men, whose hearts God had touched. 27 But the children of Belial said, How shall this man save us? And they despised him, and brought him no presents. But he held his peace.

## SAUL AS KING

11 Then Nahash the Ammonite came up, and encamped against Jabesh-gilead: and all the men of Jabesh said unto Nahash, Make a covenant with us, and we will serve thee. 2 And Nahash the Ammonite answered them, On this condition will I make a covenant with you, that I may thrust out all your right eyes, and lay it for a reproach upon all Israel. 3 And the elders of Jabesh said unto him, Give us seven days' respite, that we may send messengers unto all the coasts of Israel: and then, if there be no man to save us, we will come out to thee. 4 Then came the messengers to Gibeah of Saul, and told the tidings in the ears of the people: and all the people lifted up their voices, and wept. 5 And, behold, Saul came after the herd out of the field; and Saul said, What aileth the people that they weep? And they told him the tidings of the men of Jabesh. 6 And the Spirit of God came upon Saul when he heard those tidings, and his anger was kindled greatly. 7 And he took a yoke of oxen, and hewed them in pieces, and sent them throughout all the coasts of Israel by the hands of messengers, saying, Whosoever cometh not forth after Saul and after Samuel, so shall it be done unto his oxen. And the fear of the Lord fell on the people, and they came out with one consent. 8 And when he numbered them in Bezek, the children of Israel were three hundred thousand, and the men of Judah thirty thousand. 9 And they said unto the messengers that came, Thus shall ye say unto the men of Jabesh-gilead, To-morrow, by that time the sun be hot, ye shall have help. And the messengers came and showed it to the men of Jabesh; and they were glad. 10 Therefore the men of Jabesh said, To-morrow we will come out unto you, and ye shall do with us all that seemeth good unto you.

11 And it was so on the morrow, that Saul put the people in three companies; and they came into the midst of the host in the morning watch, and slew the Ammonites until the heat of the day: and it came to pass, that they which remained were scattered, so that two of them were not left together. 12 And the people said unto Samuel, Who is he that said, Shall Saul reign over us? bring the men, that we may put them to death. 13 And Saul said, There shall not a man be put to death this day: for to-day the Lord hath wrought salvation in Israel. 14 Then said Samuel to the people, Come, and let us go to Gilgal, and renew the kingdom there. 15 And all the people went to Gilgal, and there they made Saul king before the Lord in Gilgal; and there they sacrificed sacrifices of peace offerings before the Lord; and there Saul and all the men of Israel rejoiced greatly.

12 And Samuel said unto all Israel, Behold, I have hearkened unto your voice in all that ye said unto me, and have made a king over you. 2 And now, behold, the king walketh before you: and I am old and grayheaded; and, behold, my sons are with you: and I have walked before you from my childhood unto this day. 3 Behold, here I am: witness against me before the Lord, and before his anointed: whose ox have I taken? or whose ass have I taken? or whom have I defrauded? whom have I oppressed? or of whose hand have I received any bribe to blind mine eyes therewith? and I will restore it you. 4 And they said, Thou hast not defrauded us, nor oppressed us, neither hast thou taken aught of any man's hand. 5 And he said unto them, The Lord is witness against you, and his anointed is witness this day, that ye have not found aught in my hand. And they answered, He is witness.

6 And Samuel said unto the people, It is the Lord that advanced Moses and Aaron, and that brought your fathers up out of the land of Egypt. 7 Now therefore stand still, that I may reason with you before the Lord of all the righteous acts of the Lord, which he did to you and to your fathers. 8 When Jacob was come into Egypt, and your fathers cried unto the Lord, then the Lord sent Moses and Aaron, which brought forth your fathers out of Egypt, and made them dwell in this place. 9 And when they forgat the Lord their God, he sold them into the hand of Sisera, captain of the host of Hazor, and into the hand of the Philistines, and into the hand of the king of Moab, and they fought against them. 10 And they cried unto the Lord, and said, We have sinned, because we have forsaken the Lord, and have served Baalim and Ashtaroth: but now deliver us out of the hand of our enemies, and we will serve thee. 11 And the Lord sent Jerubbaal, and Bedan, and Jephthah, and Samuel, and delivered you out of the hand of your enemies on every side, and ye dwelt safe. 12 And when ye saw that Nahash the king of the children of Ammon came against you, ye said unto me, Nay; but a king shall reign over us: when the Lord your God was your king. 13 Now therefore, behold the king whom ye have chosen, and whom ye have desired! and, behold, the Lord hath set a king over you. 14 If ye will fear the Lord, and serve him, and obey his voice, and not rebel against the commandment of the Lord; then shall both ye and also the king that reigneth over you continue following the Lord your God: 15 But if ye will not obey the voice of the Lord, but rebel against the commandment of the Lord; then shall the hand of the Lord be against you, as it was against your fathers. 16 Now therefore stand and see this great thing, which the Lord will do before your eyes. 17 Is it not wheat harvest to-day? I will call unto the Lord, and he shall send thunder and rain; that ye may perceive and see that your wickedness is great, which ye have done in the sight of the Lord, in asking you a king.

18 So Samuel called unto the Lord; and the Lord sent thunder and rain that day: and all the people greatly feared the Lord and Samuel. 19 And all the people said unto Samuel, Pray for thy servants unto

the Lord thy God, that we die not: for we have added unto all our sins this evil, to ask us a king. 20 And Samuel said unto the people, Fear not: ye have done all this wickedness: yet turn not aside from following the Lord, but serve the Lord with all your heart; 21 And turn ye not aside: for then should ye go after vain things, which cannot profit nor deliver; for they are vain. 22 For the Lord will not forsake his people for his great name's sake: because it hath pleased the Lord to make you his people. 23 Moreover as for me, God forbid that I should sin against the Lord in ceasing to pray for you: but I will teach you the good and the right way: 24 Only fear the Lord, and serve him in truth with all your heart: for consider how great things he hath done for you. 25 But if ye shall still do wickedly, ye shall be consumed, both ye and your king.

13 Saul reigned one year; and when he had reigned two years over Israel, 2 Saul chose him three thousand men of Israel; whereof two thousand were with Saul in Michmash and in mount Beth-el, and a thousand were with Jonathan in Gibeah of Benjamin: and the rest of the people he sent every man to his tent. 3 And Jonathan smote the garrison of the Philistines that was in Geba, and the Philistines heard of it. And Saul blew the trumpet throughout all the land, saying, Let the Hebrews hear. 4 And all Israel heard say that Saul had smitten a garrison of the Philistines, and that Israel also was had in abomination with the Philistines. And the people were called together after Saul to Gilgal.

5 And the Philistines gathered themselves together to fight with Israel, thirty thousand chariots, and six thousand horsemen, and people as the sand which is on the seashore in multitude: and they came up, and pitched in Michmash, eastward from Beth-aven. 6 When the men of Israel saw that they were in a strait, (for the people were distressed,) then the people did hide themselves in caves, and in thickets, and in rocks, and in high places, and in pits. 7 And some of the Hebrews went over Jordan to the land of Gad and Gilead. As for Saul, he was yet in Gilgal, and all the people followed him trembling.

8 And he tarried seven days, according to the set time that Samuel had appointed: but Samuel came not to Gilgal; and the people were scattered from him. 9 And Saul said, Bring hither a burnt offering to me, and peace offerings. And he offered the burnt offering. 10 And it came to pass, that as soon as he had made an end of offering the burnt offering, behold, Samuel came; and Saul went out to meet him, that he might salute him. 11 And Samuel said, What hast thou done? And Saul said, Because I saw that the people were scattered from me, and that thou camest not within the days appointed, and that the Philistines gathered themselves together at Michmash; 12 Therefore said I, The Philistines will come down now upon me to Gilgal, and I have not made supplication unto the Lord: I forced myself therefore, and offered a burnt offering. 13 And Samuel said to Saul, Thou hast

done foolishly: thou hast not kept the commandment of the Lord thy God, which he commanded thee: for now would the Lord have established thy kingdom upon Israel for ever. 14 But now thy kingdom shall not continue: the Lord hath sought him a man after his own heart, and the Lord hath commanded him to be captain over his people, because thou hast not kept that which the Lord commanded thee. 15 And Samuel arose, and gat him up from Gilgal unto Gibeah of Benjamin.

And Saul numbered the people that were present with him, about six hundred men. 16 And Saul, and Jonathan his son, and the people that were present with them, abode in Gibeah of Benjamin: but the Philistines encamped in Michmash. 17 And the spoilers came out of the camp of the Philistines in three companies: one company turned unto the way that leadeth to Ophrah, unto the land of Shual: 18 And another company turned the way to Beth-horon: and another company turned to the way of the border that looketh to the valley of Zeboim toward the wilderness.

19 Now there was no smith found throughout all the land of Israel: for the Philistines said, Lest the Hebrews make them swords or spears: 20 But all the Israelites went down to the Philistines, to sharpen every man his share, and his coulter, and his axe, and his mattock. 21 Yet they had a file for the mattocks, and for the coulters, and for the forks, and for the axes, and to sharpen the goads. 22 So it came to pass in the day of battle, that there was neither sword nor spear found in the hand of any of the people that were with Saul and Jonathan: but with Saul and with Jonathan his son was there found. 23 And the garrison of the Philistines went out to the passage of Michmash.

14 Now it came to pass upon a day, that Jonathan the son of Saul said unto the young man that bare his armor, Come, and let us go over to the Philistines' garrison, that is on the other side. But he told not his father. 2 And Saul tarried in the uttermost part of Gibeah under a pomegranate tree which is in Migron: and the people that were with him were about six hundred men; 3 And Ahiah, the son of Ahitub, I-chabod's brother, the son of Phinehas, the son of Eli, the Lord's priest in Shiloh, wearing an ephod. And the people knew not that Jonathan was gone. 4 And between the passages, by which Jonathan sought to go over unto the Philistines' garrison, there was a sharp rock on the one side, and a sharp rock on the other side: and the name of the one was Bozez, and the name of the other Seneh. 5 The forefront of the one was situate northward over against Michmash, and the other southward over against Gibeah.

6 And Jonathan said to the young man that bare his armor, Come, and let us go over unto the garrison of these uncircumcised: it may be that the Lord will work for us: for there is no restraint to the Lord to save by many or by few. 7 And his armor-bearer said unto him, Do all that is in thy heart: turn thee; behold, I am with thee accord-

ing to thy heart. 8 Then said Jonathan, Behold, we will pass over unto these men, and we will discover ourselves unto them. 9 If they say thus unto us, Tarry until we come to you; then we will stand still in our place, and will not go up unto them. 10 But if they say thus, Come up unto us; then we will go up: for the Lord hath delivered them into our hand; and this shall be a sign unto us. 11 And both of them discovered themselves unto the garrison of the Philistines: and the Philistines said, Behold, the Hebrews come forth out of the holes where they had hid themselves. 12 And the men of the garrison answered Jonathan and his armor-bearer, and said, Come up to us, and we will show you a thing. And Jonathan said unto his armor-bearer, Come up after me: for the Lord hath delivered them into the hand of Israel. 13 And Jonathan climbed up upon his hands and upon his feet, and his armor-bearer after him: and they fell before Jonathan; and his armor-bearer slew after him. 14 And that first slaughter, which Jonathan and his armor-bearer made, was about twenty men, within as it were a half acre of land, which a yoke of oxen might plow. 15 And there was trembling in the host, in the field, and among all the people: the garrison, and the spoilers, they also trembled, and the earth quaked: so it was a very great trembling. 16 And the watchmen of Saul in Gibeah of Benjamin looked; and, behold, the multitude melted away, and they went on beating down one another.

17 Then said Saul unto the people that were with him, Number now, and see who is gone from us. And when they had numbered, behold, Jonathan and his armor-bearer were not there. 18 And Saul said unto Ahiah, Bring hither the ark of God. For the ark of God was at that time with the children of Israel. 19 And it came to pass, while Saul talked unto the priest, that the noise that was in the host of the Philistines went on and increased: and Saul said unto the priest, Withdraw thine hand. 20 And Saul and all the people that were with him assembled themselves, and they came to the battle: and, behold, every man's sword was against his fellow, and there was a very great discomfiture. 21 Moreover, the Hebrews that were with the Philistines before that time, which went up with them into the camp from the country round about, even they also turned to be with the Israelites that were with Saul and Jonathan. 22 Likewise all the men of Israel which had hid themselves in mount Ephraim, when they heard that the Philistines fled, even they also followed hard after them in the battle. 23 So the Lord saved Israel that day: and the battle passed over unto Beth-aven.

24 And the men of Israel were distressed that day: for Saul had adjured the people, saying, Cursed be the man that eateth any food until evening, that I may be avenged on mine enemies. So none of the people tasted any food. 25 And all they of the land came to a wood; and there was honey upon the ground. 26 And when the people were come into the wood, behold, the honey dropped; but no man put his hand to his mouth: for the people feared the oath. 27 But Jonathan heard not when his father charged the people with the oath:

wherefore he put forth the end of the rod that was in his hand, and dipped it in a honeycomb, and put his hand to his mouth; and his eyes were enlightened. 28 Then answered one of the people, and said, Thy father straitly charged the people with an oath, saying, Cursed be the man that eateth any food this day. And the people were faint. 29 Then said Jonathan, My father hath troubled the land: see, I pray you, how mine eyes have been enlightened, because I tasted a little of this honey. 30 How much more, if haply the people had eaten freely to-day of the spoil of their enemies which they found? for had there not been now a much greater slaughter among the Philistines? 31 And they smote the Philistines that day from Michmash to Aijalon: and the people were very faint. 32 And the people flew upon the spoil, and took sheep, and oxen, and calves, and slew them on the ground: and the people did eat them with the blood. 33 Then they told Saul, saying, Behold, the people sin against the Lord, in that they eat with the blood. And he said, Ye have transgressed: roll a great stone unto me this day. 34 And Saul said, Disperse yourselves among the people, and say unto them, Bring me hither every man his ox, and every man his sheep, and slay them here, and eat; and sin not against the Lord in eating with the blood. And all the people brought every man his ox with him that night, and slew them there. 35 And Saul built an altar unto the Lord: the same was the first altar that he built unto the Lord.

36 And Saul said, Let us go down after the Philistines by night, and spoil them until the morning light, and let us not leave a man of them. And they said, Do whatsoever seemeth good unto thee. Then said the priest, Let us draw near hither unto God. 37 And Saul asked counsel of God, Shall I go down after the Philistines? wilt thou deliver them into the hand of Israel? But he answered him not that day. 38 And Saul said, Draw ye near hither, all the chief of the people: and know and see wherein this sin hath been this day. 39 For, as the Lord liveth, which saveth Israel, though it be in Jonathan my son, he shall surely die. But there was not a man among all the people that answered him. 40 Then said he unto all Israel, Be ye on one side, and I and Jonathan my son will be on the other side. And the people said unto Saul, Do what seemeth good unto thee. 41 Therefore Saul said unto the Lord God of Israel, Give a perfect lot. And Saul and Jonathan were taken: but the people escaped. 42 And Saul said, Cast lots between me and Jonathan my son. And Jonathan was taken. 43 Then Saul said to Jonathan, Tell me what thou hast done. And Jonathan told him, and said, I did but taste a little honey with the end of the rod that was in mine hand, and, lo, I must die. 44 And Saul answered, God do so and more also: for thou shalt surely die, Jonathan. 45 And the people said unto Saul, Shall Jonathan die, who hath wrought this great salvation in Israel? God forbid: as the Lord liveth, there shall not one hair of his head fall to the ground; for he hath wrought with God this day. So the people rescued Jonathan, that he died not. 46

Then Saul went up from following the Philistines: and the Philistines went to their own place.

47 So Saul took the kingdom over Israel, and fought against all his enemies on every side, against Moab, and against the children of Ammon, and against Edom, and against the kings of Zobah, and against the Philistines: and whithersoever he turned himself, he vexed them. 48 And he gathered a host, and smote the Amalekites, and delivered Israel out of the hands of them that spoiled them.

49 Now the sons of Saul were Jonathan, and Ishui, and Melchishua: and the names of his two daughters were these; the name of the firstborn Merab, and the name of the younger Michal: 50 And the name of Saul's wife was Ahinoam, the daughter of Ahimaaz: and the name of the captain of his host was Abner, the son of Ner, Saul's uncle. 51 And Kish was the father of Saul; and Ner the father of Abner was the son of Abiel.

52 And there was sore war against the Philistines all the days of Saul: and when Saul saw any strong man, or any valiant man, he took him unto him.

15 Samuel also said unto Saul, The Lord sent me to anoint thee to be king over his people, over Israel: now therefore hearken thou unto the voice of the words of the Lord. 2 Thus saith the Lord of hosts, I remember that which Amalek did to Israel, how he laid wait for him in the way, when he came up from Egypt. 3 Now go and smite Amalek, and utterly destroy all that they have, and spare them not; but slay both man and woman, infant and suckling, ox and sheep, camel and ass.

4 And Saul gathered the people together, and numbered them in Telaim, two hundred thousand footmen, and ten thousand men of Judah. 5 And Saul came to a city of Amalek, and laid wait in the valley. 6 And Saul said unto the Kenites, Go, depart, get you down from among the Amalekites, lest I destroy you with them: for ye showed kindness to all the children of Israel, when they came up out of Egypt. So the Kenites departed from among the Amalekites. 7 And Saul smote the Amalekites from Havilah until thou comest to Shur, that is over against Egypt. 8 And he took Agag the king of the Amalekites alive, and utterly destroyed all the people with the edge of the sword. 9 But Saul and the people spared Agag, and the best of the sheep, and of the oxen, and of the fatlings, and the lambs, and all that was good, and would not utterly destroy them: but every thing that was vile and refuse, that they destroyed utterly.

10 Then came the word of the Lord unto Samuel, saying, 11 It repenteth me that I have set up Saul to be king: for he is turned back from following me, and hath not performed my commandments. And it grieved Samuel; and he cried unto the Lord all night. 12 And when Samuel rose early to meet Saul in the morning, it was told Samuel, saying, Saul came to Carmel, and, behold, he set him up a place, and is

gone about, and passed on, and gone down to Gilgal. 13 And Samuel came to Saul: and Saul said unto him, Blessed be thou of the Lord: I have performed the commandment of the Lord. 14 And Samuel said, What meaneth then this bleating of the sheep in mine ears, and the lowing of the oxen which I hear? 15 And Saul said, They have brought them from the Amalekites: for the people spared the best of the sheep and of the oxen, to sacrifice unto the Lord thy God; and the rest we have utterly destroyed. 16 Then Samuel said unto Saul, Stay, and I will tell thee what the Lord hath said to me his night. And he said unto him, Say on.

17 And Samuel said, When thou wast little in thine own sight, wast thou not made the head of the tribes of Israel, and the Lord anointed thee king over Israel? 18 And the Lord sent thee on a journey, and said, Go and utterly destroy the sinners the Amalekites, and fight against them until they be consumed. 19 Wherefore then didst thou not obey the voice of the Lord, but didst fly upon the spoil, and didst evil in the sight of the Lord? 20 And Saul said unto Samuel, Yea, I have obeyed the voice of the Lord, and have gone the way which the Lord sent me, and have brought Agag the king of Amalek, and have utterly destroyed the Amalekites. 21 But the people took of the spoil, sheep and oxen, the chief of the things which should have been utterly destroyed, to sacrifice unto the Lord thy God in Gilgal. 22 And Samuel said,

> Hath the Lord as great delight in burnt offerings and sacrifices,
> As in obeying the voice of the Lord?
> Behold, to obey is better than sacrifice,
> And to hearken than the fat of rams.
> 23 For rebellion is as the sin of witchcraft,
> And stubbornness is as iniquity and idolatry.

Because thou hast rejected the word of the Lord, he hath also rejected thee from being king. 24 And Saul said unto Samuel, I have sinned: for I have transgressed the commandment of the Lord, and thy words: because I feared the people, and obeyed their voice. 25 Now therefore, I pray thee, pardon my sin, and turn again with me, that I may worship the Lord. 26 And Samuel said unto Saul, I will not return with thee: for thou hast rejected the word of the Lord, and the Lord hath rejected thee from being king over Israel. 27 And as Samuel turned about to go away, he laid hold upon the skirt of his mantle, and it rent. 28 And Samuel said unto him, The Lord hath rent the kingdom of Israel from thee this day, and hath given it to a neighbor of thine, that is better than thou. 29 And also the Strength of Israel will not lie nor repent: for he is not a man, that he should repent. 30 Then he said, I have sinned: yet honor me now, I pray thee, before the elders of my people, and before Israel, and turn again with me, that I may worship the Lord thy God. 31 So Samuel turned again after Saul; and Saul worshipped the Lord.

32 Then said Samuel, Bring ye hither to me Agag the king of the

Amalekites. And Agag came unto him delicately. And Agag said, Surely the bitterness of death is past. 33 And Samuel said,

As thy sword hath made women childless,
So shall thy mother be childless among women.

And Samuel hewed Agag in pieces before the Lord in Gilgal.

34 Then Samuel went to Ramah; and Saul went up to his house to Gibeah of Saul. 35 And Samuel came no more to see Saul until the day of his death: nevertheless Samuel mourned for Saul: and the Lord repented that he had made Saul king over Israel.

## THE YOUNG DAVID

16 And the Lord said unto Samuel, How long wilt thou mourn for Saul, seeing I have rejected him from reigning over Israel? fill thine horn with oil, and go, I will send thee to Jesse the Bethlehemite: for I have provided me a king among his sons. 2 And Samuel said, How can I go? if Saul hear it, he will kill me. And the Lord said, Take a heifer with thee, and say, I am come to sacrifice to the Lord. 3 And call Jesse to the sacrifice, and I will show thee what thou shalt do: and thou shalt anoint unto me him whom I name unto thee. 4 And Samuel did that which the Lord spake, and came to Bethlehem. And the elders of the town trembled at his coming, and said, Comest thou peaceably? 5 And he said, Peaceably: I am come to sacrifice unto the Lord: sanctify yourselves, and come with me to the sacrifice. And he sanctified Jesse and his sons, and called them to the sacrifice. 6 And it came to pass, when they were come, that he looked on Eliab, and said, Surely the Lord's anointed is before him. 7 But the Lord said unto Samuel, Look not on his countenance, or on the height of his stature; because I have refused him: for the Lord seeth not as man seeth; for man looketh on the outward appearance, but the Lord looketh on the heart. 8 Then Jesse called Abinadab, and made him pass before Samuel. And he said, Neither hath the Lord chosen this. 9 Then Jesse made Shammah to pass by. And he said, Neither hath the Lord chosen this. 10 Again, Jesse made seven of his sons to pass before Samuel. And Samuel said unto Jesse, The Lord hath not chosen these. 11 And Samuel said unto Jesse, Are here all thy children? And he said, There remaineth yet the youngest, and, behold, he keepeth the sheep. And Samuel said unto Jesse, Send and fetch him: for we will not sit down till he come hither. 12 And he sent, and brought him in. Now he was ruddy, and withal of a beautiful countenance, and goodly to look to. And the Lord said, Arise, anoint him: for this is he. 13 Then Samuel took the horn of oil, and anointed him in the midst of his brethren: and the Spirit of the Lord came upon David from that day forward. So Samuel rose up, and went to Ramah.

14 But the Spirit of the Lord departed from Saul, and an evil spirit from the Lord troubled him. 15 And Saul's servants said unto him, Behold now, an evil spirit from God troubleth thee. 16 Let our

lord now command thy servants, which are before thee, to seek out a man, who is a cunning player on a harp: and it shall come to pass, when the evil spirit from God is upon thee, that he shall play with his hand, and thou shalt be well. 17 And Saul said unto his servants, Provide me now a man that can play well, and bring him to me. 18 Then answered one of the servants, and said, Behold, I have seen a son of Jesse the Bethlehemite, that is cunning in playing, and a mighty valiant man, and a man of war, and prudent in matters, and a comely person, and the Lord is with him. 19 Wherefore Saul sent messengers unto Jesse, and said, Send me David thy son, which is with the sheep. 20 And Jesse took an ass laden with bread, and a bottle of wine, and a kid, and sent them by David his son unto Saul. 21 And David came to Saul, and stood before him: and he loved him greatly; and he became his armor-bearer. 22 And Saul sent to Jesse, saying, Let David, I pray thee, stand before me; for he hath found favor in my sight. 23 And it came to pass, when the evil spirit from God was upon Saul, that David took a harp, and played with his hand: so Saul was refreshed, and was well, and the evil spirit departed from him.

17 Now the Philistines gathered together their armies to battle, and were gathered together at Shochoh, which belongeth to Judah, and pitched between Shochoh and Azekah, in Ephes-dammim. 2 And Saul and the men of Israel were gathered together, and pitched by the valley of Elah, and set the battle in array against the Philistines. 3 And the Philistines stood on a mountain on the one side, and Israel stood on a mountain on the other side: and there was a valley between them. 4 And there went out a champion out of the camp of the Philistines, named Goliath, of Gath, whose height was six cubits and a span. 5 And he had a helmet of brass upon his head, and he was armed with a coat of mail; and the weight of the coat was five thousand shekels of brass. 6 And he had greaves of brass upon his legs, and a target of brass between his shoulders. 7 And the staff of his spear was like a weaver's beam; and his spear's head weighed six hundred shekels of iron: and one bearing a shield went before him. 8 And he stood and cried unto the armies of Israel, and said unto them, Why are ye come out to set your battle in array? am not I a Philistine, and ye servants to Saul? choose you a man for you, and let him come down to me. 9 If he be able to fight with me, and to kill me, then will we be your servants: but if I prevail against him, and kill him, then shall ye be our servants, and serve us. 10 And the Philistine said, I defy the armies of Israel this day; give me a man, that we may fight together. 11 When Saul and all Israel heard those words of the Philistine, they were dismayed, and greatly afraid.

12 Now David was the son of that Ephrathite of Bethlehemjudah, whose name was Jesse; and he had eight sons: and the man went among men for an old man in the days of Saul. 13 And the three eldest sons of Jesse went and followed Saul to the battle: and the names

of his three sons that went to the battle were Eliab the firstborn, and next unto him Abinadab, and the third Shammah. 14 And David was the youngest: and the three eldest followed Saul. 15 But David went and returned from Saul to feed his father's sheep at Bethlehem. 16 And the Philistine drew near morning and evening, and presented himself forty days.

17 And Jesse said unto David his son, Take now for thy brethren an ephah of this parched corn, and these ten loaves, and run to the camp to thy brethren; 18 And carry these ten cheeses unto the captain of their thousand, and look how thy brethren fare, and take their pledge. 19 Now Saul, and they, and all the men of Israel, were in the valley of Elah, fighting with the Philistines. 20 And David rose up early in the morning, and left the sheep with a keeper, and took, and went, as Jesse had commanded him; and he came to the trench, as the host was going forth to the fight, and shouted for the battle. 21 For Israel and the Philistines had put the battle in array, army against army. 22 And David left his carriage in the hand of the keeper of the carriage, and ran into the army, and came and saluted his brethren. 23 And as he talked with them, behold, there came up the champion, the Philistine of Gath, Goliath by name, out of the armies of the Philistines, and spake according to the same words: and David heard them. 24 And all the men of Israel, when they saw the man, fled from him, and were sore afraid. 25 And the men of Israel said, Have ye seen this man that is come up? surely to defy Israel is he come up: and it shall be, that the man who killeth him, the king will enrich him with great riches, and will give him his daughter, and make his father's house free in Israel.

26 And David spake to the men that stood by him, saying, What shall be done to the man that killeth this Philistine, and taketh away the reproach from Israel? for who is this uncircumcised Philistine, that he should defy the armies of the living God? 27 And the people answered him after this manner, saying, So shall it be done to the man that killeth him. 28 And Eliab his eldest brother heard when he spake unto the men; and Eliab's anger was kindled against David, and he said, Why camest thou down hither? and with whom hast thou left those few sheep in the wilderness? I know thy pride, and the naughtiness of thine heart; for thou art come down that thou mightest see the battle. 29 And David said, What have I now done? Is there not a cause? 30 And he turned from him toward another, and spake after the same manner: and the people answered him again after the former manner. 31 And when the words were heard which David spake, they rehearsed them before Saul: and he sent for him.

32 And David said to Saul, Let no man's heart fail because of him; thy servant will go and fight with this Philistine. 33 And Saul said to David, Thou art not able to go against this Philistine to fight with him: for thou art but a youth, and he a man of war from his youth. 34 And David said unto Saul, Thy servant kept his father's sheep, and there came a lion, and a bear, and took a lamb out of the flock:

35 And I went out after him, and smote him, and delivered it out of his mouth: and when he arose against me, I caught him by his beard, and smote him, and slew him. 36 Thy servant slew both the lion and the bear: and this uncircumcised Philistine shall be as one of them, seeing he hath defied the armies of the living God. 37 David said moreover, The Lord that delivered me out of the paw of the lion, and out of the paw of the bear, he will deliver me out of the hand of this Philistine. And Saul said unto David, Go, and the Lord be with thee. 38 And Saul armed David with his armor, and he put a helmet of brass upon his head; also he armed him with a coat of mail. 39 And David girded his sword upon his armor, and he assayed to go; for he had not proved it. And David said unto Saul, I cannot go with these; for I have not proved them. And David put them off him. 40 And he took his staff in his hand, and chose him five smooth stones out of the brook, and put them in a shepherd's bag which he had, even in a scrip; and his sling was in his hand: and he drew near to the Philistine.

41 And the Philistine came on and drew near unto David; and the man that bare the shield went before him. 42 And when the Philistine looked about, and saw David, he disdained him: for he was but a youth, and ruddy, and of a fair countenance. 43 And the Philistine said unto David, Am I a dog, that thou comest to me with staves? And the Philistine cursed David by his gods. 44 And the Philistine said to David, Come to me, and I will give thy flesh unto the fowls of the air, and to the beasts of the field. 45 Then said David to the Philistine, Thou comest to me with a sword, and with a spear, and with a shield: but I come to thee in the name of the Lord of hosts, the God of the armies of Israel, whom thou hast defied. 46 This day will the Lord deliver thee into mine hand; and I will smite thee, and take thine head from thee; and I will give the carcasses of the host of the Philistines this day unto the fowls of the air, and to the wild beasts of the earth; that all the earth may know that there is a God in Israel. 47 And all this assembly shall know that the Lord saveth not with sword and spear: for the battle is the Lord's, and he will give you into our hands. 48 And it came to pass, when the Philistine arose, and came and drew nigh to meet David, that David hasted, and ran toward the army to meet the Philistine. 49 And David put his hand in his bag, and took thence a stone, and slang it, and smote the Philistine in his forehead, that the stone sunk into his forehead; and he fell upon his face to the earth. 50 So David prevailed over the Philistine with a sling and with a stone, and smote the Philistine, and slew him; but there was no sword in the hand of David. 51 Therefore David ran, and stood upon the Philistine, and took his sword, and drew it out of the sheath thereof, and slew him, and cut off his head therewith. And when the Philistines saw their champion was dead, they fled. 52 And the men of Israel and of Judah arose, and shouted, and pursued the Philistines, until thou come to the valley, and to the gates of Ekron. And the wounded of the Philistines fell down by the way to

Shaaraim, even unto Gath, and unto Ekron. 53 And the children of Israel returned from chasing after the Philistines, and they spoiled their tents. 54 And David took the head of the Philistine, and brought it to Jerusalem; but he put his armor in his tent.

55 And when Saul saw David go forth against the Philistine, he said unto Abner, the captain of the host, Abner, whose son is this youth? And Abner said, As thy soul liveth, O king, I cannot tell. 56 And the king said, Inquire thou whose son the stripling is. 57 And as David returned from the slaughter of the Philistine, Abner took him, and brought him before Saul with the head of the Philistine in his hand. 58 And Saul said to him, Whose son art thou, thou young man? And David answered, I am the son of thy servant Jesse the Bethlehemite.

## DAVID AND JONATHAN

18 And it came to pass, when he had made an end of speaking unto Saul, that the soul of Jonathan was knit with the soul of David, and Jonathan loved him as his own soul. 2 And Saul took him that day, and would let him go no more home to his father's house. 3 Then Jonathan and David made a covenant, because he loved him as his own soul. 4 And Jonathan stripped himself of the robe that was upon him, and gave it to David, and his garments, even to his sword, and to his bow, and to his girdle. 5 And David went out whithersoever Saul sent him, and behaved himself wisely: and Saul set him over the men of war, and he was accepted in the sight of all the people, and also in the sight of Saul's servants.

6 And it came to pass as they came, when David was returned from the slaughter of the Philistine, that the women came out of all cities of Israel, singing and dancing, to meet king Saul, with tabrets, with joy, and with instruments of music. 7 And the women answered one another as they played, and said,

Saul hath slain his thousands,
And David his ten thousands.

8 And Saul was very wroth, and the saying displeased him; and he said, They have ascribed unto David ten thousands, and to me they have ascribed but thousands: and what can he have more but the kingdom? 9 And Saul eyed David from that day and forward.

10 And it came to pass on the morrow, that the evil spirit from God came upon Saul, and he prophesied in the midst of the house: and David played with his hand, as at other times: and there was a javelin in Saul's hand. 11 And Saul cast the javelin; for he said, I will smite David even to the wall with it. And David avoided out of his presence twice. 12 And Saul was afraid of David, because the Lord was with him, and was departed from Saul. 13 Therefore Saul removed him from him, and made him his captain over a thousand; and he went out and came in before the people. 14 And David behaved himself wisely in all his ways; and the Lord was with him. 15 Wherefore when Saul saw that he behaved himself very wisely, he was

afraid of him. 16 But all Israel and Judah loved David, because he
went out and came in before them.

17 And Saul said to David, Behold my elder daughter Merab, her
will I give thee to wife: only be thou valiant for me, and fight the
Lord's battles. For Saul said, Let not mine hand be upon him, but
let the hand of the Philistines be upon him. 18 And David said unto
Saul, Who am I? and what is my life, or my father's family in Israel,
that I should be son-in-law to the king? 19 But it came to pass at the
time when Merab Saul's daughter should have been given to David,
that she was given unto Adriel the Meholathite to wife. 20 And
Michal Saul's daughter loved David: and they told Saul, and the thing
pleased him. 21 And Saul said, I will give him her, that she may be a
snare to him, and that the hand of the Philistines may be against
him. Wherefore Saul said to David, Thou shalt this day be my son-in-
law in the one of the twain. 22 And Saul commanded his servants,
saying, Commune with David secretly, and say, Behold, the king hath
delight in thee, and all his servants love thee: now therefore be the
king's son-in-law. 23 And Saul's servants spake those words in the
ears of David. And David said, Seemeth it to you a light thing to be
a king's son-in-law, seeing that I am a poor man, and lightly esteemed?
24 And the servants of Saul told him, saying, On this manner spake
David. 25 And Saul said, Thus shall ye say to David, The king
desireth not any dowry, but a hundred foreskins of the Philistines, to
be avenged of the king's enemies. But Saul thought to make David
fall by the hand of the Philistines. 26 And when his servants told
David these words, it pleased David well to be the king's son-in-law:
and the days were not expired. 27 Wherefore David arose and went,
he and his men, and slew of the Philistines two hundred men; and
David brought their foreskins, and they gave them in full tale to the
king, that he might be the king's son-in-law. And Saul gave him
Michal his daughter to wife. 28 And Saul saw and knew that the Lord
was with David, and that Michal Saul's daughter loved him. 29 And
Saul was yet the more afraid of David; and Saul became David's enemy
continually.

30 Then the princes of the Philistines went forth: and it came to
pass, after they went forth, that David behaved himself more wisely
than all the servants of Saul; so that his name was much set by.

19 And Saul spake to Jonathan his son, and to all his servants, that
they should kill David. 2 But Jonathan Saul's son delighted much in
David: and Jonathan told David, saying, Saul my father seeketh to kill
thee: now therefore, I pray thee, take heed to thyself until the morning
and abide in a secret place, and hide thyself: 3 And I will go out and
stand beside my father in the field where thou art, and I will commune with my father of thee; and what I see, that I will tell thee.

4 And Jonathan spake good of David unto Saul his father, and said
unto him, Let not the king sin against his servant, against David;

because he hath not sinned against thee, and because his works have been to thee-ward very good: 5 For he did put his life in his hand, and slew the Philistine, and the Lord wrought a great salvation for all Israel: thou sawest it, and didst rejoice: wherefore then wilt thou sin against innocent blood, to slay David without a cause? 6 And Saul hearkened unto the voice of Jonathan: and Saul sware, As the Lord liveth, he shall not be slain. 7 And Jonathan called David, and Jonathan showed him all those things. And Jonathan brought David to Saul, and he was in his presence, as in times past.

8 And there was war again: and David went out, and fought with the Philistines, and slew them with a great slaughter; and they fled from him. 9 And the evil spirit from the Lord was upon Saul, as he sat in his house with his javelin in his hand: and David played with his hand. 10 And Saul sought to smite David even to the wall with the javelin; but he slipped away out of Saul's presence, and he smote the javelin into the wall: and David fled, and escaped that night. 11 Saul also sent messengers unto David's house, to watch him, and to slay him in the morning: and Michal David's wife told him, saying, If thou save not thy life to-night, to-morrow thou shalt be slain. 12 So Michal let David down through a window: and he went, and fled, and escaped. 13 And Michal took an image, and laid it in the bed, and put a pillow of goats' hair for his bolster, and covered it with a cloth. 14 And when Saul sent messengers to take David, she said, He is sick. 15 And Saul sent the messengers again to see David, saying, Bring him up to me in the bed, that I may slay him. 16 And when the messengers were come in, behold, there was an image in the bed, with a pillow of goats' hair for his bolster. 17 And Saul said unto Michal, Why hast thou deceived me so, and sent away mine enemy, that he is escaped? And Michal answered Saul, He said unto me, Let me go; why should I kill thee?

18 So David fled, and escaped, and came to Samuel to Ramah, and told him all that Saul had done to him. And he and Samuel went and dwelt in Naioth. 19 And it was told Saul, saying, Behold, David is at Naioth in Ramah. 20 And Saul sent messengers to take David: and when they saw the company of the prophets prophesying, and Samuel standing as appointed over them, the Spirit of God was upon the messengers of Saul, and they also prophesied. 21 And when it was told Saul, he sent other messengers, and they prophesied likewise. And Saul sent messengers again the third time, and they prophesied also. 22 Then went he also to Ramah, and came to a great well that is in Sechu: and he asked and said, Where are Samuel and David? And one said, Behold, they be at Naioth in Ramah. 23 And he went thither to Naioth in Ramah: and the Spirit of God was upon him also, and he went on, and prophesied, until he came to Naioth in Ramah. 24 And he stripped off his clothes also, and prophesied before Samuel in like manner, and lay down naked all that day and all that night. Wherefore they say, Is Saul also among the prophets?

20 And David fled from Naioth in Ramah, and came and said before Jonathan, What have I done? what is mine iniquity? and what is my sin before thy father, that he seeketh my life? 2 And he said unto him, God forbid; thou shalt not die: behold, my father will do nothing either great or small, but that he will show it me: and why should my father hide this thing from me? it is not so. 3 And David sware moreover, and said, Thy father certainly knoweth that I have found grace in thine eyes; and he saith, Let not Jonathan know this, lest he be grieved: but truly, as the Lord liveth, and as thy soul liveth, there is but a step between me and death. 4 Then said Jonathan unto David, Whatsoever thy soul desireth, I will even do it for thee. 5 And David said unto Jonathan, Behold, to-morrow is the new moon, and I should not fail to sit with the king at meat: but let me go, that I may hide myself in the field unto the third day at even. 6 If thy father at all miss me, then say, David earnestly asked leave of me that he might run to Bethlehem his city: for there is a yearly sacrifice there for all the family. 7 If he say thus, It is well; thy servant shall have peace: but if he be very wroth, then be sure that evil is determined by him. 8 Therefore thou shalt deal kindly with thy servant; for thou hast brought thy servant into a covenant of the Lord with thee: notwithstanding, if there be in me iniquity, slay me thyself; for why shouldest thou bring me to thy father? 9 And Jonathan said, Far be it from thee: for if I knew certainly that evil were determined by my father to come upon thee, then would not I tell it thee? 10 Then said David to Jonathan, Who shall tell me? or what if thy father answer thee roughly? 11 And Jonathan said unto David, Come, and let us go out into the field. And they went out both of them into the field.

12 And Jonathan said unto David, O Lord God of Israel, when I have sounded my father about to-morrow any time, or the third day, and, behold, if there be good toward David, and I then send not unto thee, and show it thee; 13 The Lord do so and much more to Jonathan: but if it please my father to do thee evil, then I will show it thee, and send thee away, that thou mayest go in peace: and the Lord be with thee, as he hath been with my father. 14 And thou shalt not only while yet I live show me the kindness of the Lord, that I die not: 15 But also thou shalt not cut off thy kindness from my house for ever: no, not when the Lord hath cut off the enemies of David every one from the face of the earth. 16 So Jonathan made a covenant with the house of David, saying, Let the Lord even require it at the hand of David's enemies. 17 And Jonathan caused David to swear again, because he loved him: for he loved him as he loved his own soul.

18 Then Jonathan said to David, To-morrow is the new moon: and thou shalt be missed, because thy seat will be empty. 19 And when thou hast stayed three days, then thou shalt go down quickly, and come to the place where thou didst hide thyself when the business was in hand, and shalt remain by the stone Ezel. 20 And I will shoot three arrows on the side thereof, as though I shot at a mark. 21 And, behold,

I will send a lad, saying, Go, find out the arrows. If I expressly say unto the lad, Behold, the arrows are on this side of thee, take them; then come thou: for there is peace to thee, and no hurt; as the Lord liveth. 22 But if I say thus unto the young man, Behold, the arrows are beyond thee; go thy way: for the Lord hath sent thee away. 23 And as touching the matter which thou and I have spoken of, behold, the Lord be between thee and me for ever.

24 So David hid himself in the field: and when the new moon was come, the king sat him down to eat meat. 25 And the king sat upon his seat, as at other times, even upon a seat by the wall: and Jonathan arose, and Abner sat by Saul's side, and David's place was empty. 26 Nevertheless Saul spake not any thing that day: for he thought, Something hath befallen him, he is not clean; surely he is not clean. 27 And it came to pass on the morrow, which was the second day of the month, that David's place was empty: and Saul said unto Jonathan his son, Wherefore cometh not the son of Jesse to meat, neither yesterday, nor to-day? 28 And Jonathan answered Saul, David earnestly asked leave of me to go to Bethlehem: 29 And he said, Let me go, I pray thee; for our family hath a sacrifice in the city; and my brother, he hath commanded me to be there: and now, if I have found favor in thine eyes, let me get away, I pray thee, and see my brethren. Therefore he cometh not unto the king's table.

30 Then Saul's anger was kindled against Jonathan, and he said unto him, Thou son of the perverse rebellious woman, do not I know that thou hast chosen the son of Jesse to thine own confusion, and unto the confusion of thy mother's nakedness? 31 For as long as the son of Jesse liveth upon the ground, thou shalt not be established, nor thy kingdom. Wherefore now send and fetch him unto me, for he shall surely die. 32 And Jonathan answered Saul his father, and said unto him, Wherefore shall he be slain? what hath he done? 33 And Saul cast a javelin at him to smite him: whereby Jonathan knew that it was determined of his father to slay David. 34 So Jonathan arose from the table in fierce anger, and did eat no meat the second day of the month: for he was grieved for David, because his father had done him shame.

35 And it came to pass in the morning, that Jonathan went out into the field at the time appointed with David, and a little lad with him. 36 And he said unto his lad, Run, find out now the arrows which I shoot. And as the lad ran, he shot an arrow beyond him. 37 And when the lad was come to the place of the arrow which Jonathan had shot, Jonathan cried after the lad, and said, Is not the arrow beyond thee? 38 And Jonathan cried after the lad, Make speed, haste, stay not. And Jonathan's lad gathered up the arrows, and came to his master. 39 But the lad knew not any thing: only Jonathan and David knew the matter. 40 And Jonathan gave his artillery[1] unto his lad, and said unto him, Go, carry them to the city. 41 And as soon as the

---

[1] I.e., bow and arrows.

lad was gone, David arose out of a place toward the south, and fell on his face to the ground, and bowed himself three times: and they kissed one another, and wept one with another, until David exceeded. 42 And Jonathan said to David, Go in peace, forasmuch as we have sworn both of us in the name of the Lord, saying, The Lord be between me and thee, and between my seed and thy seed for ever. And he arose and departed: and Jonathan went into the city.

## DAVID AS AN OUTLAW

21 Then came David to Nob to Ahimelech the priest: and Ahimelech was afraid at the meeting of David, and said unto him, Why art thou alone, and no man with thee? 2 And David said unto Ahimelech the priest, The king hath commanded me a business, and hath said unto me, Let no man know any thing of the business whereabout I send thee, and what I have commanded thee: and I have appointed my servants to such and such a place. 3 Now therefore what is under thine hand? give me five loaves of bread in mine hand, or what there is present. 4 And the priest answered David, and said, There is no common bread under mine hand, but there is hallowed bread; if the young men have kept themselves at least from women. 5 And David answered the priest, and said unto him, Of a truth women have been kept from us about these three days, since I came out, and the vessels of the young men are holy, and the bread is in a manner common, yea, though it were sanctified this day in the vessel. 6 So the priest gave him hallowed bread: for there was no bread there but the showbread, that was taken from before the Lord, to put hot bread in the day when it was taken away. 7 Now a certain man of the servants of Saul was there that day, detained before the Lord; and his name was Doeg, an Edomite, the chiefest of the herdmen that belonged to Saul. 8 And David said unto Ahimelech, And is there not here under thine hand spear or sword? for I have neither brought my sword nor my weapons with me, because the king's business required haste. 9 And the priest said, The sword of Goliath the Philistine, whom thou slewest in the valley of Elah, behold, it is here wrapped in a cloth behind the ephod: if thou wilt take that, take it: for there is no other save that here. And David said, There is none like that; give it me. 10 And David arose, and fled that day for fear of Saul, and went to Achish the king of Gath.

11 And the servants of Achish said unto him, Is not this David the king of the land? did they not sing one to another of him in dances, saying,

> Saul hath slain his thousands,
> And David his ten thousands?

12 And David laid up these words in his heart, and was sore afraid of Achish the king of Gath. 13 And he changed his behavior before them, and feigned himself mad in their hands, and scrabbled on the doors of the gate, and let his spittle fall down upon his beard. 14 Then

said Achish unto his servants, Lo, ye see the man is mad: wherefore then have ye brought him to me? 15 Have I need of madmen, that ye have brought this fellow to play the madman in my presence? shall this fellow come into my house?

22 David therefore departed thence, and escaped to the cave Adullam: and when his brethren and all his father's house heard it, they went down thither to him. 2 And every one that was in distress, and every one that was in debt, and every one that was discontented, gathered themselves unto him; and he became a captain over them: and there were with him about four hundred men.

3 And David went thence to Mizpeh of Moab: and he said unto the king of Moab, Let my father and my mother, I pray thee, come forth, and be with you, till I know what God will do for me. 4 And he brought them before the king of Moab: and they dwelt with him all the while that David was in the hold. 5 And the prophet Gad said unto David, Abide not in the hold; depart, and get thee into the land of Judah. Then David departed, and came into the forest of Hareth.

6 When Saul heard that David was discovered, and the men that were with him, (now Saul abode in Gibeah under a tree in Ramah, having his spear in his hand, and all his servants were standing about him;) 7 Then Saul said unto his servants that stood about him, Hear now, ye Benjamites; will the son of Jesse give every one of you fields and vineyards, and make you all captains of thousands, and captains of hundreds; 8 That all of you have conspired against me, and there is none that showeth me that my son hath made a league with the son of Jesse, and there is none of you that is sorry for me, or showeth unto me that my son hath stirred up my servant against me, to lie in wait, as at this day? 9 Then answered Doeg the Edomite, which was set over the servants of Saul, and said, I saw the son of Jesse coming to Nob, to Ahimelech the son of Ahitub. 10 And he inquired of the Lord for him, and gave him victuals, and gave him the sword of Goliath the Philistine.

11 Then the king sent to call Ahimelech the priest, the son of Ahitub, and all his father's house, the priests that were in Nob: and they came all of them to the king. 12 And Saul said, Hear now, thou son of Ahitub. And he answered, Here I am, my lord. 13 And Saul said unto him, Why have ye conspired against me, thou and the son of Jesse, in that thou hast given him bread, and a sword, and hast inquired of God for him, that he should rise against me, to lie in wait, as at this day? 14 Then Ahimelech answered the king, and said, And who is so faithful among all thy servants as David, which is the king's son-in-law, and goeth at thy bidding, and is honorable in thine house? 15 Did I then begin to inquire of God for him? be it far from me: let not the king impute any thing unto his servant, nor to all the house of my father: for thy servant knew nothing of all this, less or more. 16 And the king said, Thou shalt surely die, Ahimelech, thou, and all thy father's house. 17 And the king said unto the footmen that

stood about him, Turn, and slay the priests of the Lord; because their hand also is with David, and because they knew when he fled, and did not show it to me. But the servants of the king would not put forth their hand to fall upon the priests of the Lord. 18 And the king said to Doeg, Turn thou, and fall upon the priests. And Doeg the Edomite turned, and he fell upon the priests, and slew on that day fourscore and five persons that did wear a linen ephod. 19 And Nob, the city of the priests, smote he with the edge of the sword, both men and women, children and sucklings, and oxen, and asses, and sheep, with the edge of the sword.

20 And one of the sons of Ahimelech the son of Ahitub, named Abiathar, escaped, and fled after David. 21 And Abiathar showed David that Saul had slain the Lord's priests. 22 And David said unto Abiathar, I knew it that day, when Doeg the Edomite was there, that he would surely tell Saul: I have occasioned the death of all the persons of thy father's house. 23 Abide thou with me, fear not: for he that seeketh my life seeketh thy life: but with me thou shalt be in safeguard.

23 Then they told David, saying, Behold, the Philistines fight against Keilah, and they rob the threshingfloors. 2 Therefore David inquired of the Lord, saying, Shall I go and smite these Philistines? And the Lord said unto David, Go, and smite the Philistines, and save Keilah. 3 And David's men said unto him, Behold, we be afraid here in Judah: how much more then if we come to Keilah against the armies of the Philistines? 4 Then David inquired of the Lord yet again. And the Lord answered him and said, Arise, go down to Keilah; for I will deliver the Philistines into thine hand. 5 So David and his men went to Keilah, and fought with the Philistines, and brought away their cattle, and smote them with a great slaughter. So David saved the inhabitants of Keilah.

6 And it came to pass, when Abiathar the son of Ahimelech fled to David to Keilah, that he came down with an ephod in his hand. 7 And it was told Saul that David was come to Keilah. And Saul said, God hath delivered him into mine hand; for he is shut in, by entering into a town that hath gates and bars. 8 And Saul called all the people together to war, to go down to Keilah, to besiege David and his men. 9 And David knew that Saul secretly practised mischief against him; and he said to Abiathar the priest, Bring hither the ephod. 10 Then said David, O Lord God of Israel, thy servant hath certainly heard that Saul seeketh to come to Keilah, to destroy the city for my sake. 11 Will the men of Keilah deliver me up into his hand? will Saul come down, as thy servant hath heard? O Lord God of Israel, I beseech thee, tell thy servant. And the Lord said, He will come down. 12 Then said David, Will the men of Keilah deliver me and my men into the hand of Saul? And the Lord said, They will deliver thee up. 13 Then David and his men, which were about six hundred, arose and

departed out of Keilah, and went whithersoever they could go. And it was told Saul that David was escaped from Keilah; and he forbare to go forth.

14 And David abode in the wilderness in strongholds, and remained in a mountain in the wilderness of Ziph. And Saul sought him every day, but God delivered him not into his hand. 15 And David saw that Saul was come out to seek his life: and David was in the wilderness of Ziph in a wood. 16 And Jonathan Saul's son arose, and went to David into the wood, and strengthened his hand in God. 17 And he said unto him, Fear not: for the hand of Saul my father shall not find thee; and thou shalt be king over Israel, and I shall be next unto thee; and that also Saul my father knoweth. 18 And they two made a covenant before the Lord: and David abode in the wood, and Jonathan went to his house.

19 Then came up the Ziphites to Saul to Gibeah, saying, Doth not David hide himself with us in strongholds in the wood, in the hill of Hachilah, which is on the south of Jeshimon? 20 Now therefore, O king, come down according to all the desire of thy soul to come down; and our part shall be to deliver him into the king's hand. 21 And Saul said, Blessed be ye of the Lord; for ye have compassion on me. 22 Go, I pray you, prepare yet, and know and see his place where his haunt is, and who hath seen him there: for it is told me that he dealeth very subtilely. 23 See therefore, and take knowledge of all the lurking places where he hideth himself, and come ye again to me with the certainty, and I will go with you: and it shall come to pass, if he be in the land, that I will search him out throughout all the thousands of Judah.

24 And they arose, and went to Ziph before Saul: but David and his men were in the wilderness of Maon, in the plain on the south of Jeshimon. 25 Saul also and his men went to seek him. And they told David: wherefore he came down into a rock, and abode in the wilderness of Maon. And when Saul heard that, he pursued after David in the wilderness of Maon. 26 And Saul went on this side of the mountain, and David and his men on that side of the mountain: and David made haste to get away for fear of Saul; for Saul and his men compassed David and his men round about to take them. 27 But there came a messenger unto Saul, saying, Haste thee, and come; for the Philistines have invaded the land. 28 Wherefore Saul returned from pursuing after David, and went against the Philistines: therefore they called that place Sela-hammahlekoth. 29 And David went up from thence, and dwelt in strongholds at En-gedi.

24 And it came to pass, when Saul was returned from following the Philistines, that it was told him, saying, Behold, David is in the wilderness of En-gedi. 2 Then Saul took three thousand chosen men out of all Israel, and went to seek David and his men upon the rocks of the wild goats. 3 And he came to the sheepcotes by the way, where

was a cave; and Saul went in to cover his feet: and David and his men remained in the sides of the cave. 4 And the men of David said unto him, Behold the day of which the Lord said unto thee, Behold, I will deliver thine enemy into thine hand, that thou mayest do to him as it shall seem good unto thee. Then David arose, and cut off the skirt of Saul's robe privily. 5 And it came to pass afterward, that David's heart smote him, because he had cut off Saul's skirt. 6 And he said unto his men, The Lord forbid that I should do this thing unto my master, the Lord's anointed, to stretch forth mine hand against him, seeing he is the anointed of the Lord. 7 So David stayed his servants with these words, and suffered them not to rise against Saul. But Saul rose up out of the cave, and went on his way.

8 David also arose afterward, and went out of the cave, and cried after Saul, saying, My lord the king. And when Saul looked behind him, David stooped with his face to the earth, and bowed himself. 9 And David said to Saul, Wherefore hearest thou men's words, saying, Behold, David seeketh thy hurt? 10 Behold, this day thine eyes have seen how that the Lord hath delivered thee to-day into mine hand in the cave: and some bade me kill thee: but mine eye spared thee; and I said, I will not put forth mine hand against my lord; for he is the Lord's anointed. 11 Moreover, my father, see, yea, see the skirt of thy robe in my hand: for in that I cut off the skirt of thy robe, and killed thee not, know thou and see that there is neither evil nor transgression in mine hand, and I have not sinned against thee; yet thou huntest my soul to take it. 12 The Lord judge between me and thee, and the Lord avenge me of thee: but mine hand shall not be upon thee. 13 As saith the proverb of the ancients, Wickedness proceedeth from the wicked: but mine hand shall not be upon thee. 14 After whom is the king of Israel come out? after whom dost thou pursue? after a dead dog, after a flea. 15 The Lord therefore be judge, and judge between me and thee, and see, and plead my cause, and deliver me out of thine hand.

16 And it came to pass, when David had made an end of speaking these words unto Saul, that Saul said, Is this thy voice, my son David? And Saul lifted up his voice, and wept. 17 And he said to David, Thou art more righteous than I: for thou hast rewarded me good, whereas I have rewarded thee evil. 18 And thou hast showed this day how that thou hast dealt well with me: forasmuch as when the Lord had delivered me into thine hand, thou killedst me not. 19 For if a man find his enemy, will he let him go well away? wherefore the Lord reward thee good for that thou hast done unto me this day. 20 And now, behold, I know well that thou shalt surely be king, and that the kingdom of Israel shall be established in thine hand. 21 Swear now therefore unto me by the Lord, that thou wilt not cut off my seed after me, and that thou wilt not destroy my name out of my father's house. 22 And David sware unto Saul. And Saul went home; but David and his men gat them up unto the hold.

25 And Samuel died; and all the Israelites were gathered together, and lamented him, and buried him in his house at Ramah. And David arose, and went down to the wilderness of Paran.

2 And there was a man in Maon, whose possessions were in Carmel; and the man was very great, and he had three thousand sheep, and a thousand goats: and he was shearing his sheep in Carmel. 3 Now the name of the man was Nabal, and the name of his wife Abigail; and she was a woman of good understanding, and of a beautiful countenance: but the man was churlish and evil in his doings; and he was of the house of Caleb. 4 And David heard in the wilderness that Nabal did shear his sheep. 5 And David sent out ten young men, and David said unto the young men, Get you up to Carmel, and go to Nabal, and greet him in my name: 6 And thus shall ye say to him that liveth in prosperity, Peace be both to thee, and peace be to thine house, and peace be unto all that thou hast. 7 And now I have heard that thou hast shearers: now thy shepherds which were with us, we hurt them not, neither was there aught missing unto them, all the while they were in Carmel. 8 Ask thy young men, and they will show thee. Wherefore let the young men find favor in thine eyes; for we come in a good day: give, I pray thee, whatsoever cometh to thine hand unto thy servants, and to thy son David. 9 And when David's young men came, they spake to Nabal according to all those words in the name of David, and ceased.

10 And Nabal answered David's servants, and said, Who is David? and who is the son of Jesse? there be many servants nowadays that break away every man from his master. 11 Shall I then take my bread, and my water, and my flesh that I have killed for my shearers, and give it unto men, whom I know not whence they be? 12 So David's young men turned their way, and went again, and came and told him all those sayings. 13 And David said unto his men, Gird ye on every man his sword. And they girded on every man his sword; and David also girded on his sword: and there went up after David about four hundred men; and two hundred abode by the stuff.

14 But one of the young men told Abigail, Nabal's wife, saying, Behold, David sent messengers out of the wilderness to salute our master; and he railed on them. 15 But the men were very good unto us, and we were not hurt, neither missed we any thing, as long as we were conversant with them, when we were in the fields. 16 They were a wall unto us both by night and day, all the while we were with them keeping the sheep. 17 Now therefore know and consider what thou wilt do; for evil is determined against our master, and against all his household: for he is such a son of Belial, that a man cannot speak to him.

18 Then Abigail made haste, and took two hundred loaves, and two bottles of wine, and five sheep ready dressed, and five measures of parched corn, and a hundred clusters of raisins, and two hundred cakes

of figs, and laid them on asses. 19 And she said unto her servants, Go
on before me; behold, I come after you. But she told not her husband
Nabal. 20 And it was so, as she rode on the ass, that she came down
by the covert of the hill, and, behold, David and his men came down
against her; and she met them. 21 Now David had said, Surely in vain
have I kept all that this fellow hath in the wilderness, so that nothing
was missed of all that pertained unto him: and he hath requited me
evil for good. 22 So and more also do God unto the enemies of David,
if I leave of all that pertain to him by the morning light any that
pisseth against the wall.

23 And when Abigail saw David, she hasted, and lighted off the
ass, and fell before David on her face, and bowed herself to the ground,
24 And fell at his feet, and said, Upon me, my lord, upon me let this
iniquity be: and let thine handmaid, I pray thee, speak in thine audience, and hear the words of thine handmaid. 25 Let not my lord, I
pray thee, regard this man of Belial, even Nabal: for as his name is,
so is he; Nabal is his name, and folly is with him: but I thine handmaid saw not the young men of my lord, whom thou didst send.
26 Now therefore, my lord, as the Lord liveth, and as thy soul liveth,
seeing the Lord hath withholden thee from coming to shed blood,
and from avenging thyself with thine own hand, now let thine enemies,
and they that seek evil to my lord, be as Nabal. 27 And now this
blessing which thine handmaid hath brought unto my lord, let it even
be given unto the young men that follow my lord. 28 I pray thee,
forgive the trespass of thine handmaid: for the Lord will certainly
make my lord a sure house; because my lord fighteth the battles of the
Lord, and evil hath not been found in thee all thy days. 29 Yet a man
is risen to pursue thee, and to seek thy soul: but the soul of my lord
shall be bound in the bundle of life with the Lord thy God; and the
souls of thine enemies, them shall he sling out, as out of the middle
of a sling. 30 And it shall come to pass, when the Lord shall have
done to my lord according to all the good that he hath spoken concerning thee, and shall have appointed thee ruler over Israel; 31 That
this shall be no grief unto thee, nor offense of heart unto my lord,
either that thou hast shed blood causeless, or that my lord hath
avenged himself: but when the Lord shall have dealt well with my
lord, then remember thine handmaid.

32 And David said to Abigail, Blessed be the Lord God of Israel,
which sent thee this day to meet me: 33 And blessed be thy advice,
and blessed be thou, which hast kept me this day from coming to shed
blood, and from avenging myself with mine own hand. 34 For in very
deed, as the Lord God of Israel liveth, which hath kept me back from
hurting thee, except thou hadst hasted and come to meet me, surely
there had not been left unto Nabal by the morning light any that
pisseth against the wall. 35 So David received of her hand that which
she had brought him, and said unto her, Go up in peace to thine
house; see, I have hearkened to thy voice, and have accepted thy
person.

36 And Abigail came to Nabal; and, behold, he held a feast in his house, like the feast of a king; and Nabal's heart was merry within him, for he was very drunken: wherefore she told him nothing, less or more, until the morning light. 37 But it came to pass in the morning, when the wine was gone out of Nabal, and his wife had told him these things, that his heart died within him, and he became as a stone. 38 And it came to pass about ten days after, that the Lord smote Nabal, that he died.

39 And when David heard that Nabal was dead, he said, Blessed be the Lord, that hath pleaded the cause of my reproach from the hand of Nabal, and hath kept his servant from evil: for the Lord hath returned the wickedness of Nabal upon his own head. And David sent and communed with Abigail, to take her to him to wife. 40 And when the servants of David were come to Abigail to Carmel, they spake unto her, saying, David sent us unto thee, to take thee to him to wife. 41 And she arose, and bowed herself on her face to the earth, and said, Behold, let thine handmaid be a servant to wash the feet of the servants of my lord. 42 And Abigail hasted, and arose, and rode upon an ass, with five damsels of hers that went after her; and she went after the messengers of David, and became his wife.

43 David also took Ahinoam of Jezreel; and they were also both of them his wives. 44 But Saul had given Michal his daughter, David's wife, to Phalti the son of Laish, which was of Gallim.

26 And the Ziphites came unto Saul to Gibeah, saying, Doth not David hide himself in the hill of Hachilah, which is before Jeshimon? 2 Then Saul arose, and went down to the wilderness of Ziph, having three thousand chosen men of Israel with him, to seek David in the wilderness of Ziph. 3 And Saul pitched in the hill of Hachilah, which is before Jeshimon, by the way. But David abode in the wilderness, and he saw that Saul came after him into the wilderness. 4 David therefore sent out spies, and understood that Saul was come in very deed. 5 And David arose, and came to the place where Saul had pitched: and David beheld the place where Saul lay, and Abner the son of Ner, the captain of his host: and Saul lay in the trench, and the people pitched round about him.

6 Then answered David and said to Ahimelech the Hittite, and to Abishai the son of Zeruiah, brother to Joab, saying, Who will go down with me to Saul to the camp? And Abishai said, I will go down with thee. 7 So David and Abishai came to the people by night: and, behold, Saul lay sleeping within the trench, and his spear stuck in the ground at his bolster: but Abner and the people lay round about him. 8 Then said Abishai to David, God hath delivered thine enemy into thine hand this day: now therefore let me smite him, I pray thee, with the spear even to the earth at once, and I will not smite him the second time. 9 And David said to Abishai, Destroy him not: for who can stretch forth his hand against the Lord's anointed, and be guiltless? 10 David said furthermore, As the Lord liveth, the Lord shall

smite him; or his day shall come to die; or he shall descend into battle, and perish. 11 The Lord forbid that I should stretch forth mine hand against the Lord's anointed: but, I pray thee, take thou now the spear that is at his bolster, and the cruse of water, and let us go. 12 So David took the spear and the cruse of water from Saul's bolster; and they gat them away, and no man saw it, nor knew it, neither awaked: for they were all asleep; because a deep sleep from the Lord was fallen upon them.

13 Then David went over to the other side, and stood on the top of a hill afar off; a great space being between them: 14 And David cried to the people, and to Abner the son of Ner, saying, Answerest thou not, Abner? Then Abner answered and said, Who art thou that criest to the king? 15 And David said to Abner, Art not thou a valiant man? and who is like to thee in Israel? wherefore then hast thou not kept thy lord the king? for there came one of the people in to destroy the king thy lord. 16 This thing is not good that thou hast done. As the Lord liveth, ye are worthy to die, because ye have not kept your master, the Lord's anointed. And now see where the king's spear is, and the cruse of water that was at his bolster.

17 And Saul knew David's voice, and said, Is this thy voice, my son David? And David said, It is my voice, my lord, O king. 18 And he said, Wherefore doth my lord thus pursue after his servant? for what have I done? or what evil is in mine hand? 19 Now therefore, I pray thee, let my lord the king hear the words of his servant. If the Lord have stirred thee up against me, let him accept an offering: but if they be the children of men, cursed be they before the Lord; for they have driven me out this day from abiding in the inheritance of the Lord, saying, Go, serve other gods. 20 Now therefore, let not my blood fall to the earth before the face of the Lord: for the king of Israel is come out to seek a flea, as when one doth hunt a partridge in the mountains.

21 Then said Saul, I have sinned: return, my son David; for I will no more do thee harm, because my soul was precious in thine eyes this day: behold, I have played the fool, and have erred exceedingly. 22 And David answered and said, Behold the king's spear! and let one of the young men come over and fetch it. 23 The Lord render to every man his righteousness and his faithfulness: for the Lord delivered thee into my hand to-day, but I would not stretch forth mine hand against the Lord's anointed. 24 And, behold, as thy life was much set by this day in mine eyes, so let my life be much set by in the eyes of the Lord, and let him deliver me out of all tribulation. 25 Then Saul said to David, Blessed be thou, my son David: thou shalt both do great things, and also shalt still prevail. So David went on his way, and Saul returned to his place.

27 And David said in his heart, I shall now perish one day by the hand of Saul: there is nothing better for me than that I should speedily escape into the land of the Philistines; and Saul shall despair of me, to seek me any more in any coast of Israel: so shall I escape out of

his hand. 2 And David arose, and he passed over with the six hundred men that were with him unto Achish, the son of Maoch, king of Gath. 3 And David dwelt with Achish at Gath, he and his men, every man with his household, even David with his two wives, Ahinoam the Jezreelitess, and Abigail the Carmelitess, Nabal's wife. 4 And it was told Saul that David was fled to Gath: and he sought no more again for him.

5 And David said unto Achish, If I have now found grace in thine eyes, let them give me a place in some town in the country, that I may dwell there: for why should thy servant dwell in the royal city with thee? 6 Then Achish gave him Ziklag that day: wherefore Ziklag pertaineth unto the kings of Judah unto this day.

7 And the time that David dwelt in the country of the Philistines was a full year and four months. 8 And David and his men went up, and invaded the Geshurites, and the Gezrites, and the Amalekites: for those nations were of old the inhabitants of the land, as thou goest to Shur, even unto the land of Egypt. 9 And David smote the land, and left neither man nor woman alive, and took away the sheep, and the oxen, and the asses, and the camels, and the apparel, and returned, and came to Achish. 10 And Achish said, Whither have ye made a road to-day? And David said, Against the south of Judah, and against the south of the Jerahmeelites, and against the south of the Kenites. 11 And David saved neither man nor woman alive, to bring tidings to Gath, saying, Lest they should tell on us, saying, So did David, and so will be his manner all the while he dwelleth in the country of the Philistines. 12 And Achish believed David, saying, He hath made his people Israel utterly to abhor him; therefore he shall be my servant for ever.

28 And it came to pass in those days, that the Philistines gathered their armies together for warfare, to fight with Israel. And Achish said unto David, Know thou assuredly, that thou shalt go out with me to battle, thou and thy men. 2 And David said to Achish, Surely thou shalt know what thy servant can do. And Achish said to David, Therefore will I make thee keeper of mine head for ever.

3 Now Samuel was dead, and all Israel had lamented him, and buried him in Ramah, even in his own city. And Saul had put away those that had familiar spirits, and the wizards, out of the land. 4 And the Philistines gathered themselves together, and came and pitched in Shunem: and Saul gathered all Israel together, and they pitched in Gilboa. 5 And when Saul saw the host of the Philistines, he was afraid, and his heart greatly trembled. 6 And when Saul inquired of the Lord, the Lord answered him not, neither by dreams, nor by Urim, nor by prophets.

7 Then said Saul unto his servants, Seek me a woman that hath a familiar spirit, that I may go to her, and inquire of her. And his servants said to him, Behold, there is a woman that hath a familiar spirit at En-dor. 8 And Saul disguised himself, and put on other

raiment, and he went, and two men with him, and they came to the woman by night: and he said, I pray thee, divine unto me by the familiar spirit, and bring me him up, whom I shall name unto thee. 9 And the woman said unto him, Behold, thou knowest what Saul hath done, how he hath cut off those that have familiar spirits, and the wizards, out of the land: wherefore then layest thou a snare for my life, to cause me to die? 10 And Saul sware to her by the Lord, saying, As the Lord liveth, there shall no punishment happen to thee for this thing. 11 Then said the woman, Whom shall I bring up unto thee? And he said, Bring me up Samuel. 12 And when the woman saw Samuel, she cried with a loud voice: and the woman spake to Saul, saying, Why hast thou deceived me? for thou art Saul. 13 And the king said unto her, Be not afraid: for what sawest thou? And the woman said unto Saul, I saw gods ascending out of the earth. 14 And he said unto her, What form is he of? And she said, An old man cometh up; and he is covered with a mantle. And Saul perceived that it was Samuel, and he stooped with his face to the ground, and bowed himself.

15 And Samuel said to Saul, Why hast thou disquieted me, to bring me up? And Saul answered, I am sore distressed; for the Philistines make war against me, and God is departed from me, and answereth me no more, neither by prophets, nor by dreams: therefore I have called thee, that thou mayest make known unto me what I shall do. 16 Then said Samuel, Wherefore then dost thou ask of me, seeing the Lord is departed from thee, and is become thine enemy? 17 And the Lord hath done to him, as he spake by me: for the Lord hath rent the kingdom out of thine hand, and given it to thy neighbor, even to David: 18 Because thou obeyedst not the voice of the Lord, nor executedst his fierce wrath upon Amalek, therefore hath the Lord done this thing unto thee this day. 19 Moreover the Lord will also deliver Israel with thee into the hand of the Philistines: and to-morrow shalt thou and thy sons be with me: the Lord also shall deliver the host of Israel into the hand of the Philistines.

20 Then Saul fell straightway all along on the earth, and was sore afraid, because of the words of Samuel; and there was no strength in him; for he had eaten no bread all the day, nor all the night. 21 And the woman came unto Saul, and saw that he was sore troubled, and said unto him, Behold, thine handmaid hath obeyed thy voice, and I have put my life in my hand, and have hearkened unto thy words which thou spakest unto me. 22 Now therefore, I pray thee, hearken thou also unto the voice of thine handmaid, and let me set a morsel of bread before thee; and eat, that thou mayest have strength, when thou goest on thy way. 23 But he refused, and said, I will not eat. But his servants, together with the woman, compelled him; and he hearkened unto their voice. So he arose from the earth, and sat upon the bed. 24 And the woman had a fat calf in the house; and she hasted, and killed it, and took flour, and kneaded it, and did bake unleavened bread thereof: 25 And she brought it before Saul, and

before his servants; and they did eat. Then they rose up, and went away that night.

**29** Now the Philistines gathered together all their armies to Aphek: and the Israelites pitched by a fountain which is in Jezreel. 2 And the lords of the Philistines passed on by hundreds, and by thousands: but David and his men passed on in the rearward with Achish. 3 Then said the princes of the Philistines, What do these Hebrews here? And Achish said unto the princes of the Philistines, Is not this David, the servant of Saul the king of Israel, which hath been with me these days, or these years, and I have found no fault in him since he fell unto me unto this day? 4 And the princes of the Philistines were wroth with him; and the princes of the Philistines said unto him, Make this fellow return, that he may go again to his place which thou hast appointed him, and let him not go down with us to battle, lest in the battle he be an adversary to us: for wherewith should he reconcile himself unto his master? should it not be with the heads of these men? 5 Is not this David, of whom they sang one to another in dances, saying

Saul slew his thousands,
And David his ten thousands?

6 Then Achish called David, and said unto him, Surely, as the Lord liveth, thou hast been upright, and thy going out and thy coming in with me in the host is good in my sight: for I have not found evil in thee since the day of thy coming unto me unto this day: nevertheless the lords favor thee not. 7 Wherefore now return, and go in peace, that thou displease not the lords of the Philistines. 8 And David said unto Achish, But what have I done? and what hast thou found in thy servant so long as I have been with thee unto this day, that I may not go fight against the enemies of my lord the king? 9 And Achish answered and said to David, I know that thou art good in my sight, as an angel of God: notwithstanding, the princes of the Philistines have said, He shall not go up with us to the battle. 10 Wherefore now rise up early in the morning with thy master's servants that are come with thee: and as soon as ye be up early in the morning, and have light, depart. 11 So David and his men rose up early to depart in the morning, to return into the land of the Philistines. And the Philistines went up to Jezreel.

**30** And it came to pass, when David and his men were come to Ziklag on the third day, that the Amalekites had invaded the south, and Ziklag, and smitten Ziklag, and burned it with fire; 2 And had taken the women captives, that were therein: they slew not any, either great or small, but carried them away, and went on their way. 3 So David and his men came to the city, and, behold, it was burned with fire; and their wives, and their sons, and their daughters, were taken captives. 4 Then David and the people that were with him lifted up their voice and wept, until they had no more power to weep. 5 And David's two wives were taken captives, Ahinoam the Jezreelitess, and

Abigail the wife of Nabal the Carmelite. 6 And David was greatly distressed; for the people spake of stoning him, because the soul of all the people was grieved, every man for his sons and for his daughters: but David encouraged himself in the Lord his God.

7 And David said to Abiathar the priest, Ahimelech's son, I pray thee, bring me hither the ephod. And Abiathar brought thither the ephod to David. 8 And David inquired at the Lord, saying, Shall I pursue after this troop? shall I overtake them? And he answered him, Pursue: for thou shalt surely overtake them, and without fail recover all. 9 So David went, he and the six hundred men that were with him, and came to the brook Besor, where those that were left behind stayed. 10 But David pursued, he and four hundred men: for two hundred abode behind, which were so faint that they could not go over the brook Besor.

11 And they found an Egyptian in the field, and brought him to David, and gave him bread, and he did eat; and they made him drink water; 12 And they gave him a piece of a cake of figs, and two clusters of raisins: and when he had eaten, his spirit came again to him: for he had eaten no bread, nor drunk any water, three days and three nights. 13 And David said unto him, To whom belongest thou? and whence art thou? And he said, I am a young man of Egypt, servant to an Amalekite; and my master left me, because three days agone I fell sick. 14 We made an invasion upon the south of the Cherethites, and upon the coast which belongeth to Judah, and upon the south of Caleb; and we burned Ziklag with fire. 15 And David said to him, Canst thou bring me down to this company? And he said, Swear unto me by God, that thou wilt neither kill me, nor deliver me into the hands of my master, and I will bring thee down to this company.

16 And when he had brought him down, behold, they were spread abroad upon all the earth, eating and drinking, and dancing, because of all the great spoil that they had taken out of the land of the Philistines, and out of the land of Judah. 17 And David smote them from the twilight even unto the evening of the next day: and there escaped not a man of them, save four hundred young men, which rode upon camels, and fled. 18 And David recovered all that the Amalekites had carried away: and David rescued his two wives. 19 And there was nothing lacking to them, neither small nor great, neither sons nor daughters, neither spoil, nor any thing that they had taken to them: David recovered all. 20 And David took all the flocks and the herds, which they drave before those other cattle, and said, This is David's spoil.

21 And David came to the two hundred men, which were so faint that they could not follow David, whom they had made also to abide at the brook Besor: and they went forth to meet David, and to meet the people that were with him: and when David came near to the people, he saluted them. 22 Then answered all the wicked men, and men of Belial, of those that went with David, and said, Because they went not with us, we will not give them aught of the spoil that we

have recovered, save to every man his wife and his children, that they may lead them away, and depart. 23 Then said David, Ye shall not do so, my brethren, with that which the Lord hath given us, who hath preserved us, and delivered the company that came against us into our hand. 24 For who will hearken unto you in this matter? but as his part is that goeth down to the battle, so shall his part be that tarrieth by the stuff: they shall part alike. 25 And it was so from that day forward, that he made it a statute and an ordinance for Israel unto this day.

26 And when David came to Ziklag, he sent of the spoil unto the elders of Judah, even to his friends, saying, Behold a present for you of the spoil of the enemies of the Lord; 27 To them which were in Beth-el, and to them which were in south Ramoth, and to them which were in Jattir, 28 And to them which were in Aroer, and to them which were in Siphmoth, and to them which were in Eshtemoa, 29 And to them which were in Rachal, and to them which were in the cities of the Jerahmeelites, and to them which were in the cities of the Kenites, 30 And to them which were in Hormah, and to them which were in Chor-ashan, and to them which were in Athach, 31 And to them which were in Hebron, and to all the places where David himself and his men were wont to haunt.

## THE DEATH OF SAUL

31 Now the Philistines fought against Israel: and the men of Israel fled from before the Philistines, and fell down slain in mount Gilboa. 2 And the Philistines followed hard upon Saul and upon his sons; and the Philistines slew Jonathan, and Abinadab, and Melchi-shua, Saul's sons. 3 And the battle went sore against Saul, and the archers hit him; and he was sore wounded of the archers. 4 Then said Saul unto his armor-bearer, Draw thy sword, and thrust me through therewith; lest these uncircumcised come and thrust me through, and abuse me. But his armor-bearer would not; for he was sore afraid. Therefore Saul took a sword, and fell upon it. 5 And when his armor-bearer saw that Saul was dead, he fell likewise upon his sword, and died with him. 6 So Saul died, and his three sons, and his armor-bearer, and all his men, that same day together. 7 And when the men of Israel that were on the other side of the valley, and they that were on the other side Jordan, saw that the men of Israel fled, and that Saul and his sons were dead, they forsook the cities, and fled; and the Philistines came and dwelt in them.

8 And it came to pass on the morrow, when the Philistines came to strip the slain, that they found Saul and his three sons fallen in mount Gilboa. 9 And they cut off his head, and stripped off his armor, and sent into the land of the Philistines round about, to publish it in the house of their idols, and among the people. 10 And they put his armor in the house of Ashtaroth: and they fastened his body to the wall of Beth-shan. 11 And when the inhabitants of Jabesh-gilead heard

of that which the Philistines had done to Saul, 12 All the valiant men arose, and went all night, and took the body of Saul and the bodies of his sons from the wall of Beth-shan, and came to Jabesh, and burnt them there. 13 And they took their bones, and buried them under a tree at Jabesh, and fasted seven days.

# Second Samuel

### DAVID'S LAMENT

1 Now it came to pass after the death of Saul, when David was returned from the slaughter of the Amalekites, and David had abode two days in Ziklag; 2 It came even to pass on the third day, that, behold, a man came out of the camp from Saul with his clothes rent, and earth upon his head: and so it was, when he came to David, that he fell to the earth, and did obeisance. 3 And David said unto him, From whence comest thou? And he said unto him, Out of the camp of Israel am I escaped. 4 And David said unto him, How went the matter? I pray thee, tell me. And he answered, That the people are fled from the battle, and many of the people also are fallen and dead; and Saul and Jonathan his son are dead also. 5 And David said unto the young man that told him, How knowest thou that Saul and Jonathan his son be dead? 6 And the young man that told him said, As I happened by chance upon mount Gilboa, behold, Saul leaned upon his spear; and, lo, the chariots and horsemen followed hard after him. 7 And when he looked behind him, he saw me, and called unto me. And I answered, Here am I. 8 And he said unto me, Who art thou? And I answered him, I am an Amalekite. 9 He said unto me again, Stand, I pray thee, upon me, and slay me: for anguish is come upon me, because my life is yet whole in me. 10 So I stood upon him, and slew him, because I was sure that he could not live after that he was fallen: and I took the crown that was upon his head, and the bracelet that was on his arm, and have brought them hither unto my lord.

11 Then David took hold on his clothes, and rent them; and likewise all the men that were with him: 12 And they mourned, and wept, and fasted until even, for Saul, and for Jonathan his son, and for the people of the Lord, and for the house of Israel; because they were fallen by the sword. 13 And David said unto the young man that told him, Whence art thou? And he answered, I am the son of a stranger, an Amalekite. 14 And David said unto him, How wast thou not afraid to stretch forth thine hand to destroy the Lord's anointed? 15 And David called one of the young men, and said, Go near, and fall upon him. And he smote him that he died. 16 And David said unto him, Thy blood be upon thy head; for thy mouth hath testified against thee, saying, I have slain the Lord's anointed.

17 And David lamented with this lamentation over Saul and over

Jonathan his son: 18 (Also he bade them teach the children of Judah the use of the bow: behold, it is written in the book of Jasher:)
19 The beauty of Israel is slain upon thy high places:
How are the mighty fallen!
20 Tell it not in Gath,
Publish it not in the streets of Askelon;
Lest the daughters of the Philistines rejoice,
Lest the daughters of the uncircumcised triumph.
21 Ye mountains of Gilboa,
Let there be no dew, neither let there be rain, upon you,
Nor fields of offerings:
For there the shield of the mighty is vilely cast away,
The shield of Saul, as though he had not been anointed with oil.
22 From the blood of the slain,
From the fat of the mighty,
The bow of Jonathan turned not back,
And the sword of Saul returned not empty.
23 Saul and Jonathan were lovely and pleasant in their lives,
And in their death they were not divided:
They were swifter than eagles,
They were stronger than lions.
24 Ye daughters of Israel, weep over Saul,
Who clothed you in scarlet, with other delights;
Who put on ornaments of gold upon your apparel.
25 How are the mighty fallen in the midst of the battle!
O Jonathan, thou wast slain in thine high places.
26 I am distressed for thee, my brother Jonathan:
Very pleasant hast thou been unto me:
Thy love to me was wonderful,
Passing the love of women.
27 How are the mighty fallen,
And the weapons of war perished!

## TWO KINGS IN ISRAEL

2 And it came to pass after this, that David inquired of the Lord, saying, Shall I go up into any of the cities of Judah? And the Lord said unto him, Go up. And David said, Whither shall I go up? And he said, Unto Hebron. 2 So David went up thither, and his two wives also, Ahinoam the Jezreelitess, and Abigail Nabal's wife the Carmelite. 3 And his men that were with him did David bring up, every man with his household: and they dwelt in the cities of Hebron. 4 And the men of Judah came, and there they anointed David king over the house of Judah.

And they told David, saying, That the men of Jabesh-gilead were they that buried Saul. 5 And David sent messengers unto the men of Jabesh-gilead, and said unto them, Blessed be ye of the Lord, that ye

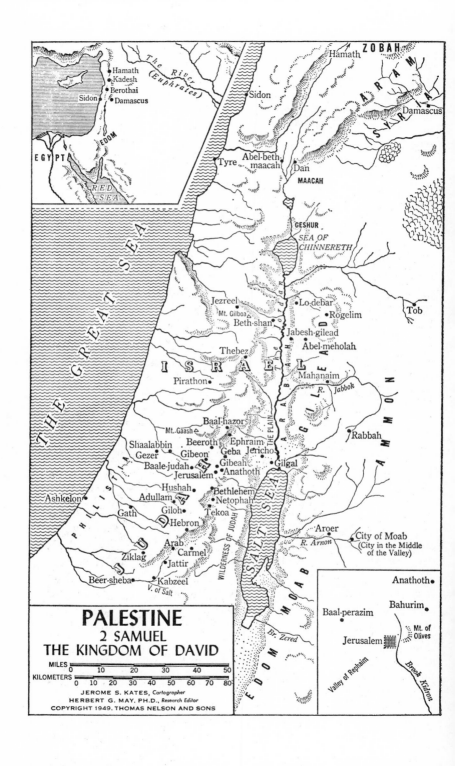

ZOBAH

Hamath
Kadesh
Berothai
Sidon
Damascus

EGYPT

EDOM

RED SEA

The River (Euphrates)

Sidon

Hamath

A R A M

S Y R I A

Damascus

Tyre

Abel-beth-maacah

Dan

MAACAH

GESHUR

SEA OF CHINNERETH

Jezreel
Mt. Gilboa
Beth-shan

Lo-debar
Rogelim

Tob

Jabesh-gilead
Abel-meholah

Thebez

I S R A E L

Pirathon

Mahanaim

G I L E A D

R. Jabbok

A M M O N

Baal-hazor
Mt. Gaash

Beeroth

Ephraim

Shaalabbin
Gezer
Gibeon
Geba
Jericho

Baale-judah
Gibeah
Gilgal

Jerusalem
Anathoth

Rabbah

Hushah

Bethlehem
Netophah

Ashkelon

Adullam
Giloh
Tekoa

Gath
Hebron

P H I L I S T I A

J U D A H

Arab
Carmel

Ziklag

Jattir

Aroer

R. Arnon

City of Moab
(City in the Middle of the Valley)

Beer-sheba
Kabzeel

V. of Salt

WILDERNESS OF JUDAH

SALT SEA

THE PLAIN

ARABAH

The Jordan

E D O M

M O A B

Br. Zered

THE GREAT SEA

## PALESTINE
## 2 SAMUEL
## THE KINGDOM OF DAVID

MILES
0        10        20        30        40        50
KILOMETERS
0   10   20   30   40   50   60   70   80

JEROME S. KATES, Cartographer
HERBERT G. MAY, PH.D., Research Editor
COPYRIGHT 1949, THOMAS NELSON AND SONS

Anathoth

Bahurim

Baal-perazim

Mt. of Olives

Jerusalem

Valley of Rephaim

Brook Kidron

have showed this kindness unto your lord, even unto Saul, and have buried him. 6 And now the Lord show kindness and truth unto you: and I also will requite you this kindness, because ye have done this thing. 7 Therefore now let your hands be strengthened, and be ye valiant: for your master Saul is dead, and also the house of Judah have anointed me king over them.

8 But Abner the son of Ner, captain of Saul's host, took Ish-bosheth the son of Saul, and brought him over to Mahanaim; 9 And made him king over Gilead, and over the Ashurites, and over Jezreel, and over Ephraim, and over Benjamin, and over all Israel. 10 Ish-bosheth Saul's son was forty years old when he began to reign over Israel, and reigned two years. But the house of Judah followed David. 11 And the time that David was king in Hebron over the house of Judah was seven years and six months.

12 And Abner the son of Ner, and the servants of Ish-bosheth the son of Saul, went out from Mahanaim to Gibeon. 13 And Joab the son of Zeruiah, and the servants of David, went out, and met together by the pool of Gibeon: and they sat down, the one on the one side of the pool, and the other on the other side of the pool. 14 And Abner said to Joab, Let the young men now arise, and play before us. And Joab said, Let them arise. 15 Then there arose and went over by number twelve of Benjamin, which pertained to Ish-bosheth the son of Saul, and twelve of the servants of David. 16 And they caught every one his fellow by the head, and thrust his sword in his fellow's side; so they fell down together: wherefore that place was called Helkath-hazzurim, which is in Gibeon. 17 And there was a very sore battle that day; and Abner was beaten, and the men of Israel, before the servants of David.

18 And there were three sons of Zeruiah there, Joab, and Abishai, and Asahel: and Asahel was as light of foot as a wild roe. 19 And Asahel pursued after Abner; and in going he turned not to the right hand nor to the left from following Abner. 20 Then Abner looked behind him, and said, Art thou Asahel? And he answered, I am. 21 And Abner said to him, Turn thee aside to thy right hand or to thy left, and lay thee hold on one of the young men, and take thee his armor. But Asahel would not turn aside from following of him. 22 And Abner said again to Asahel, Turn thee aside from following me: wherefore should I smite thee to the ground? how then should I hold up my face to Joab thy brother? 23 Howbeit he refused to turn aside: wherefore Abner with the hinder end of the spear smote him under the fifth rib, that the spear came out behind him; and he fell down there, and died in the same place: and it came to pass, that as many as came to the place where Asahel fell down and died stood still.

24 Joab also and Abishai pursued after Abner: and the sun went down when they were come to the hill of Ammah, that lieth before Giah by the way of the wilderness of Gibeon. 25 And the children of Benjamin gathered themselves together after Abner, and became one troop, and stood on the top of a hill. 26 Then Abner called to Joab,

and said, Shall the sword devour for ever? knowest thou not that it will be bitterness in the latter end? how long shall it be then, ere thou bid the people return from following their brethren? 27 And Joab said, As God liveth, unless thou hadst spoken, surely then in the morning the people had gone up every one from following his brother. 28 So Joab blew a trumpet, and all the people stood still, and pursued after Israel no more, neither fought they any more. 29 And Abner and his men walked all that night through the plain, and passed over Jordan, and went through all Bithron, and they came to Mahanaim.

30 And Joab returned from following Abner: and when he had gathered all the people together, there lacked of David's servants nineteen men and Asahel. 31 But the servants of David had smitten of Benjamin, and of Abner's men, so that three hundred and threescore men died. 32 And they took up Asahel, and buried him in the sepulchre of his father, which was in Bethlehem. And Joab and his men went all night, and they came to Hebron at break of day.

3 Now there was long war between the house of Saul and the house of David: but David waxed stronger and stronger, and the house of Saul waxed weaker and weaker.

2 And unto David were sons born in Hebron: and his firstborn was Amnon, of Ahinoam the Jezreelitess; 3 And his second, Chileab, of Abigail the wife of Nabal the Carmelite; and the third, Absalom the son of Maacah the daughter of Talmai king of Geshur; 4 And the fourth, Adonijah the son of Haggith; and the fifth, Shephatiah the son of Abital; 5 And the sixth, Ithream, by Eglah David's wife. These were born to David in Hebron.

6 And it came to pass, while there was war between the house of Saul and the house of David, that Abner made himself strong for the house of Saul. 7 And Saul had a concubine, whose name was Rizpah, the daughter of Aiah: and Ish-bosheth said to Abner, Wherefore hast thou gone in unto my father's concubine? 8 Then was Abner very wroth for the words of Ish-bosheth, and said, Am I a dog's head, which against Judah do show kindness this day unto the house of Saul thy father, to his brethren, and to his friends, and have not delivered thee into the hand of David, that thou chargest me to-day with a fault concerning this woman? 9 So do God to Abner, and more also, except, as the Lord hath sworn to David, even so I do to him; 10 To translate the kingdom from the house of Saul, and to set up the throne of David over Israel and over Judah, from Dan even to Beer-sheba. 11 And he could not answer Abner a word again, because he feared him.

12 And Abner sent messengers to David on his behalf, saying, Whose is the land? saying also, Make thy league with me, and, behold, my hand shall be with thee, to bring about all Israel unto thee. 13 And he said, Well; I will make a league with thee: but one thing I require of thee, that is, Thou shalt not see my face, except thou first bring

Michal Saul's daughter, when thou comest to see my face. 14 And David sent messengers to Ish-bosheth Saul's son, saying, Deliver me my wife Michal, which I espoused to me for a hundred foreskins of the Philistines. 15 And Ish-bosheth sent, and took her from her husband, even from Phaltiel the son of Laish. 16 And her husband went with her along weeping behind her to Bahurim. Then said Abner unto him, Go, return. And he returned.

17 And Abner had communication with the elders of Israel, saying, Ye sought for David in times past to be king over you: 18 Now then do it: for the Lord hath spoken of David, saying, By the hand of my servant David I will save my people Israel out of the hand of the Philistines, and out of the hand of all their enemies. 19 And Abner also spake in the ears of Benjamin: and Abner went also to speak in the ears of David in Hebron all that seemed good to Israel, and that seemed good to the whole house of Benjamin. 20 So Abner came to David to Hebron, and twenty men with him. And David made Abner and the men that were with him a feast. 21 And Abner said unto David, I will arise and go, and will gather all Israel unto my lord the king, that they may make a league with thee, and that thou mayest reign over all that thine heart desireth. And David sent Abner away; and he went in peace.

22 And, behold, the servants of David and Joab came from pursuing a troop, and brought in a great spoil with them: but Abner was not with David in Hebron; for he had sent him away, and he was gone in peace. 23 When Joab and all the host that was with him were come, they told Joab, saying, Abner the son of Ner came to the king, and he hath sent him away, and he is gone in peace. 24 Then Joab came to the king, and said, What hast thou done? behold, Abner came unto thee; why is it that thou hast sent him away, and he is quite gone? 25 Thou knowest Abner the son of Ner, that he came to deceive thee, and to know thy going out and thy coming in, and to know all that thou doest. 26 And when Joab was come out from David, he sent messengers after Abner, which brought him again from the well of Sirah: but David knew it not.

27 And when Abner was returned to Hebron, Joab took him aside in the gate to speak with him quietly, and smote him there under the fifth rib, that he died, for the blood of Asahel his brother. 28 And afterward when David heard it, he said, I and my kingdom are guiltless before the Lord for ever from the blood of Abner the son of Ner. 29 Let it rest on the head of Joab; and on all his father's house; and let there not fail from the house of Joab one that hath an issue, or that is a leper, or that leaneth on a staff, or that falleth on the sword, or that lacketh bread. 30 So Joab and Abishai his brother slew Abner, because he had slain their brother Asahel at Gibeon in the battle.

31 And David said to Joab, and to all the people that were with him, Rend your clothes, and gird you with sackcloth, and mourn before Abner. And king David himself followed the bier. 32 And they buried

Abner in Hebron: and the king lifted up his voice, and wept at the grave of Abner; and all the people wept. 33 And the king lamented over Abner, and said,

> Died Abner as a fool dieth?

34 Thy hands were not bound,
> Nor thy feet put into fetters:
> As a man falleth before wicked men, so fellest thou.

And all the people wept again over him. 35 And when all the people came to cause David to eat meat while it was yet day, David sware, saying, So do God to me, and more also, if I taste bread, or aught else, till the sun be down. 36 And all the people took notice of it, and it pleased them: as whatsoever the king did pleased all the people. 37 For all the people and all Israel understood that day that it was not of the king to slay Abner the son of Ner. 38 And the king said unto his servants, Know ye not that there is a prince and a great man fallen this day in Israel? 39 And I am this day weak, though anointed king; and these men the sons of Zeruiah be too hard for me: the Lord shall reward the doer of evil according to his wickedness.

4    And when Saul's son heard that Abner was dead in Hebron, his hands were feeble, and all the Israelites were troubled. 2 And Saul's son had two men that were captains of bands: the name of the one was Baanah, and the name of the other Rechab, the sons of Rimmon a Beerothite, of the children of Benjamin: (for Beeroth also was reckoned to Benjamin: 3 And the Beerothites fled to Gittaim, and were sojourners there until this day.)

4 And Jonathan, Saul's son, had a son that was lame of his feet. He was five years old when the tidings came of Saul and Jonathan out of Jezreel, and his nurse took him up, and fled: and it came to pass, as she made haste to flee, that he fell, and became lame. And his name was Mephibosheth.

5 And the sons of Rimmon the Beerothite, Rechab and Baanah, went, and came about the heat of the day to the house of Ish-bosheth, who lay on a bed at noon. 6 And they came thither into the midst of the house, as though they would have fetched wheat; and they smote him under the fifth rib: and Rechab and Baanah his brother escaped. 7 For when they came into the house, he lay on his bed in his bedchamber, and they smote him, and slew him, and beheaded him, and took his head, and gat them away through the plain all night. 8 And they brought the head of Ish-bosheth unto David to Hebron, and said to the king, Behold the head of Ish-bosheth the son of Saul thine enemy, which sought thy life; and the Lord hath avenged my lord the king this day of Saul, and of his seed. 9 And David answered Rechab and Baanah his brother, the sons of Rimmon the Beerothite, and said unto them, As the Lord liveth, who hath redeemed my soul out of all adversity, 10 When one told me, saying, Behold, Saul is dead, thinking to have brought good tidings, I took hold of him, and slew him in Ziklag, who thought that I would have given him a reward for his

tidings: 11 How much more, when wicked men have slain a right-eous person in his own house upon his bed? shall I not therefore now require his blood of your hand, and take you away from the earth? 12 And David commanded his young men, and they slew them, and cut off their hands and their feet, and hanged them up over the pool in Hebron. But they took the head of Ish-bosheth, and buried it in the sepulchre of Abner in Hebron.

## DAVID RULES ALL ISRAEL

5 Then came all the tribes of Israel to David unto Hebron, and spake, saying, Behold, we are thy bone and thy flesh. 2 Also in time past, when Saul was king over us, thou wast he that leddest out and broughtest in Israel: and the Lord said to thee, Thou shalt feed my people Israel, and thou shalt be a captain over Israel. 3 So all the elders of Israel came to the king to Hebron; and king David made a league with them in Hebron before the Lord: and they anointed David king over Israel.

4 David was thirty years old when he began to reign, and he reigned forty years. 5 In Hebron he reigned over Judah seven years and six months: and in Jerusalem he reigned thirty and three years over all Israel and Judah.

6 And the king and his men went to Jerusalem unto the Jebusites, the inhabitants of the land: which spake unto David, saying, Except thou take away the blind and the lame, thou shalt not come in hither: thinking, David cannot come in hither. 7 Nevertheless, David took the stronghold of Zion: the same is the city of David. 8 And David said on that day, Whosoever getteth up to the gutter, and smiteth the Jebusites, and the lame and the blind, that are hated of David's soul, he shall be chief and captain. Wherefore they said, The blind and the lame shall not come into the house. 9 So David dwelt in the fort, and called it the city of David. And David built round about from Millo and inward. 10 And David went on, and grew great, and the Lord God of hosts was with him.

11 And Hiram king of Tyre sent messengers to David, and cedar trees, and carpenters, and masons: and they built David a house. 12 And David perceived that the Lord had established him king over Israel, and that he had exalted his kingdom for his people Israel's sake.

13 And David took him more concubines and wives out of Jerusalem, after he was come from Hebron: and there were yet sons and daughters born to David. 14 And these be the names of those that were born unto him in Jerusalem; Shammuah, and Shobab, and Nathan, and Solomon, 15 Ibhar also, and Elishua, and Nepheg, and Japhia, 16 And Elishama, and Eliada, and Eliphalet.

17 But when the Philistines heard that they had anointed David king over Israel, all the Philistines came up to seek David; and David heard of it, and went down to the hold. 18 The Philistines also came and spread themselves in the valley of Rephaim. 19 And David in-

quired of the Lord, saying, Shall I go up to the Philistines? wilt thou deliver them into mine hand? And the Lord said unto David, Go up: for I will doubtless deliver the Philistines into thine hand. 20 And David came to Baal-perazim, and David smote them there, and said, The Lord hath broken forth upon mine enemies before me, as the breach of waters. Therefore he called the name of that place Baal-perazim. 21 And there they left their images, and David and his men burned them.

22 And the Philistines came up yet again, and spread themselves in the valley of Rephaim. 23 And when David inquired of the Lord, he said, Thou shalt not go up; but fetch a compass behind them, and come upon them over against the mulberry trees. 24 And let it be, when thou hearest the sound of a going in the tops of the mulberry trees, that then thou shalt bestir thyself: for then shall the Lord go out before thee, to smite the host of the Philistines. 25 And David did so, as the Lord had commanded him; and smote the Philistines from Geba until thou come to Gazer.

6 Again, David gathered together all the chosen men of Israel, thirty thousand. 2 And David arose, and went with all the people that were with him from Baale of Judah, to bring up from thence the ark of God, whose name is called by the name of the Lord of hosts that dwelleth between the cherubim. 3 And they set the ark of God upon a new cart, and brought it out of the house of Abinadab that was in Gibeah: and Uzzah and Ahio, the sons of Abinadab, drave the new cart. 4 And they brought it out of the house of Abinadab which was at Gibeah, accompanying the ark of God: and Ahio went before the ark. 5 And David and all the house of Israel played before the Lord on all manner of instruments made of fir wood, even on harps, and on psalteries, and on timbrels, and on cornets, and on cymbals.

6 And when they came to Nachon's threshingfloor, Uzzah put forth his hand to the ark of God, and took hold of it; for the oxen shook it. 7 And the anger of the Lord was kindled against Uzzah, and God smote him there for his error; and there he died by the ark of God. 8 And David was displeased, because the Lord had made a breach upon Uzzah: and he called the name of the place Perez-uzzah to this day. 9 And David was afraid of the Lord that day, and said, How shall the ark of the Lord come to me? 10 So David would not remove the ark of the Lord unto him into the city of David: but David carried it aside into the house of Obed-edom the Gittite. 11 And the ark of the Lord continued in the house of Obed-edom the Gittite three months: and the Lord blessed Obed-edom, and all his household.

12 And it was told king David, saying, The Lord hath blessed the house of Obed-edom, and all that pertaineth unto him, because of the ark of God. So David went and brought up the ark of God from the house of Obed-edom into the city of David with gladness. 13 And it was so, that when they that bare the ark of the Lord had gone six paces, he sacrificed oxen and fatlings. 14 And David danced before

the Lord with all his might; and David was girded with a linen ephod. 15 So David and all the house of Israel brought up the ark of the Lord with shouting, and with the sound of the trumpet.

16 And as the ark of the Lord came into the city of David, Michal Saul's daughter looked through a window, and saw king David leaping and dancing before the Lord; and she despised him in her heart. 17 And they brought in the ark of the Lord, and set it in his place, in the midst of the tabernacle that David had pitched for it: and David offered burnt offerings and peace offerings before the Lord. 18 And as soon as David had made an end of offering burnt offerings and peace offerings, he blessed the people in the name of the Lord of hosts. 19 And he dealt among all the people, even among the whole multitude of Israel, as well to the women as men, to every one a cake of bread, and a good piece of flesh, and a flagon of wine. So all the people departed every one to his house.

20 Then David returned to bless his household. And Michal the daughter of Saul came out to meet David, and said, How glorious was the king of Israel to-day, who uncovered himself to-day in the eyes of the handmaids of his servants, as one of the vain fellows shamelessly uncovereth himself! 21 And David said unto Michal, It was before the Lord, which chose me before thy father, and before all his house, to appoint me ruler over the people of the Lord, over Israel: therefore will I play before the Lord. 22 And I will yet be more vile than thus, and will be base in mine own sight: and of the maidservants which thou hast spoken of, of them shall I be had in honor. 23 Therefore Michal the daughter of Saul had no child unto the day of her death.

7 And it came to pass, when the king sat in his house, and the Lord had given him rest round about from all his enemies; 2 That the king said unto Nathan the prophet, See now, I dwell in a house of cedar, but the ark of God dwelleth within curtains. 3 And Nathan said to the king, Go, do all that is in thine heart; for the Lord is with thee. 4 And it came to pass that night, that the word of the Lord came unto Nathan, saying, 5 Go and tell my servant David, Thus saith the Lord, Shalt thou build me a house for me to dwell in? 6 Whereas I have not dwelt in any house since the time that I brought up the children of Israel out of Egypt, even to this day, but have walked in a tent and in a tabernacle. 7 In all the places wherein I have walked with all the children of Israel spake I a word with any of the tribes of Israel, whom I commanded to feed my people Israel, saying, Why build ye not me a house of cedar? 8 Now therefore so shalt thou say unto my servant David, Thus saith the Lord of hosts, I took thee from the sheepcote, from following the sheep, to be ruler over my people, over Israel: 9 And I was with thee whithersoever thou wentest, and have cut off all thine enemies out of thy sight, and have made thee a great name, like unto the name of the great men that are in the earth. 10 Moreover I will appoint a place for my people Israel, and will plant them, that they may dwell in a place of their own, and move no more; neither

207

shall the children of wickedness afflict them any more, as beforetime, 11 And as since the time that I commanded judges to be over my people Israel, and have caused thee to rest from all thine enemies. Also the Lord telleth thee that he will make thee a house. 12 And when thy days be fulfilled, and thou shalt sleep with thy fathers, I will set up thy seed after thee, which shall proceed out of thy bowels, and I will establish his kingdom. 13 He shall build a house for my name, and I will stablish the throne of his kingdom for ever. 14 I will be his father, and he shall be my son. If he commit iniquity, I will chasten him with the rod of men, and with the stripes of the children of men: 15 But my mercy shall not depart away from him, as I took it from Saul, whom I put away before thee. 16 And thine house and thy kingdom shall be established for ever before thee: thy throne shall be established for ever. 17 According to all these words, and according to all this vision, so did Nathan speak unto David.

18 Then went king David in, and sat before the Lord, and he said, Who am I, O Lord God? and what is my house, that thou hast brought me hitherto? 19 And this was yet a small thing in thy sight, O Lord God; but thou hast spoken also of thy servant's house for a great while to come. And is this the manner of man, O Lord God? 20 And what can David say more unto thee? for thou, Lord God, knowest thy servant. 21 For thy word's sake, and according to thine own heart, hast thou done all these great things, to make thy servant know them. 22 Wherefore thou art great, O Lord God: for there is none like thee, neither is there any God besides thee, according to all that we have heard with our ears. 23 And what one nation in the earth is like thy people, even like Israel, whom God went to redeem for a people to himself, and to make him a name, and to do for you great things and terrible, for thy land, before thy people, which thou redeemedst to thee from Egypt, from the nations and their gods? 24 For thou hast confirmed to thyself thy people Israel to be a people unto thee for ever: and thou, Lord, art become their God. 25 And now, O Lord God, the word that thou hast spoken concerning thy servant, and concerning his house, establish it for ever, and do as thou hast said. 26 And let thy name be magnified for ever, saying, The Lord of hosts is the God over Israel: and let the house of thy servant David be established before thee. 27 For thou, O Lord of hosts, God of Israel, hast revealed to thy servant, saying, I will build thee a house: therefore hath thy servant found in his heart to pray this prayer unto thee. 28 And now, O Lord God, thou art that God, and thy words be true, and thou hast promised this goodness unto thy servant: 29 Therefore now let it please thee to bless the house of thy servant, that it may continue for ever before thee: for thou, O Lord God, hast spoken it: and with thy blessing let the house of thy servant be blessed for ever.

8 And after this it came to pass, that David smote the Philistines, and subdued them: and David took Metheg-ammah out of the hand of the Philistines.

2 And he smote Moab, and measured them with a line, casting them down to the ground. And so the Moabites became David's servants, and brought gifts.

3 David smote also Hadadezer, the son of Rehob, king of Zobah, as he went to recover his border at the river Euphrates. 4 And David took from him a thousand chariots, and seven hundred horsemen, and twenty thousand footmen: and David houghed all the chariot horses, but reserved of them for a hundred chariots. 5 And when the Syrians of Damascus came to succor Hadadezer king of Zobah, David slew of the Syrians two and twenty thousand men. 6 Then David put garrisons in Syria of Damascus: and the Syrians became servants to David, and brought gifts. And the Lord preserved David whithersoever he went. 7 And David took the shields of gold that were on the servants of Hadadezer, and brought them to Jerusalem. 8 And from Betah, and from Berothai, cities of Hadadezer, king David took exceeding much brass.

9 When Toi king of Hamath heard that David had smitten all the host of Hadadezer, 10 Then Toi sent Joram his son unto king David, to salute him, and to bless him, because he had fought against Hadadezer, and smitten him: for Hadadezer had wars with Toi. And Joram brought with him vessels of silver, and vessels of gold, and vessels of brass: 11 Which also king David did dedicate unto the Lord, with the silver and gold that he had dedicated of all nations which he subdued; 12 Of Syria, and of Moab, and of the children of Ammon, and of the Philistines, and of Amalek, and of the spoil of Hadadezer, son of Rehob, king of Zobah. 13 And David gat him a name when he returned from smiting of the Syrians in the valley of salt, being eighteen thousand men. 14 And he put garrisons in Edom; throughout all Edom put he garrisons, and all they of Edom became David's servants. And the Lord preserved David whithersoever he went.

15 And David reigned over all Israel; and David executed judgment and justice unto all his people. 16 And Joab the son of Zeruiah was over the host; and Jehoshaphat the son of Ahilud was recorder; 17 And Zadok the son of Ahitub, and Ahimelech the son of Abiathar, were the priests; and Seraiah was the scribe; 18 And Benaiah the son of Jehoiada was over both the Cherethites and the Pelethites; and David's sons were chief rulers.

9 And David said, Is there yet any that is left of the house of Saul, that I may show him kindness for Jonathan's sake? 2 And there was of the house of Saul a servant whose name was Ziba. And when they had called him unto David, the king said unto him, Art thou Ziba? And he said, Thy servant is he. 3 And the king said, Is there not yet any of the house of Saul, that I may show the kindness of God unto him? And Ziba said unto the king, Jonathan hath yet a son, which is lame on his feet. 4 And the king said unto him, Where is he? And Ziba said unto the king, Behold, he is in the house of Machir, the son of Ammiel, in Lo-debar. 5 Then king David sent, and fetched him out

of the house of Machir, the son of Ammiel, from Lo-debar. 6 Now when Mephibosheth, the son of Jonathan, the son of Saul, was come unto David, he fell on his face, and did reverence. And David said, Mephibosheth. And he answered, Behold thy servant! 7 And David said unto him, Fear not: for I will surely show thee kindness for Jonathan thy father's sake, and will restore thee all the land of Saul thy father; and thou shalt eat bread at my table continually. 8 And he bowed himself, and said, What is thy servant, that thou shouldest look upon such a dead dog as I am?

9 Then the king called to Ziba, Saul's servant, and said unto him, I have given unto thy master's son all that pertained to Saul and to all his house. 10 Thou therefore, and thy sons, and thy servants, shall till the land for him, and thou shalt bring in the fruits, that thy master's son may have food to eat: but Mephibosheth thy master's son shall eat bread alway at my table. Now Ziba had fifteen sons and twenty servants. 11 Then said Ziba unto the king, According to all that my lord the king hath commanded his servant, so shall thy servant do. As for Mephibosheth, said the king, he shall eat at my table, as one of the king's sons. 12 And Mephibosheth had a young son, whose name was Micha. And all that dwelt in the house of Ziba were servants unto Mephibosheth. 13 So Mephibosheth dwelt in Jerusalem: for he did eat continually at the king's table; and was lame on both his feet.

10 And it came to pass after this, that the king of the children of Ammon died, and Hanun his son reigned in his stead. 2 Then said David, I will show kindness unto Hanun the son of Nahash, as his father showed kindness unto me. And David sent to comfort him by the hand of his servants for his father. And David's servants came into the land of the children of Ammon. 3 And the princes of the children of Ammon said unto Hanun their lord, Thinkest thou that David doth honor thy father, that he hath sent comforters unto thee? hath not David rather sent his servants unto thee, to search the city, and to spy it out, and to overthrow it? 4 Wherefore Hanun took David's servants, and shaved off the one half of their beards, and cut off their garments in the middle, even to their buttocks, and sent them away. 5 When they told it unto David, he sent to meet them, because the men were greatly ashamed: and the king said, Tarry at Jericho until your beards be grown, and then return.

6 And when the children of Ammon saw that they stank before David, the children of Ammon sent and hired the Syrians of Beth-rehob, and the Syrians of Zoba, twenty thousand footmen, and of king Maacah a thousand men, and of Ish-tob twelve thousand men. 7 And when David heard of it, he sent Joab, and all the host of the mighty men. 8 And the children of Ammon came out, and put the battle in array at the entering in of the gate: and the Syrians of Zoba, and of Rehob, and Ish-tob, and Maacah, were by themselves in the field.

9 When Joab saw that the front of the battle was against him before

and behind, he chose of all the choice men of Israel, and put them in array against the Syrians: 10 And the rest of the people he delivered into the hand of Abishai his brother, that he might put them in array against the children of Ammon. 11 And he said, If the Syrians be too strong for me, then thou shalt help me: but if the children of Ammon be too strong for thee, then I will come and help thee. 12 Be of good courage, and let us play the men for our people, and for the cities of our God: and the Lord do that which seemeth him good. 13 And Joab drew nigh, and the people that were with him, unto the battle against the Syrians: and they fled before him. 14 And when the children of Ammon saw that the Syrians were fled, then fled they also before Abishai, and entered into the city. So Joab returned from the children of Ammon, and came to Jerusalem.

15 And when the Syrians saw that they were smitten before Israel, they gathered themselves together. 16 And Hadarezer sent, and brought out the Syrians that were beyond the river; and they came to Helam: and Shobach the captain of the host of Hadarezer went before them. 17 And when it was told David, he gathered all Israel together, and passed over Jordan, and came to Helam. And the Syrians set themselves in array against David, and fought with him. 18 And the Syrians fled before Israel; and David slew the men of seven hundred chariots of the Syrians, and forty thousand horsemen, and smote Shobach the captain of their host, who died there. 19 And when all the kings that were servants to Hadarezer saw that they were smitten before Israel, they made peace with Israel, and served them. So the Syrians feared to help the children of Ammon any more.

## DAVID AND BATHSHEBA

11 And it came to pass, after the year was expired, at the time when kings go forth to battle, that David sent Joab, and his servants with him, and all Israel; and they destroyed the children of Ammon, and besieged Rabbah. But David tarried still at Jerusalem.

2 And it came to pass in an eveningtide, that David arose from off his bed, and walked upon the roof of the king's house: and from the roof he saw a woman washing herself; and the woman was very beautiful to look upon. 3 And David sent and inquired after the woman. And one said, Is not this Bath-sheba, the daughter of Eliam, the wife of Uriah the Hittite? 4 And David sent messengers, and took her; and she came in unto him, and he lay with her; for she was purified from her uncleanness: and she returned unto her house. 5 And the woman conceived, and sent and told David, and said, I am with child.

6 And David sent to Joab, saying, Send me Uriah the Hittite. And Joab sent Uriah to David. 7 And when Uriah was come unto him, David demanded of him how Joab did, and how the people did, and how the war prospered. 8 And David said to Uriah, Go down to thy house, and wash thy feet. And Uriah departed out of the king's house,

and there followed him a mess of meat from the king. 9 But Uriah slept at the door of the king's house with all the servants of his lord, and went not down to his house. 10 And when they had told David, saying, Uriah went not down unto his house, David said unto Uriah, Camest thou not from thy journey? why then didst thou not go down unto thine house? 11 And Uriah said unto David, The ark, and Israel, and Judah, abide in tents; and my lord Joab, and the servants of my lord, are encamped in the open fields; shall I then go into mine house, to eat and to drink, and to lie with my wife? as thou livest, and as thy soul liveth, I will not do this thing. 12 And David said to Uriah, Tarry here to-day also, and to-morrow I will let thee depart. So Uriah abode in Jerusalem that day, and the morrow. 13 And when David had called him, he did eat and drink before him; and he made him drunk: and at even he went out to lie on his bed with the servants of his lord, but went not down to his house.

14 And it came to pass in the morning, that David wrote a letter to Joab, and sent it by the hand of Uriah. 15 And he wrote in the letter, saying, Set ye Uriah in the forefront of the hottest battle, and retire ye from him, that he may be smitten, and die. 16 And it came to pass, when Joab observed the city, that he assigned Uriah unto a place where he knew that valiant men were. 17 And the men of the city went out, and fought with Joab: and there fell some of the people of the servants of David; and Uriah the Hittite died also. 18 Then Joab sent and told David all the things concerning the war; 19 And charged the messenger, saying, When thou hast made an end of telling the matters of the war unto the king, 20 And if so be that the king's wrath arise, and he say unto thee, Wherefore approached ye so nigh unto the city when ye did fight? knew ye not that they would shoot from the wall? 21 Who smote Abimelech the son of Jerubbesheth? did not a woman cast a piece of a millstone upon him from the wall, that he died in Thebaz? why went ye nigh the wall? then say thou, Thy servant Uriah the Hittite is dead also.

22 So the messenger went, and came and showed David all that Joab had sent him for. 23 And the messenger said unto David, Surely the men prevailed against us, and came out unto us into the field, and we were upon them even unto the entering of the gate. 24 And the shooters shot from off the wall upon thy servants; and some of the king's servants be dead, and thy servant Uriah the Hittite is dead also. 25 Then David said unto the messenger, Thus shalt thou say unto Joab, Let not this thing displease thee, for the sword devoureth one as well as another: make thy battle more strong against the city, and overthrow it: and encourage thou him.

26 And when the wife of Uriah heard that Uriah her husband was dead, she mourned for her husband. 27 And when the mourning was past, David sent and fetched her to his house, and she became his wife, and bare him a son. But the thing that David had done displeased the Lord.

12 And the Lord sent Nathan unto David. And he came unto him, and said unto him, There were two men in one city; the one rich, and the other poor. 2 The rich man had exceeding many flocks and herds: 3 But the poor man had nothing, save one little ewe lamb, which he had bought and nourished up: and it grew up together with him, and with his children; it did eat of his own meat, and drank of his own cup, and lay in his bosom, and was unto him as a daughter. 4 And there came a traveler unto the rich man, and he spared to take of his own flock and of his own herd, to dress for the wayfaring man that was come unto him; but took the poor man's lamb, and dressed it for the man that was come to him. 5 And David's anger was greatly kindled against the man; and he said to Nathan, As the Lord liveth, the man that hath done this thing shall surely die: 6 And he shall restore the lamb fourfold, because he did this thing, and because he had no pity.

7 And Nathan said to David, Thou art the man. Thus saith the Lord God of Israel, I anointed thee king over Israel, and I delivered thee out of the hand of Saul; 8 And I gave thee thy master's house, and thy master's wives into thy bosom, and gave thee the house of Israel and of Judah; and if that had been too little, I would moreover have given unto thee such and such things. 9 Wherefore hast thou despised the commandment of the Lord, to do evil in his sight? thou hast killed Uriah the Hittite with the sword, and hast taken his wife to be thy wife, and hast slain him with the sword of the children of Ammon. 10 Now therefore the sword shall never depart from thine house; because thou hast despised me, and hast taken the wife of Uriah the Hittite to be thy wife. 11 Thus saith the Lord, Behold, I will raise up evil against thee out of thine own house, and I will take thy wives before thine eyes, and give them unto thy neighbor, and he shall lie with thy wives in the sight of this sun. 12 For thou didst it secretly: but I will do this thing before all Israel, and before the sun. 13 And David said unto Nathan, I have sinned against the Lord. And Nathan said unto David, The Lord also hath put away thy sin; thou shalt not die. 14 Howbeit, because by this deed thou hast given great occasion to the enemies of the Lord to blaspheme, the child also that is born unto thee shall surely die. 15 And Nathan departed unto his house.

And the Lord struck the child that Uriah's wife bare unto David, and it was very sick. 16 David therefore besought God for the child; and David fasted, and went in, and lay all night upon the earth. 17 And the elders of his house arose, and went to him, to raise him up from the earth: but he would not, neither did he eat bread with them. 18 And it came to pass on the seventh day, that the child died. And the servants of David feared to tell him that the child was dead: for they said, Behold, while the child was yet alive, we spake unto him, and he would not hearken unto our voice: how will he then vex him-

self, if we tell him that the child is dead? 19 But when David saw
that his servants whispered, David perceived that the child was dead:
therefore David said unto his servants, Is the child dead? And they
said, He is dead. 20 Then David arose from the earth, and washed,
and anointed himself, and changed his apparel, and came into the
house of the Lord, and worshipped: then he came to his own house;
and when he required, they set bread before him, and he did eat.
21 Then said his servants unto him, What thing is this that thou hast
done? thou didst fast and weep for the child, while it was alive; but
when the child was dead, thou didst rise and eat bread. 22 And he said,
While the child was yet alive, I fasted and wept: for I said, Who
can tell whether God will be gracious to me, that the child may live?
23 But now he is dead, wherefore should I fast? can I bring him back
again? I shall go to him, but he shall not return to me. 24 And David
comforted Bath-Sheba his wife, and went in unto her, and lay with
her: and she bare a son, and he called his name Solomon: and the
Lord loved him.

26 And Joab fought against Rabbah of the children of Ammon,
and took the royal city. 27 And Joab sent messengers to David, and
said, I have fought against Rabbah, and have taken the city of waters.
28 Now therefore gather the rest of the people together, and encamp
against the city, and take it: lest I take the city, and it be called after
my name. 29 And David gathered all the people together, and went
to Rabbah, and fought against it, and took it. 30 And he took their
king's crown from off his head, the weight whereof was a talent of
gold with the precious stones: and it was set on David's head. And
he brought forth the spoil of the city in great abundance. 31 And he
brought forth the people that were therein, and put them under saws,
and under harrows of iron, and under axes of iron, and made them
pass through the brickkiln:[1] and thus did he unto all the cities of the
children of Ammon. So David and all the people returned unto Jerusalem.

13   And it came to pass after this, that Absalom the son of David
had a fair sister, whose name was Tamar; and Amnon the son of David
loved her. 2 And Amnon was so vexed, that he fell sick for his sister
Tamar; for she was a virgin; and Amnon thought it hard for him to
do any thing to her. 3 But Amnon had a friend, whose name was
Jonadab, the son of Shimeah David's brother: and Jonadab was a very
subtile man. 4 And he said unto him, Why art thou, being the king's
son, lean from day to day? wilt thou not tell me? And Amnon said
unto him, I love Tamar, my brother Absalom's sister. 5 And Jonadab
said unto him, Lay thee down on thy bed, and make thyself sick: and
when thy father cometh to see thee, say unto him, I pray thee, let my

---

[1] This verse is badly mistranslated. The Revised Standard Version and
others give the correct sense — namely, that David put his captives to work
with saws, harrows, and axes, and that he made them operate the brick
furnaces. The prisoners were put to work, not tortured and killed.

sister Tamar come, and give me meat, and dress the meat in my sight, that I may see it, and eat it at her hand. 6 So Amnon lay down, and made himself sick: and when the king was come to see him, Amnon said unto the king, I pray thee, let Tamar my sister come, and make me a couple of cakes in my sight, that I may eat at her hand.

7 Then David sent home to Tamar, saying, Go now to thy brother Amnon's house, and dress him meat. 8 So Tamar went to her brother Amnon's house; and he was laid down. And she took flour, and kneaded it, and made cakes in his sight, and did bake the cakes. 9 And she took a pan, and poured them out before him; but he refused to eat. And Amnon said, Have out all men from me. And they went out every man from him. 10 And Amnon said unto Tamar, Bring the meat into the chamber, that I may eat of thine hand. And Tamar took the cakes which she had made, and brought them into the chamber to Amnon her brother. 11 And when she had brought them unto him to eat, he took hold of her, and said unto her, Come lie with me, my sister. 12 And she answered him, Nay, my brother, do not force me; for no such thing ought to be done in Israel: do not thou this folly. 13 And I, whither shall I cause my shame to go? and as for thee, thou shalt be as one of the fools in Israel. Now therefore, I pray thee, speak unto the king; for he will not withhold me from thee. 14 Howbeit he would not hearken unto her voice: but, being stronger than she, forced her, and lay with her.

15 Then Amnon hated her exceedingly; so that the hatred wherewith he hated her was greater than the love wherewith he had loved her. And Amnon said unto her, Arise, be gone. 16 And she said unto him, There is no cause: this evil in sending me away is greater than the other that thou didst unto me. But he would not hearken unto her. 17 Then he called his servant that ministered unto him, and said, Put now this woman out from me, and bolt the door after her. 18 And she had a garment of divers colors upon her: for with such robes were the king's daughters that were virgins appareled. Then his servant brought her out, and bolted the door after her. 19 And Tamar put ashes on her head, and rent her garment of divers colors that was on her, and laid her hand on her head, and went on crying.

20 And Absalom her brother said unto her, Hath Amnon thy brother been with thee? but hold now thy peace, my sister: he is thy brother; regard not this thing. So Tamar remained desolate in her brother Absalom's house. 21 But when king David heard of all these things, he was very wroth. 22 And Absalom spake unto his brother Amnon neither good nor bad: for Absalom hated Amnon, because he had forced his sister Tamar.

23 And it came to pass after two full years, that Absalom had sheep-shearers in Baal-hazor, which is beside Ephraim: and Absalom invited all the king's sons. 24 And Absalom came to the king, and said, Behold now, thy servant hath sheepshearers; let the king, I beseech thee, and his servants go with thy servant. 25 And the king said to Absalom, Nay, my son, let us not all now go, lest we be chargeable unto thee.

And he pressed him: howbeit he would not go, but blessed him. 26 Then said Absalom, If not, I pray thee, let my brother Amnon go with us. And the king said unto him, Why should he go with thee? 27 But Absalom pressed him, that he let Amnon and all the king's sons go with him. 28 Now Absalom had commanded his servants, saying, Mark ye now when Amnon's heart is merry with wine, and when I say unto you, Smite Amnon; then kill him, fear not: have not I commanded you? be courageous, and be valiant. 29 And the servants of Absalom did unto Amnon as Absalom had commanded. Then all the king's sons arose, and every man gat him up upon his mule, and fled.

30 And it came to pass, while they were in the way, that tidings came to David, saying, Absalom hath slain all the king's sons, and there is not one of them left. 31 Then the king arose, and tare his garments, and lay on the earth; and all his servants stood by with their clothes rent. 32 And Jonadab, the son of Shimeah David's brother, answered and said, Let not my lord suppose that they have slain all the young men the king's sons; for Amnon only is dead: for by the appointment of Absalom this hath been determined from the day that he forced his sister Tamar. 33 Now therefore let not my lord the king take the thing to his heart, to think that all the king's sons are dead: for Amnon only is dead.

34 But Absalom fled. And the young man that kept the watch lifted up his eyes, and looked, and, behold, there came much people by the way of the hillside behind him. 35 And Jonadab said unto the king, Behold, the king's sons come: as thy servant said, so it is. 36 And it came to pass, as soon as he had made an end of speaking, that, behold, the king's sons came, and lifted up their voice and wept: and the king also and all his servants wept very sore.

37 But Absalom fled, and went to Talmai, the son of Ammihud, king of Geshur. And David mourned for his son every day. 38 So Absalom fled, and went to Geshur, and was there three years. 39 And the soul of king David longed to go forth unto Absalom: for he was comforted concerning Amnon, seeing he was dead.

### DAVID AND ABSALOM

14 Now Joab the son of Zeruiah perceived that the king's heart was toward Absalom. 2 And Joab sent to Tekoah, and fetched thence a wise woman, and said unto her, I pray thee, feign thyself to be a mourner, and put on now mourning apparel, and anoint not thyself with oil, but be as a woman that had a long time mourned for the dead: 3 And come to the king, and speak on this manner unto him. So Joab put the words in her mouth.

4 And when the woman of Tekoah spake to the king, she fell on her face to the ground, and did obeisance, and said, Help, O king. 5 And the king said unto her, What aileth thee? And she answered, I am indeed a widow woman, and mine husband is dead. 6 And thy hand-

maid had two sons, and they two strove together in the field, and there was none to part them, but the one smote the other, and slew him. 7 And, behold, the whole family is risen against thine handmaid, and they said, Deliver him that smote his brother, that we may kill him, for the life of his brother whom he slew; and we will destroy the heir also: and so they shall quench my coal which is left, and shall not leave to my husband neither name nor remainder upon the earth.

8 And the king said unto the woman, Go to thine house, and I will give charge concerning thee. 9 And the woman of Tekoah said unto the king, My lord, O king, the iniquity be on me, and on my father's house: and the king and his throne be guiltless. 10 And the king said, Whosoever saith aught unto thee, bring him to me, and he shall not touch thee any more. 11 Then said she, I pray thee, let the king remember the Lord thy God, that thou wouldest not suffer the revengers of blood to destroy any more, lest they destroy my son. And he said, As the Lord liveth, there shall not one hair of thy son fall to the earth.

12 Then the woman said, Let thine handmaid, I pray thee, speak one word unto my lord the king. And he said, Say on. 13 And the woman said, Wherefore then hast thou thought such a thing against the people of God? for the king doth speak this thing as one which is faulty, in that the king doth not fetch home again his banished. 14 For we must needs die, and are as water spilt on the ground, which cannot be gathered up again; neither doth God respect any person; yet doth he devise means, that his banished be not expelled from him. 15 Now therefore that I am come to speak of this thing unto my lord the king, it is because the people have made me afraid: and thy handmaid said, I will now speak unto the king; it may be that the king will perform the request of his handmaid. 16 For the king will hear, to deliver his handmaid out of the hand of the man that would destroy me and my son together out of the inheritance of God. 17 Then thine handmaid said, The word of my lord the king shall now be comfortable: for as an angel of God, so is my lord the king to discern good and bad: therefore the Lord thy God will be with thee.

18 Then the king answered and said unto the woman, Hide not from me, I pray thee, the thing that I shall ask thee. And the woman said, Let my lord the king now speak. 19 And the king said, Is not the hand of Joab with thee in all this? And the woman answered and said, As thy soul liveth, my lord the king, none can turn to the right hand or to the left from aught that my lord the king hath spoken: for thy servant Joab, he bade me, and he put all these words in the mouth of thine handmaid: 20 To fetch about this form of speech hath thy servant Joab done this thing: and my lord is wise, according to the wisdom of an angel of God, to know all things that are in the earth.

21 And the king said unto Joab, Behold now, I have done this thing: go therefore, bring the young man Absalom again. 22 And Joab fell to the ground on his face, and bowed himself, and thanked the king: and Joab said, To-day thy servant knoweth that I have found grace

in thy sight, my lord, O king, in that the king hath fulfilled the request of his servant. 23 So Joab arose and went to Geshur, and brought Absalom to Jerusalem. 24 And the king said, Let him turn to his own house, and let him not see my face. So Absalom returned to his own house, and saw not the king's face. 25 But in all Israel there was none to be so much praised as Absalom for his beauty: from the sole of his foot even to the crown of his head there was no blemish in him. 26 And when he polled his head, (for it was at every year's end that he polled it; because the hair was heavy on him, therefore he polled it:) he weighed the hair of his head at two hundred shekels after the king's weight. 27 And unto Absalom there were born three sons, and one daughter, whose name was Tamar: she was a woman of a fair countenance.

28 So Absalom dwelt two full years in Jerusalem, and saw not the king's face. 29 Therefore Absalom sent for Joab, to have sent him to the king; but he would not come to him: and when he sent again the second time, he would not come. 30 Therefore he said unto his servants, See, Joab's field is near mine, and he hath barley there; go and set it on fire. And Absalom's servants set the field on fire. 31 Then Joab arose, and came to Absalom unto his house, and said unto him, Wherefore have thy servants set my field on fire? 32 And Absalom answered Joab, Behold, I sent unto thee, saying, Come hither, that I may send thee to the king, to say, Wherefore am I come from Geshur? it had been good for me to have been there still: now therefore let me see the king's face; and if there be any iniquity in me, let him kill me. 33 So Joab came to the king, and told him: and when he had called for Absalom, he came to the king, and bowed himself on his face to the ground before the king: and the king kissed Absalom.

15 And it came to pass after this, that Absalom prepared him chariots and horses, and fifty men to run before him. 2 And Absalom rose up early, and stood beside the way of the gate; and it was so, that when any man that had a controversy came to the king for judgment, then Absalom called unto him, and said, Of what city art thou? And he said, Thy servant is of one of the tribes of Israel. 3 And Absalom said unto him, See, thy matters are good and right; but there is no man deputed of the king to hear thee. 4 Absalom said moreover, Oh that I were made judge in the land, that every man which hath any suit or cause might come unto me, and I would do him justice! 5 And it was so, that when any man came nigh to him to do him obeisance, he put forth his hand, and took him, and kissed him. 6 And on this manner did Absalom to all Israel that came to the king for judgment: so Absalom stole the hearts of the men of Israel.

7 And it came to pass after forty[1] years, that Absalom said unto the king, I pray thee, let me go and pay my vow, which I have vowed unto the Lord, in Hebron. 8 For thy servant vowed a vow while I

---

[1] The true reading is "four."

abode at Geshur in Syria, saying, If the Lord shall bring me again indeed to Jerusalem, then I will serve the Lord. 9 And the king said unto him, Go in peace. So he arose, and went to Hebron. 10 But Absalom sent spies throughout all the tribes of Israel, saying, As soon as ye hear the sound of the trumpet, then ye shall say, Absalom reigneth in Hebron. 11 And with Absalom went two hundred men out of Jerusalem, that were called; and they went in their simplicity, and they knew not any thing. 12 And Absalom sent for Ahithophel the Gilonite, David's counselor, from his city, even from Giloh, while he offered sacrifices. And the conspiracy was strong; for the people increased continually with Absalom.

13 And there came a messenger to David, saying, The hearts of the men of Israel are after Absalom. 14 And David said unto all his servants that were with him at Jerusalem, Arise, and let us flee; for we shall not else escape from Absalom: make speed to depart, lest he overtake us suddenly, and bring evil upon us, and smite the city with the edge of the sword. 15 And the king's servants said unto the king, Behold, thy servants are ready to do whatsoever my lord the king shall appoint. 16 And the king went forth, and all his household after him. And the king left ten women, which were concubines, to keep the house. 17 And the king went forth, and all the people after him, and tarried in a place that was far off. 18 And all his servants passed on beside him; and all the Cherethites, and all the Pelethites, and all the Gittites, six hundred men which came after him from Gath, passed on before the king.

19 Then said the king to Ittai the Gittite, Wherefore goest thou also with us? return to thy place, and abide with the king: for thou art a stranger, and also an exile. 20 Whereas thou camest but yesterday, should I this day make thee go up and down with us? seeing I go whither I may, return thou, and take back thy brethren: mercy and truth be with thee. 21 And Ittai answered the king, and said, As the Lord liveth, and as my lord the king liveth, surely in what place my lord the king shall be, whether in death or life, even there also will thy servant be. 22 And David said to Ittai, Go and pass over. And Ittai the Gittite passed over, and all his men, and all the little ones that were with him. 23 And all the country wept with a loud voice, and all the people passed over: the king also himself passed over the brook Kidron, and all the people passed over, toward the way of the wilderness.

24 And lo Zadok also, and all the Levites were with him, bearing the ark of the covenant of God: and they set down the ark of God; and Abiathar went up, until all the people had done passing out of the city. 25 And the king said unto Zadok, Carry back the ark of God into the city: if I shall find favor in the eyes of the Lord, he will bring me again, and show me both it, and his habitation: 26 But if he thus say, I have no delight in thee; behold, here am I, let him do to me as seemeth good unto him. 27 The king said also unto Zadok the priest, Art not thou a seer? return into the city in peace, and your two sons

with you, Ahimaaz thy son, and Jonathan the son of Abiathar. 28 See, I will tarry in the plain of the wilderness, until there come word from you to certify me. 29 Zadok therefore and Abiathar carried the ark of God again to Jerusalem: and they tarried there.

30 And David went up by the ascent of mount Olivet, and wept as he went up, and had his head covered, and he went barefoot: and all the people that was with him covered every man his head, and they went up, weeping as they went up. 31 And one told David, saying, Ahithophel is among the conspirators with Absalom. And David said, O Lord, I pray thee, turn the counsel of Ahithophel into foolishness. 32 And it came to pass, that when David was come to the top of the mount, where he worshipped God, behold, Hushai the Archite came to meet him with his coat rent, and earth upon his head: 33 Unto whom David said, If thou passest on with me, then thou shalt be a burden unto me: 34 But if thou return to the city, and say unto Absalom, I will be thy servant, O king; as I have been thy father's servant hitherto, so will I now also be thy servant: then mayest thou for me defeat the counsel of Ahithophel. 35 And hast thou not there with thee Zadok and Abiathar the priests? therefore it shall be, that what thing soever thou shalt hear out of the king's house, thou shalt tell it to Zadok and Abiathar the priests. 36 Behold, they have there with them their two sons, Ahimaaz Zadok's son, and Jonathan Abiathar's son; and by them ye shall send unto me every thing that ye can hear. 37 So Hushai David's friend came into the city, and Absalom came into Jerusalem.

16 And when David was a little past the top of the hill, behold, Ziba the servant of Mephibosheth met him, with a couple of asses saddled, and upon them two hundred loaves of bread, and a hundred bunches of raisins, and a hundred of summer fruits, and a bottle of wine. 2 And the king said unto Ziba, What meanest thou by these? And Ziba said, The asses be for the king's household to ride on; and the bread and summer fruit for the young men to eat; and the wine, that such as be faint in the wilderness may drink. 3 And the king said, And where is thy master's son? And Ziba said unto the king, Behold, he abideth at Jerusalem: for he said, To-day shall the house of Israel restore me the kingdom of my father. 4 Then said the king to Ziba, Behold, thine are all that pertained unto Mephibosheth. And Ziba said, I humbly beseech thee that I may find grace in thy sight, my lord, O king.

5 And when king David came to Bahurim, behold, thence came out a man of the family of the house of Saul, whose name was Shimei, the son of Gera: he came forth, and cursed still as he came. 6 And he cast stones at David, and at all the servants of king David: and all the people and all the mighty men were on his right hand and on his left. 7 And thus said Shimei when he cursed, Come out, come out, thou bloody man, and thou man of Belial. 8 The Lord hath returned upon thee all the blood of the house of Saul, in whose stead thou hast

reigned; and the Lord hath delivered the kingdom into the hand of Absalom thy son: and, behold, thou art taken in thy mischief, because thou art a bloody man.

9 Then said Abishai the son of Zeruiah unto the king, Why should this dead dog curse my lord the king? let me go over, I pray thee, and take off his head. 10 And the king said, What have I to do with you, ye sons of Zeruiah? so let him curse, because the Lord hath said unto him, Curse David. Who shall then say, Wherefore hast thou done so? 11 And David said to Abishai, and to all his servants, Behold, my son, which came forth of my bowels, seeketh my life: how much more now may this Benjamite do it? let him alone, and let him curse; for the Lord hath bidden him. 12 It may be that the Lord will look on mine affliction, and that the Lord will requite me good for his cursing this day. 13 And as David and his men went by the way, Shimei went along on the hillside over against him, and cursed as he went, and threw stones at him, and cast dust. 14 And the king, and all the people that were with him, came weary, and refreshed themselves there.

15 And Absalom, and all the people the men of Israel, came to Jerusalem, and Ahithophel with him. 16 And it came to pass, when Hushai the Archite, David's friend, was come unto Absalom, that Hushai said unto Absalom, God save the king, God save the king. 17 And Absalom said to Hushai, Is this thy kindness to thy friend? why wentest thou not with thy friend? 18 And Hushai said unto Absalom, Nay; but whom the Lord, and this people, and all the men of Israel, choose, his will I be, and with him will I abide. 19 And again, whom should I serve? should I not serve in the presence of his son? as I have served in thy father's presence, so will I be in thy presence.

20 Then said Absalom to Ahithophel, Give counsel among you what we shall do. 21 And Ahithophel said unto Absalom, Go in unto thy father's concubines, which he hath left to keep the house; and all Israel shall hear that thou art abhorred of thy father: then shall the hands of all that are with thee be strong. 22 So they spread Absalom a tent upon the top of the house; and Absalom went in unto his father's concubines in the sight of all Israel. 23 And the counsel of Ahithophel, which he counseled in those days, was as if a man had inquired at the oracle of God: so was all the counsel of Ahithophel both with David and with Absalom.

17 Moreover Ahithophel said unto Absalom, Let me now choose out twelve thousand men, and I will arise and pursue after David this night: 2 And I will come upon him while he is weary and weak-handed, and will make him afraid: and all the people that are with him shall flee; and I will smite the king only: 3 And I will bring back all the people unto thee: the man whom thou seekest is as if all returned: so all the people shall be in peace. 4 And the saying pleased Absalom well, and all the elders of Israel.

5 Then said Absalom, Call now Hushai the Archite also, and let us hear likewise what he saith. 6 And when Hushai was come to Absalom, Absalom spake unto him, saying, Ahithophel hath spoken after this manner: shall we do after his saying? if not, speak thou. 7 And Hushai said unto Absalom, The counsel that Ahithophel hath given is not good at this time. 8 For, said Hushai, thou knowest thy father and his men, that they be mighty men, and they be chafed in their minds, as a bear robbed of her whelps in the field: and thy father is a man of war, and will not lodge with the people. 9 Behold, he is hid now in some pit, or in some other place: and it will come to pass, when some of them be overthrown at the first, that whosoever heareth it will say, There is a slaughter among the people that follow Absalom. 10 And he also that is valiant, whose heart is as the heart of a lion, shall utterly melt: for all Israel knoweth that thy father is a mighty man, and they which be with him are valiant men. 11 Therefore I counsel that all Israel be generally gathered unto thee, from Dan even to Beer-sheba, as the sand that is by the sea for multitude; and that thou go to battle in thine own person. 12 So shall we come upon him in some place where he shall be found, and we will light upon him as the dew falleth on the ground: and of him and of all the men that are with him there shall not be left so much as one. 13 Moreover if he be gotten into a city, then shall all Israel bring ropes to that city, and we will draw it into the river, until there be not one small stone found there. 14 And Absalom and all the men of Israel said, The counsel of Hushai the Archite is better than the counsel of Ahithophel. For the Lord had appointed to defeat the good counsel of Ahithophel, to the intent that the Lord might bring evil upon Absalom.

15 Then said Hushai unto Zadok and to Abiathar the priests, Thus and thus did Ahithophel counsel Absalom and the elders of Israel; and thus and thus have I counseled. 16 Now therefore send quickly, and tell David, saying, Lodge not this night in the plains of the wilderness, but speedily pass over; lest the king be swallowed up, and all the people that are with him. 17 Now Jonathan and Ahimaaz stayed by En-rogel; for they might not be seen to come into the city: and a wench went and told them; and they went and told king David. 18 Nevertheless, a lad saw them, and told Absalom: but they went both of them away quickly, and came to a man's house in Bahurim, which had a well in his court; whither they went down. 19 And the woman took and spread a covering over the well's mouth, and spread ground corn thereon; and the thing was not known. 20 And when Absalom's servants came to the woman to the house, they said, Where is Ahimaaz and Jonathan? And the woman said unto them, They be gone over the brook of water. And when they had sought and could not find them, they returned to Jerusalem.

21 And it came to pass, after they were departed, that they came up out of the well, and went and told king David, and said unto David, Arise, and pass quickly over the water: for thus hath Ahithophel

counseled against you. 22 Then David arose, and all the people that were with him, and they passed over Jordan: by the morning light there lacked not one of them that was not gone over Jordan.

23 And when Ahithophel saw that his counsel was not followed, he saddled his ass, and arose, and gat him home to his house, to his city, and put his household in order, and hanged himself, and died, and was buried in the sepulchre of his father.

24 Then David came to Mahanaim. And Absalom passed over Jordan, he and all the men of Israel with him. 25 And Absalom made Amasa captain of the host instead of Joab: which Amasa was a man's son, whose name was Ithra an Israelite, that went in to Abigail the daughter of Nahash, sister to Zeruiah Joab's mother. 26 So Israel and Absalom pitched in the land of Gilead.

27 And it came to pass, when David was come to Mahanaim, that Shobi the son of Nahash of Rabbah of the children of Ammon, and Machir the son of Ammiel of Lo-debar, and Barzillai the Gileadite of Rogelim, 28 Brought beds, and basins, and earthen vessels, and wheat, and barley, and flour, and parched corn, and beans, and lentils, and parched pulse, 29 And honey, and butter, and sheep, and cheese of kine, for David, and for the people that were with him, to eat: for they said, The people is hungry, and weary, and thirsty, in the wilderness.

18 And David numbered the people that were with him, and set captains of thousands and captains of hundreds over them. 2 And David sent forth a third part of the people under the hand of Joab, and a third part under the hand of Abishai the son of Zeruiah, Joab's brother, and a third part under the hand of Ittai the Gittite. And the king said unto the people, I will surely go forth with you myself also. 3 But the people answered, Thou shalt not go forth: for if we flee away, they will not care for us; neither if half of us die, will they care for us: but now thou art worth ten thousand of us: therefore now it is better that thou succor us out of the city. 4 And the king said unto them, What seemeth you best I will do. And the king stood by the gate side, and all the people came out by hundreds and by thousands. 5 And the king commanded Joab and Abishai and Ittai, saying, Deal gently for my sake with the young man, even with Absalom. And all the people heard when the king gave all the captains charge concerning Absalom.

6 So the people went out into the field against Israel: and the battle was in the wood of Ephraim; 7 Where the people of Israel were slain before the servants of David, and there was there a great slaughter that day of twenty thousand men. 8 For the battle was there scattered over the face of all the country: and the wood devoured more people that day than the sword devoured.

9 And Absalom met the servants of David. And Absalom rode upon a mule, and the mule went under the thick boughs of a great oak, and his head caught hold of the oak, and he was taken up between the

heaven and the earth; and the mule that was under him went away. 10 And a certain man saw it, and told Joab, and said, Behold, I saw Absalom hanged in an oak. 11 And Joab said unto the man that told him, And, behold, thou sawest him, and why didst thou not smite him there to the ground? and I would have given thee ten shekels of silver, and a girdle. 12 And the man said unto Joab, Though I should receive a thousand shekels of silver in mine hand, yet would I not put forth mine hand against the king's son: for in our hearing the king charged thee and Abishai and Ittai, saying, Beware that none touch the young man Absalom. 13 Otherwise I should have wrought falsehood against mine own life: for there is no matter hid from the king, and thou thyself wouldest have set thyself against me. 14 Then said Joab, I may not tarry thus with thee. And he took three darts in his hand, and thrust them through the heart of Absalom, while he was yet alive in the midst of the oak. 15 And ten young men that bare Joab's armor compassed about and smote Absalom, and slew him. 16 And Joab blew the trumpet, and the people returned from pursuing after Israel: for Joab held back the people. 17 And they took Absalom, and cast him into a great pit in the wood, and laid a very great heap of stones upon him: and all Israel fled every one to his tent.

18 Now Absalom in his lifetime had taken and reared up for himself a pillar, which is in the king's dale: for he said, I have no son to keep my name in remembrance: and he called the pillar after his own name: and it is called unto this day, Absalom's place.

19 Then said Ahimaaz the son of Zadok, Let me now run, and bear the king tidings, how that the Lord hath avenged him of his enemies. 20 And Joab said unto him, Thou shalt not bear tidings this day, but thou shalt bear tidings another day: but this day thou shalt bear no tidings, because the king's son is dead. 21 Then said Joab to Cushi, Go tell the king what thou hast seen. And Cushi bowed himself unto Joab, and ran. 22 Then said Ahimaaz the son of Zadok yet again to Joab, But howsoever, let me, I pray thee, also run after Cushi. And Joab said, Wherefore wilt thou run, my son, seeing that thou hast no tidings ready? 23 But howsoever, said he, let me run. And he said unto him, Run. Then Ahimaaz ran by the way of the plain, and overran Cushi.

24 And David sat between the two gates: and the watchman went up to the roof over the gate unto the wall, and lifted up his eyes, and looked, and behold a man running alone. 25 And the watchman cried, and told the king. And the king said, If he be alone, there is tidings in his mouth. And he came apace, and drew near. 26 And the watchman saw another man running: and the watchman called unto the porter, and said, Behold another man running alone. And the king said, He also bringeth tidings. 27 And the watchman said, Methinketh the running of the foremost is like the running of Ahimaaz the son of Zadok. And the king said, He is a good man, and cometh with good tidings.

28 And Ahimaaz called, and said unto the king, All is well. And he fell down to the earth upon his face before the king, and said, Blessed be the Lord thy God, which hath delivered up the men that lifted up their hand against my lord the king. 29 And the king said, Is the young man Absalom safe? And Ahimaaz answered, When Joab sent the king's servant, and me thy servant, I saw a great tumult, but I knew not what it was. 30 And the king said unto him, Turn aside, and stand here. And he turned aside, and stood still.

31 And, behold, Cushi came; and Cushi said, Tidings, my lord the king: for the Lord hath avenged thee this day of all them that rose up against thee. 32 And the king said unto Cushi, Is the young man Absalom safe? And Cushi answered, The enemies of my lord the king, and all that rise against thee to do thee hurt, be as that young man is. 33 And the king was much moved, and went up to the chamber over the gate, and wept: and as he went, thus he said, O my son Absalom! my son, my son Absalom! would God I had died for thee, O Absalom, my son, my son!

## DAVID RESUMES THE THRONE

19 And it was told Joab, Behold, the king weepeth and mourneth for Absalom. 2 And the victory that day was turned into mourning unto all the people: for the people heard say that day how the king was grieved for his son. 3 And the people gat them by stealth that day into the city, as people being ashamed steal away when they flee in battle. 4 But the king covered his face, and the king cried with a loud voice, O my son Absalom! O Absalom, my son, my son! 5 And Joab came into the house to the king, and said, Thou hast shamed this day the faces of all thy servants, which this day have saved thy life, and the lives of thy sons and of thy daughters, and the lives of thy wives, and the lives of thy concubines; 6 In that thou lovest thine enemies, and hatest thy friends. For thou hast declared this day, that thou regardest neither princes nor servants: for this day I perceive, that if Absalom had lived, and all we had died this day, then it had pleased thee well. 7 Now therefore arise, go forth, and speak comfortably unto thy servants: for I swear by the Lord, if thou go not forth, there will not tarry one with thee this night: and that will be worse unto thee than all the evil that befell thee from thy youth until now. 8 Then the king arose, and sat in the gate. And they told unto all the people, saying, Behold, the king doth sit in the gate. And all the people came before the king: for Israel had fled every man to his tent.

9 And all the people were at strife throughout all the tribes of Israel, saying, The king saved us out of the hand of our enemies, and he delivered us out of the hand of the Philistines; and now he is fled out of the land for Absalom. 10 And Absalom, whom we anointed over us, is dead in battle. Now therefore why speak ye not a word of bringing the king back?

11 And king David sent to Zadok and to Abiathar the priests, saying, Speak unto the elders of Judah, saying, Why are ye the last to bring the king back to his house? seeing the speech of all Israel is come to the king, even to his house. 12 Ye are my brethren, ye are my bones and my flesh: wherefore then are ye the last to bring back the king? 13 And say ye to Amasa, Art thou not of my bone, and of my flesh? God do so to me, and more also, if thou be not captain of the host before me continually in the room of Joab. 14 And he bowed the heart of all the men of Judah, even as the heart of one man; so that they sent this word unto the king, Return thou, and all thy servants.

15 So the king returned, and came to Jordan. And Judah came to Gilgal, to go to meet the king, to conduct the king over Jordan. 16 And Shimei the son of Gera, a Benjamite, which was of Bahurim, hasted and came down with the men of Judah to meet king David. 17 And there were a thousand men of Benjamin with him, and Ziba the servant of the house of Saul, and his fifteen sons and his twenty servants with him; and they went over Jordan before the king. 18 And there went over a ferryboat to carry over the king's household, and to do what he thought good. And Shimei the son of Gera fell down before the king, as he was come over Jordan; 19 And said unto the king, Let not my lord impute iniquity unto me, neither do thou remember that which thy servant did perversely the day that my lord the king went out of Jerusalem, that the king should take it to his heart. 20 For thy servant doth know that I have sinned: therefore, behold, I am come the first this day of all the house of Joseph to go down to meet my lord the king.

21 But Abishai the son of Zeruiah answered and said, Shall not Shimei be put to death for this, because he cursed the Lord's anointed? 22 And David said, What have I to do with you, ye sons of Zeruiah, that ye should this day be adversaries unto me? shall there any man be put to death this day in Israel? for do not I know that I am this day king over Israel? 23 Therefore the king said unto Shimei, Thou shalt not die. And the king sware unto him.

24 And Mephibosheth the son of Saul came down to meet the king, and had neither dressed his feet, nor trimmed his beard, nor washed his clothes, from the day the king departed until the day he came again in peace. 25 And it came to pass, when he was come to Jerusalem to meet the king, that the king said unto him, Wherefore wentest not thou with me, Mephibosheth? 26 And he answered, My lord, O king, my servant deceived me: for thy servant said, I will saddle me an ass, that I may ride thereon, and go to the king; because thy servant is lame. 27 And he hath slandered thy servant unto my lord the king; but my lord the king is as an angel of God: do therefore what is good in thine eyes. 28 For all of my father's house were but dead men before my lord the king: yet didst thou set thy servant among them that did eat at thine own table. What right therefore have I yet to cry any more unto the king? 29 And the king said unto him, Why speak-

est thou any more of thy matters? I have said, Thou and Ziba divide the land. 30 And Mephibosheth said unto the king, Yea, let him take all, forasmuch as my lord the king is come again in peace unto his own house.

31 And Barzillai the Gileadite came down from Rogelim, and went over Jordan with the king, to conduct him over Jordan. 32 Now Barzillai was a very aged man, even fourscore years old: and he had provided the king of sustenance while he lay at Mahanaim; for he was a very great man. 33 And the king said unto Barzillai, Come thou over with me, and I will feed thee with me in Jerusalem. 34 And Barzillai said unto the king, How long have I to live, that I should go up with the king unto Jerusalem? 35 I am this day fourscore years old: and can I discern between good and evil? can thy servant taste what I eat or what I drink? can I hear any more the voice of singing men and singing women? wherefore then should thy servant be yet a burden unto my lord the king? 36 Thy servant will go a little way over Jordan with the king: and why should the king recompense it me with such a reward? 37 Let thy servant, I pray thee, turn back again, that I may die in mine own city, and be buried by the grave of my father and of my mother. But behold thy servant Chimham; let him go over with my lord the king; and do to him what shall seem good unto thee. 38 And the king answered, Chimham shall go over with me, and I will do to him that which shall seem good unto thee: and whatsoever thou shalt require of me, that will I do for thee. 39 And all the people went over Jordan. And when the king was come over, the king kissed Barzillai, and blessed him; and he returned unto his own place.

40 Then the king went on to Gilgal, and Chimham went on with him: and all the people of Judah conducted the king, and also half the people of Israel. 41 And, behold, all the men of Israel came to the king, and said unto the king, Why have our brethren the men of Judah stolen thee away, and have brought the king, and his household, and all David's men with him, over Jordan? 42 And all the men of Judah answered the men of Israel, Because the king is near of kin to us: wherefore then be ye angry for this matter? have we eaten at all of the king's cost? or hath he given us any gift? 43 And the men of Israel answered the men of Judah, and said, We have ten parts in the king, and we have also more right in David than ye: why then did ye despise us, that our advice should not be first had in bringing back our king? And the words of the men of Judah were fiercer than the words of the men of Israel.

20 And there happened to be there a man of Belial, whose name was Sheba, the son of Bichri, a Benjamite: and he blew a trumpet, and said,

> We have no part in David,
> Neither have we inheritance in the son of Jesse:
> Every man to his tents, O Israel.

2 So every man of Israel went up from after David, and followed Sheba the son of Bichri: but the men of Judah clave unto their king, from Jordan even to Jerusalem.

3 And David came to his house at Jerusalem; and the king took the ten women his concubines, whom he had left to keep the house, and put them in ward, and fed them, but went not in unto them. So they were shut up unto the day of their death, living in widowhood.

4 Then said the king of Amasa, Assemble me the men of Judah within three days, and be thou here present. 5 So Amasa went to assemble the men of Judah: but he tarried longer than the set time which he had appointed him. 6 And David said to Abishai, Now shall Sheba the son of Bichri do us more harm than did Absalom: take thou thy lord's servants, and pursue after him, lest he get him fenced cities, and escape us. 7 And there went out after him Joab's men, and the Cherethites, and the Pelethites, and all the mighty men: and they went out of Jerusalem, to pursue after Sheba the son of Bichri. 8 When they were at the great stone which is in Gibeon, Amasa went before them. And Joab's garment that he had put on was girded unto him, and upon it a girdle with a sword fastened upon his loins in the sheath thereof; and as he went forth it fell out. 9 And Joab said to Amasa, Art thou in health, my brother? And Joab took Amasa by the beard with the right hand to kiss him. 10 But Amasa took no heed to the sword that was in Joab's hand: so he smote him therewith in the fifth rib, and shed out his bowels to the ground, and struck him not again; and he died.

So Joab and Abishai his brother pursued after Sheba the son of Bichri. 11 And one of Joab's men stood by him, and said, He that favoreth Joab, and he that is for David, let him go after Joab. 12 And Amasa wallowed in blood in the midst of the highway. And when the man saw that all the people stood still, he removed Amasa out of the highway into the field, and cast a cloth upon him, when he saw that every one that came by him stood still. 13 When he was removed out of the highway, all the people went on after Joab, to pursue after Sheba the son of Bichri.

14 And he went through all the tribes of Israel unto Abel, and to Beth-maachah, and all the Berites: and they were gathered together, and went also after him. 15 And they came and besieged him in Abel of Beth-maachah, and they cast up a bank against the city, and it stood in the trench: and all the people that were with Joab battered the wall, to throw it down. 16 Then cried a wise woman out of the city, Hear, hear; say, I pray you, unto Joab, Come near hither, that I may speak with thee. 17 And when he was come near unto her, the woman said, Art thou Joab? And he answered, I am he. Then she said unto him, Hear the words of thine handmaid. And he answered, I do hear. 18 Then she spake, saying, They were wont to speak in old time, saying, They shall surely ask counsel at Abel: and so they ended the matter. 19 I am one of them that are peaceable and faithful in

Israel: thou seekest to destroy a city and a mother in Israel: why wilt thou swallow up the inheritance of the Lord? 20 And Joab answered and said, Far be it, far be it from me, that I should swallow up or destroy. 21 The matter is not so: but a man of mount Ephraim, Sheba the son of Bichri by name, hath lifted up his hand against the king, even against David: deliver him only, and I will depart from the city. And the woman said unto Joab, Behold, his head shall be thrown to thee over the wall. 22 Then the woman went unto all the people in her wisdom: and they cut off the head of Sheba the son of Bichri, and cast it out to Joab. And he blew a trumpet, and they retired from the city, every man to his tent. And Joab returned to Jerusalem unto the king.

23 Now Joab was over all the host of Israel: and Benaiah the son of Jehoiada was over the Cherethites and over the Pelethites: 24 And Adoram was over the tribute: and Jehoshaphat the son of Ahilud was recorder: 25 And Sheva was scribe: and Zadok and Abiathar were the priests: 26 And Ira also the Jairite was a chief ruler about David.

21 Then there was a famine in the days of David three years, year after year; and David inquired of the Lord. And the Lord answered, It is for Saul, and for his bloody house, because he slew the Gibeonites. 2 And the king called the Gibeonites, and said unto them; (now the Gibeonites were not of the children of Israel, but of the remnant of the Amorites; and the children of Israel had sworn unto them: and Saul sought to slay them in his zeal to the children of Israel and Judah:) 3 Wherefore David said unto the Gibeonites, What shall I do for you? and wherewith shall I make the atonement, that ye may bless the inheritance of the Lord? 4 And the Gibeonites said unto him, We will have no silver nor gold of Saul, nor of his house; neither for us shalt thou kill any man in Israel. And he said, What ye shall say, that will I do for you. 5 And they answered the king, The man that consumed us, and that devised against us that we should be destroyed from remaining in any of the coasts of Israel, 6 Let seven men of his sons be delivered unto us, and we will hang them up unto the Lord in Gibeah of Saul, whom the Lord did choose. And the king said, I will give them.

7 But the king spared Mephibosheth, the son of Jonathan the son of Saul, because of the Lord's oath that was between them, between David and Jonathan the son of Saul. 8 But the king took the two sons of Rizpah the daughter of Aiah, whom she bare unto Saul, Armoni and Mephibosheth; and the five sons of Michal the daughter of Saul, whom she brought up for Adriel the son of Barzillai the Meholathite: 9 And he delivered them into the hands of the Gibeonites, and they hanged them in the hill before the Lord: and they fell all seven together, and were put to death in the days of harvest, in the first days, in the beginning of barley harvest.

10 And Rizpah the daughter of Aiah took sackcloth, and spread it

for her upon the rock, from the beginning of harvest until water dropped upon them out of heaven, and suffered neither the birds of the air to rest on them by day, nor the beasts of the field by night. 11 And it was told David what Rizpah the daughter of Aiah, the concubine of Saul, had done. 12 And David went and took the bones of Saul and the bones of Jonathan his son from the men of Jabesh-gilead, which had stolen them from the street of Beth-shan, where the Philistines had hanged them, when the Philistines had slain Saul in Gilboa: 13 And he brought up from thence the bones of Saul and the bones of Jonathan his son; and they gathered the bones of them that were hanged. 14 And the bones of Saul and Jonathan his son buried they in the country of Benjamin in Zelah, in the sepulchre of Kish his father: and they performed all that the king commanded. And after that God was entreated for the land.

15 Moreover the Philistines had yet war again with Israel; and David went down, and his servants with him, and fought against the Philistines: and David waxed faint. 16 And Ishbi-benob, which was of the sons of the giant, the weight of whose spear weighed three hundred shekels of brass in weight, he being girded with a new sword, thought to have slain David. 17 But Abishai the son of Zeruiah succored him, and smote the Philistine, and killed him. Then the men of David sware unto him, saying, Thou shalt go no more out with us to battle, that thou quench not the light of Israel.

18 And it came to pass after this, that there was again a battle with the Philistines at Gob: then Sibbechai the Hushathite slew Saph, which was of the sons of the giant. 19 And there was again a battle in Gob with the Philistines, where Elhanan the son of Jaare-oregim, a Bethlehemite, slew the brother of Goliath the Gittite, the staff of whose spear was like a weaver's beam. 20 And there was yet a battle in Gath, where was a man of great stature, that had on every hand six fingers, and on every foot six toes, four and twenty in number; and he also was born to the giant. 21 And when he defied Israel, Jonathan the son of Shimeah the brother of David slew him. 22 These four were born to the giant in Gath, and fell by the hand of David, and by the hand of his servants.

22    And David spake unto the Lord the words of this song, in the day that the Lord had delivered him out of the hand of all his enemies, and out of the hand of Saul: 2 And he said,
   The Lord is my rock, and my fortress, and my deliverer;
   3 The God of my rock; in him will I trust:
   He is my shield, and the horn of my salvation, my high tower, and my refuge,
   My saviour; thou savest me from violence.
   4 I will call on the Lord, who is worthy to be praised:
   So shall I be saved from mine enemies.
   5 When the waves of death compassed me,
   The floods of ungodly men made me afraid;

6 The sorrows of hell compassed me about;
The snares of death prevented me.
7 In my distress I called upon the Lord,
And cried to my God:
And he did hear my voice out of his temple,
And my cry did enter into his ears.
8 Then the earth shook and trembled;
The foundations of heaven moved
And shook, because he was wroth.
9 There went up a smoke out of his nostrils,
And fire out of his mouth devoured:
Coals were kindled by it.
10 He bowed the heavens also, and came down;
And darkness was under his feet.
11 And he rode upon a cherub, and did fly:
And he was seen upon the wings of the wind.
12 And he made darkness pavilions round about him,
Dark waters, and thick clouds of the skies.
13 Through the brightness before him
Were coals of fire kindled.
14 The Lord thundered from heaven,
And the Most High uttered his voice.
15 And he sent out arrows, and scattered them;
Lightning, and discomfited them.
16 And the channels of the sea appeared,
The foundations of the world were discovered,
At the rebuking of the Lord,
At the blast of the breath of his nostrils.
17 He sent from above, he took me;
He drew me out of many waters:
18 He delivered me from my strong enemy,
And from them that hated me: for they were too strong for
me.
19 They prevented me in the day of my calamity:
But the Lord was my stay.
20 He brought me forth also into a large place:
He delivered me, because he delighted in me.
21 The Lord rewarded me according to my righteousness;
According to the cleanness of my hands hath he recompensed
me.
22 For I have kept the ways of the Lord,
And have not wickedly departed from my God.
23 For all his judgments were before me:
And as for his statutes, I did not depart from them.
24 I was also upright before him,
And have kept myself from mine iniquity.
25 Therefore the Lord hath recompensed me according to my
righteousness;

According to my cleanness in his eyesight.
26 With the merciful thou wilt show thyself merciful,
And with the upright man thou wilt show thyself upright.
27 With the pure thou wilt show thyself pure;
And with the froward thou wilt show thyself unsavory.
28 And the afflicted people thou wilt save:
But thine eyes are upon the haughty, that thou mayest bring
them down.
29 For thou art my lamp, O Lord:
And the Lord will lighten my darkness.
30 For by thee I have run through a troop:
By my God have I leaped over a wall.
31 As for God, his way is perfect;
The word of the Lord is tried:
He is a buckler to all them that trust in him.
32 For who is God, save the Lord?
And who is a rock, save our God?
33 God is my strength and power;
And he maketh my way perfect.
34 He maketh my feet like hinds' feet;
And setteth me upon my high places.
35 He teacheth my hands to war;
So that a bow of steel is broken by mine arms.
36 Thou hast also given me the shield of thy salvation:
And thy gentleness hath made me great.
37 Thou hast enlarged my steps under me;
So that my feet did not slip.
38 I have pursued mine enemies, and destroyed them;
And turned not again until I had consumed them.
39 And I have consumed them, and wounded them, that they
could not arise:
Yea, they are fallen under my feet.
40 For thou hast girded me with strength to battle:
Them that rose up against me hast thou subdued under me.
41 Thou hast also given me the necks of mine enemies,
That I might destroy them that hate me.
42 They looked, but there was none to save;
Even unto the Lord, but he answered them not.
43 Then did I beat them as small as the dust of the earth:
I did stamp them as the mire of the street, and did spread
them abroad.
44 Thou also hast delivered me from the strivings of my people,
Thou hast kept me to be head of the heathen:
A people which I knew not shall serve me.
45 Strangers shall submit themselves unto me:
As soon as they hear, they shall be obedient unto me.
46 Strangers shall fade away,
And they shall be afraid out of their close places.

47 The Lord liveth; and blessed be my rock;
And exalted be the God of the rock of my salvation.
48 It is God that avengeth me,
And that bringeth down the people under me,
49 And that bringeth me forth from mine enemies:
Thou also hast lifted me up on high above them that rose up
against me:
Thou hast delivered me from the violent man.
50 Therefore I will give thanks unto thee, O Lord, among the
heathen,
And I will sing praises unto thy name.
51 He is the tower of salvation for his king:
And showeth mercy to his anointed,
Unto David, and to his seed for evermore.

### DAVID'S LAST SONG

23    Now these be the last words of David.
David the son of Jesse said,
And the man who was raised up on high,
The anointed of the God of Jacob,
And the sweet psalmist of Israel, said,
2 The Spirit of the Lord spake by me,
And his word was in my tongue.
3 The God of Israel said,
The Rock of Israel spake to me,
He that ruleth over men must be just,
Ruling in the fear of God.
4 And he shall be as the light of the morning, when the sun
riseth,
Even a morning without clouds;
As the tender grass springing out of the earth
By clear shining after rain.
5 Although my house be not so with God;
Yet he hath made with me an everlasting covenant,
Ordered in all things, and sure:
For this is all my salvation, and all my desire,
Although he make it not to grow.
6 But the sons of Belial shall be all of them as thorns thrust
away,
Because they cannot be taken with hands:
7 But the man that shall touch them
Must be fenced with iron and the staff of a spear;
And they shall be utterly burned with fire in the same place.

# *First Kings*

## THE DEATH OF DAVID

1 Now king David was old and stricken in years; and they covered him with clothes, but he gat no heat. 2 Wherefore his servants said unto him, Let there be sought for my lord the king a young virgin: and let her stand before the king, and let her cherish him, and let her lie in thy bosom, that my lord the king may get heat. 3 So they sought for a fair damsel throughout all the coasts of Israel, and found Abishag a Shunammite, and brought her to the king. 4 And the damsel was very fair, and cherished the king, and ministered to him: but the king knew her not.

5 Then Adonijah the son of Haggith exalted himself, saying, I will be king: and he prepared him chariots and horsemen, and fifty men to run before him. 6 And his father had not displeased him at any time in saying, Why hast thou done so? and he also was a very goodly man; and his mother bare him after Absalom. 7 And he conferred with Joab the son of Zeruiah, and with Abiathar the priest: and they following Adonijah helped him. 8 But Zadok the priest, and Benaiah the son of Jehoiada, and Nathan the prophet, and Shimei, and Rei, and the mighty men which belonged to David, were not with Adonijah. 9 And Adonijah slew sheep and oxen and fat cattle by the stone of Zoheleth, which is by En-rogel, and called all his brethren the king's sons, and all the men of Judah the king's servants: 10 But Nathan the prophet, and Benaiah, and the mighty men, and Solomon his brother, he called not.

11 Wherefore Nathan spake unto Bath-sheba the mother of Solomon, saying, Hast thou not heard that Adonijah the son of Haggith doth reign, and David our lord knoweth it not? 12 Now therefore come, let me, I pray thee, give thee counsel, that thou mayest save thine own life, and the life of thy son Solomon. 13 Go and get thee in unto king David, and say unto him, Didst not thou, my lord, O king, swear unto thine handmaid, saying, Assuredly Solomon thy son shall reign after me, and he shall sit upon my throne? why then doth Adonijah reign? 14 Behold, while thou yet talkest there with the king, I also will come in after thee, and confirm thy words.

15 And Bath-sheba went in unto the king into the chamber: and the king was very old; and Abishag the Shunammite ministered unto the king. 16 And Bath-sheba bowed, and did obeisance unto the king. And the king said, What wouldest thou? 17 And she said unto him, My lord, thou swarest by the Lord thy God unto thine handmaid, saying, Assuredly Solomon thy son shall reign after me, and he shall sit upon my throne. 18 And now, behold, Adonijah reigneth; and now, my lord the king, thou knowest it not: 19 And he hath slain oxen and fat cattle and sheep in abundance, and hath called all the sons of the

king, and Abiathar the priest, and Joab the captain of the host: but Solomon thy servant hath he not called. 20 And thou, my lord, O king, the eyes of all Israel are upon thee, that thou shouldest tell them who shall sit on the throne of my lord the king after him. 21 Otherwise it shall come to pass, when my lord the king shall sleep with his fathers, that I and my son Solomon shall be counted offenders.

22 And, lo, while she yet talked with the king, Nathan the prophet also came in. 23 And they told the king, saying, Behold Nathan the prophet. And when he was come in before the king, he bowed himself before the king with his face to the ground. 24 And Nathan said, My lord, O king, hast thou said, Adonijah shall reign after me, and he shall sit upon my throne? 25 For he is gone down this day, and hath slain oxen and fat cattle and sheep in abundance, and hath called all the king's sons, and the captains of the host, and Abiathar the priest; and, behold, they eat and drink before him, and say, God save king Adonijah. 26 But me, even me thy servant, and Zadok the priest, and Benaiah the son of Jehoiada, and thy servant Solomon, hath he not called. 27 Is this thing done by my lord the king, and thou hast not showed it unto thy servant, who should sit on the throne of my lord the king after him?

28 Then king David answered and said, Call me Bath-sheba. And she came into the king's presence, and stood before the king. 29 And the king sware, and said, As the Lord liveth, that hath redeemed my soul out of all distress, 30 Even as I sware unto thee by the Lord God of Israel, saying, Assuredly Solomon thy son shall reign after me, and he shall sit upon my throne in my stead; even so will I certainly do this day. 31 Then Bath-sheba bowed with her face to the earth, and did reverence to the king, and said, Let my lord king David live for ever.

32 And king David said, Call me Zadok the priest, and Nathan the prophet, and Benaiah the son of Jehoiada. And they came before the king. 33 The king also said unto them, Take with you the servants of your lord, and cause Solomon my son to ride upon mine own mule, and bring him down to Gihon: 34 And let Zadok the priest and Nathan the prophet anoint him there king over Israel: and blow ye with the trumpet, and say, God save king Solomon. 35 Then ye shall come up after him, that he may come and sit upon my throne; for he shall be king in my stead: and I have appointed him to be ruler over Israel and over Judah. 36 And Benaiah the son of Jehoiada answered the king, and said, Amen: the Lord God of my lord the king say so too. 37 As the Lord hath been with my lord the king, even so be he with Solomon, and make his throne greater than the throne of my lord king David.

38 So Zadok the priest, and Nathan the prophet, and Benaiah the son of Jehoiada, and the Cherethites, and the Pelethites, went down, and caused Solomon to ride upon king David's mule, and brought him to Gihon. 39 And Zadok the priest took a horn of oil out of the tabernacle, and anointed Solomon. And they blew the trumpet; and all

the people said, God save king Solomon. 40 And all the people came up after him, and the people piped with pipes, and rejoiced with great joy, so that the earth rent with the sound of them.

41 And Adonijah and all the guests that were with him heard it as they had made an end of eating. And when Joab heard the sound of the trumpet, he said, Wherefore is this noise of the city being in an uproar? 42 And while he yet spake, behold, Jonathan the son of Abiathar the priest came: and Adonijah said unto him, Come in; for thou art a valiant man, and bringest good tidings. 43 And Jonathan answered and said to Adonijah, Verily our lord king David hath made Solomon king. 44 And the king hath sent with him Zadok the priest, and Nathan the prophet, and Benaiah the son of Jehoiada, and the Cherethites, and the Pelethites, and they have caused him to ride upon the king's mule: 45 And Zadok the priest and Nathan the prophet have anointed him king in Gihon: and they are come up from thence rejoicing, so that the city rang again. This is the noise that ye have heard. 46 And also Solomon sitteth on the throne of the kingdom. 47 And moreover the king's servants came to bless our lord king David, saying, God make the name of Solomon better than thy name, and make his throne greater than thy throne. And the king bowed himself upon the bed. 48 And also thus said the king, Blessed be the Lord God of Israel, which hath given one to sit on my throne this day, mine eyes even seeing it.

49 And all the guests that were with Adonijah were afraid, and rose up, and went every man his way. 50 And Adonijah feared because of Solomon, and arose, and went, and caught hold on the horns of the altar. 51 And it was told Solomon, saying, Behold, Adonijah feareth king Solomon: for, lo, he hath caught hold on the horns of the altar, saying, Let king Solomon swear unto me to-day that he will not slay his servant with the sword. 52 And Solomon said, If he will show himself a worthy man, there shall not a hair of him fall to the earth: but if wickedness shall be found in him, he shall die. 53 So king Solomon sent, and they brought him down from the altar. And he came and bowed himself to king Solomon: and Solomon said unto him, Go to thine house.

2 Now the days of David drew nigh that he should die; and he charged Solomon his son, saying, 2 I go the way of all the earth: be thou strong therefore, and show thyself a man; 3 And keep the charge of the Lord thy God, to walk in his ways, to keep his statutes, and his commandments, and his judgments, and his testimonies, as it is written in the law of Moses, that thou mayest prosper in all that thou doest, and whithersoever thou turnest thyself: 4 That the Lord may continue his word which he spake concerning me, saying, If thy children take heed to their way, to walk before me in truth with all their heart and with all their soul, there shall not fail thee (said he) a man on the throne of Israel. 5 Moreover thou knowest also what Joab the son of Zeruiah did to me, and what he did to the two captains of the

hosts of Israel, unto Abner the son of Ner, and unto Amasa the son of Jether, whom he slew, and shed the blood of war in peace, and put the blood of war upon his girdle that was about his loins, and in his shoes that were on his feet. 6 Do therefore according to thy wisdom, and let not his hoar head go down to the grave in peace. 7 But show kindness unto the sons of Barzillai the Gileadite, and let them be of those that eat at thy table: for so they came to me when I fled because of Absalom thy brother. 8 And, behold, thou hast with thee Shimei the son of Gera, a Benjamite of Bahurim, which cursed me with a grievous curse in the day when I went to Mahanaim: but he came down to meet me at Jordan, and I sware to him by the Lord, saying, I will not put thee to death with the sword. 9 Now therefore hold him not guiltless: for thou art a wise man, and knowest what thou oughtest to do unto him; but his hoar head bring thou down to the grave with blood.

10 So David slept with his fathers, and was buried in the city of David. 11 And the days that David reigned over Israel were forty years: seven years reigned he in Hebron, and thirty and three years reigned he in Jerusalem.

# The Age of Kings:
## *First and Second Kings*

David's son, Solomon, was able to consolidate his father's gains, and under him Israel reached its zenith of wealth and power. Solomon established many foreign alliances and contracted many diplomatic marriages, yet he lacked his father's ability to accept a heathen person without allowing heathen religion to infiltrate Israel. For all his vaunted wisdom, Solomon did not succeed in establishing a lasting regime, and after him the country was divided into northern and southern kingdoms, known respectively as Israel and Judah. The general tendency under the succeeding kings was towards moral and religious corruption, though there were remarkable reforms. The story moves swiftly, and is peopled by a number of clearly and impressively drawn characters.

## *First Kings*

### SOLOMON AND HIS GLORY

2 12 Then sat Solomon upon the throne of David his father; and his kingdom was established greatly. 13 And Adonijah the son of Haggith came to Bath-sheba the mother of Solomon. And she said, Comest thou peaceably? And he said, Peaceably. 14 He said moreover, I have somewhat to say unto thee. And she said, Say on. 15 And he said, Thou knowest that the kingdom was mine, and that all Israel set their faces on me, that I should reign: howbeit the kingdom is turned about, and is become my brother's: for it was his from the Lord. 16 And now I ask one petition of thee, deny me not. And she said unto him, Say on. 17 And he said, Speak, I pray thee, unto Solomon the king, (for he will not say thee nay,) that he give me Abishag the Shunammite to wife. 18 And Bath-sheba said, Well; I will speak for thee unto the king.

19 Bath-sheba therefore went unto king Solomon, to speak unto him for Adonijah. And the king rose up to meet her, and bowed himself unto her, and sat down on his throne, and caused a seat to be set for the king's mother; and she sat on his right hand. 20 Then she said, I desire one small petition of thee; I pray thee, say me not nay. And the king said unto her, Ask on, my mother; for I will not say thee

nay. 21 And she said, Let Abishag the Shunammite be given to Adonijah thy brother to wife. 22 And king Solomon answered and said unto his mother, And why dost thou ask Abishag the Shunammite for Adonijah? ask for him the kingdom also; for he is mine elder brother; even for him, and for Abiathar the priest, and for Joab the son of Zeruiah. 23 Then king Solomon sware by the Lord, saying, God do so to me, and more also, if Adonijah have not spoken this word against his own life. 24 Now therefore, as the Lord liveth, which hath established me, and set me on the throne of David my father, and who hath made me a house, as he promised, Adonijah shall be put to death this day. 25 And king Solomon sent by the hand of Benaiah the son of Jehoiada; and he fell upon him that he died.

26 And unto Abiathar the priest said the king, Get thee to Anathoth, unto thine own fields; for thou art worthy of death: but I will not at this time put thee to death, because thou barest the ark of the Lord God before David my father, and because thou hast been afflicted in all wherein my father was afflicted. 27 So Solomon thrust out Abiathar from being priest unto the Lord; that he might fulfil the word of the Lord, which he spake concerning the house of Eli in Shiloh.

28 Then tidings came to Joab: for Joab had turned after Adonijah, though he turned not after Absalom. And Joab fled unto the tabernacle of the Lord, and caught hold on the horns of the altar. 29 And it was told king Solomon that Joab was fled unto the tabernacle of the Lord; and, behold, he is by the altar. Then Solomon sent Benaiah the son of Jehoiada, saying, Go, fall upon him. 30 And Benaiah came to the tabernacle of the Lord, and said unto him, Thus saith the king, Come forth. And he said, Nay; but I will die here. And Benaiah brought the king word again, saying, Thus said Joab, and thus he answered me. 31 And the king said unto him, Do as he hath said, and fall upon him, and bury him; that thou mayest take away the innocent blood, which Joab shed, from me, and from the house of my father. 32 And the Lord shall return his blood upon his own head, who fell upon two men more righteous and better than he, and slew them with the sword, my father David not knowing thereof, to wit, Abner the son of Ner, captain of the host of Israel, and Amasa the son of Jether, captain of the host of Judah. 33 Their blood shall therefore return upon the head of Joab, and upon the head of his seed for ever: but upon David, and upon his seed, and upon his house, and upon his throne, shall there be peace for ever from the Lord. 34 So Benaiah the son of Jehoiada went up, and fell upon him, and slew him: and he was buried in his own house in the wilderness. 35 And the king put Benaiah the son of Jehoiada in his room over the host: and Zadok the priest did the king put in the room of Abiathar.

36 And the king sent and called for Shimei, and said unto him, Build thee a house in Jerusalem, and dwell there, and go not forth thence any whither. 37 For it shall be, that on the day thou goest out, and passest over the brook Kidron, thou shalt know for certain that

thou shalt surely die: thy blood shall be upon thine own head. 38 And Shimei said unto the king, The saying is good: as my lord the king hath said, so will thy servant do. And Shimei dwelt in Jerusalem many days.

39 And it came to pass at the end of three years, that two of the servants of Shimei ran away unto Achish son of Maachah king of Gath. And they told Shimei, saying, Behold, thy servants be in Gath. 40 And Shimei arose, and saddled his ass, and went to Gath to Achish to seek his servants: and Shimei went, and brought his servants from Gath. 41 And it was told Solomon that Shimei had gone from Jerusalem to Gath, and was come again. 42 And the king sent and called for Shimei, and said unto him, Did I not make thee to swear by the Lord, and protested unto thee, saying, Know for a certain, on the day thou goest out, and walkest abroad any whither, that thou shalt surely die? and thou saidst unto me, The word that I have heard is good. 43 Why then hast thou not kept the oath of the Lord, and the commandment that I have charged thee with? 44 The king said moreover to Shimei, Thou knowest all the wickedness which thine heart is privy to, that thou didst to David my father; therefore the Lord shall return thy wickedness upon thine own head: 45 And king Solomon shall be blessed, and the throne of David shall be established before the Lord for ever. 46 So the king commanded Benaiah the son of Jehoiada; which went out, and fell upon him, that he died. And the kingdom was established in the hand of Solomon.

3 And Solomon made affinity with Pharaoh king of Egypt, and took Pharaoh's daughter, and brought her into the city of David, until he had made an end of building his own house, and the house of the Lord, and the wall of Jerusalem round about. 2 Only the people sacrificed in high places, because there was no house built unto the name of the Lord, until those days. 3 And Solomon loved the Lord, walking in the statutes of David his father: only he sacrificed and burnt incense in high places.

4 And the king went to Gibeon to sacrifice there; for that was the great high place: a thousand burnt offerings did Solomon offer upon that altar.

5 In Gibeon the Lord appeared to Solomon in a dream by night: and God said, Ask what I shall give thee. 6 And Solomon said, Thou hast showed unto thy servant David my father great mercy, according as he walked before thee in truth, and in righteousness, and in uprightness of heart with thee; and thou hast kept for him this great kindness, that thou hast given him a son to sit on his throne, as it is this day. 7 And now, O Lord my God, thou hast made thy servant king instead of David my father: and I am but a little child: I know not how to go out or come in. 8 And thy servant is in the midst of thy people which thou hast chosen, a great people, that cannot be numbered nor counted for multitude. 9 Give therefore thy servant an understanding heart to judge thy people, that I may discern between

good and bad: for who is able to judge this thy so great a people? 10 And the speech pleased the Lord, that Solomon had asked this thing. 11 And God said unto him, Because thou hast asked this thing, and hast not asked for thyself long life; neither hast asked riches for thyself, nor hast asked the life of thine enemies; but hast asked for thyself understanding to discern judgment; 12, Behold, I have done according to thy word: lo, I have given thee a wise and an understanding heart; so that there was none like thee before thee, neither after thee shall any arise like unto thee. 13 And I have also given thee that which thou hast not asked, both riches, and honor: so that there shall not be any among the kings like unto thee all thy days. 14 And if thou wilt walk in my ways, to keep my statutes and my commandments, as thy father David did walk, then I will lengthen thy days. 15 And Solomon awoke; and, behold, it was a dream. And he came to Jerusalem, and stood before the ark of the covenant of the Lord, and offered up burnt offerings, and offered peace offerings, and made a feast to all his servants.

16 Then came there two women, that were harlots, unto the king, and stood before him. 17 And the one woman said, O my lord, I and this woman dwell in one house; and I was delivered of a child with her in the house. 18 And it came to pass the third day after that I was delivered, that this woman was delivered also: and we were together; there was no stranger with us in the house, save we two in the house. 19 And this woman's child died in the night; because she overlaid it. 20 And she arose at midnight, and took my son from beside me, while thine handmaid slept, and laid it in her bosom, and laid her dead child in my bosom. 21 And when I rose in the morning to give my child suck, behold, it was dead: but when I had considered it in the morning, behold, it was not my son, which I did bear. 22 And the other woman said, Nay; but the living is my son, and the dead is thy son. And this said, No; but the dead is thy son, and the living is my son. Thus they spake before the king.

23 Then said the king, The one saith, This is my son that liveth, and thy son is the dead: and the other saith, Nay; but thy son is the dead, and my son is the living. 24 And the king said, Bring me a sword. And they brought a sword before the king. 25 And the king said, Divide the living child in two, and give half to the one, and half to the other. 26 Then spake the woman whose the living child was unto the king, for her bowels yearned upon her son, and she said, O my lord, give her the living child, and in no wise slay it. But the other said, Let it be neither mine nor thine, but divide it. 27 Then the king answered and said, Give her the living child, and in no wise slay it: she is the mother thereof. 28 And all Israel heard of the judgment which the king had judged; and they feared the king: for they saw that the wisdom of God was in him to do judgment.

4 So king Solomon was king over all Israel. 7 And Solomon had twelve officers over all Israel, which provided victuals for the king and

his household: each man his month in a year made provision. 21 And Solomon reigned over all kingdoms from the river unto the land of the Philistines, and unto the border of Egypt: they brought presents, and served Solomon all the days of his life.

22 And Solomon's provision for one day was thirty measures of fine flour, and threescore measures of meal, 23 Ten fat oxen, and twenty oxen out of the pastures, and a hundred sheep, besides harts, and roebucks, and fallow deer, and fatted fowl. 24 For he had dominion over all the region on this side the river, from Tiphsah even to Azzah, over all the kings on this side the river: and he had peace on all sides round about him. 25 And Judah and Israel dwelt safely, every man under his vine and under his fig tree, from Dan even to Beer-sheba, all the days of Solomon.

26 And Solomon had forty thousand stalls of horses for his chariots, and twelve thousand horsemen. 27 And those officers provided victuals for king Solomon, and for all that came unto king Solomon's table, every man in his month: they lacked nothing. 28 Barley also and straw for the horses and dromedaries brought they unto the place where the officers were, every man according to his charge.

29 And God gave Solomon wisdom and understanding exceeding much, and largeness of heart, even as the sand that is on the seashore. 30 And Solomon's wisdom excelled the wisdom of all the children of the east country, and all the wisdom of Egypt. 31 For he was wiser than all men; than Ethan the Ezrahite, and Heman, and Chalcol, and Darda, the sons of Mahol: and his fame was in all nations round about. 32 And he spake three thousand proverbs: and his songs were a thousand and five. 33 And he spake of trees, from the cedar tree that is in Lebanon even unto the hyssop that springeth out of the wall: he spake also of beasts, and of fowl, and of creeping things, and of fishes. 34 And there came of all people to hear the wisdom of Solomon, from all kings of the earth, which had heard of his wisdom.

## BUILDING THE TEMPLE

5 And Hiram king of Tyre sent his servants unto Solomon; for he had heard that they had anointed him king in the room of his father: for Hiram was ever a lover of David. 2 And Solomon sent to Hiram, saying, 3 Thou knowest how that David my father could not build a house unto the name of the Lord his God, for the wars which were about him on every side, until the Lord put them under the soles of his feet. 4 But now the Lord my God hath given me rest on every side, so that there is neither adversary nor evil occurrent. 5 And, behold, I purpose to build a house unto the name of the Lord my God, as the Lord spake unto David my father, saying, Thy son, whom I will set upon thy throne in thy room, he shall build a house unto my name. 6 Now therefore command thou that they hew me cedar trees out of Lebanon; and my servants shall be with thy servants: and unto thee will I give hire for thy servants according to all that thou shalt appoint:

for thou knowest that there is not among us any that can skill to hew timber like unto the Sidonians.

7 And it came to pass, when Hiram heard the words of Solomon, that he rejoiced greatly, and said, Blessed be the Lord this day, which hath given unto David a wise son over this great people. 8 And Hiram sent to Solomon, saying, I have considered the things which thou sentest to me for: and I will do all thy desire concerning timber of cedar, and concerning timber of fir. 9 My servants shall bring them down from Lebanon unto the sea; and I will convey them by sea in floats unto the place that thou shalt appoint me, and will cause them to be discharged there, and thou shalt receive them: and thou shalt accomplish my desire, in giving food for my household. 10 So Hiram gave Solomon cedar trees and fir trees according to all his desire. 11 And Solomon gave Hiram twenty thousand measures of wheat for food to his household, and twenty measures of pure oil: thus gave Solomon to Hiram year by year. 12 And the Lord gave Solomon wisdom, as he promised him: and there was peace between Hiram and Solomon; and they two made a league together.

13 And king Solomon raised a levy out of all Israel; and the levy was thirty thousand men. 14 And he sent them to Lebanon, ten thousand a month by courses: a month they were in Lebanon, and two months at home: and Adoniram was over the levy. 15 And Solomon had threescore and ten thousand that bare burdens, and fourscore thousand hewers in the mountains; 16 Besides the chief of Solomon's officers which were over the work, three thousand and three hundred, which ruled over the people that wrought in the work. 17 And the king commanded, and they brought great stones, costly stones, and hewed stones, to lay the foundation of the house. 18 And Solomon's builders and Hiram's builders did hew them, and the stonesquarers: so they prepared timber and stones to build the house.

6 11 And the word of the Lord came to Solomon, saying, 12 Concerning this house which thou art in building, if thou wilt walk in my statutes, and execute my judgments, and keep all my commandments to walk in them; then will I perform my word with thee, which I spake unto David thy father: 13 And I will dwell among the children of Israel, and will not forsake my people Israel. 14 So Solomon built the house, and finished it.

7 51 So was ended all the work that king Solomon made for the house of the Lord. And Solomon brought in the things which David his father had dedicated; even the silver, and the gold, and the vessels, did he put among the treasures of the house of the Lord.

8 Then Solomon assembled the elders of Israel, and all the heads of the tribes, the chief of the fathers of the children of Israel, unto king Solomon in Jerusalem, that they might bring up the ark of the covenant of the Lord out of the city of David, which is Zion. 2 And

all the men of Israel assembled themselves unto king Solomon at the feast in the month Ethanim, which is the seventh month. 3 And all the elders of Israel came, and the priests took up the ark. 4 And they brought up the ark of the Lord, and the tabernacle of the congregation, and all the holy vessels that were in the tabernacle, even those did the priests and the Levites bring up. 5 And king Solomon, and all the congregation of Israel, that were assembled unto him, were with him before the ark, sacrificing sheep and oxen, that could not be told nor numbered for multitude. 6 And the priests brought in the ark of the covenant of the Lord unto his place, into the oracle of the house, to the most holy place, even under the wings of the cherubim. 7 For the cherubim spread forth their two wings over the place of the ark, and the cherubim covered the ark and the staves thereof above. 9 There was nothing in the ark save the two tables of stone, which Moses put there at Horeb, when the Lord made a covenant with the children of Israel, when they came out of the land of Egypt. 10 And it came to pass, when the priests were come out of the holy place, that the cloud filled the house of the Lord, 11 So that the priests could not stand to minister because of the cloud: for the glory of the Lord had filled the house of the Lord.

12 Then spake Solomon,
The Lord said that he would dwell in the thick darkness.
13 I have surely built thee a house to dwell in,
A settled place for thee to abide in for ever.

27 But will God indeed dwell on the earth? behold, the heaven and heaven of heavens cannot contain thee; how much less this house that I have builded? 28 Yet have thou respect unto the prayer of thy servant, and to his supplication, O Lord my God, to hearken unto the cry and to the prayer, which thy servant prayeth before thee to-day: 29 That thine eyes may be open toward this house night and day, even toward the place of which thou hast said, My name shall be there: that thou mayest hearken unto the prayer which thy servant shall make toward this place. 30 And hearken thou to the supplication of thy servant, and of thy people Israel, when they shall pray toward this place: and hear thou in heaven thy dwelling place: and when thou hearest, forgive.

9 And it came to pass, when Solomon had finished the building of the house of the Lord, and the king's house, and all Solomon's desire which he was pleased to do, 2 That the Lord appeared to Solomon the second time, as he had appeared unto him at Gibeon. 3 And the Lord said unto him, I have heard thy prayer and thy supplication, that thou hast made before me: I have hallowed this house, which thou hast built, to put my name there for ever; and mine eyes and mine heart shall be there perpetually. 4 And if thou wilt walk before me, as David thy father walked, in integrity of heart, and in uprightness, to do according to all that I have commanded thee, and wilt keep my statutes and my judgments; 5 Then I will establish the

throne of thy kingdom upon Israel for ever, as I promised to David thy father, saying, There shall not fail thee a man upon the throne of Israel. 6 But if ye shall at all turn from following me, ye or your children, and will not keep my commandments and my statutes which I have set before you, but go and serve other gods, and worship them; 7 Then will I cut off Israel out of the land which I have given them; and this house, which I have hallowed for my name, will I cast out of my sight; and Israel shall be a proverb and a byword among all people: 8 And at this house, which is high, every one that passeth by it shall be astonished, and shall hiss; and they shall say, Why hath the Lord done thus unto this land, and to this house? 9 And they shall answer, Because they forsook the Lord their God, who brought forth their fathers out of the land of Egypt, and have taken hold upon other gods, and have worshipped them, and served them: therefore hath the Lord brought upon them all this evil.

## SOLOMON'S FAME AND FALL

10 And when the queen of Sheba heard of the fame of Solomon concerning the name of the Lord, she came to prove him with hard questions. 2 And she came to Jerusalem with a very great train, with camels that bare spices, and very much gold, and precious stones: and when she was come to Solomon, she communed with him of all that was in her heart. 3 And Solomon told her all her questions: there was not any thing hid from the king, which he told her not. 4 And when the queen of Sheba had seen all Solomon's wisdom, and the house that he had built, 5 And the meat of his table, and the sitting of his servants, and the attendance of his ministers, and their apparel, and his cupbearers, and his ascent by which he went up unto the house of the Lord; there was no more spirit in her. 6 And she said to the king, It was a true report that I heard in mine own land of thy acts and of thy wisdom. 7 Howbeit I believed not the words, until I came, and mine eyes had seen it; and, behold, the half was not told me: thy wisdom and prosperity exceedeth the fame which I heard. 8 Happy are thy men, happy are these thy servants, which stand continually before thee, and that hear thy wisdom. 9 Blessed be the Lord thy God, which delighted in thee, to set thee on the throne of Israel: because the Lord loved Israel for ever, therefore made he thee king, to do judgment and justice. 10 And she gave the king a hundred and twenty talents of gold, and of spices very great store, and precious stones: there came no more such abundance of spices as these which the queen of Sheba gave to king Solomon. 11 And the navy also of Hiram, that brought gold from Ophir, brought in from Ophir great plenty of almug trees, and precious stones. 12 And the king made of the almug trees pillars for the house of the Lord, and for the king's house, harps also and psalteries for singers: there came no such almug trees, nor were seen unto this day. 13 And king Solomon gave unto the queen of Sheba all her desire, whatsoever she asked, besides that

which Solomon gave her of his royal bounty. So she turned and went to her own country, she and her servants.

23 So king Solomon exceeded all the kings of the earth for riches and for wisdom. 24 And all the earth sought to Solomon, to hear his wisdom, which God had put in his heart. 25 And they brought every man his present, vessels of silver, and vessels of gold, and garments, and armor, and spices, horses, and mules, a rate year by year.

26 And Solomon gathered together chariots and horsemen: and he had a thousand and four hundred chariots, and twelve thousand horsemen, whom he bestowed in the cities for chariots, and with the king at Jerusalem. 27 And the king made silver to be in Jerusalem as stones, and cedars made he to be as the sycamore trees that are in the vale, for abundance.

11 But king Solomon loved many strange women, together with the daughter of Pharaoh, women of the Moabites, Ammonites, Edomites, Zidonians, and Hittites; 2 Of the nations concerning which the Lord said unto the children of Israel, Ye shall not go in to them, neither shall they come in unto you: for surely they will turn away your heart after their gods: Solomon clave unto these in love. 3 And he had seven hundred wives, princesses, and three hundred concubines: and his wives turned away his heart. 4 For it came to pass, when Solomon was old, that his wives turned away his heart after other gods: and his heart was not perfect with the Lord his God, as was the heart of David his father. 5 For Solomon went after Ashtoreth the goddess of the Zidonians, and after Milcom the abomination of the Ammonites. 6 And Solomon did evil in the sight of the Lord, and went not fully after the Lord, as did David his father. 7 Then did Solomon build a high place for Chemosh, the abomination of Moab, in the hill that is before Jerusalem, and for Molech, the abomination of the children of Ammon. 8 And likewise did he for all his strange wives, which burnt incense and sacrificed unto their gods.

9 And the Lord was angry with Solomon, because his heart was turned from the Lord God of Israel, which had appeared unto him twice, 10 And had commanded him concerning this thing, that he should not go after other gods: but he kept not that which the Lord commanded. 11 Wherefore the Lord said unto Solomon, Forasmuch as this is done of thee, and thou hast not kept my covenant and my statutes, which I have commanded thee, I will surely rend the kingdom from thee, and will give it to thy servant. 12 Notwithstanding, in thy days I will not do it for David thy father's sake: but I will rend it out of the hand of thy son. 13 Howbeit I will not rend away all the kingdom; but will give one tribe to thy son for David my servant's sake, and for Jerusalem's sake which I have chosen.

26 And Jeroboam the son of Nebat, an Ephrathite of Zereda, Solomon's servant, whose mother's name was Zeruah, a widow woman, even he lifted up his hand against the king. 27 And this was the cause that he lifted up his hand against the king: Solomon built

Millo, and repaired the breaches of the city of David his father. 28 And the man Jeroboam was a mighty man of valor: and Solomon seeing the young man that he was industrious, he made him ruler over all the charge of the house of Joseph. 29 And it came to pass at that time when Jeroboam went out of Jerusalem, that the prophet Ahijah the Shilonite found him in the way; and he had clad himself with a new garment; and they two were alone in the field: 30 And Ahijah caught the new garment that was on him, and rent it in twelve pieces: 31 And he said to Jeroboam, Take these ten pieces: for thus saith the Lord, the God of Israel, Behold, I will rend the kingdom out of the hand of Solomon, and will give ten tribes to thee: 32 (But he shall have one tribe for my servant David's sake, and for Jerusalem's sake, the city which I have chosen out of all the tribes of Israel:) 33 Because that they have forsaken me, and have worshipped Ashtoreth the goddess of the Zidonians, Chemosh the god of the Moabites, and Milcom the god of the children of Ammon, and have not walked in my ways, to do that which is right in mine eyes, and to keep my statutes and my judgments, as did David his father. 34 Howbeit I will not take the whole kingdom out of his hand: but I will make him prince all the days of his life for David my servant's sake, whom I chose, because he kept my commandments and my statutes: 35 But I will take the kingdom out of his son's hand, and will give it unto thee, even ten tribes. 36 And unto his son will I give one tribe, that David my servant may have a light alway before me in Jerusalem, the city which I have chosen me to put my name there. 37 And I will take thee, and thou shalt reign according to all that thy soul desireth, and shalt be king over Israel. 38 And it shall be, if thou wilt hearken unto all that I command thee, and wilt walk in my ways, and do that is right in my sight, to keep my statutes and my commandments, as David my servant did; that I will be with thee, and build thee a sure house, as I built for David, and will give Israel unto thee. 39 And I will for this afflict the seed of David, but not for ever.

40 Solomon sought therefore to kill Jeroboam. And Jeroboam arose, and fled into Egypt, unto Shishak king of Egypt, and was in Egypt until the death of Solomon.

42 And the time that Solomon reigned in Jerusalem over all Israel was forty years. 43 And Solomon slept with his fathers, and was buried in the city of David his father: and Rehoboam his son reigned in his stead.

## THE KINGDOM DIVIDED

12 And Rehoboam went to Shechem: for all Israel were come to Shechem to make him king. 2 And it came to pass, when Jeroboam the son of Nebat, who was yet in Egypt, heard of it, (for he was fled from the presence of king Solomon, and Jeroboam dwelt in Egypt,) 3 That they sent and called him. And Jeroboam and all the congregation of Israel came, and spake unto Rehoboam, saying,

4 Thy father made our yoke grievous: now therefore make thou the grievous service of thy father, and his heavy yoke which he put upon us, lighter, and we will serve thee. 5 And he said unto them, Depart yet for three days, then come again to me. And the people departed.

6 And king Rehoboam consulted with the old men, that stood before Solomon his father while he yet lived, and said, How do ye advise that I may answer this people? 7 And they spake unto him, saying, If thou wilt be a servant unto this people this day, and wilt serve them, and answer them, and speak good words to them, then they will be thy servants for ever. 8 But he forsook the counsel of the old men, which they had given him, and consulted with the young men that were grown up with him, and which stood before him: 9 And he said unto them, What counsel give ye that we may answer this people, who have spoken to me, saying, Make the yoke which thy father did put upon us lighter? 10 And the young men that were grown up with him spake unto him, saying, Thus shalt thou speak unto this people that spake unto thee, saying, Thy father made our yoke heavy, but make thou it lighter unto us; thus shalt thou say unto them, My little finger shall be thicker than my father's loins. 11 And now whereas my father did lade you with a heavy yoke, I will add to your yoke: my father hath chastised you with whips, but I will chastise you with scorpions.

12 So Jeroboam and all the people came to Rehoboam the third day, as the king had appointed, saying, Come to me again the third day. 13 And the king answered the people roughly, and forsook the old men's counsel that they gave him; 14 And spake to them after the counsel of the young men, saying, My father made your yoke heavy, and I will add to your yoke: my father also chastised you with whips, but I will chastise you with scorpions. 15 Wherefore the king hearkened not unto the people; for the cause was from the Lord, that he might perform his saying, which the Lord spake by Ahijah the Shilonite unto Jeroboam the son of Nebat.

16 So when all Israel saw that the king hearkened not unto them, the people answered the king, saying,

> What portion have we in David?
> Neither have we inheritance in the son of Jesse:
> To your tents, O Israel:
> Now see to thine own house, David.

So Israel departed unto their tents. 17 But as for the children of Israel which dwelt in the cities of Judah, Rehoboam reigned over them. 18 Then king Rehoboam sent Adoram, who was over the tribute; and all Israel stoned him with stones, that he died. Therefore king Rehoboam made speed to get him up to his chariot, to flee to Jerusalem. 19 So Israel rebelled against the house of David unto this day. 20 And it came to pass, when all Israel heard that Jeroboam was come again, that they sent and called him unto the congregation, and made him king over all Israel: there was none that followed the house of David, but the tribe of Judah only.

21 And when Rehoboam was come to Jerusalem, he assembled all

the house of Judah, with the tribe of Benjamin, a hundred and four-score thousand chosen men, which were warriors, to fight against the house of Israel, to bring the kingdom again to Rehoboam the son of Solomon. 22 But the word of God came unto Shemaiah the man of God, saying, 23 Speak unto Rehoboam, the son of Solomon, king of Judah, and unto all the house of Judah and Benjamin, and to the remnant of the people, saying,

24 Thus saith the Lord, Ye shall not go up, nor fight against your brethren the children of Israel: return every man to his house; for this thing is from me. They hearkened therefore to the word of the Lord, and returned to depart, according to the word of the Lord.

25 Then Jeroboam built Shechem in mount Ephraim, and dwelt therein; and went out from thence, and built Penuel. 26 And Jeroboam said in his heart, Now shall the kingdom return to the house of David: 27 If this people go up to do sacrifice in the house of the Lord at Jerusalem, then shall the heart of this people turn again unto their lord, even unto Rehoboam king of Judah, and they shall kill me, and go again to Rehoboam king of Judah. 28 Whereupon the king took counsel, and made two calves of gold, and said unto them, It is too much for you to go up to Jerusalem: behold thy gods, O Israel, which brought thee up out of the land of Egypt. 29 And he set the one in Beth-el, and the other put he in Dan. 30 And this thing became a sin: for the people went to worship before the one, even unto Dan. 31 And he made a house of high places, and made priests of the lowest of the people, which were not of the sons of Levi. 32 And Jeroboam ordained a feast in the eighth month, on the fifteenth day of the month, like unto the feast that is in Judah, and he offered upon the altar. So did he in Beth-el, sacrificing unto the calves that he had made: and he placed in Beth-el the priests of the high places which he had made. 33 So he offered upon the altar which he had made in Beth-el the fifteenth day of the eighth month, even in the month which he had devised of his own heart; and ordained a feast unto the children of Israel: and he offered upon the altar, and burnt incense.

13 And, behold, there came a man of God out of Judah by the word of the Lord unto Beth-el: and Jeroboam stood by the altar to burn incense. 2 And he cried against the altar in the word of the Lord, and said, O altar, altar, thus saith the Lord; Behold, a child shall be born unto the house of David, Josiah by name; and upon thee shall he offer the priests of the high places that burn incense upon thee, and men's bones shall be burnt upon thee. 3 And he gave a sign the same day, saying, This is the sign which the Lord hath spoken; Behold, the altar shall be rent, and the ashes that are upon it shall be poured out. 4 And it came to pass, when king Jeroboam heard the saying of the man of God, which had cried against the altar in Beth-el, that he put forth his hand from the altar, saying, Lay hold on him. And his hand, which he put forth against him, dried up, so that he could not pull it in again to him. 5 The altar also was rent, and the ashes poured

out from the altar, according to the sign which the man of God had given by the word of the Lord. 6 And the king answered and said unto the man of God, Entreat now the face of the Lord thy God, and pray for me, that my hand may be restored me again. And the man of God besought the Lord, and the king's hand was restored him again, and became as it was before. 7 And the king said unto the man of God, Come home with me, and refresh thyself, and I will give thee a reward. 8 And the man of God said unto the king, If thou wilt give me half thine house, I will not go in with thee, neither will I eat bread nor drink water in this place: 9 For so was it charged me by the word of the Lord, saying, Eat no bread, nor drink water, nor turn again by the same way that thou camest. 10 So he went another way, and returned not by the way that he came to Beth-el.

11 Now there dwelt an old prophet in Beth-el; and his sons came and told him all the works that the man of God had done that day in Beth-el: the words which he had spoken unto the king, them they told also to their father. 12 And their father said unto them, What way went he? For his sons had seen what way the man of God went, which came from Judah. 13 And he said unto his sons, Saddle me the ass. So they saddled him the ass: and he rode thereon, 14 And went after the man of God, and found him sitting under an oak: and he said unto him, Art thou the man of God that camest from Judah? And he said, I am. 15 Then he said unto him, Come home with me, and eat bread. 16 And he said, I may not return with thee, nor go in with thee: neither will I eat bread nor drink water with thee in this place: 17 For it was said to me by the word of the Lord, Thou shalt eat no bread nor drink water there, nor turn again to go by the way that thou camest. 18 He said unto him, I am a prophet also as thou art; and an angel spake unto me by the word of the Lord, saying, Bring him back with thee into thine house, that he may eat bread and drink water. But he lied unto him. 19 So he went back with him, and did eat bread in his house, and drank water.

20 And it came to pass, as they sat at the table, that the word of the Lord came unto the prophet that brought him back: 21 And he cried unto the man of God that came from Judah, saying, Thus saith the Lord, Forasmuch as thou hast disobeyed the mouth of the Lord, and hast not kept the commandment which the Lord thy God commanded thee, 22 But camest back, and hast eaten bread and drunk water in the place, of the which the Lord did say to thee, Eat no bread, and drink no water; thy carcass shall not come unto the sepulchre of thy fathers. 23 And it came to pass, after he had eaten bread, and after he had drunk, that he saddled for him the ass, to wit, for the prophet whom he had brought back. 24 And when he was gone, a lion met him by the way, and slew him: and his carcass was cast in the way, and the ass stood by it, the lion also stood by the carcass. 25 And, behold, men passed by, and saw the carcass cast in the way, and the lion standing by the carcass: and they came and told it in the city where the old prophet dwelt.

26 And when the prophet that brought him back from the way heard thereof, he said, It is the man of God, who was disobedient unto the word of the Lord: therefore the Lord hath delivered him unto the lion, which hath torn him, and slain him, according to the word of the Lord, which he spake unto him. 27 And he spake to his sons, saying, Saddle me the ass. And they saddled him. 28 And he went and found his carcass cast in the way, and the ass and the lion standing by the carcass: the lion had not eaten the carcass, nor torn the ass. 29 And the prophet took up the carcass of the man of God, and laid it upon the ass, and brought it back: and the old prophet came to the city, to mourn and to bury him. 30 And he laid his carcass in his own grave; and they mourned over him, saying, Alas, my brother! 31 And it came to pass, after he had buried him, that he spake to his sons, saying, When I am dead, then bury me in the sepulchre wherein the man of God is buried; lay my bones beside his bones: 32 For the saying which he cried by the word of the Lord against the altar in Beth-el, and against all the houses of the high places which are in the cities of Samaria, shall surely come to pass.

33 After this thing Jeroboam returned not from his evil way, but made again of the lowest of the people priests of the high places: whosoever would, he consecrated him, and he became one of the priests of the high places. 34 And this thing became sin unto the house of Jeroboam, even to cut it off, and to destroy it from off the face of the earth.

14 At that time Abijah the son of Jeroboam fell sick. 2 And Jeroboam said to his wife, Arise, I pray thee, and disguise thyself, that thou be not known to be the wife of Jeroboam; and get thee to Shiloh: behold, there is Ahijah the prophet, which told me that I should be king over this people. 3 And take with thee ten loaves, and cracknels, and a cruse of honey, and go to him: he shall tell thee what shall become of the child. 4 And Jeroboam's wife did so, and arose, and went to Shiloh, and came to the house of Ahijah. But Ahijah could not see; for his eyes were set by reason of his age. 5 And the Lord said unto Ahijah, Behold, the wife of Jeroboam cometh to ask a thing of thee for her son; for he is sick: thus and thus shalt thou say unto her: for it shall be, when she cometh in, that she shall feign herself to be another woman.

6 And it was so, when Ahijah heard the sound of her feet, as she came in at the door, that he said, Come in, thou wife of Jeroboam; why feignest thou thyself to be another? for I am sent to thee with heavy tidings. 7 Go, tell Jeroboam, Thus saith the Lord God of Israel, Forasmuch as I exalted thee from among the people, and made thee prince over my people Israel, 8 And rent the kingdom away from the house of David, and gave it thee: and yet thou hast not been as my servant David, who kept my commandments, and who followed me with all his heart, to do that only which was right in mine eyes; 9 But hast done evil above all that were before thee: for thou hast

gone and made thee other gods, and molten images, to provoke me to anger, and hast cast me behind thy back: 10 Therefore, behold, I will bring evil upon the house of Jeroboam, and will cut off from Jeroboam him that pisseth against the wall, and him that is shut up and left in Israel, and will take away the remnant of the house of Jeroboam, as a man taketh away dung, till it be all gone. 11 Him that dieth of Jeroboam in the city shall the dogs eat; and him that dieth in the field shall the fowls of the air eat: for the Lord hath spoken it. 12 Arise thou therefore, get thee to thine own house: and when thy feet enter into the city, the child shall die. 13 And all Israel shall mourn for him, and bury him: for he only of Jeroboam shall come to the grave, because in him there is found some good thing toward the Lord God of Israel in the house of Jeroboam. 14 Moreover the Lord shall raise him up a king over Israel, who shall cut off the house of Jeroboam that day: but what? even now. 15 For the Lord shall smite Israel, as a reed is shaken in the water, and he shall root up Israel out of this good land, which he gave to their fathers, and shall scatter them beyond the river, because they have made their groves, provoking the Lord to anger. 16 And he shall give Israel up because of the sins of Jeroboam, who did sin, and who made Israel to sin.

17 And Jeroboam's wife arose, and departed, and came to Tirzah: and when she came to the threshold of the door, the child died; 18 And they buried him; and all Israel mourned for him, according to the word of the Lord, which he spake by the hand of his servant Ahijah the prophet.

20 And the days which Jeroboam reigned were two and twenty years: and he slept with his fathers, and Nadab his son reigned in his stead.

21 And Rehoboam the son of Solomon reigned in Judah. Rehoboam was forty and one years old when he began to reign, and he reigned seventeen years in Jerusalem, the city which the Lord did choose out of all the tribes of Israel, to put his name there. And his mother's name was Naamah an Ammonitess. 22 And Judah did evil in the sight of the Lord, and they provoked him to jealousy with their sins which they had committed, above all that their fathers had done. 23 For they also built them high places, and images, and groves, on every high hill, and under every green tree. 24 And there were also sodomites in the land: and they did according to all the abominations of the nations which the Lord cast out before the children of Israel.

25 And it came to pass in the fifth year of king Rehoboam, that Shishak king of Egypt came up against Jerusalem: 26 And he took away the treasures of the house of the Lord, and the treasures of the king's house; he even took away all: and he took away all the shields of gold which Solomon had made. 27 And king Rehoboam made in their stead brazen shields, and committed them unto the hands of the chief of the guard, which kept the door of the king's house. 28 And it was so, when the king went into the house of the Lord, that the guard bare them, and brought them back into the guard chamber.

15    9 And in the twentieth year of Jeroboam king of Israel reigned
Asa over Judah. 10 And forty and one years reigned he in Jerusalem.
And his mother's name was Maachah, the daughter of Abishalom.
11 And Asa did that which was right in the eyes of the Lord, as did
David his father. 12 And he took away the sodomites out of the land,
and removed all the idols that his fathers had made. 13 And also
Maachah his mother, even her he removed from being queen, because
she had made an idol in a grove; and Asa destroyed her idol, and
burnt it by the brook Kidron. 14 But the high places were not removed: nevertheless Asa's heart was perfect with the Lord all his days.

### ELIJAH, AHAB, AND JEZEBEL

16    29 And in the thirty and eighth year of Asa king of Judah
began Ahab the son of Omri to reign over Israel: and Ahab the son
of Omri reigned over Israel in Samaria twenty and two years. 30 And
Ahab the son of Omri did evil in the sight of the Lord above all that
were before him. 31 And it came to pass, as if it had been a light
thing for him to walk in the sins of Jeroboam the son of Nebat, that
he took to wife Jezebel the daughter of Ethbaal king of the Zidonians,
and went and served Baal, and worshipped him. 32 And he reared up
an altar for Baal in the house of Baal, which he had built in Samaria.
33 And Ahab made a grove; and Ahab did more to provoke the Lord
God of Israel to anger than all the kings of Israel that were before him.
    34 In his days did Hiel the Beth-elite build Jericho: he laid the
foundation thereof in Abiram his firstborn, and set up the gates thereof
in his youngest son Segub, according to the word of the Lord, which
he spake by Joshua the son of Nun.

17    And Elijah the Tishbite, who was of the inhabitants of Gilead,
said unto Ahab, As the Lord God of Israel liveth, before whom I
stand, there shall not be dew nor rain these years, but according to
my word. 2 And the word of the Lord came unto him, saying, 3 Get
thee hence, and turn thee eastward, and hide thyself by the brook
Cherith, that is before Jordan. 4 And it shall be, that thou shalt drink
of the brook; and I have commanded the ravens to feed thee there.
5 So he went and did according unto the word of the Lord: for he
went and dwelt by the brook Cherith, that is before Jordan. 6 And
the ravens brought him bread and flesh in the morning, and bread
and flesh in the evening; and he drank of the brook. 7 And it came
to pass after a while, that the brook dried up, because there had been
no rain in the land.
    8 And the word of the Lord came unto him, saying, 9 Arise, get
thee to Zarephath, which belongeth to Zidon, and dwell there: behold,
I have commanded a widow woman there to sustain thee. 10 So he
arose and went to Zarephath. And when he came to the gate of the
city, behold, the widow woman was there gathering of sticks: and he

called to her, and said, Fetch me, I pray thee, a little water in a vessel, that I may drink. 11 And as she was going to fetch it, he called to her, and said, Bring me, I pray thee, a morsel of bread in thine hand. 12 And she said, As the Lord thy God liveth, I have not a cake, but a handful of meal in a barrel, and a little oil in a cruse: and, behold, I am gathering two sticks, that I may go in and dress it for me and my son, that we may eat it, and die. 13 And Elijah said unto her, Fear not; go and do as thou hast said: but make me thereof a little cake first, and bring it unto me, and after make for thee and for thy son. 14 For thus saith the Lord God of Israel, The barrel of meal shall not waste, neither shall the cruse of oil fail, until the day that the Lord sendeth rain upon the earth. 15 And she went and did according to the saying of Elijah: and she, and he, and her house, did eat many days. 16 And the barrel of meal wasted not, neither did the cruse of oil fail, according to the word of the Lord, which he spake by Elijah.

17 And it came to pass after these things, that the son of the woman, the mistress of the house, fell sick; and his sickness was so sore, that there was no breath left in him. 18 And she said unto Elijah, What have I to do with thee, O thou man of God? art thou come unto me to call my sin to remembrance, and to slay my son? 19 And he said unto her, Give me thy son. And he took him out of her bosom, and carried him up into a loft, where he abode, and laid him upon his own bed. 20 And he cried unto the Lord, and said, O Lord my God, hast thou also brought evil upon the widow with whom I sojourn, by slaying her son? 21 And he stretched himself upon the child three times, and cried unto the Lord, and said, O Lord my God, I pray thee, let this child's soul come into him again. 22 And the Lord heard the voice of Elijah; and the soul of the child came into him again, and he revived. 23 And Elijah took the child, and brought him down out of the chamber into the house, and delivered him unto his mother: and Elijah said, See, thy son liveth. 24 And the woman said to Elijah, Now by this I know that thou art a man of God, and that the word of the Lord in thy mouth is truth.

18    And it came to pass after many days, that the word of the Lord came to Elijah in the third year, saying, Go, show thyself unto Ahab; and I will send rain upon the earth. 2 And Elijah went to show himself unto Ahab.

And there was a sore famine in Samaria. 3 And Ahab called Obadiah, which was the governor of his house. (Now Obadiah feared the Lord greatly: 4 For it was so, when Jezebel cut off the prophets of the Lord, that Obadiah took a hundred prophets, and hid them by fifty in a cave, and fed them with bread and water.) 5 And Ahab said unto Obadiah, Go into the land, unto all fountains of water, and unto all brooks: peradventure we may find grass to save the horses and mules alive, that we lose not all the beasts. 6 So they divided the land between them to pass throughout it: Ahab went one way by himself, and Obadiah went another way by himself.

7 And as Obadiah was in the way, behold, Elijah met him: and he knew him, and fell on his face, and said, Art thou that my lord Elijah? 8 And he answered him, I am: go, tell thy lord, Behold, Elijah is here. 9 And he said, What have I sinned, that thou wouldest deliver thy servant into the hand of Ahab, to slay me? 10 As the Lord thy God liveth, there is no nation or kingdom, whither my lord hath not sent to seek thee: and when they said, He is not there; he took an oath of the kingdom and nation, that they found thee not. 11 And now thou sayest, Go, tell thy lord, Behold, Elijah is here. 12 And it shall come to pass, as soon as I am gone from thee, that the Spirit of the Lord shall carry thee whither I know not; and so when I come and tell Ahab, and he cannot find thee, he shall slay me: but I thy servant fear the Lord from my youth. 13 Was it not told my lord what I did when Jezebel slew the prophets of the Lord, how I hid a hundred men of the Lord's prophets by fifty in a cave, and fed them with bread and water? 14 And now thou sayest, Go, tell thy lord, Behold, Elijah is here: and he shall slay me. 15 And Elijah said, As the Lord of hosts liveth, before whom I stand, I will surely show myself unto him to-day.

16 So Obadiah went to meet Ahab, and told him: and Ahab went to meet Elijah. 17 And it came to pass, when Ahab saw Elijah, that Ahab said unto him, Art thou he that troubleth Israel? 18 And he answered, I have not troubled Israel; but thou, and thy father's house, in that ye have forsaken the commandments of the Lord, and thou hast followed Baalim. 19 Now therefore send, and gather to me all Israel unto mount Carmel, and the prophets of Baal four hundred and fifty, and the prophets of the groves four hundred, which eat at Jezebel's table.

20 So Ahab sent unto all the children of Israel, and gathered the prophets together unto mount Carmel. 21 And Elijah came unto all the people, and said, How long halt ye between two opinions? if the Lord be God, follow him: but if Baal, then follow him. And the people answered him not a word. 22 Then said Elijah unto the people, I, even I only, remain a prophet of the Lord; but Baal's prophets are four hundred and fifty men. 23 Let them therefore give us two bullocks; and let them choose one bullock for themselves, and cut it in pieces, and lay it on wood, and put no fire under: and I will dress the other bullock, and lay it on wood, and put no fire under: 24 And call ye on the name of your gods, and I will call on the name of the Lord: and the God that answereth by fire, let him be God. And all the people answered and said, It is well spoken.

25 And Elijah said unto the prophets of Baal, Choose you one bullock for yourselves, and dress it first; for ye are many; and call on the name of your gods, but put no fire under. 26 And they took the bullock which was given them, and they dressed it, and called on the

name of Baal from morning even until noon, saying, O Baal, hear us. But there was no voice, nor any that answered. And they leaped upon the altar which was made. 27 And it came to pass at noon, that Elijah mocked them, and said, Cry aloud: for he is a god; either he is talking, or he is pursuing, or he is in a journey, or peradventure he sleepeth, and must be awaked. 28 And they cried aloud, and cut themselves after their manner with knives and lancets, till the blood gushed out upon them. 29 And it came to pass, when midday was past, and they prophesied until the time of the offering of the evening sacrifice, that there was neither voice, nor any to answer, nor any that regarded.

30 And Elijah said unto all the people, Come near unto me. And all the people came near unto him. And he repaired the altar of the Lord that was broken down. 31 And Elijah took twelve stones, according to the number of the tribes of the sons of Jacob, unto whom the word of the Lord came, saying, Israel shall be thy name: 32 And with the stones he built an altar in the name of the Lord: and he made a trench about the altar, as great as would contain two measures of seed. 33 And he put the wood in order, and cut the bullock in pieces, and laid him on the wood, and said, Fill four barrels with water, and pour it on the burnt sacrifice, and on the wood. 34 And he said, Do it the second time. And they did it the second time. And he said, Do it the third time. And they did it the third time. 35 And the water ran round about the altar; and he filled the trench also with water. 36 And it came to pass at the time of the offering of the evening sacrifice, that Elijah the prophet came near, and said, Lord God of Abraham, Isaac, and of Israel, let it be known this day that thou art God in Israel, and that I am thy servant, and that I have done all these things at thy word. 37 Hear me, O Lord, hear me, that this people may know that thou art the Lord God, and that thou hast turned their heart back again. 38 Then the fire of the Lord fell, and consumed the burnt sacrifice, and the wood, and the stones, and the dust, and licked up the water that was in the trench. 39 And when all the people saw it, they fell on their faces: and they said, The Lord, he is the God; the Lord, he is the God. 40 And Elijah said unto them, Take the prophets of Baal; let not one of them escape. And they took them: and Elijah brought them down to the brook Kishon, and slew them there.

41 And Elijah said unto Ahab, Get thee up, eat and drink; for there is a sound of abundance of rain. 42 So Ahab went up to eat and to drink. And Elijah went up to the top of Carmel; and he cast himself down upon the earth, and put his face between his knees. 43 And said to his servant, Go up now, look toward the sea. And he went up, and looked, and said, There is nothing. And he said, Go again seven times. 44 And it came to pass at the seventh time, that he said, Behold, there ariseth a little cloud out of the sea, like a man's hand. And he said, Go up, say unto Ahab, Prepare thy chariot, and get thee down, that the rain stop thee not. 45 And it came to pass in the mean while, that the heaven was black with clouds and wind, and there

was a great rain. And Ahab rode, and went to Jezreel. 46 And the hand of the Lord was on Elijah; and he girded up his loins, and ran before Ahab to the entrance of Jezreel.

19 And Ahab told Jezebel all that Elijah had done, and withal how he had slain all the prophets with the sword. 2 Then Jezebel sent a messenger unto Elijah, saying, So let the gods do to me, and more also, if I make not thy life as the life of one of them by to-morrow about this time. 3 And when he saw that, he arose, and went for his life, and came to Beer-sheba, which belongeth to Judah, and left his servant there. 4 But he himself went a day's journey into the wilderness, and came and sat down under a juniper tree: and he requested for himself that he might die; and said, It is enough; now, O Lord, take away my life; for I am not better than my fathers. 5 And as he lay and slept under a juniper tree, behold, then an angel touched him, and said unto him, Arise and eat. 6 And he looked, and, behold, there was a cake baked on the coals, and a cruse of water at his head. And he did eat and drink, and laid him down again. 7 And the angel of the Lord came again the second time, and touched him, and said, Arise and eat; because the journey is too great for thee. 8 And he arose, and did eat and drink, and went in the strength of that meat forty days and forty nights unto Horeb the mount of God.

9 And he came thither unto a cave, and lodged there; and, behold, the word of the Lord came to him, and he said unto him, What doest thou here, Elijah? 10 And he said, I have been very jealous for the Lord God of hosts: for the children of Israel have forsaken thy covenant, thrown down thine altars, and slain thy prophets with the sword; and I, even I only, am left; and they seek my life, to take it away. 11 And he said, Go forth, and stand upon the mount before the Lord. And, behold, the Lord passed by, and a great and strong wind rent the mountains, and brake in pieces the rocks before the Lord; but the Lord was not in the wind: and after the wind an earthquake; but the Lord was not in the earthquake: 12 And after the earthquake a fire; but the Lord was not in the fire: and after the fire a still small voice. 13 And it was so, when Elijah heard it, that he wrapped his face in his mantle, and went out, and stood in the entering in of the cave. And, behold, there came a voice unto him, and said, What doest thou here, Elijah? 14 And he said, I have been very jealous for the Lord God of hosts: because the children of Israel have forsaken thy covenant, thrown down thine altars, and slain thy prophets with the sword; and I, even I only, am left; and they seek my life, to take it away.

15 And the Lord said unto him, Go, return on thy way to the wilderness of Damascus: and when thou comest, anoint Hazael to be king over Syria: 16 And Jehu the son of Nimshi shalt thou anoint to be king over Israel: and Elisha the son of Shaphat of Abel-meholah shalt thou anoint to be prophet in thy room. 17 And it shall come to pass, that him that escapeth the sword of Hazael shall Jehu slay:

and him that escapeth from the sword of Jehu shall Elisha slay. 18 Yet I have left me seven thousand in Israel, all the knees which have not bowed unto Baal, and every mouth which hath not kissed him.

19 So he departed thence, and found Elisha the son of Shaphat, who was plowing with twelve yoke of oxen before him, and he with the twelfth: and Elijah passed by him, and cast his mantle upon him. 20 And he left the oxen, and ran after Elijah, and said, Let me, I pray thee, kiss my father and my mother, and then I will follow thee. And he said unto him, Go back again: for what have I done to thee? 21 And he returned back from him, and took a yoke of oxen, and slew them, and boiled their flesh with the instruments of the oxen, and gave unto the people, and they did eat. Then he arose, and went after Elijah, and ministered unto him.

20   And Ben-hadad the king of Syria gathered all his host together: and there were thirty and two kings with him, and horses, and chariots: and he went up and besieged Samaria, and warred against it. 2 And he sent messengers to Ahab king of Israel into the city, and said unto him, Thus saith Ben-hadad, 3 Thy silver and thy gold is mine; thy wives also and thy children, even the goodliest, are mine. 4 And the king of Israel answered and said, My lord, O king, according to thy saying, I am thine, and all that I have. 5 And the messengers came again, and said, Thus speaketh Ben-hadad, saying, Although I have sent unto thee, saying, Thou shalt deliver me thy silver, and thy gold, and thy wives, and thy children; 6 Yet I will send my servants unto thee to-morrow about this time, and they shall search thine house, and the houses of thy servants; and it shall be, that whatsoever is pleasant in thine eyes, they shall put it in their hand, and take it away.

7 Then the king of Israel called all the elders of the land, and said, Mark, I pray you, and see how this man seeketh mischief: for he sent unto me for my wives, and for my children, and for my silver, and for my gold; and I denied him not. 8 And all the elders and all the people said unto him, Hearken not unto him, nor consent. 9 Wherefore he said unto the messengers of Ben-hadad, Tell my lord the king, All that thou didst send for to thy servant at the first I will do: but this thing I may not do. And the messengers departed, and brought him word again. 10 And Ben-hadad sent unto him, and said, The gods do so unto me, and more also, if the dust of Samaria shall suffice for handfuls for all the people that follow me. 11 And the king of Israel answered and said, Tell him, Let not him that girdeth on his harness boast himself as he that putteth it off. 12 And it came to pass, when Ben-hadad heard this message, as he was drinking, he and the kings in the pavilions, that he said unto his servants, Set yourselves in array. And they set themselves in array against the city.

13 And, behold, there came a prophet unto Ahab king of Israel, saying, Thus saith the Lord, Hast thou seen all this great multitude? behold, I will deliver it into thine hand this day; and thou shalt know that I am the Lord. 14 And Ahab said, By whom? And he said,

Thus saith the Lord, Even by the young men of the princes of the provinces. Then he said, Who shall order the battle? And he answered, Thou. 15 Then he numbered the young men of the princes of the provinces, and they were two hundred and thirty-two: and after them he numbered all the people, even all the children of Israel, being seven thousand.

16 And they went out at noon. But Ben-hadad was drinking himself drunk in the pavilions, he and the kings, the thirty and two kings that helped him. 17 And the young men of the princes of the provinces went out first; and Ben-hadad sent out, and they told him, saying, There are men come out of Samaria. 18 And he said, Whether they be come out for peace, take them alive; or whether they be come out for war, take them alive. 19 So these young men of the princes of the provinces came out of the city, and the army which followed them. 20 And they slew every one his man: and the Syrians fled; and Israel pursued them: and Ben-hadad the king of Syria escaped on a horse with the horsemen. 21 And the king of Israel went out, and smote the horses and chariots, and slew the Syrians with a great slaughter. 22 And the prophet came to the king of Israel, and said unto him, Go, strengthen thyself, and mark, and see what thou doest: for at the return of the year the king of Syria will come up against thee.

23 And the servants of the king of Syria said unto him, Their gods are gods of the hills; therefore they were stronger than we; but let us fight against them in the plain, and surely we shall be stronger than they. 24 And do this thing, Take the kings away, every man out of his place, and put captains in their rooms: 25 And number thee an army, like the army that thou hast lost, horse for horse, and chariot for chariot: and we will fight against them in the plain, and surely we shall be stronger than they. And he hearkened unto their voice, and did so.

26 And it came to pass at the return of the year, that Ben-hadad numbered the Syrians, and went up to Aphek, to fight against Israel. 27 And the children of Israel were numbered, and were all present, and went against them: and the children of Israel pitched before them like two little flocks of kids; but the Syrians filled the country. 28 And there came a man of God, and spake unto the king of Israel, and said, Thus saith the Lord, Because the Syrians have said, The Lord is God of the hills, but he is not God of the valleys, therefore will I deliver all this great multitude into thine hand, and ye shall know that I am the Lord. 29 And they pitched one over against the other seven days. And so it was, that in the seventh day the battle was joined: and the children of Israel slew of the Syrians a hundred thousand footmen in one day. 30 But the rest fled to Aphek, into the city; and there a wall fell upon twenty and seven thousand of the men that were left. And Ben-hadad fled, and came into the city, into an inner chamber.

31 And his servants said unto him, Behold now, we have heard that the kings of the house of Israel are merciful kings: let us, I pray thee,

put sackcloth on our loins, and ropes upon our heads, and go out to the king of Israel: peradventure he will save thy life. 32 So they girded sackcloth on their loins, and put ropes on their heads, and came to the king of Israel, and said, Thy servant Ben-hadad saith, I pray thee, let me live. And he said, Is he yet alive? he is my brother. 33 Now the men did diligently observe whether any thing would come from him, and did hastily catch it: and they said, Thy brother Ben-hadad. Then he said, Go ye, bring him. Then Ben-hadad came forth to him; and he caused him to come up into the chariot. 34 And Ben-hadad said unto him, The cities, which my father took from thy father, I will restore; and thou shalt make streets for thee in Damascus, as my father made in Samaria. Then said Ahab, I will send thee away with this covenant. So he made a covenant with him, and sent him away.

35 And a certain man of the sons of the prophets said unto his neighbor in the word of the Lord, Smite me, I pray thee. And the man refused to smite him. 36 Then said he unto him, Because thou hast not obeyed the voice of the Lord, behold, as soon as thou art departed from me, a lion shall slay thee. And as soon as he was departed from him, a lion found him, and slew him. 37 Then he found another man, and said, Smite me, I pray thee. And the man smote him, so that in smiting he wounded him. 38 So the prophet departed, and waited for the king by the way, and disguised himself with ashes upon his face. 39 And as the king passed by, he cried unto the king: and he said, Thy servant went out into the midst of the battle; and, behold, a man turned aside, and brought a man unto me, and said, Keep this man: if by any means he be missing, then shall thy life be for his life, or else thou shalt pay a talent of silver. 40 And as thy servant was busy here and there, he was gone. And the king of Israel said unto him, So shall thy judgment be; thyself hast decided it. 41 And he hasted, and took the ashes away from his face; and the king of Israel discerned him that he was of the prophets. 42 And he said unto him, Thus saith the Lord, Because thou hast let go out of thy hand a man whom I appointed to utter destruction, therefore thy life shall go for his life, and thy people for his people. 43 And the king of Israel went to his house heavy and displeased, and came to Samaria.

21  And it came to pass after these things, that Naboth the Jezreelite had a vineyard, which was in Jezreel, hard by the palace of Ahab king of Samaria. 2 And Ahab spake unto Naboth, saying, Give me thy vineyard, that I may have it for a garden of herbs, because it is near unto my house: and I will give thee for it a better vineyard than it; or, if it seem good to thee, I will give thee the worth of it in money. 3 And Naboth said to Ahab, The Lord forbid it me, that I should give the inheritance of my fathers unto thee. 4 And Ahab came into his house heavy and displeased because of the word which Naboth the Jezreelite had spoken to him: for he had said, I will not give thee the inheritance of my fathers. And he laid him down upon his bed, and turned away his face, and would eat no bread.

5 But Jezebel his wife came to him, and said unto him, Why is thy spirit so sad, that thou eatest no bread? 6 And he said unto her, Because I spake unto Naboth the Jezreelite, and said unto him, Give me thy vineyard for money; or else, if it please thee, I will give thee another vineyard for it: and he answered, I will not give thee my vineyard. 7 And Jezebel his wife said unto him, Dost thou now govern the kingdom of Israel? arise, and eat bread, and let thine heart be merry: I will give thee the vineyard of Naboth the Jezreelite. 8 So she wrote letters in Ahab's name, and sealed them with his seal, and sent the letters unto the elders and to the nobles that were in his city, dwelling with Naboth. 9 And she wrote in the letters, saying, Proclaim a fast, and set Naboth on high among the people: 10 And set two men, sons of Belial, before him, to bear witness against him, saying, Thou didst blaspheme God and the king. And then carry him out, and stone him, that he may die.

11 And the men of his city, even the elders and the nobles who were the inhabitants in his city, did as Jezebel had sent unto them, and as it was written in the letters which she had sent unto them. 12 They proclaimed a fast, and set Naboth on high among the people. 13 And there came in two men, children of Belial, and sat before him: and the men of Belial witnessed against him, even against Naboth, in the presence of the people, saying, Naboth did blaspheme God and the king. Then they carried him forth out of the city, and stoned him with stones, that he died. 14 Then they sent to Jezebel, saying, Naboth is stoned, and is dead. 15 And it came to pass, when Jezebel heard that Naboth was stoned, and was dead, that Jezebel said to Ahab, Arise, take possession of the vineyard of Naboth the Jezreelite, which he refused to give thee for money: for Naboth is not alive, but dead. 16 And it came to pass, when Ahab heard that Naboth was dead, that Ahab rose up to go down to the vineyard of Naboth the Jezreelite, to take possession of it.

17 And the word of the Lord came to Elijah the Tishbite, saying, 18 Arise, go down to meet Ahab king of Israel, which is in Samaria: behold, he is in the vineyard of Naboth, whither he is gone down to possess it. 19 And thou shalt speak unto him, saying, Thus saith the Lord, Hast thou killed, and also taken possession? And thou shalt speak unto him, saying, Thus saith the Lord, In the place where dogs licked the blood of Naboth shall dogs lick thy blood, even thine. 20 And Ahab said to Elijah, Hast thou found me, O mine enemy? And he answered, I have found thee: because thou hast sold thyself to work evil in the sight of the Lord. 21 Behold, I will bring evil upon thee, and will take away thy posterity, and will cut off from Ahab him that pisseth against the wall, and him that is shut up and left in Israel, 22 And will make thine house like the house of Jeroboam the son of Nebat, and like the house of Baasha the son of Ahijah, for the provocation wherewith thou hast provoked me to anger, and made Israel to sin. 23 And of Jezebel also spake the Lord, saying, The dogs shall eat Jezebel by the wall of Jezreel. 24 Him that

dieth of Ahab in the city the dogs shall eat; and him that dieth in the field shall the fowls of the air eat. 25 But there was none like unto Ahab, which did sell himself to work wickedness in the sight of the Lord, whom Jezebel his wife stirred up. 26 And he did very abominably in following idols, according to all things as did the Amorites, whom the Lord cast out before the children of Israel.

27 And it came to pass, when Ahab heard those words, that he rent his clothes, and put sackcloth upon his flesh, and fasted, and lay in sackcloth, and went softly. 28 And the word of the Lord came to Elijah the Tishbite, saying, 29 Seest thou how Ahab humbleth himself before me? because he humbleth himself before me, I will not bring the evil in his days: but in his son's days will I bring the evil upon his house.

### FALSE PROPHETS AND TRUE

22 And they continued three years without war between Syria and Israel. 2 And it came to pass in the third year, that Jehoshaphat the king of Judah came down to the king of Israel. 3 And the king of Israel said unto his servants, Know ye that Ramoth in Gilead is ours, and we be still, and take it not out of the hand of the king of Syria? 4 And he said unto Jehoshaphat, Wilt thou go with me to battle to Ramoth-gilead? And Jehoshaphat said to the king of Israel, I am as thou art, my people as thy people, my horses as thy horses.

5 And Jehoshaphat said unto the king of Israel, Inquire, I pray thee, at the word of the Lord to-day. 6 Then the king of Israel gathered the prophets together, about four hundred men, and said unto them, Shall I go against Ramoth-gilead to battle, or shall I forbear? And they said, Go up; for the Lord shall deliver it into the hand of the king. 7 And Jehoshaphat said, Is there not here a prophet of the Lord besides, that we might inquire of him? 8 And the king of Israel said unto Jehoshaphat, There is yet one man, Micaiah the son of Imlah, by whom we may inquire of the Lord: but I hate him; for he doth not prophesy good concerning me, but evil. And Jehoshaphat said, Let not the king say so. 9 Then the king of Israel called an officer, and said, Hasten hither Micaiah the son of Imlah. 10 And the king of Israel and Jehoshaphat the king of Judah sat each on his throne, having put on their robes, in a void place in the entrance of the gate of Samaria; and all the prophets prophesied before them. 11 And Zedekiah the son of Chenaanah made him horns of iron: and he said, Thus saith the Lord, With these shalt thou push the Syrians, until thou have consumed them. 12 And all the prophets prophesied so, saying, Go up to Ramoth-gilead, and prosper: for the Lord shall deliver it into the king's hand.

13 And the messenger that was gone to call Micaiah spake unto him, saying, Behold now, the words of the prophets declare good unto the king with one mouth: let thy word, I pray thee, be like the word of one of them, and speak that which is good. 14 And Micaiah said,

As the Lord liveth, what the Lord saith unto me, that will I speak. 15 So he came to the king. And the king said unto him, Micaiah, shall we go against Ramoth-gilead to battle, or shall we forbear? And he answered him, Go, and prosper: for the Lord shall deliver it into the hand of the king. 16 And the king said unto him, How many times shall I adjure thee that thou tell me nothing but that which is true in the name of the Lord? 17 And he said, I saw all Israel scattered upon the hills, as sheep that have not a shepherd: and the Lord said, These have no master: let them return every man to his house in peace. 18 And the king of Israel said unto Jehoshaphat, Did I not tell thee that he would prophesy no good concerning me, but evil? 19 And he said, Hear thou therefore the word of the Lord: I saw the Lord sitting on his throne, and all the host of heaven standing by him on his right hand and on his left. 20 And the Lord said, Who shall persuade Ahab, that he may go up and fall at Ramoth-gilead? And one said on this manner, and another said on that manner. 21 And there came forth a spirit, and stood before the Lord, and said, I will persuade him. 22 And the Lord said unto him, Wherewith? And he said, I will go forth, and I will be a lying spirit in the mouth of all his prophets. And he said, Thou shalt persuade him, and prevail also: go forth, and do so. 23 Now therefore, behold, the Lord hath put a lying spirit in the mouth of all these thy prophets, and the Lord hath spoken evil concerning thee.

24 But Zedekiah the son of Chenaanah went near, and smote Micaiah on the cheek, and said, Which way went the Spirit of the Lord from me to speak unto thee? 25 And Micaiah said, Behold, thou shalt see in that day, when thou shalt go into an inner chamber to hide thyself. 26 And the king of Israel said, Take Micaiah, and carry him back unto Amon the governor of the city, and to Joash the king's son; 27 And say, Thus saith the king, Put this fellow in the prison, and feed him with bread of affliction and with water of affliction, until I come in peace. 28 And Micaiah said, If thou return at all in peace, the Lord hath not spoken by me. And he said, Hearken, O people, every one of you.

29 So the king of Israel and Jehoshaphat the king of Judah went up to Ramoth-gilead. 30 And the king of Israel said unto Jehoshaphat, I will disguise myself, and enter into the battle; but put thou on thy robes. And the king of Israel disguised himself, and went into the battle. 31 But the king of Syria commanded his thirty and two captains that had rule over his chariots, saying, Fight neither with small nor great, save only with the king of Israel. 32 And it came to pass, when the captains of the chariots saw Jehoshaphat, that they said, Surely it is the king of Israel. And they turned aside to fight against him: and Jehoshaphat cried out. 33 And it came to pass, when the captains of the chariots perceived that it was not the king of Israel, that they turned back from pursuing him. 34 And a certain man drew a bow at a venture, and smote the king of Israel between the joints of the harness: wherefore he said unto the driver of his chariot, Turn

thine hand, and carry me out of the host; for I am wounded. 35 And the battle increased that day: and the king was stayed up in his chariot against the Syrians, and died at even: and the blood ran out of the wound into the midst of the chariot. 36 And there went a proclamation throughout the host about the going down of the sun, saying, Every man to his city, and every man to his own country.

37 So the king died, and was brought to Samaria; and they buried the king in Samaria. 38 And one washed the chariot in the pool of Samaria; and the dogs licked up his blood; and they washed his armor; according unto the word of the Lord which he spake.

# Second Kings

## ELISHA SUCCEEDS ELIJAH

2 And it came to pass, when the Lord would take up Elijah into heaven by a whirlwind, that Elijah went with Elisha from Gilgal. 2 And Elijah said unto Elisha, Tarry here, I pray thee; for the Lord hath sent me to Beth-el. And Elisha said unto him, As the Lord liveth, and as thy soul liveth, I will not leave thee. So they went down to Beth-el. 3 And the sons of the prophets that were at Beth-el came forth to Elisha, and said unto him, Knowest thou that the Lord will take away thy master from thy head to-day? And he said, Yea, I know it; hold ye your peace. 4 And Elijah said unto him, Elisha, tarry here, I pray thee; for the Lord hath sent me to Jericho. And he said, As the Lord liveth, and as thy soul liveth, I will not leave thee. So they came to Jericho. 5 And the sons of the prophets that were at Jericho came to Elisha, and said unto him, Knowest thou that the Lord will take away thy master from thy head to-day? And he answered, Yea, I know it; hold ye your peace. 6 And Elijah said unto him, Tarry, I pray thee, here; for the Lord hath sent me to Jordan. And he said, As the Lord liveth, and as thy soul liveth, I will not leave thee. And they two went on.

7 And fifty men of the sons of the prophets went, and stood to view afar off: and they two stood by Jordan. 8 And Elijah took his mantle, and wrapped it together, and smote the waters, and they were divided hither and thither, so that they two went over on dry ground. 9 And it came to pass, when they were gone over, that Elijah said unto Elisha, Ask what I shall do for thee, before I be taken away from thee. And Elisha said, I pray thee, let a double portion of thy spirit be upon me. 10 And he said, Thou hast asked a hard thing: nevertheless, if thou see me when I am taken from thee, it shall be so unto thee; but if not, it shall not be so. 11 And it came to pass, as they still went on, and talked, that, behold, there appeared a chariot of fire, and horses of fire, and parted them both asunder; and Elijah went up by a whirlwind into heaven.

12 And Elisha saw it, and he cried, My father, my father, the chariot of Israel, and the horsemen thereof! And he saw him no more: and he took hold of his own clothes, and rent them in two pieces. 13 He took up also the mantle of Elijah that fell from him, and went back, and stood by the bank of Jordan; 14 And he took the mantle of Elijah that fell from him, and smote the waters, and said, Where is the Lord God of Elijah? And when he also had smitten the waters, they parted hither and thither: and Elisha went over.

5 Now Naaman, captain of the host of the king of Syria, was a great man with his master, and honorable, because by him the Lord had given deliverance unto Syria: he was also a mighty man in valor, but he was a leper. 2 And the Syrians had gone out by companies, and had brought away captive out of the land of Israel a little maid; and she waited on Naaman's wife. 3 And she said unto her mistress, Would God my lord were with the prophet that is in Samaria! for he would recover him of his leprosy. 4 And one went in, and told his lord, saying, Thus and thus said the maid that is of the land of Israel. 5 And the king of Syria said, Go to, go, and I will send a letter unto the king of Israel. And he departed, and took with him ten talents of silver, and six thousand pieces of gold, and ten changes of raiment. 6 And he brought the letter to the king of Israel, saying, Now when this letter is come unto thee, behold, I have therewith sent Naaman my servant to thee, that thou mayest recover him of his leprosy. 7 And it came to pass, when the king of Israel had read the letter, that he rent his clothes, and said, Am I God, to kill and to make alive, that this man doth send unto me to recover a man of his leprosy? Wherefore consider, I pray you, and see how he seeketh a quarrel against me.

8 And it was so, when Elisha the man of God had heard that the king of Israel had rent his clothes, that he sent to the king, saying, Wherefore hast thou rent thy clothes? let him come now to me, and he shall know that there is a prophet in Israel. 9 So Naaman came with his horses and with his chariot, and stood at the door of the house of Elisha. 10 And Elisha sent a messenger unto him, saying, Go and wash in Jordan seven times, and thy flesh shall come again to thee, and thou shalt be clean. 11 But Naaman was wroth, and went away, and said, Behold, I thought, He will surely come out to me, and stand, and call on the name of the Lord his God, and strike his hand over the place, and recover the leper. 12 Are not Abana and Pharpar, rivers of Damascus, better than all the waters of Israel? may I not wash in them, and be clean? So he turned and went away in a rage. 13 And his servants came near, and spake unto him, and said, My father, if the prophet had bid thee do some great thing, wouldest thou not have done it? how much rather then, when he saith to thee, Wash, and be clean? 14 Then went he down, and dipped himself seven times in Jordan, according to the saying of the man of God: and his flesh came again like unto the flesh of a little child, and he was clean.

15 And he returned to the man of God, he and all his company, and came, and stood before him: and he said, Behold, now I know that there is no God in all the earth, but in Israel: now therefore, I pray thee, take a blessing of thy servant. 16 But he said, As the Lord liveth, before whom I stand, I will receive none. And he urged him to take it; but he refused. 17 And Naaman said, Shall there not then, I pray thee, be given to thy servant two mules' burden of earth? for thy servant will henceforth offer neither burnt offering nor sacrifice unto other gods, but unto the Lord. 18 In this thing the Lord pardon thy servant, that when my master goeth into the house of Rimmon to worship there, and he leaneth on my hand, and I bow myself in the house of Rimmon: when I bow down myself in the house of Rimmon, the Lord pardon thy servant in this thing. 19 And he said unto him, Go in peace. So he departed from him a little way.

20 But Gehazi, the servant of Elisha the man of God, said, Behold, my master hath spared Naaman this Syrian, in not receiving at his hands that which he brought: but, as the Lord liveth, I will run after him, and take somewhat of him. 21 So Gehazi followed after Naaman. And when Naaman saw him running after him, he lighted down from the chariot to meet him, and said, Is all well? 22 And he said, All is well. My master hath sent me, saying, Behold, even now there be come to me from mount Ephraim two young men of the sons of the prophets: give them, I pray thee, a talent of silver, and two changes of garments. 23 And Naaman said, Be content, take two talents. And he urged him, and bound two talents of silver in two bags, with two changes of garments, and laid them upon two of his servants; and they bare them before him. 24 And when he came to the tower, he took them from their hand, and bestowed them in the house: and he let the men go, and they departed. 25 But he went in, and stood before his master. And Elisha said unto him, Whence comest thou, Gehazi? And he said, Thy servant went no whither. 26 And he said unto him, Went not mine heart with thee, when the man turned again from his chariot to meet thee? Is it a time to receive money, and to receive garments, and oliveyards, and vineyards, and sheep, and oxen, and menservants, and maidservants? 27 The leprosy therefore of Naaman shall cleave unto thee, and unto thy seed for ever. And he went out from his presence a leper as white as snow.

6 8 Then the king of Syria warred against Israel, and took counsel with his servants, saying, In such and such a place shall be my camp. 9 And the man of God sent unto the king of Israel, saying, Beware that thou pass not such a place; for thither the Syrians are come down. 10 And the king of Israel sent to the place which the man of God told him and warned him of, and saved himself there, not once nor twice. 11 Therefore the heart of the king of Syria was sore troubled for this thing; and he called his servants, and said unto them, Will ye not show me which of us is for the king of Israel? 12 And one of his servants said, None, my lord, O king: but Elisha, the prophet that is

in Israel, telleth the king of Israel the words that thou speakest in thy bedchamber. 13 And he said, Go and spy where he is, that I may send and fetch him. And it was told him, saying, Behold, he is in Dothan.

14 Therefore sent he thither horses, and chariots, and a great host: and they came by night, and compassed the city about. 15 And when the servant of the man of God was risen early, and gone forth, behold, a host compassed the city both with horses and chariots. And his servant said unto him, Alas, my master! how shall we do? 16 And he answered, Fear not: for they that be with us are more than they that be with them. 17 And Elisha prayed, and said, Lord, I pray thee, open his eyes, that he may see. And the Lord opened the eyes of the young man; and he saw: and, behold, the mountain was full of horses and chariots of fire round about Elisha. 18 And when they came down to him, Elisha prayed unto the Lord, and said, Smite this people, I pray thee, with blindness. And he smote them with blindness according to the word of Elisha. 19 And Elisha said unto them, This is not the way, neither is this the city: follow me, and I will bring you to the man whom ye seek. But he led them to Samaria.

20 And it came to pass, when they were come into Samaria, that Elisha said, Lord, open the eyes of these men, that they may see. And the Lord opened their eyes, and they saw; and, behold, they were in the midst of Samaria. 21 And the king of Israel said unto Elisha, when he saw them, My father, shall I smite them? shall I smite them? 22 And he answered, Thou shalt not smite them: wouldest thou smite those whom thou hast taken captive with thy sword and with thy bow? set bread and water before them, that they may eat and drink, and go to their master. 23 And he prepared great provision for them: and when they had eaten and drunk, he sent them away, and they went to their master. So the bands of Syria came no more into the land of Israel.

# The Age of Prophets: *Second Kings and the Prophets*

The death of King Ahab, whose wickedness the prophet Elijah had so courageously exposed, did not bring an end to the moral and religious decay of Israel. The rot which had already entered deeply into the fiber of the nation continued to eat away at it. Idolatry and injustice were compounded from reign to reign.

Under these circumstances, in the eighth century B.C., the ancient Biblical role of the prophet asserted itself with such force and vigor as virtually to become a new phenomenon. We have already seen the important place of the prophet Nathan under David, and of Elijah and Micaiah under Ahab, but the activities of these prophets were still contained within the narrative accounts of the historical books. Now, however, the prophets assume such an important role that entire books are developed under their names. Even the minor prophets are given more attention in the Old Testament than are the more important kings of the eighth, seventh, and sixth centuries. We are therefore justified in referring to these centuries as The Age of Prophets.

A number of popular misconceptions about the prophets should be dispelled at the outset. In the first place, they are not to be regarded as primarily "predictors," for the prediction of the future was only a minor part of their function, which was basically concerned with a call to repentance and reform which would prevent disaster. Nor were they merely social malcontents who delighted in the prestige which came to them as critics, for instead of prestige they were more often greeted with abuse and contempt. Again, though they were without exception very practical men, they did not regard their message as the product of their own wise and experienced human judgment, but saw themselves as instruments of God. And finally, they were not mere parrots of God, mechanical voices recording and repeating a message, but were intensely individual personalities who could, as Jeremiah did, dispute with God even as they served him. Their messages were essentially similar, but each man spoke with individual emphases, with distinctive power and beauty, and in his own accents. Together, they have contributed more of value to the individual and social conscience of the modern world than even the ancient Greek philosophers, great as were their contributions.

Wherever possible in the following passages material from Second Kings is placed side by side with related material from the prophets, so as to provide a meaningful continuity.

## Jeroboam II and Amos

Our first example of the work of the eighth-century prophets comes in the criticism of King Jeroboam II and his Northern Kingdom by Amos the herdsman of Tekoa. Though little attention is given to this king in the historical books of the Old Testament, we know from what is said there and from what has been discovered elsewhere that his reign was a period of great wealth and power for Israel. At the court and among the ruling classes there was a pervasive sense of euphoria, but the prophet Amos saw more deeply. The brief treatment of Jeroboam II in Second Kings is given below, followed by passages selected from the book of Amos.

# Second Kings

**14** 23 In the fifteenth year of Amaziah the son of Joash king of Judah, Jeroboam the son of Joash king of Israel began to reign in Samaria, and reigned forty and one years. 24 And he did that which was evil in the sight of the Lord: he departed not from all the sins of Jeroboam the son of Nebat, who made Israel to sin. 25 He restored the coast of Israel from the entering of Hamath unto the sea of the plain.

# Amos

**1** The words of Amos, who was among the herdmen of Tekoa, which he saw concerning Israel in the days of Uzziah king of Judah, and in the days of Jeroboam the son of Joash king of Israel, two years before the earthquake. 2 And he said,

> The Lord will roar from Zion,
> And utter his voice from Jerusalem;
> And the habitations of the shepherds shall mourn,
> And the top of Carmel shall wither.

**2** 4 Thus saith the Lord;
> For three transgressions of Judah,
> And for four, I will not turn away the punishment thereof;
> Because they have despised the law of the Lord,
> And have not kept his commandments,

269

And their lies caused them to err,
After the which their fathers have walked:
5 But I will send a fire upon Judah,
And it shall devour the palaces of Jerusalem.
6 Thus saith the Lord;
For three transgressions of Israel,
And for four, I will not turn away the punishment thereof;
Because they sold the righteous for silver,
And the poor for a pair of shoes;
7 That pant after the dust of the earth on the head of the poor,
And turn aside the way of the meek:
And a man and his father will go in unto the same maid,
To profane my holy name:
8 And they lay themselves down upon clothes laid to pledge
By every altar,
And they drink the wine of the condemned
In the house of their god.
9 Yet destroyed I the Amorite before them,
Whose height was like the height of the cedars,
And he was strong as the oaks;
Yet I destroyed his fruit from above,
And his roots from beneath.
10 Also I brought you up from the land of Egypt,
And led you forty years through the wilderness,
To possess the land of the Amorite.
11 And I raised up of your sons for prophets,
And of your young men for Nazarites.
Is it not even thus, O ye children of Israel?
Saith the Lord.
12 But ye gave the Nazarites wine to drink;
And commanded the prophets, saying, Prophesy not.
13 Behold, I am pressed under you,
As a cart is pressed that is full of sheaves.
14 Therefore the flight shall perish from the swift,
And the strong shall not strengthen his force,
Neither shall the mighty deliver himself:
15 Neither shall he stand that handleth the bow;
And he that is swift of foot shall not deliver himself:
Neither shall he that rideth the horse deliver himself.
16 And he that is courageous among the mighty
Shall flee away naked in that day,
Saith the Lord.

4 Hear this word, ye kine of Bashan,
That are in the mountain of Samaria,
Which oppress the poor, which crush the needy,
Which say to their masters, Bring, and let us drink.
2 The Lord God hath sworn by his holiness,

That, lo, the days shall come upon you,
That he will take you away with hooks,
And your posterity with fishhooks.

12 Therefore thus will I do unto thee, O Israel:
And because I will do this unto thee,
Prepare to meet thy God, O Israel.

13 For, lo, he that formeth the mountains, and createth the wind,
And declareth unto man what is his thought,
That maketh the morning darkness,
And treadeth upon the high places of the earth,
The Lord, The God of hosts, is his name.

5    7 Ye who turn judgment to wormwood,
And leave off righteousness in the earth,

8 Seek him that maketh the seven stars and Orion,
And turneth the shadow of death into the morning,
And maketh the day dark with night:
That calleth for the waters of the sea,
And poureth them out upon the face of the earth:
The Lord is his name:

9 That strengtheneth the spoiled against the strong,
So that the spoiled shall come against the fortress.

10 They hate him that rebuketh in the gate,
And they abhor him that speaketh uprightly.

11 Forasmuch therefore as your treading is upon the poor,
And ye take from him burdens of wheat:
Ye have built houses of hewn stone,
But ye shall not dwell in them;
Ye have planted pleasant vineyards,
But ye shall not drink wine of them.

12 For I know your manifold transgressions
And your mighty sins:
They afflict the just, they take a bribe,
And they turn aside the poor in the gate from their right.

18 Woe unto you that desire the day of the Lord![1]
To what end is it for you?
The day of the Lord is darkness, and not light.

19 As if a man did flee from a lion,
And a bear met him;
Or went into the house, and leaned his hand on the wall,
And a serpent bit him.

20 Shall not the day of the Lord be darkness, and not light?
Even very dark, and no brightness in it?

21 I hate, I despise your feast days,

[1] The "day" of the Lord, or of God's judgment with rewards and penalties, was often regarded as a time when the Jewish nation would be exalted. Amos, like other prophets, here declares that on this "day" God will condemn the Jews for their wickedness.

271

And I will not smell in your solemn assemblies.
22 Though ye offer me burnt offerings and your meat offerings,
I will not accept them;
Neither will I regard the peace offerings of your fat beasts.
23 Take thou away from me the noise of thy songs;
For I will not hear the melody of thy viols.
24 But let judgment run down as waters,
And righteousness as a mighty stream.

6      Woe to them that are at ease in Zion,
And trust in the mountain of Samaria,
4 That lie upon beds of ivory,
And stretch themselves upon their couches,
And eat the lambs out of the flock,
And the calves out of the midst of the stall;
5 That chant to the sound of the viol,
And invent to themselves instruments of music, like David;
6 That drink wine in bowls,
And anoint themselves with the chief ointments:
But they are not grieved for the affliction of Joseph.

7    7 Thus he showed me: and, behold, the Lord stood upon a wall made by a plumbline, with a plumbline in his hand. 8 And the Lord said unto me, Amos, what seest thou? And I said, A plumbline. Then said the Lord,

Behold, I will set a plumbline in the midst of my people Israel:
I will not again pass by them any more:
9 And the high places of Isaac shall be desolate,
And the sanctuaries of Israel shall be laid waste;
And I will rise against the house of Jeroboam with the sword.

10 Then Amaziah, the priest of Beth-el sent to Jeroboam king of Israel, saying, Amos hath conspired against thee in the midst of the house of Israel: the land is not able to bear all his words. 11 For thus Amos saith, Jeroboam shall die by the sword, and Israel shall surely be led away captive out of their own land. 12 Also Amaziah said unto Amos, O thou seer, go, flee thee away into the land of Judah, and there eat bread, and prophesy there: 13 But prophesy not again any more at Beth-el: for it is the king's chapel, and it is the king's court. 14 Then answered Amos, and said to Amaziah, I was no prophet, neither was I a prophet's son; but I was a herdman, and a gatherer of sycamore fruit: 15 And the Lord took me as I followed the flock, and the Lord said unto me, Go, prophesy unto my people Israel. 16 Now therefore hear thou the word of the Lord.

8    4 Hear this, O ye that swallow up the needy,
Even to make the poor of the land to fail,
5 Saying, When will the new moon be gone, that we may sell corn?

And the sabbath, that we may set forth wheat,
Making the ephah small, and the shekel great,
And falsifying the balances by deceit?
6 That we may buy the poor for silver;
And the needy for a pair of shoes;
Yea, and sell the refuse of the wheat?
7 The Lord hath sworn by the excellency of Jacob,
Surely I will never forget any of their works.
8 Shall not the land tremble for this,
And every one mourn that dwelleth therein?
And it shall rise up wholly as a flood;
And it shall be cast out and drowned, as by the flood of Egypt.
9 And it shall come to pass in that day,
Saith the Lord God,
That I will cause the sun to go down at noon,
And I will darken the earth in the clear day:
10 And I will turn your feasts into mourning,
And all your songs into lamentations;
And I will bring up sackcloth upon all loins,
And baldness upon every head;
And I will make it as the mourning of an only son,
And the end thereof as a bitter day.
11 Behold, the days come,
Saith the Lord God,
That I will send a famine in the land,
Not a famine of bread,
Nor a thirst for water,
But of hearing the words of the Lord:
12 And they shall wander from sea to sea,
And from the north even to the east,
They shall run to and fro to seek the word of the Lord,
And shall not find it.
13 In that day shall the fair virgins
And young men faint for thirst.
14 They that swear by the sin of Samaria,
And say, Thy god, O Dan, liveth;
And, The manner of Beer-sheba liveth;
Even they shall fall, and never rise up again.

## Hosea, Gomer, and the Latter Plight of Israel

The destruction of Israel was foretold by the prophets, and never more graphically than by Hosea. In typical Hebrew fashion, he dramatizes his word from God — but in a unique way. He declares that he has married a prostitute of one of the Canaanite fertility rites, and that despite her "whoredoms" he continues to love her and seek her faithfulness to him. Whether the situa-

273

tion as described was actual or allegorical we do not know, but the point was dramatically clear, and the parallel to Israel's "whoredoms" against God was unmistakable. At the end, there is still the hope of return and reconciliation. The passage begins with Hosea's address to the children of his marriage, and concludes with stating the analogy with Israel's plight.

# *Hosea*

2 Say ye unto your brethren, Ammi; and to your sisters, Ruhamah.
2 Plead with your mother, plead;
For she is not my wife, neither am I her husband:
Let her therefore put away her whoredoms out of her sight,
And her adulteries from between her breasts;
3 Lest I strip her naked,
And set her as in the day that she was born,
And make her as a wilderness,
And set her like a dry land,
And slay her with thirst.
4 And I will not have mercy upon her children;
For they be the children of whoredoms.
5 For their mother hath played the harlot:
She that conceived them hath done shamefully;
For she said, I will go after my lovers,
That give me my bread and my water,
My wool and my flax, mine oil and my drink.
6 Therefore, behold, I will hedge up thy ways with thorns,
And make a wall,
That she shall not find her paths.
7 And she shall follow after her lovers, but she shall not overtake them;
And she shall seek them, but shall not find them:
Then shall she say, I will go and return to my first husband;
For then was it better with me than now.
8 For she did not know that I gave her
Corn, and wine, and oil,
And multiplied her silver and gold,
Which they prepared for Baal.
9 Therefore will I return, and take away my corn in the time thereof,
And my wine in the season thereof,
And will recover my wool and my flax
Given to cover her nakedness.
10 And now will I discover her lewdness in the sight of her lovers,
And none shall deliver her out of mine hand.

11 I will also cause all her mirth to cease,
   Her feast days, her new moons, and her sabbaths,
   And all her solemn feasts.
12 And I will destroy her vines and her fig trees,
   Whereof she hath said, There are my rewards
   That my lovers have given me:
   And I will make them a forest,
   And the beasts of the field shall eat them.
13 And I will visit upon her the days of Baalim,
   Wherein she burned incense to them,
   And she decked herself with her earrings and her jewels,
   And she went after her lovers,
   And forgat me, saith the Lord.
14 Therefore, behold, I will allure her,
   And bring her into the wilderness,
   And speak comfortably unto her.
15 And I will give her her vineyards from thence,
   And the valley of Achor for a door of hope:
   And she shall sing there, as in the days of her youth,
   And as in the day when she came up out of the land of Egypt.
16 And it shall be at that day, saith the Lord,
   That thou shalt call me Ishi;
   And shalt call me no more Baali.[1]
17 For I will take away the names of Baalim out of her mouth,
   And they shall no more be remembered by their name.
18 And in that day will I make a covenant for them
   With the beasts of the field, and with the fowls of heaven,
   And with the creeping things of the ground:
   And I will break the bow and the sword and the battle out
      of the earth,
   And will make them to lie down safely.
19 And I will betroth thee unto me for ever;
   Yea, I will betroth thee unto me in righteousness, and in
      judgment,
   And in loving-kindness, and in mercies.
20 I will even betroth thee unto me in faithfulness:
   And thou shalt know the Lord.
21 And it shall come to pass in that day,
   I will hear, saith the Lord, I will hear the heavens,
   And they shall hear the earth;
22 And the earth shall hear the corn, and the wine, and the oil;
   And they shall hear Jezreel.

---

[1] "Baali" and "Ishi" both convey similar meanings of husband and lord, but "Baali" will no longer be applied to God because of the pagan associations of the word with the cult of Baal. Of the two words, "Ishi" may imply a more intimate relationship.

23 And I will sow her unto me in the earth;
And I will have mercy upon her that had not obtained mercy;
And I will say to them which were not my people, Thou art
my people;
And they shall say, Thou art my God.

3  Then said the Lord unto me, Go yet, love a woman beloved of
her friend, yet an adulteress, according to the love of the Lord toward
the children of Israel, who look to other gods, and love flagons of wine.
2 So I bought her to me for fifteen pieces of silver, and for a homer of
barley, and a half homer of barley: 3 And I said unto her, Thou shalt
abide for me many days; thou shalt not play the harlot, and thou shalt
not be for another man: so will I also be for thee. 4 For the children
of Israel shall abide many days without a king, and without a prince,
and without a sacrifice, and without an image, and without an ephod,
and without teraphim: 5 Afterward shall the children of Israel return,
and seek the Lord their God, and David their king; and shall fear the
Lord and his goodness in the latter days.

## The Destruction and Captivity of Israel

*Despite the prophetic mission, the degeneracy of the Northern
Kingdom continued without abatement after the time of Jeroboam II and Amos, until the people became too corrupt to maintain their independence. The final captivity under the Assyrians
occurred in the years 722–721 B.C., and is described here.*

# *Second Kings*

17  In the twelfth year of Ahaz king of Judah began Hoshea the
son of Elah to reign in Samaria over Israel nine years. 2 And he did
that which was evil in the sight of the Lord, but not as the kings of
Israel that were before him. 3 Against him came up Shalmaneser
king of Assyria; and Hoshea became his servant, and gave him presents.
4 And the king of Assyria found conspiracy in Hoshea: for he had
sent messengers to So king of Egypt, and brought no present to the
king of Assyria, as he had done year by year: therefore the king of
Assyria shut him up, and bound him in prison. 5 Then the king of
Assyria came up throughout all the land, and went up to Samaria,
and besieged it three years. 6 In the ninth year of Hoshea the king of
Assyria took Samaria, and carried Israel away into Assyria, and placed
them in Halah and in Habor by the river of Gozan, and in the cities of
the Medes.
7 For so it was, that the children of Israel had sinned against the
Lord their God, which had brought them up out of the land of

Egypt, from under the hand of Pharaoh king of Egypt, and had feared other gods, 8 And walked in the statutes of the heathen, whom the Lord cast out from before the children of Israel, and of the kings of Israel, which they had made. 9 And the children of Israel did secretly those things that were not right against the Lord their God, and they built them high places in all their cities, from the tower of the watchmen to the fenced city. 10 And they set them up images and groves in every high hill, and under every green tree: 11 And there they burnt incense in all the high places, as did the heathen whom the Lord carried away before them; and wrought wicked things to provoke the Lord to anger: 12 For they served idols, whereof the Lord had said unto them, Ye shall not do this thing. 13 Yet the Lord testified against Israel, and against Judah, by all the prophets, and by all the seers, saying, Turn ye from your evil ways, and keep my commandments and my statutes, according to all the law which I commanded your fathers, and which I sent to you by my servants the prophets. 14 Notwithstanding, they would not hear, but hardened their necks, like to the neck of their fathers, that did not believe in the Lord their God. 15 And they rejected his statutes, and his covenant that he made with their fathers, and his testimonies which he testified against them; and they followed vanity, and became vain, and went after the heathen that were round about them, concerning whom the Lord had charged them, that they should not do like them. 16 And they left all the commandments of the Lord their God, and made them molten images, even two calves, and made a grove, and worshipped all the host of heaven, and served Baal. 17 And they caused their sons and their daughters to pass through the fire, and used divination and enchantments, and sold themselves to do evil in the sight of the Lord, to provoke him to anger. 18 Therefore the Lord was very angry with Israel, and removed them out of his sight: there was none left but the tribe of Judah only. 19 Also Judah kept not the commandments of the Lord their God, but walked in the statutes of Israel which they made. 20 And the Lord rejected all the seed of Israel, and afflicted them, and delivered them into the hand of spoilers, until he had cast them out of his sight. 21 For he rent Israel from the house of David; and they made Jeroboam the son of Nebat king: and Jeroboam drave Israel from following the Lord, and made them sin a great sin. 22 For the children of Israel walked in all the sins of Jeroboam which he did; they departed not from them; 23 Until the Lord removed Israel out of his sight, as he had said by all his servants the prophets. So was Israel carried away out of their own land to Assyria unto this day.

## The Role of Assyria

*The destruction of the Northern Kingdom by Assyria was not regarded as a happening merely of chance or of fortune. As an instrument of God, Assyria served to punish the wickedness of*

Israel and of Judah, but Assyria itself stood under the judgment of God and would be dealt with by God for its arrogance and cruelty. In the Biblical view, one evil is often used as a scourge upon another, when men refuse to honor God and each other. Isaiah gives a classical statement of the case in connection with Assyria. Then follows Zephaniah's prophecy of God's destruction of Assyria.

# Isaiah

10  5 O Assyrian, the rod of mine anger,
     And the staff in their hand is mine indignation.
   6 I will send him against a hypocritical nation,
     And against the people of my wrath will I give him a charge,
     To take the spoil, and to take the prey,
     And to tread them down like the mire of the streets.
   7 Howbeit he meaneth not so,
     Neither doth his heart think so;
     But it is in his heart to destroy
     And cut off nations not a few.
   8 For he saith,
     Are not my princes altogether kings?
12 Wherefore it shall come to pass, that, when the Lord hath performed his whole work upon mount Zion and on Jerusalem, I will punish the fruit of the stout heart of the king of Assyria, and the glory of his high looks. 13 For he saith,
     By the strength of my hand I have done it,
     And by my wisdom; for I am prudent:
     And I have removed the bounds of the people,
     And have robbed their treasures,
     And I have put down the inhabitants like a valiant man:
  14 And my hand hath found as a nest the riches of the people:
     And as one gathereth eggs that are left,
     Have I gathered all the earth;
     And there was none that moved the wing,
     Or opened the mouth, or peeped.
  15 Shall the axe boast itself against him that heweth therewith?
     Or shall the saw magnify itself against him that shaketh it?
     As if the rod should shake itself against them that lift it up,
     Or as if the staff should lift up itself, as if it were no wood.
  16 Therefore shall the Lord, the Lord of hosts,
     Send among his fat ones leanness;
     And under his glory he shall kindle a burning
     Like the burning of a fire.

# Zephaniah

**2** 13 And he will stretch out his hand against the north,
And destroy Assyria;
And will make Nineveh a desolation,
And dry like a wilderness.
14 And flocks shall lie down in the midst of her,
All the beasts of the nations:
Both the cormorant and the bittern
Shall lodge in the upper lintels of it;
Their voice shall sing in the windows;
Desolation shall be in the thresholds:
For he shall uncover the cedar work.
15 This is the rejoicing city
That dwelt carelessly,
That said in her heart,
I am, and there is none besides me:
How is she become a desolation,
A place for beasts to lie down in!
Every one that passeth by her shall hiss,
And wag his hand.

## Judah: King Uzziah

*With the end of the Northern Kingdom, Second Kings and the
prophetic books alike concentrate primarily upon the Southern
Kingdom of Judah. Below, we pick up these treatments with the
reign of King Azariah (referred to by Isaiah as Uzziah), who was
a younger contemporary of Jeroboam II, and carry on without
further direct reference to the Northern Kingdom.*

# Second Kings

**15** In the twenty and seventh year of Jeroboam king of Israel began
Azariah son of Amaziah king of Judah to reign. 2 Sixteen years old was
he when he began to reign, and he reigned two and fifty years in
Jerusalem. And his mother's name was Jecholiah of Jerusalem. 3 And
he did that which was right in the sight of the Lord, according to all
that his father Amaziah had done; 4 Save that the high places were
not removed: the people sacrificed and burnt incense still on the high
places. 5 And the Lord smote the king, so that he was a leper unto
the day of his death, and dwelt in a several[1] house. And Jotham the

---

[1] Separate.

king's son was over the house, judging the people of the land. 7 So Azariah slept with his fathers; and they buried him with his fathers in the city of David: and Jotham his son reigned in his stead.

## Judah's Relative Virtue

*The Southern Kingdom of Judah fairly consistently preserved a higher degree of faithfulness than did Israel, yet relative righteousness was not enough. A clear and majestic declaration of the righteousness of God who demands righteousness among men is found in Isaiah's description of his call to be a prophet. (Uzziah here is another name for King Azariah of Judah.)*

# Isaiah

6 In the year that king Uzziah died I saw also the Lord sitting upon a throne, high and lifted up, and his train filled the temple. 2 Above it stood the seraphim: each one had six wings; with twain he covered his face, and with twain he covered his feet, and with twain he did fly. 3 And one cried unto another, and said,
Holy, holy, holy, is the Lord of hosts:
The whole earth is full of his glory.
4 And the posts of the door moved at the voice of him that cried, and the house was filled with smoke. 5 Then said I,
Woe is me! for I am undone;
Because I am a man of unclean lips,
And I dwell in the midst of a people of unclean lips:
For mine eyes have seen the King,
The Lord of hosts.
6 Then flew one of the seraphim unto me, having a live coal in his hand, which he had taken with the tongs from off the altar: 7 And he laid it upon my mouth, and said,
Lo, this hath touched thy lips;
And thine iniquity is taken away,
And thy sin purged.
8 Also I heard the voice of the Lord, saying,
Whom shall I send,
And who will go for us?
Then said I, Here am I; send me.

## King Jotham

*Though King Jotham "did that which was right," as the account in Second Kings given below indicates, the condition of*

Judah as a whole was nonetheless marked by religious hypocrisy and practical injustice. In the following passages Isaiah attacks the substitution of religious observances for the true service of God, the exploitation of the poor to support useless and fashionable luxury, and then summarizes the Lord's case against Judah in the parable of the vineyard.

# Second Kings

**15** 32 [Then] began Jotham the son of Uzziah king of Judah to reign. 33 Five and twenty years old was he when he began to reign, and he reigned sixteen years in Jerusalem. And his mother's name was Jerusha, the daughter of Zadok. 34 And he did that which was right in the sight of the Lord: he did according to all that his father Uzziah had done. 35 Howbeit the high places were not removed: the people sacrificed and burned incense still in the high places. He built the higher gate of the house of the Lord.

# Isaiah

**1** 10 Hear the word of the Lord,
　　Ye rulers of Sodom;
　　Give ear unto the law of our God,
　　Ye people of Gomorrah.[1]
11 To what purpose is the multitude of your sacrifices unto me?
　　Saith the Lord:
　　I am full of the burnt offerings of rams,
　　And the fat of fed beasts;
　　And I delight not
　　In the blood of bullocks, or of lambs, or of he goats.
12 When ye come to appear before me,
　　Who hath required this at your hand,
　　To tread my courts?
13 Bring no more vain oblations;
　　Incense is an abomination unto me;
　　The new moons and sabbaths, the calling of assemblies,
　　I cannot away with;[2]
　　It is iniquity, even the solemn meeting.
14 Your new moons and your appointed feasts
　　My soul hateth:

---

[1] God here addresses the chosen people as though they were the wicked citizens of Sodom and Gomorrah.
[2] I.e., I cannot endure.

They are a trouble unto me;
I am weary to bear them.
15 And when ye spread forth your hands,
I will hide mine eyes from you;
Yea, when ye make many prayers,
I will not hear:
Your hands are full of blood.
16 Wash ye, make you clean;
Put away the evil of your doings
From before mine eyes;
Cease to do evil;
17 Learn to do well;
Seek judgment, relieve the oppressed,
Judge the fatherless, plead for the widow.
18 Come now, and let us reason together,
Saith the Lord:
Though your sins be as scarlet,
They shall be as white as snow;
Though they be red like crimson,
They shall be as wool.
19 If ye be willing and obedient,
Ye shall eat the good of the land:
20 But if ye refuse and rebel,
Ye shall be devoured with the sword:
For the mouth of the Lord hath spoken it.

3   13 The Lord standeth up to plead,
And standeth to judge the people.
14 The Lord will enter into judgment
With the ancients of his people, and the princes thereof:
For ye have eaten up the vineyard;
The spoil of the poor is in your houses.
15 What mean ye that ye beat my people to pieces,
And grind the faces of the poor?
Saith the Lord God of hosts.
16 Moreover the Lord saith,
Because the daughters of Zion are haughty,
And walk with stretched forth necks
And wanton eyes,
Walking and mincing as they go,
And making a tinkling with their feet:
17 Therefore the Lord will smite with a scab
The crown of the head of the daughters of Zion,
And the Lord will discover their secret parts.
18 In that day the Lord will take away the bravery of their tinkling ornaments about their feet, and their cauls, and their round tires like the moon. 19 The chains, and the bracelets, and the mufflers, 20 The

bonnets, and the ornaments of the legs, and the headbands, and the tablets, and the earrings, 21 The rings, and nose jewels, 22 The changeable suits of apparel, and the mantles, and the wimples, and the crisping pins, 23 The glasses, and the fine linen, and the hoods, and the veils. 24 And it shall come to pass, that

> Instead of sweet smell there shall be stink;
> And instead of a girdle a rent;
> And instead of well set hair baldness;
> And instead of a stomacher a girding of sackcloth;
> And burning instead of beauty.

25 Thy men shall fall by the sword,
> And thy mighty in the war.

26 And her gates shall lament and mourn;
> And she being desolate shall sit upon the ground.

5  20 Woe unto them that call evil good,
> And good evil;
> That put darkness for light,
> And light for darkness;
> That put bitter for sweet,
> And sweet for bitter!

21 Woe unto them that are wise in their own eyes,
> And prudent in their own sight!

22 Woe unto them that are mighty to drink wine,
> And men of strength to mingle strong drink:

23 Which justify the wicked for reward,
> And take away the righteousness of the righteous from him!

24 Therefore as the fire devoureth the stubble,
> And the flame consumeth the chaff,
> So their root shall be as rottenness,
> And their blossom shall go up as dust:
> Because they have cast away the law of the Lord of hosts,
> And despised the word of the Holy One of Israel.

# The Prophet Micah

*Jeremiah 26:18–19 says that Micah's work was under King Hezekiah, whose reforms Micah supported in a major way. The opening verse of the prophecy, on the other hand, relates Micah's work also to the two reigns preceding Hezekiah's, including that of Jotham, as well as to the time of Hezekiah. One thing is clear, however, and this is that whether under good or evil kings, Judah was in great need of reform among its princes, leaders, and people. In the prophecies preserved in the book of Micah, we find both judgment and hope.*

# *Micah*

1 The word of the Lord that came to Micah the Morasthite in the days of Jotham, Ahaz, and Hezekiah, kings of Judah, which he saw concerning Samaria and Jerusalem.

2     Woe to them that devise iniquity,
    And work evil upon their beds!
    When the morning is light, they practise it,
    Because it is in the power of their hand.
  2 And they covet fields, and take them by violence;
    And houses, and take them away:
    So they oppress a man and his house,
    Even a man and his heritage.

3     And I said, Hear, I pray you, O heads of Jacob,
    And ye princes of the house of Israel;
    Is it not for you to know judgment?
  2 Who hate the good, and love the evil;
    Who pluck off their skin from off them,
    And their flesh from off their bones;
  3 Who also eat the flesh of my people,
    And flay their skin from off them;
    And they break their bones,
    And chop them in pieces, as for the pot,
    And as flesh within the caldron.
  4 Then shall they cry unto the Lord,
    But he will not hear them:
    He will even hide his face from them at that time,
    As they have behaved themselves ill in their doings.
  9 Hear this, I pray you, ye heads of the house of Jacob,
    And princes of the house of Israel,
    That abhor judgment, and pervert all equity.
 10 They build up Zion with blood,
    And Jerusalem with iniquity.
 11 The heads thereof judge for reward,
    And the priests thereof teach for hire,
    And the prophets thereof divine for money:
    Yet will they lean upon the Lord, and say,
    Is not the Lord among us?
    None evil can come upon us.
 12 Therefore shall Zion for your sake be plowed as a field,
    And Jerusalem shall become heaps,
    And the mountain of the house as the high places of the
      forest.

4   But in the last days it shall come to pass,
    That the mountain of the house of the Lord shall be estab-
        lished in the top of the mountains,
    And it shall be exalted above the hills;
    And people shall flow unto it.
2   And many nations shall come, and say,
    Come, and let us go up to the mountain of the Lord,
    And to the house of the God of Jacob;
    And he will teach us of his ways,
    And we will walk in his paths:
    For the law shall go forth of Zion,
    And the word of the Lord from Jerusalem.
3   And he shall judge among many people,
    And rebuke strong nations afar off;
    And they shall beat their swords into plowshares,
    And their spears into pruning hooks:
    Nation shall not lift up a sword against nation,
    Neither shall they learn war any more.
4   But they shall sit every man under his vine and under his fig
        tree;
    And none shall make them afraid:
    For the mouth of the Lord of hosts hath spoken it.

6   Hear ye now what the Lord saith;
    Arise, contend thou before the mountains,
    And let the hills hear thy voice.
2   Hear ye, O mountains, the Lord's controversy,
    And ye strong foundations of the earth:
    For the Lord hath a controversy with his people,
    And he will plead with Israel.
3   O my people, what have I done unto thee?
    And wherein have I wearied thee?
    Testify against me.
4   For I brought thee up out of the land of Egypt,
    And redeemed thee out of the house of servants;
    And I sent before thee Moses, Aaron, and Miriam.
5   O my people, remember now what Balak king of Moab
        consulted,
    And what Balaam the son of Beor answered him
    From Shittim unto Gilgal;
    That ye may know the righteousness of the Lord.
6   Wherewith shall I come before the Lord,
    And bow myself before the high God?
    Shall I come before him with burnt offerings,
    With calves of a year old?
7   Will the Lord be pleased with thousands of rams,

Or with ten thousands of rivers of oil?
Shall I give my firstborn for my transgression,
The fruit of my body for the sin of my soul?
8 He hath showed thee, O man, what is good;
And what doth the Lord require of thee,
But to do justly, and to love mercy,
And to walk humbly with thy God?

7

7 Therefore I will look unto the Lord;
I will wait for the God of my salvation:
My God will hear me.
8 Rejoice not against me, O mine enemy:
When I fall, I shall arise;
When I sit in darkness, the Lord shall be a light unto me.
9 I will bear the indignation of the Lord, because I have sinned
against him,
Until he plead my cause, and execute judgment for me:
He will bring me forth to the light, and I shall behold his
righteousness.
18 Who is a God like unto thee, that pardoneth iniquity,
And passeth by the transgression of the remnant of his her-
itage?
He retaineth not his anger for ever,
Because he delighteth in mercy.
19 He will turn again, he will have compassion upon us;
He will subdue our iniquities;
And thou wilt cast all their sins into the depths of the sea.
20 Thou wilt perform the truth to Jacob, and the mercy to
Abraham,
Which thou hast sworn unto our fathers from the days of old.

## The Reforming Reign of King Hezekiah

*Under the prophetic stimulus, King Hezekiah led in many re-
forms and in preserving the Southern Kingdom from the threats
of Assyria.*

# Second Kings

18 Now it came to pass in the third year of Hoshea son of Elah
king of Israel, that Hezekiah the son of Ahaz king of Judah began to
reign. 2 Twenty and five years old was he when he began to reign;
and he reigned twenty and nine years in Jerusalem. His mother's name
also was Abi, the daughter of Zachariah. 3 And he did that which

was right in the sight of the Lord, according to all that David his father did. 4 He removed the high places, and brake the images, and cut down the groves, and brake in pieces the brazen serpent that Moses had made: for unto those days the children of Israel did burn incense to it: and he called it Nehushtan. 5 He trusted in the Lord God of Israel; so that after him was none like him among all the kings of Judah, nor any that were before him. 6 For he clave to the Lord, and departed not from following him, but kept his commandments, which the Lord commanded Moses. 7 And the Lord was with him; and he prospered whithersoever he went forth: and he rebelled against the king of Assyria, and served him not. 8 He smote the Philistines, even unto Gaza, and the borders thereof, from the tower of the watchmen to the fenced city.

13 Now in the fourteenth year of king Hezekiah did Sennacherib king of Assyria come up against all the fenced cities of Judah, and took them. 14 And Hezekiah king of Judah sent to the king of Assyria to Lachish, saying, I have offended; return from me: that which thou puttest on me will I bear. And the king of Assyria appointed unto Hezekiah king of Judah three hundred talents of silver and thirty talents of gold. 15 And Hezekiah gave him all the silver that was found in the house of the Lord, and in the treasures of the king's house. 16 At that time did Hezekiah cut off the gold from the doors of the temple of the Lord, and from the pillars which Hezekiah king of Judah had overlaid, and gave it to the king of Assyria.

17 And the king of Assyria sent Tartan and Rabsaris and Rabshakeh from Lachish to king Hezekiah with a great host against Jerusalem: and they went up and came to Jerusalem. And when they were come up, they came and stood by the conduit of the upper pool, which is in the highway of the fuller's field. 18 And when they had called to the king, there came out to them Eliakim the son of Hilkiah, which was over the household, and Shebna the scribe, and Joah the son of Asaph the recorder.

19 And Rab-shakeh said unto them, Speak ye now to Hezekiah, Thus saith the great king, the king of Assyria, What confidence is this wherein thou trustest? 20 Thou sayest, (but they are but vain words,) I have counsel and strength for the war. Now on whom dost thou trust, that thou rebellest against me? 21 Now, behold, thou trustest upon the staff of this bruised reed, even upon Egypt, on which if a man lean, it will go into his hand, and pierce it: so is Pharaoh king of Egypt unto all that trust on him. 22 But if ye say unto me, We trust in the Lord our God: is not that he, whose high places and whose altars Hezekiah hath taken away, and hath said to Judah and Jerusalem, Ye shall worship before this altar in Jerusalem? 23 Now therefore, I pray thee, give pledges to my lord the king of Assyria, and I will deliver thee two thousand horses, if thou be able on thy part to set riders upon them. 24 How then wilt thou turn away the face of one captain of the least of my master's servants, and put thy trust on Egypt

for chariots and for horsemen? 25 Am I now come up without the Lord against this place to destroy it? The Lord said to me, Go up against this land, and destroy it.

26 Then said Eliakim the son of Hilkiah, and Shebna, and Joah, unto Rab-shakeh, Speak, I pray thee, to thy servants in the Syrian language; for we understand it: and talk not with us in the Jews' language in the ears of the people that are on the wall. 27 But Rabshakeh said unto them, Hath my master sent me to thy master, and to thee, to speak these words? hath he not sent me to the men which sit on the wall, that they may eat their own dung, and drink their own piss with you? 28 Then Rab-shakeh stood and cried with a loud voice in the Jews' language, and spake, saying, Hear the word of the great king, the king of Assyria: 29 Thus saith the king, Let not Hezekiah deceive you: for he shall not be able to deliver you out of his hand: 30 Neither let Hezekiah make you trust in the Lord, saying, The Lord will surely deliver us, and this city shall not be delivered into the hand of the king of Assyria. 31 Hearken not to Hezekiah: for thus saith the king of Assyria, Make an agreement with me by a present, and come out to me, and then eat ye every man of his own vine, and every one of his fig tree, and drink ye every one the waters of his cistern: 32 Until I come and take you away to a land like your own land, a land of corn and wine, a land of bread and vineyards, a land of oil olive and of honey, that ye may live, and not die: and hearken not unto Hezekiah, when he persuadeth you, saying, The Lord will deliver us. 33 Hath any of the gods of the nations delivered at all his land out of the hand of the king of Assyria? 34 Where are the gods of Hamath, and of Arpad? where are the gods of Sepharvaim, Hena, and Ivah? have they delivered Samaria out of mine hand? 35 Who are they among all the gods of the countries, that have delivered their country out of mine hand, that the Lord should deliver Jerusalem out of mine hand?

36 But the people held their peace, and answered him not a word: for the king's commandment was, saying, Answer him not. 37 Then came Eliakim the son of Hilkiah, which was over the household, and Shebna the scribe, and Joah the son of Asaph the recorder, to Hezekiah with their clothes rent, and told him the words of Rab-shakeh.

19 And it came to pass, when king Hezekiah heard it, that he rent his clothes, and covered himself with sackcloth, and went into the house of the Lord. 2 And he sent Eliakim, which was over the household, and Shebna the scribe, and the elders of the priests, covered with sackcloth, to Isaiah the prophet the son of Amoz. 3 And they said unto him, Thus saith Hezekiah, This day is a day of trouble, and of rebuke, and blasphemy: for the children are come to the birth, and there is not strength to bring forth. 4 It may be the Lord thy God will hear all the words of Rab-shakeh, whom the king of Assyria his master hath sent to reproach the living God; and will reprove the words which the Lord thy God hath heard: wherefore lift up thy prayer

for the remnant that are left. 5 So the servants of king Hezekiah came to Isaiah. 6 And Isaiah said unto them, Thus shall ye say to your master, Thus saith the Lord, Be not afraid of the words which thou hast heard, with which the servants of the king of Assyria have blasphemed me. 7 Behold, I will send a blast upon him, and he shall hear a rumor, and shall return to his own land; and I will cause him to fall by the sword in his own land.

8 So Rab-shakeh returned, and found the king of Assyria warring against Libnah: for he had heard that he was departed from Lachish. 9 And when he heard say of Tirhakah king of Ethiopia, Behold, he is come out to fight against thee; he sent messengers again unto Hezekiah, saying, 10 Thus shall ye speak to Hezekiah king of Judah, saying, Let not thy God in whom thou trustest deceive thee, saying, Jerusalem shall not be delivered into the hand of the king of Assyria. 11 Behold, thou hast heard what the kings of Assyria have done to all lands, by destroying them utterly: and shalt thou be delivered? 12 Have the gods of the nations delivered them which my fathers have destroyed; as Gozan, and Haran, and Rezeph, and the children of Eden which were in Thelasar? 13 Where is the king of Hamath, and the king of Arpad, and the king of the city of Sepharvaim, of Hena, and Ivah?

14 And Hezekiah received the letter of the hand of the messengers, and read it: and Hezekiah went up into the house of the Lord, and spread it before the Lord. 15 And Hezekiah prayed before the Lord, and said, O Lord God of Israel, which dwellest between the cherubim, thou art the God, even thou alone, of all the kingdoms of the earth; thou hast made heaven and earth. 16 Lord, bow down thine ear, and hear: open, Lord, thine eyes, and see: and hear the words of Sennacherib, which hath sent him to reproach the living God. 17 Of a truth, Lord, the kings of Assyria have destroyed the nations and their lands, 18 And have cast their gods into the fire: for they were no gods, but the work of men's hands, wood and stone: therefore they have destroyed them. 19 Now therefore, O Lord our God, I beseech thee, save thou us out of his hand, that all the kingdoms of the earth may know that thou art the Lord God, even thou only.

20 Then Isaiah the son of Amoz sent to Hezekiah, saying, Thus saith the Lord God of Israel, That which thou hast prayed to me against Sennacherib king of Assyria I have heard. 21 This is the word that the Lord hath spoken concerning him;

The virgin the daughter of Zion
Hath despised thee, and laughed thee to scorn;
The daughter of Jerusalem
Hath shaken her head at thee.
22 Whom hast thou reproached and blasphemed?
And against whom hast thou exalted thy voice,
And lifted up thine eyes on high?
Even against the Holy One of Israel.
23 By thy messengers thou hast reproached the Lord,

And hast said, With the multitude of my chariots
I am come up to the height of the mountains,
To the sides of Lebanon,
And will cut down the tall cedar trees thereof,
And the choice fir trees thereof:
And I will enter into the lodgings of his borders,
And into the forest of his Carmel.

24 I have digged and drunk
Strange waters,
And with the sole of my feet have I dried up
All the rivers of besieged places.

25 Hast thou not heard
Long ago how I have done it,
And of ancient times that I have formed it?
Now have I brought it to pass,
That thou shouldest be to lay waste
Fenced cities into ruinous heaps.

26 Therefore their inhabitants were of small power,
They were dismayed and confounded;
They were as the grass of the field,
And as the green herb,
As the grass on the housetops,
And as corn blasted before it be grown up.

27 But I know thy abode, and thy going out, and thy coming in,
And thy rage against me.

28 Because thy rage against me
And thy tumult is come up into mine ears,
Therefore I will put my hook in thy nose,
And my bridle in thy lips,
And I will turn thee back by the way
By which thou camest.

33 By the way that he came, by the same shall he return, and shall not come into this city, saith the Lord. 34 For I will defend this city, to save it, for mine own sake, and for my servant David's sake.

35 And it came to pass that night, that the angel of the Lord went out, and smote in the camp of the Assyrians a hundred fourscore and five thousand: and when they arose early in the morning, behold, they were all dead corpses.

20   12 At that time Berodach-baladan, the son of Baladan, king of Babylon, sent letters and a present unto Hezekiah: for he had heard that Hezekiah had been sick. 13 And Hezekiah hearkened unto them, and showed them all the house of his precious things, the silver, and the gold, and the spices, and the precious ointment, and all the house of his armor, and all that was found in his treasures: there was nothing in his house, nor in all his dominion, that Hezekiah showed them not. 14 Then came Isaiah the prophet unto king Hezekiah, and said unto

him, What said these men? and from whence came they unto thee? And Hezekiah said, They are come from a far country, even from Babylon. 15 And he said, What have they seen in thine house? And Hezekiah answered, All the things that are in mine house have they seen: there is nothing among my treasures that I have not showed them.

16 And Isaiah said unto Hezekiah, Hear the word of the Lord. 17 Behold, the days come, that all that is in thine house, and that which thy fathers have laid up in store unto this day, shall be carried unto Babylon: nothing shall be left, saith the Lord. 18 And of thy sons that shall issue from thee, which thou shalt beget, shall they take away; and they shall be eunuchs in the palace of the king of Babylon. 19 Then said Hezekiah unto Isaiah, Good is the word of the Lord which thou hast spoken. And he said, Is it not good, if peace and truth be in my days? 21 And Hezekiah slept with his fathers: and Manasseh his son reigned in his stead.

## Isaiah on Alliances

*Despite the words of the prophets and the examples of history, the Southern Kingdom repeatedly put its trust in powerful political alliances in a world of shifting balances of power, rather than in thoroughgoing reform of itself. Isaiah regarded such alliances as an escape mechanism which deluded the people into ignoring their major problems. In the following passages he declared them to be "a covenant with death" and an evasion of the crying need for increasing in the strength of righteousness.*

# Isaiah

28 14 Wherefore hear the word of the Lord, ye scornful men,
That rule this people which is in Jerusalem.
15 Because ye have said, We have made a covenant with death,
And with hell are we at agreement;
When the overflowing scourge shall pass through, it shall not
come unto us:
For we have made lies our refuge,
And under falsehood have we hid ourselves:

30 Woe to the rebellious children, saith the Lord,
That take counsel, but not of me;
And that cover with a covering, but not of my Spirit,
That they may add sin to sin:
2 That walk to go down into Egypt,

And have not asked at my mouth;
To strengthen themselves in the strength of Pharaoh,
And to trust in the shadow of Egypt!
3 Therefore shall the strength of Pharaoh be your shame,
And the trust in the shadow of Egypt your confusion.
4 For his princes were at Zoan,
And his ambassadors came to Hanes.
5 They were all ashamed of a people that could not profit them,
Nor be a help nor profit,
But a shame, and also a reproach.
7 For the Egyptians shall help in vain, and to no purpose:
Therefore have I cried concerning this, Their strength is to
sit still.
8 Now go, write it before them in a table,
And note it in a book,
That it may be for the time to come
For ever and ever:
9 That this is a rebellious people, lying children,
Children that will not hear the law of the Lord:
10 Which say to the seers, See not;
And to the prophets, Prophesy not unto us right things,
Speak unto us smooth things, prophesy deceits:
11 Get you out of the way,
Turn aside out of the path,
Cause the Holy One of Israel to cease from before us.
12 Wherefore thus saith the Holy One of Israel,
Because ye despise this word,
And trust in oppression and perverseness,
And stay thereon:
13 Therefore this iniquity shall be to you
As a breach ready to fall, swelling out in a high wall,
Whose breaking cometh suddenly at an instant.
14 And he shall break it as the breaking of the potters' vessel
that is broken in pieces;
He shall not spare:
So that there shall not be found in the bursting of it a sherd
To take fire from the hearth,
Or to take water withal out of the pit.
15 For thus saith the Lord God, the Holy One of Israel;
In returning and rest shall ye be saved;
In quietness and in confidence shall be your strength:
And ye would not.
16 But ye said, No; for we will flee upon horses;
Therefore shall ye flee:
And, We will ride upon the swift;
Therefore shall they that pursue you be swift.
17 One thousand shall flee at the rebuke of one;
At the rebuke of five shall ye flee:

Till ye be left as a beacon upon the top of a mountain,
And as an ensign on a hill.

## The Prophetic Hope

*Isaiah did far more than denounce, however, as the following
passages indicate. Whether these assurances were addressed to
particular events within the lifetime of Isaiah or expressed some
more distant hope for the future is open to disagreement. They
do, however, represent an important element in the prophetic
tradition, and they were taken by early Christians as foreshadow-
ings of Christ and the Messianic Kingdom.*

# *Isaiah*

2    The word that Isaiah the son of Amoz saw concerning Judah
and Jerusalem.
   2 And it shall come to pass in the last days,
      That the mountain of the Lord's house shall be established in
         the top of the mountains,
      And shall be exalted above the hills;
      And all nations shall flow unto it.
   3 And many people shall go and say,
      Come ye, and let us go up to the mountain of the Lord,
      To the house of the God of Jacob;
      And he will teach us of his ways,
      And we will walk in his paths:
      For out of Zion shall go forth the law,
      And the word of the Lord from Jerusalem.
   4 And he shall judge among the nations,
      And shall rebuke many people:
      And they shall beat their swords into plowshares,
      And their spears into pruning hooks:
      Nation shall not lift up sword against nation,
      Neither shall they learn war any more.

9    2 The people that walked in darkness
      Have seen a great light:
      They that dwell in the land of the shadow of death,
      Upon them hath the light shined.
   3 Thou hast multiplied the nation,
      And not increased the joy:
      They joy before thee according to the joy in harvest,
      And as men rejoice when they divide the spoil.
   4 For thou hast broken the yoke of his burden,

And the staff of his shoulder,
The rod of his oppressor,
As in the day of Midian.
5 For every battle of the warrior is with confused noise,
And garments rolled in blood;
But this shall be with burning and fuel of fire.
6 For unto us a child is born,
Unto us a son is given:
And the government shall be upon his shoulder:
And his name shall be called
Wonderful, Counselor, The mighty God,
The everlasting Father, The Prince of Peace.
7 Of the increase of his government and peace
There shall be no end,
Upon the throne of David, and upon his kingdom,
To order it, and to establish it
With judgment and with justice
From henceforth even for ever.
The zeal of the Lord of hosts will perform this.

11   And there shall come forth a rod out of the stem of Jesse,
And a Branch shall grow out of his roots:
2 And the Spirit of the Lord shall rest upon him,
The spirit of wisdom and understanding,
The spirit of counsel and might,
The spirit of knowledge and of the fear of the Lord;
3 And shall make him of quick understanding in the fear of the
Lord:
And he shall not judge after the sight of his eyes,
Neither reprove after the hearing of his ears:
4 But with righteousness shall he judge the poor,
And reprove with equity for the meek of the earth:
And he shall smite the earth with the rod of his mouth,
And with the breath of his lips shall he slay the wicked.
5 And righteousness shall be the girdle of his loins,
And faithfulness the girdle of his reins.
6 The wolf also shall dwell with the lamb,
And the leopard shall lie down with the kid;
And the calf and the young lion and the fatling together;
And a little child shall lead them.
7 And the cow and the bear shall feed;
Their young ones shall lie down together:
And the lion shall eat straw like the ox.
8 And the sucking child shall play on the hole of the asp,
And the weaned child shall put his hand on the cockatrice'
den.
9 They shall not hurt nor destroy
In all my holy mountain:

For the earth shall be full of the knowledge of the Lord,
As the waters cover the sea.
10 And in that day there shall be a root of Jesse,
Which shall stand for an ensign of the people;
To it shall the Gentiles seek:
And his rest shall be glorious.

## King Manasseh and King Amon

*The reforming reign of King Hezekiah was followed by the rule of his son Manasseh, which along with the short succeeding reign of Amon was one of the worst periods in Biblical history.*

# Second Kings

21 Manasseh was twelve years old when he began to reign, and reigned fifty and five years in Jerusalem. And his mother's name was Hephzi-bah. 2 And he did that which was evil in the sight of the Lord, after the abominations of the heathen, whom the Lord cast out before the children of Israel. 3 For he built up again the high places which Hezekiah his father had destroyed; and he reared up altars for Baal, and made a grove, as did Ahab king of Israel; and worshipped all the host of heaven, and served them. 4 And he built altars in the house of the Lord, of which the Lord said, In Jerusalem will I put my name. 5 And he built altars for all the host of heaven in the two courts of the house of the Lord. 6 And he made his son pass through the fire, and observed times, and used enchantments, and dealt with familiar spirits and wizards: he wrought much wickedness in the sight of the Lord, to provoke him to anger. 7 And he set a graven image of the grove that he had made in the house, of which the Lord said to David, and to Solomon his son, In this house, and in Jerusalem, which I have chosen out of all the tribes of Israel, will I put my name for ever: 8 Neither will I make the feet of Israel move any more out of the land which I gave their fathers; only if they will observe to do according to all that I have commanded them, and according to all the law that my servant Moses commanded them. 9 But they hearkened not: and Manasseh seduced them to do more evil than did the nations whom the Lord destroyed before the children of Israel.

10 And the Lord spake by his servants the prophets, saying, 11 Because Manasseh king of Judah hath done these abominations, and hath done wickedly above all that the Amorites did, which were before him, and hath made Judah also to sin with his idols: 12 Therefore thus saith the Lord God of Israel, Behold, I am bringing such evil upon Jerusalem and Judah, that whosoever heareth of it, both his ears shall tingle. 13 And I will stretch over Jerusalem the line of Samaria,

and the plummet of the house of Ahab: and I will wipe Jerusalem as a man wipeth a dish, wiping it, and turning it upside down. 14 And I will forsake the remnant of mine inheritance, and deliver them into the hand of their enemies; and they shall become a prey and a spoil to all their enemies; 15 Because they have done that which was evil in my sight, and have provoked me to anger, since the day their fathers came forth out of Egypt, even unto this day.

16 Moreover Manasseh shed innocent blood very much, till he had filled Jerusalem from one end to another; besides his sin wherewith he made Judah to sin, in doing that which was evil in the sight of the Lord.

18 And Manasseh slept with his fathers, and was buried in the garden of his own house, in the garden of Uzza: and Amon his son reigned in his stead. 19 Amon was twenty and two years old when he began to reign, and he reigned two years in Jerusalem. And his mother's name was Meshullemeth, the daughter of Haruz of Jotbah. 20 And he did that which was evil in the sight of the Lord, as his father Manasseh did. 21 And he walked in all the way that his father walked in, and served the idols that his father served, and worshipped them: 22 And he forsook the Lord God of his fathers, and walked not in the way of the Lord. 23 And the servants of Amon conspired against him, and slew the king in his own house. 24 And the people of the land slew all them that had conspired against king Amon; and the people of the land made Josiah his son king in his stead.

## The Prophet Zephaniah

*Despite the evils which were rampant under kings Manasseh and Amon, the people of Judah persisted in regarding themselves as invulnerable to God's anger, and looked forward to "the day of the Lord" as a glorious triumph for themselves. Prophets repeatedly repudiated such false confidence, and none more graphically than Zephaniah, who was himself evidently a descendant of the reforming King Hezekiah. In the dies irae (day of wrath) passage given below, the words seem to have come from Zephaniah a few years before his young cousin King Josiah began his great reforms, and some forty years before the great Babylonian captivity of his people.*

# Zephaniah

1   7 Hold thy peace at the presence of the Lord God:
     For the day of the Lord is at hand:
     For the Lord hath prepared a sacrifice,
     He hath bid his guests.

8 And it shall come to pass in the day of the Lord's sacrifice,
   That I will punish the princes, and the king's children,
   And all such as are clothed with strange apparel.
9 In the same day also will I punish all those that leap on the
   threshold,
   Which fill their masters' houses with violence and deceit.
10 And it shall come to pass in that day, saith the Lord,
   That there shall be the noise of a cry from the fish gate,
   And a howling from the second,
   And a great crashing from the hills.
11 Howl, ye inhabitants of Maktesh,
   For all the merchant people are cut down;
   All they that bear silver are cut off.
12 And it shall come to pass at that time,
   That I will search Jerusalem with candles,
   And punish the men that are settled on their lees:
   That say in their heart,
   The Lord will not do good, neither will he do evil.
13 Therefore, their goods shall become a booty,
   And their houses a desolation:
   They shall also build houses, but not inhabit them;
   And they shall plant vineyards, but not drink the wine thereof.
14 The great day of the Lord is near,
   It is near, and hasteth greatly,
   Even the voice of the day of the Lord:
   The mighty man shall cry there bitterly.
15 That day is a day of wrath,
   A day of trouble and distress,
   A day of wasteness and desolation,
   A day of darkness and gloominess,
   A day of clouds and thick darkness,
16 A day of the trumpet and alarm
   Against the fenced cities,
   And against the high towers.
17 And I will bring distress upon men,
   That they shall walk like blind men,
   Because they have sinned against the Lord:
   And their blood shall be poured out as dust,
   And their flesh as the dung.
18 Neither their silver nor their gold
   Shall be able to deliver them
   In the day of the Lord's wrath.

## Josiah, the Last Reforming King

*Josiah was the last great king of Judah. He was twenty-six
years old when the high priest discovered a book which appears to*

297

have been at least a part of the present Deuteronomy. Under the impetus provided by this rediscovery of ancient laws and precepts, Josiah led a reform movement of considerable vitality, but unfortunately it was still a case of too little and too late. From the prophets we learn that for the mass of the Jewish people and princes, the reforms were at best of but superficial influence. When Josiah died in battle with the invading Egyptian pharaoh, the son who succeeded him reigned for only three months before being taken captive to Egypt. Thereafter came the deluge.

# Second Kings

22 Josiah was eight years old when he began to reign, and he reigned thirty and one years in Jerusalem. And his mother's name was Jedidah, the daughter of Adaiah of Boscath. 2 And he did that which was right in the sight of the Lord, and walked in all the way of David his father, and turned not aside to the right hand or to the left.

3 And it came to pass in the eighteenth year of king Josiah, that the king sent Shaphan the son of Azaliah, the son of Meshullam, the scribe, to the house of the Lord, saying, 4 Go up to Hilkiah the high priest, that he may sum the silver which is brought into the house of the Lord, which the keepers of the door have gathered of the people: 5 And let them deliver it into the hand of the doers of the work, that have the oversight of the house of the Lord: and let them give it to the doers of the work, which is in the house of the Lord, to repair the breaches of the house, 6 Unto carpenters, and builders, and masons, and to buy timber and hewn stone to repair the house. 7 Howbeit, there was no reckoning made with them of the money that was delivered into their hand, because they dealt faithfully.

8 And Hilkiah the high priest said unto Shaphan the scribe, I have found the book of the law in the house of the Lord. And Hilkiah gave the book to Shaphan, and he read it. 9 And Shaphan the scribe came to the king, and brought the king word again, and said, Thy servants have gathered the money that was found in the house, and have delivered it into the hand of them that do the work, that have the oversight of the house of the Lord. 10 And Shaphan the scribe showed the king, saying, Hilkiah the priest hath delivered me a book. And Shaphan read it before the king. 11 And it came to pass, when the king had heard the words of the book of the law, that he rent his clothes. 12 And the king commanded Hilkiah the priest, and Ahikam the son of Shaphan, and Achbor the son of Michaiah, and Shaphan the scribe, and Asahia a servant of the king's, saying, 13 Go ye, inquire of the Lord for me, and for the people, and for all Judah, concerning the words of this book that is found: for great is the wrath of the Lord that is kindled against us, because our fathers have not

hearkened unto the words of this book, to do according unto all that which is written concerning us.

14 So Hilkiah the priest, and Ahikam, and Achbor, and Shaphan, and Asahiah, went unto Huldah the prophetess, the wife of Shallum the son of Tikvah, the son of Harhas, keeper of the wardrobe; (now she dwelt in Jerusalem in the college;) and they communed with her. 15 And she said unto them, Thus saith the Lord God of Israel, Tell the man that sent you to me, 16 Thus saith the Lord, Behold, I will bring evil upon this place, and upon the inhabitants thereof, even all the words of the book which the king of Judah hath read: 17 Because they have forsaken me, and have burned incense unto other gods, that they might provoke me to anger with all the works of their hands; therefore my wrath shall be kindled against this place, and shall not be quenched. 18 But to the king of Judah which sent you to inquire of the Lord, thus shall ye say to him, Thus saith the Lord God of Israel, As touching the words which thou hast heard; 19 Because thine heart was tender, and thou hast humbled thyself before the Lord, when thou heardest what I spake against this place, and against the inhabitants thereof, that they should become a desolation and a curse, and hast rent thy clothes, and wept before me; I also have heard thee, saith the Lord. 20 Behold therefore, I will gather thee unto thy fathers, and thou shalt be gathered into thy grave in peace; and thine eyes shall not see all the evil which I will bring upon this place. And they brought the king word again.

23 And the king sent, and they gathered unto him all the elders of Judah and of Jerusalem. 2 And the king went up into the house of the Lord, and all the men of Judah and all the inhabitants of Jerusalem with him, and the priests, and the prophets, and all the people, both small and great: and he read in their ears all the words of the book of the covenant which was found in the house of the Lord. 3 And the king stood by a pillar, and made a covenant before the Lord, to walk after the Lord, and to keep his commandments and his testimonies and his statutes with all their heart and all their soul, to perform the words of this covenant that were written in this book. And all the people stood to the covenant.

4 And the king commanded Hilkiah the high priest, and the priests of the second order, and the keepers of the door, to bring forth out of the temple of the Lord all the vessels that were made for Baal, and for the grove, and for all the host of heaven: and he burned them without Jerusalem in the fields of Kidron, and carried the ashes of them unto Beth-el. 5 And he put down the idolatrous priests, whom the kings of Judah had ordained to burn incense in the high places in the cities of Judah, and in the places round about Jerusalem; them also that burned incense unto Baal, to the sun, and to the moon, and to the planets, and to all the host of heaven. 6 And he brought out the grove from the house of the Lord, without Jerusalem, unto the brook

Kidron, and burned it at the brook Kidron, and stamped it small to powder, and cast the powder thereof upon the graves of the children of the people. 7 And he brake down the houses of the sodomites, that were by the house of the Lord, where the women wove hangings for the grove. 8 And he brought all the priests out of the cities of Judah, and defiled the high places where the priests had burned incense, from Geba to Beer-sheba, and brake down the high places of the gates that were in the entering in of the gate of Joshua the governor of the city, which were on a man's left hand at the gate of the city. 9 Nevertheless the priests of the high places came not up to the altar of the Lord in Jerusalem, but they did eat of the unleavened bread among their brethren. 10 And he defiled Topheth, which is in the valley of the children of Hinnom, that no man might make his son or his daughter to pass through the fire to Molech. 11 And he took away the horses that the kings of Judah had given to the sun, at the entering in of the house of the Lord, by the chamber of Nathan-melech the chamberlain, which was in the suburbs, and burned the chariots of the sun with fire. 12 And the altars that were on the top of the upper chamber of Ahaz, which the kings of Judah had made, and the altars which Manasseh had made in the two courts of the house of the Lord, did the king beat down, and brake them down from thence, and cast the dust of them into the brook Kidron. 13 And the high places that were before Jerusalem, which were on the right hand of the mount of corruption, which Solomon the king of Israel had builded for Ashtoreth the abomination of the Zidonians, and for Chemosh the abomination of the Moabites, and for Milcom the abomination of the children of Ammon, did the king defile. 14 And he brake in pieces the images, and cut down the groves, and filled their places with the bones of men.[1]

15 Moreover the altar that was at Beth-el, and the high place which Jeroboam the son of Nebat, who made Israel to sin, had made, both that altar and the high place he brake down, and burned the high place, and stamped it small to powder, and burned the grove. 16 And as Josiah turned himself, he spied the sepulchres that were there in the mount, and sent, and took the bones out of the sepulchres, and burned them upon the altar, and polluted it, according to the word of the Lord which the man of God proclaimed, who proclaimed these words. 17 Then he said, What title is that that I see? And the men of the city told him, It is the sepulchre of the man of God, which came from Judah, and proclaimed these things that thou hast done against the altar of Beth-el. 18 And he said, Let him alone; let no man move his bones. So they let his bones alone, with the bones of the prophet that came out of Samaria. 19 And all the houses also of the high places that were in the cities of Samaria, which the kings of Israel had made to provoke the Lord to anger, Josiah took away, and did to

[1] The holy places of the Baal cult were thus dishonored and defiled by scattering dead men's bones over them.

them according to all the acts that he had done in Beth-el. 20 And he slew all the priests of the high places that were there upon the altars, and burned men's bones upon them, and returned to Jerusalem.

21 And the king commanded all the people, saying, Keep the passover unto the Lord your God, as it is written in the book of this covenant. 22 Surely there was not holden such a passover from the days of the judges that judged Israel, nor in all the days of the kings of Israel, nor of the kings of Judah; 23 But in the eighteenth year of king Josiah, wherein this passover was holden to the Lord in Jerusalem. 24 Moreover the workers with familiar spirits, and the wizards, and the images, and the idols, and all the abominations that were spied in the land of Judah and in Jerusalem, did Josiah put away, that he might perform the words of the law, which were written in the book that Hilkiah the priest found in the house of the Lord. 25 And like unto him was there no king before him, that turned to the Lord with all his heart, and with all his soul, and with all his might, according to all the law of Moses; neither after him arose there any like him.

26 Notwithstanding, the Lord turned not from the fierceness of his great wrath, wherewith his anger was kindled against Judah, because of all the provocations that Manasseh had provoked him withal. 27 And the Lord said, I will remove Judah also out of my sight, as I have removed Israel, and will cast off this city Jerusalem which I have chosen, and the house of which I said, My name shall be there.

29 In his days Pharaoh-nechoh king of Egypt went up against the king of Assyria to the river Euphrates: and king Josiah went against him; and he slew him[1] at Megiddo, when he had seen him. 30 And his servants carried him in a chariot dead from Megiddo, and brought him to Jerusalem, and buried him in his own sepulchre. And the people of the land took Jehoahaz the son of Josiah, and anointed him, and made him king in his father's stead.

31 Jehoahaz was twenty and three years old when he began to reign; and he reigned three months in Jerusalem. And his mother's name was Hamutal, the daughter of Jeremiah of Libnah. 32 And he did that which was evil in the sight of the Lord, according to all that his fathers had done. 33 And Pharaoh-nechoh put him in bands at Riblah in the land of Hamath, that he might not reign in Jerusalem; and put the land to a tribute of a hundred talents of silver, and a talent of gold. 34 And Pharaoh-nechoh made Eliakim the son of Josiah king in the room of Josiah his father, and turned his name to Jehoiakim, and took Jehoahaz away: and he came to Egypt, and died there. 35 And Jehoiakim gave the silver and the gold to Pharaoh; but he taxed the land to give the money according to the commandment of Pharaoh: he exacted the silver and the gold of the people of the land, of every one according to his taxation, to give it unto Pharaoh-nechoh.

---

[1] I.e., Pharaoh killed Josiah.

301

## Last Years of Judah

*In the Biblical account the dramatic catastrophe moves swiftly. The first and second sieges of Jerusalem by the Babylonians, along with the first and second mass deportations into Babylon, are recounted with great economy: "So Judah was carried away out of their land." Under the three kings Jehoiakim, Jehoiachin, and Zedekiah, the "holy history" of the chosen people appeared, on the surface at least, to have come to an end.*

## *Second Kings*

**23** 36 Jehoiakim was twenty and five years old when he began to reign; and he reigned eleven years in Jerusalem. And his mother's name was Zebudah, the daughter of Pedaiah of Rumah. 37 And he did that which was evil in the sight of the Lord, according to all that his fathers had done.

**24** In his days Nebuchadnezzar king of Babylon came up, and Jehoiakim became his servant three years: then he turned and rebelled against him. 2 And the Lord sent against him bands of the Chaldees, and bands of the Syrians, and bands of the Moabites, and bands of the children of Ammon, and sent them against Judah to destroy it, according to the word of the Lord, which he spake by his servants the prophets. 3 Surely at the commandment of the Lord came this upon Judah, to remove them out of his sight, for the sins of Manasseh, according to all that he did; 4 And also for the innocent blood that he shed: for he filled Jerusalem with innocent blood; which the Lord would not pardon.

6 So Jehoiakim slept with his fathers: and Jehoiachin his son reigned in his stead. 7 And the king of Egypt came not again any more out of his land: for the king of Babylon had taken from the river of Egypt unto the river Euphrates all that pertained to the king of Egypt.

8 Jehoiachin was eighteen years old when he began to reign, and he reigned in Jerusalem three months. And his mother's name was Nehushta, the daughter of Elnathan of Jerusalem. 9 And he did that which was evil in the sight of the Lord, according to all that his father had done. 10 At that time the servants of Nebuchadnezzar king of Babylon came up against Jerusalem, and the city was besieged. 11 And Nebuchadnezzar king of Babylon came against the city, and his servants did besiege it. 12 And Jehoiachin the king of Judah went out to the king of Babylon, he, and his mother, and his servants, and his princes, and his officers: and the king of Babylon took him in the eighth year of his reign. 13 And he carried out thence all the treasures

of the house of the Lord, and the treasures of the king's house, and cut in pieces all the vessels of gold which Solomon king of Israel had made in the temple of the Lord, as the Lord had said. 14 And he carried away all Jerusalem, and all the princes, and all the mighty men of valor, even ten thousand captives, and all the craftsmen and smiths: none remained, save the poorest sort of the people of the land. 15 And he carried away Jehoiachin to Babylon, and the king's mother, and the king's wives, and his officers, and the mighty of the land, those carried he into captivity from Jerusalem to Babylon. 16 And all the men of might, even seven thousand, and craftsmen and smiths a thousand, all that were strong and apt for war, even them the king of Babylon brought captive to Babylon. 17 And the king of Babylon made Mattaniah his father's brother king in his stead, and changed his name to Zedekiah.

18 Zedekiah was twenty and one years old when he began to reign, and he reigned eleven years in Jerusalem. And his mother's name was Hamutal, the daughter of Jeremiah of Libnah. 19 And he did that which was evil in the sight of the Lord, according to all that Jehoiakim had done. 20 For through the anger of the Lord it came to pass in Jerusalem and Judah, until he had cast them out from his presence, that Zedekiah rebelled against the king of Babylon.

25 And it came to pass in the ninth year of his reign, in the tenth month, in the tenth day of the month, that Nebuchadnezzar king of Babylon came, he, and all his host, against Jerusalem, and pitched against it; and they built forts against it round about. 2 And the city was besieged unto the eleventh year of king Zedekiah. 3 And on the ninth day of the fourth month the famine prevailed in the city, and there was no bread for the people of the land. 4 And the city was broken up, and all the men of war fled by night by the way of the gate between two walls, which is by the king's garden: (now the Chaldees were against the city round about:) and the king went the way toward the plain. 5 And the army of the Chaldees pursued after the king, and overtook him in the plains of Jericho: and all his army were scattered from him. 6 So they took the king, and brought him up to the king of Babylon to Riblah; and they gave judgment upon him. 7 And they slew the sons of Zedekiah before his eyes, and put out the eyes of Zedekiah and bound him with fetters of brass, and carried him to Babylon.

8 And in the fifth month, on the seventh day of the month, which is the nineteenth year of king Nebuchadnezzar king of Babylon, came Nebuzar-adan, captain of the guard, a servant of the king of Babylon, unto Jerusalem: 9 And he burnt the house of the Lord, and the king's house, and all the houses of Jerusalem, and every great man's house burnt he with fire. 10 And all the army of the Chaldees, that were with the captain of the guard, brake down the walls of Jerusalem round about. 11 Now the rest of the people that were left in the city, and the fugitives that fell away to the king of Babylon, with

the remnant of the multitude, did Nebuzar-adan the captain of the guard carry away. 12 But the captain of the guard left of the poor of the land to be vinedressers and husbandmen.

21 So Judah was carried away out of their land.

## Jeremiah: Introduction

The outstanding figure of this period of history was the prophet Jeremiah. More intimate details are known to us about Jeremiah's life and work than about that of any other prophet, or indeed of almost any other man of the ancient world. Born in the time of Josiah, whom he admired, his principal work was carried out under Josiah's successors Jehoiakim, Jehoiachin, and Zedekiah, the last independent kings of Judah, who reigned between 609 and 587 B.C. After the Babylonian capture of Jerusalem in 598 under King Jehoiachin, many of the Jews were carried into captivity in Babylon. Slightly over a decade later, after King Zedekiah's rebellion against the Babylonian overlords, Jerusalem was totally destroyed and the final Babylonian captivity began.

It was in these most troubled times that Jeremiah discharged his prophetic mission. From Jeremiah's own words, and from the comments of his secretary Baruch, we gain an intimate and moving picture of this final period of decay and destruction.

Jeremiah's prophetic call is described in the first selection below. Thereafter comes a section drawn together from various passages to indicate the general style and tenor of his message. Then follow particular episodes under separate headings.

# *Jeremiah*

### JEREMIAH'S PROPHETIC CALL

1 The words of Jeremiah the son of Hilkiah, of the priests that were in Anathoth in the land of Benjamin: 2 To whom the word of the Lord came in the days of Josiah the son of Amon king of Judah, in the thirteenth year of his reign. 3 It came also in the days of Jehoiakim the son of Josiah king of Judah, unto the end of the eleventh year of Zedekiah the son of Josiah king of Judah, unto the carrying away of Jerusalem captive in the fifth month.

4 Then the word of the Lord came unto me, saying,

5 Before I formed thee in the belly I knew thee;
> And before thou camest forth out of the womb I sanctified thee,
> And I ordained thee a prophet unto the nations.

6 Then said I, Ah, Lord God! behold, I cannot speak: for I am a child.
7 But the Lord said unto me,
> Say not, I am a child:
> For thou shalt go to all that I shall send thee,
> And whatsoever I command thee thou shalt speak.
> 8 Be not afraid of their faces:
> For I am with thee to deliver thee,
> Saith the Lord.

9 Then the Lord put forth his hand, and touched my mouth. And the Lord said unto me,
> Behold, I have put my words in thy mouth.
> 10 See, I have this day set thee over the nations and over the kingdoms,
> To root out, and to pull down,
> And to destroy, and to throw down,
> To build, and to plant.

## JEREMIAH'S GENERAL MESSAGE

2  Moreover the word of the Lord came to me, saying,
> 4 Hear ye the word of the Lord, O house of Jacob,
> And all the families of the house of Israel:
> 5 Thus saith the Lord,
> What iniquity have your fathers found in me,
> That they are gone far from me,
> And have walked after vanity,
> And are become vain?
> 6 Neither said they,
> Where is the Lord that brought us up
> Out of the land of Egypt,
> That led us through the wilderness,
> Through a land of deserts and of pits,
> Through a land of drought, and of the shadow of death,
> Through a land that no man passed through,
> And where no man dwelt?
> 7 And I brought you into a plentiful country,
> To eat the fruit thereof and the goodness thereof;
> But when ye entered, ye defiled my land,
> And made mine heritage an abomination.
> 8 The priests said not,
> Where is the Lord?
> And they that handle the law knew me not:
> The pastors also transgressed against me,
> And the prophets prophesied by Baal,
> And walked after things that do not profit.
> 13 For my people have committed two evils;
> They have forsaken me the fountain of living waters,

And hewed them out cisterns,
Broken cisterns, that can hold no water.
19 Thine own wickedness shall correct thee,
And thy backslidings shall reprove thee:
Know therefore and see that it is an evil thing and bitter,
That thou hast forsaken the Lord thy God,
And that my fear is not in thee,
Saith the Lord God of hosts.
20 For of old time I have broken thy yoke,
And burst thy bands;
And thou saidst, I will not transgress;
When upon every high hill
And under every green tree
Thou wanderest, playing the harlot.
21 Yet I had planted thee a noble vine,
Wholly a right seed:
How then art thou turned into the degenerate plant
Of a strange vine unto me?
22 For though thou wash thee with nitre,
And take thee much soap,
Yet thine iniquity is marked before me,
Saith the Lord God.

3 22 Return, ye backsliding children,
And I will heal your backslidings.
Behold, we come unto thee;
For thou art the Lord our God.
23 Truly in vain is salvation hoped for from the hills,
And from the multitude of mountains:
Truly in the Lord our God
Is the salvation of Israel.
24 For shame hath devoured
The labor of our fathers from our youth;
Their flocks and their herds,
Their sons and their daughters.
25 We lie down in our shame,
And our confusion covereth us:
For we have sinned against the Lord our God,
We and our fathers,
From our youth even unto this day,
And have not obeyed
The voice of the Lord our God.

4 If thou wilt return, O Israel,
Saith the Lord,
Return unto me:
And if thou wilt put away thine abominations out of my
sight,

Then shalt thou not remove.
2 And thou shalt swear, The Lord liveth,
In truth, in judgment, and in righteousness;
And the nations shall bless themselves in him,
And in him shall they glory.
3 For thus saith the Lord to the men of Judah and Jerusalem,
Break up your fallow ground,
And sow not among thorns.
4 Circumcise yourselves to the Lord,
And take away the foreskins of your heart,
Ye men of Judah and inhabitants of Jerusalem;
Lest my fury come forth like fire,
And burn that none can quench it,
Because of the evil of your doings.

5    26 For among my people are found wicked men:
They lay wait, as he that setteth snares;
They set a trap, they catch men.
27 As a cage is full of birds,
So are their houses full of deceit:
Therefore they are become great, and waxen rich.
28 They are waxen fat, they shine:
Yea, they overpass the deeds of the wicked:
They judge not the cause, the cause of the fatherless,
Yet they prosper;
And the right of the needy do they not judge.

## The Temple Sermon and After

*Jeremiah's Temple Sermon came early in the reign of Jehoi-*
*akim, and was followed by further messages, all to no avail. In*
*the fourth year of Jehoiakim, matters came to a climax when*
*Jeremiah made a direct prediction of the Babylonian conquest of*
*Jerusalem and was forbidden to speak again. At some point dur-*
*ing this period he was even placed in the stocks. Accounts of*
*these incidents are given below.*

# *Jeremiah*

### THE TEMPLE SERMON

7    The word that came to Jeremiah from the Lord, saying, 2 Stand
in the gate of the Lord's house, and proclaim there this word, and
say, Hear the word of the Lord, all ye of Judah, that enter in at these
gates to worship the Lord. 3 Thus saith the Lord of hosts, the God
of Israel,

307

Amend your ways and your doings, and I will cause you to dwell in this place. 4 Trust ye not in lying words, saying, The temple of the Lord, The temple of the Lord, The temple of the Lord, are these. 5 For if ye thoroughly amend your ways and your doings; if ye thoroughly execute judgment between a man and his neighbor; 6 If ye oppress not the stranger, the fatherless, and the widow, and shed not innocent blood in this place, neither walk after other gods to your hurt; 7 Then will I cause you to dwell in this place, in the land that I gave to your fathers, for ever and ever.

8 Behold, ye trust in lying words, that cannot profit. 9 Will ye steal, murder, and commit adultery, and swear falsely, and burn incense unto Baal, and walk after other gods whom ye know not; 10 And come and stand before me in this house, which is called by my name, and say, We are delivered to do all these abominations? 11 Is this house, which is called by my name, become a den of robbers in your eyes? Behold, even I have seen it, saith the Lord.

12 But go ye now unto my place which was in Shiloh, where I set my name at the first, and see what I did to it for the wickedness of my people Israel. 13 And now, because ye have done all these works, saith the Lord, and I spake unto you, rising up early and speaking, but ye heard not; and I called you, but ye answered not; 14 Therefore will I do unto this house, which is called by my name, wherein ye trust, and unto the place which I gave to you and to your fathers, as I have done to Shiloh. 15 And I will cast you out of my sight, as I have cast out all your brethren, even the whole seed of Ephraim. 16 Therefore pray not thou for this people, neither lift up cry nor prayer for them, neither make intercession to me: for I will not hear thee.

17 Seest thou not what they do in the cities of Judah and in the streets of Jerusalem? 18 The children gather wood, and the fathers kindle the fire, and the women knead their dough, to make cakes to the queen of heaven, and to pour out drink offerings unto other gods, that they may provoke me to anger. 19 Do they provoke me to anger? saith the Lord: do they not provoke themselves to the confusion of their own faces? 20 Therefore thus saith the Lord God; Behold, mine anger and my fury shall be poured out upon this place, upon man, and upon beast, and upon the trees of the field, and upon the fruit of the ground; and it shall burn, and shall not be quenched.

21 Thus saith the Lord of hosts, the God of Israel; Put your burnt offerings unto your sacrifices, and eat flesh. 22 For I spake not unto your fathers, nor commanded them in the day that I brought them out of the land of Egypt, concerning burnt offerings or sacrifices: 23 But this thing commanded I them, saying, Obey my voice, and I will be your God, and ye shall be my people: and walk ye in all the ways that I have commanded you, that it may be well unto you. 24 But they hearkened not, nor inclined their ear, but walked in the counsels and in the imagination of their evil heart, and went backward, and not forward. 25 Since the day that your fathers came forth

out of the land of Egypt unto this day, I have even sent unto you all my servants the prophets, daily rising up early and sending them: 26 Yet they hearkened not unto me, nor inclined their ear, but hardened their neck: they did worse than their fathers.

27 Therefore thou shalt speak all these words unto them; but they will not hearken to thee: thou shalt also call unto them; but they will not answer thee. 28 But thou shalt say unto them,

> This is a nation that obeyeth not
> The voice of the Lord their God,
> Nor receiveth correction:
> Truth is perished,
> And is cut off from their mouth.

## 26

8 Now it came to pass, when Jeremiah had made an end of speaking all that the Lord had commanded him to speak unto all the people, that the priests and the prophets and all the people took him, saying, Thou shalt surely die. 9 Why hast thou prophesied in the name of the Lord, saying, This house shall be like Shiloh, and this city shall be desolate without an inhabitant? And all the people were gathered against Jeremiah in the house of the Lord.

10 When the princes of Judah heard these things, then they came up from the king's house unto the house of the Lord, and sat down in the entry of the new gate of the Lord's house. 11 Then spake the priests and the prophets unto the princes and to all the people, saying, This man is worthy to die; for he hath prophesied against this city, as ye have heard with your ears. 12 Then spake Jeremiah unto all the princes and to all the people, saying, The Lord sent me to prophesy against this house and against this city all the words that ye have heard. 13 Therefore now amend your ways and your doings, and obey the voice of the Lord your God; and the Lord will repent him of the evil that he hath pronounced against you. 14 As for me, behold, I am in your hand: do with me as seemeth good and meet unto you. 15 But know ye for certain, that if ye put me to death, ye shall surely bring innocent blood upon yourselves, and upon this city, and upon the inhabitants thereof: for of a truth the Lord hath sent me unto you to speak all these words in your ears.

16 Then said the princes and all the people unto the priests and to the prophets; This man is not worthy to die: for he hath spoken to us in the name of the Lord our God. 17 Then rose up certain of the elders of the land, and spake to all the assembly of the people, saying, 18 Micah the Morasthite prophesied in the days of Hezekiah king of Judah, and spake to all the people of Judah, saying, Thus saith the Lord of hosts;

> Zion shall be plowed like a field,
> And Jerusalem shall become heaps,
> And the mountain of the house as the high places of a forest.

19 Did Hezekiah king of Judah and all Judah put him at all to death? did he not fear the Lord, and besought the Lord, and the Lord re-

pented him of the evil which he had pronounced against them? Thus might we procure great evil against our souls.

20 And there was also a man that prophesied in the name of the Lord, Urijah the son of Shemaiah of Kirjath-jearim, who prophesied against this city and against this land according to all the words of Jeremiah: 21 And when Jehoiakim the king, with all his mighty men, and all the princes, heard his words, the king sought to put him to death: but when Urijah heard it, he was afraid, and fled, and went into Egypt; 22 And Jehoiakim the king sent men into Egypt, namely, Elnathan the son of Achbor, and certain men with him into Egypt. 23 And they fetched forth Urijah out of Egypt, and brought him unto Jehoiakim the king; who slew him with the sword, and cast his dead body into the graves of the common people. 24 Nevertheless, the hand of Ahikam the son of Shaphan was with Jeremiah, that they should not give him into the hand of the people and put him to death.

## THE BABYLONIAN CAPTIVITY PREDICTED

25 The word that came to Jeremiah concerning all the people of Judah, in the fourth year of Jehoiakim the son of Josiah king of Judah, that was the first year of Nebuchadrezzar king of Babylon; 2 The which Jeremiah the prophet spake unto all the people of Judah, and to all the inhabitants of Jerusalem, saying,

3 From the thirteenth year of Josiah the son of Amon king of Judah, even unto this day, that is the three and twentieth year, the word of the Lord hath come unto me, and I have spoken unto you, rising early and speaking; but ye have not hearkened. 4 And the Lord hath sent unto you all his servants the prophets, rising early and sending them; but ye have not hearkened, nor inclined your ear to hear. 5 They said, Turn ye again now every one from his evil way, and from the evil of your doings, and dwell in the land that the Lord hath given unto you and to your fathers for ever and ever: 6 And go not after other gods to serve them, and to worship them, and provoke me not to anger with the works of your hands; and I will do you no hurt. 7 Yet ye have not hearkened unto me, saith the Lord; that ye might provoke me to anger with the works of your hands to your own hurt.

8 Therefore thus saith the Lord of hosts; Because ye have not heard my words, 9 Behold, I will send and take all the families of the north, saith the Lord, and Nebuchadrezzar the king of Babylon, my servant, and will bring them against this land, and against the inhabitants thereof, and against all these nations round about, and will utterly destroy them, and make them an astonishment, and a hissing, and perpetual desolations. 10 Moreover I will take from them the voice of mirth, and the voice of gladness, the voice of the bridegroom, and the voice of the bride, the sound of the millstones, and the light of the candle. 11 And this whole land shall be a desolation, and an

astonishment; and these nations shall serve the king of Babylon seventy years. 12 And it shall come to pass, when seventy years are accomplished, that I will punish the king of Babylon, and that nation, saith the Lord, for their iniquity, and the land of the Chaldeans, and will make it perpetual desolations. 13 And I will bring upon that land all my words which I have pronounced against it, even all that is written in this book, which Jeremiah hath prophesied against all the nations. 14 For many nations and great kings shall serve themselves of them also: and I will recompense them according to their deeds, and according to the works of their own hands.

36 And it came to pass in the fourth year of Jehoiakim the son of Josiah king of Judah, that this word came unto Jeremiah from the Lord, saying, 2 Take thee a roll of a book, and write therein all the words that I have spoken unto thee against Israel, and against Judah, and against all the nations, from the day I spake unto thee, from the days of Josiah, even unto this day. 3 It may be that the house of Judah will hear all the evil which I purpose to do unto them; that they may return every man from his evil way; that I may forgive their iniquity and their sin.

4 Then Jeremiah called Baruch the son of Neriah: and Baruch wrote from the mouth of Jeremiah all the words of the Lord, which he had spoken unto him, upon a roll of a book. 5 And Jeremiah commanded Baruch, saying, I am shut up; I cannot go into the house of the Lord: 6 Therefore go thou, and read in the roll, which thou hast written from my mouth, the words of the Lord in the ears of the people in the Lord's house upon the fasting day: and also thou shalt read them in the ears of all Judah that come out of their cities. 7 It may be they will present their supplication before the Lord, and will return every one from his evil way: for great is the anger and the fury that the Lord hath pronounced against this people. 8 And Baruch the son of Neriah did according to all that Jeremiah the prophet commanded him, reading in the book the words of the Lord in the Lord's house.

9 And it came to pass in the fifth year of Jehoiakim the son of Josiah king of Judah, in the ninth month, that they proclaimed a fast before the Lord to all the people in Jerusalem, and to all the people that came from the cities of Judah unto Jerusalem. 10 Then read Baruch in the book the words of Jeremiah in the house of the Lord, in the chamber of Gemariah the son of Shaphan the scribe, in the higher court, at the entry of the new gate of the Lord's house, in the ears of all the people. 11 When Michaiah the son of Gemariah, the son of Shaphan, had heard out of the book all the words of the Lord, 12 Then he went down into the king's house, into the scribe's chamber: and, lo, all the princes sat there, even Elishama the scribe, and Delaiah the son of Shemaiah, and Elnathan the son of Achbor, and Gemariah the

son of Shaphan, and Zedekiah the son of Hananiah, and all the princes. 13 Then Michaiah declared unto them all the words that he had heard, when Baruch read the book in the ears of the people. 14 Therefore all the princes sent Jehudi the son of Nethaniah, the son of Shelemiah, the son of Cushi, unto Baruch, saying, Take in thine hand the roll wherein thou hast read in the ears of the people, and come. So Baruch the son of Neriah took the roll in his hand, and came unto them. 15 And they said unto him, Sit down now, and read it in our ears. So Baruch read it in their ears. 16 Now it came to pass, when they had heard all the words, they were afraid both one and other, and said unto Baruch, We will surely tell the king of all these words. 17 And they asked Baruch, saying, Tell us now, How didst thou write all these words at his mouth? 18 Then Baruch answered them, He pronounced all these words unto me with his mouth, and I wrote them with ink in the book. 19 Then said the princes unto Baruch, Go, hide thee, thou and Jeremiah; and let no man know where ye be.

20 And they went in to the king into the court, but they laid up the roll in the chamber of Elishama the scribe, and told all the words in the ears of the king. 21 So the king sent Jehudi to fetch the roll; and he took it out of Elishama the scribe's chamber. And Jehudi read it in the ears of the king, and in the ears of all the princes which stood beside the king. 22 Now the king sat in the winter house in the ninth month: and there was a fire on the hearth burning before him. 23 And it came to pass, that when Jehudi had read three or four leaves, he cut it with the penknife, and cast it into the fire that was on the hearth, until all the roll was consumed in the fire that was on the hearth. 24 Yet they were not afraid, nor rent their garments, neither the king, nor any of his servants that heard all these words. 25 Nevertheless Elnathan and Delaiah and Gemariah had made intercession to the king that he would not burn the roll; but he would not hear them. 26 But the king commanded Jerahmeel the son of Hammelech, and Seraiah the son of Azriel, and Shelemiah the son of Abdeel, to take Baruch the scribe and Jeremiah the prophet: but the Lord hid them.

27 Then the word of the Lord came to Jeremiah, after that the king had burned the roll, and the words which Baruch wrote at the mouth of Jeremiah, saying, 28 Take thee again another roll, and write in it all the former words that were in the first roll, which Jehoiakim the king of Judah hath burned. 29 And thou shalt say to Jehoiakim king of Judah, Thus saith the Lord; Thou hast burned this roll, saying, Why hast thou written therein, saying, The king of Babylon shall certainly come and destroy this land, and shall cause to cease from thence man and beast? 30 Therefore thus saith the Lord of Jehoiakim king of Judah; He shall have none to sit upon the throne of David: and his dead body shall be cast out in the day to the heat, and in the night to the frost. 31 And I will punish him and his seed and his servants for their iniquity; and I will bring upon them, and upon the inhabitants

of Jerusalem, and upon the men of Judah, all the evil that I have pronounced against them; but they hearkened not.

32 Then took Jeremiah another roll, and gave it to Baruch the scribe, the son of Neriah; who wrote therein from the mouth of Jeremiah all the words of the book which Jehoiakim king of Judah had burned in the fire: and there were added besides unto them many like words.

## JEREMIAH IN THE STOCKS

20 Now Pashur the son of Immer the priest, who was also chief governor in the house of the Lord, heard that Jeremiah prophesied these things. 2 Then Pashur smote Jeremiah the prophet, and put him in the stocks that were in the high gate of Benjamin, which was by the house of the Lord. 3 And it came to pass on the morrow, that Pashur brought forth Jeremiah out of the stocks. Then said Jeremiah unto him, The Lord hath not called thy name Pashur, but Magormissabib.[1] 4 For thus saith the Lord, Behold, I will make thee a terror to thyself, and to all thy friends: and they shall fall by the sword of their enemies, and thine eyes shall behold it: and I will give all Judah into the hand of the king of Babylon, and he shall carry them captive into Babylon, and shall slay them with the sword. 5 Moreover I will deliver all the strength of this city, and all the labors thereof, and all the precious things thereof, and all the treasures of the kings of Judah will I give into the hand of their enemies, which shall spoil them, and take them, and carry them to Babylon. 6 And thou, Pashur, and all that dwell in thine house, shall go into captivity: and thou shalt come to Babylon, and there thou shalt die, and shalt be buried there, thou, and all thy friends, to whom thou hast prophesied lies.

## Jeremiah's Confessions

*To those around him, Jeremiah seemed a man of indomitable courage, whose resolution never wavered even under total rejection, scorn, abuse, and physical persecution. In reality, however, he was deeply sensitive to the ill will his message brought upon him. Far from being a mere parrot of God, he cried out in protest to God against having to assume the role to which he had been called. .Sometimes he would pray for those who persecuted him, and always he knew that what he spoke was for their good, but he could also call down curses upon them. A number of passages from Jeremiah's "confessions" are brought together here.*

[1] Jeremiah denounces Pashur by declaring that his name is changed, and by giving him a new name which means "a terror on all sides."

# *Jeremiah*

**20** 7 O Lord, thou hast deceived me, and I was deceived:
Thou art stronger than I, and hast prevailed:
I am in derision daily,
Every one mocketh me
8 For since I spake, I cried out,
I cried violence and spoil;
Because the word of the Lord was made
A reproach unto me, and a derision, daily.
9 Then I said, I will not make mention of him,
Nor speak any more in his name
But his word was in mine heart as a burning fire
Shut up in my bones,
And I was weary with forbearing,
And I could not stay.

**15** 10 Woe is me, my mother, that thou hast borne me
A man of strife and a man of contention to the whole earth!
I have neither lent on usury, nor men have lent to me on
usury;
Yet every one of them doth curse me.
15 O Lord, thou knowest:
Remember me, and visit me,
And revenge me of my persecutors;
Take me not away in thy long-suffering:
Know that for thy sake I have suffered rebuke.
16 Thy words were found, and I did eat them;
And thy word was unto me the joy and rejoicing of mine
heart:
For I am called by thy name,
O Lord God of hosts.
17 I sat not in the assembly of the mockers, nor rejoiced;
I sat alone because of thy hand:
For thou hast filled me with indignation.
18 Why is my pain perpetual,
And my wound incurable, which refuseth to be healed?
Wilt thou be altogether unto me as a liar,
And as waters that fail?
19 Therefore thus saith the Lord,
If thou return, then will I bring thee again,
And thou shalt stand before me:
And if thou take forth the precious from the vile,
Thou shalt be as my mouth:
Let them return unto thee;
But return not thou unto them.

20 And I will make thee unto this people
A fenced brazen wall:
And they shall fight against thee,
But they shall not prevail against thee:
For I am with thee
To save thee and to deliver thee,
Saith the Lord.
21 And I will deliver thee out of the hand of the wicked,
And I will redeem thee out of the hand of the terrible.

17   9 The heart is deceitful above all things, and desperately wicked:
Who can know it?
14 Heal me, O Lord, and I shall be healed;
Save me, and I shall be saved:
For thou art my praise.
15 Behold, they say unto me,
Where is the word of the Lord?
Let it come now.
16 As for me, I have not hastened from being a pastor to follow
thee:[1]
Neither have I desired the woeful day; thou knowest:
That which came out of my lips was right before thee.
17 Be not a terror unto me:
Thou art my hope in the day of evil.
18 Let them be confounded that persecute me, but let not me
be confounded:
Let them be dismayed, but let not me be dismayed:
Bring upon them the day of evil,
And destroy them with double destruction.

## False Prophets

*Not the least of Jeremiah's troubles came from the false
prophets and comfortable priests who, in their own self-seeking,
found that telling people what they wanted to hear was more
profitable than telling them the truth.*

## *Jeremiah*

14   13 Then said I, Ah, Lord God! behold, the prophets say unto
them, Ye shall not see the sword, neither shall ye have famine; but I
will give you assured peace in this place. 14 Then the Lord said unto
me, The prophets prophesy lies in my name: I sent them not, neither

---

[1] I.e., Jeremiah has not fled his vocation as a pastor serving God.

315

have I commanded them, neither spake unto them: they prophesy
unto you a false vision and divination, and a thing of nought, and the
deceit of their heart.

8  10 From the prophet even unto the priest
Every one dealeth falsely.
11 For they have healed the hurt of the daughter of my people
slightly,
Saying, Peace, peace; when there is no peace.
12 Were they ashamed when they had committed abomination?
Nay, they were not at all ashamed,
Neither could they blush.
15 We looked for peace, but no good came;
And for a time of health, and behold trouble!
21 For the hurt of the daughter of my people am I hurt;
I am black; astonishment hath taken hold on me.
22 Is there no balm in Gilead?
Is there no physician there?
Why then is not the health
Of the daughter of my people recovered?

9  1 Oh that my head were waters,
And mine eyes a fountain of tears,
That I might weep day and night
For the slain of the daughter of my people!

23 15 Therefore thus saith the Lord of hosts concerning the
prophets;
Behold, I will feed them with wormwood,
And make them drink the water of gall:
For from the prophets of Jerusalem
Is profaneness gone forth into all the land.
16 Thus saith the Lord of hosts,
Hearken not unto the words of the prophets that prophesy
unto you;
They make you vain:
They speak a vision of their own heart,
And not out of the mouth of the Lord.
17 They say still unto them that despise me,
The Lord hath said, Ye shall have peace;
And they say unto every one that walketh after the imagina-
tion of his own heart,
No evil shall come upon you.
22 But if they had stood in my counsel,
And had caused my people to hear my words,
Then they should have turned them from their evil way,
And from the evil of their doings.

## Final Judgment of King Jehoiakim

*Jehoiakim's reign had been marked by the king's concern for his own luxury rather than for the welfare of his people, by oppression, injustice, and idolatry. The final judgment of Jehoiakim, after his death, is given below.*

# *Jeremiah*

**22** 13 Woe unto him that buildeth his house by unrighteousness,
And his chambers by wrong;
That useth his neighbor's service without wages,
And giveth him not for his work;
14 That saith, I will build me a wide house
And large chambers,
And cutteth him out windows;
And it is ceiled with cedar,
And painted with vermilion.
15 Shalt thou reign, because thou closest thyself in cedar?
Did not thy father eat and drink,
And do judgment and justice,
And then it was well with him?
16 He judged the cause of the poor and needy;
Then it was well with him:
Was not this to know me?
Saith the Lord.
17 But thine eyes and thine heart
Are not but for thy covetousness,
And for to shed innocent blood,
And for oppression, and for violence, to do it.
18 Therefore thus saith the Lord concerning Jehoiakim the son
of Josiah king of Judah;
They shall not lament for him, saying,
Ah my brother! or, Ah sister!
They shall not lament for him, saying,
Ah lord! or, Ah his glory!
19 He shall be buried with the burial of an ass,
Drawn and cast forth beyond the gates of Jerusalem.
20 Go up to Lebanon, and cry;
And lift up thy voice in Bashan,
And cry from the passages:
For all thy lovers are destroyed.
21 I spake unto thee in thy prosperity;
But thou saidst, I will not hear.

317

This hath been thy manner from thy youth,
That thou obeyedst not my voice.
22 The wind shall eat up all thy pastors,
And thy lovers shall go into captivity:
Surely then shalt thou be ashamed and confounded
For all thy wickedness.

## Zedekiah's Accession

*Between Jehoiakim and Zedekiah, there was the three-month reign of Jehoiakim's eighteen-year-old son Jehoiachin, a reign which ended with the first Babylonian capture of Jerusalem and the deportation of ten thousand Jews by the Babylonians. Before departing, the Babylonians placed Jehoiakim's brother Zedekiah upon the throne to rule Judah as their vassal. Jeremiah thereupon speaks to Zedekiah of the practical impossibility of throwing off the yoke of Babylon, whereupon he comes into immediate conflict with a representative of the false prophets. The encounter between this man, Hananiah by name, and Jeremiah is revealing. Jeremiah would like to believe that the captivity of the ten thousand will soon be over, but he will not yield to wishful thinking. He then writes to the captives, advising them to take up their normal lives in Babylon, and even to seek the good of the city to which they have been deported. The advice must have seemed revolutionary, showing as it did that God could be served anywhere, even in captivity, and not merely in the holy land of promise.*

# *Jeremiah*

27 In the beginning of the reign of Zedekiah the son of Josiah king of Judah came this word unto Jeremiah from the Lord, saying, 2 Thus saith the Lord to me; Make thee bonds and yokes, and put them upon thy neck, 3 And send them to the king of Edom, and to the king of Moab, and to the king of the Ammonites, and to the king of Tyrus, and to the king of Zidon, by the hand of the messengers which come to Jerusalem unto Zedekiah king of Judah; 4 And command them to say unto their masters, Thus saith the Lord of hosts, the God of Israel; Thus shall ye say unto your masters; 5 I have made the earth, the man and the beast that are upon the ground, by my great power and by my outstretched arm, and have given it unto whom it seemed meet unto me. 6 And now have I given all these lands into the hand of Nebuchadnezzar the king of Babylon, my servant; and the beasts of the field have I given him also to serve him. 7 And all nations shall serve him, and his son, and his son's son,

until the very time of his land come: and then many nations and great kings shall serve themselves of him. 8 And it shall come to pass, that the nation and kingdom which will not serve the same Nebuchadnezzar the king of Babylon, and that will not put their neck under the yoke of the king of Babylon, that nation will I punish, saith the Lord, with the sword, and with the famine, and with the pestilence, until I have consumed them by his hand. 9 Therefore hearken not ye to your prophets, nor to your diviners, nor to your dreamers, nor to your enchanters, nor to your sorcerers, which speak unto you, saying, Ye shall not serve the king of Babylon: 10 For they prophesy a lie unto you, to remove you far from your land; and that I should drive you out, and ye should perish. 11 But the nations that bring their neck under the yoke of the king of Babylon, and serve him, those will I let remain still in their own land, saith the Lord; and they shall till it, and dwell therein.

12 I spake also to Zedekiah king of Judah according to all these words, saying, Bring your necks under the yoke of the king of Babylon, and serve him and his people, and live. 13 Why will ye die, thou and thy people, by the sword, by the famine, and by the pestilence, as the Lord hath spoken against the nation that will not serve the king of Babylon? 14 Therefore hearken not unto the words of the prophets that speak unto you, saying, Ye shall not serve the king of Babylon: for they prophesy a lie unto you. 15 For I have not sent them, saith the Lord, yet they prophesy a lie in my name; that I might drive you out, and that ye might perish, ye, and the prophets that prophesy unto you.

16 Also I spake to the priests and to all this people, saying, Thus saith the Lord; Hearken not to the words of your prophets that prophesy unto you, saying, Behold, the vessels of the Lord's house shall now shortly be brought again from Babylon: for they prophesy a lie unto you. 17 Hearken not unto them; serve the king of Babylon, and live: wherefore should this city be laid waste?

28 And it came to pass the same year, in the beginning of the reign of Zedekiah king of Judah, in the fourth year, and in the fifth month, that Hananiah the son of Azur the prophet, which was of Gibeon, spake unto me in the house of the Lord, in the presence of the priests and of all the people, saying, 2 Thus speaketh the Lord of hosts, the God of Israel, saying, I have broken the yoke of the king of Babylon. 3 Within two full years will I bring into this place all the vessels of the Lord's house, that Nebuchadnezzar king of Babylon took away from this place, and carried them to Babylon: 4 And I will bring again to this place Jeconiah the son of Jehoiakim king of Judah, with all the captives of Judah, that went into Babylon, saith the Lord: for I will break the yoke of the king of Babylon.

5 Then the prophet Jeremiah said unto the prophet Hananiah in the presence of the priests, and in the presence of all the people that stood in the house of the Lord, 6 Even the prophet Jeremiah said,

Amen: the Lord do so: the Lord perform thy words which thou hast prophesied, to bring again the vessels of the Lord's house, and all that is carried away captive, from Babylon into this place. 7 Nevertheless, hear thou now this word that I speak in thine ears, and in the ears of all the people; 8 The prophets that have been before me and before thee of old prophesied both against many countries, and against great kingdoms, of war, and of evil, and of pestilence. 9 The prophet which prophesieth of peace, when the word of the prophet shall come to pass, then shall the prophet be known, that the Lord hath truly sent him.

10 Then Hananiah the prophet took the yoke from off the prophet Jeremiah's neck, and brake it. 11 And Hananiah spake in the presence of all the people, saying, Thus saith the Lord; Even so will I break the yoke of Nebuchadnezzar king of Babylon from the neck of all nations within the space of two full years. And the prophet Jeremiah went his way.

12 Then the word of the Lord came unto Jeremiah the prophet, after that Hananiah the prophet had broken the yoke from off the neck of the prophet Jeremiah, saying, 13 Go and tell Hananiah, saying, Thus saith the Lord; Thou hast broken the yokes of wood; but thou shalt make for them yokes of iron. 14 For thus saith the Lord of hosts, the God of Israel; I have put a yoke of iron upon the neck of all these nations, that they may serve Nebuchadnezzar king of Babylon; and they shall serve him: and I have given him the beasts of the field also.

15 Then said the prophet Jeremiah unto Hananiah the prophet, Hear now, Hananiah; The Lord hath not sent thee; but thou makest this people to trust in a lie. 16 Therefore thus saith the Lord; Behold, I will cast thee from off the face of the earth: this year thou shalt die, because thou hast taught rebellion against the Lord. 17 So Hananiah the prophet died the same year in the seventh month.

29 Now these are the words of the letter that Jeremiah the prophet sent from Jerusalem unto the residue of the elders which were carried away captives, and to the priests, and to the prophets, and to all the people whom Nebuchadnezzar had carried away captive from Jerusalem to Babylon; 2 (After that Jeconiah the king, and the queen, and the eunuchs, the princes of Judah and Jerusalem, and the carpenters, and the smiths, were departed from Jerusalem;) 3 By the hand of Elasah the son of Shaphan, and Gemariah the son of Hilkiah, (whom Zedekiah king of Judah sent unto Babylon to Nebuchadnezzar king of Babylon) saying,

4 Thus saith the Lord of hosts, the God of Israel, unto all that are carried away captives, whom I have caused to be carried away from Jerusalem unto Babylon;

5 Build ye houses, and dwell in them; and plant gardens, and eat the fruit of them; 6 Take ye wives, and beget sons and daughters; and take wives for your sons, and give your daughters to husbands, that they may bear sons and daughters; that ye may be increased there, and

not diminished. 7 And seek the peace of the city whither I have caused you to be carried away captives, and pray unto the Lord for it: for in the peace thereof shall ye have peace.

## The Siege, and a Brief Respite

*Eventually Zedekiah follows the guidance of those who assure him that, if he rebels, God will deliver the chosen people from their enemies. When Zedekiah does rebel, the Babylonians come to besiege Jerusalem, and the final act of this particular drama draws to a close. The siege is briefly interrupted when the Babylonian forces withdraw to defeat an invading army from Egypt. The following incidents occur during this interval.*

# *Jeremiah*

37 And king Zedekiah the son of Josiah reigned instead of Coniah[1] the son of Jehoiakim, whom Nebuchadrezzar king of Babylon made king in the land of Judah. 2 But neither he, nor his servants, nor the people of the land, did hearken unto the words of the Lord, which he spake by the prophet Jeremiah.

3 And Zedekiah the king sent Jehucal the son of Shelemiah and Zephaniah the son of Maaseiah the priest to the prophet Jeremiah, saying, Pray now unto the Lord our God for us. 4 Now Jeremiah came in and went out among the people: for they had not put him into prison. 5 Then Pharaoh's army was come forth out of Egypt: and when the Chaldeans that besieged Jerusalem heard tidings of them, they departed from Jerusalem. 6 Then came the word of the Lord unto the prophet Jeremiah, saying, 7 Thus saith the Lord, the God of Israel; Thus shall ye say to the king of Judah, that sent you unto me to inquire of me; Behold, Pharoah's army, which is come forth to help you, shall return to Egypt into their own land. 8 And the Chaldeans shall come again, and fight against this city, and take it, and burn it with fire. 9 Thus saith the Lord; Deceive not yourselves, saying, The Chaldeans shall surely depart from us: for they shall not depart. 10 For though ye had smitten the whole army of the Chaldeans that fight against you, and there remained but wounded men among them, yet should they rise up every man in his tent, and burn this city with fire.

11 And it came to pass, that when the army of the Chaldeans was broken up from Jerusalem for fear of Pharaoh's army, 12 Then Jeremiah went forth out of Jerusalem to go into the land of Benjamin, to separate himself thence in the midst of the people. 13 And when he

[1] Another name for Jehoiachin.

was in the gate of Benjamin, a captain of the ward was there, whose name was Irijah, the son of Shelemiah, the son of Hananiah; and he took Jeremiah the prophet, saying, Thou fallest away to the Chaldeans. 14 Then said Jeremiah, It is false; I fall not away to the Chaldeans. But he hearkened not to him: so Irijah took Jeremiah, and brought him to the princes. 15 Wherefore the princes were wroth with Jeremiah, and smote him, and put him in prison in the house of Jonathan the scribe; for they had made that the prison.

16 When Jeremiah was entered into the dungeon, and into the cabins,[2] and Jeremiah had remained there many days; 17 Then Zedekiah the king sent, and took him out; and the king asked him secretly in his house, and said, Is there any word from the Lord? And Jeremiah said, There is: for, said he, thou shalt be delivered into the hand of the king of Babylon. 18 Moreover Jeremiah said unto king Zedekiah, What have I offended against thee, or against thy servants, or against this people, that ye have put me in prison? 19 Where are now your prophets which prophesied unto you, saying, The king of Babylon shall not come against you, nor against this land? 20 Therefore hear now, I pray thee, O my lord the king: let my supplication, I pray thee, be accepted before thee; that thou cause me not to return to the house of Jonathan the scribe, lest I die there. 21 Then Zedekiah the king commanded that they should commit Jeremiah into the court of the prison, and that they should give him daily a piece of bread out of the bakers' street, until all the bread in the city were spent. Thus Jeremiah remained in the court of the prison.

## The Treatment of the Slaves

*During the early part of the siege of Jerusalem, Zedekiah ordered the release of all Hebrew slaves. As perpetual slavery was forbidden by divine law, and as the selling of the poor into slavery "for a pair of shoes" had been strongly denounced in the prophetic messages from God, this emancipation appears to have been a rather belated attempt to avert divine punishment. As soon as the siege was lifted, however, when the Babylonians turned aside to defeat the Egyptian force already referred to, the newly freed slaves were taken back into bondage. Jeremiah denounced this pious fraud in the following passage.*

## *Jeremiah*

34   8 This is the word that came unto Jeremiah from the Lord,
· after that the king Zedekiah had made a covenant with all the people

2 I.e., prison cells.

which were at Jerusalem, to proclaim liberty unto them; 9 That every man should let his manservant, and every man his maidservant, being a Hebrew or a Hebrewess, go free; that none should serve himself of them, to wit, of a Jew his brother. 10 Now when all the princes, and all the people, which had entered into the covenant, heard that every one should let his manservant, and every one his maidservant, go free, that none should serve themselves of them any more; then they obeyed, and let them go. 11 But afterwards they turned, and caused the servants and the handmaids, whom they had let go free, to return, and brought them into subjection for servants and for handmaids. 12 Therefore the word of the Lord came to Jeremiah from the Lord, saying,

13 Thus saith the Lord, the God of Israel; I made a covenant with your fathers in the day that I brought them forth out of the land of Egypt, out of the house of bondmen, saying, 14 At the end of seven years let ye go every man his brother a Hebrew, which hath been sold unto thee; and when he hath served thee six years, thou shalt let him go free from thee: but your fathers hearkened not unto me, neither inclined their ear. 15 And ye were now turned, and had done right in my sight, in proclaiming liberty every man to his neighbor; and ye had made a covenant before me in the house which is called by my name: 16 But ye turned and polluted my name, and caused every man his servant, and every man his handmaid, whom he had set at liberty at their pleasure, to return, and brought them into subjection, to be unto you for servants and for handmaids.

17 Therefore thus saith the Lord; Ye have not hearkened unto me, in proclaiming liberty, every one to his brother, and every man to his neighbor: behold, I proclaim a liberty for you, saith the Lord, to the sword, to the pestilence, and to the famine; and I will make you to be removed into all the kingdoms of the earth. 18 And I will give the men that have transgressed my covenant, which have not performed the words of the covenant which they had made before me, when they cut the calf in twain, and passed between the parts thereof,[1] 19 The princes of Judah, and the princes of Jerusalem, the eunuchs, and the priests, and all the people of the land, which passed between the parts of the calf; 20 I will even give them into the hand of their enemies, and into the hand of them that seek their life: and their dead bodies shall be for meat unto the fowls of the heaven, and to the beasts of the earth. 21 And Zedekiah king of Judah and his princes will I give into the hand of their enemies, and into the hand of them that seek their life, and into the hand of the king of Babylon's army, which are gone up from you. 22 Behold, I will command, saith the Lord, and cause them to return to this city; and they shall fight against it, and take it, and burn it with fire: and I will make the cities of Judah a desolation without an inhabitant.

[1] A symbolic act associated with making a contract or covenant with God. See Genesis 15:10.

323

## Jeremiah in the Cistern

*The Babylonians return to the siege of Jerusalem after they
have defeated the Egyptian army. Without hope for the rulers of
Jerusalem, Jeremiah counsels the people to leave the city before
its inevitable destruction, and to surrender themselves to the en-
circling forces. Thereupon Jeremiah's powerful enemies move to
silence him permanently.*

# *Jeremiah*

38 Then Shephatiah the son of Mattan, and Gedaliah the son of
Pashur, and Jucal the son of Shelemiah, and Pashur the son of Malchiah, heard the words that Jeremiah had spoken unto all the people,
saying, 2 Thus saith the Lord, He that remaineth in this city shall die
by the sword, by the famine, and by the pestilence: but he that goeth
forth to the Chaldeans shall live; for he shall have his life for a prey,
and shall live. 3 Thus saith the Lord, This city shall surely be given
into the hand of the king of Babylon's army, which shall take it.
4 Therefore the princes said unto the king, We beseech thee, let this
man be put to death: for thus he weakeneth the hands of the men
of war that remain in this city, and the hands of all the people, in
speaking such words unto them: for this man seeketh not the welfare
of this people, but the hurt. 5 Then Zedekiah the king said, Behold,
he is in your hand: for the king is not he that can do any thing against
you. 6 Then took they Jeremiah, and cast him into the dungeon of
Malchiah the son of Hammelech, that was in the court of the prison:
and they let down Jeremiah with cords. And in the dungeon there
was no water, but mire: so Jeremiah sunk in the mire.

7 Now when Ebed-melech the Ethiopian, one of the eunuchs which
was in the king's house, heard that they had put Jeremiah in the
dungeon; the king then sitting in the gate of Benjamin; 8 Ebed-
melech went forth out of the king's house, and spake to the king,
saying, 9 My lord the king, these men have done evil in all that they
have done to Jeremiah the prophet, whom they have cast into the
dungeon; and he is like to die for hunger in the place where he is:
for there is no more bread in the city. 10 Then the king commanded
Ebed-melech the Ethiopian, saying, Take from hence thirty men with
thee, and take up Jeremiah the prophet out of the dungeon, before he
die. 11 So Ebed-melech took the men with him, and went into the
house of the king under the treasury, and took thence old cast clouts
and old rotten rags, and let them down by cords into the dungeon to
Jeremiah. 12 And Ebed-melech the Ethiopian said unto Jeremiah,
Put now these old cast clouts and rotten rags under thine armholes
under the cords. And Jeremiah did so. 13 So they drew up Jeremiah

with cords, and took him up out of the dungeon: and Jeremiah remained in the court of the prison.

## Buying a Field

*Like the other prophets, Jeremiah never presented a picture of doom without any hope. Always there was the call to repentance and reform, and the promise of restoration after the people had been purged of their wickedness. Thus even in the face of a total defeat of Judah, a defeat which he increasingly saw as inevitable, Jeremiah was willing to take what little money was available to him in the doomed city of Jerusalem and "redeem" or purchase a field which belonged to one of his cousins and lay in territory occupied by the enemy. The gesture remains a magnificent symbol of hope and promise.*

## *Jeremiah*

32 The word that came to Jeremiah from the Lord in the tenth year of Zedekiah king of Judah, which was the eighteenth year of Nebuchadrezzar. 2 For then the king of Babylon's army besieged Jerusalem: and Jeremiah the prophet was shut up in the court of the prison, which was in the king of Judah's house.

6 And Jeremiah said, The word of the Lord came unto me, saying, 7 Behold, Hanameel the son of Shallum thine uncle shall come unto thee, saying, Buy thee my field that is in Anathoth: for the right of redemption is thine to buy it. 8 So Hanameel mine uncle's son came to me in the court of the prison according to the word of the Lord, and said unto me, Buy my field, I pray thee, that is in Anathoth, which is in the country of Benjamin: for the right of inheritance is thine, and the redemption is thine; buy it for thyself. Then I knew that this was the word of the Lord. 9 And I bought the field of Hanameel my uncle's son, that was in Anathoth, and weighed him the money, even seventeen shekels of silver. 10 And I subscribed the evidence, and sealed it, and took witnesses, and weighed him the money in the balances. 11 So I took the evidence of the purchase, both that which was sealed according to the law and custom, and that which was open: 12 And I gave the evidence of the purchase unto Baruch the son of Neriah, the son of Maaseiah, in the sight of Hanameel mine uncle's son, and in the presence of the witnesses that subscribed the book of the purchase, before all the Jews that sat in the court of the prison. 13 And I charged Baruch before them, saying, 14 Thus saith the Lord of hosts, the God of Israel; Take these evidences, this evidence of the purchase, both which is sealed, and this evidence which is open; and put them in an earthen vessel, that they may continue many days.

15 For thus saith the Lord of hosts, the God of Israel; Houses and fields and vineyards shall be possessed again in this land.

36 And now therefore thus saith the Lord, the God of Israel, concerning this city, whereof ye say, It shall be delivered into the hand of the king of Babylon by the sword, and by the famine, and by the pestilence; 37 Behold, I will gather them out of all countries, whither I have driven them in mine anger, and in my fury, and in great wrath; and I will bring them again unto this place, and I will cause them to dwell safely: 38 And they shall be my people, and I will be their God: 39 And I will give them one heart, and one way, that they may fear me for ever, for the good of them, and of their children after them: 40 And I will make an everlasting covenant with them, that I will not turn away from them, to do them good; but I will put my fear in their hearts, that they shall not depart from me. 41 Yea, I will rejoice over them to do them good, and I will plant them in this land assuredly with my whole heart and with my whole soul. 42 For thus saith the Lord; Like as I have brought all this great evil upon this people, so will I bring upon them all the good that I have promised them. 43 And fields shall be bought in this land, whereof ye say, It is desolate without man or beast; it is given into the hand of the Chaldeans. 44 Men shall buy fields for money, and subscribe evidences, and seal them, and take witnesses in the land of Benjamin, and in the places about Jerusalem, and in the cities of Judah, and in the cities of the mountains, and in the cities of the valley, and in the cities of the south: for I will cause their captivity to return, saith the Lord.

## The Final Warning to Zedekiah

*Late in the siege, the king calls again for Jeremiah, and confers with him for the last time. By this point, the only hope lies in surrender, as Jeremiah once more tells the King, but to no avail.*

# *Jeremiah*

38 14 Then Zedekiah the king sent, and took Jeremiah the prophet unto him into the third entry that is in the house of the Lord: and the king said unto Jeremiah, I will ask thee a thing; hide nothing from me. 15 Then Jeremiah said unto Zedekiah, If I declare it unto thee, wilt thou not surely put me to death? and if I give thee counsel, wilt thou not hearken unto me? 16 So Zedekiah the king sware secretly unto Jeremiah, saying, As the Lord liveth, that made us this soul, I will not put thee to death, neither will I give thee into the hand of these men that seek thy life.

17 Then said Jeremiah unto Zedekiah, Thus saith the Lord, the God

of hosts, the God of Israel; If thou wilt assuredly go forth[1] unto the king of Babylon's princes, then thy soul shall live, and this city shall not be burned with fire; and thou shalt live, and thine house: 18 But if thou wilt not go forth to the king of Babylon's princes, then shall this city be given into the hand of the Chaldeans, and they shall burn it with fire, and thou shalt not escape out of their hand. 19 And Zedekiah the king said unto Jeremiah, I am afraid of the Jews that are fallen to the Chaldeans, lest they deliver me into their hand, and they mock me. 20 But Jeremiah said, They shall not deliver thee. Obey, I beseech thee, the voice of the Lord, which I speak unto thee: so it shall be well unto thee, and thy soul shall live. 21 But if thou refuse to go forth, this is the word that the Lord hath showed me: 22 And, behold, all the women that are left in the king of Judah's house shall be brought forth to the king of Babylon's princes, and those women shall say,

Thy friends have set thee on,
And have prevailed against thee:
Thy feet are sunk in the mire,
And they are turned away back.

23 So they shall bring out all thy wives and thy children to the Chaldeans: and thou shalt not escape out of their hand, but shalt be taken by the hand of the king of Babylon: and thou shalt cause this city to be burned with fire.

24 Then said Zedekiah unto Jeremiah, Let no man know of these words, and thou shalt not die. 25 But if the princes hear that I have talked with thee, and they come unto thee, and say unto thee, Declare unto us now what thou hast said unto the king, hide it not from us, and we will not put thee to death; also what the king said unto thee: 26 Then thou shalt say unto them, I presented my supplication before the king, that he would not cause me to return to Jonathan's house, to die there. 27 Then came all the princes unto Jeremiah, and asked him: and he told them according to all these words that the king had commanded. So they left off speaking with him; for the matter was not perceived. 28 So Jeremiah abode in the court of the prison until the day that Jerusalem was taken: and he was there when Jerusalem was taken.

# The End of the Southern Kingdom

*The destruction of Judah follows swiftly, and the Babylonians take many of the people into captivity. They do, however, leave a "remnant" behind, under the governorship of Gedaliah, and the land is divided among the poorer classes. But one of the royal heirs, Ishmael, and a faction of the dispossessed nobility rebel*

[1] I.e., surrender and make peace.

327

against Gedaliah and assassinate him and others in a futile blood bath. *After the assassin has fled, the leaders of the "remnant" consult Jeremiah as to whether they, too, should abandon the land, and go to Egypt. Jeremiah counsels them to remain in their land and seek to rebuild it according to the will of God. If they do so in righteousness, they will again have peace and can reconstruct a righteous community. The leaders of the remnant ignore this advice, however, and elect to return to Egypt. The action is highly significant, representing the total and ultimate rejection of all that God had done for Israel since bringing them out of the first Egyptian bondage. Now they choose to return — a complete apostasy. It is clear that the return is a repudiation of the true God in favor of idolatrous worship. From this apostasy, only a very few will extricate themselves to re-enter the land of promise. Exodus has been re-enacted in reverse, and Judah no longer exists. Jeremiah has predicted the return out of Babylon of a purified people — but not again from Egypt.*

# *Jeremiah*

39 In the ninth year of Zedekiah king of Judah, in the tenth month, came Nebuchadrezzar king of Babylon and all his army against Jerusalem, and they besieged it. 2 And in the eleventh year of Zedekiah, in the fourth month, the ninth day of the month, the city was broken up. 3 And all the princes of the king of Babylon came in, and sat in the middle gate, even Nergal-sharezer, Samgar-nebo, Sarsechim, Rab-saris, Nergal-sharezer, Rab-mag, with all the residue of the princes of the king of Babylon.

4 And it came to pass, that when Zedekiah the king of Judah saw them, and all the men of war, then they fled, and went forth out of the city by night, by the way of the king's garden, by the gate betwixt the two walls: and he went out the way of the plain. 5 But the Chaldeans' army pursued after them, and overtook Zedekiah in the plains of Jericho: and when they had taken him, they brought him up to Nebuchadnezzar king of Babylon to Riblah in the land of Hamath, where he gave judgment upon him. 6 Then the king of Babylon slew the sons of Zedekiah in Riblah before his eyes: also the king of Babylon slew all the nobles of Judah. 7 Moreover he put out Zedekiah's eyes, and bound him with chains, to carry him to Babylon. 8 And the Chaldeans burned the king's house, and the houses of the people, with fire, and brake down the walls of Jerusalem. 9 Then Nebuzar-adan the captain of the guard carried away captive into Babylon the remnant of the people that remained in the city, and those that fell away, that fell to him, with the rest of the people that remained. 10 But Nebuzar-adan the captain of the guard left of the poor of the people, which had

nothing, in the land of Judah, and gave them vineyards and fields at the same time. 11 Now Nebuchadrezzar king of Babylon gave charge concerning Jeremiah to Nebuzar-adan the captain of the guard, saying, 12 Take him, and look well to him, and do him no harm; but do unto him even as he shall say unto thee. 13 So Nebuzar-adan the captain of the guard sent, and Nebushasban, Rab-saris, and Nergal-sharezer, Rab-mag, and all the king of Babylon's princes; 14 Even they sent, and took Jeremiah out of the court of the prison, and committed him unto Gedaliah the son of Ahikam the son of Shaphan, that he should carry him home: so he dwelt among the people.

44 The word that came to Jeremiah concerning all the Jews which dwell in the land of Egypt, which dwell at Migdol, and at Tahpanhes, and at Noph, and in the country of Pathros, saying, 2 Thus saith the Lord of hosts, the God of Israel; Ye have seen all the evil that I have brought upon Jerusalem, and upon all the cities of Judah; and, behold, this day they are a desolation, and no man dwelleth therein; 3 Because of their wickedness which they have committed to provoke me to anger, in that they went to burn incense, and to serve other gods, whom they knew not, neither they, ye, nor your fathers. 4 Howbeit I sent unto you all my servants the prophets, rising early and sending them, saying, Oh, do not this abominable thing that I hate. 5 But they hearkened not, nor inclined their ear to turn from their wickedness, to burn no incense unto other gods. 6 Wherefore my fury and mine anger was poured forth, and was kindled in the cities of Judah and in the streets of Jerusalem; and they are wasted and desolate, as at this day. 7 Therefore now thus saith the Lord, the God of hosts, the God of Israel; Wherefore commit ye this great evil against your souls, to cut off from you man and woman, child and suckling, out of Judah, to leave you none to remain; 8 In that ye provoke me unto wrath with the works of your hands, burning incense unto other gods in the land of Egypt, whither ye be gone to dwell, that ye might cut yourselves off, and that ye might be a curse and a reproach among all the nations of the earth? 9 Have ye forgotten the wickedness of your fathers, and the wickedness of the kings of Judah, and the wickedness of their wives, and your own wickedness, and the wickedness of your wives, which they have committed in the land of Judah, and in the streets of Jerusalem? 10 They are not humbled even unto this day, neither have they feared, nor walked in my law, nor in my statutes, that I set before you and before your fathers.

11 Therefore thus saith the Lord of hosts, the God of Israel; Behold, I will set my face against you for evil, and to cut off all Judah. 12 And I will take the remnant of Judah, that have set their faces to go into the land of Egypt to sojourn there, and they shall all be consumed, and fall in the land of Egypt; they shall even be consumed by the sword and by the famine: they shall die, from the least even unto the

greatest, by the sword and by the famine: and they shall be an execration, and an astonishment, and a curse, and a reproach. 13 For I will punish them that dwell in the land of Egypt, as I have punished Jerusalem, by the sword, by the famine, and by the pestilence: 14 So that none of the remnant of Judah, which are gone into the land of Egypt to sojourn there, shall escape or remain, that they should return into the land of Judah, to the which they have a desire to return to dwell there.

# Exile and Return:
## The Prophets and Nehemiah

### Captivity and Release: Two Psalms

Poetry was integrally related to the total experience of the Biblical people. Below are two psalms concerning the Babylonian captivity and release from it. Nowhere in the literature of the world is the pathos of exile more beautifully expressed than in Psalm 137, though at the end the elegiac quality turns into the bitterness of imprecation. An entirely different mood is conveyed in Psalm 126, which celebrates the return of the captives and hope for a new age.

## Psalms

137    By the rivers of Babylon,
There we sat down, yea, we wept,
When we remembered Zion.
2 We hanged our harps
Upon the willows in the midst thereof.
3 For there they that carried us away captive required of us a
    song;
And they that wasted us required of us mirth, saying,
Sing us one of the songs of Zion.
4 How shall we sing the Lord's song
In a strange land?
5 If I forget thee, O Jerusalem,
Let my right hand forget her cunning.
6 If I do not remember thee,
Let my tongue cleave to the roof of my mouth;
If I prefer not Jerusalem
Above my chief joy.
7 Remember, O Lord, the children of Edom
In the day of Jerusalem;
Who said, Rase it, rase it,
Even to the foundation thereof.
8 O daughter of Babylon, who art to be destroyed;

Happy shall he be, that rewardeth thee
As thou hast served us.
9 Happy shall he be, that taketh and dasheth
Thy little ones against the stones.

126  When the Lord turned again the captivity of Zion,
We were like them that dream.
2 Then was our mouth filled with laughter,
And our tongue with singing:
Then said they among the heathen,
The Lord hath done great things for them.
3 The Lord hath done great things for us;
Whereof we are glad.
4 Turn again our captivity, O Lord,
As the streams in the south.
5 They that sow in tears
Shall reap in joy.
6 He that goeth forth and weepeth, bearing precious seed,
Shall doubtless come again with rejoicing, bringing his sheaves
with him.

## A Prophet in Exile: *Ezekiel*

*Ezekiel was taken into exile with the first group, which was removed by the Babylonians in 597 B.C. He strove to reform and re-fashion the exilic community. As a part of this mission, he asserted that men were not to be condemned for the sins of their fathers: although their nation had been uprooted because of earlier sins, they could themselves now repent and still serve God. He also prophesied the revival of Israel as a people, in the magnificent vision of the valley of dry bones.*

# *Ezekiel*

18  The word of the Lord came unto me again, saying, 2 What mean ye, that ye use this proverb concerning the land of Israel, saying,
The fathers have eaten sour grapes,
And the children's teeth are set on edge?
3 As I live, saith the Lord God, ye shall not have occasion any more to use this proverb in Israel. 4 Behold, all souls are mine; as the soul of the father, so also the soul of the son is mine: the soul that sinneth, it shall die.
5 But if a man be just, and do that which is lawful and right, 6 And hath not eaten upon the mountains, neither hath lifted up his eyes to the idols of the house of Israel, neither hath defiled his neigh-

bor's wife, neither hath come near to a menstruous woman, 7 And hath not oppressed any, but hath restored to the debtor his pledge, hath spoiled none by violence, hath given his bread to the hungry, and hath covered the naked with a garment; 8 He that hath not given forth upon usury, neither hath taken any increase, that hath withdrawn his hand from iniquity, hath executed true judgment between man and man, 9 Hath walked in my statutes, and hath kept my judgments, to deal truly; he is just, he shall surely live, saith the Lord God.

10 If he beget a son that is a robber, a shedder of blood, and that doeth the like to any one of these things, 11 And that doeth not any of those duties, but even hath eaten upon the mountains, and defiled his neighbor's wife, 12 Hath oppressed the poor and needy, hath spoiled by violence, hath not restored the pledge, and hath lifted up his eyes to the idols, hath committed abomination, 13 Hath given forth upon usury, and hath taken increase: shall he then live? he shall not live: he hath done all these abominations; he shall surely die; his blood shall be upon him.

14 Now, lo, if he beget a son, that seeth all his father's sins which he hath done, and considereth, and doeth not such like, 15 That hath not eaten upon the mountains, neither hath lifted up his eyes to the idols of the house of Israel, hath not defiled his neighbor's wife, 16 Neither hath oppressed any, hath not withholden the pledge, neither hath spoiled by violence, but hath given his bread to the hungry, and hath covered the naked with a garment, 17 That hath taken off his hand from the poor, that hath not received usury nor increase, hath executed my judgments, hath walked in my statutes; he shall not die for the iniquity of his father, he shall surely live. 18 As for his father, because he cruelly oppressed, spoiled his brother by violence, and did that which is not good among his people, lo, even he shall die in his iniquity. 19 Yet say ye, Why? doth not the son bear the iniquity of the father? When the son hath done that which is lawful and right, and hath kept all my statutes, and hath done them, he shall surely live. 20 The soul that sinneth, it shall die. The son shall not bear the iniquity of the father, neither shall the father bear the iniquity of the son: the righteousness of the righteous shall be upon him, and the wickedness of the wicked shall be upon him.

21 But if the wicked will turn from all his sins that he hath committed, and keep all my statutes, and do that which is lawful and right, he shall surely live, he shall not die. 22 All his transgressions that he hath committed, they shall not be mentioned unto him: in his righteousness that he hath done he shall live. 23 Have I any pleasure at all that the wicked should die? saith the Lord God: and not that he should return from his ways, and live?

24 But when the righteous turneth away from his righteousness, and committeth iniquity, and doeth according to all the abominations that the wicked man doeth, shall he live? All his righteousness that he hath done shall not be mentioned: in his trespass that he hath trespassed, and in his sin that he hath sinned, in them shall he die.

25 Yet ye say, The way of the Lord is not equal. Hear now, O house of Israel; Is not my way equal? are not your ways unequal? 26 When a righteous man turneth away from his righteousness, and committeth iniquity, and dieth in them; for his iniquity that he hath done shall he die. 27 Again, when the wicked man turneth away from his wickedness that he hath committed, and doeth that which is lawful and right, he shall save his soul alive. 28 Because he considereth, and turneth away from all his transgressions that he hath committed, he shall surely live, he shall not die. 29 Yet saith the house of Israel, The way of the Lord is not equal. O house of Israel, are not my ways equal? are not your ways unequal? 30 Therefore I will judge you, O house of Israel, every one according to his ways, saith the Lord God. Repent, and turn yourselves from all your transgressions; so iniquity shall not be your ruin. 31 Cast away from you all your transgressions, whereby ye have transgressed; and make you a new heart and a new spirit: for why will ye die, O house of Israel? 32 For I have no pleasure in the death of him that dieth, saith the Lord God: wherefore turn yourselves, and live ye.

33  10 Therefore, O thou son of man, speak unto the house of Israel; Thus ye speak, saying, If our transgressions and our sins be upon us, and we pine away in them, how should we then live? 11 Say unto them, As I live, saith the Lord God, I have no pleasure in the death of the wicked; but that the wicked turn from his way and live: turn ye, turn ye from your evil ways; for why will ye die, O house of Israel?

12 Therefore, thou son of man, say unto the children of thy people, The righteousness of the righteous shall not deliver him in the day of his transgression: as for the wickedness of the wicked, he shall not fall thereby in the day that he turneth from his wickedness; neither shall the righteous be able to live for his righteousness in the day that he sinneth. 13 When I shall say to the righteous, that he shall surely live; if he trust to his own righteousness, and commit iniquity, all his righteousness shall not be remembered; but for his iniquity that he hath committed, he shall die for it. 14 Again, when I say unto the wicked, Thou shalt surely die; if he turn from his sin, and do that which is lawful and right; 15 If the wicked restore the pledge, give again that he had robbed, walk in the statutes of life, without committing iniquity; he shall surely live, he shall not die. 16 None of his sins that he hath committed shall be mentioned unto him: he hath done that which is lawful and right; he shall surely live.

37  The hand of the Lord was upon me, and carried me out in the Spirit of the Lord, and set me down in the midst of the valley which was full of bones, 2 And caused me to pass by them round about: and, behold, there were very many in the open valley; and, lo, they were very dry. 3 And he said unto me, Son of man, can these bones

live? And I answered, O Lord God, thou knowest. 4 Again he said unto me, Prophesy upon these bones, and say unto them, O ye dry bones, hear the word of the Lord. 5 Thus saith the Lord God unto these bones; Behold, I will cause breath to enter into you, and ye shall live: 6 And I will lay sinews upon you, and will bring up flesh upon you, and cover you with skin, and put breath in you, and ye shall live; and ye shall know that I am the Lord. 7 So I prophesied as I was commanded: and as I prophesied, there was a noise, and behold a shaking, and the bones came together, bone to his bone. 8 And when I beheld, lo, the sinews and the flesh came up upon them, and the skin covered them above: but there was no breath in them. 9 Then said he unto me, Prophesy unto the wind, prophesy, son of man, and say to the wind, Thus saith the Lord God; Come from the four winds, O breath, and breathe upon these slain, that they may live. 10 So I prophesied as he commanded me, and the breath came into them, and they lived, and stood up upon their feet, an exceeding great army.

11 Then he said unto me, Son of man, these bones are the whole house of Israel: behold, they say, Our bones are dried, and our hope is lost: we are cut off for our parts. 12 Therefore prophesy and say unto them, Thus saith the Lord God; Behold, O my people, I will open your graves, and cause you to come up out of your graves, and bring you into the land of Israel. 13 And ye shall know that I am the Lord, when I have opened your graves, O my people, and brought you up out of your graves, 14 And shall put my Spirit in you, and ye shall live, and I shall place you in your own land: then shall ye know that I the Lord have spoken it, and performed it, saith the Lord.

# A Prince in Exile: *Daniel*

*The book of Daniel is set in the days of the great exile, but it was composed several centuries later. In this instance, as at some other places in the Bible, which is generally careful of historical accuracy, the writer seems more intent upon making certain points than upon presenting a reliable account of events as they happened in a past age. The magnificent narratives of the first six chapters of this book convey a pervasive sense of faithfulness and of hope. The seventh chapter treats various symbols of unjust oppression and wickedness which will be overcome by "one like the Son of man" who, acting for the Ancient of Days, will establish an everlasting community; while the final chapter looks forward to the resurrection of the dead and the wondrous establishment of a truly holy community. These elements contributed greatly to the Jewish expectation of a coming messiah or savior who would found a pure new kingdom "which shall not be destroyed," all of which has quite direct bearing upon the New Testament conception of Christ.*

# Daniel

## THE FOUR PRINCES

1 In the third year of the reign of Jehoiakim king of Judah came Nebuchadnezzar king of Babylon unto Jerusalem, and besieged it. 2 And the Lord gave Jehoiakim king of Judah into his hand, with part of the vessels of the house of God: which he carried into the land of Shinar to the house of his god; and he brought the vessels into the treasure house of his god. 3 And the king spake unto Ashpenaz the master of his eunuchs, that he should bring certain of the children of Israel, and of the king's seed, and of the princes; 4 Children in whom was no blemish, but well-favored, and skilful in all wisdom, and cunning in knowledge, and understanding science, and such as had ability in them to stand in the king's palace, and whom they might teach the learning and the tongue of the Chaldeans. 5 And the king appointed them a daily provision of the king's meat, and of the wine which he drank: so nourishing them three years, that at the end thereof they might stand before the king. 6 Now among these were of the children of Judah, Daniel, Hananiah, Mishael, and Azariah: 7 Unto whom the prince of the eunuchs gave names: for he gave unto Daniel the name of Belteshazzar; and to Hananiah, of Shadrach; and to Mishael, of Meshach; and to Azariah, of Abed-nego.

8 But Daniel purposed in his heart that he would not defile himself with the portion of the king's meat, nor with the wine which he drank: therefore he requested of the prince of the eunuchs that he might not defile himself. 9 Now God had brought Daniel into favor and tender love with the prince of the eunuchs. 10 And the prince of the eunuchs said unto Daniel, I fear my lord the king, who hath appointed your meat and your drink: for why should he see your faces worse liking than the children which are of your sort? then shall ye make me endanger my head to the king. 11 Then said Daniel to Melzar, whom the prince of the eunuchs had set over Daniel, Hananiah, Mishael, and Azariah, 12 Prove thy servants, I beseech thee, ten days; and let them give us pulse to eat, and water to drink. 13 Then let our countenances be looked upon before thee, and the countenance of the children that eat of the portion of the king's meat: and as thou seest, deal with thy servants. 14 So he consented to them in this matter, and proved them ten days. 15 And at the end of ten days their countenances appeared fairer and fatter in flesh than all the children which did eat the portion of the king's meat. 16 Thus Melzar took away the portion of their meat, and the wine that they should drink; and gave them pulse.

17 As for these four children, God gave them knowledge and skill in all learning and wisdom: and Daniel had understanding in all visions

and dreams. 18 Now at the end of the days that the king had said he should bring them in, then the prince of the eunuchs brought them in before Nebuchadnezzar. 19 And the king communed with them; and among them all was found none like Daniel, Hananiah, Mishael, and Azariah: therefore stood they before the king. 20 And in all matters of wisdom and understanding, that the king inquired of them, he found them ten times better than all the magicians and astrologers that were in all his realm. 21 And Daniel continued even unto the first year of king Cyrus.

## NEBUCHADNEZZAR'S DREAM

2   And in the second year of the reign of Nebuchadnezzar, Nebuchadnezzar dreamed dreams, wherewith his spirit was troubled, and his sleep brake from him. 2 Then the king commanded to call the magicians, and the astrologers, and the sorcerers, and the Chaldeans, for to show the king his dreams. So they came and stood before the king. 3 And the king said unto them, I have dreamed a dream, and my spirit was troubled to know the dream. 4 Then spake the Chaldeans to the king in Syriac, O king, live for ever: tell thy servants the dream, and we will show the interpretation. 5 The king answered and said to the Chaldeans, The thing is gone from me: if ye will not make known unto me the dream, with the interpretation thereof, ye shall be cut in pieces, and your houses shall be made a dunghill. 6 But if ye show the dream, and the interpretation thereof, ye shall receive of me gifts and rewards and great honor: therefore show me the dream, and the interpretation thereof. 7 They answered again and said, Let the king tell his servants the dream, and we will show the interpretation of it. 8 The king answered and said, I know of certainty that ye would gain the time, because ye see the thing is gone from me. 9 But if ye will not make known unto me the dream, there is but one decree for you: for ye have prepared lying and corrupt words to speak before me, till the time be changed: therefore tell me the dream, and I shall know that ye can show me the interpretation thereof. 10 The Chaldeans answered before the king, and said, There is not a man upon the earth that can show the king's matter: therefore there is no king, lord, nor ruler, that asked such things at any magician, or astrologer, or Chaldean. 11 And it is a rare thing that the king requireth, and there is none other that can show it before the king, except the gods, whose dwelling is not with flesh. 12 For this cause the king was angry and very furious, and commanded to destroy all the wise men of Babylon. 13 And the decree went forth that the wise men should be slain; and they sought Daniel and his fellows to be slain.

14 Then Daniel answered with counsel and wisdom to Arioch the captain of the king's guard, which was gone forth to slay the wise men of Babylon: 15 He answered and said to Arioch the king's captain, Why is the decree so hasty from the king? Then Arioch made the

thing known to Daniel. 16 Then Daniel went in, and desired of the king that he would give him time, and that he would show the king the interpretation.

17 Then Daniel went to his house, and made the thing known to Hananiah, Mishael, and Azariah, his companions: 18 That they would desire mercies of the God of heaven concerning this secret; that Daniel and his fellows should not perish with the rest of the wise men of Babylon. 19 Then was the secret revealed unto Daniel in a night vision. Then Daniel blessed the God of heaven. 20 Daniel answered and said,

> Blessed be the name of God
> For ever and ever:
> For wisdom and might are his:

21 And he changeth the times and the seasons:
> He removeth kings, and setteth up kings:
> He giveth wisdom unto the wise,
> And knowledge to them that know understanding:

22 He revealeth the deep and secret things:
> He knoweth what is in the darkness,
> And the light dwelleth with him.

23 I thank thee, and praise thee,
> O thou God of my fathers,
> Who hast given me wisdom and might,
> And hast made known unto me what we desired of thee:
> For thou hast now made known unto us the king's matter.

24 Therefore Daniel went in unto Arioch, whom the king had ordained to destroy the wise men of Babylon: he went and said thus unto him; Destroy not the wise men of Babylon: bring me in before the king, and I will show unto the king the interpretation.

25 Then Arioch brought in Daniel before the king in haste, and said thus unto him, I have found a man of the captives of Judah, that will make known unto the king the interpretation. 26 The king answered and said to Daniel, whose name was Belteshazzar, Art thou able to make known unto me the dream which I have seen, and the interpretation thereof? 27 Daniel answered in the presence of the king, and said, The secret which the king hath demanded cannot the wise men, the astrologers, the magicians, the soothsayers, show unto the king: 28 But there is a God in heaven that revealeth secrets, and maketh known to the king Nebuchadnezzar what shall be in the latter days. Thy dream, and the visions of thy head upon thy bed, are these; 29 As for thee, O king, thy thoughts came into thy mind upon thy bed, what should come to pass hereafter: and he that revealeth secrets maketh known to thee what shall come to pass. 30 But as for me, this secret is not revealed to me for any wisdom that I have more than any living, but for their sakes that shall make known the interpretation to the king, and that thou mightest know the thoughts of thy heart.

31 Thou, O king, sawest, and behold a great image. This great image, whose brightness was excellent, stood before thee; and the

form thereof was terrible. 32 This image's head was of fine gold, his breast and his arms of silver, his belly and his thighs of brass, 33 His legs of iron, his feet part of iron and part of clay. 34 Thou sawest till that a stone was cut out without hands, which smote the image upon his feet that were of iron and clay, and brake them to pieces. 35 Then was the iron, the clay, the brass, the silver, and the gold, broken to pieces together, and became like the chaff of the summer threshing-floors; and the wind carried them away, that no place was found for them: and the stone that smote the image became a great mountain, and filled the whole earth.

36 This is the dream; and we will tell the interpretation thereof before the king. 37 Thou, O king, art a king of kings: for the God of heaven hath given thee a kingdom, power, and strength, and glory. 38 And wheresoever the children of men dwell, the beasts of the field and the fowls of the heaven hath he given into thine hand, and hath made thee ruler over them all. Thou art this head of gold. 39 And after thee shall arise another kingdom inferior to thee, and another third kingdom of brass, which shall bear rule over all the earth. 40 And the fourth kingdom shall be strong as iron: forasmuch as iron breaketh in pieces and subdueth all things: and as iron that breaketh all these, shall it break in pieces and bruise. 41 And whereas thou sawest the feet and toes, part of potters' clay, and part of iron, the kingdom shall be divided; but there shall be in it of the strength of the iron, forasmuch as thou sawest the iron mixed with miry clay. 42 And as the toes of the feet were part of iron, and part of clay, so the kingdom shall be partly strong, and partly broken. 43 And whereas thou sawest iron mixed with miry clay, they shall mingle themselves with the seed of men: but they shall not cleave one to another, even as iron is not mixed with clay. 44 And in the days of these kings shall the God of heaven set up a kingdom, which shall never be destroyed: and the kingdom shall not be left to other people, but it shall break in pieces and consume all these kingdoms, and it shall stand for ever. 45 Forasmuch as thou sawest that the stone was cut out of the mountain without hands, and that it brake in pieces the iron, the brass, the clay, the silver, and the gold; the great God hath made known to the king what shall come to pass hereafter: and the dream is certain, and the interpretation thereof sure.

46 Then the king Nebuchadnezzar fell upon his face, and worshipped Daniel, and commanded that they should offer an oblation and sweet odors unto him. 47 The king answered unto Daniel, and said, Of a truth it is, that your God is a God of gods, and a Lord of kings, and a revealer of secrets, seeing thou couldest reveal this secret. 48 Then the king made Daniel a great man, and gave him many great gifts, and made him ruler over the whole province of Babylon, and chief of the governors over all the wise men of Babylon. 49 Then Daniel requested of the king, and he set Shadrach, Meshach, and Abed-nego, over the affairs of the province of Babylon: but Daniel sat in the gate of the king.

### THE FIERY FURNACE

3 Nebuchadnezzar the king made an image of gold, whose height was threescore cubits, and the breadth thereof six cubits: he set it up in the plain of Dura, in the province of Babylon. 2 Then Nebuchadnezzar the king sent to gather together the princes, the governors, and the captains, the judges, the treasurers, the counselors, the sheriffs, and all the rulers of the provinces, to come to the dedication of the image which Nebuchadnezzar the king had set up. 3 Then the princes, the governors, and captains, the judges, the treasurers, the counselors, the sheriffs, and all the rulers of the provinces, were gathered together unto the dedication of the image that Nebuchadnezzar the king had set up; and they stood before the image that Nebuchadnezzar had set up. 4 Then a herald cried aloud, To you it is commanded, O people, nations, and languages, 5 That at what time ye hear the sound of the cornet, flute, harp, sackbut, psaltery, dulcimer, and all kinds of music, ye fall down and worship the golden image that Nebuchadnezzar the king hath set up: 6 And whoso falleth not down and worshippeth shall the same hour be cast into the midst of a burning fiery furnace. 7 Therefore at that time, when all the people heard the sound of the cornet, flute, harp, sackbut, psaltery, and all kinds of music, all the people, the nations, and the languages, fell down and worshipped the golden image that Nebuchadnezzar the king had set up.

8 Wherefore at that time certain Chaldeans came near, and accused the Jews. 9 They spake and said to the king Nebuchadnezzar, O king, live for ever. 10 Thou, O king, hast made a decree, that every man that shall hear the sound of the cornet, flute, harp, sackbut, psaltery, and dulcimer, and all kinds of music, shall fall down and worship the golden image: 11 And whoso falleth not down and worshippeth, that he should be cast into the midst of a burning fiery furnace. 12 There are certain Jews whom thou hast set over the affairs of the province of Babylon, Shadrach, Meshach, and Abed-nego; these men, O king, have not regarded thee: they serve not thy gods, nor worship the golden image which thou hast set up.

13 Then Nebuchadnezzar in his rage and fury commanded to bring Shadrach, Meshach, and Abed-nego. Then they brought these men before the king. 14 Nebuchadnezzar spake and said unto them, Is it true, O Shadrach, Meshach, and Abed-nego? do not ye serve my gods, nor worship the golden image which I have set up? 15 Now if ye be ready that at what time ye hear the sound of the cornet, flute, harp, sackbut, psaltery, and dulcimer, and all kinds of music, ye fall down and worship the image which I have made; well: but if ye worship not, ye shall be cast the same hour into the midst of a burning fiery furnace; and who is that God that shall deliver you out of my hands? 16 Shadrach, Meshach, and Abed-nego, answered and said to the king, O Nebuchadnezzar, we are not careful to answer thee in this matter. 17 If it be so, our God whom we serve is able to deliver us from the burning fiery furnace, and he will deliver us out of thine hand, O king.

18 But if not, be it known unto thee, O king, that we will not serve thy gods, nor worship the golden image which thou hast set up.

19 Then was Nebuchadnezzar full of fury, and the form of his visage was changed against Shadrach, Meshach, and Abed-nego: therefore he spake, and commanded that they should heat the furnace one seven times more than it was wont to be heated. 20 And he commanded the most mighty men that were in his army to bind Shadrach, Meshach, and Abed-nego, and to cast them into the burning fiery furnace. 21 Then these men were bound in their coats, their hose, and their hats, and their other garments, and were cast into the midst of the burning fiery furnace. 22 Therefore because the king's commandment was urgent, and the furnace exceeding hot, the flame of the fire slew those men that took up Shadrach, Meshach, and Abed-nego. 23 And these three men, Shadrach, Meshach, and Abed-nego, fell down bound into the midst of the burning fiery furnace.

24 Then Nebuchadnezzar the king was astonished, and rose up in haste, and spake, and said unto his counselors, Did not we cast three men bound into the midst of the fire? They answered and said unto the king, True, O king. 25 He answered and said, Lo, I see four men loose, walking in the midst of the fire, and they have no hurt; and the form of the fourth is like the Son of God.

26 Then Nebuchadnezzar came near to the mouth of the burning fiery furnace, and spake, and said, Shadrach, Meshach, and Abed-nego, ye servants of the most high God, come forth, and come hither. Then Shadrach, Meshach, and Abed-nego, came forth of the midst of the fire. 27 And the princes, governors, and captains, and the king's counselors, being gathered together, saw these men, upon whose bodies the fire had no power, nor was a hair of their head singed, neither were their coats changed, nor the smell of fire had passed on them.

28 Then Nebuchadnezzar spake, and said, Blessed be the God of Shadrach, Meshach, and Abed-nego, who hath sent his angel, and delivered his servants that trusted in him, and have changed the king's word, and yielded their bodies, that they might not serve nor worship any god, except their own God. 29 Therefore I make a decree, That every people, nation, and language, which speak any thing amiss against the God of Shadrach, Meshach, and Abed-nego, shall be cut in pieces, and their houses shall be made a dunghill; because there is no other God that can deliver after this sort. 30 Then the king promoted Shadrach, Meshach, and Abed-nego, in the province of Babylon.

## THE KING'S MADNESS

4 Nebuchadnezzar the king, unto all people, nations, and languages, that dwell in all the earth; Peace be multiplied unto you. 2 I thought it good to show the signs and wonders that the high God hath wrought toward me.

3 How great are his signs!
And how mighty are his wonders!

His kingdom is an everlasting kingdom,
And his dominion is from generation to generation.

4 I Nebuchadnezzar was at rest in mine house, and flourishing in my palace: 5 I saw a dream which made me afraid, and the thoughts upon my bed and the visions of my head troubled me. 6 Therefore made I a decree to bring in all the wise men of Babylon before me, that they might make known unto me the interpretation of the dream. 7 Then came in the magicians, the astrologers, the Chaldeans, and the soothsayers: and I told the dream before them; but they did not make known unto me the interpretation thereof. 8 But at the last Daniel came in before me, whose name was Belteshazzar, according to the name of my god, and in whom is the spirit of the holy gods: and before him I told the dream, saying, 9 O Belteshazzar, master of the magicians, because I know that the spirit of the holy gods is in thee, and no secret troubleth thee, tell me the visions of my dream that I have seen, and the interpretation thereof. 10 Thus were the visions of mine head in my bed; I saw,

And behold a tree in the midst of the earth,
And the height thereof was great.

11 The tree grew, and was strong,
And the height thereof reached unto heaven,
And the sight thereof to the end of all the earth:

12 The leaves thereof were fair, and the fruit thereof much,
And in it was meat for all:
The beasts of the field had shadow under it,
And the fowls of the heaven dwelt in the boughs thereof,
And all flesh was fed of it.

13 I saw in the visions of my head upon my bed, and, behold, a watcher and a holy one came down from heaven; 14 He cried aloud, and said thus,

Hew down the tree, and cut off his branches,
Shake off his leaves, and scatter his fruit:
Let the beasts get away from under it,
And the fowls from his branches:

15 Nevertheless, leave the stump of his roots in the earth,
Even with a band of iron and brass, in the tender grass of the field;
And let it be wet with the dew of heaven,
And let his portion be with the beasts in the grass of the earth:

16 Let his heart be changed from man's,
And let a beast's heart be given unto him;
And let seven times pass over him.

17 This matter is by the decree of the watchers,
And the demand by the word of the holy ones:
To the intent that the living may know
That the Most High ruleth in the kingdom of men,
And giveth it to whomsoever he will,
And setteth up over it the basest of men.

18 This dream I king Nebuchadnezzar have seen. Now thou, O Belteshazzar, declare the interpretation thereof, forasmuch as all the wise men of my kingdom are not able to make known unto me the interpretation: but thou art able; for the spirit of the holy gods is in thee.

19 Then Daniel, whose name was Belteshazzar, was astonished for one hour, and his thoughts troubled him. The king spake, and said, Belteshazzar, let not the dream, or the interpretation thereof, trouble thee. Belteshazzar answered and said, My lord, the dream be to them that hate thee, and the interpretation thereof to thine enemies. 20 The tree that thou sawest, which grew, and was strong, whose height reached unto the heaven, and the sight thereof to all the earth; 21 Whose leaves were fair, and the fruit thereof much, and in it was meat for all; under which the beasts of the field dwelt, and upon whose branches the fowls of the heaven had their habitation: 22 It is thou, O king, that art grown and become strong: for thy greatness is grown, and reacheth unto heaven, and thy dominion to the end of the earth. 23 And whereas the king saw a watcher and a holy one coming down from heaven, and saying, Hew the tree down, and destroy it; yet leave the stump of the roots thereof in the earth, even with a band of iron and brass, in the tender grass of the field; and let it be wet with the dew of heaven, and let his portion be with the beasts of the field, till seven times pass over him; 24 This is the interpretation, O king, and this is the decree of the Most High, which is come upon my lord the king: 25 That they shall drive thee from men, and thy dwelling shall be with the beasts of the field, and they shall make thee to eat grass as oxen, and they shall wet thee with the dew of heaven, and seven times shall pass over thee, till thou know that the Most High ruleth in the kingdom of men, and giveth it to whomsoever he will. 26 And whereas they commanded to leave the stump of the tree roots; thy kingdom shall be sure unto thee, after that thou shalt have known that the heavens do rule. 27 Wherefore, O king, let my counsel be acceptable unto thee, and break off thy sins by righteousness, and thine iniquities by showing mercy to the poor; if it may be a lengthening of thy tranquillity.

28 All this came upon the king Nebuchadnezzar. 29 At the end of twelve months he walked in the palace of the kingdom of Babylon. 30 The king spake, and said, Is not this great Babylon, that I have built for the house of the kingdom by the might of my power, and for the honor of my majesty? 31 While the word was in the king's mouth, there fell a voice from heaven, saying, O King Nebuchadnezzar, to thee it is spoken; The kingdom is departed from thee. 32 And they shall drive thee from men, and thy dwelling shall be with the beasts of the field: they shall make thee to eat grass as oxen, and seven times shall pass over thee, until thou know that the Most High ruleth in the kingdom of men, and giveth to it whomsoever he will. 33 The same hour was the thing fulfilled upon Nebuchadnezzar: and he was driven from men, and did eat grass as oxen, and his body was wet with the

dew of heaven, till his hairs were grown like eagles' feathers, and his nails like birds' claws.

34 And at the end of the days I Nebuchadnezzar lifted up mine eyes unto heaven, and mine understanding returned unto me, and I blessed the Most High, and I praised and honored him that liveth for ever,

> Whose dominion is an everlasting dominion,
> And his kingdom is from generation to generation:
> 35 And all the inhabitants of the earth are reputed as nothing:
> And he doeth according to his will in the army of heaven,
> And among the inhabitants of the earth:
> And none can stay his hand,
> Or say unto him, What doest thou?

36 At the same time my reason returned unto me; and for the glory of my kingdom, mine honor and brightness returned unto me; and my counselors and my lords sought unto me; and I was established in my kingdom, and excellent majesty was added unto me. 37 Now I Nebuchadnezzar praise and extol and honor the King of heaven, all whose works are truth, and his ways judgment: and those that walk in pride he is able to abase.

## BELSHAZZAR'S FEAST

5 Belshazzar the king made a great feast to a thousand of his lords, and drank wine before the thousand. 2 Belshazzar, while he tasted the wine, commanded to bring the golden and silver vessels which his father Nebuchadnezzar had taken out of the temple which was in Jerusalem; that the king and his princes, his wives and his concubines, might drink therein. 3 Then they brought the golden vessels that were taken out of the temple of the house of God which was at Jerusalem; and the king and his princes, his wives and his concubines, drank in them. 4 They drank wine, and praised the gods of gold, and of silver, of brass, of iron, of wood, and of stone. 5 In the same hour came forth fingers of a man's hand, and wrote over against the candlestick upon the plaster of the wall of the king's palace: and the king saw the part of the hand that wrote. 6 Then the king's countenance was changed, and his thoughts troubled him, so that the joints of his loins were loosed, and his knees smote one against another. 7 The king cried aloud to bring in the astrologers, the Chaldeans, and the soothsayers. And the king spake, and said to the wise men of Babylon, Whosoever shall read this writing, and show me the interpretation thereof, shall be clothed with scarlet, and have a chain of gold about his neck, and shall be the third ruler in the kingdom. 8 Then came in all the king's wise men: but they could not read the writing, nor make known to the king the interpretation thereof. 9 Then was king Belshazzar greatly troubled, and his countenance was changed in him, and his lords were astonished. 10 Now the queen, by reason of the words of the king and his lords, came into the banquet house: and the queen

spake and said, O king, live for ever: let not thy thoughts trouble thee, nor let thy countenance be changed: 11 There is a man in thy kingdom, in whom is the spirit of the holy gods; and in the days of thy father light and understanding and wisdom, like the wisdom of the gods, was found in him; whom the king Nebuchadnezzar thy father, the king, I say, thy father, made master of the magicians, astrologers, Chaldeans, and soothsayers; 12 Forasmuch as an excellent spirit, and knowledge, and understanding, interpreting of dreams, and showing of hard sentences, and dissolving of doubts, were found in the same Daniel, whom the king named Belteshazzar: now let Daniel be called, and he will show the interpretation.

13 Then was Daniel brought in before the king. And the king spake and said unto Daniel, Art thou that Daniel, which art of the children of the captivity of Judah, whom the king my father brought out of Jewry? 14 I have even heard of thee, that the spirit of the gods is in thee, and that light and understanding and excellent wisdom is found in thee. 15 And now the wise men, the astrologers, have been brought in before me, that they should read this writing, and make known unto me the interpretation thereof: but they could not show the interpretation of the thing: 16 And I have heard of thee, that thou canst make interpretations, and dissolve doubts: now if thou canst read the writing, and make known to me the interpretation thereof, thou shalt be clothed with scarlet, and have a chain of gold about thy neck, and shalt be the third ruler in the kingdom.

17 Then Daniel answered and said before the king, Let thy gifts be to thyself, and give thy rewards to another; yet I will read the writing unto the king and make known to him the interpretation. 18 O thou king, the most high God gave Nebuchadnezzar thy father a kingdom, and majesty, and glory, and honor: 19 And for the majesty that he gave him, all people, nations, and languages, trembled and feared before him: whom he would he slew; and whom he would he kept alive; and whom he would he set up; and whom he would he put down. 20 But when his heart was lifted up, and his mind hardened in pride, he was deposed from his kingly throne, and they took his glory from him: 21 And he was driven from the sons of men; and his heart was made like the beasts, and his dwelling was with the wild asses: they fed him with grass like oxen, and his body was wet with the dew of heaven; till he knew that the most high God ruled in the kingdom of men, and that he appointeth over it whomsoever he will. 22 And thou his son, O Belshazzar, hast not humbled thine heart, though thou knewest all this; 23 But hast lifted up thyself against the Lord of heaven, and they have brought the vessels of his house before thee, and thou and thy lords, thy wives and thy concubines, have drunk wine in them; and thou hast praised the gods of silver, and gold, of brass, iron, wood, and stone, which see not, nor hear, nor know: and the God in whose hand thy breath is, and whose are all thy ways, hast thou not glorified: 24 Then was the part of the hand sent from him; and this writing was written.

25 And this is the writing that was written, MENE, MENE, TEKEL, UPHARSIN. 26 This is the interpretation of the thing: MENE; God hath numbered thy kingdom, and finished it. 27 TEKEL; Thou art weighed in the balances, and art found wanting. 28 PERES; Thy kingdom is divided, and given to the Medes and Persians. 29 Then commanded Belshazzar, and they clothed Daniel with scarlet, and put a chain of gold about his neck, and made a proclamation concerning him, that he should be the third ruler in the kingdom. 30 In that night was Belshazzar the king of the Chaldeans slain. 31 And Darius the Median took the kingdom, being about threescore and two years old.

## DANIEL IN THE LIONS' DEN

6 It pleased Darius to set over the kingdom a hundred and twenty princes, which should be over the whole kingdom; 2 And over these three presidents; of whom Daniel was first: that the princes might give accounts unto them, and the king should have no damage. 3 Then this Daniel was preferred above the presidents and princes, because an excellent spirit was in him; and the king thought to set him over the whole realm.

4 Then the presidents and princes sought to find occasion against Daniel concerning the kingdom; but they could find none occasion nor fault; forasmuch as he was faithful, neither was there any error or fault found in him. 5 Then said these men, We shall not find any occasion against this Daniel, except we find it against him concerning the law of his God. 6 Then these presidents and princes assembled together to the king, and said thus unto him, King Darius, live for ever. 7 All the presidents of the kingdom, the governors, and the princes, the counselors, and the captains, have consulted together to establish a royal statute, and to make a firm decree, that whosoever shall ask a petition of any God or man for thirty days, save of thee, O king, he shall be cast into the den of lions. 8 Now, O king, establish the decree, and sign the writing, that it be not changed, according to the law of the Medes and Persians, which altereth not. 9 Wherefore king Darius signed the writing and the decree.

10 Now when Daniel knew that the writing was signed, he went into his house; and, his windows being open in his chamber toward Jerusalem, he kneeled upon his knees three times a day, and prayed, and gave thanks before his God, as he did aforetime. 11 Then these men assembled, and found Daniel praying and making supplication before his God. 12 Then they came near, and spake before the king concerning the king's decree; Hast thou not signed a decree, that every man that shall ask a petition of any God or man within thirty days, save of thee, O king, shall be cast into the den of lions? The king answered and said, The thing is true, according to the law of the Medes and Persians, which altereth not. 13 Then answered they and said before the king, That Daniel, which is of the children of the

captivity of Judah, regardeth not thee, O king, nor the decree that thou hast signed, but maketh his petition three times a day. 14 Then the king, when he heard these words, was sore displeased with himself, and set his heart on Daniel to deliver him: and he labored till the going down of the sun to deliver him. 15 Then these men assembled unto the king, and said unto the king, Know, O king, that the law of the Medes and Persians is, That no decree nor statute which the king establisheth may be changed. 16 Then the king commanded, and they brought Daniel, and cast him into the den of lions. Now the king spake and said unto Daniel, Thy God whom thou servest continually, he will deliver thee. 17 And a stone was brought, and laid upon the mouth of the den; and the king sealed it with his own signet, and with the signet of his lords; that the purpose might not be changed concerning Daniel.

18 Then the king went to his palace, and passed the night fasting: neither were instruments of music brought before him: and his sleep went from him. 19 Then the king arose very early in the morning, and went in haste unto the den of lions. 20 And when he came to the den, he cried with a lamentable voice unto Daniel: and the king spake and said to Daniel, O Daniel, servant of the living God, is thy God, whom thou servest continually, able to deliver thee from the lions? 21 Then said Daniel unto the king, O king, live for ever. 22 My God hath sent his angel, and hath shut the lions' mouths, that they have not hurt me: forasmuch as before him innocency was found in me; and also before thee, O king, have I done no hurt. 23 Then was the king exceeding glad for him, and commanded that they should take Daniel up out of the den. So Daniel was taken up out of the den, and no manner of hurt was found upon him, because he believed in his God. 24 And the king commanded, and they brought those men which had accused Daniel, and they cast them into the den of lions, them, their children, and their wives; and the lions had the mastery of them, and brake all their bones in pieces or ever they came at the bottom of the den.

25 Then king Darius wrote unto all people, nations, and languages, that dwell in all the earth; Peace be multiplied unto you. 26 I make a decree, That in every dominion of my kingdom men tremble and fear before the God of Daniel:

> For he is the living God,
> And steadfast for ever,
> And his kingdom that which shall not be destroyed,
> And his dominion shall be even unto the end.

27 He delivereth and rescueth,
> And he worketh signs and wonders
> In heaven and in earth,
> Who hath delivered Daniel from the power of the lions.

28 So this Daniel prospered in the reign of Darius, and in the reign of Cyrus the Persian.

## VISION OF THE SON OF MAN

7 In the first year of Belshazzar king of Babylon, Daniel had a dream and visions of his head upon his bed: then he wrote the dream, and told the sum of the matters. 2 Daniel spake and said, I saw in my vision by night, and, behold, the four winds of the heaven strove upon the great sea. 3 And four great beasts came up from the sea, diverse one from another. 4 The first was like a lion, and had eagle's wings: I beheld till the wings thereof were plucked, and it was lifted up from the earth, and made stand upon the feet as a man, and a man's heart was given to it. 5 And behold another beast, a second, like to a bear, and it raised up itself on one side, and it had three ribs in the mouth of it between the teeth of it: and they said thus unto it, Arise, devour much flesh. 6 After this I beheld, and lo another, like a leopard, which had upon the back of it four wings of a fowl; the beast had also four heads; and dominion was given to it. 7 After this I saw in the night visions, and behold a fourth beast, dreadful and terrible, and strong exceedingly; and it had great iron teeth: it devoured and brake in pieces, and stamped the residue with the feet of it: and it was diverse from all the beasts that were before it; and it had ten horns. 8 I considered the horns, and, behold, there came up among them another little horn, before whom there were three of the first horns plucked up by the roots: and, behold, in this horn were eyes like the eyes of man, and a mouth speaking great things.
    9 I beheld

      Till the thrones were cast down,
      And the Ancient of days did sit,
      Whose garment was white as snow,
      And the hair of his head like the pure wool:
      His throne was like the fiery flame,
      And his wheels as burning fire.
    10 A fiery stream issued
      And came forth from before him:
      Thousand thousands ministered unto him,
      And ten thousand times ten thousand stood before him:
      The judgment was set,
      And the books were opened.

11 I beheld then, because of the voice of the great words which the horn spake: I beheld even till the beast was slain, and his body destroyed, and given to the burning flame. 12 As concerning the rest of the beasts, they had their dominion taken away: yet their lives were prolonged for a season and time.
    13 I saw in the night visions,
      And, behold, one like the Son of man
      Came with the clouds of heaven,
      And came to the Ancient of days,
      And they brought him near before him.
    14 And there was given him dominion,

And glory, and a kingdom,
That all people, nations, and languages,
Should serve him:
His dominion is an everlasting dominion, which shall not pass
away,
And his kingdom that which shall not be destroyed.

15 I Daniel was grieved in my spirit in the midst of my body, and the visions of my head troubled me. 16 I came near unto one of them that stood by, and asked him the truth of all this. So he told me, and made me know the interpretation of the things. 17 These great beasts, which are four, are four kings, which shall arise out of the earth. 18 But the saints of the Most High shall take the kingdom, and possess the kingdom for ever, even for ever and ever. 19 Then I would know the truth of the fourth beast, which was diverse from all the others, exceeding dreadful, whose teeth were of iron, and his nails of brass; which devoured, brake in pieces, and stamped the residue with his feet; 20 And of the ten horns that were in his head, and of the other which came up, and before whom three fell; even of that horn that had eyes, and a mouth that spake very great things, whose look was more stout than his fellows. 21 I beheld, and the same horn made war with the saints, and prevailed against them; 22 Until the Ancient of days came, and judgment was given to the saints of the Most High; and the time came that the saints possessed the kingdom. 23 Thus he said, The fourth beast shall be the fourth kingdom upon earth, which shall be diverse from all kingdoms, and shall devour the whole earth, and shall tread it down, and break it in pieces. 24 And the ten horns out of this kingdom are ten kings that shall arise: and another shall rise after them; and he shall be diverse from the first, and he shall subdue three kings. 25 And he shall speak great words against the Most High, and shall wear out the saints of the Most High, and think to change times and laws: and they shall be given into his hand until a time and times and the dividing of time. 26 But the judgment shall sit, and they shall take away his dominion, to consume and to destroy it unto the end.

## THE FINAL TRIUMPH

12 And at that time shall Michael stand up, the great prince which standeth for the children of thy people: and there shall be a time of trouble, such as never was since there was a nation even to that same time: and at that time thy people shall be delivered, every one that shall be found written in the book. 2 And many of them that sleep in the dust of the earth shall awake, some to everlasting life, and some to shame and everlasting contempt. 3 And they that be wise shall shine as the brightness of the firmament; and they that turn many to right-eousness, as the stars for ever and ever. 4 But thou, O Daniel, shut up the words, and seal the book, even to the time of the end: many shall run to and fro, and knowledge shall be increased.

5 Then I Daniel looked, and, behold, there stood other two, the one on this side of the bank of the river, and the other on that side of the bank of the river. 6 And one said to the man clothed in linen, which was upon the waters of the river, How long shall it be to the end of these wonders? 7 And I heard the man clothed in linen, which was upon the waters of the river, when he held up his right hand and his left hand unto heaven, and sware by him that liveth for ever, that it shall be for a time, times, and a half; and when he shall have accomplished to scatter the power of the holy people, all these things shall be finished.

8 And I heard, but I understood not: then said I, O my Lord, what shall be the end of these things? 9 And he said, Go thy way, Daniel: for the words are closed up and sealed till the time of the end. 10 Many shall be purified, and made white, and tried; but the wicked shall do wickedly: and none of the wicked shall understand; but the wise shall understand. 11 And from the time that the daily sacrifice shall be taken away, and the abomination that maketh desolate set up, there shall be a thousand two hundred and ninety days. 12 Blessed is he that waiteth, and cometh to the thousand three hundred and five and thirty days. 13 But go thou thy way till the end be: for thou shalt rest, and stand in thy lot at the end of the days.

## A New Vision: *Zechariah*

*Some two generations after the removal of the inhabitants of Judah into the Babylonian captivity, a number of them were freed by the Persians and allowed to return to Jerusalem. The actual return and the rebuilding of the city covered a number of years, but in the early days the prophet Zechariah conveyed a new vision of Jerusalem's greatness. The vision looks forward to a universal mission for the chosen people.*

# *Zechariah*

1 In the eighth month, in the second year of Darius, came the word of the Lord unto Zechariah, the son of Berechiah, the son of Iddo the prophet, saying, 2 The Lord hath been sore displeased with your fathers. 3 Therefore say thou unto them, Thus saith the Lord of hosts; Turn ye unto me, saith the Lord of hosts, and I will turn unto you, saith the Lord of hosts. 4 Be ye not as your fathers, unto whom the former prophets have cried, saying, Thus saith the Lord of hosts; Turn ye now from your evil ways, and from your evildoings: but they did not hear, nor hearken unto me, saith the Lord. 5 Your fathers, where are they? and the prophets, do they live for ever? 6 But my words and my statutes, which I commanded my servants the prophets,

did they not take hold of your fathers? and they returned and said, Like as the Lord of hosts thought to do unto us, according to our ways, and according to our doings, so hath he dealt with us.

7  8 And the word of the Lord came unto Zechariah, saying, 9 Thus speaketh the Lord of hosts, saying, Execute true judgment, and show mercy and compassions every man to his brother: 10 And oppress not the widow, nor the fatherless, the stranger, nor the poor; and let none of you imagine evil against his brother in your heart.

8  Again the word of the Lord of hosts came to me, saying, 2 Thus saith the Lord of hosts; I was jealous for Zion with great jealousy, and I was jealous for her with great fury.

3 Thus saith the Lord; I am returned unto Zion, and will dwell in the midst of Jerusalem: and Jerusalem shall be called A city of truth; and the mountain of the Lord of hosts, The holy mountain.

4 Thus saith the Lord of hosts; There shall yet old men and old women dwell in the streets of Jerusalem, and every man with his staff in his hand for very age. 5 And the streets of the city shall be full of boys and girls playing in the streets thereof.

6 Thus saith the Lord of hosts; If it be marvelous in the eyes of the remnant of this people in these days, should it also be marvelous in mine eyes? saith the Lord of hosts.

7 Thus saith the Lord of hosts; Behold, I will save my people from the east country, and from the west country.

## Return to Jerusalem: *Nehemiah*

*The return of the exiles and the rebuilding of Jerusalem are recounted in the books of Ezra and Nehemiah, of which we have chosen selections from the latter. Nehemiah was an intensely serious leader, all of whose energies were focused upon the one great work of rebuilding Jerusalem and re-establishing his people. He lacked the passionate nature of a Moses or a David, and his account of his work displays none of the human and even endearing qualities of these men. In the face of threats and dangers, he held steadfastly to his purpose, and though he had none of the romantic aura of a great hero, in his own rather prosaic way he accomplished a heroic task.*

# *Nehemiah*

### NEHEMIAH AND THE EMPEROR

1  The words of Nehemiah the son of Hachaliah.
And it came to pass in the month Chisleu, in the twentieth year, as I was in Shushan the palace, 2 That Hanani, one of my brethren,

came, he and certain men of Judah; and I asked them concerning the Jews that had escaped, which were left of the captivity, and concerning Jerusalem. 3 And they said unto me, The remnant that are left of the captivity there in the province are in great affliction and reproach: the wall of Jerusalem also is broken down, and the gates thereof are burned with fire.

4 And it came to pass, when I heard these words, that I sat down and wept, and mourned certain days, and fasted, and prayed before the God of heaven, 5 And said, I beseech thee, O Lord God of heaven, the great and terrible God, that keepeth covenant and mercy for them that love him and observe his commandments: 6 Let thine ear now be attentive, and thine eyes open, that thou mayest hear the prayer of thy servant, which I pray before thee now, day and night, for the children of Israel thy servants, and confess the sins of the children of Israel, which we have sinned against thee: both I and my father's house have sinned. 7 We have dealt very corruptly against thee, and have not kept the commandments, nor the statutes, nor the judgments, which thou commandedst thy servant Moses. 8 Remember, I beseech thee, the word that thou commandedst thy servant Moses, saying, If ye transgress, I will scatter you abroad among the nations: 9 But if ye turn unto me, and keep my commandments, and do them; though there were of you cast out unto the uttermost part of the heaven, yet will I gather them from thence, and will bring them unto the place that I have chosen to set my name there. 10 Now these are thy servants and thy people, whom thou hast redeemed by thy great power, and by thy strong hand. 11 O Lord, I beseech thee, let now thine ear be attentive to the prayer of thy servant, and to the prayer of thy servants, who desire to fear thy name: and prosper, I pray thee, thy servant this day, and grant him mercy in the sight of this man. For I was the king's cupbearer.

2 And it came to pass in the month Nisan, in the twentieth year of Artaxerxes the king, that wine was before him: and I took up the wine, and gave it unto the king. Now I had not been beforetime sad in his presence. 2 Wherefore the king said unto me, Why is thy countenance sad, seeing thou art not sick? this is nothing else but sorrow of heart. Then I was very sore afraid, 3 And said unto the king, Let the king live for ever: why should not my countenance be sad, when the city, the place of my fathers' sepulchres, lieth waste, and the gates thereof are consumed with fire? 4 Then the king said unto me, For what dost thou make request? So I prayed to the God of heaven. 5 And I said unto the king, If it please the king, and if thy servant have found favor in thy sight, that thou wouldest send me unto Judah, unto the city of my fathers' sepulchres, that I may build it. 6 And the king said unto me, (the queen also sitting by him,) For how long shall thy journey be? and when wilt thou return? So it pleased the king to send me; and I set him a time. 7 Moreover I said unto the king, If it please the king, let letters be given me to the governors beyond the river,

that they may convey me over till I come into Judah; 8 And a letter unto Asaph the keeper of the king's forest, that he may give me timber to make beams for the gates of the palace which appertained to the house, and for the wall of the city, and for the house that I shall enter into. And the king granted me, according to the good hand of my God upon me.

9 Then I came to the governors beyond the river, and gave them the king's letters. Now the king had sent captains of the army and horsemen with me. 10 When Sanballat the Horonite, and Tobiah the servant, the Ammonite, heard of it, it grieved them exceedingly that there was come a man to seek the welfare of the children of Israel. 11 So I came to Jerusalem, and was there three days. 12 And I arose in the night, I and some few men with me; neither told I any man what my God had put in my heart to do at Jerusalem: neither was there any beast with me, save the beast that I rode upon. 13 And I went out by night by the gate of the valley, even before the dragon well, and to the dung port, and viewed the walls of Jerusalem, which were broken down, and the gates thereof were consumed with fire. 14 Then I went on to the gate of the fountain, and to the king's pool: but there was no place for the beast that was under me to pass. 15 Then went I up in the night by the brook, and viewed the wall, and turned back, and entered by the gate of the valley, and so returned. 16 And the rulers knew not whither I went, or what I did; neither had I as yet told it to the Jews, nor to the priests, nor to the nobles, nor to the rulers, nor to the rest that did the work.

17 Then said I unto them, Ye see the distress that we are in, how Jerusalem lieth waste, and the gates thereof are burned with fire: come, and let us build up the wall of Jerusalem, that we be no more a reproach. 18 Then I told them of the hand of my God which was good upon me; as also the king's words that he had spoken unto me. And they said, Let us rise up and build. So they strengthened their hands for this good work. 19 But when Sanballat the Horonite, and Tobiah the servant, the Ammonite, and Geshem the Arabian, heard it, they laughed us to scorn, and despised us, and said, What is this thing that ye do? will ye rebel against the king? 20 Then answered I them, and said unto them, The God of heaven, he will prosper us; therefore we his servants will arise and build: but ye have no portion, nor right, nor memorial, in Jerusalem.

## REBUILDING JERUSALEM'S WALLS

3 Then Eliashib the high priest rose up with his brethren the priests, and they builded the sheep gate; they sanctified it, and set up the doors of it; even unto the tower of Meah they sanctified it, unto the tower of Hananeel. 2 And next unto him builded the men of Jericho. And next to them builded Zaccur the son of Imri. 3 But the fish gate did the sons of Hassenaah build, who also laid the beams thereof, and set up the doors thereof, the locks thereof, and the bars thereof.

28 From above the horse gate repaired the priests, every one over against his house. 29 After them repaired Zadok the son of Immer over against his house. After him repaired Shemaiah the son of Shechaniah, the keeper of the east gate. 30 After him repaired Hananiah the son of Shelemiah, and Hanun the sixth son of Zalaph, another piece. After him repaired Meshullam the son of Berechiah over against his chamber. 31 After him repaired Malchiah the goldsmith's son unto the place of the Nethinim, and of the merchants, over against the gate Miphkad, and to the going up of the corner. 32 And between the going up of the corner unto the sheep gate repaired the goldsmiths and the merchants.

4 But it came to pass, that when Sanballat heard that we builded the wall, he was wroth, and took great indignation, and mocked the Jews. 2 And he spake before his brethren and the army of Samaria, and said, What do these feeble Jews? will they fortify themselves? will they sacrifice? will they make an end in a day? will they revive the stones out of the heaps of the rubbish which are burned? 3 Now Tobiah the Ammonite was by him, and he said, Even that which they build, if a fox go up, he shall even break down their stone wall. 4 Hear, O our God; for we are despised: and turn their reproach upon their own head, and give them for a prey in the land of captivity: 5 And cover not their iniquity, and let not their sin be blotted out from before thee: for they have provoked thee to anger before the builders. 6 So built we the wall; and all the wall was joined together unto the half thereof: for the people had a mind to work.

7 But it came to pass, that when Sanballat, and Tobiah, and the Arabians, and the Ammonites, and the Ashdodites, heard that the walls of Jerusalem were made up, and that the breaches began to be stopped, then they were very wroth, 8 And conspired all of them together to come and to fight against Jerusalem, and to hinder it. 9 Nevertheless we made our prayer unto our God, and set a watch against them day and night, because of them. 10 And Judah said, The strength of the bearers of burdens is decayed, and there is much rubbish; so that we are not able to build the wall. 11 And our adversaries said, They shall not know, neither see, till we come in the midst among them, and slay them, and cause the work to cease. 12 And it came to pass, that when the Jews which dwelt by them came, they said unto us ten times, From all places whence ye shall return unto us they will be upon you. 13 Therefore set I in the lower places behind the wall, and on the higher places, I even set the people after their families with their swords, their spears, and their bows. 14 And I looked, and rose up, and said unto the nobles, and to the rulers, and to the rest of the people, Be not ye afraid of them: remember the Lord, which is great and terrible, and fight for your brethren, your sons, and your daughters, your wives, and your houses.

15 And it came to pass, when our enemies heard that it was known unto us, and God had brought their counsel to nought, that we returned

all of us to the wall, every one unto his work. 16 And it came to pass from that time forth, that the half of my servants wrought in the work, and the other half of them held both the spears, the shields, and the bows, and the habergeons; and the rulers were behind all the house of Judah. 17 They which builded on the wall, and they that bare burdens, with those that laded, every one with one of his hands wrought in the work, and with the other hand held a weapon. 18 For the builders, every one had his sword girded by his side, and so builded. And he that sounded the trumpet was by me. 19 And I said unto the nobles, and to the rulers, and to the rest of the people, The work is great and large, and we are separated upon the wall, one far from another. 20 In what place therefore ye hear the sound of the trumpet, resort ye thither unto us: our God shall fight for us.

21 So we labored in the work: and half of them held the spears from the rising of the morning till the stars appeared. 22 Likewise at the same time said I unto the people, Let every one with his servant lodge within Jerusalem, that in the night they may be a guard to us, and labor on the day. 23 So neither I, nor my brethren, nor my servants, nor the men of the guard which followed me, none of us put off our clothes, saving that every one put them off for washing.

## ESTABLISHING SOCIAL JUSTICE

5 And there was a great cry of the people and of their wives against their brethren the Jews. 2 For there were that said, We, our sons, and our daughters, are many: therefore we take up corn for them, that we may eat, and live. 3 Some also there were that said, We have mortgaged our lands, vineyards, and houses, that we might buy corn, because of the dearth. 4 There were also that said, We have borrowed money for the king's tribute, and that upon our lands and vineyards. 5 Yet now our flesh is as the flesh of our brethren, our children as their children: and, lo, we bring into bondage our sons and our daughters to be servants, and some of our daughters are brought into bondage already: neither is it in our power to redeem them; for other men have our lands and vineyards.

6 And I was very angry when I heard their cry and these words. 7 Then I consulted with myself, and I rebuked the nobles, and the rulers, and said unto them, Ye exact usury, every one of his brother. And I set a great assembly against them. 8 And I said unto them, We, after our ability, have redeemed our brethren the Jews, which were sold unto the heathen; and will ye even sell your brethren? or shall they be sold unto us? Then held they their peace, and found nothing to answer. 9 Also I said, It is not good that ye do: ought ye not to walk in the fear of our God because of the reproach of the heathen our enemies? 10 I likewise, and my brethren, and my servants, might exact of them money and corn: I pray you, let us leave off this usury. 11 Restore, I pray you, to them, even this day, their lands, their vineyards, their oliveyards, and their houses, also the hundredth part of the

money, and of the corn, the wine, and the oil, that ye exact of them. 12 Then said they, We will restore them, and will require nothing of them; so will we do as thou sayest. Then I called the priests, and took an oath of them, that they should do according to this promise. 13 Also I shook my lap, and said, So God shake out every man from his house, and from his labor, that performeth not this promise, even thus be he shaken out, and emptied. And all the congregation said, Amen, and praised the Lord. And the people did according to this promise.

14 Moreover from the time that I was appointed to be their governor in the land of Judah, from the twentieth year even unto the two and thirtieth year of Artaxerxes the king, that is, twelve years, I and my brethren have not eaten the bread of the governor. 15 But the former governors that had been before me were chargeable unto the people, and had taken of them bread and wine, besides forty shekels of silver; yea, even their servants bare rule over the people: but so did not I, because of the fear of God. 16 Yea, also I continued in the work of this wall, neither bought we any land: and all my servants were gathered thither unto the work. 17 Moreover there were at my table a hundred and fifty of the Jews and rulers, besides those that came unto us from among the heathen that are about us. 18 Now that which was prepared for me daily was one ox and six choice sheep; also fowls were prepared for me, and once in ten days store of all sorts of wine: yet for all this required not I the bread of the governor, because the bondage was heavy upon this people. 19 Think upon me, my God, for good, according to all that I have done for this people.

## PLOTS AND THREATS

6 Now it came to pass, when Sanballat, and Tobiah, and Geshem the Arabian, and the rest of our enemies, heard that I had builded the wall, and that there was no breach left therein; (though at that time I had not set up the doors upon the gates;) 2 That Sanballat and Geshem sent unto me, saying, Come, let us meet together in some one of the villages in the plain of Ono. But they thought to do me mischief. 3 And I sent messengers unto them, saying, I am doing a great work, so that I cannot come down: why should the work cease, whilst I leave it, and come down to you? 4 Yet they sent unto me four times after this sort; and I answered them after the same manner. 5 Then sent Sanballat his servant unto me in like manner the fifth time with an open letter in his hand; 6 Wherein was written, It is reported among the heathen, and Gashmu saith it, that thou and the Jews think to rebel: for which cause thou buildest the wall, that thou mayest be their king, according to these words. 7 And thou hast also appointed prophets to preach of thee at Jerusalem, saying, There is a king in Judah: and now shall it be reported to the king according to these words. Come now therefore, and let us take counsel together. 8 Then I sent unto him, saying, There are no such things done as thou sayest,

but thou feignest them out of thine own heart. 9 For they all made us afraid, saying, Their hands shall be weakened from the work, that it be not done. Now therefore, O God, strengthen my hands.

10 Afterward I came unto the house of Shemaiah the son of Delaiah the son of Mehetabeel, who was shut up; and he said, Let us meet together in the house of God, within the temple, and let us shut the doors of the temple: for they will come to slay thee; yea, in the night will they come to slay thee. 11 And I said, Should such a man as I flee? and who is there, that, being as I am, would go into the temple to save his life? I will not go in. 12 And, lo, I perceived that God had not sent him; but that he pronounced this prophecy against me: for Tobiah and Sanballat had hired him. 13 Therefore was he hired, that I should be afraid, and do so, and sin, and that they might have matter for an evil report, that they might reproach me. 14 My God, think thou upon Tobiah and Sanballat according to these their works, and on the prophetess Noadiah, and the rest of the prophets, that would have put me in fear.

15 So the wall was finished in the twenty and fifth day of the month Elul, in fifty and two days. 16 And it came to pass, that when all our enemies heard thereof, and all the heathen that were about us saw these things, they were much cast down in their own eyes: for they perceived that this work was wrought of our God. 17 Moreover in those days the nobles of Judah sent many letters unto Tobiah, and the letters of Tobiah came unto them. 18 For there were many in Judah sworn unto him, because he was the son-in-law of Shechaniah the son of Arah; and his son Johanan had taken the daughter of Meshullam the son of Berechiah. 19 Also they reported his good deeds before me, and uttered my words to him. And Tobiah sent letters to put me in fear.

7 Now it came to pass, when the wall was built, and I had set up the doors, and the porters and the singers and the Levites were appointed, 2 That I gave my brother Hanani, and Hananiah the ruler of the palace, charge over Jerusalem: for he was a faithful man, and feared God above many. 3 And I said unto them, Let not the gates of Jerusalem be opened until the sun be hot; and while they stand by, let them shut the doors, and bar them: and appoint watches of the inhabitants of Jerusalem, every one in his watch, and every one to be over against his house. 4 Now the city was large and great: but the people were few therein, and the houses were not builded.

66 The whole congregation together was forty and two thousand three hundred and threescore, 67 Besides their manservants and their maidservants, of whom there were seven thousand three hundred thirty and seven: and they had two hundred forty and five singing men and singing women. 68 Their horses, seven hundred thirty and six: their mules, two hundred forty and five: 69 Their camels, four hundred thirty and five: six thousand seven hundred and twenty asses.

70 And some of the chief of the fathers gave unto the work. The Tirshatha[1] gave to the treasure a thousand drams of gold, fifty basins, five hundred and thirty priests' garments. 71 And some of the chief of the fathers gave to the treasure of the work twenty thousand drams of gold, and two thousand and two hundred pounds of silver. 72 And that which the rest of the people gave was twenty thousand drams of gold, and two thousand pounds of silver, and threescore and seven priests' garments.

73 So the priests, and the Levites, and the porters, and the singers, and some of the people, and the Nethinim, and all Israel, dwelt in their cities; and when the seventh month came, the children of Israel were in their cities.

## THE LAW RE-ESTABLISHED

8 And all the people gathered themselves together as one man into the street that was before the water gate; and they spake unto Ezra the scribe to bring the book of the law of Moses, which the Lord had commanded to Israel. 2 And Ezra the priest brought the law before the congregation both of men and women, and all that could hear with understanding, upon the first day of the seventh month. 3 And he read therein before the street that was before the water gate from the morning until midday, before the men and the women, and those that could understand; and the ears of all the people were attentive unto the book of the law. 4 And Ezra the scribe stood upon a pulpit of wood, which they had made for the purpose; and beside him stood Mattithiah, and Shema, and Anaiah, and Urijah, and Hilkiah, and Maaseiah, on his right hand; and on his left hand, Pedaiah, and Mishael, and Malchiah, and Hashum, and Hashbadana, Zechariah, and Meshullam. 5 And Ezra opened the book in the sight of all the people; (for he was above all the people;) and when he opened it, all the people stood up: 6 And Ezra blessed the Lord, the great God. And all the people answered, Amen, Amen, with lifting up their hands: and they bowed their heads, and worshipped the Lord with their faces to the ground. 7 Also Jeshua, and Bani, and Sherebiah, Jamin, Akkub, Shabbethai, Hodijah, Maaseiah, Kelita, Azariah, Jozabad, Hanan, Pelaiah, and the Levites, caused the people to understand the law: and the people stood in their place. 8 So they read in the book in the law of God distinctly, and gave the sense, and caused them to understand the reading.

9 And Nehemiah, which is the Tirshatha, and Ezra the priest the scribe, and the Levites that taught the people, said unto all the people, This day is holy unto the Lord your God; mourn not, nor weep. For all the people wept, when they heard the words of the law. 10 Then he said unto them, Go your way, eat the fat, and drink the sweet, and send portions unto them for whom nothing is prepared: for this day

---

[1] Governor, i.e., Nehemiah.

is holy unto our Lord: neither be ye sorry; for the joy of the Lord is your strength. 11 So the Levites stilled all the people, saying, Hold your peace, for the day is holy; neither be ye grieved. 12 And all the people went their way to eat, and to drink, and to send portions, and to make great mirth, because they had understood the words that were declared unto them.

9 Now in the twenty and fourth day of this month the children of Israel were assembled with fasting, and with sackclothes, and earth upon them. 2 And the seed of Israel separated themselves from all strangers, and stood and confessed their sins, and the iniquities of their fathers. 3 And they stood up in their place, and read in the book of the law of the Lord their God one fourth part of the day; and another fourth part they confessed, and worshipped the Lord their God. 5 Then the Levites, Jeshua, and Kadmiel, Bani, Hashabniah, Sherebiah, Hodijah, Shebaniah, and Pethahiah, said, Stand up and bless the Lord your God for ever and ever: and blessed be thy glorious name, which is exalted above all blessing and praise.

32 Now therefore, our God, the great, the mighty, and the terrible God, who keepest covenant and mercy, let not all the trouble seem little before thee, that hath come upon us, on our kings, on our princes, and on our priests, and on our prophets, and on our fathers, and on all thy people, since the time of the kings of Assyria unto this day. 33 Howbeit thou art just in all that is brought upon us; for thou hast done right, but we have done wickedly: 34 Neither have our kings, our princes, our priests, nor our fathers, kept thy law, nor hearkened unto thy commandments and thy testimonies, wherewith thou didst testify against them. 35 For they have not served thee in their kingdom, and in thy great goodness that thou gavest them, and in the large and fat land which thou gavest before them, neither turned they from their wicked works. 36 Behold, we are servants this day, and for the land that thou gavest unto our fathers to eat the fruit thereof and the good thereof, behold, we are servants in it: 37 And it yieldeth much increase unto the kings whom thou hast set over us because of our sins: also they have dominion over our bodies, and over our cattle, at their pleasure, and we are in great distress. 38 And because of all this we make a sure covenant, and write it; and our princes, Levites, and priests, seal unto it.

10 28 And the rest of the people, the priests, the Levites, the porters, the singers, the Nethinim, and all they that had separated themselves from the people of the lands unto the law of God, their wives, their sons, and their daughters, every one having knowledge, and having understanding; 29 They clave to their brethren, their nobles, and entered into a curse, and into an oath, to walk in God's law, which was given by Moses the servant of God, and to observe and do all the commandments of the Lord our Lord, and his judgments and his statutes; 30 And that we would not give our daughters unto the

people of the land, nor take their daughters for our sons: 31 And if the people of the land bring ware or any victuals on the sabbath day to sell, that we would not buy it of them on the sabbath, or on the holy day: and that we would leave the seventh year, and the exaction of every debt.

12  27 And at the dedication of the wall of Jerusalem they sought the Levites out of all their places, to bring them to Jerusalem, to keep the dedication with gladness, both with thanksgiving, and with singing, with cymbals, psalteries, and with harps. 28 And the sons of the singers gathered themselves together, both out of the plain country round about Jerusalem, and from the villages of Netophathi; 29 Also from the house of Gilgal, and out of the fields of Geba and Azmaveth: for the singers had builded them villages round about Jerusalem. 30 And the priests and the Levites purified themselves, and purified the people, and the gates, and the wall.

31 Then I brought up the princes of Judah upon the wall, and appointed two great companies of them that gave thanks. 43 Also that day they offered great sacrifices, and rejoiced: for God had made them rejoice with great joy: the wives also and the children rejoiced: so that the joy of Jerusalem was heard even afar off.

13  On that day they read in the book of Moses in the audience of the people; and therein was found written, that the Ammonite and the Moabite should not come into the congregation of God for ever; 2 Because they met not the children of Israel with bread and with water, but hired Balaam against them, that he should curse them: howbeit our God turned the curse into a blessing. 3 Now it came to pass, when they had heard the law, that they separated from Israel all the mixed multitude.

### CONTINUING NEED OF REFORM

4 And before this, Eliashib the priest, having the oversight of the chamber of the house of our God, was allied unto Tobiah: 5 And he had prepared for him a great chamber, where aforetime they laid the meat offerings, the frankincense, and the vessels, and the tithes of the corn, the new wine, and the oil, which was commanded to be given to the Levites, and the singers, and the porters; and the offerings of the priests. 6 But in all this time was not I at Jerusalem: for in the two and thirtieth year of Artaxerxes king of Babylon came I unto the king, and after certain days obtained I leave of the king: 7 And I came to Jerusalem, and understood of the evil that Eliashib did for Tobiah, in preparing him a chamber in the courts of the house of God. 8 And it grieved me sore: therefore I cast forth all the household stuff of Tobiah out of the chamber. 9 Then I commanded, and they cleansed the chambers: and thither brought I again the vessels of the house of God, with the meat offering and the frankincense.

10 And I perceived that the portions of the Levites had not been given them: for the Levites and the singers, that did the work, were fled every one to his field. 11 Then contended I with the rulers, and said, Why is the house of God forsaken? And I gathered them together, and set them in their place. 12 Then brought all Judah the tithe of the corn and the new wine and the oil unto the treasuries. 13 And I made treasurers over the treasuries, Shelemiah the priest, and Zadok the scribe, and of the Levites, Pedaiah: and next to them was Hanan the son of Zaccur, the son of Mattaniah: for they were counted faithful, and their office was to distribute unto their brethren. 14 Remember me, O my God, concerning this, and wipe not out my good deeds that I have done for the house of my God, and for the offices thereof.

15 In those days saw I in Judah some treading winepresses on the sabbath, and bringing in sheaves, and lading asses; as also wine, grapes, and figs, and all manner of burdens, which they brought into Jerusalem on the sabbath day: and I testified against them in the day wherein they sold victuals. 16 There dwelt men of Tyre also therein, which brought fish, and all manner of ware, and sold on the sabbath unto the children of Judah, and in Jerusalem. 17 Then I contended with the nobles of Judah, and said unto them, What evil thing is this that ye do, and profane the sabbath day? 18 Did not your fathers thus, and did not our God bring all this evil upon us, and upon this city? yet ye bring more wrath upon Israel by profaning the sabbath.

19 And it came to pass, that when the gates of Jerusalem began to be dark before the sabbath, I commanded that the gates should be shut, and charged that they should not be opened till after the sabbath: and some of my servants set I at the gates, that there should no burden be brought in on the sabbath day. 20 So the merchants and sellers of all kind of ware lodged without Jerusalem once or twice. 21 Then I testified against them, and said unto them, Why lodge ye about the wall? if ye do so again, I will lay hands on you. From that time forth came they no more on the sabbath. 22 And I commanded the Levites, that they should cleanse themselves, and that they should come and keep the gates, to sanctify the sabbath day. Remember me, O my God, concerning this also, and spare me according to the greatness of thy mercy.

23 In those days also saw I Jews that had married wives of Ashdod, of Ammon, and of Moab: 24 And their children spake half in the speech of Ashdod, and could not speak in the Jews' language, but according to the language of each people. 25 And I contended with them, and cursed them, and smote certain of them, and plucked off their hair, and made them swear by God, saying, Ye shall not give your daughters unto their sons, nor take their daughters unto your sons, or for yourselves. 26 Did not Solomon king of Israel sin by these things? yet among many nations was there no king like him, who was beloved of his God, and God made him king over all Israel: neverthe-

less even him did outlandish women cause to sin. 27 Shall we then hearken unto you to do all this great evil, to transgress against our God in marrying strange wives?

28 And one of the sons of Joiada, the son of Eliashib the high priest, was son-in-law to Sanballat the Horonite: therefore I chased him from me. 29 Remember them, O my God, because they have defiled the priesthood, and the covenant of the priesthood, and of the Levites.

30 Thus cleansed I them from all strangers, and appointed the wards of the priests and the Levites, every one in his business; 31 And for the wood offering, at times appointed, and for the firstfruits. Remember me, O my God, for good.

# A Mission to Assyria: *Jonah*

*Jonah differs from the other prophetic books in that it is a book about a prophet, and not a collection of prophetic addresses. Written after the return of the Jews from exile, it is an extended parable on the relation of men and nations to God. Here we must recall that Nineveh, "that great city," to which God sends Jonah, was the capital of the Assyrians who had destroyed the Northern Kingdom of Israel. From beginning to end, then, the small book of Jonah shows God's concern for nations other than the chosen people. It is against this divine concern that Jonah rebels, assuming to himself a greater knowledge of good and evil than he is willing to credit to God. The events described in the parable have about them a fine comic quality, as Jonah's attitudes are subjected to the most telling satire. Underlying and pervading the entire account, however, is an intensely serious and even sublime consciousness of the faithfulness owed to God by an individual man and by the Jewish community as a bearer of God's blessings to all mankind. After the return of the exiles to Jerusalem, there was the strictest observation of the ceremonial and civil law, and the sternest measures were taken to prevent an infiltration of idolatry into the Judaic cult, as we have seen in the book of Nehemiah. The author of Jonah was in no sense suggesting that the Jews should repudiate their refusal to worship foreign gods; what he was stressing was the obligation of the chosen people to carry the message of the true God to foreigners. His position was essentially that of Isaiah 49:6*

*I will also give thee for a light to the Gentiles,*
*That thou mayest be my salvation to the end of the earth.*

*But though his position was essentially the same, his literary method was radically different, as a reading of his short book will show.*

# Jonah

1 Now the word of the Lord came unto Jonah the son of Amittai, saying, 2 Arise, go to Nineveh, that great city, and cry against it; for their wickedness is come up before me. 3 But Jonah rose up to flee unto Tarshish from the presence of the Lord, and went down to Joppa; and he found a ship going to Tarshish: so he paid the fare thereof, and went down into it, to go with them unto Tarshish from the presence of the Lord.

4 But the Lord sent out a great wind into the sea, and there was a mighty tempest in the sea, so that the ship was like to be broken. 5 Then the mariners were afraid, and cried every man unto his god, and cast forth the wares that were in the ship into the sea, to lighten it of them. But Jonah was gone down into the sides of the ship; and he lay, and was fast asleep. 6 So the shipmaster came to him, and said unto him, What meanest thou, O sleeper? arise, call upon thy God, if so be that God will think upon us, that we perish not. 7 And they said every one to his fellow, Come, and let us cast lots, that we may know for whose cause this evil is upon us. So they cast lots, and the lot fell upon Jonah. 8 Then said they unto him, Tell us, we pray thee, for whose cause this evil is upon us; What is thine occupation? and whence comest thou? what is thy country? and of what people art thou? 9 And he said unto them, I am a Hebrew; and I fear the Lord, the God of heaven, which hath made the sea and the dry land. 10 Then were the men exceedingly afraid, and said unto him, Why hast thou done this? For the men knew that he fled from the presence of the Lord, because he had told them.

11 Then said they unto him, What shall we do unto thee, that the sea may be calm unto us? for the sea wrought, and was tempestuous. 12 And he said unto them, Take me up, and cast me forth into the sea; so shall the sea be calm unto you: for I know that for my sake this great tempest is upon you. 13 Nevertheless the men rowed hard to bring it to the land; but they could not: for the sea wrought, and was tempestuous against them. 14 Wherefore they cried unto the Lord, and said, We beseech thee, O Lord, we beseech thee, let us not perish for this man's life, and lay not upon us innocent blood: for thou, O Lord, hast done as it pleased thee. 15 So they took up Jonah, and cast him forth into the sea: and the sea ceased from her raging. 16 Then the men feared the Lord exceedingly, and offered a sacrifice unto the Lord, and made vows.

17 Now the Lord had prepared a great fish to swallow up Jonah. And Jonah was in the belly of the fish three days and three nights.

2 Then Jonah prayed unto the Lord his God out of the fish's belly, 2 And said,

     I cried by reason of mine affliction

Unto the Lord, and he heard me;
Out of the belly of hell cried I,
And thou heardest my voice.
3 For thou hadst cast me into the deep,
In the midst of the seas;
And the floods compassed me about:
All thy billows and thy waves passed over me.
4 Then I said, I am cast out of thy sight;
Yet I will look again toward thy holy temple.
5 The waters compassed me about, even to the soul:
The depth closed me round about,
The weeds were wrapped about my head.
6 I went down to the bottoms of the mountains;
The earth with her bars was about me for ever:
Yet hast thou brought up my life from corruption,
O Lord my God.
7 When my soul fainted within me
I remembered the Lord:
And my prayer came in unto thee,
Into thine holy temple.
8 They that observe lying vanities
Forsake their own mercy.
9 But I will sacrifice unto thee
With the voice of thanksgiving;
I will pay that that I have vowed.
Salvation is of the Lord.
10 And the Lord spake unto the fish, and it vomited out Jonah upon the dry land.

3 And the word of the Lord came unto Jonah the second time, saying, 2 Arise, go unto Nineveh, that great city, and preach unto it the preaching that I bid thee. 3 So Jonah arose, and went unto Nineveh, according to the word of the Lord. Now Nineveh was an exceeding great city of three days' journey. 4 And Jonah began to enter into the city a day's journey, and he cried, and said, Yet forty days, and Nineveh shall be overthrown.

5 So the people of Nineveh believed God, and proclaimed a fast, and put on sackcloth, from the greatest of them even to the least of them. 6 For word came unto the king of Nineveh, and he arose from his throne, and he laid his robe from him, and covered him with sackcloth, and sat in ashes. 7 And he caused it to be proclaimed and published through Nineveh by the decree of the king of his nobles, saying, Let neither man nor beast, herd nor flock, taste any thing: let them not feed, nor drink water: 8 But let man and beast be covered with sackcloth, and cry mightily unto God: yea, let them turn every one from his evil way, and from the violence that is in their hands. 9 Who can tell if God will turn and repent, and turn away from his fierce anger, that we perish not?

10 And God saw their works, that they turned from their evil way; and God repented of the evil, that he had said that he would do unto them; and he did it not.

4 But it displeased Jonah exceedingly, and he was very angry. 2 And he prayed unto the Lord, and said, I pray thee, O Lord, was not this my saying, when I was yet in my country? Therefore I fled before unto Tarshish: for I knew that thou art a gracious God, and merciful, slow to anger, and of great kindness, and repentest thee of the evil. 3 Therefor now, O Lord, take, I beseech thee, my life from me; for it is better for me to die than to live. 4 Then said the Lord, Doest thou well to be angry?

5 So Jonah went out of the city, and sat on the east side of the city, and there made him a booth, and sat under it in the shadow, till he might see what would become of the city. 6 And the Lord God prepared a gourd, and made it to come up over Jonah, that it might be a shadow over his head, to deliver him from his grief. So Jonah was exceeding glad of the gourd. 7 But God prepared a worm when the morning rose the next day, and it smote the gourd that it withered. 8 And it came to pass, when the sun did arise, that God prepared a vehement east wind; and the sun beat upon the head of Jonah, that he fainted, and wished in himself to die, and said, It is better for me to die than to live. 9 And God said to Jonah, Doest thou well to be angry for the gourd? And he said, I do well to be angry, even unto death. 10 Then said the Lord, Thou hast had pity on the gourd, for the which thou hast not labored, neither madest it grow; which came up in a night, and perished in a night: 11 And should not I spare Nineveh, that great city, wherein are more than sixscore thousand persons that cannot discern between their right hand and their left hand; and also much cattle?

## The Latest Prophet: *Malachi*

*After the initial zeal and righteousness evinced upon the return to Jerusalem, there was another falling away, especially evident among the priests. It is to this situation that Malachi, the last of the Old Testament prophets, addressed himself.*

# *Malachi*

1 The burden of the word of the Lord to Israel by Malachi.
  2 I have loved you, saith the Lord.
    Yet ye say, Wherein hast thou loved us?
  6 A son honoreth his father, and a servant his master:
    If then I be a father, where is mine honor?

And if I be a master, where is my fear?
Saith the Lord of hosts unto you,
O priests, that despise my name.
And ye say, Wherein have we despised thy name?
7 Ye offer polluted bread upon mine altar;
And ye say, Wherein have we polluted thee?
In that ye say, The table of the Lord is contemptible.
8 And if ye offer the blind for sacrifice, is it not evil?
And if ye offer the lame and sick, is it not evil?
Offer it now unto thy governor;
Will he be pleased with thee, or accept thy person?
Saith the Lord of hosts.
10 Who is there even among you that would shut the doors for
 nought?
Neither do ye kindle fire on mine altar for nought.
I have no pleasure in you,
Saith the Lord of hosts,
Neither will I accept an offering at your hand.
11 For, from the rising of the sun even unto the going down of
 the same,
My name shall be great among the Gentiles;
And in every place incense shall be offered unto my name,
And a pure offering:
For my name shall be great among the heathen,
Saith the Lord of hosts.
12 But ye have profaned it, in that ye say,
The table of the Lord is polluted;
And the fruit thereof, even his meat, is contemptible.
13 Ye said also, Behold, what a weariness is it!
And ye have snuffed at it,
Saith the Lord of hosts;
And ye brought that which was torn, and the lame, and the
 sick;
Thus ye brought an offering:
Should I accept this of your hand?
Saith the Lord.

2    And now, O ye priests, this commandment is for you.
2 If ye will not hear, and if ye will not lay it to heart,
To give glory unto my name,
Saith the Lord of hosts,
I will even send a curse upon you,
And I will curse your blessings:
Yea, I have cursed them already,
Because ye do not lay it to heart.
8 But ye are departed out of the way;
Ye have caused many to stumble at the law;

Ye have corrupted the covenant of Levi,
Saith the Lord of hosts.
9 Therefore have I also made you
Contemptible and base before all the people,
According as ye have not kept my ways,
But have been partial in the law.
17 Ye have wearied the Lord with your words.
Yet ye say, Wherein have we wearied him?
When ye say, Every one that doeth evil is good in the sight
of the Lord,
And he delighteth in them;
Or, Where is the God of judgment?

3
Behold, I will send my messenger, and he shall prepare the
way before me:
And the Lord, whom ye seek, shall suddenly come to his
temple,
Even the messenger of the covenant, whom ye delight in:
Behold, he shall come,
Saith the Lord of hosts.
2 But who may abide the day of his coming?
And who shall stand when he appeareth?
For he is like a refiner's fire, and like fullers' soap:
3 And he shall sit as a refiner and purifier of silver:
And he shall purify the sons of Levi, and purge them as gold
and silver,
That they may offer unto the Lord an offering in righteousness.
4 Then shall the offering of Judah and Jerusalem be pleasant
unto the Lord,
As in the days of old, and as in former years.
5 And I will come near to you to judgment;
And I will be a swift witness
Against the sorcerers, and against the adulterers, and against
false swearers,
And against those that oppress the hireling in his wages,
The widow, and the fatherless,
And that turn aside the stranger from his right, and fear not
me,
Saith the Lord of hosts.

4
For, behold, the day cometh, that shall burn as an oven;
And all the proud, yea, and all that do wickedly, shall be
stubble:
And the day that cometh shall burn them up,
Saith the Lord of hosts,
That it shall leave them neither root nor branch.
2 But unto you that fear my name

Shall the Sun of righteousness arise with healing in his wings;
And ye shall go forth, and grow up as calves of the stall.
3 And ye shall tread down the wicked;
For they shall be ashes under the soles of your feet
In the day that I shall do this,
Saith the Lord of hosts.
4 Remember ye the law of Moses my servant,
Which I commanded unto him in Horeb for all Israel,
With the statutes and judgments.
5 Behold, I will send you Elijah the prophet
Before the coming of the great and dreadful day of the Lord:
6 And he shall turn the heart of the fathers to the children,
And the heart of the children to their fathers,
Lest I come and smite the earth with a curse.

# Various Writings

## Lyrics of Religious Devotion: *The Psalms*

The Psalms were the lyric prayers of a poetic people. Intimately connected with the rituals of the Jewish religion, they often contain antiphonal responses in which different voices or groups of voices address each other in the course of a single psalm; if this structural device is kept in mind, readers will have little difficulty in interpreting the shifts from one speaker to another in the course of the lyric developments. The psalms cover the full gamut of human emotions, but they most prominently illustrate the freedom which the devout Hebrew felt in his access to God under the most varied circumstances. Albert Einstein summarized another central theme of the psalms as "a sort of intoxicated joy and amazement at the beauty and grandeur of the world, of which man can just form a faint notion."[1]

## *Psalms*

1   Blessed is the man that walketh not in the counsel of the
    ungodly,
    Nor standeth in the way of sinners,
    Nor sitteth in the seat of the scornful.
2 But his delight is in the law of the Lord;
    And in his law doth he meditate day and night.
3 And he shall be like a tree planted by the rivers of water,
    That bringeth forth his fruit in his season;
    His leaf also shall not wither;
    And whatsoever he doeth shall prosper.
4 The ungodly are not so:
    But are like the chaff which the wind driveth away.
5 Therefore the ungodly shall not stand in the judgment,
    Nor sinners in the congregation of the righteous.
6 For the Lord knoweth the way of the righteous:
    But the way of the ungodly shall perish.

2   Why do the heathen rage,
    And the people imagine a vain thing?

[1] *The World as I See It* (New York: Philosophical Library, 1949), p. 91.

2 The kings of the earth set themselves,
  And the rulers take counsel together,
  Against the Lord, and against his Anointed, saying,
3 Let us break their bands asunder,
  And cast away their cords from us.
4 He that sitteth in the heavens shall laugh:
  The Lord shall have them in derision.
5 Then shall he speak unto them in his wrath,
  And vex them in his sore displeasure.
6 Yet have I set my King
  Upon my holy hill of Zion.
7 I will declare the decree:
  The Lord hath said unto me, Thou art my Son;
  This day have I begotten thee.
8 Ask of me,
  And I shall give thee the heathen for thine inheritance,
  And the uttermost parts of the earth for thy possession.
9 Thou shalt break them with a rod of iron;
  Thou shalt dash them in pieces like a potter's vessel.
10 Be wise now therefore, O ye kings:
  Be instructed, ye judges of the earth.
11 Serve the Lord with fear,
  And rejoice with trembling.
12 Kiss the Son, lest he be angry,
  And ye perish from the way,
  When his wrath is kindled but a little.
  Blessed are all they that put their trust in him.

## 11

In the Lord put I my trust:
  How say ye to my soul,
  Flee as a bird to your mountain?
2 For, lo, the wicked bend their bow,
  They make ready their arrow upon the string,
  That they may privily shoot at the upright in heart.
3 If the foundations be destroyed,
  What can the righteous do?
4 The Lord is in his holy temple,
  The Lord's throne is in heaven:
  His eyes behold,
  His eyelids try, the children of men.
5 The Lord trieth the righteous:
  But the wicked and him that loveth violence his soul hateth.
6 Upon the wicked he shall rain snares, fire and brimstone,
  And a horrible tempest: this shall be the portion of their cup.
7 For the righteous Lord loveth righteousness;
  His countenance doth behold the upright.

14 The fool hath said in his heart, There is no God.
They are corrupt, they have done abominable works,
There is none that doeth good.
2 The Lord looked down from heaven upon the children of
men,
To see if there were any that did understand, and seek God.
3 They are all gone aside, they are all together become filthy:
There is none that doeth good, no, not one.
4 Have all the workers of iniquity no knowledge?
Who eat up my people as they eat bread,
And call not upon the Lord.
5 There were they in great fear:
For God is in the generation of the righteous.
6 Ye have shamed the counsel of the poor,
Because the Lord is his refuge.
7 Oh that the salvation of Israel were come out of Zion!
When the Lord bringeth back the captivity of his people,
Jacob shall rejoice, and Israel shall be glad.

15 Lord, who shall abide in thy tabernacle?
Who shall dwell in thy holy hill?
2 He that walketh uprightly, and worketh righteousness,
And speaketh the truth in his heart.
3 He that backbiteth not with his tongue,
Nor doeth evil to his neighbor,
Nor taketh up a reproach against his neighbor.
4 In whose eyes a vile person is contemned;
But he honoreth them that fear the Lord.
He that sweareth to his own hurt, and changeth not.
5 He that putteth not out his money to usury,
Nor taketh reward against the innocent.
He that doeth these things shall never be moved.

16 Preserve me, O God: for in thee do I put my trust.
2 O my soul, thou hast said unto the Lord, Thou art my Lord:
My goodness extendeth not to thee;
3 But to the saints that are in the earth,
And to the excellent, in whom is all my delight.
4 Their sorrows shall be multiplied that hasten after another
god:
Their drink offerings of blood will I not offer,
Nor take up their names into my lips.
5 The Lord is the portion of mine inheritance and of my cup:
Thou maintainest my lot.
6 The lines are fallen unto me in pleasant places;
Yea, I have a goodly heritage.

7 I will bless the Lord, who hath given me counsel:
My reins also instruct me in the night seasons.
8 I have set the Lord always before me:
Because he is at my right hand, I shall not be moved.
9 Therefore my heart is glad, and my glory rejoiceth:
My flesh also shall rest in hope.
10 For thou wilt not leave my soul in hell;
Neither wilt thou suffer thine Holy One to see corruption.
11 Thou wilt show me the path of life:
In thy presence is fulness of joy;
At thy right hand there are pleasures for evermore.

19    The heavens declare the glory of God;
And the firmament showeth his handiwork.
2 Day unto day uttereth speech,
And night unto night showeth knowledge.
3 There is no speech nor language,
Where their voice is not heard.
4 Their line is gone out through all the earth,
And their words to the end of the world.
In them hath he set a tabernacle for the sun,
5 Which is as a bridegroom coming out of his chamber,
And rejoiceth as a strong man to run a race.
6 His going forth is from the end of the heaven,
And his circuit unto the ends of it:
And there is nothing hid from the heat thereof.
7 The law of the Lord is perfect, converting the soul:
The testimony of the Lord is sure, making wise the simple.
8 The statutes of the Lord are right, rejoicing the heart:
The commandment of the Lord is pure, enlightening the eyes.
9 The fear of the Lord is clean, enduring for ever:
The judgments of the Lord are true and righteous altogether.
10 More to be desired are they than gold, yea, than much fine
gold:
Sweeter also than honey and the honeycomb.
11 Moreover by them is thy servant warned:
And in keeping of them there is great reward.
12 Who can understand his errors?
Cleanse thou me from secret faults.
13 Keep back thy servant also from presumptuous sins;
Let them not have dominion over me:
Then shall I be upright,
And I shall be innocent from the great transgression.
14 Let the words of my mouth, and the meditation of my heart,
Be acceptable in thy sight,
O Lord, my strength, and my redeemer.

22 My God, my God, why hast thou forsaken me?
Why art thou so far from helping me, and from the words of
my roaring?
2 O my God, I cry in the daytime, but thou hearest not;
And in the night season, and am not silent.
3 But thou art holy,
O thou that inhabitest the praises of Israel.
4 Our fathers trusted in thee:
They trusted, and thou didst deliver them.
5 They cried unto thee, and were delivered:
They trusted in thee, and were not confounded.
6 But I am a worm, and no man;
A reproach of men, and despised of the people.
7 All they that see me laugh me to scorn:
They shoot out the lip, they shake the head, saying,
8 He trusted on the Lord that he would deliver him:
Let him deliver him, seeing he delighted in him.
9 But thou art he that took me out of the womb:
Thou didst make me hope when I was upon my mother's
breasts.
10 I was cast upon thee from the womb:
Thou art my God from my mother's belly.
11 Be not far from me;
For trouble is near;
For there is none to help.
12 Many bulls have compassed me:
Strong bulls of Bashan have beset me round.
13 They gaped upon me with their mouths,
As a ravening and a roaring lion.
14 I am poured out like water,
And all my bones are out of joint:
My heart is like wax;
It is melted in the midst of my bowels.
15 My strength is dried up like a potsherd;
And my tongue cleaveth to my jaws;
And thou hast brought me into the dust of death.
16 For dogs have compassed me:
The assembly of the wicked have inclosed me:
They pierced my hands and my feet.
17 I may tell all my bones:
They look and stare upon me.
18 They part my garments among them,
And cast lots upon my vesture.
19 But be not thou far from me, O Lord:
O my strength, haste thee to help me.
20 Deliver my soul from the sword;
My darling from the power of the dog.

21 Save me from the lion's mouth:
For thou hast heard me from the horns of the unicorns.
22 I will declare thy name unto my brethren:
In the midst of the congregation will I praise thee.
23 Ye that fear the Lord, praise him;
All ye the seed of Jacob, glorify him;
And fear him, all ye the seed of Israel.
24 For he hath not despised nor abhorred the affliction of the afflicted;
Neither hath he hid his face from him;
But when he cried unto him, he heard.
25 My praise shall be of thee in the great congregation:
I will pay my vows before them that fear him.
26 The meek shall eat and be satisfied:
They shall praise the Lord that seek him:
Your heart shall live for ever.
27 All the ends of the world shall remember and turn unto the Lord:
And all the kindreds of the nations shall worship before thee.
28 For the kingdom is the Lord's:
And he is the governor among the nations.
29 All they that be fat upon earth shall eat and worship:
All they that go down to the dust shall bow before him:
And none can keep alive his own soul.
30 A seed shall serve him;
It shall be accounted to the Lord for a generation.
31 They shall come, and shall declare his righteousness
Unto a people that shall be born, that he hath done this.

23    The Lord is my shepherd; I shall not want.
2 He maketh me to lie down in green pastures:
He leadeth me beside the still waters.
3 He restoreth my soul:
He leadeth me in the paths of righteousness for his name's sake.
4 Yea, though I walk through the valley of the shadow of death,
I will fear no evil: for thou art with me;
Thy rod and thy staff they comfort me.
5 Thou preparest a table before me in the presence of mine enemies:
Thou anointest my head with oil; my cup runneth over.
6 Surely goodness and mercy shall follow me all the days of my life:
And I will dwell in the house of the Lord for ever.

24    The earth is the Lord's, and the fulness thereof;
The world, and they that dwell therein.
2 For he hath founded it upon the seas,

And established it upon the floods.
3 Who shall ascend into the hill of the Lord?
 Or who shall stand in his holy place?
4 He that hath clean hands, and a pure heart;
 Who hath not lifted up his soul unto vanity,
 Nor sworn deceitfully.
5 He shall receive the blessing from the Lord,
 And righteousness from the God of his salvation.
6 This is the generation of them that seeks him,
 That seek thy face, O Jacob.    Selah.
7 Lift up your heads, O ye gates;
 And be ye lifted up, ye everlasting doors;
 And the King of glory shall come in.
8 Who is this King of glory?
 The Lord strong and mighty,
 The Lord mighty in battle.
9 Lift up your heads, O ye gates;
 Even lift them up, ye everlasting doors;
 And the King of glory shall come in.
10 Who is this King of glory?
 The Lord of hosts,
 He is the King of glory.    Selah.

27    The Lord is my light and my salvation; whom shall I fear?
 The Lord is the strength of my life; of whom shall I be
 afraid?
2 When the wicked, even mine enemies and my foes,
 Came upon me to eat up my flesh,
 They stumbled and fell.
3 Though a host should encamp against me,
 My heart shall not fear:
 Though war should rise against me,
 In this will I be confident.
4 One thing have I desired of the Lord, that will I seek after;
 That I may dwell in the house of the Lord all the days of my
 life,
 To behold the beauty of the Lord, and to inquire in his
 temple.
5 For in the time of trouble he shall hide me in his pavilion:
 In the secret of his tabernacle shall he hide me;
 He shall set me up upon a rock.
6 And now shall mine head be lifted up above mine enemies
 round about me:
 Therefore will I offer in his tabernacle sacrifices of joy;
 I will sing, yea, I will sing praises unto the Lord.
7 Hear, O Lord, when I cry with my voice:
 Have mercy also upon me, and answer me.
8 When thou saidst, Seek ye my face;

375

My heart said unto thee,
Thy face, Lord, will I seek.
9 Hide not thy face far from me;
Put not thy servant away in anger:
Thou hast been my help;
Leave me not, neither forsake me,
O God of my salvation.
10 When my father and my mother forsake me,
Then the Lord will take me up.
11 Teach me thy way, O Lord,
And lead me in a plain path,
Because of mine enemies.
12 Deliver me not over unto the will of mine enemies:
For false witnesses are risen up against me,
And such as breathe out cruelty.
13 I had fainted, unless I had believed to see the goodness of
the Lord
In the land of the living.
14 Wait on the Lord:
Be of good courage, and he shall strengthen thine heart:
Wait, I say, on the Lord.

**30** I will extol thee, O Lord; for thou hast lifted me up,
And hast not made my foes to rejoice over me.
2 O Lord my God, I cried unto thee, and thou hast healed me.
3 O Lord, thou hast brought up my soul from the grave:
Thou hast kept me alive, that I should not go down to the pit.
4 Sing unto the Lord, O ye saints of his,
And give thanks at the remembrance of his holiness.
5 For his anger endureth but a moment;
In his favor is life:
Weeping may endure for a night,
But joy cometh in the morning.
6 And in my prosperity I said,
I shall never be moved.
7 Lord, by thy favor thou hast made my mountain to stand
strong:
Thou didst hide thy face, and I was troubled.
8 I cried to thee, O Lord;
And unto the Lord I made supplication.
9 What profit is there in my blood, when I go down to the pit?
Shall the dust praise thee? shall it declare thy truth?
10 Hear, O Lord, and have mercy upon me:
Lord, be thou my helper.
11 Thou hast turned for me my mourning into dancing:
Thou hast put off my sackcloth, and girded me with gladness;

12 To the end that my glory may sing praise to thee, and not
be silent.
O Lord my God, I will give thanks unto thee for ever.

**34** I will bless the Lord at all times:
His praise shall continually be in my mouth.
2 My soul shall make her boast in the Lord:
The humble shall hear thereof, and be glad.
3 O magnify the Lord with me,
And let us exalt his name together.
4 I sought the Lord, and he heard me,
And delivered me from all my fears.
5 They looked unto him, and were lightened:
And their faces were not ashamed.
6 This poor man cried, and the Lord heard him,
And saved him out of all his troubles.
7 The angel of the Lord encampeth round about them that fear
him,
And delivereth them.
8 O taste and see that the Lord is good:
Blessed is the man that trusteth in him.
9 O fear the Lord, ye his saints:
For there is no want to them that fear him.
10 The young lions do lack, and suffer hunger:
But they that seek the Lord shall not want any good thing.
11 Come, ye children, hearken unto me:
I will teach you the fear of the Lord.
12 What man is he that desireth life,
And loveth many days, that he may see good?
13 Keep thy tongue from evil,
And thy lips from speaking guile.
14 Depart from evil, and do good;
Seek peace, and pursue it.
15 The eyes of the Lord are upon the righteous,
And his ears are open unto their cry.
16 The face of the Lord is against them that do evil,
To cut off the remembrance of them from the earth.
17 The righteous cry, and the Lord heareth,
And delivereth them out of all their troubles.
18 The Lord is nigh unto them that are of a broken heart;
And saveth such as be of a contrite spirit.
19 Many are the afflictions of the righteous:
But the Lord delivereth him out of them all.
20 He keepeth all his bones:
Not one of them is broken.
21 Evil shall slay the wicked:
And they that hate the righteous shall be desolate.

22 The Lord redeemeth the soul of his servants:
And none of them that trust in him shall be desolate.

39
I said, I will take heed to my ways,
That I sin not with my tongue:
I will keep my mouth with a bridle,
While the wicked is before me.
2 I was dumb with silence,
I held my peace, even from good;
And my sorrow was stirred.
3 My heart was hot within me;
While I was musing the fire burned:
Then spake I with my tongue,
4 Lord, make me to know mine end,
And the measure of my days, what it is;
That I may know how frail I am.
5 Behold, thou hast made my days as a handbreadth;
And mine age is as nothing before thee:
Verily every man at his best state is altogether vanity.
Selah.
6 Surely every man walketh in a vain show:
Surely they are disquieted in vain:
He heapeth up riches, and knoweth not who shall gather
them.
7 And now, Lord, what wait I for?
My hope is in thee.
8 Deliver me from all my transgressions:
Make me not the reproach of the foolish.
9 I was dumb, I opened not my mouth;
Because thou didst it.
10 Remove thy stroke away from me:
I am consumed by the blow of thine hand.
11 When thou with rebukes doth correct man for iniquity,
Thou makest his beauty to consume away like a moth:
Surely every man is vanity.     Selah.
12 Hear my prayer, O Lord,
And give ear unto my cry;
Hold not thy peace at my tears:
For I am a stranger with thee,
And a sojourner, as all my fathers were.
13 O spare me, that I may recover strength,
Before I go hence, and be no more.

42
As the hart panteth after the water brooks,
So panteth my soul after thee, O God.
2 My soul thirsteth for God, for the living God:
When shall I come and appear before God?

3 My tears have been my meat day and night,
While they continually say unto me, Where is thy God?
4 When I remember these things, I pour out my soul in me:
For I had gone with the multitude, I went with them to the
house of God,
With the voice of joy and praise, with a multitude that kept
holyday.
5 Why art thou cast down, O my soul?
And why art thou disquieted in me?
Hope thou in God: for I shall yet praise him
For the help of his countenance.
6 O my God, my soul is cast down within me:
Therefore will I remember thee from the land of Jordan,
And of the Hermonites, from the hill Mizar.
7 Deep calleth unto deep at the noise of thy waterspouts:
All thy waves and thy billows are gone over me.
8 Yet the Lord will command his loving-kindness in the day-
time,
And in the night his song shall be with me,
And my prayer unto the God of my life.
9 I will say unto God my rock, Why hast thou forgotten me?
Why go I mourning because of the oppression of the enemy?
10 As with a sword in my bones, mine enemies reproach me;
While they say daily unto me, Where is thy God?
11 Why art thou cast down, O my soul?
And why art thou disquieted within me?
Hope thou in God: for I shall yet praise him,
Who is the health of my countenance, and my God.

**46** God is our refuge and strength,
A very present help in trouble.
2 Therefore will not we fear, though the earth be removed,
And though the mountains be carried into the midst of the
sea;
3 Though the waters thereof roar and be troubled,
Though the mountains shake with the swelling thereof.
Selah.
4 There is a river, the streams whereof shall make glad the city
of God,
The holy place of the tabernacles of the Most High.
5 God is in the midst of her; she shall not be moved:
God shall help her, and that right early.
6 The heathen raged, the kingdoms were moved:
He uttered his voice, the earth melted.
7 The Lord of hosts is with us;
The God of Jacob is our refuge.    Selah.
8 Come, behold the works of the Lord,

What desolations he hath made in the earth.
9 He maketh wars to cease unto the end of the earth;
He breaketh the bow, and cutteth the spear in sunder;
He burneth the chariot in the fire.
10 Be still, and know that I am God:
I will be exalted among the heathen, I will be exalted in the earth.
11 The Lord of hosts is with us;
The God of Jacob is our refuge.    Selah.

50      The mighty God, even the Lord, hath spoken, and called the earth
From the rising of the sun unto the going down thereof.
2 Out of Zion, the perfection of beauty,
God hath shined.
3 Our God shall come, and shall not keep silence:
A fire shall devour before him,
And it shall be very tempestuous round about him.
4 He shall call to the heavens from above,
And to the earth, that he may judge his people.
5 Gather my saints together unto me;
Those that have made a covenant with me by sacrifice.
6 And the heavens shall declare his righteousness:
For God is judge himself.    Selah.
7 Hear, O my people, and I will speak;
O Israel, and I will testify against thee:
I am God, even thy God.
8 I will not reprove thee for thy sacrifices
Or thy burnt offerings, to have been continually before me.
9 I will take no bullock out of thy house,
Nor he goats out of thy folds:
10 For every beast of the forest is mine,
And the cattle upon a thousand hills.
11 I know all the fowls of the mountains:
And the wild beasts of the field are mine.
12 If I were hungry, I would not tell thee:
For the world is mine, and the fulness thereof.
13 Will I eat the flesh of bulls,
Or drink the blood of goats?
14 Offer unto God thanksgiving;
And pay thy vows unto the Most High:
15 And call upon me in the day of trouble:
I will deliver thee, and thou shalt glorify me.
16 But unto the wicked God saith,
What hast thou to do to declare my statutes,
Or that thou shouldest take my covenant in thy mouth?
17 Seeing thou hatest instruction,
And castest my words behind thee.

18 When thou sawest a thief, then thou consentedst with him,
   And hast been partaker with adulterers.
19 Thou givest thy mouth to evil,
   And thy tongue frameth deceit.
20 Thou sittest and speakest against thy brother;
   Thou slanderest thine own mother's son.
21 These things hast thou done, and I kept silence;
   Thou thoughtest that I was altogether such a one as thyself:
   But I will reprove thee, and set them in order before thine
      eyes.
22 Now consider this, ye that forget God,
   Lest I tear you in pieces, and there be none to deliver.
23 Whoso offereth praise glorifieth me:
   And to him that ordereth his conversation aright
   Will I show the salvation of God.

51    Have mercy upon me, O God, according to thy loving-kind-
      ness:
   According unto the multitude of thy tender mercies blot out
      my transgressions.
 2 Wash me thoroughly from mine iniquity,
   And cleanse me from my sin.
 3 For I acknowledge my transgressions:
   And my sin is ever before me.
 4 Against thee, thee only, have I sinned,
   And done this evil in thy sight:
   That thou mightest be justified when thou speakest,
   And be clear when thou judgest.
 5 Behold, I was shapen in iniquity;
   And in sin did my mother conceive me.
 6 Behold, thou desirest truth in the inward parts:
   And in the hidden part thou shalt make me to know wisdom.
 7 Purge me with hyssop, and I shall be clean:
   Wash me, and I shall be whiter than snow.
 8 Make me to hear joy and gladness;
   That the bones which thou hast broken may rejoice.
 9 Hide thy face from my sins,
   And blot out all mine iniquities.
10 Create in me a clean heart, O God;
   And renew a right spirit within me.
11 Cast me not away from thy presence;
   And take not thy Holy Spirit from me.
12 Restore unto me the joy of thy salvation;
   And uphold me with thy free Spirit.
13 Then will I teach transgressors thy ways;
   And sinners shall be converted unto thee.
14 Deliver me from bloodguiltiness, O God, thou God of my
      salvation:

And my tongue shall sing aloud of thy righteousness.
15 O Lord, open thou my lips;
And my mouth shall show forth thy praise.
16 For thou desirest not sacrifice; else would I give it:
Thou delightest not in burnt offering.
17 The sacrifices of God are a broken spirit:
A broken and a contrite heart, O God, thou wilt not despise.
18 Do good in thy good pleasure unto Zion:
Build thou the walls of Jerusalem.
19 Then shalt thou be pleased with the sacrifices of righteousness,
with burnt offering and whole burnt offering:
Then shall they offer bullocks upon thine altar.

67 God be merciful unto us, and bless us;
And cause his face to shine upon us;    Selah.
2 That thy way may be known upon earth,
Thy saving health among all nations.
3 Let the people praise thee, O God;
Let all the people praise thee.
4 O let the nations be glad and sing for joy:
For thou shalt judge the people righteously,
And govern the nations upon earth.    Selah.
5 Let the people praise thee, O God;
Let all the people praise thee.
6 Then shall the earth yield her increase;
And God, even our own God, shall bless us.
7 God shall bless us;
And all the ends of the earth shall fear him.

82 God standeth in the congregation of the mighty;
He judgeth among the gods.
2 How long will ye judge unjustly,
And accept the persons of the wicked?    Selah.
3 Defend the poor and fatherless:
Do justice to the afflicted and needy.
4 Deliver the poor and needy:
Rid them out of the hand of the wicked.
5 They know not, neither will they understand;
They walk on in darkness:
All the foundations of the earth are out of course.
6 I have said, Ye are gods;
And all of you are children of the Most High.
7 But ye shall die like men,
And fall like one of the princes.
8 Arise, O God, judge the earth:
For thou shalt inherit all nations.

**84** How amiable are thy tabernacles, O Lord of hosts!
2 My soul longeth, yea, even fainteth for the courts of the Lord:
My heart and my flesh crieth out for the living God.
3 Yea, the sparrow hath found a house,
And the swallow a nest for herself,
Where she may lay her young,
Even thine altars, O Lord of hosts,
My King, and my God.
4 Blessed are they that dwell in thy house:
They will be still praising thee.    Selah.
5 Blessed is the man whose strength is in thee;
In whose heart are the ways of them.
6 Who passing through the valley of Baca[1] make it a well;
The rain also filleth the pools.
7 They go from strength to strength,
Every one of them in Zion appeareth before God.
8 O Lord God of hosts, hear my prayer:
Give ear, O God of Jacob.    Selah.
9 Behold, O God our shield,
And look upon the face of thine anointed.
10 For a day in thy courts is better than a thousand.
I had rather be a doorkeeper in the house of my God,
Than to dwell in the tents of wickedness.
11 For the Lord God is a sun and shield:
The Lord will give grace and glory:
No good thing will he withhold from them that walk up-
rightly.
12 O Lord of hosts,
Blessed is the man that trusteth in thee.

**90** Lord, thou hast been our dwelling place in all generations.
2 Before the mountains were brought forth,
Or ever thou hadst formed the earth and the world,
Even from everlasting to everlasting, thou art God.
3 Thou turnest man to destruction;
And sayest, Return, ye children of men.
4 For a thousand years in thy sight
Are but as yesterday when it is past,
And as a watch in the night.
5 Thou carriest them away as with a flood; they are as a sleep:
In the morning they are like grass which groweth up.
6 In the morning it flourisheth, and groweth up;
In the evening it is cut down, and withereth.
7 For we are consumed by thine anger,
And by thy wrath are we troubled.

[1] A desert place or wilderness.

8 Thou hast set our iniquities before thee,
  Our secret sins in the light of thy countenance.
9 For all our days are passed away in thy wrath:
  We spend our years as a tale that is told.
10 The days of our years are threescore years and ten;
  And if by reason of strength they be fourscore years,
  Yet is their strength labor and sorrow;
  For it is soon cut off, and we fly away.
11 Who knoweth the power of thine anger?
  Even according to thy fear, so is thy wrath.
12 So teach us to number our days,
  That we may apply our hearts unto wisdom.
13 Return, O Lord, how long?
  And let it repent thee concerning thy servants.
14 O satisfy us early with thy mercy;
  That we may rejoice and be glad all our days.
15 Make us glad according to the days wherein thou hast afflicted
  us,
  And the years wherein we have seen evil.
16 Let thy work appear unto thy servants,
  And thy glory unto their children.
17 And let the beauty of the Lord our God be upon us:
  And establish thou the work of our hands upon us;
  Yea, the work of our hands establish thou it.

**91** He that dwelleth in the secret place of the Most High
  Shall abide under the shadow of the Almighty.
2 I will say of the Lord, He is my refuge and my fortress:
  My God; in him will I trust.
3 Surely he shall deliver thee from the snare of the fowler,
  And from the noisome pestilence.
4 He shall cover thee with his feathers,
  And under his wings shalt thou trust:
  His truth shall be thy shield and buckler.
5 Thou shalt not be afraid for the terror by night;
  Nor for the arrow that flieth by day;
6 Nor for the pestilence that walketh in darkness;
  Nor for the destruction that wasteth at noonday.
7 A thousand shall fall at thy side,
  And ten thousand at thy right hand;
  But it shall not come nigh thee.
8 Only with thine eyes shalt thou behold
  And see the reward of the wicked.
9 Because thou hast made the Lord, which is my refuge,
  Even the Most High, thy habitation;
10 There shall no evil befall thee,
  Neither shall any plague come nigh thy dwelling.
11 For he shall give his angels charge over thee,

To keep thee in all thy ways.
12 They shall bear thee up in their hands,
Lest thou dash thy foot against a stone.
13 Thou shalt tread upon the lion and adder:
The young lion and the dragon shalt thou trample under feet.
14 Because he hath set his love upon me, therefore will I deliver him:
I will set him on high, because he hath known my name.
15 He shall call upon me, and I will answer him:
I will be with him in trouble;
I will deliver him, and honor him.
16 With long life will I satisfy him,
And show him my salvation.

95   O come, let us sing unto the Lord:
Let us make a joyful noise to the rock of our salvation.
2 Let us come before his presence with thanksgiving,
And make a joyful noise unto him with psalms.
3 For the Lord is a great God,
And a great King above all gods.
4 In his hand are the deep places of the earth:
The strength of the hills is his also.
5 The sea is his, and he made it:
And his hands formed the dry land.
6 O come, let us worship and bow down:
Let us kneel before the Lord our maker.
7 For he is our God;
And we are the people of his pasture, and the sheep of his hand.
To-day if ye will hear his voice,
8 Harden not your heart, as in the provocation,
And as in the day of temptation in the wilderness:
9 When your fathers tempted me,
Proved me, and saw my work.
10 Forty years long was I grieved with this generation,
And said, It is a people that do err in their heart,
And they have not known my ways:
11 Unto whom I sware in my wrath
That they should not enter into my rest.

96   O sing unto the Lord a new song:
Sing unto the Lord, all the earth.
2 Sing unto the Lord, bless his name;
Show forth his salvation from day to day.
3 Declare his glory among the heathen,
His wonders among all people.
4 For the Lord is great, and greatly to be praised:
He is to be feared above all gods.

5 For all the gods of the nations are idols:
But the Lord made the heavens.
6 Honor and majesty are before him:
Strength and beauty are in his sanctuary.
7 Give unto the Lord, O ye kindreds of the people,
Give unto the Lord glory and strength.
8 Give unto the Lord the glory due unto his name:
Bring an offering, and come into his courts.
9 O worship the Lord in the beauty of holiness:
Fear before him, all the earth.
10 Say among the heathen that the Lord reigneth:
The world also shall be established that it shall not be moved:
He shall judge the people righteously.
11 Let the heavens rejoice, and let the earth be glad;
Let the sea roar, and the fulness thereof.
12 Let the field be joyful, and all that is therein:
Then shall all the trees of the wood rejoice
13 Before the Lord: for he cometh,
For he cometh to judge the earth:
He shall judge the world with righteousness,
And the people with his truth.

**98**   O sing unto the Lord a new song;
For he hath done marvelous things:
His right hand, and his holy arm, hath gotten him the victory.
2 The Lord hath made known his salvation:
His righteousness hath he openly showed in the sight of the
heathen.
3 He hath remembered his mercy and his truth toward the
house of Israel:
All the ends of the earth have seen the salvation of our God.
4 Make a joyful noise unto the Lord, all the earth:
Make a loud noise, and rejoice, and sing praise.
5 Sing unto the Lord with the harp;
With the harp, and the voice of a psalm.
6 With trumpets and sound of cornet
Make a joyful noise before the Lord, the King.
7 Let the sea roar, and the fulness thereof;
The world, and they that dwell therein.
8 Let the floods clap their hands:
Let the hills be joyful together
9 Before the Lord; for he cometh to judge the earth:
With righteousness shall he judge the world,
And the people with equity.

**100**   Make a joyful noise unto the Lord, all ye lands.
2 Serve the Lord with gladness:
Come before his presence with singing.

3 Know ye that the Lord he is God:
It is he that hath made us, and not we ourselves;
We are his people, and the sheep of his pasture.
4 Enter into his gates with thanksgiving,
And into his courts with praise:
Be thankful unto him, and bless his name.
5 For the Lord is good; his mercy is everlasting;
And his truth endureth to all generations.

**102** Hear my prayer, O Lord,
And let my cry come unto thee.
2 Hide not thy face from me in the day when I am in trouble;
Incline thine ear unto me:
In the day when I call answer me speedily.
3 For my days are consumed like smoke,
And my bones are burned as a hearth.
4 My heart is smitten, and withered like grass;
So that I forget to eat my bread.
5 By reason of the voice of my groaning
My bones cleave to my skin.
6 I am like a pelican of the wilderness:
I am like an owl of the desert.
7 I watch, and am
As a sparrow alone upon the housetop.
8 Mine enemies reproach me all the day;
And they that are mad against me are sworn against me.
9 For I have eaten ashes like bread,
And mingled my drink with weeping,
10 Because of thine indignation and thy wrath:
For thou hast lifted me up, and cast me down.
11 My days are like a shadow that declineth;
And I am withered like grass.
12 But thou, O Lord, shalt endure for ever;
And thy remembrance unto all generations.
13 Thou shalt arise, and have mercy upon Zion:
For the time to favor her, yea, the set time, is come.
14 For thy servants take pleasure in her stones,
And favor the dust thereof.
15 So the heathen shall fear the name of the Lord,
And all the kings of the earth thy glory.
16 When the Lord shall build up Zion,
He shall appear in his glory.
17 He will regard the prayer of the destitute,
And not despise their prayer.
18 This shall be written for the generation to come:
And the people which shall be created shall praise the Lord.
19 For he hath looked down from the height of his sanctuary;
From heaven did the Lord behold the earth;

20 To hear the groaning of the prisoner;
To loose those that are appointed to death;
21 To declare the name of the Lord in Zion,
And his praise in Jerusalem;
22 When the people are gathered together,
And the kingdoms, to serve the Lord.
23 He weakened my strength in the way;
He shortened my days.
24 I said, O my God, take me not away in the midst of my
days:
Thy years are throughout all generations.
25 Of old hast thou laid the foundation of the earth:
And the heavens are the work of thy hands.
26 They shall perish, but thou shalt endure:
Yea, all of them shall wax old like a garment;
As a vesture shalt thou change them, and they shall be
changed:
27 But thou art the same,
And thy years shall have no end.
28 The children of thy servants shall continue,
And their seed shall be established before thee.

103 Bless the Lord, O my soul:
And all that is within me, bless his holy name.
2 Bless the Lord, O my soul,
And forget not all his benefits:
3 Who forgiveth all thine iniquities;
Who healeth all thy diseases;
4 Who redeemeth thy life from destruction;
Who crowneth thee with loving-kindness and tender mercies;
5 Who satisfieth thy mouth with good things;
So that thy youth is renewed like the eagle's.
6 The Lord executeth righteousness
And judgment for all that are oppressed.
7 He made known his ways unto Moses,
His acts unto the children of Israel.
8 The Lord is merciful and gracious,
Slow to anger, and plenteous in mercy.
9 He will not always chide:
Neither will he keep his anger for ever.
10 He hath not dealt with us after our sins;
Nor rewarded us according to our iniquities.
11 For as the heaven is high above the earth,
So great is his mercy toward them that fear him.
12 As far as the east is from the west,
So far hath he removed our transgressions from us.
13 Like as a father pitieth his children,
So the Lord pitieth them that fear him.

14 For he knoweth our frame;
   He remembereth that we are dust.
15 As for man, his days are as grass:
   As a flower of the field, so he flourisheth.
16 For the wind passeth over it, and it is gone;
   And the place thereof shall know it no more.
17 But the mercy of the Lord is from everlasting to everlasting
      upon them that fear him,
   And his righteousness unto children's children;
18 To such as keep his covenant,
   And to those that remember his commandments to do them.
19 The Lord hath prepared his throne in the heavens;
   And his kingdom ruleth over all.
20 Bless the Lord, ye his angels,
   That excel in strength, that do his commandments,
   Hearkening unto the voice of his word.
21 Bless ye the Lord, all ye his hosts;
   Ye ministers of his, that do his pleasure.
22 Bless the Lord, all his works
   In all places of his dominion:
   Bless the Lord, O my soul.

104   Bless the Lord, O my soul.
   O Lord my God, thou art very great;
   Thou art clothed with honor and majesty:
2 Who coverest thyself with light as with a garment:
   Who stretchest out the heavens like a curtain:
3 Who layeth the beams of his chambers in the waters:
   Who maketh the clouds his chariot:
   Who walketh upon the wings of the wind:
4 Who maketh his angels spirits;
   His ministers a flaming fire:
5 Who laid the foundations of the earth,
   That it should not be removed for ever.
6 Thou coveredst it with the deep as with a garment:
   The waters stood above the mountains.
7 At thy rebuke they fled;
   At the voice of thy thunder they hasted away.
8 They go up by the mountains; they go down by the valleys
   Unto the place which thou hast founded for them.
9 Thou hast set a bound that they may not pass over;
   That they turn not again to cover the earth.
10 He sendeth the springs into the valleys,
   Which run among the hills.
11 They give drink to every beast of the field:
   The wild asses quench their thirst.
12 By them shall the fowls of the heaven have their habitation,
   Which sing among the branches.

13 He watereth the hills from his chambers:
The earth is satisfied with the fruit of thy works.
14 He causeth the grass to grow for the cattle,
And herb for the service of man:
That he may bring forth food out of the earth;
15 And wine that maketh glad the heart of man,
And oil to make his face to shine,
And bread which strengtheneth man's heart.
16 The trees of the Lord are full of sap;
The cedars of Lebanon, which he hath planted;
17 Where the birds make their nests:
As for the stork, the fir trees are her house.
18 The high hills are a refuge for the wild goats;
And the rocks for the conies.
19 He appointed the moon for seasons:
The sun knoweth his going down.
20 Thou makest darkness, and it is night:
Wherein all the beasts of the forest do creep forth.
21 The young lions roar after their prey,
And seek their meat from God.
22 The sun ariseth, they gather themselves together,
And lay them down in their dens.
23 Man goeth forth unto his work
And to his labor until the evening.
24 O Lord, how manifold are thy works!
In wisdom hast thou made them all:
The earth is full of thy riches.
25 So is this great and wide sea,
Wherein are things creeping innumerable,
Both small and great beasts.
26 There go the ships:
There is that leviathan, whom thou hast made to play
therein.
27 These wait all upon thee;
That thou mayest give them their meat in due season.
28 That thou givest them they gather:
Thou openest thine hand, they are filled with good.
29 Thou hidest thy face, they are troubled:
Thou takest away their breath, they die,
And return to their dust.
30 Thou sendest forth thy spirit, they are created:
And thou renewest the face of the earth.
31 The glory of the Lord shall endure for ever:
The Lord shall rejoice in his works.
32 He looketh on the earth, and it trembleth:
He toucheth the hills, and they smoke.
33 I will sing unto the Lord as long as I live:
I will sing praise to my God while I have my being.

34 My meditation of him shall be sweet:
I will be glad in the Lord.
35 Let the sinners be consumed out of the earth,
And let the wicked be no more.
Bless thou the Lord, O my soul.
Praise ye the Lord.

107 O give thanks unto the Lord, for he is good:
For his mercy endureth for ever.
2 Let the redeemed of the Lord say so,
Whom he hath redeemed from the hand of the enemy;
3 And gathered them out of the lands,
From the east, and from the west,
From the north, and from the south.
4 They wandered in the wilderness in a solitary way;
They found no city to dwell in.
5 Hungry and thirsty,
Their soul fainted in them.
6 Then they cried unto the Lord in their trouble,
And he delivered them out of their distresses.
7 And he led them forth by the right way,
That they might go to a city of habitation.
8 Oh that men would praise the Lord for his goodness,
And for his wonderful works to the children of men!
9 For he satisfieth the longing soul,
And filleth the hungry soul with goodness.
10 Such as sit in darkness and in the shadow of death,
Being bound in affliction and iron;
11 Because they rebelled against the words of God,
And contemned the counsel of the Most High:
12 Therefore he brought down their heart with labor;
They fell down, and there was none to help.
13 Then they cried unto the Lord in their trouble,
And he saved them out of their distresses.
14 He brought them out of darkness and the shadow of death,
And brake their bands in sunder.
15 Oh that men would praise the Lord for his goodness,
And for his wonderful works to the children of men!
16 For he hath broken the gates of brass,
And cut the bars of iron in sunder.
17 Fools, because of their transgression,
And because of their iniquities, are afflicted.
18 Their soul abhorreth all manner of meat;
And they draw near unto the gates of death.
19 Then they cry unto the Lord in their trouble,
And he saveth them out of their distresses.
20 He sent his word, and healed them,
And delivered them from their destructions.

21 Oh that men would praise the Lord for his goodness,
And for his wonderful works to the children of men!
22 And let them sacrifice the sacrifices of thanksgiving,
And declare his works with rejoicing.
23 They that go down to the sea in ships,
That do business in great waters;
24 These see the works of the Lord,
And his wonders in the deep.
25 For he commandeth, and raiseth the stormy wind,
Which lifteth up the waves thereof.
26 They mount up to the heaven, they go down again to the
depths:
Their soul is melted because of trouble.
27 They reel to and fro, and stagger like a drunken man,
And are at their wit's end.
28 Then they cry unto the Lord in their trouble,
And he bringeth them out of their distresses.
29 He maketh the storm a calm,
So that the waves thereof are still.
30 Then are they glad because they be quiet;
So he bringeth them unto their desired haven.
31 Oh that men would praise the Lord for his goodness,
And for his wonderful works to the children of men!
32 Let them exalt him also in the congregation of the people,
And praise him in the assembly of the elders.
33 He turneth rivers into a wilderness,
And the watersprings into dry ground;
34 A fruitful land into barrenness,
For the wickedness of them that dwell therein.
35 He turneth the wilderness into a standing water,
And dry ground into watersprings.
36 And there he maketh the hungry to dwell,
That they may prepare a city for habitation;
37 And sow the fields, and plant vineyards,
Which may yield fruits of increase.
38 He blesseth them also, so that they are multiplied greatly;
And suffereth not their cattle to decrease.
39 Again, they are minished and brought low
Through oppression, affliction, and sorrow.
40 He poureth contempt upon princes,
And causeth them to wander in the wilderness, where there
is no way.
41 Yet setteth he the poor on high from affliction,
And maketh him families like a flock.
42 The righteous shall see it, and rejoice:
And all iniquity shall stop her mouth.
43 Whoso is wise, and will observe these things,
Even they shall understand the loving-kindness of the Lord.

114  When Israel went out of Egypt,
     The house of Jacob from a people of strange language;
  2 Judah was his sanctuary,
    And Israel his dominion.
  3 The sea saw it, and fled:
    Jordan was driven back.
  4 The mountains skipped like rams,
    And the little hills like lambs.
  5 What ailed thee, O thou sea, that thou fleddest?
    Thou Jordan, that thou wast driven back?
  6 Ye mountains, that ye skipped like rams;
    And ye little hills, like lambs?
  7 Tremble, thou earth, at the presence of the Lord,
    At the presence of the God of Jacob;
  8 Which turned the rock into a standing water,
    The flint into a fountain of waters.

115  Not unto us, O Lord, not unto us,
     But unto thy name give glory,
     For thy mercy, and for thy truth's sake.
  2 Wherefore should the heathen say,
    Where is now their God?
  3 But our God is in the heavens:
    He hath done whatsoever he hath pleased.
  4 Their idols are silver and gold,
    The work of men's hands.
  5 They have mouths, but they speak not:
    Eyes have they, but they see not:
  6 They have ears, but they hear not:
    Noses have they, but they smell not:
  7 They have hands, but they handle not:
    Feet have they, but they walk not:
    Neither speak they through their throat.
  8 They that make them are like unto them;
    So is every one that trusteth in them.
  9 O Israel, trust thou in the Lord:
    He is their help and their shield.
 10 O house of Aaron, trust in the Lord:
    He is their help and their shield.
 11 Ye that fear the Lord, trust in the Lord:
    He is their help and their shield.
 12 The Lord hath been mindful of us: he will bless us;
    He will bless the house of Israel;
    He will bless the house of Aaron.
 13 He will bless them that fear the Lord,
    Both small and great.

14 The Lord shall increase you more and more,
   You and your children.
15 Ye are blessed of the Lord
   Which made heaven and earth.
16 The heaven, even the heavens, are the Lord's:
   But the earth hath he given to the children of men.
17 The dead praise not the Lord,
   Neither any that go down into silence.
18 But we will bless the Lord
   From this time forth and for evermore.
   Praise the Lord.

121   I will lift up mine eyes unto the hills,
      From whence cometh my help.
   2 My help cometh from the Lord,
      Which made heaven and earth.
   3 He will not suffer thy foot to be moved:
      He that keepeth thee will not slumber.
   4 Behold, he that keepeth Israel
      Shall neither slumber nor sleep.
   5 The Lord is thy keeper:
      The Lord is thy shade upon thy right hand.
   6 The sun shall not smite thee by day,
      Nor the moon by night.
   7 The Lord shall preserve thee from all evil:
      He shall preserve thy soul.
   8 The Lord shall preserve thy going out and thy coming in
      From this time forth, and even for evermore.

122   I was glad when they said unto me,
      Let us go into the house of the Lord.
   2 Our feet shall stand
      Within thy gates, O Jerusalem.
   3 Jerusalem is builded
      As a city that is compact together:
   4 Whither the tribes go up, the tribes of the Lord,
      Unto the testimony of Israel,
      To give thanks unto the name of the Lord.
   5 For there are set thrones of judgment,
      The thrones of the house of David.
   6 Pray for the peace of Jerusalem:
      They shall prosper that love thee.
   7 Peace be within thy walls,
      And prosperity within thy palaces.
   8 For my brethren and companions' sakes,
      I will now say, Peace be within thee.
   9 Because of the house of the Lord our God
      I will seek thy good.

**124**   If it had not been the Lord who was on our side,
Now may Israel say;
2 If it had not been the Lord who was on our side,
When men rose up against us:
3 Then they had swallowed us up quick,
When their wrath was kindled against us:
4 Then the waters had overwhelmed us,
The stream had gone over our soul:
5 Then the proud waters
Had gone over our soul.
6 Blessed be the Lord,
Who hath not given us as a prey to their teeth.
7 Our soul is escaped as a bird out of the snare of the fowlers:
The snare is broken, and we are escaped.
8 Our help is in the name of the Lord,
Who made heaven and earth.

**125**   They that trust in the Lord
Shall be as mount Zion, which cannot be removed,
But abideth for ever.
2 As the mountains are round about Jerusalem,
So the Lord is round about his people
From henceforth even for ever.
3 For the rod of the wicked shall not rest upon the lot of the
righteous;
Lest the righteous put forth their hands unto iniquity.
4 Do good, O Lord, unto those that be good,
And to them that are upright in their hearts.
5 As for such as turn aside unto their crooked ways,
The Lord shall lead them forth with the workers of iniquity:
But peace shall be upon Israel.

**126**   [See page 332.]

**127**   Except the Lord build the house,
They labor in vain that build it:
Except the Lord keep the city,
The watchman waketh but in vain.
2 It is vain for you to rise up early,
To sit up late,
To eat the bread of sorrows:
For so he giveth his beloved sleep.
3 Lo, children are a heritage of the Lord:
And the fruit of the womb is his reward.
4 As arrows are in the hand of a mighty man;
So are children of the youth.
5 Happy is the man that hath his quiver full of them:

They shall not be ashamed,
But they shall speak with the enemies in the gate.

**130** Out of the depths have I cried unto thee, O Lord.
2 Lord, hear my voice:
Let thine ears be attentive
To the voice of my supplications.
3 If thou, Lord, shouldest mark iniquities,
O, Lord, who shall stand?
4 But there is forgiveness with thee,
That thou mayest be feared.
5 I wait for the Lord, my soul doth wait,
And in his word do I hope.
6 My soul waiteth for the Lord
More than they that watch for the morning:
I say, more than they that watch for the morning.
7 Let Israel hope in the Lord:
For with the Lord there is mercy,
And with him is plenteous redemption.
8 And he shall redeem Israel
From all his iniquities.

**133** Behold, how good and how pleasant it is
For brethren to dwell together in unity!
2 It is like the precious ointment upon the head,
That ran down upon the beard,
Even Aaron's beard:
That went down to the skirts of his garments;
3 As the dew of Hermon,
And as the dew that descended upon the mountains of Zion:
For there the Lord commanded the blessing,
Even life for evermore.

**136** O give thanks unto the Lord; for he is good:
For his mercy endureth for ever.
2 O give thanks unto the God of gods:
For his mercy endureth for ever.
3 O give thanks to the Lord of lords:
For his mercy endureth for ever.
4 To him who alone doeth great wonders:
For his mercy endureth for ever.
5 To him that by wisdom made the heavens:
For his mercy endureth for ever.
6 To him that stretched out the earth above the waters:
For his mercy endureth for ever.
7 To him that made great lights:
For his mercy endureth for ever:

8 The sun to rule by day:
For his mercy endureth for ever:
9 The moon and stars to rule by night:
For his mercy endureth for ever.
10 To him that smote Egypt in their firstborn:
For his mercy endureth for ever:
11 And brought out Israel from among them:
For his mercy endureth for ever:
12 With a strong hand, and with a stretched out arm:
For his mercy endureth for ever.
13 To him which divided the Red sea into parts:
For his mercy endureth for ever:
14 And made Israel to pass through the midst of it:
For his mercy endureth for ever:
15 But overthrew Pharaoh and his host in the Red sea:
For his mercy endureth for ever.
16 To him which led his people through the wilderness:
For his mercy endureth for ever.
17 To him which smote great kings:
For his mercy endureth for ever:
18 And slew famous kings:
For his mercy endureth for ever:
19 Sihon king of the Amorites:
For his mercy endureth for ever:
20 And Og the king of Bashan:
For his mercy endureth for ever:
21 And gave their land for a heritage:
For his mercy endureth for ever:
22 Even a heritage unto Israel his servant:
For his mercy endureth for ever.
23 Who remembered us in our low estate:
For his mercy endureth for ever:
24 And hath redeemed us from our enemies:
For his mercy endureth for ever.
25 Who giveth food to all flesh:
For his mercy endureth for ever.
26 O give thanks unto the God of heaven:
For his mercy endureth for ever.

137 [See pages 331–32.]

139 O Lord, thou hast searched me, and known me.
2 Thou knowest my downsitting and mine uprising;
Thou understandest my thought afar off.
3 Thou compassest my path and my lying down,
And art acquainted with all my ways.
4 For there is not a word in my tongue,
But, lo, O Lord, thou knowest it altogether.

5 Thou hast beset me behind and before,
And laid thine hand upon me.
6 Such knowledge is too wonderful for me;
It is high, I cannot attain unto it.
7 Whither shall I go from thy Spirit?
Or whither shall I flee from thy presence?
8 If I ascend up into heaven, thou art there:
If I make my bed in hell, behold, thou art there.
9 If I take the wings of the morning,
And dwell in the uttermost parts of the sea;
10 Even there shall thy hand lead me,
And thy right hand shall hold me.
11 If I say, Surely the darkness shall cover me;
Even the night shall be light about me.
12 Yea, the darkness hideth not from thee;
But the night shineth as the day:
The darkness and the light are both alike to thee.
13 For thou hast possessed my reins:
Thou hast covered me in my mother's womb.
14 I will praise thee; for I am fearfully and wonderfully made:
Marvelous are thy works;
And that my soul knoweth right well.
15 My substance was not hid from thee
When I was made in secret,
And curiously wrought in the lowest parts of the earth.
16 Thine eyes did see my substance, yet being unperfect;
And in thy book all my members were written,
Which in continuance were fashioned,
When as yet there was none of them.
17 How precious also are thy thoughts unto me, O God!
How great is the sum of them!
18 If I should count them, they are more in number than the
sand:
When I awake, I am still with thee.
19 Surely thou wilt slay the wicked, O God:
Depart from me therefore, ye bloody men.
20 For they speak against thee wickedly,
And thine enemies take thy name in vain.
21 Do not I hate them, O Lord, that hate thee?
And am not I grieved with those that rise up against thee?
22 I hate them with perfect hatred:
I count them mine enemies.
23 Search me, O God, and know my heart:
Try me, and know my thoughts:
24 And see if there be any wicked way in me,
And lead me in the way everlasting.

148 Praise ye the Lord.
Praise ye the Lord from the heavens:
Praise him in the heights.
2 Praise ye him, all his angels:
Praise ye him, all his hosts.
3 Praise ye him, sun and moon:
Praise him, all ye stars of light.
4 Praise him, ye heavens of heavens,
And ye waters that be above the heavens.
5 Let them praise the name of the Lord:
For he commanded, and they were created.
6 He hath also stablished them for ever and ever:
He hath made a decree which shall not pass.
7 Praise the Lord from the earth,
Ye dragons, and all deeps:
8 Fire, and hail; snow, and vapor;
Stormy wind fulfilling his word:
9 Mountains, and all hills;
Fruitful trees, and all cedars:
10 Beasts, and all cattle;
Creeping things, and flying fowl:
11 Kings of the earth, and all people;
Princes, and all judges of the earth:
12 Both young men, and maidens;
Old men, and children:
13 Let them praise the name of the Lord:
For his name alone is excellent;
His glory is above the earth and heaven.
14 He also exalteth the horn of his people,
The praise of all his saints;
Even of the children of Israel, a people near unto him.
Praise ye the Lord.

150 Praise ye the Lord.
Praise God in his sanctuary:
Praise him in the firmament of his power.
2 Praise him for his mighty acts:
Praise him according to his excellent greatness.
3 Praise him with the sound of the trumpet:
Praise him with the psaltery and harp.
4 Praise him with the timbrel and dance:
Praise him with stringed instruments and organs.
5 Praise him upon the loud cymbals:
Praise him upon the high sounding cymbals.
6 Let every thing that hath breath praise the Lord.
Praise ye the Lord.

## Lyrics of Human Love: *The Song of Songs*

The Song of Songs seems to have reached its present form in the third century B.C., and was probably composed by joining together a number of passionate love lyrics of uncertain origin. The result of this process is that we are not always certain as to who is speaking, except as the Hebrew gender gives us a key. The central character is certainly a beautiful young woman of dark complexion, but scholars differ as to whether she is addressed by one lover (the interpretation followed here), or by this lover and also by an unsuccessful suitor. In addition, there are verses which cannot be ascribed to any of these individuals, and which are best regarded as comments made by a "chorus" of "the daughters of Jerusalem." For the convenience of readers, the lines are ascribed to various speakers in accord with one judgment of responsible scholarship, but other ascriptions are also possible. Solomon was certainly not the author of the poem as it stands, and whether he is the principal male character is also open to question, though to me at least it seems likely that the young man here was cast as Solomon. The poem contains clear evidence of the Biblical ideal of love between man and wife, and has also been interpreted by Jewish and Christian readers as symbolically representing the love between God and his faithful people.

# *The Song of Songs*

1 The song of songs, which is Solomon's.

### Maiden:

2 Let him kiss me with the kisses of his mouth:
For thy love is better than wine.
3 Because of the savor of thy good ointments
Thy name is as ointment poured forth,
Therefore do the virgins love thee.
4 Draw me, we will run after thee:
The King hath brought me into his chambers:

### Chorus:

We will be glad and rejoice in thee,
We will remember thy love more than wine:
The upright love thee.

### Maiden:

5 I am black, but comely, O ye daughters of Jerusalem,
As the tent of Kedar,
As the curtains of Solomon.

400

6 Look not upon me, because I am black,
Because the sun hath looked upon me:
My mother's children were angry with me;
They made me the keeper of the vineyards;
But mine own vineyard have I not kept.
7 Tell me, O thou whom my soul loveth,
Where thou feedest, where thou makest thy flock to rest at
  noon:
For why should I be as one that turneth aside
By the flocks of thy companions?

### Youth:

8 If thou know not, O thou fairest among women,
Go thy way forth by the footsteps of the flock,
And feed thy kids beside the shepherds' tent.
9 I have compared thee, O my love,
To a company of horses in Pharaoh's chariots.
10 Thy cheeks are comely with rows of jewels,
Thy neck with chains of gold.
11 We will make thee borders of gold
With studs of silver.

### Maiden:

12 While the King sitteth at his table,
My spikenard sendeth forth the smell thereof.
13 A bundle of myrrh is my well-beloved unto me;
He shall lie all night betwixt my breasts.
14 My beloved is unto me as a cluster of camphire
In the vineyard of En-gedi.

### Youth:

15 Behold, thou art fair, my love; behold, thou art fair;
Thou hast doves' eyes.

### Maiden:

16 Behold, thou art fair, my beloved, yea, pleasant:
Also our bed is green.
17 The beams of our house are cedar,
And our rafters of fir.


2     I am the rose of Sharon,
And the lily of the valleys.

### Youth:

2 As the lily among thorns,
So is my love among the daughters.

*Maiden:*

3 As the apple tree among the trees of the wood,
So is my beloved among the sons.
I sat down under his shadow with great delight,
And his fruit was sweet to my taste.

4 He brought me to the banqueting house,
And his banner over me was love.

5 Stay me with flagons, comfort me with apples:
For I am sick of love.

6 His left hand is under my head,
And his right hand doth embrace me.

7 I charge you, O ye daughters of Jerusalem,
By the roes, and by the hinds of the field,
That ye stir not up, nor awake my love,
Till he please.

8 The voice of my beloved! behold, he cometh
Leaping upon the mountains, skipping upon the hills.

9 My beloved is like a roe or a young hart:
Behold, he standeth behind our wall,
He looketh forth at the windows,
Showing himself through the lattice.

10 My beloved spake, and said unto me,
Rise up, my love, my fair one, and come away.

11 For, lo, the winter is past,
The rain is over and gone;

12 The flowers appear on the earth;
The time of the singing of birds is come,
And the voice of the turtle is heard in our land;

13 The fig tree putteth forth her green figs,
And the vines with the tender grape give a good smell.
Arise, my love, my fair one, and come away.

14 O my dove, that art in the clefts of the rocks, in the secret
places of the stairs,
Let me see thy countenance, let me hear thy voice;
For sweet is thy voice, and thy countenance is comely.

15 Take us the foxes,
The little foxes, that spoil the vines:
For our vines have tender grapes.

16 My beloved is mine, and I am his:
He feedeth among the lilies.

17 Until the day break, and the shadows flee away,
Turn, my beloved,
And be thou like a roe or a young hart
Upon the mountains of Bether.

### Youth:

**4**
7 Thou art all fair, my love; there is no spot in thee.
8 Come with me from Lebanon, my spouse, with me from
Lebanon:
Look from the top of Amana, from the top of Shenir and
Hermon,
From the lions' dens, from the mountains of the leopards.
9 Thou hast ravished my heart, my sister, my spouse;
Thou hast ravished my heart with one of thine eyes,
With one chain of thy neck.
10 How fair is thy love, my sister, my spouse!
How much better is thy love than wine!
And the smell of thine ointments than all spices!
11 Thy lips, O my spouse, drop as the honeycomb:
Honey and milk are under thy tongue;
And the smell of thy garments is like the smell of Lebanon.
12 A garden inclosed is my sister, my spouse;
A spring shut up, a fountain sealed.
13 Thy plants are an orchard of pomegranates, with pleasant
fruits;
Camphire, with spikenard,
14 Spikenard and saffron;
Calamus and cinnamon, with all trees of frankincense;
Myrrh and aloes, with all the chief spices:
15 A fountain of gardens, a well of living waters,
And streams from Lebanon.

### Maiden:

16 Awake, O north wind; and come, thou south;
Blow upon my garden, that the spices thereof may flow out.
Let my beloved come into his garden,
And eat his pleasant fruits.

### Youth:

**5**
I am come into my garden, my sister, my spouse:
I have gathered my myrrh with my spice;
I have eaten my honeycomb with my honey;
I have drunk my wine with my milk.

### Chorus:

9 What is thy beloved more than another beloved, O thou fairest
among women?
What is thy beloved more than another beloved, that thou
dost so charge us?

### Maiden:

10 My beloved is white and ruddy,
The chiefest among ten thousand.

11 His head is as the most fine gold;
His locks are bushy, and black as a raven:
12 His eyes are as the eyes of doves by the rivers of waters,
Washed with milk, and fitly set:
13 His cheeks are as a bed of spices, as sweet flowers:
His lips like lilies, dropping sweet smelling myrrh:
14 His hands are as gold rings set with the beryl:
His belly is as bright ivory overlaid with sapphires:
15 His legs are as pillars of marble, set upon sockets of fine gold:
His countenance is as Lebanon, excellent as the cedars:
16 His mouth is most sweet: yea, he is altogether lovely.
This is my beloved, and this is my friend, O daughters of
Jerusalem.

### Chorus:

6 Whither is thy beloved gone, O thou fairest among women?
Whither is thy beloved turned aside? that we may seek him
with thee.

### Maiden:

2 My beloved is gone down into his garden, to the beds of spices,
To feed in the gardens, and to gather lilies.
3 I am my beloved's, and my beloved is mine:
He feedeth among the lilies.

### Youth:

4 Thou art beautiful, O my love, as Tirzah,
Comely as Jerusalem,
Terrible as an army with banners.
5 Turn away thine eyes from me, for they have overcome me:
Thy hair is as a flock of goats that appear from Gilead:
6 Thy teeth are as a flock of sheep which go up from the washing,
Whereof every one beareth twins, and there is not one barren
among them.
7 As a piece of a pomegranate are thy temples within thy locks.
8 There are threescore queens, and fourscore concubines,
And virgins without number.
9 My dove, my undefiled is but one;
She is the only one of her mother,
She is the choice one of her that bare her.
The daughters saw her, and blessed her;
Yea, the queens and the concubines, and they praised her.
10 Who is she that looketh forth as the morning,
Fair as the moon, clear as the sun,
And terrible as an army with banners?

### Maiden:

11 I went down into the garden of nuts
To see the fruits of the valley,

And to see whether the vine flourished, and the pomegranates
    budded.
12 Or ever I was aware,
    My soul made me like the chariots of Ammi-nadib.

### Chorus:

13 Return, return, O Shulamite;
    Return, return, that we may look upon thee.
    What will ye see in the Shulamite?
    As it were the company of two armies.

### Youth:

7

6 How fair and how pleasant art thou, O love, for delights!
7 This thy stature is like to a palm tree,
    And thy breasts to clusters of grapes.
8 I said, I will go up to the palm tree,
    I will take hold of the boughs thereof:
    Now also thy breasts shall be as clusters of the vine,
    And the smell of thy nose like apples;
9 And the roof of thy mouth like the best wine
    For my beloved, that goeth down sweetly,
    Causing the lips of those that are asleep to speak.

### Maiden:

10 I am my beloved's, and his desire is toward me.
11 Come, my beloved, let us go forth into the field;
    Let us lodge in the villages.
12 Let us get up early to the vineyards;
    Let us see if the vine flourish, whether the tender grape ap-
      pear,
    And the pomegranates bud forth:
    There will I give thee my loves.
13 The mandrakes give a smell,
    And at our gates are all manner of pleasant fruits,
    New and old,
    Which I have laid up for thee, O my beloved.

8

6 Set me as a seal upon thine heart,
    As a seal upon thine arm:
    For love is strong as death;
    Jealousy is cruel as the grave:
    The coals thereof are coals of fire,
    Which hath a most vehement flame.
7 Many waters cannot quench love,
    Neither can the floods drown it.
14 Make haste, my beloved,
    And be thou like to a roe or to a young hart
    Upon the mountains of spices.

## A Genial Skeptic: *Ecclesiastes*

The basic thrust of the Bible is toward faith in God and in the divine providence, whatever differences of accent may be found in the individual books. Against this background, the book of Ecclesiastes stands out in some contrast, with its pervasive sense of skepticism and what at times approaches an affirmation of the futility of life. The book appears to have been written after the return from Babylonian captivity and the restoration of Jerusalem. The author put the words of his book into the mouth of Solomon, as a dramatic character. His sense of the "vanity" of human existence has been echoed and re-echoed in the contemptu mundi (contempt of this world) literature of Christendom, but never so effectively as it is expressed in the words of "the preacher" himself.

# *Ecclesiastes*

1 The words of the Preacher, the son of David, king in Jerusalem.
2 Vanity of vanities, saith the Preacher,
Vanity of vanities; all is vanity.
3 What profit hath a man of all his labor
Which he taketh under the sun?
4 One generation passeth away, and another generation cometh:
But the earth abideth for ever.
5 The sun also ariseth, and the sun goeth down,
And hasteth to his place where he arose.
6 The wind goeth toward the south,
And turneth about unto the north;
It whirleth about continually,
And the wind returneth again according to his circuits.
7 All the rivers run into the sea;
Yet the sea is not full:
Unto the place from whence the rivers come,
Thither they return again.
8 All things are full of labor;
Man cannot utter it:
The eye is not satisfied with seeing,
Nor the ear filled with hearing.
9 The thing that hath been,
It is that which shall be;
And that which is done is that which shall be done:
And there is no new thing under the sun.
10 Is there any thing whereof it may be said,
See, this is new?

It hath been already of old time,
Which was before us.
11 There is no remembrance of former things;
Neither shall there be any remembrance of things that are to
come
With those that shall come after.
12 I the Preacher was king over Israel in Jerusalem. 13 And I gave my
heart to seek and search out by wisdom concerning all things that are
done under heaven: this sore travail hath God given to the sons of
man to be exercised therewith. 14 I have seen all the works that are
done under the sun; and, behold, all is vanity and vexation of spirit.
15 That which is crooked cannot be made straight:
And that which is wanting cannot be numbered.
16 I communed with mine own heart, saying, Lo, I am come to great
estate, and have gotten more wisdom than all they that have been
before me in Jerusalem: yea, my heart had great experience of wisdom
and knowledge. 17 And I gave my heart to know wisdom, and to
know madness and folly: I perceived that this also is vexation of spirit.
18 For in much wisdom is much grief:
And he that increaseth knowledge increaseth sorrow.

2 I said in mine heart, Go to now, I will prove thee with mirth;
therefore enjoy pleasure: and, behold, this also is vanity. 2 I said of
laughter, It is mad: and of mirth, What doeth it? 3 I sought in mine
heart to give myself unto wine, yet acquainting mine heart with wisdom; and to lay hold on folly, till I might see what was that good for
the sons of men, which they should do under the heaven all the days
of their life. 4 I made me great works; I builded me houses; I planted
me vineyards: 5 I made me gardens and orchards, and I planted trees
in them of all kind of fruits: 6 I made me pools of water, to water
therewith the wood that bringeth forth trees: 7 I got me servants
and maidens, and had servants born in my house; also I had great
possessions of great and small cattle above all that were in Jerusalem
before me: 8 I gathered me also silver and gold, and the peculiar
treasure of kings and of the provinces: I gat me men singers and women
singers, and the delights of the sons of men, as musical instruments,
and that of all sorts. 9 So I was great, and increased more than all
that were before me in Jerusalem: also my wisdom remained with me.
10 And whatsoever mine eyes desired I kept not from them, I withheld not my heart from any joy; for my heart rejoiced in all my labor:
and this was my portion of all my labor. 11 Then I looked on all the
works that my hands had wrought, and on the labor that I had labored
to do: and, behold, all was vanity and vexation of spirit, and there was
no profit under the sun.
12 And I turned myself to behold wisdom, and madness, and folly:
for what can the man do that cometh after the king? even that which
hath been already done. 13 Then I saw that wisdom excelleth folly,
as far as light excelleth darkness.

14 The wise man's eyes are in his head;
But the fool walketh in darkness:
and I myself perceived also that one event happeneth to them all.
15 Then said I in my heart, As it happeneth to the fool, so it happeneth even to me; and why was I then more wise? Then I said in my heart, that this also is vanity. 16 For there is no remembrance of the wise more than of the fool for ever; seeing that which now is in the days to come shall all be forgotten. And how dieth the wise man? as the fool. 17 Therefore I hated life; because the work that is wrought under the sun is grievous unto me: for all is vanity and vexation of spirit.

18 Yea, I hated all my labor which I had taken under the sun: because I should leave it unto the man that shall be after me. 19 And who knoweth whether he shall be a wise man or a fool? yet shall he have rule over all my labor wherein I have labored, and wherein I have showed myself wise under the sun. This is also vanity. 20 Therefore I went about to cause my heart to despair of all the labor which I took under the sun. 21 For there is a man whose labor is in wisdom, and in knowledge, and in equity; yet to a man that hath not labored therein shall he leave it for his portion. This also is vanity and a great evil. 22 For what hath man of all his labor, and of the vexation of his heart, wherein he hath labored under the sun? 23 For all his days are sorrows, and his travail grief; yea, his heart taketh not rest in the night. This is also vanity.

24 There is nothing better for a man, than that he should eat and drink, and that he should make his soul enjoy good in his labor. This also I saw, that it was from the hand of God. 25 For who can eat, or who else can hasten hereunto, more than I? 26 For God giveth to a man that is good in his sight, wisdom, and knowledge, and joy: but to the sinner he giveth travail, to gather and to heap up, that he may give to him that is good before God. This also is vanity and vexation of spirit.

3 To every thing there is a season,
And a time to every purpose under the heaven:
2 A time to be born, and a time to die;
A time to plant, and a time to pluck up that which is planted;
3 A time to kill, and a time to heal;
A time to break down, and a time to build up;
4 A time to weep, and a time to laugh;
A time to mourn, and a time to dance;
5 A time to cast away stones, and a time to gather stones together;
A time to embrace, and a time to refrain from embracing;
6 A time to get, and a time to lose;
A time to keep, and a time to cast away;
7 A time to rend, and a time to sew;
A time to keep silence, and a time to speak;

8 A time to love, and a time to hate;
A time of war, and a time of peace.

9 What profit hath he that worketh in that wherein he laboreth? 10 I have seen the travail, which God hath given to the sons of men to be exercised in it. 11 He hath made every thing beautiful in his time: also he hath set the world in their heart, so that no man can find out the work that God maketh from the beginning to the end. 12 I know that there is no good in them, but for a man to rejoice, and to do good in his life. 13 And also that every man should eat and drink, and enjoy the good of all his labor, it is the gift of God. 14 I know that, whatsoever God doeth, it shall be for ever: nothing can be put to it, nor any thing taken from it: and God doeth it, that men should fear before him. 15 That which hath been is now; and that which is to be hath already been; and God requireth that which is past.

16 And moreover I saw under the sun the place of judgment, that wickedness was there; and the place of righteousness, that iniquity was there. 17 I said in mine heart, God shall judge the righteous and the wicked: for there is a time there for every purpose and for every work. 18 I said in mine heart concerning the estate of the sons of men, that God might manifest them, and that they might see that they themselves are beasts. 19 For that which befalleth the sons of men befalleth beasts; even one thing befalleth them: as the one dieth, so dieth the other; yea, they have all one breath; so that a man hath no preeminence above a beast: for all is vanity. 20 All go unto one place; all are of the dust, and all turn to dust again. 21 Who knoweth the spirit of man that goeth upward, and the spirit of the beast that goeth downward to the earth? 22 Wherefore I perceive that there is nothing better, than that a man should rejoice in his own works; for that is his portion: for who shall bring him to see what shall be after him?

4 So I returned, and considered all the oppressions that are done under the sun: and behold the tears of such as were oppressed, and they had no comforter; and on the side of their oppressors there was power; but they had no comforter. 2 Wherefore I praised the dead which are already dead, more than the living which are yet alive. 3 Yea, better is he than both they, which hath not yet been, who hath not seen the evil work that is done under the sun.

9 For all this I considered in my heart even to declare all this, that the righteous, and the wise, and their works, are in the hand of God: no man knoweth either love or hatred by all that is before them. 2 All things come alike to all: there is one event to the righteous, and to the wicked; to the good and to the clean, and to the unclean; to him that sacrificeth, and to him that sacrificeth not: as is the good, so is the sinner; and he that sweareth, as he that feareth an oath. 3 This

is an evil among all things that are done under the sun, that there is
one event unto all: yea, also the heart of the sons of men is full of
evil, and madness is in their heart while they live, and after that they
go to the dead.

11 I returned, and saw under the sun, that the race is not to the
swift, nor the battle to the strong, neither yet bread to the wise, nor yet
riches to men of understanding, nor yet favor to men of skill; but time
and chance happeneth to them all. 12 For man also knoweth not his
time: as the fishes that are taken in an evil net, and as the birds that
are caught in the snare; so are the sons of men snared in an evil time,
when it falleth suddenly upon them.

11    7 Truly the light is sweet,
And a pleasant thing it is for the eyes to behold the sun:
8 But if a man live many years,
And rejoice in them all;
Yet let him remember the days of darkness;
For they shall be many.
All that cometh is vanity.
9 Rejoice, O young man, in thy youth;
And let thy heart cheer thee in the days of thy youth,
And walk in the ways of thine heart,
And in the sight of thine eyes:
But know thou, that for all these things
God will bring thee into judgment.
10 Therefore remove sorrow from thy heart,
And put away evil from thy flesh:
For childhood and youth are vanity.

12    Remember now thy Creator in the days of thy youth,
While the evil days come not,
Nor the years draw nigh, when thou shalt say,
I have no pleasure in them;
2 While the sun, or the light, or the moon,
Or the stars, be not darkened,
Nor the clouds return after the rain:
3 In the day when the keepers of the house shall tremble,
And the strong men shall bow themselves,
And the grinders cease because they are few,
And those that look out of the windows be darkened,
4 And the doors shall be shut in the streets,
When the sound of the grinding is low,
And he shall rise up at the voice of the bird,
And all the daughters of music shall be brought low;
5 Also when they shall be afraid of that which is high,
And fears shall be in the way,
And the almond tree shall flourish,

And the grasshopper shall be a burden,
And desire shall fail:
Because man goeth to his long home,
And the mourners go about the streets:
6 Or ever the silver cord be loosed,
Or the golden bowl be broken,
Or the pitcher be broken at the fountain,
Or the wheel broken at the cistern.
7 Then shall the dust return to the earth as it was:
And the spirit shall return unto God who gave it.
8 Vanity of vanities, saith the Preacher;
All is vanity.


### POSTSCRIPT

9 And moreover, because the Preacher was wise, he still taught the people knowledge; yea, he gave good heed, and sought out, and set in order many proverbs. 10 The Preacher sought to find out acceptable words: and that which was written was upright, even words of truth.

11 The words of the wise are as goads, and as nails fastened by the masters of assemblies, which are given from one shepherd. 12 And further, by these, my son, be admonished: of making many books there is no end; and much study is a weariness of the flesh.

13 Let us hear the conclusion of the whole matter: Fear God, and keep his commandments: for this is the whole duty of man. 14 For God shall bring every work into judgment, with every secret thing, whether it be good, or whether it be evil.


## The Problem of Suffering: *Job*

The presence of undeserved suffering in the world has always posed problems for thinking men. The problems might disappear entirely if only people suffered and were afflicted in strict proportion to the evil they had previously done, but it often appears that suffering is quite disproportionate to sin. It is with such questions that the book of Job is concerned, as the virtuous Job is struck down by almost total disaster. The discussions between Job and his friends, with the eventual entrance of God into the argument, form one of the most profound analyses of man's predicament in any language or culture. In this Biblical drama, the human dignity and pathos of Job stand out in sharp contrast to the nouveau riche sentimentality of the title character in Archibald MacLeish's contemporary play J.B., which is based on the story of Job.

411

# *Job*

PROLOGUE

1 There was a man in the land of Uz, whose name was Job; and that man was perfect and upright, and one that feared God, and eschewed evil. 2 And there were born unto him seven sons and three daughters. 3 His substance also was seven thousand sheep, and three thousand camels, and five hundred yoke of oxen, and five hundred she asses, and a very great household; so that this man was the greatest of all the men of the east. 4 And his sons went and feasted in their houses, every one his day; and sent and called for their three sisters to eat and to drink with them. 5 And it was so, when the days of their feasting were gone about, that Job sent and sanctified them, and rose up early in the morning, and offered burnt offerings according to the number of them all: for Job said, It may be that my sons have sinned, and cursed God in their hearts. Thus did Job continually.

6 Now there was a day when the sons of God came to present themselves before the Lord, and Satan came also among them. 7 And the Lord said unto Satan, Whence comest thou? Then Satan answered the Lord, and said, From going to and fro in the earth, and from walking up and down in it. 8 And the Lord said unto Satan, Hast thou considered my servant Job, that there is none like him in the earth, a perfect and an upright man, one that feareth God, and eschcweth evil? 9 Then Satan answered the Lord, and said, Doth Job fear God for nought? 10 Hast not thou made a hedge about him, and about his house, and about all that he hath on every side? thou hast blessed the work of his hands, and his substance is increased in the land. 11 But put forth thine hand now, and touch all that he hath, and he will curse thee to thy face. 12 And the Lord said unto Satan, Behold, all that he hath is in thy power; only upon himself put not forth thine hand. So Satan went forth from the presence of the Lord.

13 And there was a day when his sons and his daughters were eating and drinking wine in their eldest brother's house: 14 And there came a messenger unto Job, and said, The oxen were plowing, and the asses feeding beside them: 15 And the Sabeans fell upon them, and took them away; yea, they have slain the servants with the edge of the sword; and I only am escaped alone to tell thee. 16 While he was yet speaking, there came also another, and said, The fire of God is fallen from heaven, and hath burned up the sheep, and the servants, and consumed them; and I only am escaped alone to tell thee. 17 While he was yet speaking, there came also another, and said, The Chaldeans made out three bands, and fell upon the camels, and have carried them away, yea, and slain the servants with the edge of the

sword; and I only am escaped alone to tell thee. 18 While he was yet speaking, there came also another, and said, Thy sons and thy daughters were eating and drinking wine in their eldest brother's house: 19 And, behold, there came a great wind from the wilderness, and smote the four corners of the house, and it fell upon the young men, and they are dead; and I only am escaped alone to tell thee. 20 Then Job arose, and rent his mantle, and shaved his head, and fell down upon the ground, and worshipped, 21 And said,

Naked came I out of my mother's womb,
And naked shall I return thither:
The Lord gave, and the Lord hath taken away;
Blessed be the name of the Lord.

22 In all this Job sinned not, nor charged God foolishly.

2 Again there was a day when the sons of God came to present themselves before the Lord, and Satan came also among them to present himself before the Lord. 2 And the Lord said unto Satan, From whence comest thou? And Satan answered the Lord, and said, From going to and fro in the earth, and from walking up and down in it. 3 And the Lord said unto Satan, Hast thou considered my servant Job, that there is none like him in the earth, a perfect and an upright man, one that feareth God, and escheweth evil? and still he holdeth fast his integrity, although thou movedst me against him, to destroy him without cause. 4 And Satan answered the Lord, and said, Skin for skin, yea, all that a man hath will he give for his life. 5 But put forth thine hand now, and touch his bone and his flesh, and he will curse thee to thy face. 6 And the Lord said unto Satan, Behold, he is in thine hand; but save his life.

7 So went Satan forth from the presence of the Lord, and smote Job with sore boils from the sole of his foot unto his crown. 8 And he took him a potsherd to scrape himself withal; and he sat down among the ashes. 9 Then said his wife unto him, Dost thou still retain thine integrity? curse God, and die. 10 But he said unto her, Thou speakest as one of the foolish women speaketh. What? shall we receive good at the hand of God, and shall we not receive evil? In all this did not Job sin with his lips.

11 Now when Job's three friends heard of all this evil that was come upon him, they came every one from his own place; Eliphaz the Temanite, and Bildad the Shuhite, and Zophar the Naamathite: for they had made an appointment together to come to mourn with him, and to comfort him. 12 And when they lifted up their eyes afar off, and knew him not, they lifted up their voice, and wept; and they rent every one his mantle, and sprinkled dust upon their heads toward heaven. 13 So they sat down with him upon the ground seven days and seven nights, and none spake a word unto him: for they saw that his grief was very great.

## JOB'S LAMENT

3 After this opened Job his mouth, and cursed his day. 2 And Job
spake, and said,

3 Let the day perish wherein I was born,
And the night in which it was said,
There is a man child conceived.
11 Why died I not from the womb?
Why did I not give up the ghost when I came out of the belly?
20 Wherefore is light given to him that is in misery,
And life unto the bitter in soul;
21 Which long for death, but it cometh not;
And dig for it more than for hid treasures;
22 Which rejoice exceedingly,
And are glad, when they can find the grave?
23 Why is light given to a man whose way is hid,
And whom God hath hedged in?

### FIRST CYCLE OF DEBATE

#### Eliphaz

4 Then Eliphaz the Temanite answered and said,

2 If we assay to commune with thee, wilt thou be grieved?
But who can withhold himself from speaking?
3 Behold, thou hast instructed many,
And thou hast strengthened the weak hands.
4 Thy words have upholden him that was falling,
And thou hast strengthened the feeble knees.
5 But now it is come upon thee, and thou faintest;
It toucheth thee, and thou art troubled.
7 Remember, I pray thee, who ever perished, being innocent?
Or where were the righteous cut off?
8 Even as I have seen, they that plow iniquity,
And sow wickedness, reap the same.
9 By the blast of God they perish,
And by the breath of his nostrils are they consumed.

5 17 Behold, happy is the man whom God correcteth:
Therefore despise not thou the chastening of the Almighty:
18 For he maketh sore, and bindeth up:
He woundeth, and his hands make whole.
19 He shall deliver thee in six troubles:
Yea, in seven there shall no evil touch thee.
25 Thou shalt know also that thy seed shall be great,
And thine offspring as the grass of the earth.
26 Thou shalt come to thy grave in a full age,
Like as a shock of corn cometh in in his season.
27 Lo this, we have searched it, so it is;
Hear it, and know thou it for thy good.

### Job

**6** But Job answered and said,

2 Oh that my grief were thoroughly weighed,
And my calamity laid in the balances together!

8 Oh that I might have my request;
And that God would grant me the thing that I long for!

9 Even that it would please God to destroy me;
That he would let loose his hand, and cut me off!

14 To him that is afflicted pity should be showed from his friend;
But he forsaketh the fear of the Almighty.

15 My brethren have dealt deceitfully as a brook,
And as the stream of brooks they pass away;

21 For now ye are nothing;
Ye see my casting down, and are afraid.

**7** 6 My days are swifter than a weaver's shuttle,
And are spent without hope.

11 Therefore I will not refrain my mouth;
I will speak in the anguish of my spirit;
I will complain in the bitterness of my soul.

17 What is man, that thou shouldest magnify him?
And that thou shouldest set thine heart upon him?

18 And that thou shouldest visit him every morning,
And try him every moment?

19 How long wilt thou not depart from me,
Nor let me alone till I swallow down my spittle?

### Bildad

**8** Then answered Bildad the Shuhite, and said,

3 Doth God pervert judgment?
Or doth the Almighty pervert justice?

6 If thou wert pure and upright;
Surely now he would awake for thee,
And make the habitation of thy righteousness prosperous.

20 Behold, God will not cast away a perfect man,
Neither will he help the evildoers:

21 Till he fill thy mouth with laughing,
And thy lips with rejoicing.

22 They that hate thee shall be clothed with shame;
And the dwelling place of the wicked shall come to nought.

### Job

**9** Then Job answered and said,

2 I know it is so of a truth:
But how should man be just with God?

3 If he will contend with him,
He cannot answer him one of a thousand.

4 He is wise in heart, and mighty in strength:
    Who hath hardened himself against him, and hath prospered?
20 If I justify myself, mine own mouth shall condemn me:
    If I say, I am perfect, it shall also prove me perverse.
21 Though I were perfect, yet would I not know my soul:
    I would despise my life.
22 This is one thing, therefore I said it,
    He destroyeth the perfect and the wicked.
32 For he is not a man, as I am, that I should answer him,
    And we should come together in judgment.
33 Neither is there any daysman betwixt us,
    That might lay his hand upon us both.

**10**
2 I will say unto God, Do not condemn me;
    Show me wherefore thou contendest with me.
7 Thou knowest that I am not wicked;
    And there is none that can deliver out of thine hand.
8 Thine hands have made me and fashioned me
    Together round about; yet thou dost destroy me.
15 If I be wicked, woe unto me;
    And if I be righteous, yet will I not lift up my head.
    I am full of confusion; therefore see thou mine affliction;
16 For it increaseth. Thou huntest me as a fierce lion:
    And again thou showest thyself marvelous upon me.
20 Are not my days few? cease then,
    And let me alone, that I may take comfort a little,
21 Before I go whence I shall not return,
    Even to the land of darkness and the shadow of death;
22 A land of darkness, as darkness itself;
    And of the shadow of death, without any order,
    And where the light is as darkness.

### Zophar

**11** Then answered Zophar the Naamathite, and said,
3 Should thy lies make men hold their peace?
    And when thou mockest, shall no man make thee ashamed?
4 For thou hast said, My doctrine is pure,
    And I am clean in thine eyes.
5 But oh that God would speak,
    And open his lips against thee;
6 And that he would show thee the secrets of wisdom,
    That they are double to that which is!
    Know therefore that God exacteth of thee less than thine
      iniquity deserveth.

### Job

**12** And Job answered and said,
2 No doubt but ye are the people,
    And wisdom shall die with you.

3 But I have understanding as well as you;
I am not inferior to you:
Yea, who knoweth not such things as these?
4 I am as one mocked of his neighbor . . .

13     Lo, mine eye hath seen all this,
Mine ear hath heard and understood it.
2 What ye know, the same do I know also:
I am not inferior unto you.
3 Surely I would speak to the Almighty,
And I desire to reason with God.
4 But ye are forgers of lies,
Ye are all physicians of no value.
5 Oh that ye would altogether hold your peace!
And it should be your wisdom.
6 Hear now my reasoning,
And hearken to the pleadings of my lips.
7 Will ye speak wickedly for God?
And talk deceitfully for him?
8 Will ye accept his person?
Will ye contend for God?
9 Is it good that he should search you out?
Or as one man mocketh another, do ye so mock him?
10 He will surely reprove you,
If ye do secretly accept persons.
11 Shall not his excellency make you afraid?
And his dread fall upon you?
12 Your remembrances are like unto ashes,
Your bodies to bodies of clay.
13 Hold your peace, let me alone, that I may speak,
And let come on me what will.
14 Wherefore do I take my flesh in my teeth,
And put my life in mine hand?
15 Though he slay me, yet will I trust in him:
But I will maintain mine own ways before him.

## SECOND CYCLE OF DEBATE

### Eliphaz

15     Then answered Eliphaz the Temanite, and said,
2 Should a wise man utter vain knowledge,
And fill his belly with the east wind?
3 Should he reason with unprofitable talk?
Or with speeches wherewith he can do no good?
12 Why doth thine heart carry thee away?
And what do thy eyes wink at,
13 That thou turnest thy spirit against God,
And lettest such words go out of thy mouth?

## Job

16 Then Job answered and said,
    2 I have heard many such things:
       Miserable comforters are ye all.
    3 Shall vain words have an end?
       Or what emboldeneth thee that thou answerest?
    4 I also could speak as ye do:
       If your soul were in my soul's stead,
       I could heap up words against you,
       And shake mine head at you.
    5 But I would strengthen you with my mouth,
       And the moving of my lips should assuage your grief.
   11 God hath delivered me to the ungodly,
       And turned me over into the hands of the wicked.
   12 I was at ease, but he hath broken me asunder:
       He hath also taken me by my neck, and shaken me to pieces,
       And set me up for his mark.
   16 My face is foul with weeping,
       And on my eyelids is the shadow of death;
   17 Not for any injustice in mine hands:
       Also my prayer is pure.

17 11 My days are past, my purposes are broken off,
       Even the thoughts of my heart.
   13 If I wait, the grave is mine house:
       I have made my bed in the darkness.
   14 I have said to corruption, Thou art my father:
       To the worm, Thou art my mother, and my sister.
   15 And where is now my hope?
       As for my hope, who shall see it?
   16 They shall go down to the bars of the pit,
       When our rest together is in the dust.

### Bildad

18 Then answered Bildad the Shuhite, and said,
    4 He teareth himself in his anger:
       Shall the earth be forsaken for thee?
       And shall the rock be removed out of his place?
    5 Yea, the light of the wicked shall be put out,
       And the spark of his fire shall not shine.
    6 The light shall be dark in his tabernacle,
       And his candle shall be put out with him.
    7 The steps of his strength shall be straitened,
       And his own counsel shall cast him down.
    8 For he is cast into a net by his own feet,
       And he walketh upon a snare.

18 He shall be driven from light into darkness,
And chased out of the world.
19 He shall neither have son nor nephew among his people,
Nor any remaining in his dwellings.
21 Surely such are the dwellings of the wicked,
And this is the place of him that knoweth not God.

## Job

19 Then Job answered and said,
2 How long will ye vex my soul,
And break me in pieces with words?
3 These ten times have ye reproached me:
Ye are not ashamed that ye make yourselves strange to me.
14 My kinsfolk have failed,
And my familiar friends have forgotten me.
15 They that dwell in mine house, and my maids, count me for a stranger:
I am an alien in their sight.
16 I called my servant, and he gave me no answer;
I entreated him with my mouth.
17 My breath is strange to my wife,
Though I entreated for the children's sake of mine own body.
18 Yea, young children despised me;
I arose, and they spake against me.
19 All my inward friends abhorred me:
And they whom I loved are turned against me.
20 My bone cleaveth to my skin and to my flesh,
And I am escaped with the skin of my teeth.
21 Have pity upon me, have pity upon me, O ye my friends;
For the hand of God hath touched me.
22 Why do ye persecute me as God,
And are not satisfied with my flesh?
23 Oh that my words were now written!
Oh that they were printed in a book!
24 That they were graven with an iron pen and lead
In the rock for ever!
25 For I know that my Redeemer liveth,
And that he shall stand at the latter day upon the earth:
26 And though after my skin worms destroy this body,
Yet in my flesh shall I see God:
27 Whom I shall see for myself,
And mine eyes shall behold, and not another;
Though my reins be consumed within me.

## Zophar

20 Then answered Zophar the Naamathite, and said,
4 Knowest thou not this of old,
Since man was placed upon earth,

5 That the triumphing of the wicked is short,
And the joy of the hypocrite but for a moment?
6 Though his excellency mount up to the heavens,
And his head reach unto the clouds;
7 Yet he shall perish for ever like his own dung:
They which have seen him shall say, Where is he?
27 The heaven shall reveal his iniquity;
And the earth shall rise up against him.
28 The increase of his house shall depart,
And his goods shall flow away in the day of his wrath.
29 This is the portion of a wicked man from God,
And the heritage appointed unto him by God.

### Job

21 But Job answered and said,
7 Wherefore do the wicked live,
Become old, yea, are mighty in power?
8 Their seed is established in their sight with them,
And their offspring before their eyes.
9 Their houses are safe from fear,
Neither is the rod of God upon them.
10 Their bull gendereth, and faileth not;
Their cow calveth, and casteth not her calf.
11 They send forth their little ones like a flock,
And their children dance.
12 They take the timbrel and harp,
And rejoice at the sound of the organ.
13 They spend their days in wealth,
And in a moment go down to the grave.
34 How then comfort ye me in vain,
Seeing in your answers there remaineth falsehood?

### THIRD CYCLE OF DEBATE

### Eliphaz

22 Then Eliphaz the Temanite answered and said,
5 Is not thy wickedness great?
And thine iniquities infinite?
10 Therefore snares are round about thee,
And sudden fear troubleth thee;
22 Receive, I pray thee, the law from his mouth,
And lay up his words in thine heart.
23 If thou return to the Almighty, thou shalt be built up,
Thou shalt put away iniquity far from thy tabernacles.
24 Then shalt thou lay up gold as dust,
And the gold of Ophir as the stones of the brooks.
25 Yea, the Almighty shall be thy defense,
And thou shalt have plenty of silver.

### Job

**23** Then Job answered and said,

2 Even to-day is my complaint bitter:
My stroke is heavier than my groaning.

3 Oh that I knew where I might find him!
That I might come even to his seat!

4 I would order my cause before him,
And fill my mouth with arguments.

5 I would know the words which he would answer me,
And understand what he would say unto me.

6 Will he plead against me with his great power?
No; but he would put strength in me.

7 There the righteous might dispute with him;
So should I be delivered for ever from my judge.

8 Behold, I go forward, but he is not there;
And backward, but I cannot perceive him:

9 On the left hand, where he doth work, but I cannot behold him:
He hideth himself on the right hand, that I cannot see him:

10 But he knoweth the way that I take:
When he hath tried me, I shall come forth as gold.

### Bildad

**25** Then answered Bildad the Shuhite, and said,

2 Dominion and fear are with him;
He maketh peace in his high places.

3 Is there any number of his armies?
And upon whom doth not his light arise?

4 How then can man be justified with God?
Or how can he be clean that is born of a woman?

5 Behold even to the moon, and it shineth not;
Yea, the stars are not pure in his sight.

6 How much less man, that is a worm?
And the son of man, which is a worm?

### Job

**26** But Job answered and said,

7 He stretcheth out the north over the empty place,
And hangeth the earth upon nothing.

8 He bindeth up the waters in his thick clouds;
And the cloud is not rent under them.

9 He holdeth back the face of his throne,
And spreadeth his cloud upon it.

10 He hath compassed the waters with bounds,
Until the day and night come to an end.

11 The pillars of heaven tremble,
And are astonished at his reproof.

421

12 He divideth the sea with his power,
And by his understanding he smiteth through the proud.
13 By his Spirit he hath garnished the heavens;
His hand hath formed the crooked serpent.
14 Lo, these are parts of his ways;
But how little a portion is heard of him?
But the thunder of his power who can understand?

27 2 As God liveth, who hath taken away my judgment;
And the Almighty, who hath vexed my soul;
3 All the while my breath is in me,
And the spirit of God is in my nostrils;
4 My lips shall not speak wickedness,
Nor my tongue utter deceit.
5 God forbid that I should justify you:
Till I die I will not remove mine integrity from me.
6 My righteousness I hold fast, and will not let it go:
My heart shall not reproach me so long as I live.

29 2 Oh that I were as in months past,
As in the days when God preserved me;
3 When his candle shined upon my head,
And when by his light I walked through darkness;
4 As I was in the days of my youth,
When the secret of God was upon my tabernacle;
5 When the Almighty was yet with me,
When my children were about me;
6 When I washed my steps with butter,
And the rock poured me out rivers of oil;
7 When I went out to the gate through the city,
When I prepared my seat in the street!
8 The young men saw me, and hid themselves:
And the aged arose, and stood up.
9 The princes refrained talking,
And laid their hand on their mouth.
10 The nobles held their peace,
And their tongue cleaved to the roof of their mouth.
11 When the ear heard me, then it blessed me;
And when the eye saw me, it gave witness to me:
12 Because I delivered the poor that cried,
And the fatherless, and him that had none to help him.
13 The blessing of him that was ready to perish came upon me:
And I caused the widow's heart to sing for joy.
14 I put on righteousness, and it clothed me:
My judgment was as a robe and a diadem.
15 I was eyes to the blind,
And feet was I to the lame.

16 I was a father to the poor:
And the cause which I knew not I searched out.
17 And I brake the jaws of the wicked,
And plucked the spoil out of his teeth.
21 Unto me men gave ear, and waited,
And kept silence at my counsel.
22 After my words they spake not again;
And my speech dropped upon them.
25 I chose out their way, and sat chief,
And dwelt as a king in the army,
As one that comforteth the mourners.

30   But now they that are younger than I have me in derision,
Whose fathers I would have disdained to have set with the
dogs of my flock.
8 They were children of fools, yea, children of base men:
They were viler than the earth.
9 And now am I their song,
Yea, I am their byword.
10 They abhor me, they flee far from me,
And spare not to spit in my face.
29 I am a brother to dragons,
And a companion to owls.
30 My skin is black upon me,
And my bones are burned with heat.
31 My harp also is turned to mourning,
And my organ into the voice of them that weep.

31   5 If I have walked with vanity,
Or if my foot hath hasted to deceit;
6 Let me be weighed in an even balance,
That God may know mine integrity.
13 If I did despise the cause of my manservant or of my maidservant,
When they contended with me;
14 What then shall I do when God riseth up?
And when he visiteth, what shall I answer him?
15 Did not he that made me in the womb make him?
And did not one fashion us in the womb?
16 If I have withheld the poor from their desire,
Or have caused the eyes of the widow to fail;
17 Or have eaten my morsel myself alone,
And the fatherless hath not eaten thereof;
22 Then let mine arm fall from my shoulder blade,
And mine arm be broken from the bone.
35 Oh that one would hear me!
Behold, my desire is, that the Almighty would answer me,
And that mine adversary had written a book.

36 Surely I would take it upon my shoulder,
And bind it as a crown to me.
37 I would declare unto him the number of my steps;
As a prince would I go near unto him.
38 If my land cry against me,
Or that the furrows likewise thereof complain;
39 If I have eaten the fruits thereof without money,
Or have caused the owners thereof to lose their life:
40 Let thistles grow instead of wheat,
And cockle instead of barley.
The words of Job are ended.

## THE INTERVENTION OF THE LORD

### God

38   Then the Lord answered Job out of the whirlwind, and said,
2 Who is this that darkeneth counsel
By words without knowledge?
3 Gird up now thy loins like a man;
For I will demand of thee, and answer thou me.
4 Where wast thou when I laid the foundations of the earth?
Declare, if thou hast understanding.
5 Who hath laid the measures thereof, if thou knowest?
Or who hath stretched the line upon it?
6 Whereupon are the foundations thereof fastened?
Or who laid the corner stone thereof;
7 When the morning stars sang together,
And all the sons of God shouted for joy?
31 Canst thou bind the sweet influences of Pleiades,
Or loose the bands of Orion?
32 Canst thou bring forth Mazzaroth in his season?
Or canst thou guide Arcturus with his sons?

39 13 Gavest thou the goodly wings unto the peacocks?
Or wings and feathers unto the ostrich?
14 Which leaveth her eggs in the earth,
And warmeth them in the dust,
15 And forgetteth that the foot may crush them,
Or that the wild beast may break them.
19 Hast thou given the horse strength?
Hast thou clothed his neck with thunder?
20 Canst thou make him afraid as a grasshopper?
The glory of his nostrils is terrible.
21 He paweth in the valley, and rejoiceth in his strength:
He goeth on to meet the armed men.
22 He mocketh at fear, and is not affrighted;
Neither turneth he back from the sword.

26 Doth the hawk fly by thy wisdom,
And stretch her wings toward the south?
27 Doth the eagle mount up at thy command,
And make her nest on high?

**40** Moreover the Lord answered Job, and said,
2 Shall he that contendeth with the Almighty instruct him?
He that reproveth God, let him answer it.

### Job

3 Then Job answered the Lord, and said,
4 Behold, I am vile; what shall I answer thee?
I will lay mine hand upon my mouth.
5 Once have I spoken; but I will not answer:
Yea, twice; but I will proceed no further.

### God

6 Then answered the Lord unto Job out of the whirlwind, and
said,
7 Gird up thy loins now like a man:
I will demand of thee, and declare thou unto me.
8 Wilt thou also disannul my judgment?
Wilt thou condemn me, that thou mayest be righteous?
9 Hast thou an arm like God?
Or canst thou thunder with a voice like him?
10 Deck thyself now with majesty and excellency;
And array thyself with glory and beauty.
11 Cast abroad the rage of thy wrath:
And behold every one that is proud, and abase him.
12 Look on every one that is proud, and bring him low;
And tread down the wicked in their place.
13 Hide them in the dust together;
And bind their faces in secret.
14 Then will I also confess unto thee
That thine own right hand can save thee.

**41** Canst thou draw out leviathan with a hook?
Or his tongue with a cord which thou lettest down?
2 Canst thou put a hook into his nose?
Or bore his jaw through with a thorn?
3 Will he make many supplications unto thee?
Will he speak soft words unto thee?
4 Will he make a covenant with thee?
Wilt thou take him for a servant for ever?
5 Wilt thou play with him as with a bird?
Or wilt thou bind him for thy maidens?
6 Shall the companions make a banquet of him?
Shall they part him among the merchants?

31 He maketh the deep to boil like a pot:
He maketh the sea like a pot of ointment.
32 He maketh a path to shine after him;
One would think the deep to be hoary.
33 Upon earth there is not his like,
Who is made without fear.
34 He beholdeth all high things:
He is a king over all the children of pride.

## Job

**42** Then Job answered the Lord, and said,
2 I know that thou canst do every thing,
And that no thought can be withholden from thee.
3 Who is he that hideth counsel without knowledge?
Therefore have I uttered that I understood not;
Things too wonderful for me, which I knew not.
4 Hear, I beseech thee, and I will speak:
I will demand of thee, and declare thou unto me.
5 I have heard of thee by the hearing of the ear;
But now mine eye seeth thee:
6 Wherefore I abhor myself, and repent
In dust and ashes.

### EPILOGUE

7 And it was so, that after the Lord had spoken these words unto Job, the Lord said to Eliphaz the Temanite, My wrath is kindled against thee, and against thy two friends: for ye have not spoken of me the thing that is right, as my servant Job hath. 8 Therefore take unto you now seven bullocks and seven rams, and go to my servant Job, and offer up for yourselves a burnt offering; and my servant Job shall pray for you: for him will I accept: lest I deal with you after your folly, in that ye have not spoken of me the thing which is right, like my servant Job. 9 So Eliphaz the Temanite and Bildad the Shuhite and Zophar the Naamathite went, and did according as the Lord commanded them: the Lord also accepted Job. 10 And the Lord turned the captivity of Job, when he prayed for his friends: also the Lord gave Job twice as much as he had before. 11 Then came there unto him all his brethren, and all his sisters, and all they that had been of his acquaintance before, and did eat bread with him in his house: and they bemoaned him, and comforted him over all the evil that the Lord had brought upon him: every man also gave him a piece of money, and every one an earring of gold. 12 So the Lord blessed the latter end of Job more than his beginning: for he had fourteen thousand sheep, and six thousand camels, and a thousand yoke of oxen, and a thousand she asses. 13 He had also seven sons and three daughters. 14 And he called the name of the first, Jemima; and the name of the second, Kezia; and the name of the third, Keren-happuch.

15 And in all the land were no women found so fair as the daughters of Job: and their father gave them inheritance among their brethren. 16 After this lived Job a hundred and forty years, and saw his sons, and his sons' sons, even four generations. 17 So Job died, being old and full of days.

## Practical Wisdom: *Proverbs*

The book of Proverbs represents the practical branch of Biblical wisdom, but this is not all: from a concern with the most worldly prudence, the proverbs range through sagacity and piety, and even approach a kind of beatific vision in the apotheosis of Wisdom as an attribute of God. But they deal principally with practical discretion in the conduct of human life. Solomon was famed for such wisdom, and brought wise men to live in his court. His influence, and some of his proverbs, are doubtless present here, but the book as it stands is certainly not his work. For purposes of study, proverbs are here brought together from various parts of the book and grouped under common themes. One proverb often qualifies another, or even exists as a balanced antithesis to it. The book of Proverbs endures as a crystallization of reflections upon life by sages who made it their business to observe the successes and failures, pains and joys of men and nations.

# *Proverbs*

### WISDOM'S CALL

8
    Doth not wisdom cry?
    And understanding put forth her voice?
2 She standeth in the top of high places,
    By the way in the places of the paths.
3 She crieth at the gates, at the entry of the city,
    At the coming in at the doors:
4 Unto you, O men, I call;
    And my voice is to the sons of man.
5 O ye simple, understand wisdom:
    And, ye fools, be ye of an understanding heart.
6 Hear; for I will speak of excellent things;
    And the opening of my lips shall be right things.
7 For my mouth shall speak truth;
    And wickedness is an abomination to my lips.
8 All the words of my mouth are in righteousness;
    There is nothing froward or perverse in them.

9 They are all plain to him that understandeth,
And right to them that find knowledge.
10 Receive my instruction, and not silver;
And knowledge rather than choice gold.
11 For wisdom is better than rubies;
And all the things that may be desired are not to be compared
to it.
12 I wisdom dwell with prudence,
And find out knowledge of witty inventions.
13 The fear of the Lord is to hate evil:
Pride, and arrogancy, and the evil way,
And the froward mouth, do I hate.
14 Counsel is mine, and sound wisdom:
I am understanding; I have strength.
15 By me kings reign,
And princes decree justice.
16 By me princes rule,
And nobles, even all the judges of the earth.
17 I love them that love me;
And those that seek me early shall find me.
18 Riches and honor are with me;
Yea, durable riches and righteousness.
19 My fruit is better than gold, yea, than fine gold;
And my revenue than choice silver.
20 I lead in the way of righteousness,
In the midst of the paths of judgment:
21 That I may cause those that love me to inherit substance;
And I will fill their treasures.
22 The Lord possessed me in the beginning of his way,
Before his works of old.
23 I was set up from everlasting, from the beginning,
Or ever the earth was.
24 When there were no depths, I was brought forth;
When there were no fountains abounding with water.
25 Before the mountains were settled,
Before the hills was I brought forth:
26 While as yet he had not made the earth, nor the fields,
Nor the highest part of the dust of the world.
27 When he prepared the heavens, I was there:
When he set a compass upon the face of the depth:
28 When he established the clouds above:
When he strengthened the fountains of the deep:
29 When he gave to the sea his decree,
That the waters should not pass his commandment:
When he appointed the foundations of the earth:
30 Then I was by him, as one brought up with him:
And I was daily his delight,
Rejoicing always before him;

31 Rejoicing in the habitable part of his earth;
And my delights were with the sons of men.
32 Now therefore hearken unto me, O ye children:
For blessed are they that keep my ways.
33 Hear instruction, and be wise,
And refuse it not.
34 Blessed is the man that heareth me,
Watching daily at my gates,
Waiting at the posts of my doors.
35 For whoso findeth me findeth life,
And shall obtain favor of the Lord.
36 But he that sinneth against me wrongeth his own soul:
All they that hate me love death.

## EXAMPLES OF WISDOM

30 24 There be four things which are little upon the earth,
But they are exceeding wise:
25 The ants are a people not strong,
Yet they prepare their meat in the summer;
26 The conies are but a feeble folk,
Yet make they their houses in the rocks;
27 The locusts have no king,
Yet go they forth all of them by bands;
28 The spider taketh hold with her hands,
And is in kings' palaces.

## THE PRAISE OF A GOOD WOMAN

31 10 Who can find a virtuous woman?
For her price is far above rubies.
11 The heart of her husband doth safely trust in her,
So that he shall have no need of spoil.
12 She will do him good and not evil
All the days of her life.
13 She seeketh wool, and flax,
And worketh willingly with her hands.
14 She is like the merchants' ships;
She bringeth her food from afar.
15 She riseth also while it is yet night,
And giveth meat to her household,
And a portion to her maidens.
16 She considereth a field, and buyeth it:
With the fruit of her hands she planteth a vineyard.
17 She girdeth her loins with strength,
And strengtheneth her arms.
18 She perceiveth that her merchandise is good:
Her candle goeth not out by night.

19 She layeth her hands to the spindle,
And her hands hold the distaff.
20 She stretcheth out her hand to the poor;
Yea, she reacheth forth her hands to the needy.
21 She is not afraid of the snow for her household:
For all her household are clothed with scarlet.
22 She maketh herself coverings of tapestry;
Her clothing is silk and purple.
23 Her husband is known in the gates,
When he sitteth among the elders of the land.
24 She maketh fine linen, and selleth it;
And delivereth girdles unto the merchant.
25 Strength and honor are her clothing;
And she shall rejoice in time to come.
26 She openeth her mouth with wisdom;
And in her tongue is the law of kindness.
27 She looketh well to the ways of her household,
And eateth not the bread of idleness.
28 Her children arise up, and call her blessed;
Her husband also, and he praiseth her.
29 Many daughters have done virtuously,
But thou excellest them all.
30 Favor is deceitful, and beauty is vain:
But a woman that feareth the Lord, she shall be praised.
31 Give her of the fruit of her hands;
And let her own works praise her in the gates.

## ABOUT SEX

5    My son, attend unto my wisdom,
And bow thine ear to my understanding:
2 That thou mayest regard discretion,
And that thy lips may keep knowledge.
3 For the lips of a strange woman drop as a honeycomb,
And her mouth is smoother than oil:
4 But her end is bitter as wormwood,
Sharp as a two-edged sword.
5 Her feet go down to death;
Her steps take hold on hell.
6 Lest thou shouldest ponder the path of life,
Her ways are movable, that thou canst not know them.
7 Hear me now therefore, O ye children,
And depart not from the words of my mouth.
8 Remove thy way far from her,
And come not nigh the door of her house:
9 Lest thou give thine honor unto others,
And thy years unto the cruel:

10 Lest strangers be filled with thy wealth;
   And thy labors be in the house of a stranger;
11 And thou mourn at the last,
   When thy flesh and thy body are consumed,
12 And say, How have I hated instruction,
   And my heart despised reproof;
13 And have not obeyed the voice of my teachers,
   Nor inclined mine ear to them that instructed me!
14 I was almost in all evil
   In the midst of the congregation and assembly.

15 Drink waters out of thine own cistern,
   And running waters out of thine own well.
16 Let thy fountains be dispersed abroad,
   And rivers of waters in the streets.
17 Let them be only thine own,
   And not strangers' with thee.
18 Let thy fountain be blessed:
   And rejoice with the wife of thy youth.
19 Let her be as the loving hind and pleasant roe;
   Let her breasts satisfy thee at all times;
   And be thou ravished always with her love.

20 And why wilt thou, my son, be ravished with a strange woman,
   And embrace the bosom of a stranger?
21 For the ways of man are before the eyes of the Lord,
   And he pondereth all his goings.
22 His own iniquities shall take the wicked himself,
   And he shall be holden with the cords of his sins.
23 He shall die without instruction;
   And in the greatness of his folly he shall go astray.

### PARENTS AND CHILDREN

A wise son heareth his father's instruction:
But a scorner heareth not rebuke.   (13:1)

A wise son maketh a glad father:
But a foolish man despiseth his mother.   (15:20)

He that spareth his rod hateth his son:
But he that loveth him chasteneth him betimes.   (13:24)

Chasten thy son while there is hope,
And let not thy soul spare for his crying.   (19:18)

The rod and reproof give wisdom:
But a child left to himself bringeth his mother to shame.
   (29:15)

Correct thy son, and he shall give thee rest;
Yea, he shall give delight unto thy soul.   (29:17)

431

The just man walketh in his integrity:
His children are blessed after him.  (20:7)
Train up a child in the way he should go:
And when he is old, he will not depart from it.  (22:6)

## THE FAMILY

Better is little with the fear of the Lord,
Than great treasure and trouble therewith.
Better is a dinner of herbs where love is,
Than a stalled ox and hatred therewith.  (15:16–17)
Whoso rewardeth evil for good,
Evil shall not depart from his house.  (17:13)
A brother offended is harder to be won than a strong city:
And their contentions are like the bars of a castle.  (18:19)
A foolish son is the calamity of his father:
And the contentions of a wife are a continual dropping.
House and riches are the inheritance of fathers:
And a prudent wife is from the Lord.  (19:13–14)

## FRIENDSHIP

A friend loveth at all times,
And a brother is born for adversity.  (17:17)
A man that hath friends must show himself friendly:
And there is a friend that sticketh closer than a brother.
  (18:24)
Thine own friend, and thy father's friend, forsake not. . . .
  (27:10)
Faithful are the wounds of a friend;
But the kisses of an enemy are deceitful.  (27:6)

## THE SOCIAL ORDER

Where there is no vision, the people perish:
But he that keepeth the law, happy is he.  (29:18)
Where no counsel is, the people fall:
But in the multitude of counselors there is safety.  (11:14)
By the blessing of the upright the city is exalted:
But it is overthrown by the mouth of the wicked.  (11:11)
Whoso mocketh the poor reproacheth his Maker:
And he that is glad at calamities shall not be unpunished.
  (17:5)
He that oppresseth the poor reproacheth his Maker:
But he that honoreth him hath mercy on the poor.  (14:31)

He that hath pity upon the poor lendeth unto the Lord:
And that which he hath given will he pay him again.   (19:17)
Whoso stoppeth his ears at the cry of the poor,
He also shall cry himself, but shall not be heard.   (21:13)
Rob not the poor, because he is poor:
Neither oppress the afflicted in the gate:
For the Lord will plead their cause,
And spoil the soul of those that spoiled them.   (22:22-23)
Righteousness exalteth a nation:
But sin is a reproach to any people.   (14:34)

## THE SEVEN ABOMINATIONS

These six things doth the Lord hate;
Yea, seven are an abomination unto him:
A proud look, a lying tongue,
And hands that shed innocent blood,
A heart that deviseth wicked imaginations,
Feet that be swift in running to mischief,
A false witness that speaketh lies,
And he that soweth discord among brethren.   (6:16-19)

## AN EVIL GENERATION

There is a generation that curseth their father,
And doth not bless their mother.
There is a generation that are pure in their own eyes,
And yet is not washed from their filthiness.
There is a generation, O how lofty are their eyes!
And their eyelids are lifted up.
There is a generation, whose teeth are as swords,
And their jaw teeth as knives,
To devour the poor from off the earth,
And the needy from among men.   (30:11-14)

## SCORNERS AND FOOLS

Let a bear robbed of her whelps meet a man,
Rather than a fool in his folly.   (17:12)
Make no friendship with an angry man;
And with a furious man thou shalt not go;
Lest thou learn his ways,
And get a snare to thy soul.   (22:24-25)
Eat thou not the bread of him that hath an evil eye,
Neither desire thou his dainty meats:
For as he thinketh in his heart, so is he:

Eat and drink, saith he to thee;
But his heart is not with thee.
The morsel which thou hast eaten shalt thou vomit up,
And lose thy sweet words.  (23:6–8)
Confidence in an unfaithful man in time of trouble
Is like a broken tooth, and a foot out of joint.  (25:19)
Where no wood is, there the fire goeth out:
So where there is no talebearer, the strife ceaseth.
As coals are to burning coals, and wood to fire;
So is a contentious man to kindle strife.  (26:20–21)
A man that flattereth his neighbor
Spreadeth a net for his feet.  (29:5)

### AN UNRULY TONGUE

In all labor there is profit:
But the talk of the lips tendeth only to penury.  (14:23)
He that keepeth his mouth keepeth his life:
But he that openeth wide his lips shall have destruction.
  (13:3)
A soft answer turneth away wrath:
But grievous words stir up anger.  (15:1)
Boast not thyself of to-morrow;
For thou knowest not what a day may bring forth.
Let another man praise thee, and not thine own mouth;
A stranger, and not thine own lips.  (27:1–2)

### A WOMAN WITHOUT DISCRETION

As a jewel of gold in a swine's snout,
So is a fair woman which is without discretion.  (11:22)
It is better to dwell in a corner of the housetop,
Than with a brawling woman in a wide house.  (21:9)
It is better to dwell in the wilderness,
Than with a contentious and an angry woman.  (21:19)
A continual dropping in a very rainy day
And a contentious woman are alike.  (27:15)

### ON SLOTH

He also that is slothful in his work
Is brother to him that is a great waster.  (18:9)
Go to the ant, thou sluggard;
Consider her ways, and be wise:
Which having no guide,

Overseer, or ruler,
Provideth her meat in the summer,
And gathereth her food in the harvest.   (6:6–8)
I went by the field of the slothful,
And by the vineyard of the man void of understanding;
And, lo, it was all grown over with thorns,
And nettles had covered the face thereof,
And the stone wall thereof was broken down.
Then I saw, and considered it well:
I looked upon it, and received instruction.
Yet a little sleep, a little slumber,
A little folding of the hands to sleep:
So shall thy poverty come as one that traveleth;
And thy want as an armed man.   (24:30–34)


## ON OVERINDULGENCE

Hast thou found honey? eat so much as is sufficient for thee,
Lest thou be filled therewith, and vomit it.   (25:16)
Wine is a mocker, strong drink is raging:
And whosoever is deceived thereby is not wise.   (20:1)
It is not for kings, O Lemuel,
It is not for kings to drink wine;
Nor for princes strong drink:
Lest they drink, and forget the law,
And pervert the judgment of any of the afflicted.   (31:4–5)
Who hath woe? who hath sorrow?
Who hath contentions? who hath babbling?
Who hath wounds without cause?
Who hath redness of eyes?
They that tarry long at the wine;
They that go to seek mixed wine.
Look not thou upon the wine when it is red,
When it giveth his color in the cup,
When it moveth itself aright.
At the last it biteth like a serpent,
And stingeth like an adder.
Thine eyes shall behold strange women,
And thine heart shall utter perverse things.
Yea, thou shalt be as he that lieth down in the midst of the
sea,
Or as he that lieth upon the top of a mast.
They have stricken me, shalt thou say, and I was not sick;
They have beaten me, and I felt it not:
When shall I awake?
I will seek it yet again.   (23:29–35)

## MISCELLANEOUS ADVICE

There is a way which seemeth right unto a man;
But the end thereof are the ways of death.  (14:12)

The simple believeth every word:
But the prudent man looketh well to his going.  (14:15)

A wise man scaleth the city of the mighty,
And casteth down the strength of the confidence thereof.
(21:22)

My son, eat thou honey, because it is good;
And the honeycomb, which is sweet to thy taste:
So shall the knowledge of wisdom be unto thy soul:
When thou hast found it, then there shall be a reward,
And thy expectation shall not be cut off.  (24:13–14)

Answer not a fool according to his folly,
Lest thou also be like unto him.
Answer a fool according to his folly,
Lest he be wise in his own conceit.  (26:4–5)

Seest thou a man wise in his own conceit?
There is more hope of a fool than of him.  (26:12)

Whoso diggeth a pit shall fall therein:
And he that rolleth a stone, it will return upon him.  (26:27)

Iron sharpeneth iron;
So a man sharpeneth the countenance of his friend.  (27:17)

Though thou shouldest bray a fool in a mortar among wheat
with a pestle,
Yet will not his foolishness depart from him.  (27:22)

Evil men understand not judgment:
But they that seek the Lord understand all things.  (28:5)

He that rebuketh a man, afterward shall find more favor
Than he that flattereth with the tongue.  (28:23)

## SADNESS AND JOY

The heart knoweth his own bitterness;
And a stranger doth not intermeddle with his joy.  (14:10)

Even in laughter the heart is sorrowful;
And the end of that mirth is heaviness.  (14:13)

All the days of the afflicted are evil:
But he that is of a merry heart hath a continual feast.
(15:15)

## RICH AND POOR

The rich man's wealth is his strong city:
The destruction of the poor is their poverty.  (10:15)

An inheritance may be gotten hastily at the beginning;
But the end thereof shall not be blessed.  (20:21)

The rich and poor meet together:
The Lord is the maker of them all.  (22:2)

The rich ruleth over the poor,
And the borrower is servant to the lender.  (22:7)

Be thou diligent to know the state of thy flocks,
And look well to thy herds:
For riches are not for ever:
And doth the crown endure to every generation?  (27:23–24)

Better is the poor that walketh in his uprightness,
Than he that is perverse in his ways, though he be rich.
  (28:6)

### WISDOM AND FOOLISHNESS

The fear of the Lord is the beginning of wisdom:
And the knowledge of the Holy is understanding.  (9:10)

How much better is it to get wisdom than gold!
And to get understanding rather to be chosen than silver!
  (16:16)

Excellent speech becometh not a fool:
Much less do lying lips a prince.  (17:7)

Wherefore is there a price in the hand of a fool
To get wisdom, seeing he hath no heart to it?  (17:16)

He that answereth a matter before he heareth it,
It is folly and shame unto him.  (18:13)

The hearing ear, and the seeing eye,
The Lord hath made even both of them.  (20:12)

The man that wandereth out of the way of understanding
Shall remain in the congregation of the dead.  (21:16)

Seest thou a man diligent in his business?
He shall stand before kings;
He shall not stand before mean men.  (22:29)

Speak not in the ears of a fool:
For he will despise the wisdom of thy words.  (23:9)

The legs of the lame are not equal:
So is a parable in the mouth of fools.  (26:7)

As a dog returneth to his vomit,
So a fool returneth to his folly.  (26:11)

He that passeth by, and meddleth with strife belonging not
  to him,
Is like one that taketh a dog by the ears.  (26:17)

## RIGHTEOUSNESS AND WICKEDNESS

The merciful man doeth good to his own soul:
But he that is cruel troubleth his own flesh.  (11:17)
A righteous man regardeth the life of his beast:
But the tender mercies of the wicked are cruel.  (12:10)
Better is a little with righteousness,
Than great revenues without right.  (16:8)
Pride goeth before destruction,
And a haughty spirit before a fall.
Better it is to be of an humble spirit with the lowly,
Than to divide the spoil with the proud.  (16:18–19)
Bread of deceit is sweet to a man;
But afterward his mouth shall be filled with gravel.  (20:17)
A high look, and a proud heart,
And the plowing of the wicked, is sin.  (21:4)
The getting of treasures by a lying tongue
Is a vanity tossed to and fro of them that seek death.  (21:6)
A good name is rather to be chosen than great riches,
And loving favor rather than silver and gold.  (22:1)
Fret not thyself because of evil men,
Neither be thou envious at the wicked;
For there shall be no reward to the evil man;
The candle of the wicked shall be put out.  (24:19–20)
The wicked flee when no man pursueth:
But the righteous are bold as a lion.  (28:1)
A faithful man shall abound with blessings:
But he that maketh haste to be rich shall not be innocent.
  (28:20)
An unjust man is an abomination to the just:
And he that is upright in the way is abomination to the
  wicked.  (29:27)
The path of the just is as the shining light,
That shineth more and more unto the perfect day.
The way of the wicked is as darkness:
They know not at what they stumble.  (4:18–19)

## GOOD COUNSEL

The way of a fool is right in his own eyes:
But he that hearkeneth unto counsel is wise.  (12:15)
Poverty and shame shall be to him that refuseth instruction:
But he that regardeth reproof shall be honored.  (13:18)
He that refuseth instruction despiseth his own soul:
But he that heareth reproof getteth understanding.  (15:32)

He that turneth away his ear from hearing the law,
Even his prayer shall be abomination.  (28:9)

SELF-UNDERSTANDING

The fear of the Lord is the instruction of wisdom;
And before honor is humility.  (15:33)
Who can say, I have made my heart clean,
I am pure from my sin?  (20:9)
All the ways of a man are clean in his own eyes;
But the Lord weigheth the spirits.
Commit thy works unto the Lord,
And thy thoughts shall be established.  (16:2–3)
Whoso boasteth himself of a false gift
Is like clouds and wind without rain.  (25:14)
It is not good to eat much honey:
So for men to search their own glory is not glory.
He that hath no rule over his own spirit
Is like a city that is broken down, and without walls.
   (25:27–28)
He that is slow to anger is better than the mighty;
And he that ruleth his spirit than he that taketh a city.
   (16:32)

# The Greatest Prophet: *Isaiah* 40-55

The great prophetic tradition finds its noblest expression in the sustained eloquence of chapters 40-55 of Isaiah. Most scholars now believe that these chapters are to be ascribed to a second Isaiah, rather than to the first, and that they were written in Babylonian captivity just prior to the liberation of the Jews and their return to Palestine. Here monotheism and universalism attain a new majesty of expression, which brings to fruition the entire Jewish past and which clearly stands as prelude to the emergence of Christianity in the New Testament. For that reason, selections from this work are placed here, as the culmination of the Old Testament and as the primary source for the New Testament conception of Christ as the suffering servant of God and man.

## *Isaiah*

### THE MESSAGE OF JOY

40 Comfort ye, comfort ye my people,
Saith your God.
2 Speak ye comfortably to Jerusalem,
And cry unto her,
That her warfare is accomplished,
That her iniquity is pardoned:
For she hath received of the Lord's hand
Double for all her sins.
3 The voice of him that crieth in the wilderness,
Prepare ye the way of the Lord,
Make straight in the desert
A highway for our God.
4 Every valley shall be exalted,
And every mountain and hill shall be made low:
And the crooked shall be made straight,
And the rough places plain:
5 And the glory of the Lord shall be revealed,
And all flesh shall see it together:
For the mouth of the Lord hath spoken it.
6 The voice said, Cry.
And he said, What shall I cry?
All flesh is grass,
And all the goodliness thereof is as the flower of the field:

7 The grass withereth, the flower fadeth;
　Because the spirit of the Lord bloweth upon it:
　Surely the people is grass.
8 The grass withereth, the flower fadeth:
　But the word of our God shall stand for ever.
9 O Zion, that bringest good tidings,
　Get thee up into the high mountain;
　O Jerusalem, that bringest good tidings,
　Lift up thy voice with strength;
　Lift it up, be not afraid;
　Say unto the cities of Judah,
　Behold your God!
10 Behold, the Lord God will come with strong hand,
　And his arm shall rule for him:
　Behold, his reward is with him,
　And his work before him.
11 He shall feed his flock like a shepherd:
　He shall gather the lambs with his arm,
　And carry them in his bosom,
　And shall gently lead those that are with young.

### THE TRUE GOD AND THE FALSE GODS

18 To whom then will ye liken God?
　Or what likeness will ye compare unto him?
19 The workman melteth a graven image,
　And the goldsmith spreadeth it over with gold,
　And casteth silver chains.
20 He that is so impoverished that he hath no oblation
　Chooseth a tree that will not rot;
　He seeketh unto him a cunning workman
　To prepare a graven image, that shall not be moved.
21 Have ye not known? have ye not heard?
　Hath it not been told you from the beginning?
　Have ye not understood from the foundations of the earth?
22 It is he that sitteth upon the circle of the earth,
　And the inhabitants thereof are as grasshoppers;
　That stretcheth out the heavens as a curtain,
　And spreadeth them out as a tent to dwell in:
23 That bringeth the princes to nothing;
　He maketh the judges of the earth as vanity.
24 Yea, they shall not be planted;
　Yea, they shall not be sown;
　Yea, their stock shall not take root in the earth:
　And he shall also blow upon them, and they shall wither,
　And the whirlwind shall take them away as stubble.
25 To whom then will ye liken me,
　Or shall I be equal? saith the Holy One.

26 Lift up your eyes on high,
And behold who hath created these things,
That bringeth out their host by number:
He calleth them all by names
By the greatness of his might,
For that he is strong in power;
Not one faileth.

### THE CALL TO ISRAEL

27 Why sayest thou, O Jacob,
And speakest, O Israel,
My way is hid from the Lord,
And my judgment is passed over from my God?
28 Hast thou not known? hast thou not heard,
That the everlasting God, the Lord,
The Creator of the ends of the earth,
Fainteth not, neither is weary?
There is no searching of his understanding.
29 He giveth power to the faint;
And to them that have no might he increaseth strength.
30 Even the youths shall faint and be weary,
And the young men shall utterly fall:
31 But they that wait upon the Lord shall renew their strength;
They shall mount up with wings as eagles;
They shall run, and not be weary;
And they shall walk, and not faint.

### THE SERVANT OF THE LORD

42 Behold my servant, whom I uphold;
Mine elect, in whom my soul delighteth;
I have put my Spirit upon him:
He shall bring forth judgment to the Gentiles.
2 He shall not cry, nor lift up,
Nor cause his voice to be heard in the street.
3 A bruised reed shall he not break,
And the smoking flax shall he not quench:
He shall bring forth judgment unto truth.
4 He shall not fail nor be discouraged,
Till he have set judgment in the earth:
And the isles shall wait for his law.

### THE IDOL MAKERS

44 9 They that make a graven image are all of them vanity; and
their delectable things shall not profit; and they are their own witnesses; they see not, nor know; that they may be ashamed. 10 Who

442

hath formed a god, or molten a graven image that is profitable for nothing? 11 Behold, all his fellows shall be ashamed; and the workmen, they are of men: let them all be gathered together, let them stand up; yet they shall fear, and they shall be ashamed together. 12 The smith with the tongs both worketh in the coals, and fashioneth it with hammers, and worketh it with the strength of his arms: yea, he is hungry, and his strength faileth: he drinketh no water, and is faint. 13 The carpenter stretcheth out his rule; he marketh it out with a line; he fitteth it with planes, and he marketh it out with the compass, and maketh it after the figure of a man, according to the beauty of a man; that it may remain in the house. 14 He heweth him down cedars, and taketh the cypress and the oak, which he strengtheneth for himself among the trees of the forest: he planteth an ash, and the rain doth nourish it. 15 Then shall it be for a man to burn: for he will take thereof, and warm himself; yea, he kindleth it, and baketh bread; yea, he maketh a god, and worshippeth it; he maketh it a graven image, and falleth down thereto. 16 He burneth part thereof in the fire; with part thereof he eateth flesh; he roasteth roast, and is satisfied: yea, he warmeth himself, and saith, Aha, I am warm, I have seen the fire: 17 And the residue thereof he maketh a god, even his graven image: he falleth down unto it, and worshippeth it, and prayeth unto it, and saith, Deliver me; for thou art my god. 18 They have not known nor understood: for he hath shut their eyes, that they cannot see; and their hearts, that they cannot understand. 19 And none considereth in his heart, neither is there knowledge nor understanding to say, I have burned part of it in the fire; yea, also I have baked bread upon the coals thereof; I have roasted flesh, and eaten it: and shall I make the residue thereof an abomination? shall I fall down to the stock of a tree? 20 He feedeth on ashes: a deceived heart hath turned him aside, that he cannot deliver his soul, nor say, Is there not a lie in my right hand?

### THE ANOINTED GENTILE: CYRUS OF PERSIA

24 Thus saith the Lord, thy Redeemer,
And he that formed thee from the womb,
I am the Lord that maketh all things;
That stretcheth forth the heavens alone;
That spreadeth abroad the earth by myself;
28 That saith of Cyrus, He is my shepherd,
And shall perform all my pleasure:
Even saying to Jerusalem, Thou shalt be built;
And to the temple, Thy foundation shall be laid.

45 Thus saith the Lord to his anointed, to Cyrus,
Whose right hand I have holden,
To subdue nations before him;
And I will loose the loins of kings,

To open before him the two-leaved gates;
And the gates shall not be shut;
2 I will go before thee,
And make the crooked places straight:
I will break in pieces the gates of brass,
And cut in sunder the bars of iron:
3 And I will give thee the treasures of darkness,
And hidden riches of secret places,
That thou mayest know that I, the Lord, which call thee by
thy name,
Am the God of Israel.
4 For Jacob my servant's sake,
And Israel mine elect,
I have even called thee by thy name:
I have surnamed thee, though thou hast not known me.
5 I am the Lord, and there is none else,
There is no God besides me:
I girded thee, though thou hast not known me;
6 That they may know from the rising of the sun, and from the
west,
That there is none besides me.
I am the Lord, and there is none else.

### THE ACCURSED GENTILE: BABYLON

47    Come down, and sit in the dust,
O virgin daughter of Babylon,
Sit on the ground: there is no throne,
O daughter of the Chaldeans:
For thou shalt no more be called tender and delicate.
2 Take the millstones, and grind meal:
5 Sit thou silent, and get thee into darkness,
O daughter of the Chaldeans:
For thou shalt no more be called,
The lady of kingdoms.
6 I was wroth with my people,
I have polluted mine inheritance,
And given them into thine hand:
Thou didst show them no mercy;
Upon the ancient hast thou very heavily
Laid thy yoke.
7 And thou saidst,
I shall be a lady for ever:
So that thou didst not lay these things to thy heart,
Neither didst remember the latter end of it.
8 Therefore hear now this, thou that art given to pleasures,
That dwellest carelessly,

That sayest in thine heart,
I am, and none else besides me;
I shall not sit as a widow,
Neither shall I know the loss of children:
9 But these two things shall come to thee in a moment
In one day,
The loss of children, and widowhood:
They shall come upon thee in their perfection
For the multitude of thy sorceries,
And for the great abundance of thine enchantments.
10 For thou hast trusted in thy wickedness:
Thou hast said, None seeth me.
Thy wisdom and thy knowledge,
It hath perverted thee;
And thou hast said in thine heart,
I am, and none else besides me.
11 Therefore shall evil come upon thee;
Thou shalt not know from whence it riseth:
And mischief shall fall upon thee;
Thou shalt not be able to put it off:
And desolation shall come upon thee suddenly,
Which thou shalt not know.
13 Thou art wearied in the multitude of thy counsels.
Let now the astrologers, the stargazers,
The monthly prognosticators,
Stand up, and save thee
From these things that shall come upon thee.
14 Behold, they shall be as stubble;
The fire shall burn them;
They shall not deliver themselves
From the power of the flame:
There shall not be a coal to warm at,
Nor fire to sit before it.

## ISRAEL PURIFIED AND RESTORED

**48** Hear ye this, O house of Jacob,
Which are called by the name of Israel,
And are come forth out of the waters of Judah,
Which swear by the name of the Lord,
And make mention of the God of Israel,
10 Behold, I have refined thee, but not with silver;
I have chosen thee in the furnace of affliction.
12 Hearken unto me, O Jacob
And Israel, my called;
I am he; I am the first,
I also am the last.

16 Come ye near unto me, hear ye this;
   I have not spoken in secret from the beginning;
   From the time that it was, there am I:
   And now the Lord God, and his Spirit, hath sent me.

17 Thus saith the Lord, thy Redeemer,
   The Holy One of Israel;
   I am the Lord thy God
   Which teacheth thee to profit,
   Which leadeth thee by the way that thou shouldest go.

18 O that thou hadst hearkened to my commandments!
   Then had thy peace been as a river,
   And thy righteousness as the waves of the sea:

19 Thy seed also had been as the sand,
   And the offspring of thy bowels like the gravel thereof;
   His name should not have been cut off
   Nor destroyed from before me.

20 Go ye forth of Babylon,
   Flee ye from the Chaldeans,
   With a voice of singing
   Declare ye, tell this,
   Utter it even to the end of the earth;
   Say ye, The Lord hath redeemed
   His servant Jacob.

21 And they thirsted not
   When he led them through the deserts:
   He caused the waters to flow
   Out of the rock for them:
   He clave the rock also,
   And the waters gushed out.

22 There is no peace,
   Saith the Lord, unto the wicked.


## THE SERVANT OF THE LORD

49    Listen, O isles, unto me;
   And hearken, ye people, from far;
   The Lord hath called me from the womb;
   From the bowels of my mother hath he made mention of my
      name.

2 And he hath made my mouth like a sharp sword;
   In the shadow of his hand hath he hid me,
   And made me a polished shaft;
   In his quiver hath he hid me;

3 And said unto me, Thou art my servant,
   O Israel, in whom I will be glorified.

4 Then I said, I have labored in vain,
   I have spent my strength for nought, and in vain:

446

Yet surely my judgment is with the Lord,
And my work with my God.
5 And now, saith the Lord
That formed me from the womb to be his servant,
To bring Jacob again to him,
Though Israel be not gathered,
Yet shall I be glorious in the eyes of the Lord,
And my God shall be my strength.
6 And he said, It is a light thing that thou shouldest be my
servant
To raise up the tribes of Jacob,
And to restore the preserved of Israel:
I will also give thee for a light to the Gentiles,
That thou mayest be my salvation unto the end of the earth.

50  4 The Lord God hath given me
The tongue of the learned,
That I should know how to speak a word in season to him that
is weary:
He wakeneth morning by morning,
He wakeneth mine ear
To hear as the learned.
5 The Lord God hath opened mine ear,
And I was not rebellious,
Neither turned away back.
6 I gave my back to the smiters,
And my cheeks to them that plucked off the hair:
I hid not my face from shame and spitting.
7 For the Lord God will help me;
Therefore shall I not be confounded:
Therefore have I set my face like a flint,
And I know that I shall not be ashamed.
8 He is near that justifieth me;
Who will contend with me? let us stand together:
Who is mine adversary? let him come near to me.
9 Behold, the Lord God will help me;
Who is he that shall condemn me?
Lo, they all shall wax old as a garment;
The moth shall eat them up.
10 Who is among you that feareth the Lord,
That obeyeth the voice of his servant,
That walketh in darkness,
And hath no light?
Let him trust in the name of the Lord,
And stay upon his God.
11 Behold, all ye that kindle a fire,
That compass yourselves about with sparks:

Walk in the light of your fire,
And in the sparks that ye have kindled.
This shall ye have of mine hand;
Ye shall lie down in sorrow.

### THE CALL TO ISRAEL

51 Hearken to me, ye that follow after righteousness,
Ye that seek the Lord:
Look unto the rock whence ye are hewn,
And to the hole of the pit whence ye are digged.
2 Look unto Abraham your father,
And unto Sarah that bare you:
For I called him alone,
And blessed him, and increased him.
3 For the Lord shall comfort Zion:
He will comfort all her waste places;
And he will make her wilderness like Eden,
And her desert like the garden of the Lord;
Joy and gladness shall be found therein,
Thanksgiving, and the voice of melody.
7 Hearken unto me, ye that know righteousness,
The people in whose heart is my law;
Fear ye not the reproach of men,
Neither be ye afraid of their revilings.
8 For the moth shall eat them up like a garment,
And the worm shall eat them like wool:
But my righteousness shall be for ever,
And my salvation from generation to generation.

### THE BEAUTY OF GOOD TIDINGS

52 7 How beautiful upon the mountains
Are the feet of him that bringeth good tidings,
That publisheth peace;
That bringeth good tidings of good,
That publisheth salvation;
That saith unto Zion,
Thy God reigneth!
8 Thy watchmen shall lift up the voice;
With the voice together shall they sing:
For they shall see eye to eye,
When the Lord shall bring again Zion.
9 Break forth into joy, sing together,
Ye waste places of Jerusalem:
For the Lord hath comforted his people,
He hath redeemed Jerusalem.
10 The Lord hath made bare his holy arm
In the eyes of all the nations;

And all the ends of the earth shall see
The salvation of our God.
11 Depart ye, depart ye, go ye out from thence,
Touch no unclean thing;
Go ye out of the midst of her; be ye clean,
That bear the vessels of the Lord.
12 For ye shall not go out with haste,
Nor go by flight:
For the Lord will go before you;
And the God of Israel will be your rearward.

## THE SERVANT OF THE LORD

53 Who hath believed our report?
And to whom is the arm of the Lord revealed?
2 For he shall grow up before him as a tender plant,
And as a root out of a dry ground:
He hath no form nor comeliness; and when we shall see him,
There is no beauty that we should desire him.
3 He is despised and rejected of men;
A man of sorrows, and acquainted with grief:
And we hid as it were our faces from him;
He was despised, and we esteemed him not.
4 Surely he hath borne our griefs,
And carried our sorrows:
Yet we did esteem him stricken,
Smitten of God, and afflicted.
5 But he was wounded for our transgressions,
He was bruised for our iniquities:
The chastisement of our peace was upon him;
And with his stripes we are healed.
6 All we like sheep have gone astray;
We have turned every one to his own way;
And the Lord hath laid on him
The iniquity of us all.
7 He was oppressed, and he was afflicted,
Yet he opened not his mouth:
He is brought as a lamb to the slaughter,
And as a sheep before her shearers is dumb,
So he openeth not his mouth.
8 He was taken from prison and from judgment:
And who shall declare his generation?
For he was cut off out of the land of the living:
For the transgression of my people was he stricken.
9 And he made his grave with the wicked,
And with the rich in his death;
Because he had done no violence,
Neither was any deceit in his mouth.

10 Yet it pleased the Lord to bruise him; he hath put him to
grief:
When thou shalt make his soul an offering for sin,
He shall see his seed, he shall prolong his days,
And the pleasure of the Lord shall prosper in his hand.
11 He shall see of the travail of his soul, and shall be satisfied:
By his knowledge shall my righteous servant justify many;
For he shall bear their iniquities.
12 Therefore will I divide him a portion with the great,
And he shall divide the spoil with the strong;
Because he hath poured out his soul unto death:
And he was numbered with the transgressors;
And he bare the sin of many,
And made intercession for the transgressors.

## THE NEW JERUSALEM

**54**　Sing, O barren, thou that didst not bear;
Break forth into singing, and cry aloud, thou that didst not
travail with child:
For more are the children of the desolate
Than the children of the married wife, saith the Lord.
2 Enlarge the place of thy tent,
And let them stretch forth the curtains of thine habitations:
Spare not, lengthen thy cords, and strengthen thy stakes;
3 For thou shalt break forth on the right hand and on the left;
And thy seed shall inherit the Gentiles,
And make the desolate cities to be inhabited.
4 Fear not; for thou shalt not be ashamed:
Neither be thou confounded; for thou shalt not be put to
shame:
For thou shalt forget the shame of thy youth,
And shalt not remember the reproach of thy widowhood any
more.
5 For thy Maker is thine husband;
The Lord of hosts is his name;
And thy Redeemer the Holy One of Israel;
The God of the whole earth shall he be called.
6 For the Lord hath called thee
As a woman forsaken and grieved in spirit,
And a wife of youth, when thou wast refused,
Saith thy God.
7 For a small moment have I forsaken thee;
But with great mercies will I gather thee.
8 In a little wrath
I hid my face from thee for a moment;
But with everlasting kindness will I have mercy on thee,
Saith the Lord thy Redeemer.

9 For this is as the waters of Noah unto me:
For as I have sworn that the waters of Noah
Should no more go over the earth;
So have I sworn that I would not be wroth with thee,
Nor rebuke thee.

10 For the mountains shall depart,
And the hills be removed;
But my kindness shall not depart from thee,
Neither shall the covenant of my peace be removed,
Saith the Lord that hath mercy on thee.

11 O thou afflicted, tossed with tempest,
And not comforted,
Behold, I will lay thy stones with fair colors,
And lay thy foundations with sapphires.

12 And I will make thy windows of agates,
And thy gates of carbuncles,
And all thy borders of pleasant stones.

13 And all thy children shall be taught of the Lord;
And great shall be the peace of thy children.

14 In righteousness shalt thou be established:
Thou shalt be far from oppression; for thou shalt not fear:
And from terror; for it shall not come near thee.

15 Behold, they shall surely gather together, but not by me:
Whosoever shall gather together against thee shall fall for thy
sake.

16 Behold, I have created the smith
That bloweth the coals in the fire,
And that bringeth forth an instrument for his work;
And I have created the waster to destroy.

17 No weapon that is formed against thee shall prosper;
And every tongue that shall rise against thee in judgment thou
shalt condemn.
This is the heritage of the servants of the Lord,
And their righteousness is of me, saith the Lord.


### INVITATION AND PROMISE TO ALL

**55** Ho, every one that thirsteth, come ye to the waters,
And he that hath no money;
Come ye, buy, and eat;
Yea, come, buy wine and milk
Without money and without price.

2 Wherefore do ye spend money for that which is not bread?
And your labor for that which satisfieth not?
Hearken diligently unto me, and eat ye that which is good,
And let your soul delight itself in fatness.

3 Incline your ear, and come unto me:
   Hear, and your soul shall live;
   And I will make an everlasting covenant with you,
   Even the sure mercies of David.
4 Behold, I have given him for a witness to the people,
   A leader and commander to the people.
5 Behold, thou shalt call a nation that thou knowest not,
   And nations that knew not thee shall run unto thee,
   Because of the Lord thy God,
   And for the Holy One of Israel; for he hath glorified thee.
6 Seek ye the Lord while he may be found,
   Call ye upon him while he is near:
7 Let the wicked forsake his way,
   And the unrighteous man his thoughts:
   And let him return unto the Lord, and he will have mercy
      upon him;
   And to our God, for he will abundantly pardon.
8 For my thoughts are not your thoughts,
   Neither are your ways my ways, saith the Lord.
9 For as the heavens are higher than the earth,
   So are my ways higher than your ways,
   And my thoughts than your thoughts.
10 For as the rain cometh down,
   And the snow from heaven,
   And returneth not thither,
   But watereth the earth,
   And maketh it bring forth and bud,
   That it may give seed to the sower, and bread to the eater:
11 So shall my word be that goeth forth out of my mouth:
   It shall not return unto me void,
   But it shall accomplish that which I please,
   And it shall prosper in the thing whereto I sent it.
12 For ye shall go out with joy,
   And be led forth with peace:
   The mountains and the hills shall break forth before you into
      singing,
   And all the trees of the field shall clap their hands.
13 Instead of the thorn shall come up the fir tree,
   And instead of the brier shall come up the myrtle tree:
   And it shall be to the Lord for a name,
   For an everlasting sign that shall not be cut off.

*Selections from*

# THE NEW TESTAMENT

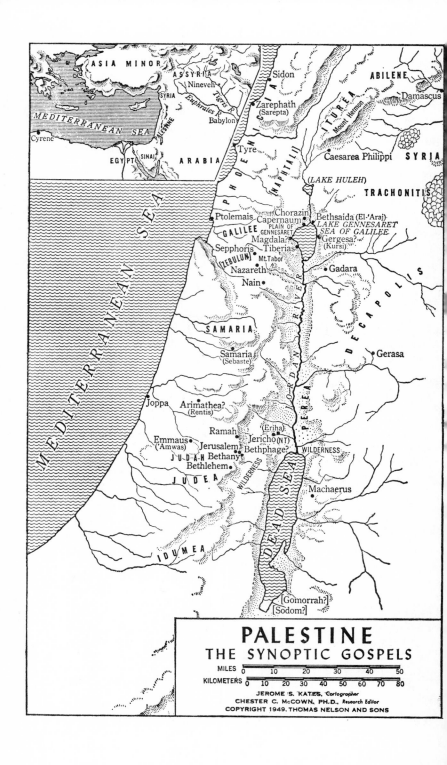

# PALESTINE
## THE SYNOPTIC GOSPELS

MILES 0 10 20 30 40 50

KILOMETERS 0 10 20 30 40 50 60 70 80

JEROME S. KATES, Cartographer
CHESTER C. McCOWN, PH.D., Research Editor
COPYRIGHT 1949, THOMAS NELSON AND SONS

# New Testament Narratives:
## Luke, John, Acts

The selections from the New Testament which are included here are divided between the forms of narrative, epistle, and apocalypse, according to the three major New Testament literary forms. There are four "gospels," or narrative books about Jesus Christ, in the New Testament. Of these, the first three — Matthew, Mark, and Luke — are called synoptic gospels, as they represent closely related treatments of the life and ministry of Christ. The gospel of John stands somewhat apart from the synoptics, and there is greater coherence between Matthew, Mark, and Luke than there is between any of these and John. Only nine percent of the synoptics coincides with John, while ninety-one percent of Mark may be found in Matthew and Luke. For reasons of its great literary skill, Luke has been chosen here from among the synoptics, and John is included as a masterly account in its own right.

Between Luke and John there are a number of differences. Luke's narrative moves forward by the meaningful placing of incidents and by the use of short passages or discussions called "pericopes." John's account, on the other hand, moves by the treatment of key themes in extended discourses, and by the almost symphonic development of governing symbols such as the world, life, light, and food and drink. Questions figure prominently in both, but play a more integral and pivotal role in Luke. Finally, the two books differ at certain points in chronology.

However great may be the differences between the gospels, the similarities are greater. Both Luke and John, as well as Matthew and Mark, are written out of firm convictions about the person of Christ. It is important to recognize this fact, and to observe that the gospels are not chronicles or annals dispassionately preserved. But to say this is not to disqualify the New Testament narratives: if the New Testament judgments of Christ are correct, then only an account written on the basis of these judgments can provide reliable insights into the original events. Throughout the gospel accounts, furthermore, there is a frank reporting of contrary judgments.

A major purpose of the gospel narratives is to provide for generations who have not been eyewitnesses and actors in the original events of Christ's work an effective contact with it. The importance of this contact is based upon the New Testament writers' judgment of Christ himself. The gospel writers did not work out the theological analyses of the Incarnation — these came as later commentaries upon what is represented in the gospels — but they unmistakably judged Christ to be the unique, ultimate, and crucial manifestation of truth about God and man. When viewed in this perspective, the very uniqueness of the union of divine and human in a single life posed the most serious literary problems for those who would give an account of what was most significant in that life.

At this point it would be well to recall and even to reread what has already been said in the general introduction about the manner in which the New Testament writers found the three primary Biblical interests in characterization brought to a focus in Christ. (See above, pages xxii ff.) Here we find concentrated the understanding of God, of humanity, and of human community. There is thus a great contraction of focus upon the single figure of Christ, but the concentration differs from that in conventional biographies, for the gospel writers regarded themselves as dealing with more than a mere man, however great. Some light is thrown upon other figures about Christ, but the intensity of the concentration upon Christ himself is such that all other personalities appear to be in the shadows. It is true that in the gospels there are flashes of individual insight, as into the personality of Peter, or Mary and Martha, or even Pilate, but these are quite incidental to the major task, which the gospel writers conceived as the characterization of God as he is revealed in Christ and of man as he should be.

This task had at least one further implication of great literary importance: on the basis of the New Testament, we cannot "identify" ourselves with Christ as in other literary works we can identify ourselves with, say, Macbeth or Cordelia — or even as we can identify with such other Biblical characters as Ruth and David, or Martha, Peter, and even Pilate. The inherent intent of the New Testament is to present Christ as sui generis, uniquely human and divine.

When we complete the gospels and move on into the book of Acts, we find ourselves on more familiar ground. Here the characters are more nearly of our own size and dimension. We see the development of these characters in clear and vital terms, under the impetus provided by their encounters with Christ. The events treated in Acts grow directly out of those earlier encounters, and are integrally related to them. The early Christians consciously conceived of themselves as continuing the work of Christ, a conception to which Paul gave brilliant expression in the metaphor which he applied to the church, "the body of Christ." All of the early Christians shared in this or some similar understanding of their role. Thus Luke wrote not only the gospel account of Christ himself but also the Acts of the Apostles, in the first verse of which he referred back to his earlier account of "all that Jesus began both to do and to teach." What Christ began in his own person, the community of Christians was to continue under the guidance of his spirit.

The book of Acts tells us much about the attitudes of early Christians to their lord. It also indicates the conscious continuity of the new community with the Old Testament, and at the same time its further expression of universal rather than racial concerns. The book is marked by great breadth of content: it includes memorable accounts of faithful martyrdom and also of scandal within the church; there are fine examples of oratory and even debate, of the clash of personalities, ideas, and cultures; and there are even touches of satire on the strolling exorcists who try to use the names of Jesus and of Paul without any commitment to either, as well as a devastating brief description of a frenzied mob shouting together for two hours, "Great is Diana of the Ephesians." Through its very variety of texture, the book conveys a vivid impression of the ongoing influence of Christ in the life of individuals and of a community. The book of Acts, however, does not have the kind of dramatic dénouement which we find at the close of the gospels, but is left open, as it were, for the future developments of the Christian community. The end of this story is written only in the prophetic vision of the New Jerusalem in the Apocalypse of Saint John, with which the New Testament is brought to its conclusion.

# *The Gospel According to Luke*

## FOREWORD

1 Forasmuch as many have taken in hand to set forth in order a declaration of those things which are most surely believed among us, 2 Even as they delivered them unto us, which from the beginning were eyewitnesses, and ministers of the word; 3 It seemed good to me also, having had perfect understanding of all things from the very first, to write unto thee in order, most excellent Theophilus, 4 That thou mightest know the certainty of those things, wherein thou hast been instructed.

## PROMISE AND PREPARATION

5 There was in the days of Herod, the king of Judea, a certain priest named Zacharias, of the course of Abia: and his wife was of the daughters of Aaron, and her name was Elisabeth. 6 And they were

both righteous before God, walking in all the commandments and ordinances of the Lord blameless. 7 And they had no child, because that Elisabeth was barren; and they both were now well stricken in years. 8 And it came to pass, that, while he executed the priest's office before God in the order of his course, 9 According to the custom of the priest's office, his lot was to burn incense when he went into the temple of the Lord. 10 And the whole multitude of the people were praying without at the time of incense. 11 And there appeared unto him an angel of the Lord standing on the right side of the altar of incense. 12 And when Zacharias saw him, he was troubled, and fear fell upon him. 13 But the angel said unto him, Fear not, Zacharias: for thy prayer is heard; and thy wife Elisabeth shall bear thee a son, and thou shalt call his name John. 14 And thou shalt have joy and gladness; and many shall rejoice at his birth. 15 For he shall be great in the sight of the Lord, and shall drink neither wine nor strong drink; and he shall be filled with the Holy Ghost, even from his mother's womb. 16 And many of the children of Israel shall he turn to the Lord their God. 17 And he shall go before him in the spirit and power of Elias,[1] to turn the hearts of the fathers to the children, and the disobedient to the wisdom of the just; to make ready a people prepared for the Lord. 18 And Zacharias said unto the angel, Whereby shall I know this? for I am an old man, and my wife well stricken in years. 19 And the angel answering said unto him, I am Gabriel, that stand in the presence of God; and am sent to speak unto thee, and to show thee these glad tidings. 20 And, behold, thou shalt be dumb, and not able to speak, until the day that these things shall be performed, because thou believest not my words, which shall be fulfilled in their season. 21 And the people waited for Zacharias, and marveled that he tarried so long in the temple. 22 And when he came out, he could not speak unto them: and they perceived that he had seen a vision in the temple; for he beckoned unto them, and remained speechless. 23 And it came to pass, that, as soon as the days of his ministration were accomplished, he departed to his own house. 24 And after those days his wife Elisabeth conceived, and hid herself five months, saying, 25 Thus hath the Lord dealt with me in the days wherein he looked on me, to take away my reproach among men.

26 And in the sixth month the angel Gabriel was sent from God unto a city of Galilee, named Nazareth, 27 To a virgin espoused to a man whose name was Joseph, of the house of David; and the virgin's name was Mary. 28 And the angel came in unto her, and said, Hail, thou that art highly favored, the Lord is with thee: blessed art thou among women. 29 And when she saw him, she was troubled at his saying, and cast in her mind what manner of salutation this should be. 30 And the angel said unto her, Fear not, Mary: for thou hast found favor with God. 31 And, behold, thou shalt conceive in thy womb, and bring forth a son, and shalt call his name Jesus. 32 He shall be

[1] A variant form of the name of the Old Testament prophet Elijah. It occurs also in Luke 4 and 9 and in John 1.

great, and shall be called the Son of the Highest; and the Lord God shall give unto him the throne of his father David: 33 And he shall reign over the house of Jacob for ever; and of his kingdom there shall be no end. 34 Then said Mary unto the angel, How shall this be, seeing I know not a man? 35 And the angel answered and said unto her, The Holy Ghost shall come upon thee, and the power of the Highest shall overshadow thee: therefore also that holy thing which shall be born of thee shall be called the Son of God. 36 And, behold, thy cousin Elisabeth, she hath also conceived a son in her old age; and this is the sixth month with her, who was called barren. 37 For with God nothing shall be impossible. 38 And Mary said, Behold the handmaid of the Lord; be it unto me according to thy word. And the angel departed from her.

39 And Mary arose in those days, and went into the hill country with haste, into a city of Juda; 40 And entered into the house of Zacharias, and saluted Elisabeth. 41 And it came to pass, that, when Elisabeth heard the salutation of Mary, the babe leaped in her womb; and Elisabeth was filled with the Holy Ghost: 42 And she spake out with a loud voice, and said, Blessed art thou among women, and blessed is the fruit of thy womb. 43 And whence is this to me, that the mother of my Lord should come to me? 44 For, lo, as soon as the voice of thy salutation sounded in mine ears, the babe leaped in my womb for joy. 45 And blessed is she that believed: for there shall be a performance of those things which were told her from the Lord. 46 And Mary said,

My soul doth magnify the Lord,

47 And my spirit hath rejoiced in God my Saviour.

48 For he hath regarded the low estate of his handmaiden:
For, behold, from henceforth all generations shall call me blessed.

49 For he that is mighty hath done to me great things;
And holy is his name.

50 And his mercy is on them that fear him
From generation to generation.

51 He hath showed strength with his arm;
He hath scattered the proud in the imagination of their hearts.

52 He hath put down the mighty from their seats,
And exalted them of low degree.

53 He hath filled the hungry with good things;
And the rich he hath sent empty away.

54 He hath holpen his servant Israel,
In remembrance of his mercy;

55 As he spake to our fathers,
To Abraham, and to his seed for ever.

56 And Mary abode with her about three months, and returned to her own house.

57 Now Elisabeth's full time came that she should be delivered; and she brought forth a son. 58 And her neighbors and her cousins heard

how the Lord had showed great mercy upon her; and they rejoiced
with her. 59 And it came to pass, that on the eighth day they came
to circumcise the child; and they called him Zacharias, after the name
of his father. 60 And his mother answered and said, Not so; but he
shall be called John. 61 And they said unto her, There is none of thy
kindred that is called by this name. 62 And they made signs to his
father, how he would have him called. 63 And he asked for a writing
table, and wrote, saying, His name is John. And they marveled all.
64 And his mouth was opened immediately, and his tongue loosed, and
he spake, and praised God. 65 And fear came on all that dwelt round
about them: and all these sayings were noised abroad throughout all
the hill country of Judea. 66 And all they that heard them laid them
up in their hearts, saying, What manner of child shall this be? And
the hand of the Lord was with him. 67 And his father Zacharias was
filled with the Holy Ghost, and prophesied, saying,

68 Blessed be the Lord God of Israel;
   For he hath visited and redeemed his people,
69 And hath raised up a horn of salvation for us
   In the house of his servant David;
70 As he spake by the mouth of his holy prophets,
   Which have been since the world began:
71 That we should be saved from our enemies,
   And from the hand of all that hate us;
72 To perform the mercy promised to our fathers,
   And to remember his holy covenant;
73 The oath which he sware to our father Abraham,
74 That he would grant unto us, that we, being delivered out of
      the hand of our enemies,
   Might serve him without fear,
75 In holiness and righteousness before him,
   All the days of our life.
76 And thou, child, shalt be called the prophet of the Highest:
   For thou shalt go before the face of the Lord
   To prepare his ways;
77 To give knowledge of salvation unto his people
   By the remission of their sins,
78 Through the tender mercy of our God;
   Whereby the dayspring from on high hath visited us,
79 To give light to them that sit in darkness and in the shadow
      of death,
   To guide our feet into the way of peace.

80 And the child grew, and waxed strong in spirit, and was in the
deserts till the day of his showing unto Israel.

2   And it came to pass in those days, that there went out a decree
from Caesar Augustus, that all the world should be taxed. 2 (And this
taxing was first made when Cyrenius was governor of Syria.) 3 And
all went to be taxed, every one into his own city. 4 And Joseph also

went up from Galilee, out of the city of Nazareth, into Judea, unto
the city of David, which is called Bethlehem, (because he was of the
house and lineage of David,) 5 To be taxed with Mary his espoused
wife, being great with child. 6 And so it was, that, while they were
there, the days were accomplished that she should be delivered. 7 And
she brought forth her firstborn son, and wrapped him in swaddling
clothes, and laid him in a manger; because there was no room for them
in the inn.

8 And there were in the same country shepherds abiding in the
field, keeping watch over their flock by night. 9 And, lo, the angel of
the Lord came upon them, and the glory of the Lord shone round
about them; and they were sore afraid. 10 And the angel said unto
them, Fear not: for, behold, I bring you good tidings of great joy,
which shall be to all people. 11 For unto you is born this day in the
city of David a Saviour, which is Christ the Lord. 12 And this shall
be a sign unto you; Ye shall find the babe wrapped in swaddling
clothes, lying in a manger. 13 And suddenly there was with the angel
a multitude of the heavenly host praising God, and saying,

14 Glory to God in the highest,
And on earth peace,
Good will toward men.

15 And it came to pass, as the angels were gone away from them into
heaven, the shepherds said one to another, Let us now go even unto
Bethlehem, and see this thing which is come to pass, which the Lord
hath made known unto us. 16 And they came with haste, and found
Mary and Joseph, and the babe lying in a manger. 17 And when they
had seen it, they made known abroad the saying which was told them
concerning this child. 18 And all they that heard it wondered at those
things which were told them by the shepherds. 19 But Mary kept all
these things, and pondered them in her heart. 20 And the shepherds
returned, glorifying and praising God for all the things that they had
heard and seen, as it was told unto them.

21 And when eight days were accomplished for the circumcising
of the child, his name was called Jesus, which was so named of the
angel before he was conceived in the womb. 22 And when the days of
her purification according to the law of Moses were accomplished, they
brought him to Jerusalem, to present him to the Lord; 23 (As it is
written in the law of the Lord, Every male that openeth the womb
shall be called holy to the Lord;) 24 And to offer a sacrifice according
to that which is said in the law of the Lord, A pair of turtledoves, or
two young pigeons. 25 And, behold, there was a man in Jerusalem,
whose name was Simeon; and the same man was just and devout,
waiting for the consolation of Israel: and the Holy Ghost was upon
him. 26 And it was revealed unto him by the Holy Ghost, that he
should not see death, before he had seen the Lord's Christ. 27 And
he came by the Spirit into the temple: and when the parents brought
in the child Jesus, to do for him after the custom of the law, 28 Then
took he him up in his arms, and blessed God, and said,

29 Lord, now lettest thou thy servant depart
In peace, according to thy word:
30 For mine eyes have seen thy salvation,
31 Which thou hast prepared before the face of all people;
32 A light to lighten the Gentiles,
And the glory of thy people Israel.

33 And Joseph and his mother marveled at those things which were spoken of him. 34 And Simeon blessed them, and said unto Mary his mother, Behold, this child is set for the fall and rising again of many in Israel; and for a sign which shall be spoken against; 35 (Yea, a sword shall pierce through thy own soul also;) that the thoughts of many hearts may be revealed. 36 And there was one Anna, a prophetess, the daughter of Phanuel, of the tribe of Aser: she was of a great age, and had lived with a husband seven years from her virginity; 37 And she was a widow of about fourscore and four years, which departed not from the temple, but served God with fastings and prayers night and day. 38 And she coming in that instant gave thanks likewise unto the Lord, and spake of him to all them that looked for redemption in Jerusalem. 39 And when they had performed all things according to the law of the Lord, they returned into Galilee, to their own city Nazareth.

40 And the child grew, and waxed strong in spirit, filled with wisdom; and the grace of God was upon him. 41 Now his parents went to Jerusalem every year at the feast of the passover. 42 And when he was twelve years old, they went up to Jerusalem after the custom of the feast. 43 And when they had fulfilled the days, as they returned, the child Jesus tarried behind in Jerusalem; and Joseph and his mother knew not of it. 44 But they, supposing him to have been in the company, went a day's journey; and they sought him among their kinfolk and acquaintance. 45 And when they found him not, they turned back again to Jerusalem, seeking him. 46 And it came to pass, that after three days they found him in the temple, sitting in the midst of the doctors, both hearing them, and asking them questions. 47 And all that heard him were astonished at his understanding and answers. 48 And when they saw him, they were amazed: and his mother said unto him, Son, why hast thou thus dealt with us? behold, thy father and I have sought thee sorrowing. 49 And he said unto them, How is it that ye sought me? wist ye not that I must be about my Father's business? 50 And they understood not the saying which he spake unto them. 51 And he went down with them, and came to Nazareth, and was subject unto them: but his mother kept all these sayings in her heart. 52 And Jesus increased in wisdom and stature, and in favor with God and man.

3 Now in the fifteenth year of the reign of Tiberius Caesar, Pontius Pilate being governor of Judea, and Herod being tetrarch of Galilee, and his brother Philip tetrarch of Iturea and of the region of Trachonitis, and Lysanias the tetrarch of Abilene, 2 Annas and Caiaphas

being the high priests, the word of God came unto John the son of Zacharias in the wilderness. 3 And he came into all the country about Jordan, preaching the baptism of repentance for the remission of sins; 4 As it is written in the book of the words of Esaias[1] the prophet, saying,

> The voice of one crying in the wilderness,
> Prepare ye the way of the Lord,
> Make his paths straight.
> 5 Every valley shall be filled,
> And every mountain and hill shall be brought low;
> And the crooked shall be made straight,
> And the rough ways shall be made smooth;
> 6 And all flesh shall see the salvation of God.

7 Then said he to the multitude that came forth to be baptized of him, O generation of vipers, who hath warned you to flee from the wrath to come? 8 Bring forth therefore fruits worthy of repentance, and begin not to say within yourselves, We have Abraham to our father: for I say unto you, That God is able of these stones to raise up children unto Abraham. 9 And now also the axe is laid unto the root of the trees: every tree therefore which bringeth not forth good fruit is hewn down, and cast into the fire.

10 And the people asked him, saying, What shall we do then? 11 He answereth and saith unto them, He that hath two coats, let him impart to him that hath none; and he that hath meat, let him do likewise. 12 Then came also publicans to be baptized, and said unto him, Master, what shall we do? 13 And he said unto them, Exact no more than that which is appointed you. 14 And the soldiers likewise demanded of him, saying, And what shall we do? And he said unto them, Do violence to no man, neither accuse any falsely; and be content with your wages. 15 And as the people were in expectation, and all men mused in their hearts of John, whether he were the Christ, or not; 16 John answered, saying unto them all, I indeed baptize you with water; but one mightier than I cometh, the latchet of whose shoes I am not worthy to unloose: he shall baptize you with the Holy Ghost and with fire: 17 Whose fan is in his hand, and he will thoroughly purge his floor, and will gather the wheat into his garner; but the chaff he will burn with fire unquenchable. 18 And many other things in his exhortation preached he unto the people. 19 But Herod the tetrarch, being reproved by him for Herodias his brother Philip's wife, and for all the evils which Herod had done, 20 Added yet this above all, that he shut up John in prison.

21 Now when all the people were baptized, it came to pass, that Jesus also being baptized, and praying, the heaven was opened, 22 And the Holy Ghost descended in a bodily shape like a dove upon him, and a voice came from heaven, which said,

[1] A variant form of the name of the Old Testament prophet Isaiah. It occurs also in Luke 4 and in John 1 and 12.

Thou art my beloved Son;
In thee I am well pleased.
23 And Jesus himself began to be about thirty years of age, being
(as was supposed) the son of Joseph, which was the son of Heli, 24
Which was the son of Matthat, which was the son of Levi, which was
the son of Melchi, which was the son of Janna, which was the son
of Joseph, 25 Which was the son of Mattathias, which was the son
of Amos, which was the son of Naum, which was the son of Esli,
which was the son of Nagge, 26 Which was the son of Maath, which
was the son of Mattathias, which was the son of Semei, which was the
son of Joseph, which was the son of Juda, 27 Which was the son of
Joanna, which was the son of Rhesa, which was the son of Zorobabel,
which was the son of Salathiel, which was the son of Neri, 28 Which
was the son of Melchi, which was the son of Addi, which was the son
of Cosam, which was the son of Elmodam, which was the son of Er,
29 Which was the son of Jose, which was the son of Eliezer, which
was the son of Jorim, which was the son of Matthat, which was the
son of Levi, 30 Which was the son of Simeon, which was the son
of Juda, which was the son of Joseph, which was the son of Jonan,
which was the son of Eliakim, 31 Which was the son of Melea,
which was the son of Menan, which was the son of Mattatha, which
was the son of Nathan, which was the son of David, 32 Which was the
son of Jesse, which was the son of Obed, which was the son of Booz,
which was the son of Salmon, which was the son of Naasson, 33
Which was the son of Aminadab, which was the son of Aram, which
was the son of Esrom, which was the son of Phares, which was the
son of Juda, 34 Which was the son of Jacob, which was the son of
Isaac, which was the son of Abraham, which was the son of Thara,
which was the son of Nachor, 35 Which was the son of Saruch,
which was the son of Ragau, which was the son of Phalec, which was
the son of Heber, which was the son of Sala, 36 Which was the son
of Cainan, which was the son of Arphaxad, which was the son of
Sem, which was the son of Noe, which was the son of Lamech, 37
Which was the son of Mathusala, which was the son of Enoch, which
was the son of Jared, which was the son of Maleleel, which was the
son of Cainan, 38 Which was the son of Enos, which was the son of
Seth, which was the son of Adam, which was the son of God.

4   And Jesus being full of the Holy Ghost returned from Jordan,
and was led by the Spirit into the wilderness, 2 Being forty days
tempted of the devil. And in those days he did eat nothing: and when
they were ended, he afterward hungered. 3 And the devil said unto
him, If thou be the Son of God, command this stone that it be made
bread. 4 And Jesus answered him, saying, It is written, That man
shall not live by bread alone, but by every word of God. 5 And the
devil, taking him up into a high mountain, showed unto him all the
kingdoms of the world in a moment of time. 6 And the devil said
unto him, All this power will I give thee, and the glory of them: for

that is delivered unto me; and to whomsoever I will, I give it. 7 If thou therefore wilt worship me, all shall be thine. 8 And Jesus answered and said unto him, Get thee behind me, Satan: for it is written, Thou shalt worship the Lord thy God, and him only shalt thou serve. 9 And he brought him to Jerusalem, and set him on a pinnacle of the temple, and said unto him, If thou be the Son of God, cast thyself down from hence: 10 For it is written,

He shall give his angels charge over thee,
To keep thee:
11 And in their hands they shall bear thee up,
Lest at any time thou dash thy foot against a stone.

12 And Jesus answering said unto him, It is said, Thou shalt not tempt the Lord thy God. 13 And when the devil had ended all the temptation, he departed from him for a season.

## THE MINISTRY LAUNCHED

14 And Jesus returned in the power of the Spirit into Galilee: and there went out a fame of him through all the region round about. 15 And he taught in their synagogues, being glorified of all. 16 And he came to Nazareth, where he had been brought up: and, as his custom was, he went into the synagogue on the sabbath day, and stood up for to read. 17 And there was delivered unto him the book of the prophet Esaias. And when he had opened the book, he found the place where it was written,

18 The Spirit of the Lord is upon me,
Because he hath anointed me
To preach the gospel to the poor;
He hath sent me to heal the broken-hearted,
To preach deliverance to the captives,
And recovering of sight to the blind,
To set at liberty them that are bruised,
19 To preach the acceptable year of the Lord.

20 And he closed the book, and he gave it again to the minister, and sat down. And the eyes of all them that were in the synagogue were fastened on him. 21 And he began to say unto them, This day is this Scripture fulfilled in your ears. 22 And all bare him witness, and wondered at the gracious words which proceeded out of his mouth. And they said, Is not this Joseph's son? 23 And he said unto them, Ye will surely say unto me this proverb, Physician, heal thyself: whatsoever we have heard done in Capernaum, do also here in thy country. 24 And he said, Verily I say unto you, No prophet is accepted in his own country. 25 But I tell you of a truth, many widows were in Israel in the days of Elias, when the heaven was shut up three years and six months, when great famine was throughout all the land; 26 But unto none of them was Elias sent, save unto Sarepta, a city of Sidon, unto a woman that was a widow. 27 And many lepers were in Israel in the time of Eliseus the prophet; and none of them was

cleansed, saving Naaman the Syrian. 28 And all they in the synagogue, when they heard these things, were filled with wrath, 29 And rose up, and thrust him out of the city, and led him unto the brow of the hill whereon their city was built, that they might cast him down headlong. 30 But he, passing through the midst of them, went his way,

31 And came down to Capernaum, a city of Galilee, and taught them on the Sabbath days. 32 And they were astonished at his doctrine: for his word was with power. 33 And in the synagogue there was a man, which had a spirit of an unclean devil, and cried out with a loud voice, 34 Saying, Let us alone; what have we to do with thee, thou Jesus of Nazareth? art thou come to destroy us? I know thee who thou art; the Holy One of God. 35 And Jesus rebuked him, saying, Hold thy peace, and come out of him. And when the devil had thrown him in the midst, he came out of him, and hurt him not. 36 And they were all amazed, and spake among themselves, saying, What a word is this! for with authority and power he commandeth the unclean spirits, and they come out. 37 And the fame of him went out into every place of the country round about.

38 And he arose out of the synagogue, and entered into Simon's house. And Simon's wife's mother was taken with a great fever; and they besought him for her. 39 And he stood over her, and rebuked the fever; and it left her: and immediately she arose and ministered unto them. 40 Now when the sun was setting, all they that had any sick with divers diseases brought them unto him; and he laid his hands on every one of them, and healed them. 41 And devils also came out of many, crying out, and saying, Thou art Christ the son of God. And he rebuking them suffered them not to speak: for they knew that he was Christ.

42 And when it was day, he departed and went into a desert place: and the people sought him, and came unto him, and stayed him, that he should not depart from them. 43 And he said unto them, I must preach the kingdom of God to other cities also: for therefore am I sent. 44 And he preached in the synagogues of Galilee.

5 And it came to pass, that, as the people pressed upon him to hear the word of God, he stood by the lake of Gennesaret, 2 And saw two ships standing by the lake: but the fishermen were gone out of them, and were washing their nets. 3 And he entered into one of the ships, which was Simon's, and prayed him that he would thrust out a little from the land. And he sat down, and taught the people out of the ship. 4 Now when he had left speaking, he said unto Simon, Launch out into the deep, and let down your nets for a draught. 5 And Simon answering said unto him, Master, we have toiled all the night, and have taken nothing: nevertheless at thy word I will let down the net. 6 And when they had this done, they inclosed a great multitude of fishes: and their net brake. 7 And they beckoned unto their partners, which were in the other ship, that they should come and help them. And they came, and filled both the ships, so that they began to sink. 8 When

Simon Peter saw it, he fell down at Jesus' knees, saying, Depart from me; for I am a sinful man, O Lord. 9 For he was astonished, and all that were with him, at the draught of the fishes which they had taken: 10 And so was also James, and John, the sons of Zebedee, which were partners with Simon. And Jesus said unto Simon, Fear not; from henceforth thou shalt catch men. 11 And when they had brought their ships to land, they forsook all, and followed him.

12 And it came to pass, when he was in a certain city, behold a man full of leprosy; who seeing Jesus fell on his face, and besought him, saying, Lord, if thou wilt, thou canst make me clean. 13 And he put forth his hand, and touched him, saying, I will: be thou clean. And immediately the leprosy departed from him. 14 And he charged him to tell no man: but go, and show thyself to the priest, and offer for thy cleansing, according as Moses commanded, for a testimony unto them. 15 But so much the more went there a fame abroad of him: and great multitudes came together to hear, and to be healed by him of their infirmities. 16 And he withdrew himself into the wilderness, and prayed.

17 And it came to pass on a certain day, as he was teaching, that there were Pharisees and doctors of the law sitting by, which were come out of every town of Galilee, and Judea, and Jerusalem: and the power of the Lord was present to heal them.

18 And, behold, men brought in a bed a man which was taken with a palsy: and they sought means to bring him in, and to lay him before him. 19 And when they could not find by what way they might bring him in because of the multitude, they went upon the housetop, and let him down through the tiling with his couch into the midst before Jesus. 20 And when he saw their faith, he said unto him, Man, thy sins are forgiven thee. 21 And the scribes and the Pharisees began to reason, saying, Who is this which speaketh blasphemies? Who can forgive sins, but God alone? 22 But when Jesus perceived their thoughts, he answering said unto them, What reason ye in your hearts? 23 Whether is easier, to say, Thy sins be forgiven thee; or to say, Rise up and walk? 24 But that ye may know that the Son of man hath power upon earth to forgive sins, (he said unto the sick of the palsy,) I say unto thee, Arise, and take up thy couch, and go into thine house. 25 And immediately he rose up before them, and took up that whereon he lay, and departed to his own house, glorifying God. 26 And they were all amazed, and they glorified God, and were filled with fear, saying, We have seen strange things to-day.

27 And after these things he went forth, and saw a publican, named Levi, sitting at the receipt of custom: and he said unto him, Follow me. 28 And he left all, rose up, and followed him. 29 And Levi made him a great feast in his own house: and there was a great company of publicans and of others that sat down with them. 30 But their scribes and Pharisees murmured against his disciples, saying, Why do ye eat and drink with publicans and sinners? 31 And Jesus answering said unto them, They that are whole need not a physician;

but they that are sick. 32 I came not to call the righteous, but sinners to repentance.

33 And they said unto him, Why do the disciples of John fast often, and make prayers, and likewise the disciples of the Pharisees; but thine eat and drink? 34 And he said unto them, Can ye make the children of the bridechamber fast, while the bridegroom is with them? 35 But the days will come, when the bridegroom shall be taken away from them, and then shall they fast in those days. 36 And he spake also a parable unto them; No man putteth a piece of a new garment upon an old; if otherwise, then both the new maketh a rent, and the piece that was taken out of the new agreeth not with the old. 37 And no man putteth new wine into old bottles; else the new wine will burst the bottles, and be spilled, and the bottles shall perish. 38 But new wine must be put into new bottles; and both are preserved. 39 No man also having drunk old wine straightway desireth new; for he saith, The old is better.

6 And it came to pass on the second sabbath after the first, that he went through the corn fields; and his disciples plucked the ears of corn, and did eat, rubbing them in their hands. 2 And certain of the Pharisees said unto them, Why do ye that which is not lawful to do on the sabbath days? 3 And Jesus answering them said, Have ye not read so much as this, what David did, when himself was ahungered, and they which were with him; 4 How he went into the house of God, and did take and eat the showbread, and gave also to them that were with him; which it is not lawful to eat but for the priests alone? 5 And he said unto them, That the Son of man is Lord also of the sabbath. 6 And it came to pass also on another sabbath, that he entered into the synagogue and taught: and there was a man whose right hand was withered. 7 And the scribes and Pharisees watched him, whether he would heal on the sabbath day; that they might find an accusation against him. 8 But he knew their thoughts, and said to the man which had the withered hand, Rise up, and stand forth in the midst. And he arose and stood forth. 9 Then said Jesus unto them, I will ask you one thing; Is it lawful on the sabbath days to do good, or to do evil? to save life, or to destroy it? 10 And looking round about upon them all, he said unto the man, Stretch forth thy hand. And he did so: and his hand was restored whole as the other. 11 And they were filled with madness; and communed one with another what they might do to Jesus.

12 And it came to pass in those days, that he went out into a mountain to pray, and continued all night in prayer to God. 13 And when it was day, he called unto him his disciples: and of them he chose twelve, whom also he named apostles; 14 Simon, (whom he also named Peter,) and Andrew his brother, James and John, Philip and Bartholomew, 15 Matthew and Thomas, James the son of Alpheus, and Simon called Zelotes, 16 And Judas the brother of James, and Judas Iscariot, which also was the traitor.

17 And he came down with them, and stood in the plain, and the company of his disciples, and a great multitude of people out of all Judea and Jerusalem, and from the seacoast of Tyre and Sidon, which came to hear him, and to be healed of their diseases; 18 And they that were vexed with unclean spirits: and they were healed. 19 And the whole multitude sought to touch him: for there went virtue out of him, and healed them all. 20 And he lifted up his eyes on his disciples, and said,

Blessed be ye poor: for yours is the kingdom of God.

21 Blessed are ye that hunger now: for ye shall be filled.

Blessed are ye that weep now: for ye shall laugh.

22 Blessed are ye, when men shall hate you, and when they shall separate you from their company, and shall reproach you, and cast out your name as evil, for the Son of man's sake. 23 Rejoice ye in that day, and leap for joy: for, behold, your reward is great in heaven: for in the like manner did their fathers unto the prophets.

24 But woe unto you that are rich! for ye have received your consolation.

25 Woe unto you that are full! for ye shall hunger.

Woe unto you that laugh now! for ye shall mourn and weep.

26 Woe unto you, when all men shall speak well of you! for so did their fathers to the false prophets.

27 But I say unto you which hear, Love your enemies, do good to them which hate you, 28 Bless them that curse you, and pray for them which despitefully use you. 29 And unto him that smiteth thee on the one cheek offer also the other; and him that taketh away thy cloak forbid not to take thy coat also. 30 Give to every man that asketh of thee; and of him that taketh away thy goods ask them not again. 31 And as ye would that men should do to you, do ye also to them likewise. 32 For if ye love them which love you, what thank have ye? for sinners also love those that love them. 33 And if ye do good to them which do good to you, what thank have ye? for sinners also do even the same. 34 And if ye lend to them of whom ye hope to receive, what thank have ye? for sinners also lend to sinners, to receive as much again. 35 But love ye your enemies, and do good, and lend, hoping for nothing again; and your reward shall be great, and ye shall be the children of the Highest: for he is kind unto the unthankful and to the evil. 36 Be ye therefore merciful, as your Father also is merciful.

37 Judge not, and ye shall not be judged: condemn not, and ye shall not be condemned: forgive, and ye shall be forgiven: 38 Give, and it shall be given unto you; good measure, pressed down, and shaken together, and running over, shall men give into your bosom. For with the same measure that ye mete withal it shall be measured to you again. 39 And he spake a parable unto them; Can the blind lead the blind? shall they not both fall into the ditch? 40 The disciple is not above his master: but every one that is perfect shall be as his master.

41 And why beholdest thou the mote that is in thy brother's eye, but perceivest not the beam that is in thine own eye? 42 Either how canst thou say to thy brother, Brother, let me pull out the mote that is in thine eye, when thou thyself beholdest not the beam that is in thine own eye? Thou hypocrite, cast out first the beam out of thine own eye, and then shalt thou see clearly to pull out the mote that is in thy brother's eye.

43 For a good tree bringeth not forth corrupt fruit; neither doth a corrupt tree bring forth good fruit. 44 For every tree is known by his own fruit. For of thorns men do not gather figs, nor of a bramble bush gather they grapes. 45 A good man out of the good treasure of his heart bringeth forth that which is good; and an evil man out of the evil treasure of his heart bringeth forth that which is evil: for of the abundance of the heart his mouth speaketh.

46 And why call ye me, Lord, Lord, and do not the things which I say? 47 Whosoever cometh to me, and heareth my sayings, and doeth them, I will show you to whom he is like: 48 He is like a man which built a house, and digged deep, and laid the foundation on a rock: and when the flood arose, the stream beat vehemently upon that house, and could not shake it; for it was founded upon a rock. 49 But he that heareth, and doeth not, is like a man that without a foundation built a house upon the earth; against which the stream did beat vehemently, and immediately it fell; and the ruin of that house was great.

7 Now when he had ended all his sayings in the audience of the people, he entered into Capernaum. 2 And a certain centurion's servant, who was dear unto him, was sick, and ready to die. 3 And when he heard of Jesus, he sent unto him the elders of the Jews, beseeching him that he would come and heal his servant. 4 And when they came to Jesus, they besought him instantly, saying, That he was worthy for whom he should do this: 5 For he loveth our nation, and he hath built us a synagogue. 6 Then Jesus went with them. And when he was now not far from the house, the centurion sent friends to him, saying unto him, Lord, trouble not thyself; for I am not worthy that thou shouldest enter under my roof: 7 Wherefore neither thought I myself worthy to come unto thee: but say in a word, and my servant shall be healed. 8 For I also am a man set under authority, having under me soldiers, and I say unto one, Go, and he goeth; and to another, Come, and he cometh; and to my servant, Do this, and he doeth it. 9 When Jesus heard these things, he marveled at him, and turned him about, and said unto the people that followed him, I say unto you, I have not found so great faith, no, not in Israel. 10 And they that were sent, returning to the house, found the servant whole that had been sick.

11 And it came to pass the day after, that he went into a city called Nain; and many of his disciples went with him, and much people. 12

Now when he came nigh to the gate of the city, behold, there was a dead man carried out, the only son of his mother, and she was a widow: and much people of the city was with her. 13 And when the Lord saw her, he had compassion on her, and said unto her, Weep not. 14 And he came and touched the bier: and they that bare him stood still. And he said, Young man, I say unto thee, Arise. 15 And he that was dead sat up, and began to speak. And he delivered him to his mother. 16 And there came a fear on all: and they glorified God, saying, That a great prophet is risen up among us; and, That God hath visited his people. 17 And this rumor of him went forth throughout all Judea, and throughout all the region round about.

18 And the disciples of John showed him of all these things. 19 And John calling unto him two of his disciples sent them to Jesus, saying, Art thou he that should come? or look we for another? 20 When the men were come unto him, they said, John Baptist hath sent us unto thee, saying, Art thou he that should come? or look we for another? 21 And in that same hour he cured many of their infirmities and plagues, and of evil spirits; and unto many that were blind he gave sight. 22 Then Jesus answering said unto them, Go your way, and tell John what things ye have seen and heard; how that the blind see, the lame walk, the lepers are cleansed, the deaf hear, the dead are raised, to the poor the gospel is preached. 23 And blessed is he, whosoever shall not be offended in me.

24 And when the messengers of John were departed, he began to speak unto the people concerning John, What went ye out into the wilderness for to see? A reed shaken with the wind? 25 But what went ye out for to see? A man clothed in soft raiment? Behold, they which are gorgeously appareled, and live delicately, are in kings' courts. 26 But what went ye out for to see? A prophet? Yea, I say unto you, and much more than a prophet. 27 This is he, of whom it is written,

Behold, I send my messenger before thy face,
Which shall prepare the way before thee.

28 For I say unto you, Among those that are born of women there is not a greater prophet than John the Baptist: but he that is least in the kingdom of God is greater than he. 29 And all the people that heard him, and the publicans, justified God, being baptized with the baptism of John. 30 But the Pharisees and lawyers rejected the counsel of God against themselves, being not baptized of him. 31 And the Lord said, Whereunto then shall I liken the men of this generation? and to what are they like? 32 They are like unto children sitting in the market place, and calling one to another, and saying,

We have piped unto you, and ye have not danced;
We have mourned to you, and ye have not wept.

33 For John the Baptist came neither eating bread nor drinking wine; and ye say, He hath a devil. 34 The Son of man is come eating and drinking; and ye say, Behold a gluttonous man, and a winebibber, a friend of publicans and sinners! 35 But wisdom is justified of all her children.

36 And one of the Pharisees desired him that he would eat with him. And he went into the Pharisee's house, and sat down to meat. 37 And, behold, a woman in the city, which was a sinner, when she knew that Jesus sat at meat in the Pharisee's house, brought an alabaster box of ointment, 38 And stood at his feet behind him weeping, and began to wash his feet with tears, and did wipe them with the hairs of her head, and kissed his feet, and anointed them with the ointment. 39 Now when the Pharisee which had bidden him saw it, he spake within himself, saying, This man, if he were a prophet, would have known who and what manner of woman this is that toucheth him; for she is a sinner. 40 And Jesus answering said unto him, Simon, I have somewhat to say unto thee. And he saith, Master, say on. 41 There was a certain creditor which had two debtors: the one owed five hundred pence, and the other fifty. 42 And when they had nothing to pay, he frankly forgave them both. Tell me therefore, which of them will love him most? 43 Simon answered and said, I suppose that he, to whom he forgave most. And he said unto him, Thou hast rightly judged. 44 And he turned to the woman, and said unto Simon, Seest thou this woman? I entered into thine house, thou gavest me no water for my feet: but she hath washed my feet with tears, and wiped them with the hairs of her head. 45 Thou gavest me no kiss: but this woman, since the time I came in, hath not ceased to kiss my feet. 46 My head with oil thou didst not anoint: but this woman hath anointed my feet with ointment. 47 Wherefore I say unto thee, Her sins, which are many, are forgiven; for she loved much: but to whom little is forgiven, the same loveth little. 48 And he said unto her, Thy sins are forgiven. 49 And they that sat at meat with him began to say within themselves, Who is this that forgiveth sins also? 50 And he said to the woman, Thy faith hath saved thee; go in peace.

8    And it came to pass afterward, that he went through every city and village, preaching and showing the glad tidings of the kingdom of God: and the twelve were with him, 2 And certain women, which had been healed of evil spirits and infirmities, Mary called Magdalene, out of whom went seven devils, 3 And Joanna the wife of Chuza Herod's steward, and Susanna, and many others, which ministered unto him of their substance.

4 And when much people were gathered together, and were come to him out of every city, he spake by a parable: 5 A sower went out to sow his seed: and as he sowed, some fell by the wayside; and it was trodden down, and the fowls of the air devoured it. 6 And some fell upon a rock; and as soon as it was sprung up, it withered away, because it lacked moisture. 7 And some fell among thorns; and the thorns sprang up with it, and choked it. 8 And other fell on good ground, and sprang up, and bare fruit a hundredfold. And when he had said these things, he cried, He that hath ears to hear, let him hear.

9 And his disciples asked him, saying, What might this parable be?

10 And he said, Unto you it is given to know the mysteries of the kingdom of God: but to others in parables;

That seeing they might not see,
And hearing they might not understand.

11 Now the parable is this: The seed is the word of God. 12 Those by the wayside are they that hear; then cometh the devil, and taketh away the word out of their hearts, lest they should believe and be saved. 13 They on the rock are they, which, when they hear, receive the word with joy; and these have no root, which for a while believe, and in time of temptation fall away. 14 And that which fell among thorns are they, which, when they have heard, go forth, and are choked with cares and riches and pleasures of this life, and bring no fruit to perfection. 15 But that on the good ground are they, which in an honest and good heart, having heard the word, keep it, and bring forth fruit with patience.

16 No man, when he hath lighted a candle, covereth it with a vessel, or putteth it under a bed; but setteth it on a candlestick, that they which enter in may see the light. 17 For nothing is secret, that shall not be made manifest; neither any thing hid, that shall not be known and come abroad. 18 Take heed therefore how ye hear: for whosoever hath, to him shall be given; and whosoever hath not, from him shall be taken even that which he seemeth to have.

19 Then came to him his mother and his brethren, and could not come at him for the press. 20 And it was told him by certain which said, Thy mother and thy brethren stand without, desiring to see thee. 21 And he answered and said unto them, My mother and my brethren are these which hear the word of God, and do it.

22 Now it came to pass on a certain day, that he went into a ship with his disciples: and he said unto them, Let us go over unto the other side of the lake. And they launched forth. 23 But as they sailed, he fell asleep: and there came down a storm of wind on the lake; and they were filled with water, and were in jeopardy. 24 And they came to him, and awoke him, saying, Master, Master, we perish. Then he arose, and rebuked the wind and the raging of the water: and they ceased, and there was a calm. 25 And he said unto them, Where is your faith? And they being afraid wondered, saying one to another, What manner of man is this! for he commandeth even the winds and water, and they obey him.

26 And they arrived at the country of the Gadarenes, which is over against Galilee. 27 And when he went forth to land, there met him out of the city a certain man, which had devils long time, and ware no clothes, neither abode in any house, but in the tombs. 28 When he saw Jesus, he cried out, and fell down before him, and with a loud voice said, What have I to do with thee, Jesus, thou Son of God most high? I beseech thee, torment me not. 29 (For he had commanded the unclean spirit to come out of the man. For oftentimes it had caught him: and he was kept bound with chains and in fetters; and

he brake the bands, and was driven of the devil into the wilderness.) 30 And Jesus asked him, saying, What is thy name? And he said, Legion: because many devils were entered into him. 31 And they besought him that he would not command them to go out into the deep. 32 And there was there a herd of many swine feeding on the mountain: and they besought him that he would suffer them to enter into them. And he suffered them. 33 Then went the devils out of the man, and entered into the swine: and the herd ran violently down a steep place into the lake, and were choked. 34 When they that fed them saw what was done, they fled, and went and told it in the city and in the country. 35 Then they went out to see what was done; and came to Jesus, and found the man, out of whom the devils were departed, sitting at the feet of Jesus, clothed, and in his right mind: and they were afraid. 36 They also which saw it told them by what means he that was possessed of the devils was healed. 37 Then the whole multitude of the country of the Gadarenes round about besought him to depart from them; for they were taken with great fear: and he went up into the ship, and returned back again. 38 Now the man, out of whom the devils were departed, besought him that he might be with him: but Jesus sent him away, saying, 39 Return to thine own house, and show how great things God hath done unto thee. And he went his way, and published throughout the whole city how great things Jesus had done unto him.

40 And it came to pass, that, when Jesus was returned, the people gladly received him: for they were all waiting for him. 41 And, behold, there came a man named Jairus, and he was a ruler of the synagogue; and he fell down at Jesus' feet, and besought him that he would come into his house: 42 For he had one only daughter, about twelve years of age, and she lay a dying. But as he went the people thronged him. 43 And a woman having an issue of blood twelve years, which had spent all her living upon physicians, neither could be healed of any, 44 Came behind him, and touched the border of his garment: and immediately her issue of blood stanched. 45 And Jesus said, Who touched me? When all denied, Peter and they that were with him said, Master, the multitude throng thee and press thee, and sayest thou, Who touched me? 46 And Jesus said, Somebody hath touched me: for I perceive that virtue is gone out of me. 47 And when the woman saw that she was not hid, she came trembling, and falling down before him, she declared unto him before all the people for what cause she had touched him, and how she was healed immediately. 48 And he said unto her, Daughter, be of good comfort: thy faith hath made thee whole; go in peace.

49 While he yet spake, there cometh one from the ruler of the synagogue's house, saying to him, Thy daughter is dead; trouble not the Master. 50 But when Jesus heard it, he answered him, saying, Fear not: believe only, and she shall be made whole. 51 And when he came into the house, he suffered no man to go in, save Peter, and James, and John, and the father and the mother of the maiden. 52

And all wept, and bewailed her: but he said, Weep not; she is not dead, but sleepeth. 53 And they laughed him to scorn, knowing that she was dead. 54 And he put them all out, and took her by the hand, and called, saying, Maid, arise. 55 And her spirit came again, and she arose straightway: and he commanded to give her meat. 56 And her parents were astonished: but he charged them that they should tell no man what was done.

9   Then he called his twelve disciples together, and gave them power and authority over all devils, and to cure diseases. 2 And he sent them to preach the kingdom of God, and to heal the sick. 3 And he said unto them, Take nothing for your journey, neither staves, nor scrip, neither bread, neither money; neither have two coats apiece. 4 And whatsoever house ye enter into, there abide, and thence depart. 5 And whosoever will not receive you, when ye go out of that city, shake off the very dust from your feet for a testimony against them. 6 And they departed, and went through the towns, preaching the gospel, and healing every where.

7 Now Herod the tetrarch heard of all that was done by him: and he was perplexed, because that it was said of some, that John was risen from the dead; 8 And of some, that Elias had appeared; and of others, that one of the old prophets was risen again. 9 And Herod said, John have I beheaded; but who is this, of whom I hear such things? And he desired to see him.

10 And the apostles, when they were returned, told him all that they had done. And he took them, and went aside privately into a desert place belonging to the city called Bethsaida. 11 And the people, when they knew it, followed him: and he received them, and spake unto them of the kingdom of God, and healed them that had need of healing. 12 And when the day began to wear away, then came the twelve, and said unto him, Send the multitude away, that they may go into the towns and country round about, and lodge, and get victuals: for we are here in a desert place. 13 But he said unto them, Give ye them to eat. And they said, We have no more but five loaves and two fishes; except we should go and buy meat for all this people. 14 For they were about five thousand men. And he said to his disciples, Make them sit down by fifties in a company. 15 And they did so, and made them all sit down. 16 Then he took the five loaves and the two fishes, and looking up to heaven, he blessed them, and brake, and gave to the disciples to set before the multitude. 17 And they did eat, and were all filled: and there was taken up of fragments that remained to them twelve baskets.

18 And it came to pass, as he was alone praying, his disciples were with him; and he asked them, saying, Whom say the people that I am? 19 They answering said, John the Baptist; but some say, Elias; and others say, that one of the old prophets is risen again. 20 He said unto them, But whom say ye that I am? Peter answering said, The Christ of God. 21 And he straitly charged them, and commanded

them to tell no man that thing; 22 Saying, The Son of man must suffer many things, and be rejected of the elders and chief priests and scribes, and be slain, and be raised the third day.

23 And he said to them all, If any man will come after me, let him deny himself, and take up his cross daily, and follow me. 24 For whosoever will save his life shall lose it: but whosoever will lose his life for my sake, the same shall save it. 25 For what is a man advantaged, if he gain the whole world, and lose himself, or be cast away? 26 For whosoever shall be ashamed of me and of my words, of him shall the Son of man be ashamed, when he shall come in his own glory, and in his Father's, and of the holy angels. 27 But I tell you of a truth, there be some standing here, which shall not taste of death, till they see the kingdom of God.

28 And it came to pass about an eight days after these sayings, he took Peter and John and James, and went up into a mountain to pray. 29 And as he prayed, the fashion of his countenance was altered, and his raiment was white and glistering. 30 And, behold, there talked with him two men, which were Moses and Elias: 31 Who appeared in glory, and spake of his decease which he should accomplish at Jerusalem. 32 But Peter and they that were with him were heavy with sleep: and when they were awake, they saw his glory, and the two men that stood with him. 33 And it came to pass, as they departed from him, Peter said unto Jesus, Master, it is good for us to be here: and let us make three tabernacles; one for thee, and one for Moses, and one for Elias: not knowing what he said. 34 While he thus spake, there came a cloud, and overshadowed them: and they feared as they entered into the cloud. 35 And there came a voice out of the cloud, saying, This is my beloved Son: hear him. 36 And when the voice was past, Jesus was found alone. And they kept it close, and told no man in those days any of those things which they had seen.

37 And it came to pass, that on the next day, when they were come down from the hill, much people met him. 38 And, behold, a man of the company cried out, saying, Master, I beseech thee, look upon my son; for he is mine only child. 39 And, lo, a spirit taketh him, and he suddenly crieth out; and it teareth him that he foameth again, and bruising him, hardly departeth from him. 40 And I besought thy disciples to cast him out; and they could not. 41 And Jesus answering said, O faithless and perverse generation, how long shall I be with you, and suffer you? Bring thy son hither. 42 And as he was yet a coming, the devil threw him down, and tare him. And Jesus rebuked the unclean spirit, and healed the child, and delivered him again to his father. 43 And they were all amazed at the mighty power of God.

But while they wondered every one at all things which Jesus did, he said unto his disciples, 44 Let these sayings sink down into your ears: for the Son of man shall be delivered into the hands of men. 45 But they understood not this saying, and it was hid from them, that they perceived it not: and they feared to ask him of that saying. 46 Then there arose a reasoning among them, which of them should be greatest. 47 And Jesus, perceiving the thought of their heart, took a child, and set him by him, 48 And said unto them, Whosoever shall receive this child in my name receiveth me; and whosoever shall receive me, receiveth him that sent me: for he that is least among you all, the same shall be great. 49 And John answered and said, Master, we saw one casting out devils in thy name; and we forbade him, because he followeth not with us. 50 And Jesus said unto him, Forbid him not: for he that is not against us is for us.

### FACING TOWARD JERUSALEM

51 And it came to pass, when the time was come that he should be received up, he steadfastly set his face to go to Jerusalem, 52 And sent messengers before his face: and they went, and entered into a village of the Samaritans, to make ready for him. 53 And they did not receive him, because his face was as though he would go to Jerusalem. 54 And when his disciples James and John saw this, they said, Lord, wilt thou that we command fire to come down from heaven, and consume them, even as Elias did? 55 But he turned, and rebuked them, and said, Ye know not what manner of spirit ye are of. 56 For the Son of man is not come to destroy men's lives, but to save them. And they went to another village.

57 And it came to pass, that, as they went in the way, a certain man said unto him, Lord, I will follow thee whithersoever thou goest. 58 And Jesus said unto him, Foxes have holes, and birds of the air have nests; but the Son of man hath not where to lay his head. 59 And he said unto another, Follow me. But he said, Lord, suffer me first to go and bury my father. 60 Jesus said unto him, Let the dead bury their dead: but go thou and preach the kingdom of God. 61 And another also said, Lord, I will follow thee; but let me first go bid them farewell, which are at home at my house. 62 And Jesus said unto him, No man, having put his hand to the plow, and looking back, is fit for the kingdom of God.

10 After these things the Lord appointed other seventy also, and sent them two and two before his face into every city and place, whither he himself would come. 2 Therefore said he unto them, The harvest truly is great, but the laborers are few: pray ye therefore the Lord of the harvest, that he would send forth laborers into his harvest. 3 Go your ways: behold, I send you forth as lambs among wolves. 4 Carry neither purse, nor scrip, nor shoes: and salute no man by the way. 5 And into whatsoever house ye enter, first say, Peace be to this house. 6 And if the son of peace be there, your peace shall rest upon it: if not, it shall turn to you again. 7 And in the same house remain, eating and drinking such things as they give: for the laborer is worthy of his hire. Go not from house to house. 8 And into whatsoever city ye enter, and they receive you, eat such things as are set before you: 9 And heal the sick that are therein, and say unto them,

The kingdom of God is come nigh unto you. 10 But into whatsoever city ye enter, and they receive you not, go your ways out into the streets of the same, and say, 11 Even the very dust of your city, which cleaveth on us, we do wipe off against you: notwithstanding, be ye sure of this, that the kingdom of God is come nigh unto you. 12 But I say unto you, that it shall be more tolerable in that day for Sodom, than for that city. 13 Woe unto thee, Chorazin! woe unto thee, Bethsaida! for if the mighty works had been done in Tyre and Sidon, which have been done in you, they had a great while ago repented, sitting in sackcloth and ashes. 14 But it shall be more tolerable for Tyre and Sidon at the judgment, than for you. 15 And thou, Capernaum, which art exalted to heaven, shalt be thrust down to hell. 16 He that heareth you heareth me; and he that despiseth you despiseth me; and he that despiseth me despiseth him that sent me. 17 And the seventy returned again with joy, saying, Lord, even the devils are subject unto us through thy name. 18 And he said unto them, I beheld Satan as lightning fall from heaven. 19 Behold, I give unto you power to tread on serpents and scorpions, and over all the power of the enemy; and nothing shall by any means hurt you. 20 Notwithstanding, in this rejoice not, that the spirits are subject unto you; but rather rejoice, because your names are written in heaven.

21 In that hour Jesus rejoiced in spirit, and said, I thank thee, O Father, Lord of heaven and earth, that thou hast hid these things from the wise and prudent, and hast revealed them unto babes: even so, Father; for so it seemed good in thy sight. 22 All things are delivered to me of my Father: and no man knoweth who the Son is, but the Father; and who the Father is, but the Son, and he to whom the Son will reveal him. 23 And he turned him unto his disciples, and said privately, Blessed are the eyes which see the things that ye see: 24 For I tell you, that many prophets and kings have desired to see those things which ye see, and have not seen them; and to hear those things which ye hear, and have not heard them.

25 And, behold, a certain lawyer stood up, and tempted him, saying, Master, what shall I do to inherit eternal life? 26 He said unto him, What is written in the law? how readest thou? 27 And he answering said, Thou shalt love the Lord thy God with all thy heart, and with all thy soul, and with all thy strength, and with all thy mind; and thy neighbor as thyself. 28 And he said unto him, Thou hast answered right: this do, and thou shalt live. 29 But he, willing to justify himself, said unto Jesus, And who is my neighbor? 30 and Jesus answering said, A certain man went down from Jerusalem to Jericho, and fell among thieves, which stripped him of his raiment, and wounded him, and departed, leaving him half dead. 31 And by chance there came down a certain priest that way; and when he saw him, he passed by on the other side. 32 And likewise a Levite, when he was at the place, came and looked on him, and passed by on the other side. 33 But a certain Samaritan, as he journeyed, came where he was; and when he saw him, he had compassion on him, 34 And went to him, and bound

up his wounds, pouring in oil and wine, and set him on his own beast, and brought him to an inn, and took care of him. 35 And on the morrow when he departed, he took out two pence, and gave them to the host, and said unto him, Take care of him: and whatsoever thou spendest more, when I come again, I will repay thee. 36 Which now of these three, thinkest thou, was neighbor unto him that fell among the thieves? 37 And he said, He that showed mercy on him. Then said Jesus unto him, Go, and do thou likewise.

38 Now it came to pass, as they went, that he entered into a certain village: and a certain woman named Martha received him into her house. 39 And she had a sister called Mary, which also sat at Jesus' feet, and heard his word. 40 But Martha was cumbered about much serving, and came to him, and said, Lord, dost thou not care that my sister hath left me to serve alone? bid her therefore that she help me. 41 And Jesus answered and said unto her, Martha, Martha, thou art careful and troubled about many things: 42 But one thing is needful; and Mary hath chosen that good part, which shall not be taken away from her.

11 And it came to pass, that, as he was praying in a certain place, when he ceased, one of his disciples said unto him, Lord, teach us to pray, as John also taught his disciples. 2 And he said unto them, When ye pray, say,

Our Father which art in heaven,
Hallowed be thy name.
Thy kingdom come.
Thy will be done,
As in heaven, so in earth.
3 Give us day by day our daily bread.
4 And forgive us our sins;
For we also forgive every one that is indebted to us.
And lead us not into temptation;
But deliver us from evil.

5 And he said unto them, Which of you shall have a friend, and shall go unto him at midnight, and say unto him, Friend, lend me three loaves; 6 For a friend of mine in his journey is come to me, and I have nothing to set before him? 7 And he from within shall answer and say, Trouble me not: the door is now shut, and my children are with me in bed; I cannot rise and give thee. 8 I say unto you, Though he will not rise and give him, because he is his friend, yet because of his importunity he will rise and give him as many as he needeth.

9 And I say unto you, Ask, and it shall be given you; seek, and ye shall find; knock, and it shall be opened unto you. 10 For every one that asketh receiveth; and he that seeketh findeth; and to him that knocketh it shall be opened. 11 If a son shall ask bread of any of you that is a father, will he give him a stone? or if he ask a fish, will he for a fish give him a serpent? 12 Or if he shall ask an egg, will he offer him a scorpion? 13 If ye then, being evil, know how to give good

gifts unto your children; how much more shall your heavenly Father give the Holy Spirit to them that ask him?

14 And he was casting out a devil, and it was dumb. And it came to pass, when the devil was gone out, the dumb spake; and the people wondered. 15 But some of them said, He casteth out devils through Beelzebub the chief of the devils. 16 And others, tempting him, sought of him a sign from heaven. 17 But he, knowing their thoughts, said unto them, Every kingdom divided against itself is brought to desolation; and a house divided against a house falleth. 18 If Satan also be divided against himself, how shall his kingdom stand? because ye say that I cast out devils through Beelzebub. 19 And if I by Beelzebub cast out devils, by whom do your sons cast them out? therefore shall they be your judges. 20 But if I with the finger of God cast out devils, no doubt the kingdom of God is come upon you. 21 When a strong man armed keepeth his palace, his goods are in peace: 22 But when a stronger than he shall come upon him, and overcome him, he taketh from him all his armor wherein he trusted, and divideth his spoils. 23 He that is not with me is against me; and he that gathereth not with me scattereth. 24 When the unclean spirit is gone out of a man, he walketh through dry places, seeking rest; and finding none, he saith, I will return unto my house whence I came out. 25 And when he cometh, he findeth it swept and garnished. 26 Then goeth he, and taketh to him seven other spirits more wicked than himself; and they enter in, and dwell there: and the last state of that man is worse than the first.

27 And it came to pass, as he spake these things, a certain woman of the company lifted up her voice, and said unto him, Blessed is the womb that bare thee, and the paps which thou hast sucked. 28 But he said, Yea, rather, blessed are they that hear the word of God, and keep it.

29 And when the people were gathered thick together, he began to say, This is an evil generation: they seek a sign; and there shall no sign be given it, but the sign of Jonas the prophet. 30 For as Jonas was a sign unto the Ninevites, so shall also the Son of man be to this generation. 31 The queen of the south shall rise up in the judgment with the men of this generation, and condemn them: for she came from the utmost parts of the earth to hear the wisdom of Solomon; and, behold, a greater than Solomon is here. 32 The men of Nineveh shall rise up in the judgment with this generation, and shall condemn it: for they repented at the preaching of Jonas; and, behold, a greater than Jonas is here. 33 No man, when he hath lighted a candle, putteth it in a secret place, neither under a bushel, but on a candlestick, that they which come in may see the light. 34 The light of the body is the eye: therefore when thine eye is single, thy whole body also is full of light; but when thine eye is evil, thy body also is full of darkness. 35 Take heed therefore, that the light which is in thee be not darkness. 36 If thy whole body therefore be full of light, having no part dark,

the whole shall be full of light, as when the bright shining of a candle doth give thee light.
37 And as he spake, a certain Pharisee besought him to dine with him: and he went in, and sat down to meat. 38 And when the Pharisee saw it, he marveled that he had not first washed before dinner. 39 And the Lord said unto him, Now do ye Pharisees make clean the outside of the cup and the platter; but your inward part is full of ravening and wickedness. 40 Ye fools, did not he, that made that which is without, make that which is within also? 41 But rather give alms of such things as ye have; and, behold, all things are clean unto you. 42 But woe unto you, Pharisees! for ye tithe mint and rue and all manner of herbs, and pass over judgment and the love of God: these ought ye to have done, and not to leave the other undone. 43 Woe unto you, Pharisees! for ye love the uppermost seats in the synagogues, and greetings in the markets. 44 Woe unto you, scribes and Pharisees, hypocrites! for ye are as graves which appear not, and the men that walk over them are not aware of them.
45 Then answered one of the lawyers, and said unto him, Master, thus saying thou reproachest us also. 46 And he said, Woe unto you also, ye lawyers! for ye lade men with burdens grievous to be borne, and ye yourselves touch not the burdens with one of your fingers. 47 Woe unto you! for ye build the sepulchres of the prophets, and your fathers killed them. 48 Truly ye bear witness that ye allow the deeds of your fathers: for they indeed killed them, and ye build their sepulchres. 49 Therefore also said the wisdom of God, I will send them prophets and apostles, and some of them they shall slay and persecute: 50 That the blood of all the prophets, which was shed from the foundation of the world, may be required of this generation; 51 From the blood of Abel unto the blood of Zacharias, which perished between the altar and the temple: verily I say unto you, It shall be required of this generation. 52 Woe unto you, lawyers! for ye have taken away the key of knowledge: ye entered not in yourselves, and them that were entering in ye hindered. 53 And as he said these things unto them, the scribes and the Pharisees began to urge him vehemently, and to provoke him to speak of many things: 54 Laying wait for him, and seeking to catch something out of his mouth, that they might accuse him.

12    In the mean time, when there were gathered together an innumerable multitude of people, insomuch that they trode one upon another, he began to say unto his disciples first of all, Beware ye of the leaven of the Pharisees, which is hypocrisy. 2 For there is nothing covered, that shall not be revealed; neither hid, that shall not be known. 3 Therefore, whatsoever ye have spoken in darkness shall be heard in the light; and that which ye have spoken in the ear in closets shall be proclaimed upon the housetops. 4 And I say unto you my friends, Be not afraid of them that kill the body, and after that have no

more that they can do. 5 But I will forewarn you whom ye shall fear:
Fear him, which after he hath killed hath power to cast into hell;
yea, I say unto you, Fear him. 6 Are not five sparrows sold for two
farthings, and not one of them is forgotten before God? 7 But even the
very hairs of your head are all numbered. Fear not therefore: ye are
of more value than many sparrows. 8 Also I say unto you, Whosoever
shall confess me before men, him shall the Son of man also confess before the angels of God: 9 But he that denieth me before men shall be
denied before the angels of God. 10 And whosoever shall speak a
word against the Son of man, it shall be forgiven him: but unto him
that blasphemeth against the Holy Ghost it shall not be forgiven.
11 And when they bring you unto the synagogues, and unto magistrates, and powers, take ye no thought how or what thing ye shall
answer, or what ye shall say: 12 For the Holy Ghost shall teach you
in the same hour what ye ought to say.

13 And one of the company said unto him, Master, speak to my
brother, that he divide the inheritance with me. 14 And he said unto
him, Man, who made me a judge or a divider over you? 15 And he
said unto them, Take heed, and beware of covetousness: for a man's
life consisteth not in the abundance of the things which he possesseth.
16 And he spake a parable unto them, saying, The ground of a certain rich man brought forth plentifully: 17 And he thought within
himself, saying, What shall I do, because I have no room where to
bestow my fruits? 18 And he said, This will I do: I will pull down
my barns, and build greater; and there will I bestow all my fruits and
my goods. 19 And I will say to my soul, Soul, thou hast much goods
laid up for many years; take thine ease, eat, drink, and be merry. 20
But God said unto him, Thou fool, this night thy soul shall be required of thee: then whose shall those things be, which thou hast provided? 21 So is he that layeth up treasure for himself, and is not rich
toward God.

22 And he said unto his disciples, Therefore I say unto you, Take no
thought for your life, what ye shall eat; neither for the body, what ye
shall put on. 23 The life is more than meat, and the body is more
than raiment. 24 Consider the ravens: for they neither sow nor reap;
which neither have storehouse nor barn; and God feedeth them: how
much more are ye better than the fowls? 25 And which of you with
taking thought can add to his stature one cubit? 26 If ye then be
not able to do that thing which is least, why take ye thought for the
rest? 27 Consider the lilies how they grow: they toil not, they spin not;
and yet I say unto you, that Solomon in all his glory was not arrayed
like one of these. 28 If then God so clothe the grass, which is to-day
in the field, and to-morrow is cast into the oven; how much more will
he clothe you, O ye of little faith? 29 And seek not ye what ye shall
eat, or what ye shall drink, neither be ye of doubtful mind. 30 For
all these things do the nations of the world seek after: and your Father
knoweth that ye have need of these things.

31 But rather seek ye the kingdom of God; and all these things shall be added unto you. 32 Fear not, little flock; for it is your Father's good pleasure to give you the kingdom. 33 Sell that ye have, and give alms; provide yourselves bags which wax not old, a treasure in the heavens that faileth not, where no thief approacheth, neither moth corrupteth. 34 For where your treasure is, there will your heart be also.

35 Let your loins be girded about, and your lights burning; 36 And ye yourselves like unto men that wait for their lord, when he will return from the wedding; that, when he cometh and knocketh, they may open unto him immediately. 37 Blessed are those servants, whom the lord when he cometh shall find watching: verily I say unto you, that he shall gird himself, and make them to sit down to meat, and will come forth and serve them. 38 And if he shall come in the second watch, or come in the third watch, and find them so, blessed are those servants. 39 And this know, that if the goodman of the house had known what hour the thief would come, he would have watched, and not have suffered his house to be broken through. 40 Be ye therefore ready also: for the Son of man cometh at an hour when ye think not.

41 Then Peter said unto him, Lord, speakest thou this parable unto us, or even to all? 42 And the Lord said, Who then is that faithful and wise steward, whom his lord shall make ruler over his household, to give them their portion of meat in due season? 43 Blessed is that servant, whom his lord when he cometh shall find so doing. 44 Of a truth I say unto you, that he will make him ruler over all that he hath. 45 But and if that servant say in his heart, My lord delayeth his coming; and shall begin to beat the menservants and maidens, and to eat and drink, and to be drunken; 46 The lord of that servant will come in a day when he looketh not for him, and at an hour when he is not aware, and will cut him in sunder, and will appoint him his portion with the unbelievers. 47 And that servant, which knew his lord's will, and prepared not himself, neither did according to his will, shall be beaten with many stripes. 48 But he that knew not, and did commit things worthy of stripes, shall be beaten with few stripes. For unto whomsoever much is given, of him shall be much required; and to whom men have committed much, of him they will ask the more.

49 I am come to send fire on the earth; and what will I, if it be already kindled? 50 But I have a baptism to be baptized with; and how am I straitened till it be accomplished! 51 Suppose ye that I am come to give peace on earth? I tell you, Nay; but rather division: 52 For from henceforth there shall be five in one house divided, three against two, and two against three. 53 The father shall be divided against the son, and the son against the father; the mother against the daughter, and the daughter against the mother; the mother-in-law against her daughter-in-law, and the daughter-in-law against her mother-in-law.

54 And he said also to the people, When ye see a cloud rise out of the west, straightway ye say, There cometh a shower; and so it is. 55 And when ye see the south wind blow, ye say, There will be heat; and it cometh to pass. 56 Ye hypocrites, ye can discern the face of the sky and of the earth; but how is it that ye do not discern this time? 57 Yea, and why even of yourselves judge ye not what is right? 58 When thou goest with thine adversary to the magistrate, as thou art in the way, give diligence that thou mayest be delivered from him; lest he hale thee to the judge, and the judge deliver thee to the officer, and the officer cast thee into prison. 59 I tell thee, thou shalt not depart thence, till thou hast paid the very last mite.

13 There were present at that season some that told him of the Galileans, whose blood Pilate had mingled with their sacrifices. 2 And Jesus answering said unto them, Suppose ye that these Galileans were sinners above all the Galileans, because they suffered such things? 3 I tell you, Nay: but, except ye repent, ye shall all likewise perish. 4 Or those eighteen, upon whom the tower in Siloam fell, and slew them, think ye that they were sinners above all men that dwelt in Jerusalem? 5 I tell you, Nay: but, except ye repent, ye shall all likewise perish.

6 He spake also this parable; A certain man had a fig tree planted in his vineyard; and he came and sought fruit thereon, and found none. 7 Then said he unto the dresser of his vineyard, Behold, these three years I come seeking fruit on this fig tree, and find none: cut it down; why cumbereth it the ground? 8 And he answering said unto him, Lord, let it alone this year also, till I shall dig about it, and dung it: 9 And if it bear fruit, well: and if not, then after that thou shalt cut it down.

10 And he was teaching in one of the synagogues on the sabbath. 11 And, behold, there was a woman which had a spirit of infirmity eighteen years, and was bowed together, and could in no wise lift up herself. 12 And when Jesus saw her, he called her to him, and said unto her, Woman, thou art loosed from thine infirmity. 13 And he laid his hands on her: and immediately she was made straight, and glorified God. 14 And the ruler of the synagogue answered with indignation, because that Jesus had healed on the sabbath day, and said unto the people, There are six days in which men ought to work: in them therefore come and be healed, and not on the sabbath day. 15 The Lord then answered him, and said, Thou hypocrite, doth not each one of you on the sabbath loose his ox or his ass from the stall, and lead him away to watering? 16 And ought not this woman, being a daughter of Abraham, whom Satan hath bound, lo, these eighteen years, be loosed from this bond on the sabbath day? 17 And when he had said these things, all his adversaries were ashamed: and all the people rejoiced for all the glorious things that were done by him.

18 Then said he, Unto what is the kingdom of God like? and whereunto shall I resemble it? 19 It is like a grain of mustard seed, which a

man took, and cast into his garden; and it grew, and waxed a great tree; and the fowls of the air lodged in the branches of it. 20 And again he said, Whereunto shall I liken the kingdom of God? 21 It is like leaven, which a woman took and hid in three measures of meal, till the whole was leavened.

22 And he went through the cities and villages, teaching, and journeying toward Jerusalem. 23 Then said one unto him, Lord, are there few that be saved? And he said unto them, 24 Strive to enter in at the strait gate: for many, I say unto you, will seek to enter in, and shall not be able. 25 When once the master of the house is risen up, and hath shut to the door, and ye begin to stand without, and to knock at the door, saying, Lord, Lord, open unto us; and he shall answer and say unto you, I know you not whence ye are: 26 Then shall ye begin to say, We have eaten and drunk in thy presence, and thou hast taught in our streets. 27 But he shall say, I tell you, I know you not whence ye are; depart from me, all ye workers of iniquity. 28 There shall be weeping and gnashing of teeth, when ye shall see Abraham, and Isaac, and Jacob, and all the prophets, in the kingdom of God, and you yourselves thrust out. 29 And they shall come from the east, and from the west, and from the north, and from the south, and shall sit down in the kingdom of God. 30 And, behold, there are last which shall be first; and there are first which shall be last.

31 The same day there came certain of the Pharisees, saying unto him, Get thee out, and depart hence; for Herod will kill thee. 32 And he said unto them, Go ye, and tell that fox, Behold, I cast out devils, and I do cures to-day and to-morrow, and the third day I shall be perfected. 33 Nevertheless I must walk to-day, and to-morrow, and the day following: for it cannot be that a prophet perish out of Jerusalem. 34 O Jerusalem, Jerusalem, which killest the prophets, and stonest them that are sent unto thee; how often would I have gathered thy children together, as a hen doth gather her brood under her wings, and ye would not! 35 Behold, your house is left unto you desolate: and verily I say unto you, Ye shall not see me, until the time come when ye shall say, Blessed is he that cometh in the name of the Lord.

14 And it came to pass, as he went into the house of one of the chief Pharisees to eat bread on the sabbath day, that they watched him. 2 And, behold, there was a certain man before him which had the dropsy. 3 And Jesus answering spake unto the lawyers and Pharisees, saying, Is it lawful to heal on the sabbath day? 4 And they held their peace. And he took him, and healed him, and let him go; 5 And answered them, saying, Which of you shall have an ass or an ox fallen into a pit, and will not straightway pull him out on the sabbath day? 6 And they could not answer him again to these things.

7 And he put forth a parable to those which were bidden, when he marked how they chose out the chief rooms; saying unto them, 8 When thou art bidden of any man to a wedding, sit not down in the highest room; lest a more honorable man than thou be bidden of

him; 9 And he that bade thee and him come and say to thee, Give this man place; and thou begin with shame to take the lowest room. 10 But when thou art bidden, go and sit down in the lowest room; that when he that bade thee cometh, he may say unto thee, Friend, go up higher: then shalt thou have worship in the presence of them that sit at meat with thee. 11 For whosoever exalteth himself shall be abased; and he that humbleth himself shall be exalted. 12 Then said he also to him that bade him, When thou makest a dinner or a supper, call not thy friends, nor thy brethren, neither thy kinsmen, nor thy rich neighbors; lest they also bid thee again, and a recompense be made thee. 13 But when thou makest a feast, call the poor, the maimed, the lame, the blind: 14 And thou shalt be blessed; for they cannot recompense thee: for thou shalt be recompensed at the resurrection of the just.

15 And when one of them that sat at meat with him heard these things, he said unto him, Blessed is he that shall eat bread in the kingdom of God. 16 Then said he unto him, A certain man made a great supper, and bade many: 17 And sent his servant at supper time to say to them that were bidden, Come; for all things are now ready. 18 And they all with one consent began to make excuse. The first said unto him, I have bought a piece of ground, and I must needs go and see it: I pray thee have me excused. 19 And another said, I have bought five yoke of oxen, and I go to prove them: I pray thee have me excused. 20 And another said, I have married a wife, and therefore I cannot come. 21 So that servant came, and showed his lord these things. Then the master of the house being angry said to his servant, Go out quickly into the streets and lanes of the city, and bring in hither the poor, and the maimed, and the halt, and the blind. 22 And the servant said, Lord, it is done as thou hast commanded, and yet there is room. 23 And the lord said unto the servant, Go out into the highways and hedges, and compel them to come in, that my house may be filled. 24 For I say unto you, That none of those men which were bidden shall taste of my supper.

25 And there went great multitudes with him: and he turned, and said unto them, 26 If any man come to me, and hate not his father, and mother, and wife, and children, and brethren, and sisters, yea, and his own life also, he cannot be my disciple. 27 And whosoever doth not bear his cross, and come after me, cannot be my disciple. 28 For which of you, intending to build a tower, sitteth not down first, and counteth the cost, whether he have sufficient to finish it? 29 Lest haply, after he hath laid the foundation, and is not able to finish it, all that behold it begin to mock him, 30 Saying, This man began to build, and was not able to finish. 31 Or what king, going to make war against another king, sitteth not down first, and consulteth whether he be able with ten thousand to meet him that cometh against him with twenty thousand? 32 Or else, while the other is yet a great way off, he sendeth an ambassage, and desireth conditions of peace. 33 So likewise, whosoever he be of you that forsaketh not all

that he hath, he cannot be my disciple. 34 Salt is good: but if the salt have lost his savor, wherewith shall it be seasoned? 35 It is neither fit for the land, nor yet for the dunghill; but men cast it out. He that hath ears to hear, let him hear.

15 Then drew near unto him all the publicans and sinners for to hear him. 2 And the Pharisees and scribes murmured, saying, This man receiveth sinners, and eateth with them. 3 And he spake this parable unto them, saying, 4 What man of you, having a hundred sheep, if he lose one of them, doth not leave the ninety and nine in the wilderness, and go after that which is lost, until he find it? 5 And when he hath found it, he layeth it on his shoulders, rejoicing. 6 And when he cometh home, he calleth together his friends and neighbors, saying unto them, Rejoice with me; for I have found my sheep which was lost. 7 I say unto you, that likewise joy shall be in heaven over one sinner that repenteth, more than over ninety and nine just persons, which need no repentance.

8 Either what woman having ten pieces of silver, if she lose one piece, doth not light a candle, and sweep the house, and seek diligently till she find it? 9 And when she hath found it, she calleth her friends and her neighbors together, saying, Rejoice with me; for I have found the piece which I had lost. 10 Likewise, I say unto you, there is joy in the presence of the angels of God over one sinner that repenteth.

11 And he said, A certain man had two sons: 12 And the younger of them said to his father, Father, give me the portion of goods that falleth to me. And he divided unto them his living. 13 And not many days after the younger son gathered all together, and took his journey into a far country, and there wasted his substance with riotous living. 14 And when he had spent all, there arose a mighty famine in that land; and he began to be in want. 15 And he went and joined himself to a citizen of that country; and he sent him into his fields to feed swine. 16 And he would fain have filled his belly with the husks that the swine did eat: and no man gave unto him. 17 And when he came to himself, he said, How many hired servants of my father's have bread enough and to spare, and I perish with hunger! 18 I will arise and go to my father, and will say unto him, Father, I have sinned against heaven, and before thee, 19 And am no more worthy to be called thy son: make me as one of thy hired servants. 20 And he arose, and came to his father. But when he was yet a great way off, his father saw him, and had compassion, and ran, and fell on his neck, and kissed him. 21 And the son said unto him, Father, I have sinned against heaven, and in thy sight, and am no more worthy to be called thy son. 22 But the father said to his servants, Bring forth the best robe, and put it on him; and put a ring on his hand, and shoes on his feet: 23 And bring hither the fatted calf, and kill it; and let us eat, and be merry: 24 For this my son was dead, and is alive again; he was lost, and is found. And they began to be merry. 25 Now his elder son was

in the field: and as he came and drew nigh to the house, he heard music and dancing. 26 And he called one of the servants, and asked what these things meant. 27 And he said unto him, Thy brother is come; and thy father hath killed the fatted calf, because he hath received him safe and sound. 28 And he was angry, and would not go in: therefore came his father out, and entreated him. 29 And he answering said to his father, Lo, these many years do I serve thee, neither transgressed I at any time thy commandment; and yet thou never gavest me a kid, that I might make merry with my friends: 30 But as soon as this thy son was come, which hath devoured thy living with harlots, thou hast killed for him the fatted calf. 31 And he said unto him, Son, thou art ever with me, and all that I have is thine. 32 It was meet that we should make merry, and be glad: for this thy brother was dead, and is alive again; and was lost, and is found.

16 And he said also unto his disciples, There was a certain rich man, which had a steward; and the same was accused unto him that he had wasted his goods. 2 And he called him, and said unto him, How is it that I hear this of thee? give an account of thy stewardship; for thou mayest be no longer steward. 3 Then the steward said within himself, What shall I do? for my lord taketh away from me the stewardship: I cannot dig; to beg I am ashamed. 4 I am resolved what to do, that, when I am put out of the stewardship, they may receive me into their houses. 5 So he called every one of his lord's debtors unto him, and said unto the first, How much owest thou unto my lord? 6 And he said, A hundred measures of oil. And he said unto him, Take thy bill, and sit down quickly, and write fifty. 7 Then said he to another, And how much owest thou? And he said, A hundred measures of wheat. And he said unto him, Take thy bill, and write fourscore. 8 And the lord commended the unjust steward, because he had done wisely: for the children of this world are in their generation wiser than the children of light. 9 And I say unto you, Make to yourselves friends of the mammon of unrighteousness; that, when ye fail, they may receive you into everlasting habitations. 10 He that is faithful in that which is least is faithful also in much: and he that is unjust in the least is unjust also in much. 11 If therefore ye have not been faithful in the unrighteous mammon, who will commit to your trust the true riches? 12 And if ye have not been faithful in that which is another man's, who shall give you that which is your own? 13 No servant can serve two masters: for either he will hate the one, and love the other; or else he will hold to the one, and despise the other. Ye cannot serve God and mammon.

14 And the Pharisees also, who were covetous, heard all these things: and they derided him. 15 And he said unto them, Ye are they which justify yourselves before men; but God knoweth your hearts: for that which is highly esteemed among men is abomination in the sight of God. 16 The law and the prophets were until John: since that time

the kingdom of God is preached, and every man presseth into it. 17 And it is easier for heaven and earth to pass, than one tittle of the law to fail. 18 Whosoever putteth away his wife, and marrieth another, committeth adultery: and whosoever marrieth her that is put away from her husband committeth adultery.

19 There was a certain rich man, which was clothed in purple and fine linen, and fared sumptuously every day: 20 And there was a certain beggar named Lazarus, which was laid at his gate, full of sores, 21 And desiring to be fed with the crumbs which fell from the rich man's table: moreover the dogs came and licked his sores. 22 And it came to pass, that the beggar died, and was carried by the angels into Abraham's bosom: the rich man also died, and was buried; 23 And in hell he lifted up his eyes, being in torments, and seeth Abraham afar off, and Lazarus in his bosom. 24 And he cried and said, Father Abraham, have mercy on me, and send Lazarus, that he may dip the tip of his finger in water, and cool my tongue; for I am tormented in this flame. 25 But Abraham said, Son, remember that thou in thy lifetime receivedst thy good things, and likewise Lazarus evil things: but now he is comforted, and thou art tormented. 26 And beside all this, between us and you there is a great gulf fixed: so that they which would pass from hence to you cannot; neither can they pass to us, that would come from thence. 27 Then he said, I pray thee therefore, father, that thou wouldest send him to my father's house: 28 For I have five brethren; that he may testify unto them, lest they also come into this place of torment. 29 Abraham saith unto him, They have Moses and the prophets; let them hear them. 30 And he said, Nay, father Abraham: but if one went unto them from the dead, they will repent. 31 And he said unto him, If they hear not Moses and the prophets, neither will they be persuaded, though one rose from the dead.

17 Then said he unto the disciples, It is impossible but that offenses will come: but woe unto him, through whom they come! 2 It were better for him that a millstone were hanged about his neck, and he cast into the sea, than that he should offend one of these little ones. 3 Take heed to yourselves: If thy brother trespass against thee, rebuke him; and if he repent, forgive him. 4 And if he trespass against thee seven times in a day, and seven times in a day turn again to thee, saying, I repent; thou shalt forgive him. 5 And the apostles said unto the Lord, Increase our faith. 6 And the Lord said, If ye had faith as a grain of mustard seed, ye might say unto this sycamine tree, Be thou plucked up by the root, and be thou planted in the sea; and it should obey you. 7 But which of you, having a servant plowing or feeding cattle, will say unto him by and by, when he is come from the field, Go and sit down to meat? 8 And will not rather say unto him, Make ready wherewith I may sup, and gird thyself, and serve me, till I have eaten and drunken; and afterward thou shalt eat and drink? 9 Doth

he thank that servant because he did the things that were commanded him? I trow not. 10 So likewise ye, when ye shall have done all those things which are commanded you, say, We are unprofitable servants: we have done that which was our duty to do.

11 And it came to pass, as he went to Jerusalem, that he passed through the midst of Samaria and Galilee. 12 And as he entered into a certain village, there met him ten men that were lepers, which stood afar off: 13 And they lifted up their voices, and said, Jesus, Master, have mercy on us. 14 And when he saw them, he said unto them, Go show yourselves unto the priests. And it came to pass, that, as they went, they were cleansed. 15 And one of them, when he saw that he was healed, turned back, and with a loud voice glorified God, 16 And fell down on his face at his feet, giving him thanks: and he was a Samaritan. 17 And Jesus answering said, Were there not ten cleansed? but where are the nine? 18 There are not found that returned to give glory to God, save this stranger. 19 And he said unto him, Arise, go thy way: thy faith hath made thee whole.

20 And when he was demanded of the Pharisees, when the kingdom of God should come, he answered them and said, The kingdom of God cometh not with observation: 21 Neither shall they say, Lo here! or, lo there! for, behold, the kingdom of God is within you. 22 And he said unto the disciples, The days will come, when ye shall desire to see one of the days of the Son of man, and ye shall not see it. 23 And they shall say to you, See here; or, see there: go not after them, nor follow them. 24 For as the lightning, that lighteneth out of the one part under heaven, shineth unto the other part under heaven; so shall also the Son of man be in his day. 25 But first must he suffer many things, and be rejected of this generation. 26 And as it was in the days of Noe, so shall it be also in the days of the Son of man. 27 They did eat, they drank, they married wives, they were given in marriage, until the day that Noe entered into the ark, and the flood came, and destroyed them all. 28 Likewise also as it was in the days of Lot; they did eat, they drank, they bought, they sold, they planted, they builded; 29 But the same day that Lot went out of Sodom it rained fire and brimstone from heaven, and destroyed them all. 30 Even thus shall it be in the day when the Son of man is revealed. 31 In that day, he which shall be upon the housetop, and his stuff in the house, let him not come down to take it away: and he that is in the field, let him likewise not return back. 32 Remember Lot's wife. 33 Whosoever shall seek to save his life shall lose it; and whosoever shall lose his life shall preserve it. 34 I tell you, in that night there shall be two men in one bed; the one shall be taken, and the other shall be left. 35 Two women shall be grinding together; the one shall be taken, and the other left. 36 Two men shall be in the field; the one shall be taken, and the other left. 37 And they answered and said unto him, Where, Lord? And he said unto them, Wheresoever the body is, thither will the eagles be gathered together.

18 And he spake a parable unto them to this end, that men ought always to pray, and not to faint; 2 Saying, There was in a city a judge, which feared not God, neither regarded man: 3 And there was a widow in that city; and she came unto him, saying, Avenge me of mine adversary. 4 And he would not for a while: but afterward he said within himself, Though I fear not God, nor regard man; 5 Yet because this widow troubleth me, I will avenge her, lest by her continual coming she weary me. 6 And the Lord said, Hear what the unjust judge saith. 7 And shall not God avenge his own elect, which cry day and night unto him, though he bear long with them? 8 I tell you that he will avenge them speedily. Nevertheless, when the Son of man cometh, shall he find faith on the earth?

9 And he spake this parable unto certain which trusted in themselves that they were righteous, and despised others: 10 Two men went up into the temple to pray; the one a Pharisee, and the other a publican. 11 The Pharisee stood and prayed thus with himself, God, I thank thee, that I am not as other men are, extortioners, unjust, adulterers, or even as this publican. 12 I fast twice in the week, I give tithes of all that I possess. 13 And the publican, standing afar off, would not lift up so much as his eyes unto heaven, but smote upon his breast, saying, God be merciful to me a sinner. 14 I tell you, this man went down to his house justified rather than the other: for every one that exalteth himself shall be abased; and he that humbleth himself shall be exalted.

15 And they brought unto him also infants, that he would touch them: but when his disciples saw it, they rebuked them. 16 But Jesus called them unto him, and said, Suffer little children to come unto me, and forbid them not: for of such is the kingdom of God. 17 Verily I say unto you, Whosoever shall not receive the kingdom of God as a little child shall in no wise enter therein.

18 And a certain ruler asked him, saying, Good Master, what shall I do to inherit eternal life? 19 And Jesus said unto him, Why callest thou me good? none is good, save one, that is, God. 20 Thou knowest the commandments, Do not commit adultery, Do not kill, Do not steal, Do not bear false witness, Honor thy father and thy mother. 21 And he said, All these have I kept from my youth up. 22 Now when Jesus heard these things, he said unto him, Yet lackest thou one thing: sell all that thou hast, and distribute unto the poor, and thou shalt have treasure in heaven: and come, follow me. 23 And when he heard this, he was very sorrowful: for he was very rich. 24 And when Jesus saw that he was very sorrowful, he said, How hardly shall they that have riches enter into the kingdom of God! 25 For it is easier for a camel to go through a needle's eye, than for a rich man to enter into the kingdom of God. 26 And they that heard it said, Who then can be saved? 27 And he said, The things which are impossible with men are possible with God. 28 Then Peter said,

Lo, we have left all, and followed thee. 29 And he said unto them, Verily I say unto you, There is no man that hath left house, or parents, or brethren, or wife, or children, for the kingdom of God's sake, 30 Who shall not receive manifold more in this present time, and in the world to come life everlasting.

31 Then he took unto him the twelve, and said unto them, Behold, we go up to Jerusalem, and all things that are written by the prophets concerning the Son of man shall be accomplished. 32 For he shall be delivered unto the Gentiles, and shall be mocked, and spitefully entreated, and spitted on: 33 And they shall scourge him, and put him to death; and the third day he shall rise again. 34 And they understood none of these things: and this saying was hid from them, neither knew they the things which were spoken.

35 And it came to pass, that as he was come nigh unto Jericho, a certain blind man sat by the wayside begging: 36 And hearing the multitude pass by, he asked what it meant. 37 And they told him, that Jesus of Nazareth passeth by. 38 And he cried, saying Jesus, thou Son of David, have mercy on me. 39 And they which went before rebuked him, that he should hold his peace: but he cried so much the more, Thou Son of David, have mercy on me. 40 And Jesus stood, and commanded him to be brought unto him: and when he was come near, he asked him, 41 Saying, What wilt thou that I shall do unto thee? And he said, Lord, that I may receive my sight. 42 And Jesus said unto him, Receive thy sight: thy faith hath saved thee. 43 And immediately he received his sight, and followed him, glorifying God: and all the people, when they saw it, gave praise unto God.

19 And Jesus entered and passed through Jericho. 2 And, behold, there was a man named Zaccheus, which was the chief among the publicans, and he was rich. 3 And he sought to see Jesus who he was; and could not for the press, because he was little of stature. 4 And he ran before, and climbed up into a sycamore tree to see him; for he was to pass that way. 5 And when Jesus came to the place, he looked up, and saw him, and said unto him, Zaccheus, make haste, and come down; for to-day I must abide at thy house. 6 And he made haste, and came down, and received him joyfully. 7 And when they saw it, they all murmured, saying, That he was gone to be guest with a man that is a sinner. 8 And Zaccheus stood, and said unto the Lord; Behold, Lord, the half of my goods I give to the poor; and if I have taken any thing from any man by false accusation, I restore him fourfold. 9 And Jesus said unto him, This day is salvation come to this house, forasmuch as he also is a son of Abraham. 10 For the Son of man is come to seek and to save that which was lost.

11 And as they heard these things, he added and spake a parable, because he was nigh to Jerusalem, and because they thought that the kingdom of God should immediately appear. 12 He said therefore, A certain nobleman went into a far country to receive for himself a kingdom, and to return. 13 And he called his ten servants, and de-

livered them ten pounds, and said unto them, Occupy till I come. 14 But his citizens hated him, and sent a message after him, saying, We will not have this man to reign over us. 15 And it came to pass, that when he was returned, having received the kingdom, then he commanded these servants to be called unto him, to whom he had given the money, that he might know how much every man had gained by trading. 16 Then came the first, saying, Lord, thy pound hath gained ten pounds. 17 And he said unto him, Well, thou good servant: because thou hast been faithful in a very little, have thou authority over ten cities. 18 And the second came, saying, Lord, thy pound hath gained five pounds. 19 And he said likewise to him, Be thou also over five cities. 20 And another came, saying, Lord, behold, here is thy pound, which I have kept laid up in a napkin: 21 For I feared thee, because thou art an austere man: thou takest up that thou layedst not down, and reapest that thou didst not sow. 22 And he saith unto him, Out of thine own mouth will I judge thee, thou wicked servant. Thou knewest that I was an austere man, taking up that I laid not down, and reaping that I did not sow: 23 Wherefore then gavest not thou my money into the bank, that at my coming I might have required mine own with usury? 24 And he said unto them that stood by, Take from him the pound, and give it to him that hath ten pounds. 25 (And they said unto him, Lord, he hath ten pounds.) 26 For I say unto you, That unto every one which hath shall be given; and from him that hath not, even that he hath shall be taken away from him. 27 But those mine enemies, which would not that I should reign over them, bring hither, and slay them before me. 28 And when he had thus spoken, he went before, ascending up to Jerusalem.

## TRIUMPHAL ENTRY

29 And it came to pass, when he was come nigh to Bethphage and Bethany, at the mount called the mount of Olives, he sent two of his disciples, 30 Saying, Go ye into the village over against you; in the which at your entering ye shall find a colt tied, whereon yet never man sat: loose him, and bring him hither. 31 And if any man ask you, Why do ye loose him? thus shall ye say unto him, Because the Lord hath need of him. 32 And they that were sent went their way, and found even as he had said unto them. 33 And as they were loosing the colt, the owners thereof said unto them, Why loose ye the colt? 34 And they said, The Lord hath need of him. 35 And they brought him to Jesus: and they cast their garments upon the colt, and they set Jesus thereon. 36 And as he went, they spread their clothes in the way. 37 And when he was come nigh, even now at the descent of the mount of Olives, the whole multitude of the disciples began to rejoice and praise God with a loud voice for all the mighty works that they had seen; 38 Saying,

Blessed be the King that cometh in the name of the Lord:
Peace in heaven, and glory in the highest.

39 And some of the Pharisees from among the multitude said unto
him, Master, rebuke thy disciples. 40 And he answered and said unto
them, I tell you that, if these should hold their peace, the stones would
immediately cry out.

41 And when he was come near, he beheld the city, and wept over
it, 42 Saying, If thou hadst known, even thou, at least in this thy day,
the things which belong unto thy peace! but now they are hid from
thine eyes. 43 For the days shall come upon thee, that thine enemies
shall cast a trench about thee, and compass thee round, and keep thee
in on every side, 44 And shall lay thee even with the ground, and
thy children within thee; and they shall not leave in thee one stone
upon another; because thou knewest not the time of thy visitation.

45 And he went into the temple, and began to cast out them that
sold therein, and them that bought; 46 Saying unto them, It is written, My house is the house of prayer; but ye have made it a den of
thieves. 47 And he taught daily in the temple. But the chief priests
and the scribes and the chief of the people sought to destroy him,
48 And could not find what they might do: for all the people were very
attentive to hear him.


20    And it came to pass, that on one of those days, as he taught the
people in the temple, and preached the gospel, the chief priests and
the scribes came upon him with the elders, 2 And spake unto him,
saying, Tell us, by what authority doest thou these things? or who is
he that gave thee this authority? 3 And he answered and said unto
them, I will also ask you one thing; and answer me: 4 The baptism
of John, was it from heaven, or of men? 5 And they reasoned with
themselves, saying, If we shall say, From heaven; he will say, Why
then believed ye him not? 6 But and if we say, Of men; all the
people will stone us: for they be persuaded that John was a prophet.
7 And they answered, that they could not tell whence it was. 8 And
Jesus said unto them, Neither tell I you by what authority I do these
things. 9 Then began he to speak to the people this parable; A certain
man planted a vineyard, and let it forth to husbandmen, and went
into a far country for a long time. 10 And at the season he sent a
servant to the husbandmen, that they should give him of the fruit
of the vineyard: but the husbandmen beat him, and sent him away
empty. 11 And again he sent another servant: and they beat him
also, and entreated him shamefully, and sent him away empty.
12 And again he sent a third: and they wounded him also, and cast
him out. 13 Then said the lord of the vineyard, What shall I do?
I will send my beloved son: it may be they will reverence him when
they see him. 14 But when the husbandmen saw him, they reasoned
among themselves, saying, This is the heir: come, let us kill him, that
the inheritance may be ours. 15 So they cast him out of the vineyard,

and killed him. What therefore shall the lord of the vineyard do unto them? 16 He shall come and destroy these husbandmen, and shall give the vineyard to others. And when they heard it, they said, God forbid. 17 And he beheld them, and said, What is this then that is written,

The stone which the builders rejected,
The same is become the head of the corner?

18 Whosoever shall fall upon that stone shall be broken; but on whomsoever it shall fall, it will grind him to powder. 19 And the chief priests and the scribes the same hour sought to lay hands on him; and they feared the people: for they perceived that he had spoken this parable against them.

20 And they watched him, and sent forth spies, which should feign themselves just men, that they might take hold of his words, that so they might deliver him unto the power and authority of the governor. 21 And they asked him, saying, Master, we know that thou sayest and teachest rightly, neither acceptest thou the person of any, but teachest the way of God truly: 22 Is it lawful for us to give tribute unto Caesar, or no? 23 But he perceived their craftiness, and said unto them, Why tempt ye me? 24 Show me a penny. Whose image and superscription hath it? They answered and said, Caesar's. 25 And he said unto them, Render therefore unto Caesar the things which be Caesar's, and unto God the things which be God's. 26 And they could not take hold of his words before the people: and they marveled at his answer, and held their peace.

27 Then came to him certain of the Sadducees, which deny that there is any resurrection; and they asked him, 28 Saying, Master, Moses wrote unto us, If any man's brother die, having a wife, and he die without children, that his brother should take his wife, and raise up seed unto his brother. 29 There were therefore seven brethren: and the first took a wife, and died without children. 30 And the second took her to wife, and he died childless. 31 And the third took her; and in like manner the seven also: and they left no children, and died. 32 Last of all the woman died also. 33 Therefore in the resurrection whose wife of them is she? for seven had her to wife. 34 And Jesus answering said unto them, The children of this world marry, and are given in marriage: 35 But they which shall be accounted worthy to obtain that world, and the resurrection from the dead, neither marry, nor are given in marriage: 36 Neither can they die any more: for they are equal unto the angels; and are the children of God, being the children of the resurrection. 37 Now that the dead are raised, even Moses showed at the bush, when he calleth the Lord the God of Abraham, and the God of Isaac, and the God of Jacob. 38 For he is not a God of the dead, but of the living: for all live unto him. 39 Then certain of the scribes answering said, Master, thou hast well said. 40 And after that they durst not ask him any question at all.

41 And he said unto them, How say they that Christ is David's son? 42 And David himself saith in the book of Psalms,

The Lord said unto my Lord,
Sit thou on my right hand,
43 Till I make thine enemies thy footstool.
44 David therefore calleth him Lord, how is he then his son? 45 Then in the audience of all the people he said unto his disciples, 46 Beware of the scribes, which desire to walk in long robes, and love greetings in the markets, and the highest seats in the synagogues, and the chief rooms at feasts; 47 Which devour widows' houses, and for a show make long prayers: the same shall receive greater damnation.

21 And he looked up, and saw the rich men casting their gifts into the treasury. 2 And he saw also a certain poor widow casting in thither two mites. 3 And he said, Of a truth I say unto you, that this poor widow hath cast in more than they all: 4 For all these have of their abundance cast in unto the offerings of God: but she of her penury hath cast in all the living that she had.

5 And as some spake of the temple, how it was adorned with goodly stones and gifts, he said, 6 As for these things which ye behold, the days will come, in the which there shall not be left one stone upon another, that shall not be thrown down. 7 And they asked him, saying, Master, but when shall these things be? and what sign will there be when these things shall come to pass? 8 And he said, Take heed that ye be not deceived: for many shall come in my name, saying, I am Christ; and the time draweth near: go ye not therefore after them. 9 But when ye shall hear of wars and commotions, be not terrified: for these things must first come to pass; but the end is not by and by. 10 Then said he unto them, Nation shall rise against nation, and kingdom against kingdom: 11 And great earthquakes shall be in divers places, and famines, and pestilences; and fearful sights and great signs shall there be from heaven. 12 But before all these, they shall lay their hands on you, and persecute you, delivering you up to the synagogues, and into prisons, being brought before kings and rulers for my name's sake. 13 And it shall turn to you for a testimony. 14 Settle it therefore in your hearts, not to meditate before what ye shall answer: 15 For I will give you a mouth and wisdom, which all your adversaries shall not be able to gainsay nor resist. 16 And ye shall be betrayed both by parents, and brethren, and kinsfolk, and friends; and some of you shall they cause to be put to death. 17 And ye shall be hated of all men for my name's sake. 18 But there shall not a hair of your head perish. 19 In your patience possess ye your souls.

20 And when ye shall see Jerusalem compassed with armies, then know that the desolation thereof is nigh. 21 Then let them which are in Judea flee to the mountains; and let them which are in the midst of it depart out; and let not them that are in the countries enter thereinto. 22 For these be the days of vengeance, that all things which are written may be fulfilled. 23 But woe unto them that are with child, and to them that give suck, in those days! for there shall be

great distress in the land, and wrath upon this people. 24 And they shall fall by the edge of the sword, and shall be led away captive into all nations: and Jerusalem shall be trodden down of the Gentiles, until the times of the Gentiles be fulfilled.

25 And there shall be signs in the sun, and in the moon, and in the stars; and upon the earth distress of nations, with perplexity; the sea and the waves roaring; 26 Men's hearts failing them for fear, and for looking after those things which are coming on the earth: for the powers of heaven shall be shaken. 27 And then shall they see the Son of man coming in a cloud with power and great glory. 28 And when these things begin to come to pass, then look up, and lift up your heads; for your redemption draweth nigh. 29 And he spake to them a parable; Behold the fig tree, and all the trees; 30 When they now shoot forth, ye see and know of your own selves that summer is now nigh at hand. 31 So likewise ye, when ye see these things come to pass, know ye that the kingdom of God is nigh at hand. 32 Verily I say unto you, This generation shall not pass away, till all be fulfilled. 33 Heaven and earth shall pass away; but my words shall not pass away.

34 And take heed to yourselves, lest at any time your hearts be overcharged with surfeiting, and drunkenness, and cares of this life, and so that day come upon you unawares. 35 For as a snare shall it come on all them that dwell on the face of the whole earth. 36 Watch ye therefore, and pray always, that ye may be accounted worthy to escape all these things that shall come to pass, and to stand before the Son of man. 37 And in the daytime he was teaching in the temple; and at night he went out, and abode in the mount that is called the mount of Olives. 38 And all the people came early in the morning to him in the temple, for to hear him.

## CRUCIFIXION AND RESURRECTION

22 Now the feast of unleavened bread drew nigh, which is called the passover. 2 And the chief priests and scribes sought how they might kill him; for they feared the people. 3 Then entered Satan into Judas surnamed Iscariot, being of the number of the twelve. 4 And he went his way, and communed with the chief priests and captains, how he might betray him unto them. 5 And they were glad, and covenanted to give him money. 6 And he promised, and sought opportunity to betray him unto them in the absence of the multitude.

7 Then came the day of unleavened bread, when the passover must be killed. 8 And he sent Peter and John, saying, Go and prepare us the passover, that we may eat. 9 And they said unto him, Where wilt thou that we prepare? 10 And he said unto them, Behold, when ye are entered into the city, there shall a man meet you, bearing a pitcher of water; follow him into the house where he entereth in. 11 And ye shall say unto the goodman of the house, The Master saith unto thee, Where is the guest chamber, where I shall eat the passover with

my disciples? 12 And he shall show you a large upper room furnished: there make ready. 13 And they went, and found as he had said unto them: and they made ready the passover.

14 And when the hour was come, he sat down, and the twelve apostles with him. 15 And he said unto them, With desire I have desired to eat this passover with you before I suffer: 16 For I say unto you, I will not any more eat thereof, until it be fulfilled in the kingdom of God. 17 And he took the cup, and gave thanks, and said, Take this, and divide it among yourselves: 18 For I say unto you, I will not drink of the fruit of the vine, until the kingdom of God shall come. 19 And he took bread, and gave thanks, and brake it, and gave unto them, saying, This is my body which is given for you: this do in remembrance of me. 20 Likewise also the cup after supper, saying, This cup is the new testament in my blood, which is shed for you. 21 But, behold, the hand of him that betrayeth me is with me on the table. 22 And truly the Son of man goeth, as it was determined: but woe unto that man by whom he is betrayed! 23 And they began to inquire among themselves, which of them it was that should do this thing.

24 And there was also a strife among them, which of them should be accounted the greatest. 25 And he said unto them, The kings of the Gentiles exercise lordship over them; and they that exercise authority upon them are called benefactors. 26 But ye shall not be so: but he that is greatest among you, let him be as the younger; and he that is chief, as he that doth serve. 27 For whether is greater, he that sitteth at meat, or he that serveth? is not he that sitteth at meat? but I am among you as he that serveth. 28 Ye are they which have continued with me in my temptations. 29 And I appoint unto you a kingdom, as my Father hath appointed unto me; 30 That ye may eat and drink at my table in my kingdom, and sit on thrones judging the twelve tribes of Israel.

31 And the Lord said, Simon, Simon, behold, Satan hath desired to have you, that he may sift you as wheat: 32 But I have prayed for thee, that thy faith fail not: and when thou art converted, strengthen thy brethren. 33 And he said unto him, Lord, I am ready to go with thee, both into prison, and to death. 34 And he said, I tell thee, Peter, the cock shall not crow this day, before that thou shalt thrice deny that thou knowest me. 35 And he said unto them, When I sent you without purse, and scrip, and shoes, lacked ye any thing? And they said, Nothing. 36 Then said he unto them, But now, he that hath a purse, let him take it, and likewise his scrip: and he that hath no sword, let him sell his garment, and buy one. 37 For I say unto you, that this that is written must yet be accomplished in me, And he was reckoned among the transgressors: for the things concerning me have an end. 38 And they said, Lord, behold, here are two swords. And he said unto them, It is enough.

39 And he came out, and went, as he was wont, to the mount of Olives; and his disciples also followed him. 40 And when he was at

the place, he said unto them, Pray that ye enter not into temptation. 41 And he was withdrawn from them about a stone's cast, and kneeled down, and prayed, 42 Saying, Father, if thou be willing, remove this cup from me: nevertheless, not my will, but thine, be done. 43 And there appeared an angel unto him from heaven, strengthening him. 44 And being in an agony he prayed more earnestly: and his sweat was as it were great drops of blood falling down to the ground. 45 And when he rose up from prayer, and was come to his disciples, he found them sleeping for sorrow, 46 And said unto them, Why sleep ye? rise and pray, lest ye enter into temptation.

47 And while he yet spake, behold a multitude, and he that was called Judas, one of the twelve, went before them, and drew near unto Jesus to kiss him. 48 But Jesus said unto him, Judas, betrayest thou the Son of man with a kiss? 49 When they which were about him saw what would follow, they said unto him, Lord, shall we smite with the sword? 50 And one of them smote the servant of the high priest, and cut off his right ear. 51 And Jesus answered and said, Suffer ye thus far. And he touched his ear, and healed him. 52 Then Jesus said unto the chief priests, and captains of the temple, and the elders, which were come to him, Be ye come out, as against a thief, with swords and staves? 53 When I was daily with you in the temple, ye stretched forth no hands against me: but this is your hour, and the power of darkness.

54 Then took they him, and led him, and brought him into the high priest's house. And Peter followed afar off. 55 And when they had kindled a fire in the midst of the hall, and were set down together, Peter sat down among them. 56 But a certain maid beheld him as he sat by the fire, and earnestly looked upon him, and said, This man was also with him. 57 And he denied him, saying, Woman, I know him not. 58 And after a little while another saw him, and said, Thou art also of them. And Peter said, Man, I am not. 59 And about the space of one hour after another confidently affirmed, saying, Of a truth this fellow also was with him; for he is a Galilean. 60 And Peter said, Man, I know not what thou sayest. And immediately, while he yet spake, the cock crew. 61 And the Lord turned, and looked upon Peter. And Peter remembered the word of the Lord, how he had said unto him, Before the cock crow, thou shalt deny me thrice. 62 And Peter went out, and wept bitterly. 63 And the men that held Jesus mocked him, and smote him. 64 And when they had blindfolded him, they struck him on the face, and asked him, saying, Prophesy, who is it that smote thee? 65 And many other things blasphemously spake they against him.

66 And as soon as it was day, the elders of the people and the chief priests and the scribes came together, and led him into their council, saying, 67 Art thou the Christ? tell us. And he said unto them, If I tell you, ye will not believe: 68 And if I also ask you, ye will not answer me, nor let me go. 69 Hereafter shall the Son of man sit on

the right hand of the power of God. 70 Then said they all, Art thou then the Son of God? And he said unto them, Ye say that I am. 71 And they said, What need we any further witness? for we ourselves have heard of his own mouth.

23 And the whole multitude of them arose, and led him unto Pilate. 2 And they began to accuse him, saying, We found this fellow perverting the nation, and forbidding to give tribute to Caesar, saying that he himself is Christ a king. 3 And Pilate asked him, saying, Art thou the King of the Jews? And he answered him and said, Thou sayest it. 4 Then said Pilate to the chief priests and to the people, I find no fault in this man. 5 And they were the more fierce, saying, He stirreth up the people, teaching throughout all Jewry, beginning from Galilee to this place. 6 When Pilate heard of Galilee, he asked whether the man were a Galilean. 7 And as soon as he knew that he belonged unto Herod's jurisdiction, he sent him to Herod, who himself also was at Jerusalem at that time.

8 And when Herod saw Jesus, he was exceeding glad: for he was desirous to see him of a long season, because he had heard many things of him; and he hoped to have seen some miracle done by him. 9 Then he questioned with him in many words; but he answered him nothing. 10 And the chief priests and scribes stood and vehemently accused him. 11 And Herod with his men of war set him at nought, and mocked him, and arrayed him in a gorgeous robe, and sent him again to Pilate. 12 And the same day Pilate and Herod were made friends together; for before they were at enmity between themselves.

13 And Pilate, when he had called together the chief priests and the rulers and the people, 14 Said unto them, Ye have brought this man unto me, as one that perverteth the people; and, behold, I, having examined him before you, have found no fault in this man touching those things whereof ye accuse him: 15 No, nor yet Herod: for I sent you to him; and, lo, nothing worthy of death is done unto him. 16 I will therefore chastise him, and release him. 17 (For of necessity he must release one unto them at the feast.) 18 And they cried out all at once, saying, Away with this man, and release unto us Barabbas: 19 (Who for a certain sedition made in the city, and for murder, was cast into prison.) 20 Pilate therefore, willing to release Jesus, spake again to them. 21 But they cried, saying, Crucify him, crucify him. 22 And he said unto them the third time, Why, what evil hath he done? I have found no cause of death in him: I will therefore chastise him, and let him go. 23 And they were instant with loud voices, requiring that he might be crucified: and the voices of them and of the chief priests prevailed. 24 And Pilate gave sentence that it should be as they required. 25 And he released unto them him that for sedition and murder was cast into prison, whom they had desired; but he delivered Jesus to their will.

26 And as they led him away, they laid hold upon one Simon, a

Cyrenian, coming out of the country, and on him they laid the cross, that he might bear it after Jesus. 27 And there followed him a great company of people, and of women, which also bewailed and lamented him. 28 But Jesus turning unto them said, Daughters of Jerusalem, weep not for me, but weep for yourselves, and for your children. 29 For, behold, the days are coming, in the which they shall say, Blessed are the barren, and the wombs that never bare, and the paps which never gave suck. 30 Then shall they begin to say to the mountains, Fall on us; and to the hills, Cover us. 31 For if they do these things in a green tree, what shall be done in the dry? 32 And there were also two others, malefactors, led with him to be put to death.

33 And when they were come to the place, which is called Calvary, there they crucified him, and the malefactors, one on the right hand, and the other on the left. 34 Then said Jesus, Father, forgive them; for they know not what they do. And they parted his raiment, and cast lots. 35 And the people stood beholding. And the rulers also with them derided him, saying, He saved others; let him save himself, if he be Christ, the chosen of God. 36 And the soldiers also mocked him, coming to him, and offering him vinegar, 37 And saying, If thou be the King of the Jews, save thyself. 38 And a superscription also was written over him in letters of Greek, and Latin, and Hebrew, THIS IS THE KING OF THE JEWS. 39 And one of the malefactors which were hanged railed on him, saying, If thou be Christ, save thyself and us. 40 But the other answering rebuked him, saying, Dost not thou fear God, seeing thou art in the same condemnation? 41 And we indeed justly; for we receive the due reward of our deeds: but this man hath done nothing amiss. 42 And he said unto Jesus, Lord, remember me when thou comest into thy kingdom. 43 And Jesus said unto him, Verily I say unto thee, To-day shalt thou be with me in paradise.

44 And it was about the sixth hour, and there was a darkness over all the earth until the ninth hour. 45 And the sun was darkened, and the veil of the temple was rent in the midst. 46 And when Jesus had cried with a loud voice, he said, Father, into thy hands I commend my spirit: and having said thus, he gave up the ghost. 47 Now when the centurion saw what was done, he glorified God, saying, Certainly this was a righteous man. 48 And all the people that came together to that sight, beholding the things which were done, smote their breasts, and returned. 49 And all his acquaintance, and the women that followed him from Galilee, stood afar off, beholding these things.

50 And, behold, there was a man named Joseph, a counselor; and he was a good man, and a just: 51 (The same had not consented to the counsel and deed of them:) he was of Arimathea, a city of the Jews; who also himself waited for the kingdom of God. 52 This man went unto Pilate, and begged the body of Jesus. 53 And he took it down, and wrapped it in linen, and laid it in a sepulchre that was hewn in stone, wherein never man before was laid. 54 And that day was the

preparation, and the sabbath drew on. 55 And the women also, which came with him from Galilee, followed after, and beheld the sepulchre, and how his body was laid. 56 And they returned, and prepared spices and ointments; and rested the sabbath day according to the commandment.

24 Now upon the first day of the week, very early in the morning, they came unto the sepulchre, bringing the spices which they had prepared, and certain others with them. 2 And they found the stone rolled away from the sepulchre. 3 And they entered in, and found not the body of the Lord Jesus. 4 And it came to pass, as they were much perplexed thereabout, behold, two men stood by them in shining garments: 5 And as they were afraid, and bowed down their faces to the earth, they said unto them, Why seek ye the living among the dead? 6 He is not here, but is risen: remember how he spake unto you when he was yet in Galilee, 7 Saying, The Son of man must be delivered into the hands of sinful men, and be crucified, and the third day rise again. 8 And they remembered his words, 9 And returned from the sepulchre, and told all these things unto the eleven, and to all the rest. 10 It was Mary Magdalene, and Joanna, and Mary. the mother of James, and other women that were with them, which told these things unto the apostles. 11 And their words seemed to them as idle tales, and they believed them not. 12 Then arose Peter, and ran unto the sepulchre; and stooping down, he beheld the linen clothes laid by themselves, and departed, wondering in himself at that which was come to pass.

13 And, behold, two of them went that same day to a village called Emmaus, which was from Jerusalem about threescore furlongs. 14 And they talked together of all these things which had happened. 15 And it came to pass, that, while they communed together and reasoned, Jesus himself drew near, and went with them. 16 But their eyes were holden that they should not know him. 17 And he said unto them, What manner of communications are these that ye have one to another, as ye walk, and are sad? 18 And the one of them, whose name was Cleopas, answering said unto him, Art thou only a stranger in Jerusalem, and hast not known the things which are come to pass there in these days? 19 And he said unto them, What things? And they said unto him, Concerning Jesus of Nazareth, which was a prophet mighty in deed and word before God and all the people: 20 And how the chief priests and our rulers delivered him to be condemned to death, and have crucified him. 21 But we trusted that it had been he which should have redeemed Israel: and beside all this, to-day is the third day since these things were done. 22 Yea, and certain women also of our company made us astonished, which were early at the sepulchre; 23 And when they found not his body, they came, saying, that they had also seen a vision of angels, which said that he was alive. 24 And certain of them which were with us went to the sepulchre, and

found it even so as the women had said: but him they saw not. 25 Then he said unto them, O fools, and slow of heart to believe all that the prophets have spoken: 26 Ought not Christ to have suffered these things, and to enter into his glory? 27 And beginning at Moses and all the prophets, he expounded unto them in all the Scriptures the things concerning himself. 28 And they drew nigh unto the village, whither they went: and he made as though he would have gone further. 29 But they constrained him, saying, Abide with us; for it is toward evening, and the day is far spent. And he went in to tarry with them. 30 And it came to pass, as he sat at meat with them, he took bread, and blessed it, and brake, and gave to them. 31 And their eyes were opened, and they knew him; and he vanished out of their sight. 32 And they said one to another, Did not our heart burn within us, while he talked with us by the way, and while he opened to us the Scriptures? 33 And they rose up the same hour, and returned to Jerusalem, and found the eleven gathered together, and them that were with them, 34 Saying, The Lord is risen indeed, and hath appeared to Simon. 35 And they told what things were done in the way, and how he was known of them in breaking of bread.

36 And as they thus spake, Jesus himself stood in the midst of them, and saith unto them, Peace be unto you. 37 But they were terrified and affrighted, and supposed that they had seen a spirit. 38 And he said unto them, Why are ye troubled? and why do thoughts arise in your hearts? 39 Behold my hands and my feet, that it is I myself: handle me, and see; for a spirit hath not flesh and bones, as ye see me have. 40 And when he had thus spoken, he showed them his hands and his feet. 41 And while they yet believed not for joy, and wondered, he said unto them, Have ye here any meat? 42 And they gave him a piece of a broiled fish, and of a honeycomb. 43 And he took it, and did eat before them. 44 And he said unto them, These are the words which I spake unto you, while I was yet with you, that all things must be fulfilled, which were written in the law of Moses, and in the prophets, and in the psalms, concerning me. 45 Then opened he their understanding, that they might understand the Scriptures, 46 And said unto them, Thus it is written, and thus it behooved Christ to suffer, and to rise from the dead the third day: 47 And that repentance and remission of sins should be preached in his name among all nations, beginning at Jerusalem. 48 And ye are witnesses of these things. 49 And, behold, I send the promise of my Father upon you: but tarry ye in the city of Jerusalem, until ye be endued with power from on high.

50 And he led them out as far as to Bethany, and he lifted up his hands, and blessed them. 51 And it came to pass, while he blessed them, he was parted from them, and carried up into heaven. 52 And they worshipped him, and returned to Jerusalem with great joy: 53 And were continually in the temple, praising and blessing God. Amen.

# *The Gospel According to John*

## FOREWORD: THE WORD MADE FLESH

1 In the beginning was the Word, and the Word was with God, and the Word was God. 2 The same was in the beginning with God. 3 All things were made by him; and without him was not any thing made that was made. 4 In him was life; and the life was the light of men. 5 And the light shineth in darkness; and the darkness comprehended it not.

6 There was a man sent from God, whose name was John. 7 The same came for a witness, to bear witness of the Light, that all men through him might believe. 8 He was not that Light, but was sent to bear witness of that Light. 9 That was the true Light, which lighteth every man that cometh into the world. 10 He was in the world, and the world was made by him, and the world knew him not. 11 He came unto his own, and his own received him not. 12 But as many as received him, to them gave he power to become the sons of God, even to them that believe on his name: 13 Which were born, not of blood, nor of the will of the flesh, nor of the will of man, but of God.

14 And the Word was made flesh, and dwelt among us, (and we beheld his glory, the glory as of the only begotten of the Father,) full of grace and truth. 15 John bare witness of him, and cried, saying, This was he of whom I spake, He that cometh after me is preferred before me; for he was before me. 16 And of his fulness have all we received, and grace for grace. 17 For the law was given by Moses, but grace and truth came by Jesus Christ. 18 No man hath seen God at any time; the only begotten Son, which is in the bosom of the Father, he hath declared him.

## EARLY EFFECT

19 And this is the record of John, when the Jews sent priests and Levites from Jerusalem to ask him, Who art thou? 20 And he confessed, and denied not; but confessed, I am not the Christ. 21 And they asked him, What then? Art thou Elias? And he saith, I am not. Art thou that Prophet? And he answered, No. 22 Then said they unto him, Who art thou? that we may give an answer to them that sent us. What sayest thou of thyself? 23 He said, I am

The voice of one crying in the wilderness,
Make straight the way of the Lord,

as said the prophet Esaias. 24 And they which were sent were of the Pharisees. 25 And they asked him, and said unto him, Why baptizest thou then, if thou be not that Christ, nor Elias, neither that Prophet? 26 John answered them, saying, I baptize with water: but there standeth one among you, whom ye know not; 27 He it is, who coming after me is preferred before me, whose shoe-latchet I am not worthy to unloose. 28 These things were done in Bethabara beyond Jordan, where John was baptizing.

29 The next day John seeth Jesus coming unto him, and saith, Behold the Lamb of God, which taketh away the sin of the world! 30 This is he of whom I said, After me cometh a man which is preferred before me; for he was before me. 31 And I knew him not: but that he should be made manifest to Israel, therefore am I come baptizing with water. 32 And John bare record, saying, I saw the Spirit descending from heaven like a dove, and it abode upon him. 33 And I knew him not: but he that sent me to baptize with water, the same said unto me, Upon whom thou shalt see the Spirit descending, and remaining on him, the same is he which baptizeth with the Holy Ghost. 34 And I saw, and bare record that this is the Son of God.

35 Again the next day after, John stood, and two of his disciples; 36 And looking upon Jesus as he walked, he saith, Behold the Lamb of God! 37 And the two disciples heard him speak, and they followed Jesus. 38 Then Jesus turned, and saw them following, and saith unto them, What seek ye? They said unto him, Rabbi, (which is to say, being interpreted, Master,) where dwellest thou? 39 He saith unto them, Come and see. They came and saw where he dwelt, and abode with him that day: for it was about the tenth hour. 40 One of the two which heard John speak, and followed him, was Andrew, Simon Peter's brother. 41 He first findeth his own brother Simon, and saith unto him, We have found the Messias, which is, being interpreted, the Christ. 42 And he brought him to Jesus. And when Jesus beheld him, he said, Thou art Simon the son of Jona: thou shalt be called Cephas, which is by interpretation, A stone.

43 The day following Jesus would go forth into Galilee, and findeth Philip, and saith unto him, Follow me. 44 Now Philip was of Bethsaida, the city of Andrew and Peter. 45 Philip findeth Nathanael, and saith unto him, We have found him, of whom Moses in the law, and the prophets, did write, Jesus of Nazareth, the son of Joseph. 46 And Nathanael said unto him, Can there any good thing come out of Nazareth? Philip saith unto him, Come and see. 47 Jesus saw Nathanael coming to him, and saith of him, Behold an Israelite indeed, in whom is no guile! 48 Nathanael saith unto him, Whence knowest thou me? Jesus answered and said unto him, Before that Philip called thee, when thou wast under the fig tree, I saw thee. 49 Nathanael answered and saith unto him, Rabbi, thou art the Son of God; thou art the King of Israel. 50 Jesus answered and said unto him, Because I said unto thee, I saw thee under the fig tree, believest thou? thou shalt see greater things than these. 51 And he saith unto him, Verily, verily, I say unto you, Hereafter ye shall see heaven open, and the angels of God ascending and descending upon the Son of man.

2 And the third day there was a marriage in Cana of Galilee; and the mother of Jesus was there: 2 And both Jesus was called, and his disciples, to the marriage. 3 And when they wanted wine, the mother

of Jesus saith unto him, They have no wine. 4 Jesus saith unto her, Woman, what have I to do with thee? mine hour is not yet come. 5 His mother saith unto the servants, Whatsoever he saith unto you, do it. 6 And there were set there six waterpots of stone, after the manner of the purifying of the Jews, containing two or three firkins apiece. 7 Jesus saith unto them, Fill the waterpots with water. And they filled them up to the brim. 8 And he saith unto them, Draw out now, and bear unto the governor of the feast. And they bare it. 9 When the ruler of the feast had tasted the water that was made wine, and knew not whence it was, (but the servants which drew the water knew,) the governor of the feast called the bridegroom, 10 And saith unto him, Every man at the beginning doth set forth good wine; and when men have well drunk, then that which is worse: but thou hast kept the good wine until now. 11 This beginning of miracles did Jesus in Cana of Galilee, and manifested forth his glory; and his disciples believed on him.

12 After this he went down to Capernaum, he, and his mother, and his brethren, and his disciples; and they continued there not many days. 13 And the Jews' passover was at hand, and Jesus went up to Jerusalem, 14 And found in the temple those that sold oxen and sheep and doves, and the changers of money sitting: 15 And when he had made a scourge of small cords, he drove them all out of the temple, and the sheep, and the oxen; and poured out the changers' money, and overthrew the tables; 16 And said unto them that sold doves, Take these things hence; make not my Father's house a house of merchandise. 17 And his disciples remembered that it was written, The zeal of thine house hath eaten me up. 18 Then answered the Jews and said unto him, What sign showest thou unto us, seeing that thou doest these things? 19 Jesus answered and said unto them, Destroy this temple, and in three days I will raise it up. 20 Then said the Jews, Forty and six years was this temple in building, and wilt thou rear it up in three days? 21 But he spake of the temple of his body. 22 When therefore he was risen from the dead, his disciples remembered that he had said this unto them; and they believed the Scripture, and the word which Jesus had said.

23 Now when he was in Jerusalem at the passover, in the feast day, many believed in his name, when they saw the miracles which he did. 24 But Jesus did not commit himself unto them, because he knew all men, 25 And needed not that any should testify of man; for he knew what was in man.

3   There was a man of the Pharisees, named Nicodemus, a ruler of the Jews: 2 The same came to Jesus by night, and said unto him, Rabbi, we know that thou art a teacher come from God: for no man can do these miracles that thou doest, except God be with him. 3 Jesus answered and said unto him, Verily, verily, I say unto thee, Except a man be born again, he cannot see the kingdom of God. 4 Nicodemus saith unto him, How can a man be born when he is old?

can he enter the second time into his mother's womb, and be born? 5 Jesus answered, Verily, Verily, I say unto thee, Except a man be born of water and of the Spirit, he cannot enter into the kingdom of God. 6 That which is born of the flesh is flesh; and that which is born of the Spirit is spirit. 7 Marvel not that I said unto thee, Ye must be born again. 8 The wind bloweth where it listeth, and thou hearest the sound thereof, but canst not tell whence it cometh, and whither it goeth: so is every one that is born of the Spirit. 9 Nicodemus answered and said unto him, How can these things be? 10 Jesus answered and said unto him, Art thou a master of Israel, and knowest not these things? 11 Verily, verily, I say unto thee, We speak that we do know, and testify that we have seen; and ye receive not our witness. 12 If I have told you earthly things, and ye believe not, how shall ye believe, if I tell you of heavenly things? 13 And no man hath ascended up to heaven, but he that came down from heaven, even the Son of man which is in heaven. 14 And as Moses lifted up the serpent in the wilderness, even so must the Son of man be lifted up: 15 That whosoever believeth in him should not perish, but have eternal life.

16 For God so loved the world, that he gave his only begotten Son, that whosoever believeth in him should not perish, but have everlasting life. 17 For God sent not his Son into the world to condemn the world; but that the world through him might be saved. 18 He that believeth on him is not condemned: but he that believeth not is condemned already, because he hath not believed in the name of the only begotten Son of God. 19 And this is the condemnation, that light is come into the world, and men loved darkness rather than light, because their deeds were evil. 20 For every one that doeth evil hateth the light, neither cometh to the light, lest his deed should be reproved. 21 But he that doeth truth cometh to the light, that his deeds may be made manifest, that they are wrought in God.

22 After these things came Jesus and his disciples into the land of Judea; and there he tarried with them, and baptized. 23 And John also was baptizing in Aenon near to Salim, because there was much water there: and they came, and were baptized. 24 For John was not yet cast into prison.

25 Then there arose a question between some of John's disciples and the Jews about purifying. 26 And they came unto John, and said unto him, Rabbi, he that was with thee beyond Jordan, to whom thou barest witness, behold, the same baptizeth, and all men come to him. 27 John answered and said, A man can receive nothing, except it be given him from heaven. 28 Ye yourselves bear me witness, that I said, I am not the Christ, but that I am sent before him. 29 He that hath the bride is the bridegroom: but the friend of the bridegroom, which standeth and heareth him, rejoiceth greatly because of the bridegroom's voice: this my joy therefore is fulfilled. 30 He must increase, but I must decrease.

31 He that cometh from above is above all: he that is of the earth

is earthly, and speaketh of the earth: he that cometh from heaven is above all. 32 And what he hath seen and heard, that he testifieth; and no man receiveth his testimony. 33 He that hath received his testimony hath set to his seal that God is true. 34 For he whom God hath sent speaketh the words of God: for God giveth not the Spirit by measure unto him. 35 The Father loveth the Son, and hath given all things into his hand. 36 He that believeth on the Son hath everlasting life: and he that believeth not the Son shall not see life; but the wrath of God abideth on him.

4 When therefore the Lord knew how the Pharisees had heard that Jesus made and baptized more disciples than John, 2 (Though Jesus himself baptized not, but his disciples,) 3 He left Judea, and departed again into Galilee. 4 And he must needs go through Samaria. 5 Then cometh he to a city of Samaria, which is called Sychar, near to the parcel of ground that Jacob gave to his son Joseph. 6 Now Jacob's well was there. Jesus therefore, being wearied with his journey, sat thus on the well: and it was about the sixth hour.

7 There cometh a woman of Samaria to draw water: Jesus saith unto her, Give me to drink. 8 (For his disciples were gone away unto the city to buy meat.) 9 Then saith the woman of Samaria unto him, How is it that thou, being a Jew, askest drink of me, which am a woman of Samaria? for the Jews have no dealings with the Samaritans. 10 Jesus answered and said unto her, If thou knewest the gift of God, and who it is that saith to thee, Give me to drink; thou wouldest have asked of him, and he would have given thee living water. 11 The woman saith unto him, Sir, thou hast nothing to draw with, and the well is deep: from whence then hast thou that living water? 12 Art thou greater than our father Jacob, which gave us the well, and drank thereof himself, and his children, and his cattle? 13 Jesus answered and said unto her, Whosoever drinketh of this water shall thirst again: 14 But whosoever drinketh of the water that I shall give him shall never thirst; but the water that I shall give him shall be in him a well of water springing up into everlasting life. 15 The woman saith unto him, Sir, give me this water, that I thirst not, neither come hither to draw.

16 Jesus saith unto her, Go, call thy husband, and come hither. 17 The woman answered and said, I have no husband. Jesus said unto her, Thou hast well said, I have no husband: 18 For thou hast had five husbands; and he whom thou now hast is not thy husband: in that saidst thou truly. 19 The woman saith unto him, Sir, I perceive that thou art a prophet. 20 Our fathers worshipped in this mountain; and ye say, that in Jerusalem is the place where men ought to worship. 21 Jesus saith unto her, Woman, believe me, the hour cometh, when ye shall neither in this mountain, nor yet at Jerusalem, worship the Father. 22 Ye worship ye know not what: we know what we worship; for salvation is of the Jews. 23 But the hour cometh, and now is, when the true worshippers shall worship the Father in spirit and in

truth: for the Father seeketh such to worship him. 24 God is a Spirit: and they that worship him must worship him in spirit and in truth. 25 The woman saith unto him, I know that Messias cometh, which is called Christ: when he is come, he will tell us all things. 26 Jesus saith unto her, I that speak unto thee am he.

27 And upon this came his disciples, and marveled that he talked with the woman: yet no man said, What seekest thou? or, Why talkest thou with her? 28 The woman then left her waterpot, and went her way into the city, and saith to the men, 29 Come, see a man, which told me all things that ever I did: is not this the Christ? 30 Then they went out of the city, and came unto him.

31 In the mean while his disciples prayed him, saying, Master, eat. 32 But he said unto them, I have meat to eat that ye know not of. 33 Therefore said the disciples one to another, Hath any man brought him aught to eat? 34 Jesus saith unto them, My meat is to do the will of him that sent me, and to finish his work. 35 Say not ye, There are yet four months, and then cometh harvest? behold, I say unto you, Lift up your eyes, and look on the fields; for they are white already to harvest. 36 And he that reapeth receiveth wages, and gathereth fruit unto life eternal: that both he that soweth and he that reapeth may rejoice together. 37 And herein is that saying true, One soweth, and another reapeth. 38 I sent you to reap that whereon ye bestowed no labor: other men labored, and ye are entered into their labors.

39 And many of the Samaritans of that city believed on him for the saying of the woman, which testified, He told me all that ever I did. 40 So when the Samaritans were come unto him, they besought him that he would tarry with them: and he abode there two days. 41 And many more believed because of his own word; 42 And said unto the woman, Now we believe, not because of thy saying: for we have heard him ourselves, and know that this is indeed the Christ, the Saviour of the world.

43 Now after two days he departed thence, and went into Galilee. 44 For Jesus himself testified, that a prophet hath no honor in his own country. 45 Then when he was come into Galilee, the Galileans received him, having seen all the things that he did at Jerusalem at the feast: for they also went unto the feast. 46 So Jesus came again into Cana of Galilee, where he made the water wine. And there was a certain nobleman, whose son was sick at Capernaum. 47 When he heard that Jesus was come out of Judea into Galilee, he went unto him, and besought him that he would come down, and heal his son: for he was at the point of death. 48 Then said Jesus unto him, Except ye see signs and wonders, ye will not believe. 49 The nobleman saith unto him, Sir, come down ere my child die. 50 Jesus saith unto him, Go thy way; thy son liveth. And the man believed the word that Jesus had spoken unto him, and he went his way. 51 And as he was now going down, his servants met him, and told him, saying, Thy son liveth. 52 Then inquired he of them the hour when he began

to amend. And they said unto him, Yesterday at the seventh hour the fever left him. 53 So the father knew that it was at the same hour, in the which Jesus said unto him, Thy son liveth: and himself believed, and his whole house. 54 This is again the second miracle that Jesus did, when he was come out of Judea into Galilee.

5 After this there was a feast of the Jews; and Jesus went up to Jerusalem. 2 Now there is at Jerusalem by the sheep market a pool, which is called in the Hebrew tongue Bethesda, having five porches. 3 In these lay a great multitude of impotent folk, of blind, halt, withered, waiting for the moving of the water. 4 For an angel went down at a certain season into the pool, and troubled the water: whosoever then first after the troubling of the water stepped in was made whole of whatsoever disease he had. 5 And a certain man was there, which had an infirmity thirty and eight years. 6 When Jesus saw him lie, and knew that he had been now a long time in that case, he saith unto him, Wilt thou be made whole? 7 The impotent man answered him, Sir, I have no man, when the water is troubled, to put me into the pool: but while I am coming, another steppeth down before me. 8 Jesus saith unto him, Rise, take up thy bed, and walk. 9 And immediately the man was made whole, and took up his bed, and walked: and on the same day was the sabbath.

10 The Jews therefore said unto him that was cured, It is the sabbath day: it is not lawful for thee to carry thy bed. 11 He answered them, He that made me whole, the same said unto me, Take up thy bed, and walk. 12 Then asked they him, What man is that which said unto thee, Take up thy bed, and walk? 13 And he that was healed wist not who it was: for Jesus had conveyed himself away, a multitude being in that place. 14 Afterward Jesus findeth him in the temple, and said unto him, Behold, thou art made whole: sin no more, lest a worse thing come unto thee. 15 The man departed, and told the Jews that it was Jesus, which had made him whole. 16 And therefore did the Jews persecute Jesus, and sought to slay him, because he had done these things on the sabbath day.

17 But Jesus answered them, My Father worketh hitherto, and I work. 18 Therefore the Jews sought the more to kill him, because he not only had broken the sabbath, but said also that God was his Father, making himself equal with God. 19 Then answered Jesus and said unto them, Verily, verily, I say unto you, The Son can do nothing of himself, but what he seeth the Father do: for what things soever he doeth, these also doeth the Son likewise. 20 For the Father loveth the Son, and showeth him all things that himself doeth: and he will show him greater works than these, that ye may marvel. 21 For as the Father raiseth up the dead, and quickeneth them; even so the Son quickeneth whom he will. 22 For the Father judgeth no man, but hath committed all judgment unto the Son: 23 That all men should honor the Son, even as they honor the Father. He that honoreth not the Son honoreth not the Father which hath sent him.

24 Verily, verily, I say unto you, He that heareth my word, and believeth on him that sent me, hath everlasting life, and shall not come into condemnation; but is passed from death unto life.

25 Verily, verily, I say unto you, The hour is coming, and now is, when the dead shall hear the voice of the Son of God: and they that hear shall live. 26 For as the Father hath life in himself; so hath he given to the Son to have life in himself; 27 And hath given him authority to execute judgment also, because he is the Son of man. 28 Marvel not at this: for the hour is coming, in the which all that are in the graves shall hear his voice, 29 And shall come forth; they that have done good, unto the resurrection of life; and they that have done evil, unto the resurrection of damnation.

30 I can of mine own self do nothing: as I hear, I judge: and my judgment is just; because I seek not mine own will, but the will of the Father which hath sent me. 31 If I bear witness of myself, my witness is not true. 32 There is another that beareth witness of me; and I know that the witness which he witnesseth of me is true. 33 Ye sent unto John, and he bare witness unto the truth. 34 But I receive not testimony from man: but these things I say, that ye might be saved. 35 He was a burning and a shining light: and ye were willing for a season to rejoice in his light. 36 But I have greater witness than that of John: for the works which the Father hath given me to finish, the same works that I do, bear witness of me, that the Father hath sent me. 37 And the Father himself, which hath sent me, hath borne witness of me. Ye have neither heard his voice at any time, nor seen his shape. 38 And ye have not his word abiding in you: for whom he hath sent, him ye believe not. 39 Search the Scriptures; for in them ye think ye have eternal life: and they are they which testify of me. 40 And ye will not come to me, that ye might have life. 41 I receive not honor from men. 42 But I know you, that ye have not the love of God in you. 43 I am come in my Father's name, and ye receive me not: if another shall come in his own name, him ye will receive. 44 How can ye believe, which receive honor one of another, and seek not the honor that cometh from God only? 45 Do not think that I will accuse you to the Father: there is one that accuseth you, even Moses, in whom ye trust. 46 For had ye believed Moses, ye would have believed me: for he wrote of me. 47 But if ye believe not his writings, how shall ye believe my words?

6 After these things Jesus went over the sea of Galilee, which is the sea of Tiberias. 2 And a great multitude followed him, because they saw his miracles which he did on them that were diseased. 3 And Jesus went up into a mountain, and there he sat with his disciples. 4 And the passover, a feast of the Jews, was nigh. 5 When Jesus then lifted up his eyes, and saw a great company come unto him, he saith unto Philip, Whence shall we buy bread, that these may eat? 6 And this he said to prove him: for he himself knew what he would do. 7 Philip answered him, Two hundred pennyworth of bread is not

sufficient for them, that every one of them may take a little. 8 One of his disciples, Andrew, Simon Peter's brother, saith unto him, 9 There is a lad here, which hath five barley loaves, and two small fishes: but what are they among so many? 10 And Jesus said, Make the men sit down. Now there was much grass in the place. So the men sat down, in number about five thousand. 11 And Jesus took the loaves; and when he had given thanks, he distributed to the disciples, and the disciples to them that were set down; and likewise of the fishes as much as they would. 12 When they were filled, he said unto his disciples, Gather up the fragments that remain, that nothing be lost. 13 Therefore they gathered them together, and filled twelve baskets with the fragments of the five barley loaves, which remained over and above unto them that had eaten. 14 Then those men, when they had seen the miracle that Jesus did, said, This is of a truth that Prophet that should come into the world. 15 When Jesus therefore perceived that they would come and take him by force, to make him a king, he departed again into a mountain himself alone.

16 And when even was now come, his disciples went down unto the sea, 17 And entered into a ship, and went over the sea toward Capernaum. And it was now dark, and Jesus was not come to them. 18 And the sea arose by reason of a great wind that blew. 19 So when they had rowed about five and twenty or thirty furlongs, they see Jesus walking on the sea, and drawing nigh unto the ship: and they were afraid. 20 But he saith unto them, It is I; be not afraid. 21 Then they willingly received him into the ship: and immediately the ship was at the land whither they went.

22 The day following, when the people, which stood on the other side of the sea, saw that there was none other boat there, save that one whereinto his disciples were entered, and that Jesus went not with his disciples into the boat, but that his disciples were gone away alone; 23 (Howbeit there came other boats from Tiberias nigh unto the place where they did eat bread, after that the Lord had given thanks:) 24 When the people therefore saw that Jesus was not there, neither his disciples, they also took shipping, and came to Capernaum, seeking for Jesus.

25 And when they had found him on the other side of the sea, they said unto him, Rabbi, when camest thou hither? 26 Jesus answered them and said, Verily, verily, I say unto you, Ye seek me, not because ye saw the miracles, but because ye did eat of the loaves, and were filled. 27 Labor not for the meat which perisheth, but for that meat which endureth unto everlasting life, which the Son of man shall give unto you: for him hath God the Father sealed. 28 Then said they unto him, What shall we do, that we might work the works of God? 29 Jesus answered and said unto them, This is the work of God, that ye believe on him whom he hath sent. 30 They said therefore unto him, What sign showest thou then, that we may see, and believe thee? what dost thou work? 31 Our fathers did eat manna in the

desert; as it is written, He gave them bread from heaven to eat.
32 Then Jesus said unto them, Verily, verily, I say unto you, Moses
gave you not that bread from heaven; but my Father giveth you the
true bread from heaven. 33 For the bread of God is he which cometh
down from heaven, and giveth life unto the world. 34 Then said they
unto him, Lord, evermore give us this bread.

35 And Jesus said unto them, I am the bread of life: he that cometh
to me shall never hunger; and he that believeth on me shall never
thirst. 36 But I said unto you, That ye also have seen me, and believe
not. 37 All that the Father giveth me shall come to me; and him
that cometh to me I will in no wise cast out. 38 For I came down
from heaven, not to do mine own will, but the will of him that sent
me. 39 And this is the Father's will which hath sent me, that of all
which he hath given me I should lose nothing, but should raise it up
again at the last day. 40 And this is the will of him that sent me, that
every one which seeth the Son, and believeth on him, may have everlasting life: and I will raise him up at the last day.

41 The Jews then murmured at him, because he said, I am the bread
which came down from heaven. 42 And they said, Is not this Jesus,
the son of Joseph, whose father and mother we know? how is it then
that he saith, I came down from heaven? 43 Jesus therefore answered
and said unto them, Murmur not among yourselves. 44 No man can
come to me, except the Father which hath sent me draw him: and I
will raise him up at the last day. 45 It is written in the prophets,
And they shall be all taught of God. Every man therefore that hath
heard, and hath learned of the Father, cometh unto me. 46 Not that
any man hath seen the Father, save he which is of God, he hath seen
the Father. 47 Verily, verily, I say unto you, He that believeth on me
hath everlasting life. 48 I am that bread of life. 49 Your fathers did
eat manna in the wilderness, and are dead. 50 This is the bread which
cometh down from heaven, that a man may eat thereof, and not die.
51 I am the living bread which came down from heaven: if any man
eat of this bread, he shall live for ever: and the bread that I will give
is my flesh, which I will give for the life of the world.

52 The Jews therefore strove among themselves, saying, How can
this man give us his flesh to eat? 53 Then Jesus said unto them,
Verily, verily, I say unto you, Except ye eat the flesh of the Son of
man, and drink his blood, ye have no life in you. 54 Whoso eateth
my flesh, and drinketh my blood, hath eternal life; and I will raise
him up at the last day. 55 For my flesh is meat indeed, and my blood
is drink indeed. 56 He that eateth my flesh, and drinketh my blood,
dwelleth in me, and I in him. 57 As the living Father hath sent me,
and I live by the Father; so he that eateth me, even he shall live by
me. 58 This is that bread which came down from heaven: not as
your fathers did eat manna, and are dead: he that eateth of this bread
shall live for ever. 59 These things said he in the synagogue, as he
taught in Capernaum.

## MOUNTING HOSTILITY

60 Many therefore of his disciples, when they had heard this, said, This is a hard saying; who can hear it? 61 When Jesus knew in himself that his disciples murmured at it, he said unto them, Doth this offend you? 62 What and if ye shall see the Son of man ascend up where he was before? 63 It is the Spirit that quickeneth; the flesh profiteth nothing: the words that I speak unto you, they are spirit, and they are life. 64 But there are some of you that believe not. For Jesus knew from the beginning who they were that believed not, and who should betray him. 65 And he said, Therefore said I unto you, that no man can come unto me, except it were given unto him of my Father.

66 From that time many of his disciples went back, and walked no more with him. 67 Then said Jesus unto the twelve, Will ye also go away? 68 Then Simon Peter answered him, Lord, to whom shall we go? thou hast the words of eternal life. 69 And we believe and are sure that thou art that Christ, the Son of the living God. 70 Jesus answered them, Have not I chosen you twelve, and one of you is a devil? 71 He spake of Judas Iscariot the son of Simon: for he it was that should betray him, being one of the twelve.

7  After these things Jesus walked in Galilee: for he would not walk in Jewry, because the Jews sought to kill him. 2 Now the Jews' feast of tabernacles was at hand. 3 His brethren therefore said unto him, Depart hence, and go into Judea, that thy disciples also may see the works that thou doest. 4 For there is no man that doeth any thing in secret, and he himself seeketh to be known openly. If thou do these things, show thyself to the world. 5 For neither did his brethren believe in him. 6 Then Jesus said unto them, My time is not yet come: but your time is always ready. 7 The world cannot hate you; but me it hateth, because I testify of it, that the works thereof are evil. 8 Go ye up unto this feast: I go not up yet unto this feast; for my time is not yet full come. 9 When he had said these words unto them, he abode still in Galilee.

10 But when his brethren were gone up, then went he also up unto the feast, not openly, but as it were in secret. 11 Then the Jews sought him at the feast, and said, Where is he? 12 And there was much murmuring among the people concerning him: for some said, He is a good man: others said, Nay; but he deceiveth the people. 13 Howbeit no man spake openly of him for fear of the Jews.

14 Now about the midst of the feast Jesus went up into the temple, and taught. 15 And the Jews marveled, saying, How knoweth this man letters, having never learned? 16 Jesus answered them, and said, My doctrine is not mine, but his that sent me. 17 If any man will do his will, he shall know of the doctrine, whether it be of God, or whether I speak of myself. 18 He that speaketh of himself seeketh his own glory: but he that seeketh his glory that sent him, the same is

true, and no unrighteousness is in him. 19 Did not Moses give you the law, and yet none of you keepeth the law? Why go ye about to kill me? 20 The people answered and said, Thou hast a devil: who goeth about to kill thee? 21 Jesus answered and said unto them, I have done one work, and ye all marvel. 22 Moses therefore gave unto you circumcision; (not because it is of Moses, but of the fathers;) and ye on the sabbath day circumcise a man. 23 If a man on the sabbath day receive circumcision, that the law of Moses should not be broken; are ye angry at me, because I have made a man every whit whole on the sabbath day? 24 Judge not according to the appearance, but judge righteous judgment.

25 Then said some of them of Jerusalem, Is not this he, whom they seek to kill? 26 But, lo, he speaketh boldly, and they say nothing unto him. Do the rulers know indeed that this is the very Christ? 27 Howbeit we know this man whence he is: but when Christ cometh, no man knoweth whence he is. 28 Then cried Jesus in the temple as he taught, saying, Ye both know me, and ye know whence I am: and I am not come of myself, but he that sent me is true, whom ye know not. 29 But I know him; for I am from him, and he hath sent me. 30 Then they sought to take him: but no man laid hands on him, because his hour was not yet come. 31 And many of the people believed on him, and said, When Christ cometh, will he do more miracles than these which this man hath done?

32 The Pharisees heard that the people murmured such things concerning him; and the Pharisees and the chief priests sent officers to take him. 33 Then said Jesus unto them, Yet a little while am I with you, and then I go unto him that sent me. 34 Ye shall seek me, and shall not find me: and where I am, thither ye cannot come. 35 Then said the Jews among themselves, Whither will he go, that we shall not find him? will he go unto the dispersed among the Gentiles, and teach the Gentiles? 36 What manner of saying is this that he said, Ye shall seek me, and shall not find me: and where I am, thither ye cannot come?

37 In the last day, that great day of the feast, Jesus stood and cried, saying, If any man thirst, let him come unto me, and drink. 38 He that believeth on me, as the Scripture hath said, out of his belly shall flow rivers of living water. 39 (But this spake he of the Spirit, which they that believe on him should receive: for the Holy Ghost was not yet given; because that Jesus was not yet glorified.)

40 Many of the people therefore, when they heard this saying, said, Of a truth this is the Prophet. 41 Others said, This is the Christ. But some said, Shall Christ come out of Galilee? 42 Hath not the Scripture said, That Christ cometh of the seed of David, and out of the town of Bethlehem, where David was? 43 So there was a division among the people because of him. 44 And some of them would have taken him; but no man laid hands on him.

45 Then came the officers to the chief priests and Pharisees; and they said unto them, Why have ye not brought him? 46 The officers

answered, Never man spake like this man. 47 Then answered them the Pharisees, Are ye also deceived? 48 Have any of the rulers or of the Pharisees believed on him? 49 But this people who knoweth not the law are cursed. 50 Nicodemus saith unto them, (he that came to Jesus by night, being one of them,) 51 Doth our law judge any man, before it hear him, and know what he doeth? 52 They answered and said unto him, Art thou also of Galilee? Search, and look: for out of Galilee ariseth no prophet.

8 53 And every man went unto his own house. 1 Jesus went unto the mount of Olives. 2 And early in the morning he came again into the temple, and all the people came unto him; and he sat down, and taught them. 3 And the scribes and Pharisees brought unto him a woman taken in adultery; and when they had set her in the midst, 4 They say unto him, Master, this woman was taken in adultery, in the very act. 5 Now Moses in the law commanded us, that such should be stoned: but what sayest thou? 6 This they said, tempting him, that they might have to accuse him. But Jesus stooped down, and with his finger wrote on the ground, as though he heard them not. 7 So when they continued asking him, he lifted up himself, and said unto them, He that is without sin among you, let him first cast a stone at her. 8 And again he stooped down, and wrote on the ground. 9 And they which heard it, being convicted by their own conscience, went out one by one, beginning at the eldest, even unto the last: and Jesus was left alone, and the woman standing in the midst. 10 When Jesus had lifted up himself, and saw none but the woman, he said unto her, Woman, where are those thine accusers? hath no man condemned thee? 11 She said, No man, Lord. And Jesus said unto her, Neither do I condemn thee: go, and sin no more.

12 Then spake Jesus again unto them, saying, I am the light of the world: he that followeth me shall not walk in darkness, but shall have the light of life. 13 The Pharisees therefore said unto him, Thou bearest record of thyself; thy record is not true. 14 Jesus answered and said unto them, Though I bear record of myself, yet my record is true: for I know whence I came, and whither I go; but ye cannot tell whence I come, and whither I go. 15 Ye judge after the flesh; I judge no man. 16 And yet if I judge, my judgment is true: for I am not alone, but I and the Father that sent me. 17 It is also written in your law, that the testimony of two men is true. 18 I am one that bear witness of myself, and the Father that sent me beareth witness of me. 19 Then said they unto him, Where is thy Father? Jesus answered, Ye neither know me, nor my Father: if ye had known me, ye should have known my Father also. 20 These words spake Jesus in the treasury, as he taught in the temple: and no man laid hands on him; for his hour was not yet come.

21 Then said Jesus again unto them, I go my way, and ye shall seek me, and shall die in your sins: whither I go, ye cannot come. 22 Then said the Jews, Will he kill himself? because he saith, Whither I go,

ye cannot come. 23 And he said unto them, Ye are from beneath; I am from above: ye are of this world; I am not of this world. 24 I said therefore unto you, that ye shall die in your sins: for if ye believe not that I am he, ye shall die in your sins. 25 Then said they unto him, Who art thou? And Jesus saith unto them, Even the same that I said unto you from the beginning. 26 I have many things to say and to judge of you: but he that sent me is true; and I speak to the world those things which I have heard of him. 27 They understood not that he spake to them of the Father. 28 Then said Jesus unto them, When ye have lifted up the Son of man, then shall ye know that I am he, and that I do nothing of myself; but as my Father hath taught me, I speak these things. 29 And he that sent me is with me: the Father hath not left me alone; for I do always those things that please him. 30 As he spake these words, many believed on him.

31 Then said Jesus to those Jews which believed on him, If ye continue in my word, then are ye my disciples indeed; 32 And ye shall know the truth, and the truth shall make you free. 33 They answered him, We be Abraham's seed, and were never in bondage to any man: how sayest thou, Ye shall be made free?

34 Jesus answered them, Verily, verily, I say unto you, Whosoever committeth sin is the servant of sin. 35 And the servant abideth not in the house for ever: but the Son abideth ever. 36 If the Son therefore shall make you free, ye shall be free indeed. 37 I know that ye are Abraham's seed; but ye seek to kill me, because my word hath no place in you. 38 I speak that which I have seen with my Father: and ye do that which ye have seen with your father.

39 They answered and said unto him, Abraham is our father. Jesus saith unto them, If ye were Abraham's children, ye would do the works of Abraham. 40 But now ye seek to kill me, a man that hath told you the truth, which I have heard of God: this did not Abraham. 41 Ye do the deeds of your father. Then said they to him, We be not born of fornication; we have one Father, even God. 42 Jesus said unto them, If God were your Father, ye would love me: for I proceeded forth and came from God; neither came I of myself, but he sent me. 43 Why do ye not understand my speech? even because ye cannot hear my word. 44 Ye are of your father the devil, and the lusts of your father ye will do: he was a murderer from the beginning, and abode not in the truth, because there is no truth in him. When he speaketh a lie, he speaketh of his own: for he is a liar, and the father of it. 45 And because I tell you the truth, ye believe me not. 46 Which of you convinceth me of sin? And if I say the truth, why do ye not believe me? 47 He that is of God heareth God's words: ye therefore hear them not, because ye are not of God.

48 Then answered the Jews, and said unto him, Say we not well that thou art a Samaritan, and hast a devil? 49 Jesus answered, I have not a devil; but I honor my Father, and ye do dishonor me. 50 And I seek not mine own glory: there is one that seeketh and judgeth. 51 Verily, verily, I say unto you, If a man keep my saying, he shall never

see death. 52 Then said the Jews unto him, Now we know that thou hast a devil. Abraham is dead, and the prophets; and thou sayest, If a man keep my saying, he shall never taste of death. 53 Art thou greater than our father Abraham, which is dead? and the prophets are dead: whom makest thou thyself? 54 Jesus answered, If I honor myself, my honor is nothing: it is my Father that honoreth me; of whom ye say, that he is your God: 55 Yet ye have not known him; but I know him: and if I should say, I know him not, I shall be a liar like unto you: but I know him, and keep his saying. 56 Your father Abraham rejoiced to see my day: and he saw it, and was glad. 57 Then said the Jews unto him, Thou art not yet fifty years old, and hast thou seen Abraham? 58 Jesus said unto them, Verily, verily, I say unto you, Before Abraham was, I am. 59 Then took they up stones to cast at him: but Jesus hid himself, and went out of the temple, going through the midst of them, and so passed by.

9 And as Jesus passed by, he saw a man which was blind from his birth. 2 And his disciples asked him, saying, Master, who did sin, this man, or his parents, that he was born blind? 3 Jesus answered, Neither hath this man sinned, nor his parents: but that the works of God should be made manifest in him. 4 I must work the works of him that sent me, while it is day: the night cometh, when no man can work. 5 As long as I am in the world, I am the light of the world. 6 When he had thus spoken, he spat on the ground, and made clay of the spittle, and he anointed the eyes of the blind man with the clay, 7 And said unto him, Go, wash in the pool of Siloam, (which is by interpretation, Sent.) He went his way therefore, and washed, and came seeing. 8 The neighbors therefore, and they which before had seen him that he was blind, said, Is not this he that sat and begged? 9 Some said, This is he: others said, He is like him: but he said, I am he. 10 Therefore said they unto him, How were thine eyes opened? 11 He answered and said, A man that is called Jesus made clay, and anointed mine eyes, and said unto me, Go to the pool of Siloam, and wash: and I went and washed, and I received sight. 12 Then said they unto him, Where is he? He said, I know not.

13 They brought to the Pharisees him that aforetime was blind. 14 And it was the sabbath day when Jesus made the clay, and opened his eyes. 15 Then again the Pharisees also asked him how he had received his sight. He said unto them, He put clay upon mine eyes, and I washed, and do see. 16 Therefore said some of the Pharisees, This man is not of God, because he keepeth not the sabbath day. Others said, How can a man that is a sinner do such miracles? And there was a division among them. 17 They say unto the blind man again, What sayest thou of him, that he hath opened thine eyes? He said, He is a prophet.

18 But the Jews did not believe concerning him, that he had been blind, and received his sight, until they called the parents of him that had received his sight. 19 And they asked them, saying, Is this your

son, who ye say was born blind? how then doth he now see? 20 His parents answered them and said, We know that this is our son, and that he was born blind: 21 But by what means he now seeth, we know not; or who hath opened his eyes, we know not: he is of age; ask him: he shall speak for himself. 22 These words spake his parents, because they feared the Jews: for the Jews had agreed already, that if any man did confess that he was Christ, he should be put out of the synagogue. 23 Therefore said his parents, He is of age; ask him.

24 Then again called they the man that was blind, and said unto him, Give God the praise: we know that this man is a sinner. 25 He answered and said, Whether he be a sinner or no, I know not: one thing I know, that, whereas I was blind, now I see. 26 Then said they to him again, What did he to thee? how opened he thine eyes? 27 He answered them, I have told you already, and ye did not hear: wherefore would ye hear it again? will ye also be his disciples? 28 Then they reviled him, and said, Thou art his disciple; but we are Moses' disciples. 29 We know that God spake unto Moses: as for this fellow, we know not from whence he is. 30 The man answered and said unto them, Why herein is a marvelous thing, that ye know not from whence he is, and yet he hath opened mine eyes. 31 Now we know that God heareth not sinners: but if any man be a worshipper of God, and doeth his will, him he heareth. 32 Since the world began was it not heard that any man opened the eyes of one that was born blind. 33 If this man were not of God, he could do nothing. 34 They answered and said unto him, Thou wast altogether born in sins, and dost thou teach us? And they cast him out.

35 Jesus heard that they had cast him out; and when he had found him, he said unto him, Dost thou believe on the Son of God? 36 He answered and said, Who is he, Lord, that I might believe on him? 37 And Jesus said unto him, Thou hast both seen him, and it is he that talketh with thee. 38 And he said, Lord, I believe. And he worshipped him. 39 And Jesus said, For judgment I am come into this world, that they which see not might see; and that they which see might be made blind. 40 And some of the Pharisees which were with him heard these words, and said unto him, Are we blind also? 41 Jesus said unto them, If ye were blind, ye should have no sin: but now ye say, We see; therefore your sin remaineth.

10 Verily, verily, I say unto you, He that entereth not by the door into the sheepfold, but climbeth up some other way, the same is a thief and a robber. 2 But he that entereth in by the door is the shepherd of the sheep. 3 To him the porter openeth; and the sheep hear his voice: and he calleth his own sheep by name, and leadeth them out. 4 And when he putteth forth his own sheep, he goeth before them, and the sheep follow him: for they know his voice. 5 And a stranger will they not follow, but will flee from him; for they know not the voice of strangers. 6 This parable spake Jesus unto them: but they understood not what things they were which he spake unto them.

7 Then said Jesus unto them again, Verily, verily, I say unto you, I am the door of the sheep. 8 All that ever came before me are thieves and robbers: but the sheep did not hear them. 9 I am the door: by me if any man enter in, he shall be saved, and shall go in and out, and find pasture. 10 The thief cometh not, but for to steal, and to kill, and to destroy: I am come that they might have life, and that they might have it more abundantly. 11 I am the good shepherd: the good shepherd giveth his life for the sheep. 12 But he that is a hireling, and not the shepherd, whose own the sheep are not, seeth the wolf coming, and leaveth the sheep, and fleeth; and the wolf catcheth them, and scattereth the sheep. 13 The hireling fleeth, because he is a hireling, and careth not for the sheep. 14 I am the good shepherd, and know my sheep, and am known of mine. 15 As the Father knoweth me, even so know I the Father: and I lay down my life for the sheep. 16 And other sheep I have, which are not of this fold: them also I must bring, and they shall hear my voice; and there shall be one fold, and one shepherd. 17 Therefore doth my Father love me, because I lay down my life, that I might take it again. 18 No man taketh it from me, but I lay it down of myself. I have power to lay it down, and I have power to take it again. This commandment have I received of my Father.

19 There was a division therefore again among the Jews for these sayings. 20 And many of them said, He hath a devil, and is mad; why hear ye him? 21 Others said, These are not the words of him that hath a devil. Can a devil open the eyes of the blind?

22 And it was at Jerusalem the feast of the dedication, and it was winter. 23 And Jesus walked in the temple in Solomon's porch. 24 Then came the Jews round about him, and said unto him, How long dost thou make us to doubt? If thou be the Christ, tell us plainly. 25 Jesus answered them, I told you, and ye believed not: the works that I do in my Father's name, they bear witness of me. 26 But ye believe not, because ye are not of my sheep, as I said unto you. 27 My sheep hear my voice, and I know them, and they follow me: 28 And I give unto them eternal life; and they shall never perish, neither shall any man pluck them out of my hand. 29 My Father, which gave them me, is greater than all; and no man is able to pluck them out of my Father's hand. 30 I and my Father are one.

31 Then the Jews took up stones again to stone him. 32 Jesus answered them, Many good works have I showed you from my Father; for which of those works do ye stone me? 33 The Jews answered him, saying, For a good work we stone thee not; but for blasphemy; and because that thou, being a man, makest thyself God. 34 Jesus answered them, Is it not written in your law, I said, Ye are gods? 35 If he called them gods, unto whom the word of God came, and the Scripture cannot be broken; 36 Say ye of him, whom the Father hath sanctified, and sent into the world, Thou blasphemest; because I said, I am the Son of God? 37 If I do not the works of my Father, believe me not. 38 But if I do, though ye believe not me, believe the

works; that ye may know, and believe, that the Father is in me, and I in him. 39 Therefore they sought again to take him; but he escaped out of their hand, 40 And went away again beyond Jordan into the place where John at first baptized; and there he abode. 41 And many resorted unto him, and said, John did no miracle: but all things that John spake of this man were true. 42 And many believed on him there.

11  Now a certain man was sick, named Lazarus, of Bethany, the town of Mary and her sister Martha. 2 (It was that Mary which anointed the Lord with ointment, and wiped his feet with her hair, whose brother Lazarus was sick.) 3 Therefore his sisters sent unto him, saying, Lord, behold, he whom thou lovest is sick. 4 When Jesus heard that, he said, This sickness is not unto death, but for the glory of God, that the Son of God might be glorified thereby.

5 Now Jesus loved Martha, and her sister, and Lazarus. 6 When he had heard therefore that he was sick, he abode two days still in the same place where he was. 7 Then after that saith he to his disciples, Let us go into Judea again. 8 His disciples say unto him, Master, the Jews of late sought to stone thee; and goest thou thither again? 9 Jesus answered, Are there not twelve hours in the day? If any man walk in the day, he stumbleth not, because he seeth the light of this world. 10 But if a man walk in the night, he stumbleth, because there is no light in him. 11 These things said he: and after that he saith unto them, Our friend Lazarus sleepeth; but I go, that I may awake him out of sleep. 12 Then said his disciples, Lord, if he sleep, he shall do well. 13 Howbeit Jesus spake of his death: but they thought that he had spoken of taking of rest in sleep. 14 Then said Jesus unto them plainly, Lazarus is dead. 15 And I am glad for your sakes that I was not there, to the intent ye may believe; nevertheless let us go unto him. 16 Then said Thomas, which is called Didymus, unto his fellow disciples, Let us also go, that we may die with him.

17 Then when Jesus came, he found that he had lain in the grave four days already. 18 Now Bethany was nigh unto Jerusalem, about fifteen furlongs off: 19 And many of the Jews came to Martha and Mary, to comfort them concerning their brother. 20 Then Martha, as soon as she heard that Jesus was coming, went and met him: but Mary sat still in the house. 21 Then said Martha unto Jesus, Lord, if thou hadst been here, my brother had not died. 22 But I know, that even now, whatsoever thou wilt ask of God, God will give it thee. 23 Jesus saith unto her, Thy brother shall rise again. 24 Martha saith unto him, I know that he shall rise again in the resurrection at the last day. 25 Jesus said unto her, I am the resurrection, and the life: he that believeth in me, though he were dead, yet shall he live: 26 And whosoever liveth and believeth in me shall never die. Believest thou this? 27 She saith unto him, Yea, Lord: I believe that thou art the Christ, the Son of God, which should come into the world.

28 And when she had so said, she went her way, and called Mary her sister secretly, saying, The Master is come, and calleth for thee.

29 As soon as she heard that, she arose quickly, and came unto him. 30 Now Jesus was not yet come into the town, but was in that place where Martha met him. 31 The Jews then which were with her in the house, and comforted her, when they saw Mary, that she rose up hastily and went out, followed her, saying, She goeth unto the grave to weep there. 32 Then when Mary was come where Jesus was, and saw him, she fell down at his feet, saying unto him, Lord, if thou hadst been here, my brother had not died. 33 When Jesus therefore saw her weeping, and the Jews also weeping which came with her, he groaned in the spirit, and was troubled, 34 And said, Where have ye laid him? They say unto him, Lord, come and see. 35 Jesus wept. 36 Then said the Jews, Behold how he loved him! 37 And some of them said, Could not this man, which opened the eyes of the blind, have caused that even this man should not have died?

38 Jesus therefore again groaning in himself cometh to the grave. It was a cave, and a stone lay upon it. 39 Jesus said, Take ye away the stone. Martha, the sister of him that was dead, saith unto him, Lord, by this time he stinketh: for he hath been dead four days. 40 Jesus saith unto her, Said I not unto thee, that, if thou wouldest believe, thou shouldest see the glory of God? 41 Then they took away the stone from the place where the dead was laid. And Jesus lifted up his eyes, and said, Father, I thank thee that thou hast heard me. 42 And I knew that thou hearest me always: but because of the people which stand by I said it, that they may believe that thou hast sent me. 43 And when he thus had spoken, he cried with a loud voice, Lazarus, come forth. 44 And he that was dead came forth, bound hand and foot with graveclothes; and his face was bound about with a napkin. Jesus saith unto them, Loose him, and let him go.

45 Then many of the Jews which came to Mary, and had seen the things which Jesus did, believed on him. 46 But some of them went their ways to the Pharisees, and told them what things Jesus had done. 47 Then gathered the chief priests and the Pharisees a council, and said, What do we? for this man doeth many miracles. 48 If we let him thus alone, all men will believe on him; and the Romans shall come and take away both our place and nation. 49 And one of them, named Caiaphas, being the high priest that same year, said unto them, Ye know nothing at all, 50 Nor consider that it is expedient for us, that one man should die for the people, and that the whole nation perish not. 51 And this spake he not of himself: but being high priest that year, he prophesied that Jesus should die for that nation; 52 And not for that nation only, but that also he should gather together in one the children of God that were scattered abroad. 53 Then from that day forth they took counsel together for to put him to death.

54 Jesus therefore walked no more openly among the Jews; but went thence unto a country near to the wilderness, into a city called Ephraim, and there continued with his disciples.

55 And the Jews' passover was nigh at hand: and many went out of the country up to Jerusalem before the passover, to purify themselves.

56 Then sought they for Jesus, and spake among themselves, as they stood in the temple, What think ye, that he will not come to the feast? 57 Now both the chief priests and the Pharisees had given a commandment, that, if any man knew where he were, he should show it, that they might take him.

12 Then Jesus six days before the passover came to Bethany, where Lazarus was which had been dead, whom he raised from the dead. 2 There they made him a supper; and Martha served: but Lazarus was one of them that sat at the table with him. 3 Then took Mary a pound of ointment of spikenard, very costly, and anointed the feet of Jesus, and wiped his feet with her hair: and the house was filled with the odor of the ointment. 4 Then saith one of his disciples, Judas Iscariot, Simon's son, which should betray him, 5 Why was not this ointment sold for three hundred pence, and given to the poor? 6 This he said, not that he cared for the poor; but because he was a thief, and had the bag, and bare what was put therein. 7 Then said Jesus, Let her alone: against the day of my burying hath she kept this. 8 For the poor always ye have with you; but me ye have not always.

9 Much people of the Jews therefore knew that he was there: and they came not for Jesus' sake only, but that they might see Lazarus also, whom he had raised from the dead. 10 But the chief priests consulted that they might put Lazarus also to death; 11 Because that by reason of him many of the Jews went away, and believed on Jesus.

12 On the next day much people that were come to the feast, when they heard that Jesus was coming to Jerusalem, 13 Took branches of palm trees, and went forth to meet him, and cried,
> Hosanna:
> Blessed is the King of Israel
> That cometh in the name of the Lord.

14 And Jesus, when he had found a young ass, sat thereon; as it is written,
> 15 Fear not, daughter of Sion:
> Behold, thy King cometh,
> Sitting on an ass's colt.

16 These things understood not his disciples at the first: but when Jesus was glorified, then remembered they that these things were written of him, and that they had done these things unto him. 17 The people therefore that was with him when he called Lazarus out of his grave, and raised him from the dead, bare record. 18 For this cause the people also met him, for that they heard that he had done this miracle. 19 The Pharisees therefore said among themselves, Perceive ye how ye prevail nothing? behold, the world is gone after him.

20 And there were certain Greeks among them that came up to worship at the feast: 21 The same came therefore to Philip, which was of Bethsaida of Galilee, and desired him, saying, Sir, we would see Jesus. 22 Philip cometh and telleth Andrew: and again Andrew and Philip tell Jesus. 23 And Jesus answered them, saying, The hour is

come, that the Son of man should be glorified. 24 Verily, verily, I say unto you, Except a corn of wheat fall into the ground and die, it abideth alone: but if it die, it bringeth forth much fruit. 25 He that loveth his life shall lose it; and he that hateth his life in this world shall keep it unto life eternal. 26 If any man serve me, let him follow me; and where I am, there shall also my servant be: if any man serve me, him will my Father honor.

27 Now is my soul troubled; and what shall I say? Father, save me from this hour: but for this cause came I unto this hour. 28 Father, glorify thy name. Then came there a voice from heaven, saying, I have both glorified it, and will glorify it again. 29 The people therefore that stood by, and heard it, said that it thundered: others said, An angel spake to him. 30 Jesus answered and said, This voice came not because of me, but for your sakes. 31 Now is the judgment of this world: now shall the prince of this world be cast out. 32 And I, if I be lifted up from the earth, will draw all men unto me. 33 This he said, signifying what death he should die. 34 The people answered him, We have heard out of the law that Christ abideth for ever: and how sayest thou, The Son of man must be lifted up? who is this Son of man? 35 Then Jesus said unto them, Yet a little while is the light with you. Walk while ye have the light, lest darkness come upon you: for he that walketh in darkness knoweth not whither he goeth. 36 While ye have light, believe in the light, that ye may be the children of light.

These things spake Jesus, and departed, and did hide himself from them. 37 But though he had done so many miracles before them, yet they believe not on him: 38 That the saying of Esaias the prophet might be fulfilled, which he spake,

Lord, who hath believed our report?
And to whom hath the arm of the Lord been revealed?

39 Therefore they could not believe, because that Esaias said again,
40 He hath blinded their eyes,
And hardened their heart;
That they should not see with their eyes,
Nor understand with their heart,
And be converted, and I should heal them.

41 These things said Esaias, when he saw his glory, and spake of him. 42 Nevertheless among the chief rulers also many believed on him; but because of the Pharisees they did not confess him, lest they should be put out of the synagogue: 43 For they loved the praise of men more than the praise of God.

44 Jesus cried and said, He that believeth on me, believeth not on me, but on him that sent me. 45 And he that seeth me seeth him that sent me. 46 I am come a light into the world, that whosoever believeth on me should not abide in darkness. 47 And if any man hear my words, and believe not, I judge him not: for I came not to judge the world, but to save the world. 48 He that rejecteth me, and receiveth not my words, hath one that judgeth him: the word that I

have spoken, the same shall judge him in the last day. 49 For I have not spoken of myself; but the Father which sent me, he gave me a commandment, what I should say, and what I should speak. 50 And I know that his commandment is life everlasting: whatsoever I speak therefore, even as the Father said unto me, so I speak.

## DEEPER INSIGHT

13 Now before the feast of the passover, when Jesus knew that his hour was come that he should depart out of this world unto the Father, having loved his own which were in the world, he loved them unto the end. 2 And supper being ended, the devil having now put into the heart of Judas Iscariot, Simon's son, to betray him; 3 Jesus knowing that the Father had given all things into his hands, and that he was come from God, and went to God; 4 He riseth from supper, and laid aside his garments; and took a towel, and girded himself. 5 After that he poureth water into a basin, and began to wash the disciples' feet, and to wipe them with the towel wherewith he was girded. 6 Then cometh he to Simon Peter: and Peter saith unto him, Lord, dost thou wash my feet? 7 Jesus answered and said unto him, What I do thou knowest not now; but thou shalt know hereafter. 8 Peter saith unto him, Thou shalt never wash my feet. Jesus answered him, If I wash thee not, thou hast no part with me. 9 Simon Peter saith unto him, Lord, not my feet only, but also my hands and my head. 10 Jesus saith to him, He that is washed needeth not save to wash his feet, but is clean every whit: and ye are clean, but not all. 11 For he knew who should betray him; therefore said he, Ye are not all clean.

12 So after he had washed their feet, and had taken his garments, and was set down again, he said unto them, Know ye what I have done to you? 13 Ye call me Master and Lord: and ye say well; for so I am. 14 If I then, your Lord and Master, have washed your feet; ye also ought to wash one another's feet. 15 For I have given you an example, that ye should do as I have done to you. 16 Verily, verily, I say unto you, The servant is not greater than his lord; neither he that is sent greater than he that sent him. 17 If ye know these things, happy are ye if ye do them. 18 I speak not of you all: I know whom I have chosen: but that the Scripture may be fulfilled,

> He that eateth bread with me
> Hath lifted up his heel against me.

19 Now I tell you before it come, that, when it is come to pass, ye may believe that I am he. 20 Verily, verily, I say unto you, He that receiveth whomsoever I send receiveth me; and he that receiveth me receiveth him that sent me.

21 When Jesus had thus said, he was troubled in spirit, and testified, and said, Verily, verily, I say unto you, that one of you shall betray me. 22 Then the disciples looked one on another, doubting of whom he spake. 23 Now there was leaning on Jesus' bosom one of his dis-

ciples, whom Jesus loved. 24 Simon Peter therefore beckoned to him, that he should ask who it should be of whom he spake. 25 He then lying on Jesus' breast saith unto him, Lord, who is it? 26 Jesus answered, He it is, to whom I shall give a sop, when I have dipped it. And when he had dipped the sop, he gave it to Judas Iscariot, the son of Simon. 27 And after the sop Satan entered into him. Then said Jesus unto him, That thou doest, do quickly. 28 Now no man at the table knew for what intent he spake this unto him. 29 For some of them thought, because Judas had the bag, that Jesus had said unto him, Buy those things that we have need of against the feast; or, that he should give something to the poor. 30 He then, having received the sop, went immediately out; and it was night.

31 Therefore, when he was gone out, Jesus said, Now is the Son of man glorified, and God is glorified in him. 32 If God be glorified in him, God shall also glorify him in himself, and shall straightway glorify him. 33 Little children, yet a little while I am with you. Ye shall seek me; and as I said unto the Jews, Whither I go, ye cannot come; so now I say to you. 34 A new commandment I give unto you, That ye love one another; as I have loved you, that ye also love one another. 35 By this shall all men know that ye are my disciples, if ye have love one to another.

36 Simon Peter said unto him, Lord, whither goest thou? Jesus answered him, Whither I go, thou canst not follow me now; but thou shalt follow me afterward. 37 Peter said unto him, Lord, why cannot I follow thee now? I will lay down my life for thy sake. 38 Jesus answered him, Wilt thou lay down thy life for my sake? Verily, verily, I say unto thee, The cock shall not crow, till thou hast denied me thrice.

14   Let not your heart be troubled: ye believe in God, believe also in me. 2 In my Father's house are many mansions: if it were not so, I would have told you. I go to prepare a place for you. 3 And if I go and prepare a place for you, I will come again, and receive you unto myself; that where I am, there ye may be also. 4 And whither I go ye know, and the way ye know. 5 Thomas saith unto him, Lord, we know not whither thou goest; and how can we know the way? 6 Jesus saith unto him, I am the way, the truth, and the life: no man cometh unto the Father, but by me. 7 If ye had known me, ye should have known my Father also: and from henceforth ye know him, and have seen him.

8 Philip saith unto him, Lord, show us the Father, and it sufficeth us. 9 Jesus saith unto him, Have I been so long time with you, and yet hast thou not known me, Philip? he that hath seen me hath seen the Father; and how sayest thou then, Show us the Father? 10 Believest thou not that I am in the Father, and the Father in me? the words that I speak unto you I speak not of myself: but the Father that dwelleth in me, he doeth the works. 11 Believe me that I am in the Father, and the Father in me: or else believe me for the very works' sake.

12 Verily, verily, I say unto you, He that believeth on me, the works that I do shall he do also; and greater works than these shall he do; because I go unto my Father. 13 And whatsoever ye shall ask in my name, that will I do, that the Father may be glorified in the Son. 14 If ye shall ask any thing in my name, I will do it.

15 If ye love me, keep my commandments. 16 And I will pray the Father, and he shall give you another Comforter, that he may abide with you for ever; 17 Even the Spirit of truth; whom the world cannot receive, because it seeth him not, neither knoweth him: but ye know him; for he dwelleth with you, and shall be in you.

18 I will not leave you comfortless: I will come to you. 19 Yet a little while, and the world seeth me no more; but ye see me: because I live, ye shall live also. 20 At that day ye shall know that I am in my Father, and ye in me, and I in you. 21 He that hath my commandments, and keepeth them, he it is that loveth me: and he that loveth me shall be loved of my Father, and I will love him, and will manifest myself to him. 22 Judas saith unto him, not Iscariot, Lord, how is it that thou wilt manifest thyself unto us, and not unto the world? 23 Jesus answered and said unto him, If a man love me, he will keep my words: and my Father will love him, and we will come unto him, and make our abode with him. 24 He that loveth me not keepeth not my sayings: and the word which ye hear is not mine, but the Father's which sent me.

25 These things have I spoken unto you, being yet present with you. 26 But the Comforter, which is the Holy Ghost, whom the Father will send in my name, he shall teach you all things, and bring all things to your remembrance, whatsoever I have said unto you. 27 Peace I leave with you, my peace I give unto you: not as the world giveth, give I unto you. Let not your heart be troubled, neither let it be afraid. 28 Ye have heard how I said unto you, I go away, and come again unto you. If ye loved me, ye would rejoice, because I said, I go unto the Father: for my Father is greater than I. 29 And now I have told you before it come to pass, that, when it is come to pass, ye might believe. 30 Hereafter I will not talk much with you: for the prince of this world cometh, and hath nothing in me. 31 But that the world may know that I love the Father; and as the Father gave me commandment, even so I do. Arise, let us go hence.

15 I am the true vine, and my Father is the husbandman. 2 Every branch in me that beareth not fruit he taketh away: and every branch that beareth fruit, he purgeth it, that it may bring forth more fruit. 3 Now ye are clean through the word which I have spoken unto you. 4 Abide in me, and I in you. As the branch cannot bear fruit of itself, except it abide in the vine; no more can ye, except ye abide in me. 5 I am the vine, ye are the branches. He that abideth in me, and I in him, the same bringeth forth much fruit: for without me ye can do nothing. 6 If a man abide not in me, he is cast forth as a branch, and is withered; and men gather them, and cast them into the fire, and

they are burned. 7 If ye abide in me, and my words abide in you, ye shall ask what ye will, and it shall be done unto you. 8 Herein is my Father glorified, that ye bear much fruit; so shall ye be my disciples.

9 As the Father hath loved me, so have I loved you: continue ye in my love. 10 If ye keep my commandments, ye shall abide in my love; even as I have kept my Father's commandments, and abide in his love. 11 These things have I spoken unto you, that my joy might remain in you, and that your joy might be full.

12 This is my commandment, That ye love one another, as I have loved you. 13 Greater love hath no man than this, that a man lay down his life for his friends. 14 Ye are my friends, if ye do whatsoever I command you. 15 Henceforth I call you not servants; for the servant knoweth not what his lord doeth: but I have called you friends; for all things that I have heard of my Father I have made known unto you. 16 Ye have not chosen me, but I have chosen you, and ordained you, that ye should go and bring forth fruit, and that your fruit should remain; that whatsoever ye shall ask of the Father in my name, he may give it you. 17 These things I command you, that ye love one another.

18 If the world hate you, ye know that it hated me before it hated you. 19 If ye were of the world, the world would love his own; but because ye are not of the world, but I have chosen you out of the world, therefore the world hateth you. 20 Remember the word that I said unto you, The servant is not greater than his lord. If they have persecuted me, they will also persecute you; if they have kept my saying, they will keep yours also. 21 But all these things will they do unto you for my name's sake, because they know not him that sent me. 22 If I had not come and spoken unto them, they had not had sin; but now they have no cloak for their sin. 23 He that hateth me hateth my Father also. 24 If I had not done among them the works which none other man did, they had not had sin: but now have they both seen and hated both me and my Father. 25 But this cometh to pass, that the word might be fulfilled that is written in their law, They hated me without a cause.

26 But when the Comforter is come, whom I will send unto you from the Father, even the Spirit of truth, which proceedeth from the Father, he shall testify of me: 27 And ye also shall bear witness, because ye have been with me from the beginning.

16 These things have I spoken unto you, that ye should not be offended. 2 They shall put you out of the synagogues: yea, the time cometh, that whosoever killeth you will think that he doeth God service. 3 And these things will they do unto you, because they have not known the Father, nor me. 4 But these things have I told you, that when the time shall come, ye may remember that I told you of them. And these things I said not unto you at the beginning, because I was with you. 5 But now I go my way to him that sent me; and none of you asketh me, Whither goest thou? 6 But because I have said

these things unto you, sorrow hath filled your heart. 7 Nevertheless I tell you the truth; It is expedient for you that I go away: for if I go not away, the Comforter will not come unto you; but if I depart, I will send him unto you. 8 And when he is come, he will reprove the world of sin, and of righteousness, and of judgment: 9 Of sin, because they believe not on me; 10 Of righteousness, because I go to my Father, and ye see me no more; 11 Of judgment, because the prince of this world is judged.

12 I have yet many things to say unto you, but ye cannot bear them now. 13 Howbeit when he, the Spirit of truth, is come, he will guide you into all truth: for he shall not speak of himself; but whatsoever he shall hear, that shall he speak: and he will show you things to come. 14 He shall glorify me: for he shall receive of mine, and shall show it unto you. 15 All things that the Father hath are mine: therefore said I, that he shall take of mine, and shall show it unto you.

16 A little while, and ye shall not see me: and again, a little while, and ye shall see me, because I go to the Father. 17 Then said some of his disciples among themselves, What is this that he saith unto us, A little while, and ye shall not see me: and again, a little while, and ye shall see me: and, Because I go to the Father? 18 They said therefore, What is this that he saith, A little while? we cannot tell what he saith. 19 Now Jesus knew that they were desirous to ask him, and said unto them, Do ye inquire among yourselves of that I said, A little while, and ye shall not see me: and again, a little while, and ye shall see me? 20 Verily, verily, I say unto you, That ye shall weep and lament, but the world shall rejoice; and ye shall be sorrowful, but your sorrow shall be turned into joy. 21 A woman when she is in travail hath sorrow, because her hour is come: but as soon as she is delivered of the child, she remembereth no more the anguish, for joy that a man is born into the world. 22 And ye now therefore have sorrow: but I will see you again, and your heart shall rejoice, and your joy no man taketh from you. 23 And in that day ye shall ask me nothing. Verily, verily, I say unto you, Whatsoever ye shall ask the Father in my name, he will give it you. 24 Hitherto have ye asked nothing in my name: ask, and ye shall receive, that your joy may be full.

25 These things have I spoken unto you in proverbs: but the time cometh, when I shall no more speak unto you in proverbs, but I shall show you plainly of the Father. 26 At that day ye shall ask in my name: and I say not unto you, that I will pray the Father for you: 27 For the Father himself loveth you, because ye have loved me, and have believed that I came out from God. 28 I came forth from the Father, and am come into the world: again, I leave the world, and go to the Father.

29 His disciples said unto him, Lo, now speakest thou plainly, and speakest no proverb. 30 Now are we sure that thou knowest all things, and needest not that any man should ask thee: by this we believe that thou camest forth from God. 31 Jesus answered them, Do ye now

believe? 32 Behold, the hour cometh, yea, is now come, that ye shall be scattered, every man to his own, and shall leave me alone: and yet I am not alone, because the Father is with me. 33 These things I have spoken unto you, that in me ye might have peace. In the world ye shall have tribulation: but be of good cheer; I have overcome the world.

17 These words spake Jesus, and lifted up his eyes to heaven, and said, Father, the hour is come; glorify thy Son, that thy Son also may glorify thee: 2 As thou hast given him power over all flesh, that he should give eternal life to as many as thou hast given him. 3 And this is life eternal, that they might know thee the only true God, and Jesus Christ, whom thou hast sent. 4 I have glorified thee on the earth: I have finished the work which thou gavest me to do. 5 And now, O Father, glorify thou me with thine own self with the glory which I had with thee before the world was.

6 I have manifested thy name unto the men which thou gavest me out of the world: thine they were, and thou gavest them me; and they have kept thy word. 7 Now they have known that all things whatsoever thou hast given me are of thee. 8 For I have given unto them the words which thou gavest me; and they have received them, and have known surely that I came out from thee, and they have believed that thou didst send me. 9 I pray for them: I pray not for the world, but for them which thou hast given me; for they are thine. 10 And all mine are thine, and thine are mine; and I am glorified in them. 11 And now I am no more in the world, but these are in the world, and I come to thee. Holy Father, keep through thine own name those whom thou hast given me, that they may be one, as we are. 12 While I was with them in the world, I kept them in thy name: those that thou gavest me I have kept, and none of them is lost, but the son of perdition; that the Scripture might be fulfilled. 13 And now come I to thee; and these things I speak in the world, that they might have my joy fulfilled in themselves. 14 I have given them thy word; and the world hath hated them, because they are not of the world, even as I am not of the world. 15 I pray not that thou shouldest take them out of the world, but that thou shouldest keep them from the evil. 16 They are not of the world, even as I am not of the world. 17 Sanctify them through thy truth: thy word is truth. 18 As thou hast sent me into the world, even so have I also sent them into the world. 19 And for their sakes I sanctify myself, that they also might be sanctified through the truth.

20 Neither pray I for these alone, but for them also which shall believe on me through their word; 21 That they all may be one; as thou, Father, art in me, and I in thee, that they also may be one in us: that the world may believe that thou hast sent me. 22 And the glory which thou gavest me I have given them; that they may be one, even as we are one: 23 I in them, and thou in me, that they may be made perfect in one; and that the world may know that thou hast sent me, and hast

loved them, as thou hast loved me. 24 Father, I will that they also, whom thou hast given me, be with me where I am; that they may behold my glory, which thou hast given me: for thou lovedst me before the foundation of the world. 25 O righteous Father, the world hath not known thee: but I have known thee, and these have known that thou hast sent me. 26 And I have declared unto them thy name, and will declare it; that the love wherewith thou hast loved me may be in them, and I in them.

## FINAL REVELATION

18 When Jesus had spoken these words, he went forth with his disciples over the brook Cedron, where was a garden, into which he entered, and his disciples. 2 And Judas also, which betrayed him, knew the place: for Jesus ofttimes resorted thither with his disciples. 3 Judas then, having received a band of men and officers from the chief priests and Pharisees, cometh thither with lanterns and torches and weapons. 4 Jesus therefore, knowing all things that should come upon him, went forth, and said unto them, Whom seek ye? 5 They answered him, Jesus of Nazareth. Jesus saith unto them, I am he. And Judas also, which betrayed him, stood with them. 6 As soon then as he had said unto them, I am he, they went backward, and fell to the ground. 7 Then asked he them again, Whom seek ye? And they said, Jesus of Nazareth. 8 Jesus answered, I have told you that I am he: if therefore ye seek me, let these go their way: 9 That the saying might be fulfilled, which he spake, Of them which thou gavest me have I lost none. 10 Then Simon Peter having a sword drew it, and smote the high priest's servant, and cut off his right ear. The servant's name was Malchus. 11 Then said Jesus unto Peter, Put up thy sword into the sheath: the cup which my Father hath given me, shall I not drink it?

12 Then the band and the captain and officers of the Jews took Jesus, and bound him, 13 And led him away to Annas first; for he was father-in-law to Caiaphas, which was the high priest that same year. 14 Now Caiaphas was he, which gave counsel to the Jews, that it was expedient that one man should die for the people.

15 And Simon Peter followed Jesus, and so did another disciple: that disciple was known unto the high priest, and went in with Jesus into the palace of the high priest.

16 But Peter stood at the door without. Then went out that other disciple, which was known unto the high priest, and spake unto her that kept the door, and brought in Peter. 17 Then saith the damsel that kept the door unto Peter, Art not thou also one of this man's disciples? He saith, I am not. 18 And the servants and officers stood there, who had made a fire of coals, for it was cold; and they warmed themselves: and Peter stood with them, and warmed himself.

19 The high priest then asked Jesus of his disciples, and of his doctrine. 20 Jesus answered him, I spake openly to the world; I ever

taught in the synagogue, and in the temple, whither the Jews always resort; and in secret have I said nothing. 21 Why askest thou me? ask them which heard me, what I have said unto them: behold, they know what I said. 22 And when he had thus spoken, one of the officers which stood by struck Jesus with the palm of his hand, saying, Answerest thou the high priest so? 23 Jesus answered him, If I have spoken evil, bear witness of the evil: but if well, why smitest thou me? 24 Now Annas had sent him bound unto Caiaphas the high priest.

25 And Simon Peter stood and warmed himself. They said therefore unto him, Art not thou also one of his disciples? He denied it, and said, I am not. 26 One of the servants of the high priest, being his kinsman whose ear Peter cut off, saith, Did not I see thee in the garden with him? 27 Peter then denied again; and immediately the cock crew.

28 Then led they Jesus from Caiaphas unto the hall of judgment: and it was early; and they themselves went not into the judgment hall, lest they should be defiled; but that they might eat the passover. 29 Pilate then went out unto them, and said, What accusation bring ye against this man? 30 They answered and said unto him, If he were not a malefactor, we would not have delivered him up unto thee. 31 Then said Pilate unto them, Take ye him, and judge him according to your law. The Jews therefore said unto him, It is not lawful for us to put any man to death: 32 That the saying of Jesus might be fulfilled, which he spake, signifying what death he should die.

33 Then Pilate entered into the judgment hall again, and called Jesus, and said unto him, Art thou the King of the Jews? 34 Jesus answered him, Sayest thou this thing of thyself, or did others tell it thee of me? 35 Pilate answered, Am I a Jew? Thine own nation and the chief priests have delivered thee unto me: what hast thou done? 36 Jesus answered, My kingdom is not of this world: if my kingdom were of this world, then would my servants fight, that I should not be delivered to the Jews: but now is my kingdom not from hence. 37 Pilate therefore said unto him, Art thou a king then? Jesus answered, Thou sayest that I am a king. To this end was I born, and for this cause came I into the world, that I should bear witness unto the truth. Every one that is of the truth heareth my voice. 38 Pilate saith unto him, What is truth?

And when he had said this, he went out again unto the Jews, and saith unto them, I find in him no fault at all. 39 But ye have a custom, that I should release unto you one at the passover: will ye therefore that I release unto you the King of the Jews? 40 Then cried they all again, saying, Not this man, but Barabbas. Now Barabbas was a robber.

19 Then Pilate therefore took Jesus, and scourged him. 2 And the soldiers platted a crown of thorns, and put it on his head, and they put on him a purple robe, 3 And said, Hail, King of the Jews! and

they smote him with their hands. 4 Pilate therefore went forth again, and saith unto them, Behold, I bring him forth to you, that ye may know that I find no fault in him. 5 Then came Jesus forth, wearing the crown of thorns, and the purple robe. And Pilate saith unto them, Behold the man! 6 When the chief priests therefore and officers saw him, they cried out, saying, Crucify him, crucify him. Pilate saith unto them, Take ye him, and crucify him: for I find no fault in him. 7 The Jews answered him, We have a law, and by our law he ought to die, because he made himself the Son of God. 8 When Pilate therefore heard that saying, he was the more afraid; 9 And went again into the judgment hall, and saith unto Jesus, Whence art thou? But Jesus gave him no answer. 10 Then saith Pilate unto him, Speakest thou not unto me? knowest thou not that I have power to crucify thee, and have power to release thee? 11 Jesus answered, Thou couldest have no power at all against me, except it were given thee from above: therefore he that delivered me unto thee hath the greater sin.

12 And from thenceforth Pilate sought to release him: but the Jews cried out, saying, If thou let this man go, thou art not Caesar's friend: whosoever maketh himself a king speaketh against Caesar. 13 When Pilate therefore heard that saying, he brought Jesus forth, and sat down in the judgment seat in a place that is called the Pavement, but in the Hebrew, Gabbatha. 14 And it was the preparation of the passover, and about the sixth hour: and he saith unto the Jews, Behold your King! 15 But they cried out, Away with him, away with him, crucify him. Pilate saith unto them, Shall I crucify your King? The chief priests answered, We have no king but Caesar. 16 Then delivered he him therefore unto them to be crucified. And they took Jesus, and led him away.

17 And he bearing his cross went forth into a place called the place of a skull, which is called in the Hebrew Golgotha: 18 Where they crucified him, and two others with him, on either side one, and Jesus in the midst. 19 And Pilate wrote a title, and put it on the cross. And the writing was, JESUS OF NAZARETH THE KING OF THE JEWS. 20 This title then read many of the Jews; for the place where Jesus was crucified was nigh to the city: and it was written in Hebrew, and Greek, and Latin. 21 Then said the chief priests of the Jews to Pilate, Write not, The King of the Jews; but that he said, I am King of the Jews. 22 Pilate answered, What I have written I have written.

23 Then the soldiers, when they had crucified Jesus, took his garments, and made four parts, to every soldier a part; and also his coat: now the coat was without seam woven from the top throughout. 24 They said therefore among themselves, Let us not rend it, but cast lots for it, whose it shall be: that the Scripture might be fulfilled, which saith,

> They parted my raiment among them,
> And for my vesture they did cast lots.

These things therefore the soldiers did.

25 Now there stood by the cross of Jesus his mother, and his mother's sister, Mary the wife of Cleophas, and Mary Magdalene. 26 When Jesus therefore saw his mother, and the disciple standing by, whom he loved, he saith unto his mother, Woman, behold thy son! 27 Then saith he to the disciple, Behold thy mother! And from that hour that disciple took her unto his own home.

28 After this, Jesus knowing that all things were now accomplished, that the Scripture might be fulfilled, saith, I thirst. 29 Now there was set a vessel full of vinegar: and they filled a sponge with vinegar, and put it upon hyssop, and put it to his mouth. 30 When Jesus therefore had received the vinegar, he said, It is finished: and he bowed his head, and gave up the ghost.

31 The Jews therefore, because it was the preparation, that the bodies should not remain upon the cross on the sabbath day, (for that sabbath day was a high day,) besought Pilate that their legs might be broken, and that they might be taken away. 32 Then came the soldiers, and brake the legs of the first, and of the other which was crucified with him. 33 But when they came to Jesus, and saw that he was dead already, they brake not his legs: 34 But one of the soldiers with a spear pierced his side, and forthwith came there out blood and water. 35 And he that saw it bare record, and his record is true; and he knoweth that he saith true, that ye might believe. 36 For these things were done, that the Scripture should be fulfilled, A bone of him shall not be broken. 37 And again another Scripture saith, They shall look on him whom they pierced.

38 And after this Joseph of Arimathea, being a disciple of Jesus, but secretly for fear of the Jews, besought Pilate that he might take away the body of Jesus: and Pilate gave him leave. He came therefore, and took the body of Jesus. 39 And there came also Nicodemus, which at the first came to Jesus by night, and brought a mixture of myrrh and aloes, about a hundred pound weight. 40 Then took they the body of Jesus, and wound it in linen clothes with the spices, as the manner of the Jews is to bury. 41 Now in the place where he was crucified there was a garden; and in the garden a new sepulchre, wherein was never man yet laid. 42 There laid they Jesus therefore because of the Jews' preparation day; for the sepulchre was nigh at hand.

20 The first day of the week cometh Mary Magdalene early, when it was yet dark, unto the sepulchre, and seeth the stone taken away from the sepulchre. 2 Then she runneth, and cometh to Simon Peter, and to the other disciple, whom Jesus loved, and saith unto them, They have taken away the Lord out of the sepulchre, and we know not where they have laid him. 3 Peter therefore went forth, and that other disciple, and came to the sepulchre. 4 So they ran both together: and the other disciple did outrun Peter, and came first to the sepulchre. 5 And he stooping down, and looking in, saw the linen clothes lying; yet went he not in. 6 Then cometh Simon Peter following him, and went into the sepulchre, and seeth the linen clothes lie, 7 And the

napkin, that was about his head, not lying with the linen clothes, but wrapped together in a place by itself. 8 Then went in also that other disciple, which came first to the sepulchre, and he saw, and believed. 9 For as yet they knew not the Scripture, that he must rise again from the dead. 10 Then the disciples went away again unto their own home.

11 But Mary stood without at the sepulchre weeping: and as she wept, she stooped down, and looked into the sepulchre, 12 And seeth two angels in white sitting, the one at the head, and the other at the feet, where the body of Jesus had lain. 13 And they say unto her, Woman, why weepest thou? She saith unto them, Because they have taken away my Lord, and I know not where they have laid him. 14 And when she had thus said, she turned herself back, and saw Jesus standing, and knew not that it was Jesus. 15 Jesus saith unto her, Woman, why weepest thou? whom seekest thou? She, supposing him to be the gardener, saith unto him, Sir, if thou have borne him hence, tell me where thou hast laid him, and I will take him away. 16 Jesus saith unto her, Mary. She turned herself, and saith unto him, Rabboni; which is to say, Master. 17 Jesus saith unto her, Touch me not; for I am not yet ascended to my Father: but go to my brethren, and say unto them, I ascend unto my Father, and your Father; and to my God, and your God. 18 Mary Magdalene came and told the disciples that she had seen the Lord, and that he had spoken these things unto her.

19 Then the same day at evening, being the first day of the week, when the doors were shut where the disciples were assembled for fear of the Jews, came Jesus and stood in the midst, and saith unto them, Peace be unto you. 20 And when he had so said, he showed unto them his hands and his side. Then were the disciples glad, when they saw the Lord. 21 Then said Jesus to them again, Peace be unto you: as my Father hath sent me, even so send I you. 22 And when he had said this, he breathed on them, and saith unto them, Receive ye the Holy Ghost: 23 Whosesoever sins ye remit, they are remitted unto them; and whosesoever sins ye retain, they are retained.

24 But Thomas, one of the twelve, called Didymus, was not with them when Jesus came. 25 The other disciples therefore said unto him, We have seen the Lord. But he said unto them, Except I shall see in his hands the print of the nails, and put my finger into the print of the nails, and thrust my hand into his side, I will not believe.

26 And after eight days again his disciples were within, and Thomas with them: then came Jesus, the doors being shut, and stood in the midst, and said, Peace be unto you. 27 Then saith he to Thomas, Reach hither thy finger, and behold my hands; and reach hither thy hand, and thrust it into my side; and be not faithless, but believing. 28 And Thomas answered and said unto him, My Lord and my God. 29 Jesus saith unto him, Thomas, because thou hast seen me, thou hast believed: blessed are they that have not seen, and yet have believed.

30 And many other signs truly did Jesus in the presence of his disciples, which are not written in this book: 31 But these are written,

that ye might believe that Jesus is the Christ, the Son of God; and that believing ye might have life through his name.

21 After these things Jesus showed himself again to the disciples at the sea of Tiberias; and on this wise showed he himself. 2 There were together Simon Peter, and Thomas called Didymus, and Nathanael of Cana in Galilee, and the sons of Zebedee, and two other of his disciples. 3 Simon Peter saith unto them, I go a fishing. They say unto him, We also go with thee. They went forth, and entered into a ship immediately; and that night they caught nothing.

4 But when the morning was now come, Jesus stood on the shore; but the disciples knew not that it was Jesus. 5 Then Jesus saith unto them, Children, have ye any meat? They answered him, No. 6 And he said unto them, Cast the net on the right side of the ship, and ye shall find. They cast therefore, and now they were not able to draw it for the multitude of fishes. 7 Therefore that disciple whom Jesus loved saith unto Peter, It is the Lord. Now when Simon Peter heard that it was the Lord, he girt his fisher's coat unto him, (for he was naked,) and did cast himself into the sea. 8 And the other disciples came in a little ship, (for they were not far from land, but as it were two hundred cubits,) dragging the net with fishes.

9 As soon then as they were come to land, they saw a fire of coals there, and fish laid thereon, and bread. 10 Jesus saith unto them, Bring of the fish which ye have now caught. 11 Simon Peter went up, and drew the net to land full of great fishes, a hundred and fifty and three: and for all there were so many, yet was not the net broken. 12 Jesus saith unto them, Come and dine. And none of the disciples durst ask him, Who art thou? knowing that it was the Lord. 13 Jesus then cometh, and taketh bread, and giveth them, and fish likewise. 14 This is now the third time that Jesus showed himself to his disciples, after that he was risen from the dead.

15 So when they had dined, Jesus saith to Simon Peter, Simon, son of Jonas, lovest thou me more than these? He saith unto him, Yea, Lord; thou knowest that I love thee. He saith unto him, Feed my lambs. 16 He saith to him again the second time, Simon, son of Jonas, lovest thou me? He saith unto him, Yea, Lord; thou knowest that I love thee. He saith unto him, Feed my sheep. 17 He saith unto him the third time, Simon, son of Jonas, lovest thou me? Peter was grieved because he said unto him the third time, Lovest thou me? And he said unto him, Lord, thou knowest all things; thou knowest that I love thee. Jesus saith unto him, Feed my sheep. 18 Verily, verily, I say unto thee, When thou wast young, thou girdedst thyself, and walkedst whither thou wouldest: but when thou shalt be old, thou shalt stretch forth thy hands, and another shall gird thee, and carry thee whither thou wouldest not. 19 This spake he, signifying by what death he should glorify God. And when he had spoken this, he saith unto him, Follow me.

20 Then Peter, turning about, seeth the disciple whom Jesus loved following; which also leaned on his breast at supper, and said, Lord, which is he that betrayeth thee? 21 Peter seeing him saith to Jesus, Lord, and what shall this man do? 22 Jesus saith unto him, If I will that he tarry till I come, what is that to thee? follow thou me. 23 Then went this saying abroad among the brethren, that that disciple should not die: yet Jesus said not unto him, He shall not die; but, If I will that he tarry till I come, what is that to thee?

24 This is the disciple which testifieth of these things, and wrote these things: and we know that his testimony is true.

25 And there are also many other things which Jesus did, the which, if they should be written every one, I suppose that even the world itself could not contain the books that should be written. Amen.

# *The Acts of the Apostles*

## THE CHURCH IN PALESTINE

1 The former treatise have I made, O Theophilus, of all that Jesus began both to do and teach, 2 Until the day in which he was taken up, after that he through the Holy Ghost had given commandments unto the apostles whom he had chosen: 3 To whom also he showed himself alive after his passion by many infallible proofs, being seen of them forty days, and speaking of the things pertaining to the kingdom of God: 4 And, being assembled together with them, commanded them that they should not depart from Jerusalem, but wait for the promise of the Father, which, saith he, ye have heard of me. 5 For John truly baptized with water; but ye shall be baptized with the Holy Ghost not many days hence.

6 When they therefore were come together, they asked of him, saying, Lord, wilt thou at this time restore again the kingdom to Israel? 7 And he said unto them, It is not for you to know the times or the seasons, which the Father hath put in his own power. 8 But ye shall receive power, after that the Holy Ghost is come upon you: and ye shall be witnesses unto me both in Jerusalem, and in all Judea, and in Samaria, and unto the uttermost part of the earth.

9 And when he had spoken these things, while they beheld, he was taken up; and a cloud received him out of their sight. 10 And while they looked steadfastly toward heaven as he went up, behold, two men stood by them in white apparel; 11 Which also said, Ye men of Galilee, why stand ye gazing up into heaven? this same Jesus, which is taken up from you into heaven, shall so come in like manner as ye have seen him go into heaven. 12 Then returned they unto Jerusalem from the mount called Olivet, which is from Jerusalem a sabbath day's journey.

2   And when the day of Pentecost was fully come, they were all with
one accord in one place. 2 And suddenly there came a sound from
heaven as of a rushing mighty wind, and it filled all the house where
they were sitting. 3 And there appeared unto them cloven tongues like
as of fire, and it sat upon each of them. 4 And they were all filled
with the Holy Ghost, and began to speak with other tongues, as the
Spirit gave them utterance.

5 And there were dwelling at Jerusalem Jews, devout men, out of
every nation under heaven. 6 Now when this was noised abroad, the
multitude came together, and were confounded, because that every
man heard them speak in his own language. 7 And they were all amazed
and marveled, saying one to another, Behold, are not all these which
speak Galileans? 8 And how hear we every man in our own tongue,
wherein we were born? 9 Parthians, and Medes, and Elamites, and
the dwellers in Mesopotamia, and in Judea, and Cappadocia, in
Pontus, and Asia, 10 Phrygia, and Pamphylia, in Egypt, and in the
parts of Libya about Cyrene, and strangers of Rome, Jews and proselytes, 11 Cretes and Arabians, we do hear them speak in our tongues
the wonderful works of God. 12 And they were all amazed, and were
in doubt, saying one to another, What meaneth this? 13 Others
mocking said, These men are full of new wine.

14 But Peter, standing up with the eleven, lifted up his voice, and
said unto them, Ye men of Judea, and all ye that dwell at Jerusalem,
be this known unto you, and hearken to my words: 15 For these are
not drunken, as ye suppose, seeing it is but the third hour of the day.
16 But this is that which was spoken by the prophet Joel;

17   And it shall come to pass in the last days, saith God,
        I will pour out of my Spirit upon all flesh:
        And your sons and your daughters shall prophesy,
        And your young men shall see visions,
        And your old men shall dream dreams:
18   And on my servants and on my handmaidens
        I will pour out in those days of my Spirit;
        And they shall prophesy:
19   And I will show wonders in heaven above, and signs in the
            earth beneath;
        Blood, and fire, and vapor of smoke:
20   The sun shall be turned into darkness,
        And the moon into blood,
        Before that great and notable day of the Lord come:
21   And it shall come to pass, that whosoever shall call on the
            name of the Lord shall be saved.

22 Ye men of Israel, hear these words; Jesus of Nazareth, a man
approved of God among you by miracles and wonders and signs, which
God did by him in the midst of you, as ye yourselves also know:
23 Him, being delivered by the determinate counsel and foreknowledge

of God, ye have taken, and by wicked hands have crucified and slain: 24 Whom God hath raised up, having loosed the pains of death: because it was not possible that he should be holden of it. 25 For David speaketh concerning him,

I foresaw the Lord always before my face;
For he is on my right hand, that I should not be moved:
26 Therefore did my heart rejoice, and my tongue was glad;
Moreover also my flesh shall rest in hope:
27 Because thou wilt not leave my soul in hell,
Neither wilt thou suffer thine Holy One to see corruption.
28 Thou hast made known to me the ways of life;
Thou shalt make me full of joy with thy countenance.

29 Men and brethren, let me freely speak unto you of the patriarch David, that he is both dead and buried, and his sepulchre is with us unto this day. 30 Therefore being a prophet, and knowing that God had sworn with an oath to him, that of the fruit of his loins, according to the flesh, he would raise up Christ to sit on his throne; 31 He, seeing this before, spake of the resurrection of Christ, that his soul was not left in hell, neither his flesh did see corruption. 32 This Jesus hath God raised up, whereof we all are witnesses. 33 Therefore being by the right hand of God exalted, and having received of the Father the promise of the Holy Ghost, he hath shed forth this, which ye now see and hear. 34 For David is not ascended into the heavens: but he saith himself,

The Lord said unto my Lord,
Sit thou on my right hand,
35 Until I make thy foes thy footstool.

36 Therefore let all the house of Israel know assuredly, that God hath made that same Jesus, whom ye have crucified, both Lord and Christ.

37 Now when they heard this, they were pricked in their heart, and said unto Peter and to the rest of the apostles, Men and brethren, what shall we do? 38 Then Peter said unto them, Repent, and be baptized every one of you in the name of Jesus Christ for the remission of sins, and ye shall receive the gift of the Holy Ghost. 39 For the promise is unto you, and to your children, and to all that are afar off, even as many as the Lord our God shall call. 40 And with many other words did he testify and exhort, saying, Save yourselves from this untoward generation. 41 Then they that gladly received his word were baptized: and the same day there were added unto them about three thousand souls.

42 And they continued steadfastly in the apostles' doctrine and fellowship, and in breaking of bread, and in prayers. 43 And fear came upon every soul: and many wonders and signs were done by the apostles. 44 And all that believed were together, and had all things common; 45 And sold their posesssions and goods, and parted them to all men, as every man had need. 46 And they, continuing daily with one accord in the temple, and breaking bread from house to

house, did eat their meat with gladness and singleness of heart, 47 Praising God, and having favor with all the people. And the Lord added to the church daily such as should be saved.

3 Now Peter and John went up together into the temple at the hour of prayer, being the ninth hour. 2 And a certain man lame from his mother's womb was carried, whom they laid daily at the gate of the temple which is called Beautiful, to ask alms of them that entered into the temple; 3 Who, seeing Peter and John about to go into the temple, asked an alms. 4 And Peter, fastening his eyes upon him with John, said, Look on us. 5 And he gave heed unto them, expecting to receive something of them. 6 Then Peter said, Silver and gold have I none; but such as I have give I thee: In the name of Jesus Christ of Nazareth rise up and walk. 7 And he took him by the right hand, and lifted him up: and immediately his feet and ankle bones received strength. 8 And he leaping up stood, and walked, and entered with them into the temple, walking, and leaping, and praising God. 9 And all the people saw him walking and praising God: 10 And they knew that it was he which sat for alms at the Beautiful gate of the temple: and they were filled with wonder and amazement at that which had happened unto him. 11 And as the lame man which was healed held Peter and John, all the people ran together unto them in the porch that is called Solomon's, greatly wondering.

12 And when Peter saw it, he answered unto the people, Ye men of Israel, why marvel ye at this? or why look ye so earnestly on us, as though by our own power or holiness we had made this man to walk? 13 The God of Abraham, and of Isaac, and of Jacob, the God of our fathers, hath glorified his Son Jesus; whom ye delivered up, and denied him in the presence of Pilate, when he was determined to let him go. 14 But ye denied the Holy One and the Just, and desired a murderer to be granted unto you; 15 And killed the Prince of life, whom God hath raised from the dead; whereof we are witnesses. 16 And his name, through faith in his name, hath made this man strong, whom ye see and know: yea, the faith which is by him hath given him this perfect soundness in the presence of you all.

17 And now, brethren, I wot that through ignorance ye did it, as did also your rulers. 18 But those things, which God before had showed by the mouth of all his prophets, that Christ should suffer, he hath so fulfilled. 19 Repent ye therefore, and be converted, that your sins may be blotted out, when the times of refreshing shall come from the presence of the Lord; 20 And he shall send Jesus Christ, which before was preached unto you: 21 Whom the heaven must receive until the times of restitution of all things, which God hath spoken by the mouth of all his holy prophets since the world began. 22 For Moses truly said unto the fathers, A Prophet shall the Lord your God raise up unto you of your brethren, like unto me; him shall ye hear in all things whatsoever he shall say unto you. 23 And it shall come to

pass, that every soul, which will not hear that Prophet, shall be destroyed from among the people. 24 Yea, and all the prophets from Samuel and those that follow after, as many as have spoken, have likewise foretold of these days. 25 Ye are the children of the prophets, and of the covenant which God made with our fathers, saying unto Abraham, And in thy seed shall all the kindreds of the earth be blessed. 26 Unto you first God, having raised up his Son Jesus, sent him to bless you, in turning away every one of you from his iniquities.

4 And as they spake unto the people, the priests, and the captain of the temple, and the Sadducees, came upon them, 2 Being grieved that they taught the people, and preached through Jesus the resurrection from the dead. 3 And they laid hands on them, and put them in hold unto the next day: for it was now eventide. 4 Howbeit many of them which heard the word believed; and the number of the men was about five thousand.

5 And it came to pass on the morrow, that their rulers, and elders, and scribes, 6 And Annas the high priest, and Caiaphas, and John, and Alexander, and as many as were of the kindred of the high priest, were gathered together at Jerusalem. 7 And when they had set them in the midst, they asked, By what power, or by what name, have ye done this? 8 Then Peter, filled with the Holy Ghost, said unto them, Ye rulers of the people, and elders of Israel, 9 If we this day be examined of the good deed done to the impotent man, by what means he is made whole; 10 Be it known unto you all, and to all the people of Israel, that by the name of Jesus Christ of Nazareth, whom ye crucified, whom God raised from the dead, even by him doth this man stand here before you whole. 11 This is the stone which was set at nought of you builders, which is become the head of the corner. 12 Neither is there salvation in any other: for there is none other name under heaven given among men, whereby we must be saved.

13 Now when they saw the boldness of Peter and John, and perceived that they were unlearned and ignorant men, they marveled; and they took knowledge of them, that they had been with Jesus. 14 And beholding the man which was healed standing with them, they could say nothing against it. 15 But when they had commanded them to go aside out of the council, they conferred among themselves, 16 Saying, What shall we do to these men? for that indeed a notable miracle hath been done by them is manifest to all them that dwell in Jerusalem; and we cannot deny it. 17 But that it spread no further among the people, let us straitly threaten them, that they speak henceforth to no man in this name. 18 And they called them, and commanded them not to speak at all nor teach in the name of Jesus. 19 But Peter and John answered and said unto them, Whether it be right in the sight of God to hearken unto you more than unto God, judge ye. 20 For we cannot but speak the things which we have seen and heard. 21 So when they had further threatened them, they let them go, finding

nothing how they might punish them, because of the people: for all men glorified God for that which was done. 22 For the man was above forty years old, on whom this miracle of healing was showed.

23 And being let go, they went to their own company, and reported all that the chief priests and elders had said unto them. 24 And when they heard that, they lifted up their voice to God with one accord, and said, Lord, thou art God, which hast made heaven, and earth, and the sea, and all that in them is; 25 Who by the mouth of thy servant David hast said,

> Why did the heathen rage,
> And the people imagine vain things?
> 26 The kings of the earth stood up,
> And the rulers were gathered together
> Against the Lord, and against his Christ.

27 For of a truth against thy holy child Jesus, whom thou hast anointed, both Herod, and Pontius Pilate, with the Gentiles, and the people of Israel, were gathered together, 28 For to do whatsoever thy hand and thy counsel determined before to be done. 29 And now, Lord, behold their threatenings: and grant unto thy servants, that with all boldness they may speak thy word, 30 By stretching forth thine hand to heal; and that signs and wonders may be done by the name of thy holy child Jesus. 31 And when they had prayed, the place was shaken where they were assembled together; and they were all filled with the Holy Ghost, and they spake the word of God with boldness.

32 And the multitude of them that believed were of one heart and of one soul: neither said any of them that aught of the things which he possessed was his own; but they had all things common. 33 And with great power gave the apostles witness of the resurrection of the Lord Jesus: and great grace was upon them all. 34 Neither was there any among them that lacked: for as many as were possessors of lands or houses sold them, and brought the prices of the things that were sold, 35 And laid them down at the apostles' feet: and distribution was made unto every man according as he had need.

36 And Joses, who by the apostles was surnamed Barnabas, (which is, being interpreted, The son of consolation,) a Levite, and of the country of Cyprus, 37 Having land, sold it, and brought the money, and laid it at the apostles' feet.

5    12 And by the hands of the apostles were many signs and wonders wrought among the people; (and they were all with one accord in Solomon's porch. 13 And of the rest durst no man join himself to them: but the people magnified them. 14 And believers were the more added to the Lord, multitudes both of men and women;) 15 Insomuch that they brought forth the sick into the streets, and laid them on beds and couches, that at the least the shadow of Peter passing by might overshadow some of them. 16 There came also a multitude

out of the cities round about unto Jerusalem, bringing sick folks, and them which were vexed with unclean spirits: and they were healed every one.

17 Then the high priest rose up, and all they that were with him, (which is the sect of the Sadducees,) and were filled with indignation, 18 And laid their hands on the apostles, and put them in the common prison. 19 But the angel of the Lord by night opened the prison doors, and brought them forth, and said, 20 Go, stand and speak in the temple to the people all the words of this life. 21 And when they heard that, they entered into the temple early in the morning, and taught. But the high priest came, and they that were with him, and called the council together, and all the senate of the children of Israel, and sent to the prison to have them brought. 22 But when the officers came, and found them not in the prison, they returned, and told, 23 Saying, The prison truly found we shut with all safety, and the keepers standing without before the doors: but when we had opened, we found no man within. 24 Now when the high priest and the captain of the temple and the chief priests heard these things, they doubted of them whereunto this would grow. 25 Then came one and told them, saying, Behold, the men whom ye put in prison are standing in the temple, and teaching the people. 26 Then went the captain with the officers, and brought them without violence: for they feared the people, lest they should have been stoned.

27 And when they had brought them, they set them before the council: and the high priest asked them, 28 Saying, Did not we straitly command you that ye should not teach in this name? and, behold, ye have filled Jerusalem with your doctrine, and intend to bring this man's blood upon us. 29 Then Peter and the other apostles answered and said, We ought to obey God rather than men. 30 The God of our fathers raised up Jesus, whom ye slew and hanged on a tree. 31 Him hath God exalted with his right hand to be a Prince and a Saviour, for to give repentance to Israel, and forgiveness of sins. 32 And we are his witnesses of these things; and so is also the Holy Ghost, whom God hath given to them that obey him.

33 When they heard that, they were cut to the heart, and took counsel to slay them. 34 Then stood there up one in the council, a Pharisee, named Gamaliel, a doctor of the law, had in reputation among all the people, and commanded to put the apostles forth a little space; 35 And said unto them, Ye men of Israel, take heed to yourselves what ye intend to do as touching these men. 36 For before these days rose up Theudas, boasting himself to be somebody; to whom a number of men, about four hundred, joined themselves: who was slain; and all, as many as obeyed him, were scattered, and brought to nought. 37 After this man rose up Judas of Galilee in the days of the taxing, and drew away much people after him: he also perished; and all, even as many as obeyed him, were dispersed. 38 And now I say unto you, Refrain from these men, and let them alone: for if this counsel or this work be of men, it will come to nought: 39 But if it be

of God, ye cannot overthrow it; lest haply ye be found even to fight against God. 40 And to him they agreed: and when they had called the apostles, and beaten them, they commanded that they should not speak in the name of Jesus, and let them go.

41 And they departed from the presence of the council, rejoicing that they were counted worthy to suffer shame for his name. 42 And daily in the temple, and in every house, they ceased not to teach and preach Jesus Christ.

6 And in those days, when the number of the disciples was multiplied, there arose a murmuring of the Grecians against the Hebrews, because their widows were neglected in the daily ministration. 2 Then the twelve called the multitude of the disciples unto them, and said, It is not reason that we should leave the word of God, and serve tables. 3 Wherefore, brethren, look ye out among you seven men of honest report, full of the Holy Ghost and wisdom, whom we may appoint over this business. 4 But we will give ourselves continually to prayer, and to the ministry of the word. 5 And the saying pleased the whole multitude: and they chose Stephen, a man full of faith and of the Holy Ghost, and Philip, and Prochorus, and Nicanor, and Timon, and Parmenas, and Nicolas a proselyte of Antioch; 6 Whom they set before the apostles: and when they had prayed, they laid their hands on them.

7 And the word of God increased; and the number of the disciples multipled in Jerusalem greatly; and a great company of the priests were obedient to the faith.

8 And Stephen, full of faith and power, did great wonders and miracles among the people. 9 Then there arose certain of the synagogue, which is called the synagogue of the Libertines, and Cyrenians, and Alexandrians, and of them of Cilicia and of Asia, disputing with Stephen. 10 And they were not able to resist the wisdom and the spirit by which he spake. 11 Then they suborned men, which said, We have heard him speak blasphemous words against Moses, and against God. 12 And they stirred up the people, and the elders, and the scribes, and came upon him, and caught him, and brought him to the council, 13 And set up false witnesses, which said, This man ceaseth not to speak blasphemous words against this holy place, and the law: 14 For we have heard him say, that this Jesus of Nazareth shall destroy this place, and shall change the customs which Moses delivered us. 15 And all that sat in the council, looking steadfastly on him, saw his face as it had been the face of an angel.

7 Then said the high priest, Are these things so? 2 And he said, Men, brethren, and fathers, hearken. . . . 51 Ye stiffnecked and uncircumcised in heart and ears, ye do always resist the Holy Ghost: as your fathers did, so do ye. 52 Which of the prophets have not your fathers persecuted? and they have slain them which showed before of the coming of the Just One; of whom ye have been now the betrayers

and murderers: 53 Who have received the law by the disposition of angels, and have not kept it.

54 When they heard these things, they were cut to the heart, and they gnashed on him with their teeth. 55 But he, being full of the Holy Ghost, looked up steadfastly into heaven, and saw the glory of God, and Jesus standing on the right hand of God, 56 And said, Behold, I see the heavens opened, and the Son of man standing on the right hand of God. 57 Then they cried out with a loud voice, and stopped their ears, and ran upon him with one accord, 58 And cast him out of the city, and stoned him: and the witnesses laid down their clothes at a young man's feet, whose name was Saul. 59 And they stoned Stephen, calling upon God, and saying, Lord Jesus, receive my spirit. 60 And he kneeled down, and cried with a loud voice, Lord, lay not this sin to their charge. And when he had said this, he fell asleep.

8 And Saul was consenting unto his death. And at that time there was a great persecution against the church which was at Jerusalem; and they were all scattered abroad throughout the regions of Judea and Samaria, except the apostles. 2 And devout men carried Stephen to his burial, and made great lamentation over him. 3 As for Saul, he made havoc of the church, entering into every house, and haling men and women committed them to prison.

4 Therefore they that were scattered abroad went every where preaching the word. 5 Then Philip went down to the city of Samaria, and preached Christ unto them. 6 And the people with one accord gave heed unto those things which Philip spake, hearing and seeing the miracles which he did. 7 For unclean spirits, crying with loud voice, came out of many that were possessed with them: and many taken with palsies, and that were lame, were healed. 8 And there was great joy in that city. 9 But there was a certain man, called Simon, which beforetime in the same city used sorcery, and bewitched the people of Samaria, giving out that himself was some great one: 10 To whom they all gave heed, from the least to the greatest, saying, This man is the great power of God. 11 And to him they had regard, because that of long time he had bewitched them with sorceries. 12 But when they believed Philip preaching the things concerning the kingdom of God, and the name of Jesus Christ, they were baptized, both men and women. 13 Then Simon himself believed also: and when he was baptized, he continued with Philip, and wondered, beholding the miracles and signs which were done.

14 Now when the apostles which were at Jerusalem heard that Samaria had received the word of God, they sent unto them Peter and John: 15 Who, when they were come down, prayed for them, that they might receive the Holy Ghost: 16 (For as yet he was fallen upon none of them: only they were baptized in the name of the Lord Jesus.) 17 Then laid they their hands on them, and they received the Holy Ghost. 18 And when Simon saw that through laying on of the apostles'

hands the Holy Ghost was given, he offered them money, 19 Saying, Give me also this power, that on whomsoever I lay hands, he may receive the Holy Ghost. 20 But Peter said unto him, Thy money perish with thee, because thou hast thought that the gift of God may be purchased with money. 21 Thou hast neither part nor lot in this matter: for thy heart is not right in the sight of God. 22 Repent therefore of this thy wickedness, and pray God, if perhaps the thought of thine heart may be forgiven thee. 23 For I perceive that thou art in the gall of bitterness, and in the bond of iniquity. 24 Then answered Simon, and said, Pray ye to the Lord for me, that none of these things which ye have spoken come upon me. 25 And they, when they had testified and preached the word of the Lord, returned to Jerusalem, and preached the gospel in many villages of the Samaritans.

26 And the angel of the Lord spake unto Philip, saying, Arise, and go toward the south, unto the way that goeth down from Jerusalem unto Gaza, which is desert. 27 And he arose and went: and, behold, a man of Ethiopia, a eunuch of great authority under Candace queen of the Ethiopians, who had the charge of all her treasure, and had come to Jerusalem for to worship, 28 Was returning, and sitting in his chariot read Esaias the prophet. 29 Then the Spirit said unto Philip, Go near, and join thyself to this chariot. 30 And Philip ran thither to him, and heard him read the prophet Esaias, and said, Understandest thou what thou readest? 31 And he said, How can I, except some man should guide me? And he desired Philip that he would come up and sit with him. 32 The place of the Scripture which he read was this,

> He was led as a sheep to the slaughter;
> And like a lamb dumb before his shearer,
> So opened he not his mouth:
> 33 In his humiliation his judgment was taken away:
> And who shall declare his generation?
> For his life is taken from the earth.

34 And the eunuch answered Philip, and said, I pray thee, of whom speaketh the prophet this? of himself, or of some other man? 35 Then Philip opened his mouth, and began at the same Scripture, and preached unto him Jesus.

36 And as they went on their way, they came unto a certain water: and the eunuch said, See, here is water; what doth hinder me to be baptized? 37 And Philip said, If thou believest with all thine heart, thou mayest. And he answered and said, I believe that Jesus Christ is the Son of God. 38 And he commanded the chariot to stand still: and they went down both into the water, both Philip and the eunuch; and he baptized him. 39 And when they were come up out of the water, the Spirit of the Lord caught away Philip, that the eunuch saw him no more: and he went on his way rejoicing. 40 But Philip was found at Azotus: and passing through he preached in all the cities, till he came to Caesarea.

9    And Saul, yet breathing out threatenings and slaughter against the disciples of the Lord, went unto the high priest, 2 And desired of him letters to Damascus to the synagogues, that if he found any of this way, whether they were men or women, he might bring them bound unto Jerusalem. 3 And as he journeyed, he came near Damascus: and suddenly there shined round about him a light from heaven: 4 And he fell to the earth, and heard a voice saying unto him, Saul, Saul, why persecutest thou me? 5 And he said, Who art thou, Lord? And the Lord said, I am Jesus whom thou persecutest: it is hard for thee to kick against the pricks. 6 And he trembling and astonished said, Lord, what wilt thou have me to do? And the Lord said unto him, Arise, and go into the city, and it shall be told thee what thou must do. 7 And the men which journeyed with him stood speechless, hearing a voice, but seeing no man. 8 And Saul arose from the earth; and when his eyes were opened, he saw no man: but they led him by the hand, and brought him into Damascus. 9 And he was three days without sight, and neither did eat nor drink.

10 And there was a certain disciple at Damascus, named Ananias; and to him said the Lord in a vision, Ananias. And he said, Behold, I am here, Lord. 11 And the Lord said unto him, Arise, and go into the street which is called Straight, and inquire in the house of Judas for one called Saul, of Tarsus: for, behold, he prayeth, 12 And hath seen in a vision a man named Ananias coming in, and putting his hand on him, that he might receive his sight. 13 Then Ananias answered, Lord, I have heard by many of this man, how much evil he hath done to thy saints at Jerusalem: 14 And here he hath authority from the chief priests to bind all that call on thy name. 15 But the Lord said unto him, Go thy way: for he is a chosen vessel unto me, to bear my name before the Gentiles, and kings, and the children of Israel: 16 For I will show him how great things he must suffer for my name's sake.

17 And Ananias went his way, and entered into the house; and putting his hands on him said, Brother Saul, the Lord, even Jesus, that appeared unto thee in the way as thou camest, hath sent me, that thou mightest receive thy sight, and be filled with the Holy Ghost. 18 And immediately there fell from his eyes as it had been scales: and he received sight forthwith, and arose, and was baptized. 19 And when he had received meat, he was strengthened. Then was Saul certain days with the disciples which were at Damascus. 20 And straightway he preached Christ in the synagogues, that he is the Son of God. 21 But all that heard him were amazed, and said; Is not this he that destroyed them which called on this name in Jerusalem, and came hither for that intent, that he might bring them bound unto the chief priests? 22 But Saul increased the more in strength, and confounded the Jews which dwelt at Damascus, proving that this is very Christ.

23 And after that many days were fulfilled, the Jews took counsel

to kill him: 24 But their laying wait was known of Saul. And they watched the gates day and night to kill him. 25 Then the disciples took him by night, and let him down by the wall in a basket.

26 And when Saul was come to Jerusalem, he assayed to join himself to the disciples: but they were all afraid of him, and believed not that he was a disciple. 27 But Barnabas took him, and brought him to the apostles, and declared unto them how he had seen the Lord in the way, and that he had spoken to him, and how he had preached boldly at Damascus in the name of Jesus. 28 And he was with them coming in and going out at Jerusalem. 29 And he spake boldly in the name of the Lord Jesus, and disputed against the Grecians: but they went about to slay him. 30 Which when the brethren knew, they brought him down to Caesarea, and sent him forth to Tarsus.

31 Then had the churches rest throughout all Judea and Galilee and Samaria, and were edified; and walking in the fear of the Lord, and in the comfort of the Holy Ghost, were multiplied.

## APPEAL TO THE GENTILES

10 There was a certain man in Caesarea called Cornelius, a centurion of the band called the Italian band, 2 A devout man, and one that feared God with all his house, which gave much alms to the people, and prayed to God always. 3 He saw in a vision evidently, about the ninth hour of the day, an angel of God coming in to him, and saying unto him, Cornelius. 4 And when he looked on him, he was afraid, and said, What is it, Lord? And he said unto him, Thy prayers and thine alms are come up for a memorial before God. 5 And now send men to Joppa, and call for one Simon, whose surname is Peter: 6 He lodgeth with one Simon a tanner, whose house is by the sea side: he shall tell thee what thou oughtest to do. 7 And when the angel which spake unto Cornelius was departed, he called two of his household servants, and a devout soldier of them that waited on him continually; 8 And when he had declared all these things unto them, he sent them to Joppa.

9 On the morrow, as they went on their journey, and drew nigh unto the city, Peter went up upon the housetop to pray about the sixth hour: 10 And he became very hungry, and would have eaten: but while they made ready, he fell into a trance, 11 And saw heaven opened, and a certain vessel descending unto him, as it had been a great sheet knit at the four corners, and let down to the earth: 12 Wherein were all manner of four-footed beasts of the earth, and wild beasts, and creeping things, and fowls of the air. 13 And there came a voice to him, Rise, Peter; kill, and eat. 14 But Peter said, Not so, Lord; for I have never eaten any thing that is common or unclean. 15 And the voice spake unto him again the second time, What God hath cleansed, that call not thou common. 16 This was done thrice: and the vessel was received up again into heaven.

17 Now while Peter doubted in himself what this vision which he had seen should mean, behold, the men which were sent from Cornelius had made inquiry for Simon's house, and stood before the gate, 18 And called, and asked whether Simon, which was surnamed Peter, were lodged there. 19 While Peter thought on the vision, the Spirit said unto him, Behold, three men seek thee. 20 Arise therefore, and get thee down, and go with them, doubting nothing: for I have sent them. 21 Then Peter went down to the men which were sent unto him from Cornelius; and said, Behold, I am he whom ye seek: what is the cause wherefore ye are come? 22 And they said, Cornelius the centurion, a just man, and one that feareth God, and of good report among all the nation of the Jews, was warned from God by a holy angel to send for thee into his house, and to hear words of thee. 23 Then called he them in, and lodged them.

And on the morrow Peter went away with them, and certain brethren from Joppa accompanied him. 24 And the morrow after they entered into Caesarea. And Cornelius waited for them, and had called together his kinsmen and near friends. 25 And as Peter was coming in, Cornelius met him, and fell down at his feet, and worshipped him. 26 But Peter took him up, saying, Stand up; I myself also am a man. 27 And as he talked with him, he went in, and found many that were come together. 28 And he said unto them, Ye know how that it is an unlawful thing for a man that is a Jew to keep company, or come unto one of another nation; but God hath showed me that I should not call any man common or unclean. 29 Therefore came I unto you without gainsaying, as soon as I was sent for: I ask therefore for what intent ye have sent for me?

30 And Cornelius said, Four days ago I was fasting until this hour; and at the ninth hour I prayed in my house, and, behold, a man stood before me in bright clothing, 31 And said, Cornelius, thy prayer is heard, and thine alms are had in remembrance in the sight of God. 32 Send therefore to Joppa, and call hither Simon, whose surname is Peter; he is lodged in the house of one Simon a tanner by the sea side: who, when he cometh, shall speak unto thee. 33 Immediately therefore I sent to thee; and thou hast well done that thou art come. Now therefore are we all here present before God, to hear all things that are commanded thee of God.

34 Then Peter opened his mouth, and said, Of a truth I perceive that God is no respecter of persons: 35 But in every nation he that feareth him, and worketh righteousness, is accepted with him. 36 The word which God sent unto the children of Israel, preaching peace by Jesus Christ: (he is Lord of all:) 37 That word, I say, ye know, which was published throughout all Judea, and began from Galilee, after the baptism which John preached; 38 How God anointed Jesus of Nazareth with the Holy Ghost and with power: who went about doing good, and healing all that were oppressed of the devil; for God was with him. 39 And we are witnesses of all things which he did both

in the land of the Jews, and in Jerusalem; whom they slew and hanged on a tree: 40 Him God raised up the third day, and showed him openly; 41 Not to all the people, but unto witnesses chosen before of God, even to us, who did eat and drink with him after he rose from the dead. 42 And he commanded us to preach unto the people, and to testify that it is he which was ordained of God to be the Judge of quick and dead. 43 To him give all the prophets witness, that through his name whosoever believeth in him shall receive remission of sins.

44 While Peter yet spake these words, the Holy Ghost fell on all them which heard the word. 45 And they of the circumcision which believed were astonished, as many as came with Peter, because that on the Gentiles also was poured out the gift of the Holy Ghost. 46 For they heard them speak with tongues, and magnify God. Then answered Peter, 47 Can any man forbid water, that these should not be baptized, which have received the Holy Ghost as well as we? 48 And he commanded them to be baptized in the name of the Lord. Then prayed them him to tarry certain days.

11 And the apostles and brethren that were in Judea heard that the Gentiles had also received the word of God. 2 And when Peter was come up to Jerusalem, they that were of the circumcision contended with him, 3 Saying, Thou wentest in to men uncircumcised, and didst eat with them. 4 But Peter rehearsed the matter from the beginning, and expounded it by order unto them. . . . 18 When they heard these things, they held their peace, and glorified God, saying, Then hath God also to the Gentiles granted repentance unto life.

19 Now they which were scattered abroad upon the persecution that arose about Stephen traveled as far as Phenice, and Cyprus, and Antioch, preaching the word to none but unto the Jews only. 20 And some of them were men of Cyprus and Cyrene, which, when they were come to Antioch, spake unto the Grecians, preaching the Lord Jesus. 21 And the hand of the Lord was with them: and a great number believed, and turned unto the Lord.

22 Then tidings of these things came unto the ears of the church which was in Jerusalem: and they sent forth Barnabas, that he should go as far as Antioch. 23 Who, when he came, and had seen the grace of God, was glad, and exhorted them all, that with purpose of heart they would cleave unto the Lord. 24 For he was a good man, and full of the Holy Ghost and of faith: and much people was added unto the Lord. 25 Then departed Barnabas to Tarsus, for to seek Saul: 26 And when he had found him, he brought him unto Antioch. And it came to pass, that a whole year they assembled themselves with the church, and taught much people. And the disciples were called Christians first in Antioch.

12 Now about that time Herod the king stretched forth his hands to vex certain of the church. 2 And he killed James the brother of John with the sword.

3 And because he saw it pleased the Jews, he proceeded further to take Peter also. (Then were the days of unleavened bread.) 4 And when he had apprehended him, he put him in prison, and delivered him to four quaternions of soldiers to keep him; intending after Easter to bring him forth to the people. 5 Peter therefore was kept in prison: but prayer was made without ceasing of the church unto God for him. 6 And when Herod would have brought him forth, the same night Peter was sleeping between two soldiers, bound with two chains: and the keepers before the door kept the prison. 7 And, behold, the angel of the Lord came upon him, and a light shined in the prison: and he smote Peter on the side, and raised him up, saying, Arise up quickly. And his chains fell off from his hands. 8 And the angel said unto him, Gird thyself, and bind on thy sandals. And so he did. And he saith unto him, Cast thy garment about thee, and follow me. 9 And he went out, and followed him; and wist not that it was true which was done by the angel; but thought he saw a vision. 10 When they were past the first and the second ward, they came unto the iron gate that leadeth unto the city; which opened to them of his own accord: and they went out, and passed on through one street; and forthwith the angel departed from him.

11 And when Peter was come to himself, he said, Now I know of a surety, that the Lord hath sent his angel, and hath delivered me out of the hand of Herod, and from all the expectation of the people of the Jews. 12 And when he had considered the thing, he came to the house of Mary the mother of John, whose surname was Mark; where many were gathered together praying. 13 And as Peter knocked at the door of the gate, a damsel came to hearken, named Rhoda. 14 And when she knew Peter's voice, she opened not the gate for gladness, but ran in, and told how Peter stood before the gate. 15 And they said unto her, Thou art mad. But she constantly affirmed that it was even so. Then said they, It is his angel. 16 But Peter continued knocking: and when they had opened the door, and saw him, they were astonished. 17 But he, beckoning unto them with the hand to hold their peace, declared unto them how the Lord had brought him out of the prison. And he said, Go show these things unto James, and to the brethren. And he departed, and went into another place.

18 Now as soon as it was day, there was no small stir among the soldiers, what was become of Peter. 19 And when Herod had sought for him, and found him not, he examined the keepers, and commanded that they should be put to death. And he went down from Judea to Caesarea, and there abode.

20 And Herod was highly displeased with them of Tyre and Sidon: but they came with one accord to him, and, having made Blastus the king's chamberlain their friend, desired peace; because their country was nourished by the king's country. 21 And upon a set day Herod, arrayed in royal apparel, sat upon his throne, and made an oration unto them. 22 And the people gave a shout, saying, It is the voice of a god, and not of a man. 23 And immediately the angel of the Lord smote

him, because he gave not God the glory: and he was eaten of worms, and gave up the ghost.

24 But the word of God grew and multiplied.

### FOCUS UPON PAUL

25 And Barnabas and Saul returned from Jerusalem, when they had fulfilled their ministry, and took with them John, whose surname was Mark.

13 Now there were in the church that was at Antioch certain prophets and teachers; as Barnabas, and Simeon that was called Niger, and Lucius of Cyrene, and Manaen, which had been brought up with Herod the tetrarch, and Saul. 2 As they ministered to the Lord, and fasted, the Holy Ghost said, Separate me Barnabas and Saul for the work whereunto I have called them. 3 And when they had fasted and prayed, and laid their hands on them, they sent them away.

4 So they, being sent forth by the Holy Ghost, departed unto Seleucia; and from thence they sailed to Cyprus. 5 And when they were at Salamis, they preached the word of God in the synagogues of the Jews: and they had also John to their minister. 6 And when they had gone through the isle unto Paphos, they found a certain sorcerer, a false prophet, a Jew, whose name was Bar-jesus: 7 Which was with the deputy of the country, Sergius Paulus, a prudent man; who called for Barnabas and Saul, and desired to hear the word of God. 8 But Elymas the sorcerer (for so is his name by interpretation) withstood them, seeking to turn away the deputy from the faith. 9 Then Saul, (who also is called Paul,) filled with the Holy Ghost, set his eyes on him, 10 And said, O full of all subtilty and all mischief, thou child of the devil, thou enemy of all righteousness, wilt thou not cease to pervert the right ways of the Lord? 11 And now, behold, the hand of the Lord is upon thee, and thou shalt be blind, not seeing the sun for a season. And immediately there fell on him a mist and a darkness; and he went about seeking some to lead him by the hand. 12 Then the deputy, when he saw what was done, believed, being astonished at the doctrine of the Lord.

13 Now when Paul and his company loosed from Paphos, they came to Perga in Pamphylia: and John departing from them returned to Jerusalem. 14 But when they departed from Perga, they came to Antioch in Pisidia, and went into the synagogue on the sabbath day, and sat down. 15 And after the reading of the law and the prophets, the rulers of the synagogue sent unto them, saying, Ye men and brethren, if ye have any word of exhortation for the people, say on. 16 Then Paul stood up, and beckoning with his hand said, . . .

26 Men and brethren, children of the stock of Abraham, and whosoever among you feareth God, to you is the word of this salvation sent. 27 For they that dwell at Jerusalem, and their rulers, because they knew him not, nor yet the voices of the prophets which are read

every sabbath day, they have fulfilled them in condemning him.
28 And though they found no cause of death in him, yet desired they
Pilate that he should be slain. 29 And when they had fulfilled all that
was written of him, they took him down from the tree, and laid him
in a sepulchre. 30 But God raised him from the dead: 31 And he
was seen many days of them which came up with him from Galilee
to Jerusalem, who are his witnesses unto the people. 32 And we declare unto you glad tidings, how that the promise which was made
unto the fathers, 33 God hath fulfilled the same unto us their children, in that he hath raised up Jesus again; as it is also written in the
second psalm,

> Thou art my Son,
> This day have I begotten thee.

34 And as concerning that he raised him up from the dead, now no
more to return to corruption, he said on this wise, I will give you the
sure mercies of David. 35 Wherefore he saith also in another psalm,

> Thou shalt not suffer thine Holy One to see corruption.

36 For David, after he had served his own generation by the will of
God, fell on sleep, and was laid unto his fathers, and saw corruption:
37 But he, whom God raised again, saw no corruption. 38 Be it known
unto you therefore, men and brethren, that through this man is
preached unto you the forgiveness of sins: 39 And by him all that
believe are justified from all things, from which ye could not be justified
by the law of Moses. 40 Beware therefore, lest that come upon you,
which is spoken of in the prophets;

> 41 Behold, ye despisers, and wonder, and perish:
> For I work a work in your days,
> A work which ye shall in no wise believe, though a man declare
> it unto you.

42 And when the Jews were gone out of the synagogue, the Gentiles
besought that these words might be preached to them the next sabbath. 43 Now when the congregation was broken up, many of the
Jews and religious proselytes followed Paul and Barnabas; who, speaking to them, persuaded them to continue in the grace of God.

44 And the next sabbath day came almost the whole city together
to hear the word of God. 45 But when the Jews saw the multitudes,
they were filled with envy, and spake against those things which were
spoken by Paul, contradicting and blaspheming. 46 Then Paul and
Barnabas waxed bold, and said, It was necessary that the word of God
should first have been spoken to you: but seeing ye put it from you,
and judge yourselves unworthy of everlasting life, lo, we turn to the
Gentiles. 47 For so hath the Lord commanded us, saying,

> I have set thee to be a light of the Gentiles,
> That thou shouldest be for salvation unto the ends of the
> earth.

48 And when the Gentiles heard this, they were glad, and glorified
the word of the Lord: and as many as were ordained to eternal life
believed. 49 And the word of the Lord was published thoughout all

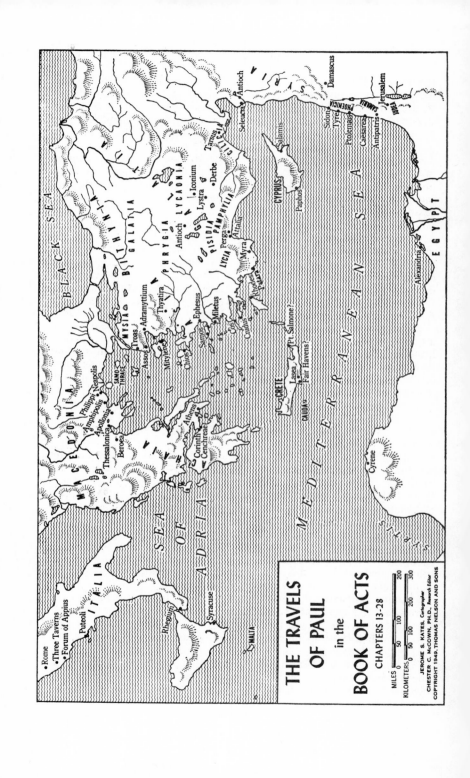

THE TRAVELS
OF PAUL
in the

BOOK OF ACTS

CHAPTERS 13-28

MILES
0    50    100         200

KILOMETERS
0    50    100    200    300

JEROME S. KATES, Cartographer
CHESTER C. McCOWN, PH.D., Research Editor
COPYRIGHT 1949, THOMAS NELSON AND SONS

the region. 50 But the Jews stirred up the devout and honorable women, and the chief men of the city, and raised persecution against Paul and Barnabas, and expelled them out of their coasts. 51 But they shook off the dust of their feet against them, and came into Iconium. 52 And the disciples were filled with joy, and with the Holy Ghost.

14 And it came to pass in Iconium, that they went both together into the synagogue of the Jews, and so spake, that a great multitude both of the Jews and also of the Greeks believed. 2 But the unbelieving Jews stirred up the Gentiles, and made their minds evil affected against the brethren. 3 Long time therefore abode they speaking boldly in the Lord, which gave testimony unto the word of his grace, and granted signs and wonders to be done by their hands. 4 But the multitude of the city was divided: and part held with the Jews, and part with the apostles. 5 And when there was an assault made both of the Gentiles, and also of the Jews with their rulers, to use them despitefully, and to stone them, 6 They were ware of it, and fled unto Lystra and Derbe, cities of Lycaonia, and unto the region that lieth round about: 7 And there they preached the gospel.

8 And there sat a certain man at Lystra, impotent in his feet, being a cripple from his mother's womb, who never had walked: 9 The same heard Paul speak: who steadfastly beholding him, and perceiving that he had faith to be healed, 10 Said with a loud voice, Stand upright on thy feet. And he leaped and walked. 11 And when the people saw what Paul had done, they lifted up their voices, saying in the speech of Lycaonia, The gods are come down to us in the likeness of men. 12 And they called Barnabas, Jupiter; and Paul, Mercurius, because he was the chief speaker. 13 Then the priest of Jupiter, which was before their city, brought oxen and garlands unto the gates, and would have done sacrifice with the people. 14 Which when the apostles, Barnabas and Paul, heard of, they rent their clothes, and ran in among the people, crying out, 15 And saying, Sirs, why do ye these things? We also are men of like passions with you, and preach unto you that ye should turn from these vanities unto the living God, which made heaven, and earth, and the sea, and all things that are therein: 16 Who in times past suffered all nations to walk in their own ways. 17 Nevertheless he left not himself without witness, in that he did good, and gave us rain from heaven, and fruitful seasons, filling our hearts with food and gladness. 18 And with these sayings scarce restrained they the people, that they had not done sacrifice unto them.

19 And there came thither certain Jews from Antioch and Iconium, who persuaded the people, and, having stoned Paul, drew him out of the city, supposing he had been dead. 20 Howbeit, as the disciples stood round about him, he rose up, and came into the city: and the next day he departed with Barnabas to Derbe.

21 And when they had preached the gospel to that city, and had taught many, they returned again to Lystra, and to Iconium, and Antioch, 22 Confirming the souls of the disciples, and exhorting them

to continue in the faith, and that we must through much tribulation enter into the kingdom of God. 23 And when they had ordained them elders in every church, and had prayed with fasting, they commended them to the Lord, on whom they believed. 24 And after they had passed throughout Pisidia, they came to Pamphylia. 25 And when they had preached the word in Perga, they went down into Attalia: 26 And thence sailed to Antioch, from whence they had been recommended to the grace of God for the work which they fulfilled. 27 And when they were come, and had gathered the church together, they rehearsed all that God had done with them, and how he had opened the door of faith unto the Gentiles. 28 And there they abode long time with the disciples.

15   And certain men which came down from Judea taught the brethren, and said, Except ye be circumcised after the manner of Moses, ye cannot be saved. 2 When therefore Paul and Barnabas had no small dissension and disputation with them, they determined that Paul and Barnabas, and certain other of them, should go up to Jerusalem unto the apostles and elders about this question. 3 And being brought on their way by the church, they passed through Phenice and Samaria, declaring the conversion of the Gentiles: and they caused great joy unto all the brethren. 4 And when they were come to Jerusalem, they were received of the church, and of the apostles and elders, and they declared all things that God had done with them. 5 But there rose up certain of the sect of the Pharisees which believed, saying, That it was needful to circumcise them, and to command them to keep the law of Moses.

6 And the apostles and elders came together for to consider of this matter. 7 And when there had been much disputing, Peter rose up, and said unto them, Men and brethren, ye know how that a good while ago God made choice among us, that the Gentiles by my mouth should hear the word of the gospel, and believe. 8 And God, which knoweth the hearts, bare them witness, giving them the Holy Ghost, even as he did unto us; 9 And put no difference between us and them, purifying their hearts by faith. 10 Now therefore why tempt ye God, to put a yoke upon the neck of the disciples, which neither our fathers nor we were able to bear? 11 But we believe that through the grace of the Lord Jesus Christ we shall be saved, even as they.

12 Then all the multitude kept silence, and gave audience to Barnabas and Paul, declaring what miracles and wonders God had wrought among the Gentiles by them.

13 And after they had held their peace, James answered, saying, Men and brethren, hearken unto me: 14 Simeon hath declared how God at the first did visit the Gentiles, to take out of them a people for his name. 15 And to this agree the words of the prophets; as it is written,

16 After this I will return,

And will build again the tabernacle of David, which is fallen
down;
And I will build again the ruins thereof,
And I will set it up:
17 That the residue of men might seek after the Lord,
And all the Gentiles, upon whom my name is called,
Saith the Lord, who doeth all these things.
18 Known unto God are all his works from the beginning of the
world.

19 Wherefore my sentence is, that we trouble not them, which from
among the Gentiles are turned to God: 20 But that we write unto
them, that they abstain from pollutions of idols, and from fornication,
and from things strangled, and from blood. 21 For Moses of old
time hath in every city them that preach him, being read in the
synagogues every sabbath day.

22 Then pleased it the apostles and elders, with the whole church,
to send chosen men of their own company to Antioch with Paul and
Barnabas; namely, Judas surnamed Barsabas, and Silas, chief men
among the brethren: 23 And they wrote letters by them after this
manner; The apostles and elders and brethren send greeting unto the
brethren which are of the Gentiles in Antioch and Syria and Cilicia:
24 Forasmuch as we have heard, that certain which went out from
us have troubled you with words, subverting your souls, saying, Ye must
be circumcised, and keep the law; to whom we gave no such commandment: 25 It seemed good unto us, being assembled with one accord, to
send chosen men unto you with our beloved Barnabas and Paul,
26 Men that have hazarded their lives for the name of our Lord Jesus
Christ. 27 We have sent therefore Judas and Silas, who shall also
tell you the same things by mouth. 28 For it seemed good to the
Holy Ghost, and to us, to lay upon you no greater burden than these
necessary things; 29 That ye abstain from meats offered to idols, and
from blood, and from things strangled, and from fornication: from
which if ye keep yourselves, ye shall do well. Fare ye well.

30 So when they were dismissed, they came to Antioch: and when
they had gathered the multitude together, they delivered the epistle:
31 Which when they had read, they rejoiced for the consolation.
32 And Judas and Silas, being prophets also themselves, exhorted the
brethren with many words, and confirmed them. 33 And after they
had tarried there a space, they were let go in peace from the brethren
unto the apostles. 34 Notwithstanding it pleased Silas to abide there
still. 35 Paul also and Barnabas continued in Antioch, teaching and
preaching the word of the Lord, with many others also.

36 And some days after, Paul said unto Barnabas, Let us go again
and visit our brethren in every city where we have preached the word
of the Lord, and see how they do. 37 And Barnabas determined to
take with them John, whose surname was Mark. 38 But Paul thought
not good to take him with them, who departed from them from

Pamphylia, and went not with them to the work. 39 And the contention was so sharp between them, that they departed asunder one from the other: and so Barnabas took Mark, and sailed unto Cyprus; 40 And Paul chose Silas, and departed, being recommended by the brethren unto the grace of God. 41 And he went through Syria and Cilicia, confirming the churches.

16 Then came he to Derbe and Lystra: and, behold, a certain disciple was there, named Timotheus, the son of a certain woman, which was a Jewess, and believed; but his father was a Greek: 2 Which was well reported of by the brethren that were at Lystra and Iconium. 3 Him would Paul have to go forth with him; and took and circumcised him because of the Jews which were in those quarters: for they knew all that his father was a Greek. 4 And as they went through the cities, they delivered them the decrees for to keep, that were ordained of the apostles and elders which were at Jerusalem. 5 And so were the churches established in the faith, and increased in number daily.

9 And a vision appeared to Paul in the night; There stood a man of Macedonia, and prayed him, saying, Come over into Macedonia, and help us. 10 And after he had seen the vision, immediately we endeavored to go into Macedonia, assuredly gathering that the Lord had called us for to preach the gospel unto them. 11 Therefore loosing from Troas, we came with a straight course to Samothracia, and the next day to Neapolis; 12 And from thence to Philippi, which is the chief city of that part of Macedonia, and a colony: and we were in that city abiding certain days.

13 And on the sabbath we went out of the city by a river side, where prayer was wont to be made; and we sat down, and spake unto the women which resorted thither. 14 And a certain woman named Lydia, a seller of purple, of the city of Thyatira, which worshipped God, heard us: whose heart the Lord opened, that she attended unto the things which were spoken of Paul. 15 And when she was baptized, and her household, she besought us, saying, If ye have judged me to be faithful to the Lord, come into my house, and abide there. And she constrained us.

16 And it came to pass, as we went to prayer, a certain damsel possessed with a spirit of divination met us, which brought her masters much gain by soothsaying: 17 The same followed Paul and us, and cried, saying, These men are the servants of the most high God, which show unto us the way of salvation. 18 And this did she many days. But Paul, being grieved, turned and said to the spirit, I command thee in the name of Jesus Christ to come out of her. And he came out the same hour.

19 And when her masters saw that the hope of their gains was gone, they caught Paul and Silas, and drew them into the market place unto the rulers, 20 And brought them to the magistrates, saying, These men, being Jews, do exceedingly trouble our city, 21 And teach customs, which are not lawful for us to receive, neither to observe, being

Romans. 22 And the multitude rose up together against them; and the magistrates rent off their clothes, and commanded to beat them.

17 Now when they had passed through Amphipolis and Apollonia, they came to Thessalonica, where was a synagogue of the Jews: 2 And Paul, as his manner was, went in unto them, and three sabbath days reasoned with them out of the Scriptures, 3 Opening and alleging, that Christ must needs have suffered, and risen again from the dead; and that this Jesus, whom I preach unto you, is Christ. 4 And some of them believed, and consorted with Paul and Silas; and of the devout Greeks a great multitude, and of the chief women not a few.

5 But the Jews which believed not, moved with envy, took unto them certain lewd fellows of the baser sort, and gathered a company, and set all the city on an uproar, and assaulted the house of Jason, and sought to bring them out to the people. 6 And when they found them not, they drew Jason and certain brethren unto the rulers of the city, crying, These that have turned the world upside down are come hither also; 7 Whom Jason hath received: and these all do contrary to the decrees of Caesar, saying that there is another king, one Jesus. 8 And they troubled the people and the rulers of the city, when they heard these things. 9 And when they had taken security of Jason, and of the others, they let them go.

10 And the brethren immediately sent away Paul and Silas by night unto Berea: who coming thither went into the synagogue of the Jews. 11 These were more noble than those in Thessalonica, in that they received the word with all readiness of mind, and searched the Scriptures daily, whether those things were so. 12 Therefore many of them believed; also of honorable women which were Greeks, and of men, not a few. 13 But when the Jews of Thessalonica had knowledge that the word of God was preached of Paul at Berea, they came thither also, and stirred up the people. 14 And then immediately the brethren sent away Paul to go as it were to the sea: but Silas and Timotheus abode there still. 15 And they that conducted Paul brought him unto Athens: and receiving a commandment unto Silas and Timotheus for to come to him with all speed, they departed.

16 Now while Paul waited for them at Athens, his spirit was stirred in him, when he saw the city wholly given to idolatry. 17 Therefore disputed he in the synagogue with the Jews, and with the devout persons, and in the market daily with them that met with him. 18 Then certain philosophers of the Epicureans, and of the Stoics, encountered him. And some said, What will this babbler say? other some, He seemeth to be a setter forth of strange gods: because he preached unto them Jesus, and the resurrection. 19 And they took him, and brought him unto Areopagus, saying, May we know what this new doctrine, whereof thou speakest, is? 20 For thou bringest certain strange things to our ears: we would know therefore what these things mean. 21 (For all the Athenians, and strangers which were there, spent their time in nothing else, but either to tell or to hear some new thing.)

22 Then Paul stood in the midst of Mars' hill, and said, Ye men of Athens, I perceive that in all things ye are too superstitious. 23 For as I passed by, and beheld your devotions, I found an altar with this inscription, To the Unknown God. Whom therefore ye ignorantly worship, him declare I unto you. 24 God that made the world and all the things therein, seeing that he is Lord of heaven and earth, dwelleth not in temples made with hands; 25 Neither is worshipped with men's hands, as though he needed any thing, seeing he giveth to all life, and breath, and all things; 26 And hath made of one blood all nations of men for to dwell on all the face of the earth, and hath determined the times before appointed, and the bounds of their habitation; 27 That they should seek the Lord, if haply they might feel after him, and find him, though he be not far from every one of us: 28 For

In him we live, and move, and have our being;
as certain also of your own poets have said,
For we are also his offspring.

29 Forasmuch then as we are the offspring of God, we ought not to think that the Godhead is like unto gold, or silver, or stone, graven by art and man's device. 30 And the times of this ignorance God winked at; but now commandeth all men every where to repent: 31 Because he hath appointed a day, in the which he will judge the world in righteousness by that man whom he hath ordained; whereof he hath given assurance unto all men, in that he hath raised him from the dead.

32 And when they heard of the resurrection of the dead, some mocked: and others said, We will hear thee again of this matter. 33 So Paul departed from among them. 34 Howbeit certain men clave unto him, and believed: among the which was Dionysius the Areopagite, and a woman named Damaris, and others with them.

18 After these things Paul departed from Athens, and came to Corinth; 2 And found a certain Jew named Aquila, born in Pontus, lately come from Italy, with his wife Priscilla, (because that Claudius had commanded all Jews to depart from Rome,) and came unto them. 3 And because he was of the same craft, he abode with them, and wrought: (for by their occupation they were tentmakers.) 4 And he reasoned in the synagogue every sabbath, and persuaded the Jews and the Greeks.

5 And when Silas and Timotheus were come from Macedonia, Paul was pressed in the spirit, and testified to the Jews that Jesus was Christ. 6 And when they opposed themselves, and blasphemed, he shook his raiment, and said unto them, Your blood be upon your own heads; I am clean: from henceforth I will go unto the Gentiles. 7 And he departed thence, and entered into a certain man's house, named Justus, one that worshipped God, whose house joined hard to the synagogue. 8 And Crispus, the chief ruler of the synagogue, believed on the Lord with all his house; and many of the Corinthians hearing believed, and were baptized. 9 Then spake the Lord to Paul in the

night by a vision, Be not afraid, but speak, and hold not thy peace: 10 For I am with thee, and no man shall set on thee to hurt thee: for I have much people in this city. 11 And he continued there a year and six months, teaching the word of God among them.

12 And when Gallio was the deputy of Achaia, the Jews made insurrection with one accord against Paul, and brought him to the judgment seat, 13 Saying, This fellow persuadeth men to worship God contrary to the law. 14 And when Paul was now about to open his mouth, Gallio said unto the Jews, If it were a matter of wrong or wicked lewdness, O ye Jews, reason would that I should bear with you: 15 But if it be a question of words and names, and of your law, look ye to it; for I will be no judge of such matters. 16 And he drave them from the judgment seat. 17 Then all the Greeks took Sosthenes, the chief ruler of the synagogue, and beat him before the judgment seat. And Gallio cared for none of those things.

18 And Paul after this tarried there yet a good while, and then took his leave of the brethren, and sailed thence into Syria, and with him Priscilla and Aquila; having shorn his head in Cenchrea: for he had a vow. 19 And he came to Ephesus, and left them there: but he himself entered into the synagogue, and reasoned with the Jews. 20 When they desired him to tarry longer time with them, he consented not; 21 But bade them farewell, saying, I must by all means keep this feast that cometh in Jerusalem: but I will return again unto you, if God will. And he sailed from Ephesus. 22 And when he had landed at Caesarea, and gone up, and saluted the church, he went down to Antioch.

23 And after he had spent some time there, he departed, and went over all the country of Galatia and Phrygia in order, strengthening all the disciples.

24 And a certain Jew named Apollos, born at Alexandria, an eloquent man, and mighty in the Scriptures, came to Ephesus. 25 This man was instructed in the way of the Lord; and being fervent in the spirit, he spake and taught diligently the things of the Lord, knowing only the baptism of John. 26 And he began to speak boldly in the synagogue: whom when Aquila and Priscilla had heard, they took him unto them, and expounded unto him the way of God more perfectly. 27 And when he was disposed to pass into Achaia, the brethren wrote, exhorting the disciples to receive him: who, when he was come, helped them much which had believed through grace: 28 For he mightily convinced the Jews, and that publicly, showing by the Scriptures that Jesus was Christ.

19 And it came to pass, that, while Apollos was at Corinth, Paul having passed through the upper coasts came to Ephesus; and finding certain disciples, 2 He said unto them, Have ye received the Holy Ghost since ye believed? And they said unto him, We have not so much as heard whether there be any Holy Ghost. 3 And he said unto them, Unto what then were ye baptized? And they said, Unto

John's baptism. 4 Then said Paul, John verily baptized with the baptism of repentance, saying unto the people, that they should believe on him which should come after him, that is, on Christ Jesus. 5 When they heard this, they were baptized in the name of the Lord Jesus. 6 And when Paul had laid his hands upon them, the Holy Ghost came on them; and they spake with tongues, and prophesied. 7 And all the men were about twelve.

8 And he went into the synagogue, and spake boldly for the space of three months, disputing and persuading the things concerning the kingdom of God. 9 But when divers were hardened, and believed not, but spake evil of that way before the multitude, he departed from them, and separated the disciples, disputing daily in the school of one Tyrannus. 10 And this continued by the space of two years; so that all they which dwelt in Asia heard the word of the Lord Jesus, both Jews and Greeks.

11 And God wrought special miracles by the hands of Paul: 12 So that from his body were brought unto the sick handkerchiefs or aprons, and the diseases departed from them, and the evil spirits went out of them.

13 Then certain of the vagabond Jews, exorcists, took upon them to call over them which had evil spirits the name of the Lord Jesus, saying, We adjure you by Jesus whom Paul preacheth. 14 And there were seven sons of one Sceva, a Jew, and chief of the priests, which did so. 15 And the evil spirit answered and said, Jesus I know, and Paul I know; but who are ye? 16 And the man in whom the evil spirit was leaped on them, and overcame them, and prevailed against them, so that they fled out of that house naked and wounded. 17 And this was known to all the Jews and Greeks also dwelling at Ephesus; and fear fell on them all, and the name of the Lord Jesus was magnified. 18 And many that believed came, and confessed, and showed their deeds. 19 Many of them also which used curious arts brought their books together, and burned them before all men: and they counted the price of them, and found it fifty thousand pieces of silver.

20 So mightily grew the word of God and prevailed.

21 After these things were ended, Paul purposed in the spirit, when he had passed through Macedonia and Achaia, to go to Jerusalem, saying, After I have been there, I must also see Rome. 22 So he sent into Macedonia two of them that ministered unto him, Timotheus and Erastus; but he himself stayed in Asia for a season.

23 And the same time there arose no small stir about that way. 24 For a certain man named Demetrius, a silversmith, which made silver shrines for Diana, brought no small gain unto the craftsmen; 25 Whom he called together with the workmen of like occupation, and said, Sirs, ye know that by this craft we have our wealth. 26 Moreover ye see and hear, that not alone at Ephesus, but almost throughout all Asia, this Paul hath persuaded and turned away much people, saying that they be no gods, which are made with hands: 27 So that not only this our craft is in danger to be set at nought; but also that

the temple of the great goddess Diana should be despised, and her magnificence should be destroyed, whom all Asia and the world worshippeth.

28 And when they heard these sayings, they were full of wrath, and cried out, saying, Great is Diana of the Ephesians. 29 And the whole city was filled with confusion: and having caught Gaius and Aristarchus, men of Macedonia, Paul's companions in travel, they rushed with one accord into the theatre. 30 And when Paul would have entered in unto the people, the disciples suffered him not. 31 And certain of the chief of Asia, which were his friends, sent unto him, desiring him that he would not adventure himself into the theatre. 32 Some therefore cried one thing, and some another: for the assembly was confused; and the more part knew not wherefore they were come together. 33 And they drew Alexander out of the multitude, the Jews putting him forward. And Alexander beckoned with the hand, and would have made his defense unto the people. 34 But when they knew that he was a Jew, all with one voice about the space of two hours cried out, Great is Diana of the Ephesians.

35 And when the townclerk had appeased the people, he said, Ye men of Ephesus, what man is there that knoweth not how that the city of the Ephesians is a worshipper of the great goddess Diana, and of the image which fell down from Jupiter? 36 Seeing then that these things cannot be spoken against, ye ought to be quiet, and to do nothing rashly. 37 For ye have brought hither these men, which are neither robbers of churches, nor yet blasphemers of your goddess. 38 Wherefore if Demetrius, and the craftsmen which are with him, have a matter against any man, the law is open, and there are deputies: let them implead one another. 39 But if ye inquire any thing concerning other matters, it shall be determined in a lawful assembly. 40 For we are in danger to be called in question for this day's uproar, there being no cause whereby we may give an account of this concourse. 41 And when he had thus spoken, he dismissed the assembly.

20 And after the uproar was ceased, Paul called unto him the disciples, and embraced them, and departed for to go into Macedonia. 7 And upon the first day of the week, when the disciples came together to break bread, Paul preached unto them, ready to depart on the morrow; and continued his speech until midnight. 8 And there were many lights in the upper chamber, where they were gathered together. 9 And there sat in a window a certain young man named Eutychus, being fallen into a deep sleep: and as Paul was long preaching, he sunk down with sleep, and fell down from the third loft, and was taken up dead. 10 And Paul went down, and fell on him, and embracing him said, Trouble not yourselves; for his life is in him. 11 When he therefore was come up again, and had broken bread, and eaten, and talked a long while, even till break of day, so he departed. 12 And they brought the young man alive, and were not a little comforted.

563

13 And we went before to ship, and sailed unto Assos, there intending to take in Paul: for so had he appointed, minding himself to go afoot. 14 And when he met with us at Assos, we took him in, and came to Mitylene. 15 And we sailed thence, and came the next day over against Chios; and the next day we arrived at Samos, and tarried at Trogyllium; and the next day we came to Miletus. 16 For Paul had determined to sail by Ephesus, because he would not spend the time in Asia: for he hasted, if it were possible for him, to be at Jerusalem the day of Pentecost.

17 And from Miletus he sent to Ephesus, and called the elders of the church. 18 And when they were come to him, he said unto them, Ye know, from the first day that I came into Asia, after what manner I have been with you at all seasons, 19 Serving the Lord with all humility of mind, and with many tears, and temptations, which befell me by the lying in wait of the Jews: 20 And how I kept back nothing that was profitable unto you, but have showed you, and have taught you publicly, and from house to house, 21 Testifying both to the Jews, and also to the Greeks, repentance toward God, and faith toward our Lord Jesus Christ. 22 And now, behold, I go bound in the spirit unto Jerusalem, not knowing the things that shall befall me there: 23 Save that the Holy Ghost witnesseth in every city, saying that bonds and afflictions abide me. 24 But none of these things move me, neither count I my life dear unto myself, so that I might finish my course with joy, and the ministry, which I have received of the Lord Jesus, to testify the gospel of the grace of God.

25 And now, behold, I know that ye all, among whom I have gone preaching the kingdom of God, shall see my face no more. 26 Wherefore I take you to record this day, that I am pure from the blood of all men. 27 For I have not shunned to declare unto you all the counsel of God. 28 Take heed therefore unto yourselves, and to all the flock, over the which the Holy Ghost hath made you overseers, to feed the church of God, which he hath purchased with his own blood. 29 For I know this, that after my departing shall grievous wolves enter in among you, not sparing the flock. 30 Also of your own selves shall men arise, speaking perverse things, to draw away disciples after them. 31 Therefore watch, and remember, that by the space of three years I ceased not to warn every one night and day with tears.

32 And now, brethren, I commend you to God, and to the word of his grace, which is able to build you up, and to give you an inheritance among all them which are sanctified. 33 I have coveted no man's silver, or gold, or apparel. 34 Yea, ye yourselves know, that these hands have ministered unto my necessities, and to them that were with me. 35 I have showed you all things, how that so laboring ye ought to support the weak, and to remember the words of the Lord Jesus, how he said, It is more blessed to give than to receive.

36 And when he had thus spoken, he kneeled down, and prayed with them all. 37 And they all wept sore, and fell on Paul's neck, and kissed him, 38 Sorrowing most of all for the words which he spake,

that they should see his face no more. And they accompanied him unto the ship.

21 And it came to pass, that after we were gotten from them, and had launched, we came with a straight course unto Coos, and the day following unto Rhodes, and from thence unto Patara: 2 And finding a ship sailing over unto Phenicia, we went aboard, and set forth. 3 Now when we had discovered Cyprus, we left it on the left hand, and sailed into Syria, and landed at Tyre: for there the ship was to unlade her burden. 4 And finding disciples, we tarried there seven days: who said to Paul through the Spirit, that he should not go up to Jerusalem. 5 And when we had accomplished those days, we departed and went our way; and they all brought us on our way, with wives and children, till we were out of the city: and we kneeled down on the shore, and prayed. 6 And when we had taken our leave one of another, we took ship; and they returned home again.

7 And when we had finished our course from Tyre, we came to Ptolemais, and saluted the brethren, and abode with them one day. 8 And the next day we that were of Paul's company departed, and came unto Caesarea; and we entered into the house of Philip the evangelist, which was one of the seven; and abode with him. 9 And the same man had four daughters, virgins, which did prophesy. 10 And as we tarried there many days, there came down from Judea a certain prophet, named Agabus. 11 And when he was come unto us, he took Paul's girdle, and bound his own hands and feet, and said, Thus saith the Holy Ghost, So shall the Jews at Jerusalem bind the man that owneth this girdle, and shall deliver him into the hands of the Gentiles. 12 And when we heard these things, both we, and they of that place, besought him not to go up to Jerusalem. 13 Then Paul answered, What mean ye to weep and to break mine heart? for I am ready not to be bound only, but also to die at Jerusalem for the name of the Lord Jesus. 14 And when he would not be persuaded, we ceased, saying, The will of the Lord be done.

15 And after those days we took up our carriages, and went up to Jerusalem. 16 There went with us also certain of the disciples of Caesarea, and brought with them one Mnason of Cyprus, an old disciple, with whom we should lodge. 17 And when we were come to Jerusalem, the brethren received us gladly. 18 And the day following Paul went in with us unto James; and all the elders were present. 19 And when he had saluted them, he declared particularly what things God had wrought among the Gentiles by his ministry. 20 And when they heard it, they glorified the Lord, and said unto him, Thou seest, brother, how many thousands of Jews there are which believe; and they are all zealous of the law: 21 And they are informed of thee, that thou teachest all the Jews which are among the Gentiles to forsake Moses, saying that they ought not to circumcise their children, neither to walk after the customs. 22 What is it therefore? the multitude must needs come together: for they will hear that

thou art come. 23 Do therefore this that we say to thee: We have four men which have a vow on them; 24 Them take, and purify thyself with them, and be at charges with them, that they may shave their heads; and all may know that those things, whereof they were informed concerning thee, are nothing; but that thou thyself also walkest orderly, and keepest the law. 25 As touching the Gentiles which believe, we have written and concluded that they observe no such thing, save only that they keep themselves from things offered to idols, and from blood, and from strangled, and from fornication. 26 Then Paul took the men, and the next day purifying himself with them entered into the temple, to signify the accomplishment of the days of purification, until that an offering should be offered for every one of them.

27 And when the seven days were almost ended, the Jews which were of Asia, when they saw him in the temple, stirred up all the people, and laid hands on him, 28 Crying out, Men of Israel, help: This is the man, that teacheth all men every where against the people, and the law, and this place: and further brought Greeks also into the temple, and hath polluted this holy place. 29 (For they had seen before with him in the city Trophimus an Ephesian, whom they supposed that Paul had brought into the temple.) 30 And all the city was moved, and the people ran together: and they took Paul, and drew him out of the temple: and forthwith the doors were shut. 31 And as they went about to kill him, tidings came unto the chief captain of the band, that all Jerusalem was in an uproar: 32 Who immediately took soldiers and centurions, and ran down unto them: and when they saw the chief captain and the soldiers, they left beating of Paul. 33 Then the chief captain came near, and took him, and commanded him to be bound with two chains; and demanded who he was, and what he had done. 34 And some cried one thing, some another, among the multitude: and when he could not know the certainty for the tumult, he commanded him to be carried into the castle. 35 And when he came upon the stairs, so it was, that he was borne of the soldiers for the violence of the people. 36 For the multitude of the people followed after, crying, Away with him.

37 And as Paul was to be led into the castle, he said unto the chief captain, May I speak unto thee? Who said, Canst thou speak Greek? 38 Art not thou that Egyptian, which before these days madest an uproar, and leddest out into the wilderness four thousand men that were murderers? 39 But Paul said, I am a man which am a Jew of Tarsus, a city in Cilicia, a citizen of no mean city: and, I beseech thee, suffer me to speak unto the people. 40 And when he had given him license, Paul stood on the stairs, and beckoned with the hand unto the people. And when there was made a great silence, he spake unto them in the Hebrew tongue, saying,

22 Men, brethren, and fathers, hear ye my defense which I make now unto you. 2 (And when they heard that he spake in the Hebrew tongue to them, they kept the more silence: and he saith,) 3 I am

verily a man which am a Jew, born in Tarsus, a city in Cilicia, yet brought up in this city at the feet of Gamaliel, and taught according to the perfect manner of the law of the fathers, and was zealous toward God, as ye all are this day. 4 And I persecuted this way unto the death, binding and delivering into prisons both men and women. 5 As also the high priest doth bear me witness, and all the estate of the elders: from whom also I received letters unto the brethren, and went to Damascus, to bring them which were there bound unto Jerusalem, for to be punished. 6 And it came to pass, that, as I made my journey, and was come nigh unto Damascus about noon, suddenly there shone from heaven a great light round about me. 7 And I fell unto the ground, and heard a voice saying unto me, Saul, Saul, why persecutest thou me? 8 And I answered, Who art thou, Lord? And he said unto me, I am Jesus of Nazareth, whom thou persecutest. 9 And they that were with me saw indeed the light, and were afraid; but they heard not the voice of him that spake to me. 10 And I said, What shall I do, Lord? And the Lord said unto me, Arise, and go into Damascus; and there it shall be told thee of all things which are appointed for thee to do. 11 And when I could not see for the glory of that light, being led by the hand of them that were with me, I came into Damascus.

12 And one Ananias, a devout man according to the law, having a good report of all the Jews which dwelt there, 13 Came unto me, and stood, and said unto me, Brother Saul, receive thy sight. And the same hour I looked up upon him. 14 And he said, The God of our fathers hath chosen thee, that thou shouldest know his will, and see that Just One, and shouldest hear the voice of his mouth. 15 For thou shalt be his witness unto all men of what thou hast seen and heard. 16 And now why tarriest thou? arise, and be baptized, and wash away thy sins, calling on the name of the Lord.

17 And it came to pass, that, when I was come again to Jerusalem, even while I prayed in the temple, I was in a trance; 18 And saw him saying unto me, Make haste, and get thee quickly out of Jerusalem: for they will not receive thy testimony concerning me. 19 And I said, Lord, they know that I imprisoned and beat in every synagogue them that believed on thee: 20 And when the blood of thy martyr Stephen was shed, I also was standing by, and consenting unto his death, and kept the raiment of them that slew him. 21 And he said unto me, Depart: for I will send thee far hence unto the Gentiles.

22 And they gave him audience unto this word, and then lifted up their voices, and said, Away with such a fellow from the earth: for it it not fit that he should live. 23 And as they cried out, and cast off their clothes, and threw dust into the air, 24 The chief captain commanded him to be brought into the castle, and bade that he should be examined by scourging; that he might know wherefore they cried so against him.

25 And as they bound him with thongs, Paul said unto the centurion that stood by, Is it lawful for you to scourge a man that is a

Roman and uncondemned? 26 When the centurion heard that, he went and told the chief captain, saying, Take heed what thou doest; for this man is a Roman. 27 Then the chief captain came, and said unto him, Tell me, art thou a Roman? He said, Yea. 28 And the chief captain answered, With a great sum obtained I this freedom. And Paul said, But I was free-born. 29 Then straightway they departed from him which should have examined him: and the chief captain also was afraid, after he knew that he was a Roman, and because he had bound him.

30 On the morrow, because he would have known the certainty wherefore he was accused of the Jews, he loosed him from his bands, and commanded the chief priests and all their council to appear, and brought Paul down, and set him before them.

23 And Paul, earnestly beholding the council, said, Men and brethren, I have lived in all good conscience before God until this day. 2 And the high priest Ananias commanded them that stood by him to smite him on the mouth. 3 Then said Paul unto him, God shall smite thee, thou whited wall: for sittest thou to judge me after the law, and commandest me to be smitten contrary to the law? 4 And they that stood by said, Revilest thou God's high priest? 5 Then said Paul, I wist not, brethren, that he was the high priest: for it is written, Thou shalt not speak evil of the ruler of thy people.

6 But when Paul perceived that the one part were Sadducees, and the other Pharisees, he cried out in the council, Men and brethren, I am a Pharisee, the son of a Pharisee: of the hope and resurrection of the dead I am called in question. 7 And when he had so said, there arose a dissension between the Pharisees and the Sadducees: and the multitude was divided. 8 For the Sadducees say that there is no resurrection, neither angel, nor spirit: but the Pharisees confess both. 9 And there arose a great cry: and the scribes that were of the Pharisees' part arose, and strove, saying, We find no evil in this man: but if a spirit or an angel hath spoken to him, let us not fight against God. 10 And when there arose a great dissension, the chief captain, fearing lest Paul should have been pulled in pieces of them, commanded the soldiers to go down, and to take him by force from among them, and to bring him into the castle.

11 And the night following the Lord stood by him, and said, Be of good cheer, Paul: for as thou hast testified of me in Jerusalem, so must thou bear witness also at Rome.

12 And when it was day, certain of the Jews banded together, and bound themselves under a curse, saying that they would neither eat nor drink till they had killed Paul. 13 And they were more than forty which had made this conspiracy. 14 And they came to the chief priests and elders, and said, We have bound ourselves under a great curse, that we will eat nothing until we have slain Paul. 15 Now therefore ye with the council signify to the chief captain that he bring him down unto you to-morrow, as though ye would inquire something

more perfectly concerning him: and we, or ever he come near, are ready to kill him.

16 And when Paul's sister's son heard of their lying in wait, he went and entered into the castle, and told Paul. 17 Then Paul called one of the centurions unto him, and said, Bring this young man unto the chief captain: for he hath a certain thing to tell him. 18 So he took him, and brought him to the chief captain, and said, Paul the prisoner called me unto him, and prayed me to bring this young man unto thee, who hath something to say unto thee. 19 Then the chief captain took him by the hand, and went with him aside privately, and asked him, What is that thou hast to tell me? 20 And he said, The Jews have agreed to desire thee that thou wouldest bring down Paul to-morrow into the council, as though they would inquire somewhat of him more perfectly. 21 But do not thou yield unto them: for there lie in wait for him of them more than forty men, which have bound themselves with an oath, that they will neither eat nor drink till they have killed him: and now are they ready, looking for a promise from thee. 22 So the chief captain then let the young man depart, and charged him, See thou tell no man that thou hast showed these things to me.

23 And he called unto him two centurions, saying, Make ready two hundred soldiers to go to Caesarea, and horsemen threescore and ten, and spearmen two hundred, at the third hour of the night; 24 And provide them beasts, that they may set Paul on, and bring him safe unto Felix the governor. 25 And he wrote a letter after this manner:

26 Claudius Lysias unto the most excellent governor Felix sendeth greeting. 27 This man was taken of the Jews, and should have been killed of them: then came I with an army, and rescued him, having understood that he was a Roman. 28 And when I would have known the cause wherefore they accused him, I brought him forth into their council: 29 Whom I perceived to be accused of questions of their law, but to have nothing laid to his charge worthy of death or of bonds. 30 And when it was told me how that the Jews laid wait for the man, I sent straightway to thee, and gave commandment to his accusers also to say before thee what they had against him. Farewell.

31 Then the soldiers, as it was commanded them, took Paul, and brought him by night to Antipatris. 32 On the morrow they left the horsemen to go with him, and returned to the castle: 33 Who, when they came to Caesarea, and delivered the epistle to the governor, presented Paul also before him. 34 And when the governor had read the letter, he asked of what province he was. And when he understood that he was of Cilicia; 35 I will hear thee, said he, when thine accusers are also come. And he commanded him to be kept in Herod's judgment hall.

24 And after five days Ananias the high priest descended with the elders, and with a certain orator named Tertullus, who informed the governor against Paul. 2 And when he was called forth, Tertullus began to accuse him, saying, Seeing that by thee we enjoy great

quietness, and that very worthy deeds are done unto this nation by thy providence, 3 We accept it always, and in all places, most noble Felix, with all thankfulness. 4 Notwithstanding, that I be not further tedious unto thee, I pray thee that thou wouldest hear us of thy clemency a few words. 5 For we have found this man a pestilent fellow, and a mover of sedition among all the Jews throughout the world, and a ringleader of the sect of the Nazarenes: 6 Who also hath gone about to profane the temple: whom we took, and would have judged according to our law. 7 But the chief captain Lysias came upon us, and with great violence took him away out of our hands, 8 Commanding his accusers to come unto thee: by examining of whom thyself mayest take knowledge of all these things, whereof we accuse him. 9 And the Jews also assented, saying that these things were so.

10 Then Paul, after that the governor had beckoned unto him to speak, answered, Forasmuch as I know that thou hast been of many years a judge unto this nation, I do the more cheerfully answer for myself: 11 Because that thou mayest understand, that there are yet but twelve days since I went up to Jerusalem for to worship. 12 And they neither found me in the temple disputing with any man, neither raising up the people, neither in the synagogues, nor in the city: 13 Neither can they prove the things whereof they now accuse me. 14 But this I confess unto thee, that after the way which they call heresy, so worship I the God of my fathers, believing all things which are written in the law and in the prophets: 15 And have hope toward God, which they themselves also allow, that there shall be a resurrection of the dead, both of the just and unjust. 16 And herein do I exercise myself, to have always a conscience void of offense toward God, and toward men. 17 Now after many years I came to bring alms to my nation, and offerings. 18 Whereupon certain Jews from Asia found me purified in the temple, neither with multitude, nor with tumult. 19 Who ought to have been here before thee, and object, if they had aught against me. 20 Or else let these same here say, if they have found any evildoing in me, while I stood before the council, 21 Except it be for this one voice, that I cried standing among them, Touching the resurrection of the dead I am called in question by you this day.

22 And when Felix heard these things, having more perfect knowledge of that way, he deferred them, and said, When Lysias the chief captain shall come down, I will know the uttermost of your matter. 23 And he commanded a centurion to keep Paul, and to let him have liberty, and that he should forbid none of his acquaintance to minister or come unto him.

24 And after certain days, when Felix came with his wife Drusilla, which was a Jewess, he sent for Paul, and heard him concerning the faith in Christ. 25 And as he reasoned of righteousness, temperance, and judgment to come, Felix trembled, and answered, Go thy way for this time; when I have a convenient season, I will call for thee. 26 He hoped also that money should have been given him of Paul,

that he might loose him: wherefore he sent for him the oftener, and communed with him. 27 But after two years Porcius Festus came into Felix' room: and Felix, willing to show the Jews a pleasure, left Paul bound.

25 Now when Festus was come into the province, after three days he ascended from Caesarea to Jerusalem. 2 Then the high priest and the chief of the Jews informed him against Paul, and besought him, 3 And desired favor against him, that he would send for him to Jerusalem, laying wait in the way to kill him. 4 But Festus answered, that Paul should be kept at Caesarea, and that he himself would depart shortly thither. 5 Let them therefore, said he, which among you are able, go down with me, and accuse this man, if there be any wickedness in him.

6 And when he had tarried among them more than ten days, he went down unto Caesarea; and the next day sitting on the judgment seat commanded Paul to be brought. 7 And when he was come, the Jews which came down from Jerusalem stood round about, and laid many and grievous complaints against Paul, which they could not prove. 8 While he answered for himself, Neither against the law of the Jews, neither against the temple, nor yet against Caesar, have I offended any thing at all. 9 But Festus, willing to do the Jews a pleasure, answered Paul, and said, Wilt thou go up to Jerusalem, and there be judged of these things before me? 10 Then said Paul, I stand at Caesar's judgment seat, where I ought to be judged: to the Jews I have done no wrong, as thou very well knowest. 11 For if I be an offender, or have committed any thing worthy of death, I refuse not to die: but if there be none of these things whereof these accuse me, no man may deliver me unto them. I appeal unto Caesar. 12 Then Festus, when he had conferred with the council, answered, Hast thou appealed unto Caesar? unto Caesar shalt thou go.

13 And after certain days king Agrippa and Bernice came unto Caesarea to salute Festus. 14 And when they had been there many days, Festus declared Paul's cause unto the king, saying, There is a certain man left in bonds by Felix: 15 About whom, when I was at Jerusalem, the chief priests and the elders of the Jews informed me, desiring to have judgment against him. 16 To whom I answered, It is not the manner of the Romans to deliver any man to die, before that he which is accused have the accusers face to face, and have license to answer for himself concerning the crime laid against him. 17 Therefore, when they were come hither, without any delay on the morrow I sat on the judgment seat, and commanded the man to be brought forth. 18 Against whom when the accusers stood up, they brought none accusation of such things as I supposed: 19 But had certain questions against him of their own superstition, and of one Jesus, which was dead, whom Paul affirmed to be alive. 20 And because I doubted of such manner of questions, I asked him whether he would go to Jerusalem, and there be judged of these matters. 21 But

when Paul had appealed to be reserved unto the hearing of Augustus, I commanded him to be kept till I might send him to Caesar. 22 Then Agrippa said unto Festus, I would also hear the man myself. To-morrow, said he, thou shalt hear him.

23 And on the morrow, when Agrippa was come, and Bernice, with great pomp, and was entered into the place of hearing, with the chief captains, and principal men of the city, at Festus' commandment Paul was brought forth. 24 And Festus said, King Agrippa, and all men which are here present with us, ye see this man, about whom all the multitude of the Jews have dealt with me, both at Jerusalem, and also here, crying that he ought not to live any longer. 25 But when I found that he had committed nothing worthy of death, and that he himself hath appealed to Augustus, I have determined to send him. 26 Of whom I have no certain thing to write unto my lord. Where-fore I have brought him forth before you, and specially before thee, O king Agrippa, that, after examination had, I might have somewhat to write. 27 For it seemeth to me unreasonable to send a prisoner, and not withal to signify the crimes laid against him.

26 Then Agrippa said unto Paul, Thou are permitted to speak for thyself. Then Paul stretched forth the hand, and answered for him-self:

2 I think myself happy, king Agrippa, because I shall answer for myself this day before thee touching all the things whereof I am ac-cused of the Jews: 3 Especially because I know thee to be expert in all customs and questions which are among the Jews: wherefore I beseech thee to hear me patiently.

4 My manner of life from my youth, which was at the first among mine own nation at Jerusalem, know all the Jews; 5 Which knew me from the beginning, if they would testify, that after the most straitest sect of our religion I lived a Pharisee. 6 And now I stand and am judged for the hope of the promise made of God unto our fathers: 7 Unto which promise our twelve tribes, instantly serving God day and night, hope to come. For which hope's sake, king Agrippa, I am accused of the Jews. 8 Why should it be thought a thing incredible with you, that God should raise the dead? 9 I verily thought with my-self, that I ought to do many things contrary to the name of Jesus of Nazareth. 10 Which thing I also did in Jerusalem: and many of the saints did I shut up in prison, having received authority from the chief priests; and when they were put to death, I gave my voice against them. 11 And I punished them oft in every synagogue, and compelled them to blaspheme; and being exceedingly mad against them, I perse-cuted them even unto strange cities.

12 Whereupon as I went to Damascus with authority and commis-sion from the chief priests, 13 At midday, O king, I saw in the way a light from heaven, above the brightness of the sun, shining round about me and them which journeyed with me. 14 And when we were all fallen to the earth, I heard a voice speaking unto me, and saying

in the Hebrew tongue, Saul, Saul, why persecutest thou me? it is hard for thee to kick against the pricks. 15 And I said, Who art thou, Lord? And he said, I am Jesus whom thou persecutest. 16 But rise, and stand upon thy feet: for I have appeared unto thee for this purpose, to make thee a minister and a witness both of these things which thou hast seen, and of those things in the which I will appear unto thee; 17 Delivering thee from the people, and from the Gentiles, unto whom now I send thee, 18 To open their eyes, and to turn them from darkness to light, and from the power of Satan unto God, that they may receive forgiveness of sins, and inheritance among them which are sanctified by faith that is in me.

19 Whereupon, O king Agrippa, I was not disobedient unto the heavenly vision: 20 But showed first unto them of Damascus, and at Jerusalem, and throughout all the coasts of Judea, and then to the Gentiles, that they should repent and turn to God, and do works meet for repentance. 21 For these causes the Jews caught me in the temple, and went about to kill me. 22 Having therefore obtained help of God, I continue unto this day, witnessing both to small and great, saying none other things than those which the prophets and Moses did say should come: 23 That Christ should suffer, and that he should be the first that should rise from the dead, and should show light unto the people, and to the Gentiles.

24 And as he thus spake for himself, Festus said with a loud voice, Paul, thou art beside thyself; much learning doth make thee mad. 25 But he said, I am not mad, most noble Festus; but speak forth the words of truth and soberness. 26 For the king knoweth of these things, before whom also I speak freely: for I am persuaded that none of these things are hidden from him; for this thing was not done in a corner. 27 King Agrippa, believest thou the prophets? I know that thou believest. 28 Then Agrippa said unto Paul, Almost thou persuadest me to be a Christian. 29 And Paul said, I would to God, that not only thou, but also all that hear me this day, were both almost, and altogether such as I am, except these bonds.

30 And when he had thus spoken, the king rose up, and the governor, and Bernice, and they that sat with them: 31 And when they were gone aside, they talked between themselves, saying, This man doeth nothing worthy of death or of bonds. 32 Then said Agrippa unto Festus, This man might have been set at liberty, if he had not appealed unto Ceasar.

27 And when it was determined that we should sail into Italy, they delivered Paul and certain other prisoners unto one named Julius, a centurion of Augustus' band. 2 And entering into a ship of Adramyttium, we launched, meaning to sail by the coasts of Asia; one Aristarchus, a Macedonian of Thessalonica, being with us. 3 And the next day we touched at Sidon. And Julius courteously entreated Paul, and gave him liberty to go unto his friends to refresh himself. 4 And when we had launched from thence, we sailed under Cyprus, because

the winds were contrary. 5 And when we had sailed over the sea of Cilicia and Pamphylia, we came to Myra, a city of Lycia. 6 And there the centurion found a ship of Alexandria sailing into Italy; and he put us therein.

7 And when we had sailed slowly many days, and scarce were come over against Cnidus, the wind not suffering us, we sailed under Crete, over against Salmone; 8 And, hardly passing it, came unto a place which is called the Fair Havens; nigh whereunto was the city of Lasea.

9 Now when much time was spent, and when sailing was now dangerous, because the fast was now already past, Paul admonished them, 10 And said unto them, Sirs, I perceive that this voyage will be with hurt and much damage, not only of the lading and ship, but also of our lives. 11 Nevertheless the centurion believed the master and the owner of the ship, more than those things which were spoken by Paul. 12 And because the haven was not commodious to winter in, the more part advised to depart thence also, if by any means they might attain to Phenice, and there to winter; which is a haven of Crete, and lieth toward the southwest and northwest. 13 And when the south wind blew softly, supposing that they had obtained their purpose, loosing thence, they sailed close by Crete.

14 But not long after there arose against it a tempestuous wind, called Euroclydon. 15 And when the ship was caught, and could not bear up into the wind, we let her drive. 16 And running under a certain island which is called Clauda, we had much work to come by the boat: 17 Which when they had taken up, they used helps, undergirding the ship; and, fearing lest they should fall into the quicksands, struck sail, and so were driven. 18 And we being exceedingly tossed with a tempest, the next day they lightened the ship; 19 And the third day we cast out with our own hands the tackling of the ship. 20 And when neither sun nor stars in many days appeared, and no small tempest lay on us, all hope that we should be saved was then taken away.

21 But after long abstinence, Paul stood forth in the midst of them, and said, Sirs, ye should have hearkened unto me, and not have loosed from Crete, and to have gained this harm and loss. 22 And now I exhort you to be of good cheer: for there shall be no loss of any man's life among you, but of the ship. 23 For there stood by me this night the angel of God, whose I am, and whom I serve, 24 Saying, Fear not, Paul; thou must be brought before Caesar: and, lo, God hath given thee all them that sail with thee. 25 Wherefore, sirs, be of good cheer: for I believe God, that it shall be even as it was told me. 26 Howbeit we must be cast upon a certain island.

27 But when the fourteenth night was come, as we were driven up and down in Adria, about midnight the shipmen deemed that they drew near to some country; 28 And sounded, and found it twenty fathoms: and when they had gone a little further, they sounded again, and found it fifteen fathoms. 29 Then fearing lest we should

have fallen upon rocks, they cast four anchors out of the stern, and wished for the day. 30 And as the shipmen were about to flee out of the ship, when they had let down the boat into the sea, under color as though they would have cast anchors out of the foreship, 31 Paul said to the centurion and to the soldiers, Except these abide in the ship, ye cannot be saved. 32 Then the soldiers cut off the ropes of the boat, and let her fall off.

33 And while the day was coming on, Paul besought them all to take meat, saying, This day is the fourteenth day that ye have tarried and continued fasting, having taken nothing. 34 Wherefore I pray you to take some meat; for this is for your health: for there shall not a hair fall from the head of any of you. 35 And when he had thus spoken, he took bread, and gave thanks to God in presence of them all; and when he had broken it, he began to eat. 36 Then were they all of good cheer, and they also took some meat. 37 And we were in all in the ship two hundred threescore and sixteen souls. 38 And when they had eaten enough, they lightened the ship, and cast out the wheat into the sea.

39 And when it was day, they knew not the land: but they discovered a certain creek with a shore, into the which they were minded, if it were possible, to thrust in the ship. 40 And when they had taken up the anchors, they committed themselves unto the sea, and loosed the rudder bands, and hoisted up the mainsail to the wind, and made toward shore. 41 And falling into a place where two seas met, they ran the ship aground; and the forepart stuck fast, and remained unmovable, but the hinder part was broken with the violence of the waves. 42 And the soldiers' counsel was to kill the prisoners, lest any of them should swim out, and escape. 43 But the centurion, willing to save Paul, kept them from their purpose; and commanded that they which could swim should cast themselves first into the sea, and get to land: 44 And the rest, some on boards, and some on broken pieces of the ship. And so it came to pass, that they escaped all safe to land.

28 And when they were escaped, then they knew that the island was called Melita. 2 And the barbarous people showed us no little kindness: for they kindled a fire, and received us every one, because of the present rain, and because of the cold. 3 And when Paul had gathered a bundle of sticks, and laid them on the fire, there came a viper out of the heat, and fastened on his hand. 4 And when the barbarians saw the venomous beast hang on his hand, they said among themselves, No doubt this man is a murderer, whom, though he hath escaped the sea, yet vengeance suffereth not to live. 5 And he shook off the beast into the fire, and felt no harm. 6 Howbeit they looked when he should have swollen, or fallen down dead suddenly: but after they had looked a great while, and saw no harm come to him, they changed their minds, and said that he was a god.

7 In the same quarters were possessions of the chief man of the island, whose name was Publius; who received us, and lodged us three

days courteously. 8 And it came to pass, that the father of Publius lay sick of a fever and of a bloody flux: to whom Paul entered in, and prayed, and laid his hands on him, and healed him. 9 So when this was done, others also, which had diseases in the island, came, and were healed: 10 Who also honored us with many honors; and when we departed, they laded us with such things as were necessary.

11 And after three months we departed in a ship of Alexandria, which had wintered in the isle, whose sign was Castor and Pollux. 12 And landing at Syracuse, we tarried there three days. 13 And from thence we fetched a compass, and came to Rhegium: and after one day the south wind blew, and we came the next day to Puteoli: 14 Where we found brethren, and were desired to tarry with them seven days: and so we went toward Rome. 15 And from thence, when the brethren heard of us, they came to meet us as far as Appii Forum, and the Three Taverns; whom when Paul saw, he thanked God, and took courage. 16 And when we came to Rome, the centurion delivered the prisoners to the captain of the guard: but Paul was suffered to dwell by himself with a soldier that kept him.

17 And it came to pass, that after three days Paul called the chief of the Jews together: and when they were come together, he said unto them, Men and brethren, though I have committed nothing against the people, or customs of our fathers, yet was I delivered prisoner from Jerusalem into the hands of the Romans: 18 Who, when they had examined me, would have let me go, because there was no cause of death in me. 19 But when the Jews spake against it, I was constrained to appeal unto Caesar; not that I had aught to accuse my nation of. 20 For this cause therefore have I called for you, to see you, and to speak with you: because that for the hope of Israel I am bound with this chain. 21 And they said unto him, We neither received letters out of Judea concerning thee, neither any of the brethren that came showed or spake any harm of thee. 22 But we desire to hear of thee what thou thinkest: for as concerning this sect, we know that every where it is spoken against.

23 And when they had appointed him a day, there came many to him into his lodging; to whom he expounded and testified the kingdom of God, persuading them concerning Jesus, both out of the law of Moses, and out of the prophets, from morning till evening. 24 And some believed the things which were spoken, and some believed not. 25 And when they agreed not among themselves, they departed, after that Paul had spoken one word, Well spake the Holy Ghost by Esaias the prophet unto our fathers, 26 Saying,

Go unto this people, and say,
Hearing ye shall hear, and shall not understand;
And seeing ye shall see, and not perceive:
27 For the heart of this people is waxed gross,
And their ears are dull of hearing,
And their eyes have they closed;
Lest they should see with their eyes,

And hear with their ears,
And understand with their heart,
And should be converted, and I should heal them.
28 Be it known therefore unto you, that the salvation of God is sent
unto the Gentiles, and that they will hear it. 29 And when he had
said these words, the Jews departed, and had great reasoning among
themselves.

30 And Paul dwelt two whole years in his own hired house, and received all that came in unto him, 31 Preaching the kingdom of God,
and teaching those things which concern the Lord Jesus Christ, with
all confidence, no man forbidding him.

# Epistles: *Romans, First Corinthians, Philippians, Galatians, James, Hebrews*

The New Testament epistles come closer than anything else in the Bible to being systematic theology, but they are not, at least in our terms. Instead of being detailed analyses of religious and ethical problems, pursued as an independent academic discipline, they are directly addressed to particular problems which arose in particular places among the emerging churches. They represent a thinking out of the implications of the Christian faith in connection with concrete issues. Printed here are selections from Paul's letters, from the letter of James, and from the anonymous Epistle to the Hebrews.

The life of the Apostle Paul, first as Saul the persecutor of the Christian community and later as the same community's leading advocate before the Gentiles, has been told in the book of Acts. The intense energy of the man carried him over much of the Mediterranean world as he sought to implant Christianity. Reared as a loyal Jew of the strictest kind, Paul was at the same time sufficiently cosmopolitan to be at ease in Athens as well as in Jerusalem. His learning was extensive, and allowed him to treat the traditions of his own people with authority while yet referring quite competently to the traditions of Classical culture. He was thus ideally suited to be the "Apostle to the Gentiles," though he never failed to appeal to the Jewish community in every city he visited. He was, furthermore, that rare figure, an intellectual with an ability to organize, so that he was able not only to convert individuals but also to establish communities with sufficient strength to survive and to grow.

Paul's writings consisted in the letters which he wrote to new churches. These letters are not of the studied and formalized Classical type, but are spontaneous, ebullient, and passionate. Their chronology is uncertain, and it is a question how many of the letters ascribed to him are actually of his authorship. The selections given below bring together a number of Pauline treatments of various important issues, or illustrate his continuous development of particular subjects.

In addition to materials drawn from Paul's letters, we also include a selection from the Epistle of James. James wrote in an excellent Greek style, which is eloquently rendered in the English of the King James Version. James' letter was made necessary by at least some popular misunderstanding of Paul's subtly balanced analysis of faith and works. James never accuses Paul of the kinds of misuse which he finds others making of Paul's teaching, but seeks to right the balance and correct a dangerously easy tendency to rely only upon orthodox belief apart from strenuous moral and social effort. The letter is a beautiful and intensely practical manual for the everyday life of Christians.

Our final selection from the New Testament epistles is taken from the last three chapters of the anonymous Letter to the Hebrews. These chapters are among the most beautiful in the Bible. First, there is a tracing of faith in terms of the great heroes of the Old Testament, coming down to the time of the writer himself; there follows an impassioned exhortation to endurance under suffering, and the whole is closed with a noble benediction.

# Epistle to the Romans

## ADVICE ON CHRISTIAN LIFE

12 I beseech you therefore, brethren, by the mercies of God, that ye present your bodies a living sacrifice, holy, acceptable unto God, which is your reasonable service. 2 And be not conformed to this world: but be ye transformed by the renewing of your mind, that ye may prove what is that good, and acceptable, and perfect will of God.

3 For I say, through the grace given unto me, to every man that is among you, not to think of himself more highly than he ought to think; but to think soberly, according as God hath dealt to every man the measure of faith. 4 For as we have many members in one body, and all members have not the same office: 5 So we, being many, are one body in Christ, and every one members one of another. 6 Having then gifts differing according to the grace that is given to us, whether prophecy, let us prophesy according to the proportion of faith; 7 Or ministry, let us wait on our ministering; or he that teacheth, on teaching; 8 Or he that exhorteth, on exhortation: he that giveth, let him do it with simplicity; he that ruleth, with diligence; he that showeth mercy, with cheerfulness.

9 Let love be without dissimulation. Abhor that which is evil; cleave to that which is good. 10 Be kindly affectioned one to another with brotherly love; in honor preferring one another; 11 Not slothful in business; fervent in spirit; serving the Lord; 12 Rejoicing in hope; patient in tribulation; continuing instant in prayer; 13 Distributing to the necessity of saints; given to hospitality.

14 Bless them which persecute you: bless, and curse not. 15 Rejoice with them that do rejoice, and weep with them that weep. 16

Be of the same mind one toward another. Mind not high things, but condescend to men of low estate. Be not wise in your own conceits. 17 Recompense to no man evil for evil. Provide things honest in the sight of all men. 18 If it be possible, as much as lieth in you, live peaceably with all men. 19 Dearly beloved, avenge not yourselves, but rather give place unto wrath: for it is written, Vengeance is mine; I will repay, saith the Lord. 20 Therefore if thine enemy hunger, feed him; if he thirst, give him drink: for in so doing thou shalt heap coals of fire on his head. 21 Be not overcome of evil, but overcome evil with good.

# First Epistle to the Corinthians

## CHARITY AND THE GIFTS OF THE SPIRIT

12 27 Now ye are the body of Christ, and members in particular. 28 And God hath set some in the church, first apostles, secondarily prophets, thirdly teachers, after that miracles, then gifts of healings, helps, governments, diversities of tongues. 29 Are all apostles? are all prophets? are all teachers? are all workers of miracles? 30 Have all the gifts of healing? do all speak with tongues? do all interpret? 31 But covet earnestly the best gifts: and yet show I unto you a more excellent way.

13 Though I speak with the tongues of men and of angels, and have not charity, I am become as sounding brass, or a tinkling cymbal. 2 And though I have the gift of prophecy, and understand all mysteries, and all knowledge; and though I have all faith, so that I could remove mountains, and have not charity, I am nothing. 3 And though I bestow all my goods to feed the poor, and though I give my body to be burned, and have not charity, it profiteth me nothing.

4 Charity suffereth long, and is kind; charity envieth not; charity vaunteth not itself, is not puffed up, 5 Doth not behave itself unseemly, seeketh not her own, is not easily provoked, thinketh no evil; 6 Rejoiceth not in iniquity, but rejoiceth in the truth; 7 Beareth all things, believeth all things, hopeth all things, endureth all things.

8 Charity never faileth: but whether there be prophecies, they shall fail; whether there be tongues, they shall cease; whether there be knowledge, it shall vanish away. 9 For we know in part, and we prophesy in part. 10 But when that which is perfect is come, then that which is in part shall be done away. 11 When I was a child, I spake as a child, I understood as a child, I thought as a child: but when I became a man, I put away childish things. 12 For now we see through a glass, darkly; but then face to face: now I know in part; but then shall I know even as also I am known. 13 And now abideth faith, hope, charity, these three; but the greatest of these is charity.

## SUMMARY OF THE GOSPEL

15 Moreover, brethren, I declare unto you the gospel which I preached unto you, which also ye have received, and wherein ye stand; 2 By which also ye are saved, if ye keep in memory what I preached unto you, unless ye have believed in vain. 3 For I delivered unto you first of all that which I also received, how that Christ died for our sins according to the Scriptures; 4 And that he was buried, and that he rose again the third day according to the Scriptures: 5 And that he was seen of Cephas, then of the twelve: 6 After that, he was seen of above five hundred brethren at once; of whom the greater part remain unto this present, but some are fallen asleep. 7 After that, he was seen of James; then of all the apostles. 8 And last of all he was seen of me also, as of one born out of due time. 9 For I am the least of the apostles, that am not meet to be called an apostle, because I persecuted the church of God. 10 But by the grace of God I am what I am: and his grace which was bestowed upon me was not in vain; but I labored more abundantly than they all: yet not I, but the grace of God which was with me. 11 Therefore whether it were I or they, so we preach, and so ye believed.

12 Now if Christ be preached that he rose from the dead, how say some among you that there is no resurrection of the dead? 13 But if there be no resurrection of the dead, then is Christ not risen: 14 And if Christ be not risen, then is our preaching vain, and your faith is also vain. 15 Yea, and we are found false witnesses of God; because we have testified of God that he raised up Christ: whom he raised not up, if so be that the dead rise not. 16 For if the dead rise not, then is not Christ raised: 17 And if Christ be not raised, your faith is vain; ye are yet in your sins. 18 Then they also which are fallen asleep in Christ are perished. 19 If in this life only we have hope in Christ, we are of all men most miserable.

20 But now is Christ risen from the dead, and become the firstfruits of them that slept. 21 For since by man came death, by man came also the resurrection of the dead. 22 For as in Adam all die, even so in Christ shall all be made alive. 23 But every man in his own order: Christ the firstfruits; afterward they that are Christ's at his coming. 24 Then cometh the end, when he shall have delivered up the kingdom to God, even the Father; when he shall have put down all rule, and all authority and power. 25 For he must reign, till he hath put all enemies under his feet. 26 The last enemy that shall be destroyed is death. 27 For he hath put all things under his feet. But when he saith, All things are put under him, it is manifest that he is excepted, which did put all things under him. 28 And when all things shall be subdued unto him, then shall the Son also himself be subject unto him that put all things under him, that God may be all in all.

29 Else what shall they do which are baptized for the dead, if the dead rise not at all? why are they then baptized for the dead? 30 And why stand we in jeopardy every hour? 31 I protest by your rejoicing

which I have in Christ Jesus our Lord, I die daily. 32 If after the manner of men I have fought with beasts at Ephesus, what advantageth it me, if the dead rise not? let us eat and drink; for to-morrow we die. 33 Be not deceived:

Evil communications corrupt good manners.

34 Awake to righteousness, and sin not; for some have not the knowledge of God: I speak this to your shame.

35 But some man will say, How are the dead raised up? and with what body do they come? 36 Thou fool, that which thou sowest is not quickened, except it die: 37 And that which thou sowest, thou sowest not that body that shall be, but bare grain, it may chance of wheat, or of some other grain: 38 But God giveth it a body as it hath pleased him, and to every seed his own body. 39 All flesh is not the same flesh: but there is one kind of flesh of men, another flesh of beasts, another of fishes, and another of birds. 40 There are also celestial bodies, and bodies terrestrial: but the glory of the celestial is one, and the glory of the terrestrial is another. 41 There is one glory of the sun, and another glory of the moon, and another glory of the stars; for one star differeth from another star in glory.

42 So also is the resurrection of the dead. It is sown in corruption, it is raised in incorruption: 43 It is sown in dishonor, it is raised in glory: it is sown in weakness, it is raised in power: 44 It is sown a natural body, it is raised a spiritual body. There is a natural body, and there is a spiritual body. 45 And so it is written, The first man Adam was made a living soul; the last Adam was made a quickening spirit. 46 Howbeit that was not first which is spiritual, but that which is natural; and afterward that which is spiritual. 47 The first man is of the earth, earthy: the second man is the Lord from heaven. 48 As is the earthy, such are they also that are earthy: and as is the heavenly, such are they also that are heavenly. 49 And as we have borne the image of the earthy, we shall also bear the image of the heavenly.

50 Now this I say, brethren, that flesh and blood cannot inherit the kingdom of God; neither doth corruption inherit incorruption. 51 Behold, I show you a mystery; We shall not all sleep, but we shall all be changed, 52 In a moment, in the twinkling of an eye, at the last trump: for the trumpet shall sound, and the dead shall be raised incorruptible, and we shall be changed. 53 For this corruptible must put on incorruption, and this mortal must put on immortality. 54 So when this corruptible shall have put on incorruption, and this mortal shall have put on immortality, then shall be brought to pass the saying that is written,

Death is swallowed up in victory.

55 O death, where is thy sting?

O grave, where is thy victory?

56 The sting of death is sin; and the strength of sin is the law. 57 But thanks be to God, which giveth us the victory through our Lord Jesus Christ.

58 Therefore, my beloved brethren, be ye steadfast, unmovable,

always abounding in the work of the Lord, forasmuch as ye know that your labor is not in vain in the Lord.

# Epistle to the Philippians

## CHRIST AS MAN'S MODEL

2 If there be therefore any consolation in Christ, if any comfort of love, if any fellowship of the Spirit, if any bowels[1] and mercies, 2 Fulfil ye my joy, that ye be likeminded, having the same love, being of one accord, of one mind. 3 Let nothing be done through strife or vainglory; but in lowliness of mind let each esteem other better than themselves. 4 Look not every man on his own things, but every man also on the things of others.

5 Let this mind be in you, which was also in Christ Jesus: 6 Who, being in the form of God, thought it not robbery to be equal with God: 7 But made himself of no reputation, and took upon him the form of a servant, and was made in the likeness of men: 8 And being found in fashion as a man, he humbled himself, and became obedient unto death, even the death of the cross. 9 Wherefore God also hath highly exalted him, and given him a name which is above every name: 10 That at the name of Jesus every knee should bow, of things in heaven, and things in earth, and things under the earth; 11 And that every tongue should confess that Jesus Christ is Lord, to the glory of God the Father.

12 Wherefore, my beloved, as ye have always obeyed, not as in my presence only, but now much more in my absence, work out your own salvation with fear and trembling: 13 For it is God which worketh in you both to will and to do of his good pleasure. 14 Do all things without murmurings and disputings: 15 That ye may be blameless and harmless, the sons of God, without rebuke, in the midst of a crooked and perverse nation, among whom ye shine as lights in the world.

# Epistle to the Galatians

## FREEDOM

5 Stand fast therefore in the liberty wherewith Christ hath made us free, and be not entangled again with the yoke of bondage. 2 Behold, I Paul say unto you, that if ye be circumcised, Christ shall profit you nothing. 3 For I testify again to every man that is circumcised,

---

[1] The bowels were regarded as the seat of the emotions in man.

that he is a debtor to do the whole law. 4 Christ is become of no effect unto you, whosoever of you are justified by the law; ye are fallen from grace. 5 For we through the Spirit wait for the hope of righteousness by faith. 6 For in Jesus Christ neither circumcision availeth any thing, nor uncircumcision; but faith which worketh by love. 7 Ye did run well; who did hinder you that ye should not obey the truth? 8 This persuasion cometh not of him that calleth you. 9 A little leaven leaveneth the whole lump. 10 I have confidence in you through the Lord, that ye will be none otherwise minded: but he that troubleth you shall bear his judgment, whosoever he be. 11 And I, brethren, if I yet preach circumcision, why do I yet suffer persecution? then is the offense of the cross ceased. 12 I would they were even cut off which trouble you.

13 For, brethren, ye have been called unto liberty; only use not liberty for an occasion to the flesh, but by love serve one another. 14 For all the law is fulfilled in one word, even in this; Thou shalt love thy neighbor as thyself. 15 But if ye bite and devour one another, take heed that ye be not consumed one of another.

16 This I say then, Walk in the Spirit, and ye shall not fulfil the lust of the flesh. 17 For the flesh lusteth against the Spirit, and the Spirit against the flesh: and these are contrary the one to the other; so that ye cannot do the things that ye would. 18 But if ye be led of the Spirit, ye are not under the law. 19 Now the works of the flesh are manifest, which are these, Adultery, fornication, uncleanness, lasciviousness, 20 Idolatry, witchcraft, hatred, variance, emulations, wrath, strife, seditions, heresies, 21 Envyings, murders, drunkenness, revelings, and such like: of the which I tell you before, as I have also told you in time past, that they which do such things shall not inherit the kingdom of God. 22 But the fruit of the Spirit is love, joy, peace, long-suffering, gentleness, goodness, faith, 23 Meekness, temperance: against such there is no law. 24 And they that are Christ's have crucified the flesh with the affections and lusts. 25 If we live in the Spirit, let us also walk in the Spirit. 26 Let us not be desirous of vainglory, provoking one another, envying one another.

# General Epistle of James

## WORKS AND FAITH

2  14 What doth it profit, my brethren, though a man say he hath faith, and have not works? can faith save him? 15 If a brother or sister be naked, and destitute of daily food, 16 And one of you say unto them, Depart in peace, be ye warmed and filled; notwithstanding ye give them not those things which are needful to the body; what doth it profit? 17 Even so faith, if it hath not works, is dead, being alone.

18 Yea, a man may say, Thou hast faith, and I have works: show me thy faith without thy works, and I will show thee my faith by my works. 19 Thou believest that there is one God; thou doest well: the devils also believe, and tremble. 20 But wilt thou know, O vain man, that faith without works is dead? 21 Was not Abraham our father justified by works, when he had offered Isaac his son upon the altar? 22 Seest thou how faith wrought with his works, and by works was faith made perfect? 23 And the Scripture was fulfilled which saith, Abraham believed God, and it was imputed unto him for righteousness: and he was called the Friend of God. 24 Ye see then how that by works a man is justified, and not by faith only. 25 Likewise also was not Rahab the harlot justified by works, when she had received the messengers, and had sent them out another way? 26 For as the body without the spirit is dead, so faith without works is dead also.

# Epistle to the Hebrews

## HEROES OF FAITH

11 Now faith is the substance of things hoped for, the evidence of things not seen. 2 For by it the elders obtained a good report. 3 Through faith we understand that the worlds were framed by the word of God, so that things which are seen were not made of things which do appear.

4 By faith Abel offered unto God a more excellent sacrifice than Cain, by which he obtained witness that he was righteous, God testifying of his gifts: and by it he being dead yet speaketh. 5 By faith Enoch was translated that he should not see death; and was not found, because God had translated him: for before his translation he had this testimony, that he pleased God. 6 But without faith it is impossible to please him: for he that cometh to God must believe that he is, and that he is a rewarder of them that diligently seek him. 7 By faith Noah, being warned of God of things not seen as yet, moved with fear, prepared an ark to the saving of his house; by the which he condemned the world, and became heir of the righteousness which is by faith.

8 By faith Abraham, when he was called to go out into a place which he should after receive for an inheritance, obeyed; and he went out, not knowing whither he went. 9 By faith he sojourned in the land of promise, as in a strange country, dwelling in tabernacles with Isaac and Jacob, the heirs with him of the same promise: 10 For he looked for a city which hath foundations, whose builder and maker is God. 11 Through faith also Sarah herself received strength to conceive seed, and was delivered of a child when she was past age, because she judged him faithful who had promised. 12 Therefore sprang there even

of one, and him as good as dead, so many as the stars of the sky in multitude, and as the sand which is by the seashore innumerable.

13 These all died in faith, not having received the promises, but having seen them afar off, and were persuaded of them, and embraced them, and confessed that they were strangers and pilgrims on the earth. 14 For they that say such things declare plainly that they seek a country. 15 And truly, if they had been mindful of that country from whence they came out, they might have had opportunity to have returned. 16 But now they desire a better country, that is, a heavenly: wherefore God is not ashamed to be called their God: for he hath prepared for them a city.

17 By faith Abraham, when he was tried, offered up Isaac: and he that had received the promises offered up his only begotten son, 18 Of whom it was said, That in Isaac shall thy seed be called: 19 Accounting that God was able to raise him up, even from the dead; from whence also he received him in a figure. 20 By faith Isaac blessed Jacob and Esau concerning things to come. 21 By faith Jacob, when he was a dying blessed both the sons of Joseph; and worshipped, leaning upon the top of his staff. 22 By faith Joseph, when he died, made mention of the departing of the children of Israel; and gave commandment concerning his bones.

23 By faith Moses, when he was born, was hid three months of his parents, because they saw he was a proper child; and they were not afraid of the king's commandment. 24 By faith Moses, when he was come to years, refused to be called the son of Pharaoh's daughter; 25 Choosing rather to suffer affliction with the people of God, than to enjoy the pleasures of sin for a season; 26 Esteeming the reproach of Christ greater riches than the treasures in Egypt: for he had respect unto the recompense of the reward. 27 By faith he forsook Egypt, not fearing the wrath of the king: for he endured, as seeing him who is invisible. 28 Through faith he kept the passover, and the sprinkling of blood, lest he that destroyed the firstborn should touch them.

29 By faith they passed through the Red sea as by dry land: which the Egyptians assaying to do were drowned. 30 By faith the walls of Jericho fell down, after they were compassed about seven days. 31 By faith the harlot Rahab perished not with them that believed not, when she had received the spies with peace.

32 And what shall I more say? for the time would fail me to tell of Gideon, and of Barak, and of Samson, and of Jephthah; of David also, and Samuel, and of the prophets: 33 Who through faith subdued kingdoms, wrought righteousness, obtained promises, stopped the mouths of lions, 34 Quenched the violence of fire, escaped the edge of the sword, out of weakness were made strong, waxed valiant in fight, turned to flight the armies of the aliens. 35 Women received their dead raised to life again: and others were tortured, not accepting deliverance; that they might obtain a better resurrection: 36 And others had trial of cruel mockings and scourgings, yea, moreover of

bonds and imprisonment: 37 They were stoned, they were sawn asunder, were tempted, were slain with the sword: they wandered about in sheepskins and goatskins; being destitute, afflicted, tormented; 38 Of whom the world was not worthy: they wandered in deserts, and in mountains, and in dens and caves of the earth.

39 And these all, having obtained a good report through faith, received not the promise: 40 God having provided some better thing for us, that they without us should not be made perfect.

12 Wherefore, seeing we also are compassed about with so great a cloud of witnesses, let us lay aside every weight. and the sin which doth so easily beset us, and let us run with patience the race that is set before us, 2 Looking unto Jesus the author and finisher of our faith; who for the joy that was set before him endured the cross, despising the shame, and is set down at the right hand of the throne of God.

3 For consider him that endured such contradiction of sinners against himself, lest ye be wearied and faint in your minds. 4 Ye have not yet resisted unto blood, striving against sin. 5 And ye have forgotten the exhortation which speaketh unto you as unto children,

My son, despise not thou the chastening of the Lord,
Nor faint when thou art rebuked of him:
6 For whom the Lord loveth he chasteneth,
And scourgeth every son whom he receiveth.

7 If ye endure chastening, God dealeth with you as with sons; for what son is he whom the father chasteneth not? 8 But if ye be without chastisement, whereof all are partakers, then are ve bastards, and not sons. 9 Furthermore, we have had fathers of our flesh which corrected us, and we gave them reverence: shall we not much rather be in subjection unto the Father of spirits, and live? 10 For they verily for a few days chastened us after their own pleasure; but he for our profit, that we might be partakers of his holiness. 11 Now no chastening for the present seemeth to be joyous, but grievous: nevertheless, afterward it yieldeth the peaceable fruit of righteousness unto them which are exercised thereby.

12 Wherefore lift up the hands which hang down. and the feeble knees; 13 And make straight paths for your feet, lest that which is lame be turned out of the way; but let it rather be healed. 14 Follow peace with all men, and holiness, without which no man shall see the Lord.

13 20 Now the God of peace, that brought again from the dead our Lord Jesus, that great shepherd of the sheep, through the blood of the everlasting covenant, 21 Make you perfect in every good work to do his will, working in you that which is well-pleasing in his sight, through Jesus Christ; to whom be glory for ever and ever. Amen.

# The End: *Revelation*

The passages printed below from the last chapters of the book of Revelation stand as the literary conclusion of the Old and New Testaments. There are elements here which are reminiscent of the Old Testament prophets, but the point of view is definitely that of the New Testament community. The conclusion is a prevision of the intended goal of history, as determined by God. As such, it stands against any view of human life and history as purposeless and meaningless, but it also implicitly contradicts the idea that men will work out their own triumphant achievement. The New Jerusalem will come, but it will not be a better engineered version of the Tower of Babel built by human efforts to rival heaven: on the contrary, it will come as God's own dénouement of human history.

In the New Jerusalem, man may know God directly: "I saw no temple therein: for the Lord God Almighty and the Lamb are the temple in it." Here, then, men "shall see his face," so that the knowledge of God will be immediate and personal. Here, too, there will be the establishment of the human personality beyond the threat of evil and of death, and the establishment of a holy community of men under God. Here there is the tree of life, for here God is "Alpha and Omega, the beginning and the end, the first and the last." The union of divine initiative and human response are preserved here as elsewhere in the Scripture: the new community is entirely a gift of God's grace, but men are nonetheless linked to this gift by their conduct in response to God's will: "Blessed are they that do his commandments, that they may have right to the tree of life, and may enter in through the gates into the city."

# *The Revelation to John*

20 11 And I saw a great white throne, and him that sat on it, from whose face the earth and the heaven fled away; and there was found no place for them. 12 And I saw the dead, small and great, stand before God; and the books were opened: and another book was opened, which is the book of life: and the dead were judged out of those things which were written in the books, according to their works.

13 And the sea gave up the dead which were in it; and death and hell delivered up the dead which were in them: and they were judged every man according to their works. 14 And death and hell were cast into the lake of fire. This is the second death. 15 And whosoever was not found written in the book of life was cast into the lake of fire.

21 And I saw a new heaven and a new earth: for the first heaven and the first earth were passed away; and there was no more sea. 2 And I John saw the holy city, new Jerusalem, coming down from God out of heaven, prepared as a bride adorned for her husband. 3 And I heard a great voice out of heaven saying, Behold, the tabernacle of God is with men, and he will dwell with them, and they shall be his people, and God himself shall be with them, and be their God. 4 And God shall wipe away all tears from their eyes; and there shall be no more death, neither sorrow, nor crying, neither shall there be any more pain: for the former things are passed away.

5 And he that sat upon the throne said, Behold, I make all things new. And he said unto me, Write: for these words are true and faithful. 6 And he said unto me, It is done. I am Alpha and Omega, the beginning and the end. I will give unto him that is athirst of the fountain of the water of life freely. 7 He that overcometh shall inherit all things; and I will be his God, and he shall be my son. 8 But the fearful, and unbelieving, and the abominable, and murderers, and whoremongers, and sorcerers, and idolaters, and all liars, shall have their part in the lake which burneth with fire and brimstone: which is the second death.

9 And there came unto me one of the seven angels which had the seven vials full of the seven last plagues, and talked with me, saying, Come hither, I will show thee the bride, the Lamb's wife. 10 And he carried me away in the spirit to a great and high mountain, and showed me that great city, the holy Jerusalem, descending out of heaven from God, 11 Having the glory of God: and her light was like unto a stone most precious, even like a jasper stone, clear as crystal; 12 And had a wall great and high, and had twelve gates, and at the gates twelve angels, and names written thereon, which are the names of the twelve tribes of the children of Israel: 13 On the east three gates; on the north three gates; on the south three gates; and on the west three gates. 14 And the wall of the city had twelve foundations, and in them the names of the twelve apostles of the Lamb.

15 And he that talked with me had a golden reed to measure the city, and the gates thereof, and the wall thereof. 16 And the city lieth foursquare, and the length is as large as the breadth: and he measured the city with the reed, twelve thousand furlongs. The length and the breadth and the height of it are equal. 17 And he measured the wall thereof, a hundred and forty and four cubits, according to the measure of a man, that is, of the angel. 18 And the building of the wall of it was of jasper: and the city was pure gold, like unto clear glass. 19 And the foundations of the wall of the city were garnished with all man-

ner of precious stones. The first foundation was jasper; the second, sapphire; the third, a chalcedony; the fourth, an emerald; 20 The fifth, sardonyx; the sixth, sardius; the seventh, chrysolite; the eighth, beryl; the ninth, a topaz; and tenth, a chrysoprasus; the eleventh, a jacinth; the twelfth, an amethyst. 21 And the twelve gates were twelve pearls; every several gate was of one pearl: and the street of the city was pure gold, as it were transparent glass.

22 And I saw no temple therein: for the Lord God Almighty and the Lamb are the temple of it. 23 And the city had no need of the sun, neither of the moon, to shine in it: for the glory of God did lighten it, and the Lamb is the light thereof. 24 And the nations of them which are saved shall walk in the light of it: and the kings of the earth do bring their glory and honor into it. 25 And the gates of it shall not be shut at all by day: for there shall be no night there. 26 And they shall bring the glory and honor of the nations into it. 27 And there shall in no wise enter into it any thing that defileth, neither whatsoever worketh abomination, or maketh a lie: but they which are written in the Lamb's book of life.

22 And he showed me a pure river of water of life, clear as crystal, proceeding out of the throne of God and of the Lamb. 2 In the midst of the street of it, and on either side of the river, was there the tree of life, which bare twelve manner of fruits, and yielded her fruit every month: and the leaves of the tree were for the healing of the nations. 3 And there shall be no more curse: but the throne of God and of the Lamb shall be in it; and his servants shall serve him: 4 And they shall see his face; and his name shall be in their foreheads. 5 And there shall be no night there; and they need no candle, neither light of the sun; for the Lord God giveth them light: and they shall reign for ever and ever.

6 And he said unto me, These sayings are faithful and true: and the Lord God of the holy prophets sent his angel to show unto his servants the things which must shortly be done. 7 Behold, I come quickly: blessed is he that keepeth the sayings of the prophecy of this book.

8 And I John saw these things, and heard them. And when I had heard and seen, I fell down to worship before the feet of the angel which showed me these things. 9 Then saith he unto me, See thou do it not: for I am thy fellow servant, and of thy brethren the prophets, and of them which keep the sayings of this book: worship God.

10 And he saith unto me, Seal not the sayings of the prophecy of this book: for the time is at hand. 11 He that is unjust, let him be unjust still: and he which is filthy, let him be filthy still: and he that is righteous, let him be righteous still: and he that is holy, let him be holy still.

12 And, behold, I come quickly; and my reward is with me, to give every man according as his work shall be. 13 I am Alpha and Omega, the beginning and the end, the first and the last.

14 Blessed are they that do his commandments, that they may have right to the tree of life, and may enter in through the gates into the city. 15 For without are dogs, and sorcerers, and whoremongers, and murderers, and idolaters, and whosoever loveth and maketh a lie.

16 I Jesus have sent mine angel to testify unto you these things in the churches. I am the root and the offspring of David, and the bright and morning star. 17 And the Spirit and the bride say, Come. And let him that heareth say, Come. And let him that is athirst come. And whosoever will, let him take the water of life freely.